GODS and GODDESSES of ANCIENT GREECE

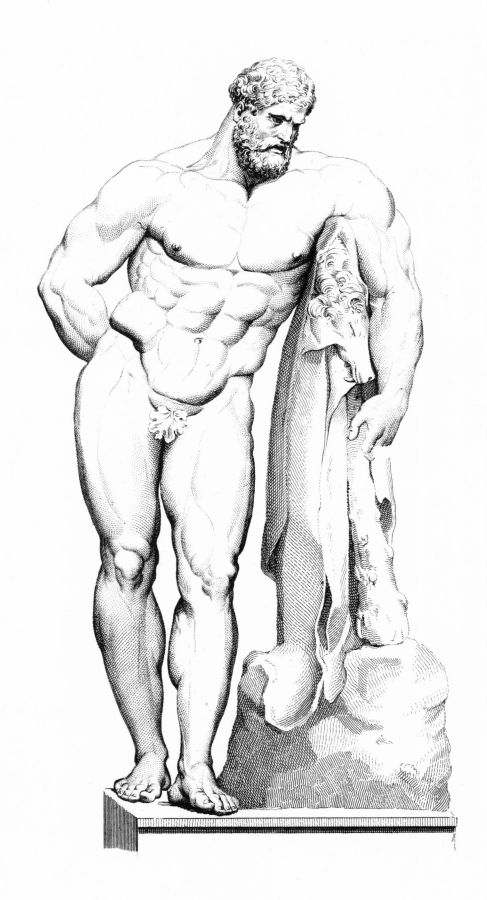

GODS and GODDESSES of ANCIENT GREECE

by Edward E. Barthell, Jr.

University of Miami Press

CORAL GABLES, FLORIDA

Copyright © 1971 by
University of Miami Press
ISBN 0–87024–165–6
Library of Congress Catalog Card No. 72–129664

Designed by Mary Lipson and Bernard Lipsky
Manufactured in the United States of America

Frontispiece: The Farnese Hercules, engraved for
Bell's New Pantheon after the faithful copy of
Giovanni Volpato & Raffaelle Morghen, by T. Cook.
Printed for John Bell, British Library,
Strand, London, February 16, 1789.

To the memory of
my Father
whose transmitted curiosity
inspired the beginning
of this book
and to my Wife
whose warm assistance
has largely contributed
to its completion

Contents

Family Charts

Acknowledgments

THE FOLLOWING QUOTATIONS from Loeb Classical Library volumes are reprinted herein by permission of the publisher, Harvard University Press:

Paragraph with reference to Athena's gift of the olive tree (page 23), from Frazer translation of *Apollodorus*.

Note 32 to chapter 3, wherein Zeus tells Ares that his brawling spirit was inherited from his mother, from Murray translation of the *Iliad*.

Paragraph describing Hermes' attempt to conceal his theft of Apollo's cattle (page 35) from Evelyn-White translation of the *Homeric Hymn to Hermes*.

Note 47 to chapter 4, a description of the palace of the Sun God, from Miller translation of *Ovid's Metamorphoses*.

Note 6 to chapter 5, a description of the wickedness of Iron Age, from Miller translation of *Ovid's Metamorphoses*.

Note 35 to chapter 6, a description of the deification of Eurypylus, from Jones translation of *Pausanias*.

Note 12 to chapter 14, a description of the Shield of Heracles, from Evelyn-White translation of *Hesiod*.

The quotation in note 12 to chapter 19 is reprinted by permission of Dodd, Mead & Company. It appears originally in G. K. Chesterton, *The Everlasting Man* (New York: Dodd, Mead & Company, 1925).

GODS and GODDESSES of ANCIENT GREECE

Introduction

SOME YEARS AGO a group of friends who were engaged in a quizzing contest were asked to state the name of the Greek goddess of love, the name of her father, and the name of her husband. The name of the goddess was variously given as Aphrodite, Cypris, or Cytherea. The name of her father was given as Zeus or Uranus; and Poseidon, Hephaestus, Ares, Hermes, Dionysus, and Anchises were each named as her husband. When he learned that every answer was a proper one, the compiler of this book decided to take a night off to correlate the interrelationships of the principal imaginary beings whom the Greeks considered as divine. The first night's research was followed by many others, until now the self-assigned task has extended over a period of almost forty years; but, as a gratifying and unexpected result, it has brought about the realization that (from the synthesized fancies of the ancients) all of the Greek deities and most of their semidivine heroes can be mythologically, and logically, tied in as members of a single family tree.

The fact of kinship, easily perceived from inspection of the genealogical charts which are a distinguishing feature of this compilation, explains many odd happenings, whose causes are only vaguely hinted at in the conventional classical accounts. Thus,

1. Oedipus unwittingly married his own mother Jocasta, with tragic results to his whole family, because his great-great-grandfather Cadmus had killed a dragon-son of the War-god Ares.

2. Pasiphae, wife of King Minos, was stricken with love for the Cretan bull, and became mother of the monstrous Minotaur, because she was a daughter of the Sun-god Helios, who had tattled to the husband of Aphrodite (the goddess of love) that his wife was unfaithful.

3. The Spartan king, Menelaus, lost his beautiful wife Helen to Trojan Paris, because his great-great-grandfather Tantalus had served his own son as edible meat to the gods.

In the slow process of investigation, it was learned that some of the more interesting mythological stories are nowhere completely detailed and, in such instances, effort has been made herein to consolidate the several parts which elsewhere are separately related. For example,

1. The ancient writers are at one in recounting that Heracles attacked the Pylians and slew their king, Neleus, together with all of his sons except Nestor; but they do not clearly explain the reason for the attack which was an earlier refusal by Neleus (contrary to the advice of Nestor), to purify Heracles of the blood guilt incurred in causing the death of his friend Iphitus.

2. The same hero, Heracles, was miraculously wafted away from the island of Cos while fighting with Chalcodon, a mere mortal whom he would surely have overcome, but the conventional accounts of the incident do not disclose that he was immediately needed to assist the Olympian gods in a great battle which they were then waging with the Giants.

3. Apollo is often referred to as Phoebus Apollo for the rarely stated reason that his maternal grandmother was one of the Titans whose name was Phoebe.

Based on the careful effort which has been expended, the compiler believes that this book, with its accompanying genealogical charts, makes an accurate reference to every consequential being of divine blood who was recognized as a part of Greek mythology, before it was added to, and perhaps distorted, by some of the later classical writers. As such, it is hoped that the book will prove entertaining and serviceable, not only to students but also to those members of the reading public who are interested in the marvelous integration of myths which has served as an inexhaustible reservoir for the literature of the past twenty-five hundred years. The book does not pretend, however, to compete with the many learned works which seek to explain the various stories, by relating their origins to primitive anthropomorphism or natural phenomena; although, in some few instances, references to such treatment have inevitably been necessary.

Despite the attempt to confine the book within the stated bounds, some persons and stories of later date have been included, simply because their prominent mention, and reiteration, by many accepted writers might require laborious explanations because of their omission. Similarly, Latin spellings have usually been adopted where names in that form have gained wide currency. For instance, the Greek for the Latin "Hercules" would literally be anglicized into "Herakles," but is actually converted to "Heracles." The Greek for Castor's twin brother is given as "Pollux," instead of a literal conversion into "Polydeukes"; "Here" is called "Hera."

The Roman, or Latin, mythology is not intended to be covered herein, as such; but, in general, it closely follows and is identified with that of the Greeks, but adds a few extra stories and deities indigenous to Italy, or conceived by patriotic writers in order to give local luster to their native land. Thus, Aeneas is transported from the burning walls of Troy across the sea to Italy, where he marries into the ruling family of Latium, thereby supplying his new country with a ready-made pedigree, which is almost the whole of Greek mythology. Some time later, his son founds the town of Alba Longa, and his

descendants continue in the kingship through Numitor; Numitor has a daughter, Rhea Silvia, who gives birth to twin sons, Romulus and Remus, and the father of her sons is Mars, the Roman god who is identified with the Greek god of war, Ares. After killing his brother, Romulus founds Rome and, at death, takes a prominent place in the Roman pantheon, alongside his originally Greek father and the Trojan ancestors of his mother. In view of the close connection between the two mythologies, references to the Latin names of the Greek divinities are given, either in the text or in the index, wherever they have been so used by authoritative sources to an extent which warrants their inclusion.

With reference to blood relationships, the difficult hurdle of contrariety has been attempted by adopting the story which appears to be best known. For example, the maiden Atalanta, in the Arcadian version of the legend, is a daughter of Iasus and is beaten in her celebrated footrace by a lover named Meilanion, who is the son of her great-uncle Amphidamas; the Boeotian legend, in other respects practically identical, makes Schoeneus her father and Hippomenes her lover. Another, and an oft-repeated, story about Atalanta relates her participation in the hunt for the Calydonian boar—a renowned event in connection wherewith she is always mentioned as a daughter of Schoeneus. Accordingly, the Boeotian version has been given preference in the text, and the Arcadian version has been relegated to a footnote.

In a few instances, missing links have been inserted without definite ancient authority but only by strict adherence to reason, based on established consanguinity or local probability. As an example, the Siamese twins, Cteatus and Eurytus, are uniformly referred to as the warriors-sons of Actor and Molione, but the descent of Molione is nowhere given; this Actor (for there were five mythical characters bearing the same name) was admittedly a great-grandson of Apollo. Another descendant of Apollo (and son of another Eurytus) was Molion, but Molione is not mentioned as his daughter. However, it seems only reasonable to consider her as such, and that she should name one of her sons for her grandfather—and she is so designated on the family chart. The fact that her name has been inserted there without express ancient authority has been indicated by a footnote. The same precedent has been followed with reference to a few others who are in the same category.

Since many references are made by the mythographers to different persons of the same name, without specifying "Eurytus Smith" or "Eurytus Jones," much confusion has naturally arisen in the course of centuries. Here, it may be appropriate to note that the historian Herodotus places Homer as having lived about 900 B.C. and that Virgil, the most renowned of the Roman poets, flourished as late as 19 B.C. Thus, a great deal of time elapsed during which many errors may have honestly occurred; but some of the apparent errors are undoubtedly traceable to the deliberate adoption by deceivers of the illustrious exploits of neighboring heroes, which are related as pertaining to their own ancestors or kinsmen bearing the same names. When we find that "Agenor" was the name of eight different men, we may readily understand the persistence of original mistakes (whether innocent or not) in the hearsay accounts of later commentators. It is believed that much of the confusion, so caused, has been eliminated by a careful checking of sources, and that the relationships as given herein have the backing of accepted authorities. The expression "checking of sources" is not intended to mean examination of original Greek and Latin texts, except in isolated instances. This work has been compiled almost wholly from reputable English translations and commentaries—a list of which appears in the bibliography.

Save only the Minotaur, as the offspring of Pasiphae, and the Idaean Dactyls as mothered by Anchiale, the genealogical charts which are inserted separately, or as parts of the text, uniformly run their descent through the paternal side, because, in many cases, the names of mothers cannot be ascertained from authoritative writings. Wherever a mother's name is missing, she has either been ignored or indicated on the charts as "Madame X."

Although the individual and localized myths may perhaps be counted by the hundreds, certain others—either in their origins or by adoption—were so generally accepted and known by all of the Greeks that they will be mentioned here briefly, notwithstanding their more detailed expansion later in the text. The more prominent of the class mentioned (which are not necessarily referred to in chronological order) are as follows:

The War of the Titans resulted in the supremacy of Zeus and his family of Olympian deities, who were the acknowledged rulers of the universe in the Heroic Age.

The Abduction of Persephone related how Hades, sovereign of the lower world, obtained his bride by carrying off the daughter of Demeter, the goddess of the harvest.

The Origin of Man, or his preservation, was attributed to the efforts of Prometheus, who brought down fire from the heavens and thereby incurred the wrath of Zeus.

The Flood of Deucalion, corresponding to the biblical inundation, related how the earth was swept clear of the impious men who dwelt in the Bronze Age.

The Adventures of Heracles, Perseus, Theseus, and Bellerophon were so geographically diversified that they became a part of the universal literature.

The Argonauts journeyed from Thessaly to the eastern end of the Euxine (the Black Sea) to bring back the Golden Fleece of the speaking ram Chrysomallus.

The Seven Against Thebes were led by the Argive king, Adrastus, to place Polyneices on the throne of Thebes, following the abdication of his unfortunate father Oedipus.

The Epigoni were the sons of the Seven Against Thebes who, ten years after the defeat of their fathers, obtained revenge by conquering the Theban citadel.

The Battle of the Lapiths and the Centaurs occurred when the biformed Centaurs assaulted the bride and her attendants at the wedding of Peirithous and Hippodameia.

The Calydonian Boar Hunt was attended by many of the earlier heroes under the leadership of the Aetolian prince, Meleager.

The Return of the Heracleidae, known also

as the Dorian Invasion, related how the descendants of Heracles, together with their Dorian allies, conquered the great southern peninsula of Greece which was known as the Peloponnesus.

The Trojan War was the most renowned action of Greek mythology, in which all of the different tribes and races consolidated their efforts and were successful in overthrowing the forces of King Priam at his Asiatic city of Troy.

The Returns related how the various Greek heroes attempted to make their way back to their homes after the fall of Troy. The principal narrative is that of Homer, known as the Odyssey, which relates the difficulties encountered by the Ithacan king, Odysseus.

Before proceeding to consider and comment individually upon the various divine and semidivine beings who compose the Greek pantheon, it is quite important to let the reader know that the compiler's reconstruction into a single, and related, family tree is actually an artificial device, but based with warrant upon authorities that are now subjected to bird's-eye inspection from the vantage coign of elapsed centuries.

Greek mythology was constantly in flux. It never anciently existed in a universally accepted form; like Topsy it "just growed up." Many myths, which at first were purely local, came to such wide currency that eventually they were comprehended within the general overall plan; but the plan itself was one conceived in the minds of only a few, among whom Hesiod and Apollodorus are perhaps the outstanding examples. Contrarily, it is certain that—owing perhaps to a lack of information, either by way of written record or hearsay—many of the later writers were wholly unaware that their added stories (conceived in plausible conjecture or deliberate imagination), were to become synthesized parts of the connected narrative herein given.

1

The Older Gods

The Four Primeval Deities

IN POINT OF TIME, the first of the deities composing the Greek pantheon was Chaos (Infinite Space).[1] Next came Gaea (Earth),[2] followed by Tartarus (the Lower World) and Eros (Love).[3] These four beings were primeval.

Chaos, a formless emergence akin to the "Deep" which preceded the biblical creation, was endowed with at least one of the mortal attributes common to the later gods: He is pictured as being made quite uncomfortable by the thunderbolts which were promiscuously tossed about in the gigantic conflict known as the War of the Titans. But, having served his purpose as the logical first of a complex family tree, the role assigned to him ultimately became as vaguely defined as the essence of his being; and recorded mythology gives to him a very minor place in that wonderful series of deified dynasties which the early Greeks established as a foundation for many of the classical stories enjoyed by all later civilized peoples.

Gaea, our "broad-bosomed Mother Earth," was conceived as a flat disk encircled by the great river Oceanus—itself unbounded, and whose waters "backward flow," because the stream flowed into itself. For this reason, no earthly trip could carry past its all-surrounding periphery. Gaea was quite naturally revered as the fruitful power sustaining universal life, and was recognized as the common ancestress of practically all of the gods and demigods comprised within the Greek theogony. Although other, and more personalized, deities of subsequent generations assumed many of the functions which were originally hers alone, yet, the old nature goddess was never wholly supplanted in the thoughts of men—for it was she who first was called "Mother."

Tartarus, next in order of the primeval beings, should not be confused with the personification, or the region, referred to under that name by the later poets in their descriptions of hell; because they usually give the title to only that division of the lower world wherein hardened sinners met their punishment after death. Our primeval Tartarus comprehended the entire lower world, and was the permanent abode of the souls of all those perished from earth, whether good or bad. As a region, its distance below Gaea's surface was equal to that covered by nine days' fall of a brazen anvil; and, upon

---

[1] The logical conception, placing Chaos as the first of the primeval deities, is that of Hesiod. Homer, admittedly earlier, makes Oceanus "father of all the gods." The so-called Orphic theogony places Cronus first, following him by Aether (Light) and Chaos, from whose union was produced a vast mundane egg; and from this egg emerged Phanes, a person of double sex, who generated the world. Apollodorus says that the first of the gods were Uranus (the Heavens) and Gaea, and Hyginus precedes Chaos with a mother, "vaporous Caligo."

[2] Gaea is sometimes shortened to Ge. Her Latin name was Tellus Mater or Terra.

[3] The Latin name for the primeval Eros was Amor. In the Orphic theogony, he was the first to spring from the mundane egg; and, according to Plato, he was the oldest of the gods.

arriving, one found it surrounded by a fence of bronze, triply reinforced with circles of darkest night. Before arrival, it was necessary to cross the river Styx in the boat of the aged and dirty ferryman Charon and to pay his carriage fare; and, for this reason, it was customary to place a silver coin in the mouth of every Greek corpse before it was buried. After the brazen gates were passed, the floor of Tartarus was not reached until a full year had run its course; because, for that long period, each newly arrived spirit was cruelly tossed about by the dark and loathsome blasts which constantly churned the entire region. Here was the dwelling place of both Night (Nyx) and Day (Hemera), who periodically passed each other at the brazen gates—the one entering always as the other left; and before those awful portals crouched the three-headed dog Cerberus, who gave welcome entrance to all new spirits, but strictly guarded against any departure which they might attempt. Nearby, stood patient Atlas, ceaselessly upholding Heaven (Uranus) and (perhaps) Earth—a penalty imposed upon him by the victorious Zeus because he was a leading, and defeated, actor in the War of the Titans. Within the Tartarean bounds dwelt not only the spirits of departed mankind, but also Death (Thanatos) and other fearsome beings[4] with ghostly forms emitting the piteous shrieks which are inseparably linked with all thoughts of the inferno. And through the endless caverns flowed the black Acheron, the wailing Cocytus, and the mysterious river Lethe, whose quaffed waters sometimes mercifully brought forgetfulness.[5]

Eros, fourth and last of the primeval deities, was the powerful personification of love—conceived as the irresistible and uniting influence responsible for reducing the conflicting ele-

ments of Chaos to the harmony and order necessary for the world's completion. He should not be confused with the later Eros, known to the Romans as Cupid, and being the mischievous, little son of Aphrodite who was in the habit of directing his love arrows to such objects as his volatile fancy suggested, without regard to the happiness or misery which he might thus create.[6] The original Eros was a serious and fundamental cause in the scheme of creation, and persisted as the force which ruled the councils of both gods and men for the ultimate and common good of all. This philosophic conception was above the level of personal amours and he, alone of the primeval deities, had no offspring to become actors in the fascinating theogony, which to the ancient Greeks was both their history and their religion.

1. The Descendants of Chaos

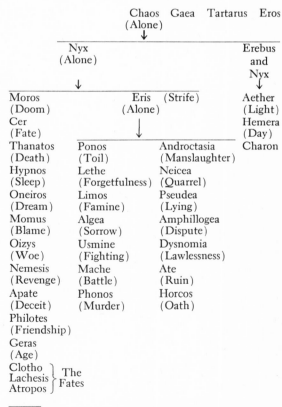

		Chaos	Gaea	Tartarus	Eros
		(Alone)			
		↓			
	Nyx				Erebus
	(Alone)				and
					Nyx
	↓				↓
Moros		Eris	(Strife)		Aether
(Doom)		(Alone)			(Light)
Cer					Hemera
(Fate)		↓			(Day)
Thanatos	Ponos		Androctasia		Charon
(Death)	(Toil)		(Manslaughter)		
Hypnos	Lethe		Neicea		
(Sleep)	(Forgetfulness)		(Quarrel)		
Oneiros	Limos		Pseudea		
(Dream)	(Famine)		(Lying)		
Momus	Algea		Amphillogea		
(Blame)	(Sorrow)		(Dispute)		
Oizys	Usmine		Dysnomia		
(Woe)	(Fighting)		(Lawlessness)		
Nemesis	Mache		Ate		
(Revenge)	(Battle)		(Ruin)		
Apate	Phonos		Horcos		
(Deceit)	(Murder)		(Oath)		
Philotes					
(Friendship)					
Geras					
(Age)					
Clotho					
Lachesis } The					
Atropos } Fates					

---

[4] Among these creatures were: the avenging Furies, who were charged with the earthly punishment of murderers and other wrongdoers; Lamia, whose perpetual task was the slaughter of little children; Empousa, a destructive monster with one foot of brass and the other of an ass; and Eurynomus, a demon who fed on the flesh of the dead.

[5] The infernal rivers Cocytus and the burning Phlegethon (Periphlegethon) are said to have flowed out of the Styx in opposite directions, reuniting to increase the channel of the Acheron. The conception that the Isles of the Blest (known also as the Elysian Fields or Plains) were a division of Tartarus was that of later poets and is not mentioned by the older writers.

[6] The later Eros, or Cupid, has nothing to do with uniting the discordant elements of the universe or with the higher sympathy which binds mankind together. He is purely the god of sensual love, who bears sway over the inhabitants of Olympus as well as over men and all other living creatures.

The offspring of Chaos were a son, Erebus, and a daughter, Nyx. Erebus was conceived as the personification of the triple circles of darkness which surrounded deep Tartarus. Nyx was the personification of night, which falls upon the physical world as the inevitable successor of Day. By seeming paradox, these murky beings were made the parents of Aether and Hemera, respectively, the pure light which the ancients presumed to exist in the stratosphere[7] and the personification of day. Perhaps more in character, they also produced Charon, the repulsive ferryman of the dead, whose eyes were "a steady flame"; and Nyx, alone, then bore children whose names are personifications of the various ills, conditions, or states of being which affect mankind. The order of their appearance (reading downward), as given by the poet Hesiod, is as follows:

Moros (Doom)	Oizys (Woe)
Cer (Fate)	Nemesis (Revenge)[8]
Thanatos (Death)	Apate (Deceit)
Hypnos (Sleep)	Philotes (Friendship)
Oneiros (Dream)	Geras (Age)
Momus (Blame)	Eris (Strife)

Nyx also bore the three Fates, whose names were Clotho, Lachesis, and Atropos. These maiden-deities were sometimes called the Destinies, the Moerae, or Parcae; and it was they who, at each birth, spun, measured, and cut off the thread of life, which immutably governed the individual lot of every person from his birth to the grave.

Eris, the goddess of strife and discord, and the last-born child of Nyx, was a daughter whose progeny were as unlovely as her title might indicate. Perhaps because no self-respecting male would care to father such a a brood, she became *sua sponte* the mother of:

Ponos (Toil)	Androctasia (Manslaughter)
Lethe (Forgetfulness)	Neicea (Quarrel)
Limos (Famine)	Pseudea (Lying)
Algea (Sorrow)	Amphillogea (Dispute)
Usmine (Fighting)	Dysnomia (Lawlessness)
Mache (Battle)	Ate (Ruin)
Phonos (Murder)	Horcos (Oath)

These children were not confined to a nursery, but were permitted to go out into the world where they immediately became unwelcome attendants upon both the immortal gods and defenseless mankind. But, some say that they were placed in a chest and later released, when Pandora's curiosity caused her to raise its lid.

2. The Descendants of Tartarus

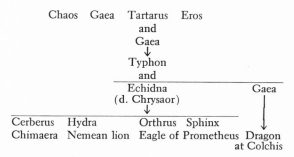

The descendants of Tartarus will next be noted, although in order of primeval emergence he was preceded by Gaea.

By Gaea, Tartarus had a son who was at once the most prodigious and fearsome monster ever brought into being. He was Typhon,[9] the demon of the whirlwind, in both size and strength surpassing the Sea itself. As he strode the earth, mountains were toppled over or crushed in by his heavy tread; and the distant stars were brushed aside from their places in the skies by the restless and angered shaking of his gigantic head, out of whose eyes and mouth flashed streams of fire hot enough to melt Mount Ossa's hardest stone. As far as the thighs he was of human shape, but on his shoulders he carried a hundred heads, which darted forth envenomed

---

[7] Between the stratosphere (?) and the earth, proceeding downward, were encountered Nephelae (Clouds) and Aër (plain Air). In later writings, they were sometimes given status as divinities, but are not mentioned in the theogony of Hesiod. Other personifications—not usually deified—were: Achlys (Misery), Aidos (Shame), Eleos (Pity), Elpis (Hope), Euphrasia (Mirth), Himeros (Desire), Hybris (Pride), Mania (Madness), Peitho (Persuasion), Sophrosyne (Discretion), and Tyche (Fortune) who later, however, became deified as early as the fifth century.

[8] Nemesis was sometimes referred to as Adrasteia, Hypnos was known to the Romans as Morpheus.

[9] Typhon was sometimes called Typhoeus. A different version relates that Hera, unaided, gave birth to the giant in retaliation for Zeus' having produced Athena from his own aching head. By the Greeks, Typhon was considered as identical with Set, an Egyptian god of evil and darkness.

serpent-tongues spraying showers of fiery brimstone. From the thighs down were huge vipers which, drawn out to full length, themselves reached to the heavens. Such a creature, as one might well imagine, was good for nothing but waste, pillage, and destruction; and, in his savage pride, he attempted to destroy even the gods themselves—and almost succeeded.

Typhon embraced Echidna, a daughter of the winged horse Chrysaor; and by her brought into being weird offspring which bulk large in mythological stories. These were:

Cerberus, the terrible three-headed dog at the bronze gates of Tartarus, which permitted no imprisoned spirit to escape from that abode of the dead;

Chimaera, a fire-breathing monster reared in the land of the mysterious Arimi, whose body (beginning at the head) was successively that of a lion, a goat, and a dragon;

Hydra, a venomous serpent of Lerna, which sprouted two extra heads whenever one was lopped off;

The Nemean lion, whose extinction was the first of the famed Twelve Labors of Heracles;

Orthrus, the two-headed hound owned by Geryon, who was himself three men grown into one;

The Eagle, which each night consumed the regrowing liver of Prometheus, while he suffered in manacles on the mountainside of Caucasus as a result of his defiance of supreme Zeus in bringing fire to mankind;

The Sphinx, a lion-bodied maiden, who dashed headlong from her rocky perch outside the gates of Boeotian Thebes when her mystic riddle was solved by young Oedipus.

The last issue of Typhon was equally monstrous. For, impregnated with a single drop of blood which fell from the giant creature's head when he was struck with a thunderbolt of Zeus, Gaea give birth to the sleepless dragon which guarded the Golden Fleece of the winged ram in the kingdom of King Aeëtes at Colchis.

Further details about the members of this grim family will be noted later in connection with various stories, primarily involving others but indirectly concerning them.

3. The Immediate Descendants of Gaea

Chaos	Gaea (Alone)	Tartarus	Eros
	↓		
Pontus (Chart 5)	Uranus (Chart 6)	Actaeus Cecrops Cranaus	

The first, and unfathered, offspring of Gaea were Pontus[10] and Uranus,[11] being, respectively, personifications of the sea and the heavens—the latter being given a dignity equal to that of his mother and "to be an ever-sure abiding place for the blessed gods."

She then bore a number of male children known as Autochthons (meaning earthborn) whose bodies, in their lower portions, were those of dragons. Of these unfathered sons, the most prominent were associated with the myths of Attica and were named Actaeus, Cecrops, and Cranaus.

The autochthons were created in legend by the imaginations of patriotic Greeks with whose cities they were inseparably connected. They will be later noted more fully, but, since they were immediate descendants of Gaea, their family chart is given here:

4. The Descendants of the Autochthons

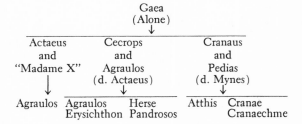

The charted autochthons were indigenous to Attica. Other legends mention Gyes in Boeotia and Lelex at Sparta.

Pontus and Gaea had two daughters named Ceto and Eurybia, and three sons named Phorcys, Nereus, and Thaumas.

---

[10] Hyginus calls Pontus a son of Aether and Gaea, and Roman mythology mentions him only as a name for the sea.

[11] Uranus was called Coelus by the Romans. According to a later legend, he had a father whose name was Acmon.

5. The Descendants of Pontus and Gaea

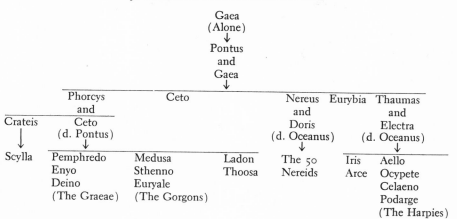

		Gaea (Alone) ↓ Pontus and Gaea ↓					
	Phorcys and	Ceto		Nereus and	Eurybia	Thaumas and	
Crateis	Ceto (d. Pontus)			Doris (d. Oceanus)		Electra (d. Oceanus)	
↓	↓			↓		↓	
Scylla	Pemphredo Enyo Deino (The Graeae)	Medusa Sthenno Euryale (The Gorgons)	Ladon Thoosa	The 50 Nereids	Iris Arce	Aello Ocypete Celaeno Podarge (The Harpies)	

Eurybia married the Titan Crius, but Ceto married her own brother, Phorcys, and their union produced a curious issue, commingling the horrible with the mysterious. They first had three daughters, known collectively as the Graeae because they had grey hair when they were born. These old crones had the figure of swans but had only one eye and one tooth in common—living tools which were passed about by hand and deposited in a coffin when not in use. Their names were Pemphredo, Enyo, and Deino.[12]

A second trinity of daughters born to Phorcys and Ceto were known as the Gorgons, and were individually named Sthenno, Euryale, and Medusa.[13] They had wings, brazen claws, and enormous teeth. Instead of hair, each wore a nest of serpents on her head. Sthenno and Euryale were immortal; but although Medusa was mortal, even after death the sight of her snaky tresses changed every spectator suddenly into stone. It was her extinction which first brought fame to the hero Perseus; and from drops of her blood, which fell into the sea when her head was cut off, sprang the winged-horses Pegasus and Chrysaor.

Ladon and Thoösa were the last two offspring of Phorcys and Ceto. Ladon was a remarkable dragon who could assume various tones of voice and was posted as guardian of the golden apples of the Hesperides. For his somewhat doubtful services (because he did not always protect the golden apples), Hera eventually translated him to the skies as the constellation Draco, which winds in and out between Lyra and the Bears.[14]

Thoösa was espoused by Poseidon and became mother of the one-eyed giant Polyphemus, a man-eating creature who will be mentioned in more detail when we come to recount the perils overcome by Odysseus on his return from the Trojan War.

By Crateïs, Phorcys had a daughter Scylla, differing greatly from the children mothered by Ceto. She was endowed with feminine charms which so attracted the Sea-god Poseidon that his wife Amphitrite became jealous and threw some magic herbs into the well where her rival was bathing. Thereupon, the innocent maiden was changed into a barking sea terror with twelve feet and six long mouths containing triple sets of teeth, and was placed on a rock between Italy and Sicily, where she often brought destruction and shipwreck to unwary mariners.

Nereus and Doris, a daughter of Oceanus, produced fifty fair daughters, known as the

---

[12] It was commonly believed that the Graeae (or Phorcides as they were called from their father's name) were marine divinities who represented personifications of the white foam of the sea.

[13] Homer mentions only Gorgo, who was a frightful phantom seen in the realm of Hades. According to some, Medusa was at first a beautiful maiden whose hair was changed into serpents by Athena, in consequence of her having been intimate with Poseidon in a temple dedicated to the stern goddess.

---

[14] A different story considers the constellation Draco as the heavenly apotheosis of the dragon-son of Ares who was slain by Cadmus.

Nereids (Neriades), whose names are given by Hesiod[15] as follows:

Actaea	Eucrante	Hippothoë	Ploto
Agave	Eudora	Laomedeia	Polynoë
Alimede	Eulimene	Leagora	Pontoporea
Amphitrite[16]	Eunice	Lysianassa	Pronoea
Autonoë	Eupompe	Melite	Proto
Cymo	Evagora	Menippe	Protomedeia
Cymodoce	Evarne	Nemertes	Psamathe
Cymothoë	Galateia	Nesaea	Sao
Doris	Galena	Neso	Speio
Doto	Glauce	Panopeia	Themisto
Dynamene	Glauconome	Pasithea	Thetis
Eione	Halia	Pherusa	Thoë
Erato	Hippothoë		

Of these beautiful sea-nymphs, Amphitrite married Poseidon and became queen of the sea; Thetis married Peleus and became mother of the warrior Achilles; and others had children whose actions will be related in subsequent pages.

Thaumas married Electra, likewise a daughter of Oceanus, and by her had six daughters—not all of whom, however, could legitimately be described as either fair or beautiful. The first of them was Iris, messenger of the gods[17] and their darling, who was sometimes considered as a personification of the rainbow. She was not only a messenger between the gods themselves, but also between the gods and mortals; and sometimes, she even initiated messages of her own.

The sisters of Iris were not so happily conceived—or treated. Arce mistakenly sided with the Titans in their losing war with Zeus and was cruelly punished by being deprived of her wings and cast into the depths of Tartarus. According to a later legend, her stripped wings were afterward given to the hero Achilles and permitted him to travel with the speed of the wind—a mythical mobility of great value.

The other sisters of Iris—four in number named Aëllo, Ocypete, Celaeno, and Podarge—were the foul Harpies,[18] who were horrid birds with the heads of maidens. As described by Aeschylus, "with breathings unapproachable they snore and forth from their eyes drippeth a loathsome rheum." In view of these rather doubtful charms, it may be surprising to learn that one of the ladies (Podarge) was able to capture the West-wind as her husband—but her children were horses.

Uranus, the second son of Gaea, by union with his mother produced the mighty dynasty known as the Titans, fated to rule imperiously for a while, but eventually to be soundly whipped and removed from both heaven and earth. In order of birth, the Titans[19] were Oceanus, Coeus, Crius, Hyperion, Iapetus, Theia,[20] Rhea,[21] Themis,[22] Mnemos-

---

[15] Homer gives a partial list of the Nereids which contains names not mentioned by Apollodorus, namely: Thaleia, Limnoreia, Iaera, Amphithoë, Dexamene, Amphinome, Callianeira, Apseudes, Callianassa, Clymene, Ianeira, Ianassa, Maera, Oreithyia, and Amatheia.

[16] Apollodorus calls Amphitrite an Oceanid. When Poseidon sued for her hand, she fled to Atlas, but her lover sent spies after her. Among them was Delphinus, who brought about her marriage to Poseidon; and the grateful god rewarded his services by placing him among the stars as the constellation which we know as the Dolphin or Job's Coffin.

[17] In the earlier poets Iris appears as a virgin goddess; but, according to later writers, she was married to Zephyrus, and became by him the mother of the second Eros (Cupid). The Odyssey does not mention her, but only Hermes, as the messenger of the gods; however, in the Iliad she appears in the role more frequently than he does. She is sometimes called Aëllopus.

[18] The Harpies were conceived as Storm-winds and, when a person suddenly disappeared from earth, it was supposed that he had been carried off by them.

[19] Apollonius Rhodius names Ophion and Eurynome as the original Titans, who first ruled from Mount Olympus.

[20] The female Titans (Titanesses) were renowned not only as mothers of illustrious children but also in their individual activities. Thus, Theia, as the mother of the Sun, the Moon, and the Dawn was herself often considered as the principle of Light to whom was attributed the brightness of her offspring.

[21] Rhea was considered as the successor of Gaea to the title of Mother Earth and was also surnamed Berecynthia and Dindymene. At Rome, under the name of Ops, she was deeply revered as the unceasing producer of all plant life and fertility. As Cybele, her worship was introduced into both Greece and Italy from Phrygia. She was said to have been tenderly attached to a handsome youth named Attis (Attys, Atys), who proved unfaithful to her and was thrown by the goddess into a fit of madness which provoked his self-destruction. In sorrow for her hasty action, she instituted a yearly mourning for him, which served as the occasion for ecstatic orgies wherein her followers—who worshipped the goddess under her surname of Agdistis—were accustomed to wound and gnash themselves in a most frightful manner.

[22] In the Homeric poems, Themis is the personification of law and order and is described as reigning in the assemblies of both men and gods. She was also considered as an ancient prophetic deity and is said to have been in possession of the Delphic oracle, as successor of

6. The Immediate Descendants of Uranus and Gaea

Gaea
(Alone)
↓
Uranus
and
Gaea
↓

Oceanus	Theia	Cronus	Brontes	Cottus	Tisiphone	Melian Nymphs
Coeus	Rhea		Arges	Briareus	Alecto	Giants
Crius	Themis		(Pyracmon)	(Aegaeon)	Megaera	
Hyperion	Mnemosyne		Steropes	Gyes	(The Furies)	
Iapetus	Phoebe		(The Cyclopes)	(The Hecatoncheires)		
	Tethys					

yne,[23] Phoebe,[24] Tethys,[25] and Cronus.[26]

Following the Titans, Gaea bore to Uranus the over-bearing Cyclopes, whose names were Brontes, Steropes, and Arges (sometimes called Pyracmon). They in all else were like gods, but one eye only was set in the middle of their foreheads; and they were accustomed to play with thunderbolts and lightning as mere tools of sport.[27]

Next, Uranus and Gaea produced "presumptuous children" called the Hecatoncheires,[28] whose names were Cottus, Briareus, and Gyes.[29] Each of these creatures had fifty heads and a hundred arms, and their strength was well-nigh irresistible.

Uranus, being none to happy about siring such enormities, hated both the Cyclopes and the Hecatoncheires and, in fear of their strength, confined them in a secret place beneath the earth from which he forbade them to return to the light of day. But Mother Gaea grieved at their imprisonment and shaped a great sickle of stone, which she gave to her youngest son Cronus for use against his father. With it he lay in ambush and, attacking Uranus, lopped off his genitals, from whose blood sprang up the avenging deities known as the Furies. Their names were Tisiphone, Alecto, and Megaera; and to them was assigned the function of relentlessly pursuing all persons who might be guilty of shedding a kinsman's blood.[30]

Other creatures, similarly born, were the Giants[31] and also the Melian nymphs who were accustomed to inhabit ash trees, from whose wood the shafts of battle spears were always made. Moreover, it is fancifully said that one drop of the god's blood, cast into the sea, pro-

---

Gaea and previous to its assumption by Apollo. She is represented in the skies as Libra, the seventh sign of the zodiac.

[23] Mnemosyne was the goddess of memory and mother of the nine Muses.

[24] According to Aeschylus, Phoebe succeeded Themis as the presiding deity at Delphi. When the oracular shrine was adopted by her grandson Apollo, he assumed the name Phoebus as an added title.

[25] In the Iliad, Tethys is pictured as such a wonderful mother that Rhea entrusted Hera's childhood education to her.

[26] Various descendants of the Titans are themselves sometimes called Titans, namely: Prometheus, Hecate, Leto, Helios, Selene, and Circe. Similarly, both Helios and Apollo—later considered gods of the sun—are sometimes referred to as Hyperion, who was their predecessor in the role.

[27] Homer paints the Cyclopes as a gigantic and lawless cannibal race of Shepherds; and in the Odyssey, where Polyphemus is named as their chief, Poseidon is called their sire. Later traditions, increasing the number to one hundred, regarded them as assistants to Hephaestus, who hammered at their fiery forges so lustily that all of the neighboring country was shaken.

[28] Since the Hecatoncheires had a hundred hands, the Romans referred to them as the Centimanes.

[29] Homer says that men called Briareus "Aegaeon." Perhaps because of his great strength, Virgil counts him

as one of the Giants who warred against the Olympians. Other writers regard him as a marine god—son of Pontus and Gaea—who lived in the Aegean Sea with his wife Cympoleia, a daughter of Poseidon and an unnamed mother.

[30] The Furies were also called the Erinnyes, the Eumenides, or the Dirae; and the surname Alastor was indiscriminately applied to each of them separately. According to the Homeric notion, they were reckoned among the inhabitants of the lower world, where they were accustomed to rest until some curse pronounced upon a criminal called them to life and activity; and the crimes which they punished were not limited to the slaying of kin, but also comprehended others of lesser degree. Aeschylus, however, limits their function to the hounding of those guilty of shedding a kinsman's blood.

[31] The names of the principal Giants (Gigantes) were: Agrius, Alcyoneus, Enceladus, Clytius, Ephialtes, Eurymedon, Eurytus, Gration, Hippolytus, Merops, Mimas, Pallas, Polybotes, Porphyrion, and Thoas.

duced Aphrodite, the goddess of love; and, owing to this legend, she was sometimes called "foam-born."

The personified Uranus, having served the usefulness for which he was created, now retires from an active part in the mythological pantheon, but only after grimly prophesying that dire retribution will surely overtake his undutiful son.

Succeeding him, the Titans raised Cronus to the throne,[32] after first liberating their monstrous brothers from the dark place of their imprisonment. Heedful of his father's prophesy, the first act of the new sovereign was to get rid of possible troublemakers, and he reimprisoned the Cyclopes and the Hecatoncheires—this time in Tartarus, where he set the huge, female dragon Campe to be their guard. Then, following the example of his sire, he took his own sister Rhea as his wife; and by her had three daughters and three sons named Hestia, Demeter, Hera, Hades, Poseidon, and Zeus, respectively.

Fearing that, he also, might be dethroned by one of his children, Cronus adopted the ghastly device of swallowing them as they were successively born. This worked very well until Rhea, *enceinte* with her sixth, decided that both Cronus and she had had enough, and went to Mother Gaea for counsel. When Zeus was about to be born, she retired with Gaea to the island of Crete where, upon birth, her child was hidden in a deep cave. Slyly, Gaea wrapped a great stone in swaddling clothes and presented it to Cronus, who promptly swallowed it in the belief that he was proceeding according to plan.

Ida and Adrasteia,[33] daughters of the Cretan king, Melisseus, were appointed as nurses for the infant and reared him on the proverbial ambrosia and nectar—supplemented with plain milk from the goat Amaltheia. For her services, as perhaps the first wetnurse, she was eventually

translated to the skies as Capricornus, the tenth sign of the zodiac; but, before her apotheosis, Zeus broke off one of her horns and gave it to the daughters of Melisseus, after endowing it with the power to become filled with whatsoever its possessors might desire. Thus, the cornucopia, or horn of plenty, was created which has been mentioned so often in literature.[34]

To keep father Cronus from discovering the deceit practiced upon him, the baby cries of the newborn child were drowned out by the Curetes, a boisterous crew of lesser divinities, who were in the habit of making loud noises on their drums and brazen cymbals so continuously that he never suspected them of anything more than plain frenzy and exuberance of spirits.[35] So, the old god continued to rule heaven and earth—with perhaps an occasional chuckle of self-satisfaction in the belief that he had warded off all possibility of his downfall.

When Zeus became fully grown he met Metis, the wisest daughter of Oceanus and, with her assistance, Cronus was induced to sip of a potion which contained a powerful emetic.[36] As a result, the great stone was disgorged, and was followed by the brothers and sisters of Zeus in the reverse order of their earlier swallowing. The stone was later set up outside the entrance to the oracle at Delphi and, for centuries, was pointed to as proving the truth of the story which we have narrated.

---

[32] Cronus was called Saturn by the Romans. To us, by a later confusion with Chronus, he is "Father Time" —the root of our "chronology."

[33] Various writers give different names to the nurses of Zeus, as their fancies may direct. Hyginus calls them Aega and Helice and, by naming Olenus—a son of Hephaestus—as their father, gives them the impossible care of their infant great-grandfather.

[34] The generally accepted tradition is that Amaltheia was the name of the she-goat that suckled the infant Zeus; but, according to some, she was a nymph who found the goat and was a daughter of Oceanus or Melisseus. Although her translation to the skies is not disputed, the horn of plenty is sometimes said to be a horn of the river Achelous, broken off by Heracles in a wrestling match for the hand of Deianeira.

[35] The Curetes of Crete were sometimes confused with the Phrygian Corybantes. They were originally three in number named Corybas, Pyrrhus, and Idaeus and were supposed to dwell on Mount Ida in Crete. In their ceremonial processions, they danced in armor, making confused noises with their drums, cymbals, and pipes; and, howling like insane persons, were in the habit of slashing their own flesh. Some writers confuse them with the mysterious Cabeiri and the Idaean Dactyls—which later were said to have been the discoverers of iron and the first to work that metal into instruments for human use.

[36] Other accounts give to Gaea, or to Thetis, credit for mixing the emetic and inducing Cronus to drink the potion in which it was concealed.

2

The Rise of Zeus to Supremacy

The War of the Titans

FURIOUS AT THE unnatural action of their father, Zeus and his brothers determined to wrest from Cronus the power which he had so cruelly abused.

A meeting was convoked on Mount Olympus in Thessaly, where Zeus announced that all who aided him should be undisturbed in their godly functions until the end of time. The first who responded was Styx, the river-goddess daughter of Oceanus—and wife of Pallas, who was a son of Crius. Although Styx was both the daughter and daughter-in-law of a Titan, she pledged herself to support Zeus' cause and promised also the powerful help of her four children, whose names were Bia (Force), Cratos (Strength), Nike (Victory), and Zelus (Emulation). This surprising offer was gladly accepted by him and, as a reward, he conferred upon the goddess the high honor of having her name used thereafter by all of the gods in giving oaths which were intended to be inviolable. The valuable assistance given by the children of Styx was in full keeping with a normal expectation from the anglicized meanings of their names, and Zeus retained all four of them ever after to be his attendants in battle.

In the war which followed,[1] all of the Titans, except Oceanus, took the part of Cronus and were assisted by Atlas and Menoetius, two of

---

[1] It was known as the Titanomachia, or War of the Titans.

7. The Descendants of Styx

Gaea
(Alone)
↓
Uranus
and
Gaea
↓
Crius
and
Eurybia
(d. Pontus)
↓
Pallas
and
Styx
(d. Oceanus)
↓

| Bia | Cratos |
| Nike | Zelus |

the four sons of Iapetus. Being perhaps more farsighted, his remaining sons—Prometheus and Epimetheus—aligned themselves with the forces of Zeus. As we shall note later, this was a rather thoughtful act and was mythologically important, if not actually necessary, in connection with the preservation of the lowly human race.

The Titans entrenched themselves in the Othrys Mountains, at the southern border of Thessaly, and Zeus established his headquarters on Mount Olympus, about fifty miles to the north. In the broad plain between, a gigantic battle was fought continuously for ten years, without either party gaining the victory. In this stalemate, Zeus remembered the cunning of

Mother Gaea, whose stratagem had preserved him from being swallowed by his father, and sought audience with her. It was her advice that he should enlist the help of the Cyclopes and Hecatoncheires, whom Cronus had previously thrust into their Tartarean dungeon. Somehow, without being apprehended, Zeus descended to the lower world, slew the guardian-dragon Campe and released her huge prisoners. The liberated creatures came storming upon the Thessalian battlefield in such haste and fury that the earth trembled as though the end of all things had come. And, the end had come for Cronus and his followers because the Cyclopes with their thunder and lightning, and the Hecatoncheires with their muscular strength, proved themselves to be just the added power necessary to vanquish the enemy. It was during the heat of this conflict that old Chaos writhed with an uneasy warmth, and far away Oceanus was deeply troubled by the boiling which was generated in his usually frigid waters.

The victorious Zeus now thrust all of the opposing Titans into Tartarus, where they were enclosed with a wall of brass, provided by Poseidon, and the Hecatoncheires were appointed to become their relentless jailers forever. Menoetius was also imprisoned with his Titan father, and his brother Atlas was punished by being forced perpetually to uphold both the heavens and the earth.[2]

The Assault of Typhon

Following the overthrow of the Titans, Zeus became the supreme sovereign (either through election or casting of lots). He appointed Poseidon to rule all the waters, delegated to Hades the government of Tartarus, and kept for himself sole dominion over earth and the heavens—with a lordly set of mansions on Mount Olympus, for use as a divine dwelling place and as a general meeting ground for all of the gods.

Just when all seemed calm, a new menace presented itself. Although Gaea had been an invaluable ally in the war against Cronus, she perhaps felt some compunction upon seeing the treatment given to the losers, for they, too, were her own grandchildren. By union with Tartarus, she produced the huge Typhon and sent him forth to destroy the forces of Zeus. After hurling kindled rocks at the gods, who were assembled on Mount Olympus, the monster moved in to tear them from their sacred habitation; and the terror-stricken deities fled to Egypt, where they changed themselves into animals in order to avoid detection and further pursuit.[3] Zeus alone remained to fight off the demon of the whirlwind whom he pelted with thunderbolts and cruelly wounded by strokes of the adamantine sickle which Gaea had originally fashioned for Cronus to use against his sire Uranus. Now Typhon fled, but Zeus followed and cornered him in Syria—only to be encircled and held powerless in the coils of the serpents which covered his enemy's lower body. Wresting the sharp sickle from the king of the gods, Typhon triumphantly cut out the sinews from his hands and feet and bore his victim, struggling but impotent, into a dark cavern in Cilicia, where he hid the sinews in a bearskin, which he set the she-dragon Delphyne to watch over. Victorious, he then lay down to rest; but, as he slept, Hermes, the quick son of Zeus, stole the sinews from the bearskin and, with the help of his half brother Aegipan, deftly refitted them to his father's useless limbs. The god, now restored to power, chased Typhon with thunderbolts

---

[2] According to Hesiod, Atlas was forced to support only the heavens; and this view appears the more logical when we learn that Heracles, in quest of the golden apples of the Hesperides, went to the land of the Hyperboreans and there temporarily relieved the giant of his burden. Ovid relates that Atlas was originally a man whom Perseus asked for shelter, as he was returning with the head of the Gorgon Medusa; and that, upon his request being refused, Perseus exhibited his trophy, which had the effect of turning his reluctant host into the stone peak of North Africa known as Mount Atlas—upon which the heavens and stars were supposed to rest. From this conceit we derive the word "atlas" for our globe.

[3] Some accounts state that Hera and Athena stood fast with Zeus when the other Olympians fled to Egypt. Aphrodite and her son Eros (Cupid) changed themselves into two fishes—a transformation installed in the heavens as Pisces, which is the twelfth sign of the zodiac. In an attempt to explain why many of the Egyptian gods were depicted as animals, it was said that they were the same with the Greek deities in their changed forms, thus acquired to escape from Typhon. However, archeological proofs show that these animal-gods were known and worshipped in Egypt many years before the Greek mythology was developed.

over sea and mountain to the island of Sicily and heaved Mount Aetna upon his frightful head. There, as all little Sicilians know, the monster still lies, with his fiery breath to this day periodically issuing forth as he ceaselessly struggles to regain his freedom.

The Battle With the Giants

The frustrated Gaea was furious at Typhon's overthrow and next sent forth, against Zeus and his Olympians, the powerful Giants (Gigantes) who had sprung from the blood of mangled Uranus as he lay stricken on her "broad bosom." These creatures were more like men than were Typhon, the Cyclopes, or the Hecatoncheires, but the lower parts of their bodies were those of scaly dragons. Their strength was such that they habitually carried huge rocks and tree trunks as weapons; and an oracle had foretold that the gods could never overcome them except with mortal help. All-knowing Gaea, aware of the prediction, created a magic herb, whose effect was intended to offset the power of the oracle; but Zeus forbade the Sun (Helios), the Moon (Selene), and the Dawn (Eos) to shine and then, before Gaea could stop him, plucked the herb from its roots and summoned Heracles—a mighty son borne to him by Alcmena under circumstances narrated later in detail. With assurance of this mortal help, the Olympians went forth to meet the attack.

The names of the principal Giants who engaged in the ensuing battle[4] were Alcyoneus, Clytius, Pallas, Gration, Porphyrion, Mimas, Polybotes, Agrius, Ephialtes, Enceladus, Hippolytus, Thoas, and Eurytus.

At the approach of the gods, the Giants fell back to the peninsula of Pallene (or Phlegra) in Chalcidice, where they had been born. Immortality had been granted to Alcyoneus so long as he fought on that country's soil. Against him, Heracles directed his first arrow, which inevitably found its mark, but, having fallen to the ground of Pallene, the Giant promptly revived

as his amazed adversary approached to complete the kill. Athena whispered to her mortal brother the secret accompanying Alcyoneus' birth, whereupon Heracles dragged him out of the peninsula into the mainland and was gratified to see his life depart. The next victim was Porphyrion, who lustfully attacked Hera, only to be slain by the simultaneous arrival of an arrow from Heracles and a thunderbolt from Zeus. Apollo then collaborated with Heracles and their dual discharge of arrows caught Ephialtes —one arrow in each eye. Eurytus was killed by Dionysus with his thyrsus (an odd sort of staff with a deadly point); and Hecate burned Clytius to death with the blazing torch which she always carried. Mimas had the misfortune to be on the receiving end of red-hot missiles of metal cast by Hephaestus; and Athena first threw the island of Sicily on Enceladus and then flayed Pallas as he tried to flee.[5] Polybotes was chased through the sea by Poseidon until he came to Cos, where the god broke off a piece of the island and buried him beneath it. Hermes, wearing the helmet of Hades which made him invisible, slew the unsuspecting Hippolytus; and Artemis shot an arrow through Gration's heart. The deadly Fates, fighting with brazen clubs, killed Agrius and Thoas; and the other Giants were destroyed with thunderbolts by Zeus and arrows by Heracles as they lay dying. Thus, all the Giants were undone, and the conquering gods returned to Mount Olympus to celebrate their victory.

Two of the Giants—Eurymedon and Merops —did not engage in the battle and lived to produce offspring who figure in later mythological stories. Their family-tree is here noted:

---

[4] It was known as the Gigantomachia.

[5] It was this martial exploit which gave to Athena the double name of Pallas Athena. Another, and rather labored, explanation is that she was sometimes called Pallas from the verb pallo (meaning "I swing") because she was constantly swinging her battleshield to ward off antagonistic influences. A third version finds the derivation of her double name in her childhood association with Pallas, a daughter of the river-god Triton, who was mortally wounded while she and the goddess engaged in a girlish play at arms.

8. The Descendants of the Giants

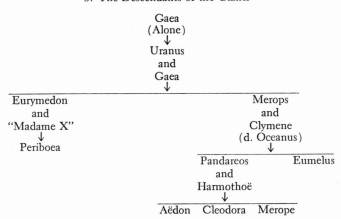

3

The Olympian Deities

ALTHOUGH ZEUS was admittedly the supreme ruler of both heaven and earth, he was assisted in the administration of their, respectively celestial and mundane, affairs by a group who were usually referred to as the greater gods or the Olympians. Like all of the divinities, their food was ambrosia, they drank only nectar, and their veins flowed with an ethereal fluid called ichor. Those conventionally considered as composing this elite assembly were:[1]

Zeus (Jupiter or Jove)
Hera (Juno) —his sister and wife
Athena (Minerva) —his daughter by Metis
Apollo ⎱—his children by Leto
Artemis (Diana) ⎰ (Latona)
Ares (Mars) ⎱
Hephaestus (Vulcan) ⎰—his children by Hera
Hebe (Juventas) ⎰
Aphrodite (Venus) —his daughter by Dione
Hermes (Mercury) —his son by Maia
Hestia (Vesta) ⎱—his sisters
Demeter (Ceres) ⎰

William Ewart Gladstone, the great English statesman, who found time in his busy life to make an exhaustive study of the myths, says that the distinctive qualities of the Olympians were that they were immortal, molded in hu-

man form, and enjoyed powers far exceeding those possessed by mortals. They were, however, liable to certain limitations of energy and knowledge—except Athena, who was never ignorant, deceived, or baffled; and they were subject to corporeal wants and human affections.

Gladstone does not include Hestia among the Olympians, but increases their number to twenty, who seem to have been given permission to ascend Mount Olympus at pleasure. In reaching this number, he adds:

Poseidon (Neptune)—brother of Zeus
Iris—daughter of Thaumas and Electra
Leto (Latona)—mother of Apollo and Artemis
Themis—daughter of Uranus and Gaea
Dione—mother of Aphrodite
Paeon—physician to the Olympians
Persephone (Proserpina)—daughter of Zeus and Demeter
Dionysus (Bacchus)—son of Zeus and Semele
Thetis—daughter of Nereus and Doris

We shall comment here individually only on those composing the conventional group of twelve; but the additional deities mentioned by Gladstone will be brought into our narrative, from time to time, as important actors on earth and as occasional visitors to heavenly Olympus.

Zeus

The circumstances attending the birth of Zeus, and his struggles with the Titans, the Giants, and Typhon have been related in chapter 2. As the presiding deity of the universe, the

---

[1] Where the Latin names for the deities differ from those used by the Greeks, they are placed in parentheses. In his scholarly *Handbook of Greek Mythology*, Professor H. J. Rose states that membership among the greater gods was anciently a matter of cult and not of mythology.

Greeks conceived Zeus to be the god who controlled the forces of nature, as well as the daily existence of men and the immortals. By shaking his fearful aegis,[2] he could produce storms, tempests, and darkness; at his command the sun and the moon paused in their courses; thunder, lightning, and rain were equally subject to his divine control. He was, therefore, often called the Thunderer, and was given many other natural appellatives, including Rainbringer (Jupiter Pluvius). From his father, he was sometimes called Cromion or Cronides.

9. The Pedigree of Zeus

Gaea
(Alone)
↓
Uranus
and
Gaea
↓
Cronus
and
Rhea
↓
Zeus

By his direction, the change of the seasons was brought about, and day followed night in regular and harmonious succession. As "father of gods and men," he settled disputes in heaven, assisted earthly princes in the just government of their peoples, and watched with paternal interest over the actions of all mortals. He rewarded truth, charity, and valor but severely punished perjury, cruelty, and cravenness. The Greeks believed that he lived with Hera in a lordly palace on Mount Olympus in Thessaly, constructed by Hephaestus of burnished gold, chased silver, and gleaming ivory. Lower on the mountain lived the other Olympians; and a third circle of mansions farther down, housed the demigods and the heroes whose earthly exploits had been rewarded by immortality. These lower dwellings were also the work of Hephaestus and their materials were of the same celestial splendor.

Zeus was first worshipped in Greece, at Dodona in Epeirus, where his voice was supposed to be heard in the rustling leaves of a giant oak tree, and was interpreted for suppliants by the priests of the shrine, who were called Selli or Helli.[3] From a number of leaden plates, which have been unearthed, advice from the oracle appears to have been sought not only by princes about their great affairs of state, but also by humbler folk concerning their more commonplace aspirations. We find one man asking for help in properly rearing his child; another inquires for a cure to bring back his lost health; and a third promises to make a handsome present to the shrine if a pending speculation in sheep should turn out well. It is fortunate that these little engraved petitions were made of lead because, had they been of more precious material they would undoubtedly have been carried off in the universal pillage which took place when Greece fell into the hands of invading barbarians.[4]

According to the historian Herodotus, an earlier shrine—dedicated to the Egyptian deity Ammon (whom the Greeks identified under the name Zeus-Ammon), their own chief god—was located at an oasis of Libya, or in the "hundred-gated" city of Egyptian Thebes.[5] However, the

---

[2] The aegis (said to be derived from the Greek word signifying "goat's skin") was made for Zeus by Hephaestus from the skin of the goat Amaltheia. It was sometimes loaned by Zeus to his favorite daughter Athena.

[3] From the name by which the Dodonean priests were called, some scholars derive the words Hellas and Hellenes—later appellatives of Greece and its inhabitants. Homer describes the Selli as "men of unwashed feet who slept on the ground."

[4] The Greeks gave the name of barbarians to all who did not speak their language.

[5] In the Bohn translation of Henry Cary, the story related by Herodotus is as follows:

"Concerning the two oracles, one in Greece, the other in Libya, the Egyptians give the following account. The priests of the Theban Jupiter say, that two women, employed in the temple, were carried away from Thebes by certain Phoenicians, and that one of them was discovered to have been sold into Libya, the other to the Greeks; and that these two women were the first who established oracles in the nations above mentioned. When I inquired how they knew this for a certainty, they answered, that they made diligent search for these women, and were never able to find them; but had afterwards heard the account they gave of them.

This, then, is the account I heard from the priests at Thebes; but the prophetesses of Dodona say, that two black pigeons flew away from Thebes in Egypt; that one of them went to Libya, and the other to them; that this last, sitting perched on an oak-tree proclaimed in a human voice, that it was fitting an oracle should be erected there to Jupiter; and that the people believed

later national seat of Zeus' worship in Greece was at Olympia in Elis. There, on a great plain, were located the stadium, in which the Olympic games were regularly held, and a magnificent temple—containing the colossal statue of the god which was modeled by Phidias in such perfection that it was accounted one of the seven wonders of the ancient world. This forty-foot image was made of gold and ivory and represented Zeus as seated on his throne. His head was crowned with an olive wreath, his right hand held the figure of Nike, the goddess of victory, and in his left hand he held his royal scepter surmounted by his sacred bird, the eagle. It is said that when the great sculptor had completed his sublime conception, the god sent a flash of lightning through the open roof of the temple to show his approval.

Hera

The place where Hera was born is variously stated, but the Aegean island of Samos was usually accorded the honor. However, in the first book of the Iliad, she herself announces that Argos, Sparta, and Mycenae are her favorite cities. She was reared by Oceanus and Tethys in their balmy dwelling place located at the

ends of the earth[6] and was nursed by the three daughters of the river-god Asterius. Without the knowledge of her parents, she was wedded to Zeus in the "garden of the gods," where Gaea created in her honor a tree of life bearing golden apples. Properly speaking, she was the only married goddess among the Olympians; and hence, was recognized as the divinity of marriage and childbirth.[7]

10. The Pedigree of Hera

Gaea
↓
Uranus
↓
Cronus
↓
Hera

With this background, Hera (especially under her Roman name of Saturnia) was often portrayed as a paragon of matronly virtues and dignity; but unfortunately, she was of a jealous disposition, which was not happily affected by the amorous peccadilloes of her great spouse; and much of her time was taken up in venting a hateful wrath on other women who attracted attention from the supreme ruler—and on their children fathered by him. Also, she was prone to quarrel over anything which she considered to be even a slight encroachment upon her queenly prerogatives; she was self-willed, proud, and sometimes deceitful; and more than once she provoked her lord and master to the use of violent language. Indeed, on one occasion, he hung her aloft in the clouds with iron anvils tied to her feet, because she had raised a storm to drive Heracles (Zeus' favored son) from his

---

this to be a divine message to them, and did accordingly. They add that the other pigeon, which flew into Libya, commanded the Libyans to found the oracle of Ammon; this also belongs to Jupiter. The priestesses of Dodona, of whom the eldest is named Promenia, the second Timarete, and the youngest Nicandra, gave this account; and the rest of the Dodonaeans, engaged in the service of the temple, agreed with them.

My opinion of these things is this: if the Phoenicians did really carry off the women employed in the temple, and sold the one of them into Libya and the other into Greece . . . this last woman, being reduced to slavery, erected a temple to Jupiter, under an oak that grew there; nothing being more natural than that she, who had been an attendant in the temple of Jupiter at Thebes, should retain the memory of it wherever she came. And after this, when she had learned the Greek language, she instituted an oracle; and she said that her sister in Libya had been sold by the same Phoenicians by whom she herself was sold.

The women, I conjecture, were called doves by the Dodoneans, because they were barbarians, and they seemed to chatter to them like birds; but after a time, when the woman spoke intelligibly to them, they presently reported that the dove had spoken with a human voice . . . . But in saying that the dove was black, they show that the woman was an Egyptian."

---

[6] The location of this ideally climated country is variously described as being in the extreme west or in the far-northern land of the Hyperboreans, who lived on an island beyond the place where the North wind (Boreas) blows. The island was both fertile and productive of every crop, grown and harvested twice a year because of the unusually balmy climate.

[7] In her role as goddess of childbirth, Hera was assisted (and sometimes supplanted) by her daughter Eileithyia, whom the Romans called Lucina. By some ancient writers, this abstract personage was multiplied into the daughters of Hera, and, with unnamed number, called the Eileithyiae. In later times, the birth function of both Hera and Eileithyia was considered as almost wholly centered in Artemis.

course, while the greatest of the gods was quietly napping.

However, Hera was greatly revered in the Peloponnesus, and the historian Herodotus attested the Greek respect for her by reciting the quaint story of Cleobis and Biton, in the following Bohn translation of Henry Cary:

When Solon had roused the attention of Croesus by relating many and happy circumstances concerning Tellus, Croesus, expecting at least to obtain the second place, asked, whom he had seen next to him. "Cleobis," said he, "and Biton, for they being natives of Argos, possessed a sufficient fortune, and withal such strength of body, that they were both alike victorious in the public games; and moreover the following story is related of them: when the Argives were celebrating a festival of Hera, it was necessary that their mother should be drawn to the temple in a chariot; but the oxen did not come from the field in time, the young men, being pressed for time, put themselves beneath the yoke, and drew the car in which their mother sate; and having conveyed it forty-five stades, they reached the temple. After they had done this in the sight of the assembled people, a most happy termination was put to their lives; and in them the Deity clearly showed, that it is better for a man to die than to live. For the men of Argos, who stood round, commended the strength of the youths, and the women blessed her as the mother of such sons; but the mother herself, transported with joy both on account of the action and its renown, stood before the image and prayed, that the goddess would grant to Cleobis and Biton, her own sons, who had so highly honored her, the greatest blessing man could receive. After this prayer, when they had sacrificed and partaken of the feast, the youths fell asleep in the temple itself, and never awoke more, but met with such a termination of life."

Athena

The first wife of Zeus was Metis, the wise daughter of Oceanus (and considered as the personification of prudence) who counseled her husband to give Cronus the magic emetic which produced the disgorgement of his brothers and sisters. When Metis was with child, Zeus was told by Gaea and Uranus that his wife would first have a daughter and, then, a son who would displace him as the supreme ruler. To circumvent this prophecy, the god proceeded to swallow her before her child was born.

When the time for birth arrived, Zeus was afflicted with a tremendous headache; Olympus shook to its deepest foundations; Gaea echoed a martial shout; Poseidon threw high his waters in foamy agitation; and Helios paused in his course through the heavens. At this climactic juncture, Prometheus struck the agonized god in the head with an axe[8] and, forthwith, from the cleft brow leapt a divine daughter—the fully grown goddess of wisdom—whom the Greeks called Athena, Pallas Athena, and the Maid.[9]

11. The Pedigree of Athena

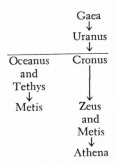

The goddess, thus born, immediately took her place in the Olympian assembly, to become distinguished as representing all that was great and noble in her sire, without exhibiting any of the mortal failings which characterized his actions in times of stress—and lovemaking. Being a direct emanation from his nobler self, she was given several of the supreme god's important prerogatives. She was permitted to hurl

---

[8] According to another account, it was Hephaestus who cleft Zeus' head; but, with an eye to chronology, those who assign the task to Prometheus appear to be the more logical.

[9] Some accounts describe Athena as "fully-armed" or "full-panoplied" as well as fully grown. These designations gave her the character of a female goddess of war. In this office, the Athenians referred to her as Athena Nike (Victory). Other surnames which they gave to her were Athena Polias (of the City), Athena Ergane (Worker), Athena Hygeia (Health), and Athena Parthenos (Virgin). She was sometimes called Tritogeneia, Trito, or Tritonis because the place of her birth was said to have been at the river Triton—in Egypt or in Boeotia; and from the Boeotian tradition, she derived the name Alalcomeneis—meaning the Powerful and identified with a local town on the banks of the river. Her Roman name—Minerva—was a personification of the noun meaning wisdom. The owl was considered her sacred bird.

the thunderbolt, she carried her own dread aegis, made from the skin of the flayed Giant Pallas,[10] she was endowed with the power of prophecy which she could bestow upon mortals, and she acted as Zeus' deputy in maintaining law, order, and justice.[11] As the patroness of art, science, and learning, she presided over all useful inventions and discoveries; and in this role, she was the supervising architect of the ship Argo and of the Wooden Horse, in which the Greeks later concealed themselves at Troy.

In addition to the many functions which she exercised in connection with general government and statecraft, Athena governed the feminine industry of spinning and weaving; and, in this department, we find perhaps the only mythological story which casts discredit upon her. Being the presiding deity, she felt that she could permit no one to rival her own handiwork; but she was challenged by her pupil Arachne, who wove a piece of tapestry, depicting the amours of the gods in such perfection that no fault could be found with its workmanship. When the humiliated goddess tore up the pattern, Arachne despairingly hanged herself. Stung with pity, Athena loosened the rope and saved the maiden's life; but the rope was changed into a cobweb and Arachne was changed into a spider.

Many other incidents, involving this greatest of the Greek goddesses, are related in the pages which follow, but it is appropriate here to add the story of her close connection with the city of Athens—named in her honor. It is thus told by Apollodorus, in the Loeb translation of Sir J. G. Frazer:

Cecrops, a son of the soil, with a body composed of man and serpent, was the first king of Attica, and the country which was formerly called Acte he named Cecropia after himself. In his time, they say, the gods resolved to take possession of cities in which each of them should receive his own peculiar worship. So Poseidon was the first that came to Attica, and with a blow of his trident on the middle of the acropolis, he produced a sea. . . . After him came Athena, and, having called on Cecrops to witness her act of taking possession, she planted an olive tree which is still shown. . . . But when the two strove for possession of the country Zeus parted them and appointed arbiters . . . the twelve gods. And in accordance with their verdict the country was adjudged to Athena, because Cecrops bore witness that she had been the first to plant the olive. Athena, therefore, called the city Athens after herself, and Poseidon in hot anger flooded the plain . . . and laid Attica under the sea.

As the guardian deity of their city, the Athenians regarded Athena with special veneration and, in the Golden Age of Pericles, erected for her worship the Parthenon, whose remains (except for the "Elgin Marbles" in the British Museum) still decorate the Acropolis. Here they placed her statue, molded by Phidias in gold and ivory, which anciently ranked second only to the massive image of Zeus at Olympia. It represented the goddess standing erect, bearing in one hand her spear and aegis, in the other the figure of Nike, the goddess of victory, with a coiled serpent at her feet.[12]

Her birthday was celebrated in the middle of summer every year, and with great pomp on

---

[10] The aegis of Athena (sometimes considered the same with that of Zeus) was covered with the scales of dragons and was bordered with serpents; and, in its center, was the fearful head of the Gorgon Medusa, which had the effect of turning all beholders into stone.

[11] At her Athenian court on the Acropolis, called the Areopagus, criminals were tried under a system of procedure which strongly indicates that the English common law found its roots there. The court scene is described by Aeschylus in his drama—the Eumenides—where Orestes is brought to trial for the murder of his adulterous mother. In the play each party makes an opening statement, a jury is empaneled, witnesses are heard for both sides, and, when the votes of the twelve jurors are found to be equally divided, the defendant is freed.

[12] After having been used by the ancient Greeks as a temple for the worship of their gods, the Parthenon (built between 447 and 432 B.C.) was appropriated for Christian worship by the Emperor Theodosius II, who removed the giant statue of Athena to his capital at Byzantium, where it inexplicably disappeared. In 1458, the conquering Turks changed the shrine into a Moslem mosque, in which their god Allah was supplicated for more than two hundred years—until, in a battle in 1645 with the Venetians, a powder store exploded and reduced the structure to the magnificent ruin of present times. Due to the action of Thomas Bruce, seventh Earl of Elgin and eleventh of Kincardine (1766–1841) (which some consider to have been an act of vandalism), the decomposing remains of some of the decorative friezes were transported to the British Museum. From these friezes, and earlier drawings of them made by a young French student, the city of Nashville, Tennessee, was able to make an accurate reconstruction of the temple, which is now one of the architectural ornaments of that southern seat of American culture.

every fourth year, at the greatest of the Athenian festivals—called the Panathenaea. The celebration was opened with musical contests and athletic events, which included races in chariots and on foot; and, appropriately enough, the prizes were usually jars of olive oil produced from groves which were sacred to the goddess. Following the contests, the principal persons of the city went in a procession to her temple on the Acropolis, where the women placed before her statue a beautiful robe embroidered for the occasion, and animals were sacrificed according to a set ritual. Returning to the city, a public banquet was spread and consumed by the governing officials, the victors in the athletic and musical contests, representatives from the colonies, and other notables who were fortunate enough as to have procured invitations. On the final day, the whole citizenry gathered around the harbor as spectators of the boat races which brought the quadrennial celebration to an end. Thus, the Athenians honored their divine protectress and themselves gained a feeling of unity which proved invaluable in later war-torn years.

Apollo

Apollo (also called Phoebus Apollo from his maternal grandmother) and his twin sister Artemis were children of Zeus who were borne to him by Leto, daughter of the Titan Coeus, on the island of Delos where, under miraculous circumstances later related, she finally found haven from the persecutions of jealous Hera. As with the birth of Athena, all nature acclaimed Apollo's appearance on the mythological stage. His island birthplace covered itself with golden flowers and was quickly encircled with swans, gracefully swimming about, while attendant nymphs filled the air with their songs of joy.

The newborn babe was given over by his mother to Themis for nursing, but, as soon as he had tasted the divine ambrosia, a wonderful thing happened. He burst from his swaddling clothes as a full-grown youth and demanded a lyre and a bow—announcing to all that thenceforth in oracles he would convey to mankind the will of his supreme father. So speaking, he was instantly wafted to Olympus and admitted to the assembly of the gods as the most glorious of

12. The Pedigree of Apollo

```
                        Gaea
                         ↓
                       Uranus
                         ↓
_____
  Rhea        Coeus          Cronus
  Phoebe       and            and
              Phoebe          Rhea
                ↓              ↓
               Leto           Zeus
                              and
                              Leto
                               ↓
                             Apollo
                             Artemis
```

all of the sons of Zeus; and, in his honor an impromptu dance ensued to the music of the newly acquired lyre which he played while "stepping high and featly."

With this rather hurried background, the young god now began a more leisurely chore—the selection of a location for his announced oracular shrine. Descending from Olympus, he inspected a number of fair places. However, none of them pleased him until he arrived at a wooded grove in Boeotia, where he laid out the foundations for his temple "wide and very long." But a nymph of the stream—variously called Telphusa, Thelpusa, or Delphusa—pointed out that the horses and mules of supplicants would make a great deal of noise while they watered at her spring, and would thereby attract attention which ought to be fixed upon the sacred temple and its treasures. Her artful sales talk produced the intended effect and induced Apollo to choose another location, farther north at Crisa below the glades of Mount Parnassus in Phocis. At this place was an ancient oracle of Gaea, guarded by a female dragon named Python, who was reputed to have reared the Giant Typhon.[13] But the young god slew the scaly creature with an arrow from his bow, and quickly set about building his shrine.[14]

---

[13] Some say that Python was the dragon set upon Leto by Hera to prevent her from coming to rest for the delivery of her twin children. In the "Furies" of Aeschylus, it is related that the oracle was successively inspired by Gaea, Themis, Phoebe, and Apollo.

[14] From Python were derived the names Pythian Apollo and Pythia or Pythoness, by which the priestesses of the shrine were called. From the same source, celebrations held quadriennially at Delphi were called the Pythian games and the place of the shrine was itself called Pytho.

In its construction, he had the help of "the countless tribes of men, who built the whole temple of wrought stones, to be sung of forever."[15] By way of chastising Telphusa for not telling him that the Python would be encountered at Crisa, he then raised a supplemental altar to himself in her precincts—thus diverting from her the worship which she had cunningly tried to retain there for herself.

While pondering what persons he should appoint to serve as ministers of his newly built oracle, Apollo spied a ship manned by some Cretans, who were sailing toward Pylus in Elis. Turning himself into a huge dolphin, he leapt to the deck of the vessel and, unresisted by the awe-struck mariners, their craft was driven by great winds until it went ashore near his temple at Crisa.[16] Here, the god revealed himself and announced to the Cretans that they were to be the keepers of his oracular altar. Because he had first appeared to them as a dolphin, they were told to worship him as Apollo Delphinius and to call his shrine-city Delphi. Thus, the chief oracle of the whole ancient world was founded: for it was consulted not only by the Greeks but also by the Egyptians, the Romans, and the rulers of the eastern countries.[17]

Being honored as the place of his birth, the whole island of Delos was consecrated to the prophetic god and, to preserve the sanctity of the spot, no one was suffered to be buried there.[18] At the foot of Mount Cynthus, a splendid temple was built, which possessed a second oracle.[19] This, too, was universally revered and was enriched with magnificent offerings from all parts of Greece as well as other nations. It is said that, when the Persians passed by on their way to attack the Greeks, they not only left the temple intact but even sent presents of gold and silver to propitiate the powerful deity whom it represented.

In addition to his preeminence as the god of prophecy, Apollo occupied other mythological roles, which appear in various stories to be related later. These roles insensibly blended into each other as may be noted from the following general classifications:

Punisher of Evil. With his bow and arrows, made for him by Hephaestus, Apollo aided Zeus in battling the insolent Giants. He shot monstrous Tityus for trying to defile Leto. Death was sent to the Greeks and their animals for their abduction of the maiden Chryseis, whose father was one of the god's priests. Lastly, Niobe was slain with her children for her boastfulness.

Averter of Evil. Supplementing his power to produce death and plague, Apollo could deliver men from them. By his oracles, he could also suggest the means for averting such calamities. In this helpful role, it was befitting that he should become the father of Asclepius, who was mythologically recognized as the master physician of mortals;[20] and confused with the Olympian healer, he was sometimes himself called Paeon.

Protector of Flocks and Herds. In addition to caring for his own celestial herds, the god—on different occasions when he was impelled by Zeus—tended the cattle of Laomedon, the

---

[15] Another story relates that the temple was built for Apollo by Agamedes and Trophonius, the skilled architect-sons of the Orchomenian king, Erginus; but, in view of the god's early appearance on the mythological scene, some surmise that they assisted only in the erection of a later addition.

[16] When Arion, an ancient bard beloved by Apollo, was about to be murdered for his treasures by a pirate crew with whom he was sailing, the god sent a dream to warn him of his danger; and, leaping overboard, he was borne safely to land by a school of dolphins.

[17] Herodotus relates that when the wealthy Lydian king Croesus sent messengers, to inquire of the oracle whether he should make war on the Persians, the reply was "That if Croesus should make war, he would destroy a mighty empire." The oracle proved true—for Croesus attacked the Persians and suffered such a defeat that his own mighty empire was destroyed.

[18] From his birth beneath Mount Cynthus on the island of Delos, Apollo was sometimes called Cynthius and Delius. Another surname—derived from his unerring bow and arrows—was Far-darter. In the Iliad, he is called

Smintheus—either as the protector or destroyer of mice; and in the dramas of the Athenian poets, he is often referred to as Loxias, a name of uncertain meaning.

[19] There were oracles or sibyls of Apollo at many other places: including one at Clarus near Colophon in Ionic Asia Minor, presided over by Mopsus; and another at Miletus in Caria, tended by the Branchidae. The god is said to have been worshipped even in the distant land of the Hyperboreans, whence his priest Abaris flew through the air, riding on an arrow, and visited foreign countries without partaking of earthly food.

[20] One or more Greek physicians—named Hippocrates and still honored in the medical fraternity—claimed their descent from Asclepius.

flocks of Admetus, and the steeds of Eumelus.

Founder and Protector of Towns. Besides his, perhaps manual, assistance given in raising the walls of Troy, Megara and his own temple at Delphi, the idea that Apollo delighted in the foundation and protection of towns stemmed from the circumstance that consultation with one of his oracles was considered to be a definite prerequisite of any successful founding.

God of Song and Music. Almost at birth, Apollo called for the lyre and began to play upon it as soon as he reached Olympus. The famed musicians of antiquity—Linus, Olen, Orpheus, Marsyas, and Musaeus were accounted as his descendants; even the poet Hesiod claimed him as the common musical ancestor of himself and Homer.[21]

Among later writers, he came to be considered as identical with the earlier Sun-god Helios; and we are told by Herodotus that the Egyptians worshipped him under the name of Horus—one of their sun-gods, who had the head of a hawk. However, to Homer and the earlier Greek writers, the older and perfectly distinct Helios (son of Hyperion) was the god of the sun; and, except for the designations of Apollo as "bright," "radiant," or "shining," no hint appears of his usurping either the role or the function of his older kinsman.

The form of Apollo was conceived as of such youthful symmetry that from it has been derived an idiom of all Indo-European languages—"as handsome as Apollo," traceable not only to the conception of the ancient Greeks but also to the beautiful statue of him which is housed in the Belvedere gallery of the Vatican. Notwithstanding the penchant for promiscuity which was his by right of divinity, the god sought to keep virginal those who announced his oracles; and when the young Pythia at Delphi was ravished by an ardent swain named Echecrates, he decreed that, thenceforth, the office should be occupied only by spinsters of an advanced age.

Artemis

The conventional story related that Artemis (the Roman Diana), was a daughter of Zeus and Leto and a twin sister of Apollo;[22] and, accordingly, she was reputed to have been born with her brother beneath Mount Cynthus on the island of Delos—hence she was sometimes called Cynthia or Delia.[23] Another, and peculiar version, however, of the legend said that she was born in the grove of Ortygia near Ephesus[24] and that her precedent birth permitted her to assist in the delivery of her brother.

13. The Pedigree of Artemis

Gaea
↓
Uranus
↓

| Rhea Phoebe | Coeus and Phoebe ↓ Leto | Cronus and Rhea ↓ Zeus and Leto ↓ Apollo Artemis |

Although she was not regarded as an oracular divinity, in many of her functions she was conceived as a sort of female Apollo. Like him, she was armed with a bow, quiver, and arrows (naturally, made by Hephaestus) and punished evil men by sending plague and death among them.[25] But her principal role was as goddess of the chase, who daily hunted with her train of lovely nymphs, over all of whom she towered by a full head.

---

[21] As leader of the Muses in their songs at various places—poetically described as the Castalian Spring, the fountain of Hippocrene, the mount of Parnassus, Mount Helicon and Pieria—Apollo took the surname Musagetes. As Averter of Evil, he was called Acestor; and as physician of mortals he was called Paion or Paean.

[22] According to a tradition which Pausanias attributes to Aeschylus, Artemis was a daughter of Zeus and Demeter. Herodotus says that the Egyptians called her the daughter of Dionysus and Isis (their Demeter).

[23] Artemis was also called Phoebe, from her maternal grandmother; on the island of Crete she was identified as Britomartis; and the Egyptians named her Bubastis. An additional Roman name was Trivia, denoting the goddess as protector of streets and highways.

[24] Under her surname of Ortygia, Artemis later supplanted Eileithyia as the goddess of childbirth.

[25] Besides assisting Apollo to destroy the Python, Tityus and Niobe, Artemis (unaided) caused the deaths of Orion, Actaeon, Chione, Broteas, and the Giant Aloads. Also, because her worship was slighted, she sent plagues against the Greeks at Aulis, Admetus at Pherae, and Oeneus at Calydon.

When wearied from her hunting, she mythologically relaxed (?) in either one of two ways: she went to Delphi and (joined by Apollo, the Muses, and the Graces) sang songs in honor of Leto, or (joined by her nymphs) she engaged in woodland dances and frolics.[26]

According to some legends, her worship originated with the Hyperboreans.[27] In Greece, however, her earliest appearance was in Arcadia, where she was regarded as the protectress of young animals and game which ranged through the forests and mountains. There, with seeming paradox, she gained her character as a mighty huntress who slaughtered rather promiscuously and regularly from her chariot drawn by four stags with golden antlers.

Since she was never conquered in love, her priests and priestesses were bound to chastity, and were severely punished for any transgression of their vows.[28]

By those who regarded Artemis as the sister of Apollo, and who regarded him as the god of the sun, it was natural that she should be deemed the successor to Selene as goddess of the "chaste" moon. When a group of Greek colonists settled in Asia Minor, they learned about an ancient divinity of Persian origin, who was represented in the two-fold character of all-pervading love and the light of heaven. Pursuant to their practice of fusing foreign deities into their own pantheon, the Greeks seized at once upon the points of resemblance, and decided that the Persian goddess was identical with their Artemis. The "Ephesian Artemis," thus adopted, included her in the character of the love which pervades all nature and penetrates everywhere; it was but a slightly farther step to believe that her presence was also felt in the mysterious Realm of the Shades, where her benign sway replaced, to a certain extent, the ancient divinity of Hecate and partly superseded Persephone as the presiding queen.

Similarly in ancient times, another band of Greeks settled in Taurica now known as the section of Crimea around Yalta. There, too, they encountered worship among the natives of a goddess whom they easily identified with Artemis as she was worshipped as the goddess of chastity. To protect her followers from foreign influence, it was decreed that all strangers, who landed or were shipwrecked on her shores, should be sacrificed upon her altar. The worship of this sanguinary divinity was brought back to Greece by some of the returning colonists[29] and, at Brauron in Attica, human victims thereafter bled freely (but perhaps did not die) under the token sacrificial knife. This revolting practice spread to other places, and is said to have continued in Sparta until the time of Lycurgus. However, the great lawgiver put an end to it by substituting in its place a whipping post—but, on occasion, the lash proved as effective as the knife in bringing honorable atonement to the young persons who were so unfortunate as to be thus consecrated.

Ares

Of the few children of Zeus who could claim Hera as their mother, probably the most important—and certainly the most odious—was Ares, the Greek god of war.[30] This wild and ungovernable deity (said to have been imported from Thrace or the land of the distant Scythians), glorified in strife for its own sake, revelled in slaughter, and was portrayed as always gloating over the desolation which he produced. Inevitably accompanying him, and filled with his own lust for violence, were his two sons, Deimos (Fear or Terror) and Phobos (Dismay or Flight from Fear). Usually his bloody train was aug-

---

[26] According to Ovid, Artemis had many suitors while she was a young maiden, but Zeus granted her plea that she might remain forever a virgin; and her companionship was confined to those of her own sex.

[27] Diodorus Siculus repeats a legend that Leto, the mother of Artemis and Apollo, was born in the island of the Hyperboreans.

[28] Comaëtho, the priestess of Artemis at her temple of Triclaria in Achaea, used the sanctuary as her bridal chamber with a youth named Melanippus. When a plague fell upon the country, the inhabitants appealed to the oracle and were told to sacrifice the unfortunate lovers on the altar of the goddess, and to follow, each year, with a similar sacrifice of the fairest youth and maiden from their city.

[29] According to Euripides, the image of the Taurican Artemis was brought to Greece by Orestes and Pylades with Iphigeneia, whom they rescued from her duties as priestess of the foreign temple.

[30] Ovid relates a later tradition that Hera, piqued at Zeus' unaided birth of Athena, conceived Ares by touching a flower.

mented by the attendance of Enyo, the murderous goddess of war (whom the Romans called Bellona).[31]

14. The Pedigree of Ares

Gaea
↓
Uranus
↓
Cronus
↓
Zeus
and
Hera
↓
Ares

As fickle as he was blustering, Ares paid no attention to the right or wrong of any cause; and, passing through contending forces like a whirlwind, he was accustomed to rush in wherever he might cause the greatest carnage. However, despite his fury, he was utterly eclipsed by the martial prowess of Athena because her efforts were directed by reason and were unswayed by her wild brother's opposition. Thus, when she assisted the hero Diomedes at the siege of Troy, he faced the sanguinary War-god in single combat and inflicted a deep wound which caused him to flee from the battlefield "roaring like ten-thousand men." The humiliated deity hastened to his supreme father to complain of his treatment, but Zeus only grudgingly permitted Paeon to heal the wound; and took pains to let it be known that his son's love of brawling was purely a maternal inheritance.[32]

Nor was it only from his sister Athena that Ares experienced humiliation. On two different occasions, he came off second-best in encounters with his mortal half brother Heracles. Firstly, when the giant Aloads—Otus and Ephialtes— once "bound him in cruel bonds" and confined him in a brazen jar, where he remained until Hermes released him after thirteen months of fuming impotence. Secondly, when Typhon assaulted the Olympians, he fled with most of the other gods to Egypt and there turned himself into a fish to escape detection by the destructive monster.

A story—first mentioned by Homer, and expanded by later writers—depicts the War-god in an even more ludicrous situation: the Sun-god Helios told Hephaestus that his wife, Aphrodite, was engaged in an intrigue with his lustful brother. Hephaestus then forged an invisible net and, placing it over his couch, announced that he was making a trip to his favored island of Lemnos; the unsuspecting lovers fell into the trap—and the net, whose meshes inextricably bound them together while they were subjected to the derisive laughter of all the gods, whom Hephaestus called in to witness their mortification.[33]

In adopting Ares, under their name of Mars, the Romans did not take over the low opinion of him which was generally held by the Greeks; but, perhaps owing to their martial instincts, they honored him as a deity second only to Zeus (their Jupiter) and related that he was the father of Romulus and Remus, who were regarded as the male ancestors of their race.

However, in one Greek story, their Ares is treated with some measure of dignity. When his daughter Alcippe was assaulted by Halirrhotaius, a son of Poseidon, he forthwith put the ravisher to death. For this action, he was summoned to appear before a tribunal of the gods, which was convened upon a hill of Athens; and, when he was acquitted by a tie vote, the name of the assembly became the Areopagus, which afterwards gained much renown as the principal Athenian court of justice.[34]

Hephaestus

Hephaestus, whom the Romans called Vulcan or Mulciber, was the son of Zeus and

---

[31] One of the surnames of Ares was Enyalius.

[32] The tongue lashing administered by Zeus is thus translated by A. T. Murray in the Loeb Classical Series: "Nay, thou renegade, sit not by me and whine. Most hateful to me art thou of all gods that dwell in Olympus; thou ever lovest strife and wars and battles. Truly thy mother's spirit is intolerably unyielding, even Hera's; her can I scarce rule with words. Therefore I deem that by her prompting thou art in this plight."

[33] Later writers say that Ares set a youth Alectryon to warn him against the approach of Helios; but the lad fell asleep and was punished by being changed into a cock—which, to retrieve his old fault, gives regular notice of the sun's approach by his crowing.

[34] Since the twelve Olympian gods composed the jury and the balloting resulted in a tie (or, according to some, seven to five), Ares was presumably given the privilege of voting for his own acquittal.

Hera,[35] who was worshipped as the god of fire—in both its beneficent and destructive aspects. Some realistic antiquarians say that he was originally a deity of the Carians, who first honored him at Lycian Olympus in southern Asia Minor, where a quantity of natural gas still escapes the soil.

15. The Pedigree of Hephaestus

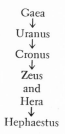

Gaea
↓
Uranus
↓
Cronus
↓
Zeus
and
Hera
↓
Hephaestus

According to Homer, he was born a lame weakling—a suggestion figuratively rationalized as the flickering and unsteady fire; and hence, he is often referred to as the Lame-god. Chagrined at her son's deformity, proud Hera cast him from Olympus when he was born; but he was tenderly caught by the sea-nymphs Eurynome and Thetis, and for nine years he remained in their marine grotto, where he wrought for his fair rescuers "much cunning handiwork, brooches, and spiral armbands, and rosettes and necklaces."

While still in exile, he made an ingenious throne of gold, with secret springs, and sent it to his mother as a supposed peace offering; but, when she mounted the regal seat, she found herself firmly entrapped.[36] Nor could the furious queen of Heaven obtain release from her undignified position until Dionysus made Hephaestus drunk, and, in that state, prevailed upon him to return to Olympus and free her.

After this episode, the Lame-god became reconciled with his mother; but he now had the misfortune to run afoul of his father's wrath—for Zeus hung Hera from the clouds for her persecution of Heracles, and Hephaestus had the foolish temerity to plead in her behalf. Nettled at this presumptuous intervention in his domestic management, the supreme ruler caught his amazed son by the foot and hurled him from Olympus for a second time. Even if he had not been lame before, one would think that the luckless deity had good reason to limp after such a repetition of his previous catastrophe. After falling for a full day through his familiar aerial course, he was again caught and was kindly received by some inhabitants of the island of Lemnos who were known as Sintians. In gratitude for their thoughtfulness, the Fire-god ever after bestowed blessings on his preservers, deemed Lemnos his favorite place on earth—and, from the incident, was often referred to as the Lemnian.

After making his way back to Mount Olympus, a second reconciliation was apparently effected, because it is related that Hephaestus now set up a divine forge on the celestial eminence and, with the aid of two golden handmaidens whom he created and animated, he wrought many wonderful works for both the gods and men. Among them, the following were particularly noted:

His own palace, shining like the stars, and enclosing his workshop, with its anvil and fire served by twenty bellows;
The palace of Helios in the land of the Ethiopians;
The watery palace of Poseidon near Aegae in Achaea;
The underground home of Orion;
The chariots of Helios, Selene, Artemis, Ares, and Cybele (Rhea);
The golden cup (or boat) of Helios;
The scepter and the aegis of Zeus;
The trident of Poseidon, and the marine chariot of Amphitrite;
The helmet of Hades;
The fruitful sickle of Demeter;
The bows, quivers, and arrows of Apollo and Artemis;

---

[35] Later traditions stated that Hera, with the help of the wind and her own imagination, give birth to Hephaestus independently because she was jealous of the unaided birth of Athena by Zeus. This story is at odds with the account which relates that Athena emerged from Zeus' head after it had been cleft by Hephaestus; but it may be harmonized with the account which considers Prometheus as the striker. The two deities of fire—Hephaestus as a personification of the element itself and Prometheus as its bringer to mankind—were sometimes worshipped at a common altar and confusion of their identities may have easily arisen.

[36] Another story relates that Hephaestus sprang from the thigh of Hera, who refused to tell him the name of his sire; and that he was forced to the stratagem of entrapping her on the golden throne in order to learn the secret of his birth.

The crown of Ariadne;
The armor of Achilles, Aeneas, and Memnon;
The shield of Heracles;
The sword of Perseus;
The necklace and robe of Harmonia;
The brass dog of Cephalus;
The gold and silver dogs of Alcinous;
The brazen-footed bulls of Aeëtes;
The brazen castanets of Athena;
The brazen Cretan Giant Talos; and,
As his masterpiece, the woman Pandora.

With the help of the Cyclopes,[37] Hephaestus forged for Zeus the fiery thunderbolts—thus giving him the name of the Thunderer, and investing the supreme father with his most powerful weapon. In appreciation, Zeus gave to his lame son the beautiful Aphrodite in marriage.[38] But this proved to be a rather questionable boon, because the lovely lady not only engaged with Ares as her paramour, but had other affairs with those of baser blood; on one occasion when Hephaestus good-naturedly took upon himself the office of cupbearer to the assembled Olympians, his disloyal partner openly joined in the burst of mirth which his clumsy efforts provoked among the gods.

The conventional representation of the Fire-god shows him as a bearded man wearing an oval cap and a cloak which leaves bare his right shoulder so that he is unimpeded in the use of the forge-hammer, which he holds in his right hand. His muscular body is supported on spindly legs, to portray his lameness. Perhaps because of his infirmity, only a few incidents are mentioned of activities which demand easy locomotion. It is related, however, that he assisted the Olympians in their war with the Giants and slew Mimas with "red-hot missiles";

in the Trojan War, he opposed himself (as a flame) to the river-god Scamander, who was hotly pursuing Achilles; by command of Zeus, he nailed Prometheus to Mount Caucasus; and, he tended the cattle of Geryon while Heracles went in search of a strayed bull.

The god of fire was worshipped in many places, but principally on the islands of Lemnos and Sicily, both containing volcanoes which were considered the emanations of his fiery breath.[39] The Lemnian earth from the place on which he was reputed to have fallen was believed to cure madness, snakebites, and hemorrhages; and, at his temple on Mount Aetna in Sicily—where a perpetual fire burned, the entrance was guarded by dogs which fawned upon righteous supplicants, but rushed upon all evil-doers and drove them away. These beliefs indicate that Hephaestus was worshipped by the Greeks (Sicily was colonized by them), primarily as the beneficent deity of fire as an element of use rather than of destruction; but in Rome, which was afflicted with many disastrous conflagrations, propitiatory sacrifices were regularly made to stay the supposed wrath of the harsh god to whom they were attributed.

Hebe

Hebe—called by the Romans Juventas—was the daughter of Zeus and Hera,[40] who was considered the personification of eternal youth under its most attractive and joyous aspect and was, naturally, among the merry celestials dancing on Olympus when Apollo first played his lyre. Her name itself means "bloom of youth" or "young maturity." At the Peloponnesian city of Sicyon, she was worshipped under the surnames of Ganymede or Dia; and, throughout Greece, she was regarded as a sort of female fountain of youth.

Her original function on Olympus was to act as cupbearer to the gods. As a royal handymaid,

---

[37] The Cyclopes who assisted Hephaestus were said to number one hundred; but the names of only three are given by Hesiod; namely: Brontes, Steropes, and Arges (which latter Virgil called Pyracmon). As previously mentioned, the Cyclopes of the Odyssey—ruled by Polyphemus—are descendants of Poseidon and are not identified with Hephaestus.

[38] Later writers add that, by the advice of Zeus, Hephaestus put poppies in Aphrodite's nectar, thereby causing her to accept his proposal while under the influence of the opiate. In the Iliad, Charis is named as his wife but in the Odyssey she is Aphrodite, and it may be surmised that Charis is her surname. However, in the "Theogony" of Hesiod, Aglaea—one of the Graces (known also as the Charities)—occupies the wifely role.

[39] The seat of Aeolus, god of the winds, was believed to be in the Liparian (Aeolian) islands near Sicily, and to have been the source of the bellows which periodically forced the smouldering volcano of Aetna into flame.

[40] A later story relates that Hera bore Hebe as a result of eating wild lettuce. Like both Hera and Aphrodite, Hebe was sometimes called Antheia, as the deity of flowers.

16. The Pedigree of Hebe

Gaea
↓
Uranus
↓
Cronus
↓
Zenus
and
Hera
↓
Hebe

17. The Pedigree of Aphrodite

Gaea
↓
Uranus
and
Gaea
↓

Oceanus	Cronus
and	and
Tethys	Rhea
↓	↓
Dione	Zeus
	and
	Dione
	↓
	Aphrodite

she also helped Hera to harness her horses and, when Ares was wounded by Diomedes, she gave her stormy brother a bath after Paeon had healed his wound. Homer's rather curt description of Hebe is that she was "queenly" and had "neat ankles"; and Hesiod mentions only her golden crown. However, we know that she was more modestly attired, because she tripped one day while pouring nectar for the gods and "indecently exposed herself." As a result, she was replaced in her duties as the Olympian cupbearer by Ganymedes, a handsome son of Tros whom Zeus sent an eagle to abduct from earth.[41]

When Heracles was given immortality, Hebe became his heavenly wife and, besides bearing him two children, she showed her affection—and her divinity—by rejuvenating his nephew Iolaus, much to the envy of several amorous goddesses whose mortal lovers were growing old.[42]

Aphrodite

Aphrodite, the goddess of love and beauty, was usually regarded as the daughter of Zeus and the Oceanid Dione. A different story related that she sprang from the sea when it received a drop of blood from the mutilated Uranus. But her surname of "Foam-born" can be harmonized with either version; because Dione, as a marine divinity, might well be

expected to bear her child beneath the waves.

According to various legends, the worship of Aphrodite was brought into Greece through Cyprus, Cythera, Crete, or Corinth by Phoenician colonists;[43] and that she was the same deity to whom, under the name of Ashtoreth (Astarte), King Solomon paid homage in his idolatrous old age.[44] In this foreign character, she was regarded as the bestower of all animal and vegetable fruitfulness and, especially at Corinth, was worshipped with the mystic rites of Adonis which were purely sensual in nature.[45] It was perhaps this disgraceful practice which caused Plato to remark that there were two Aphrodites: "the elder, having no mother, who is called the heavenly Aphrodite—she is the daughter of Uranus; the younger, who is the daughter of Zeus and Dione—her we call common."

No matter which story of her birth we may accept, the popular notion was that the bubbling waters of the sea assumed a rosy tint, and, from their depths, the goddess of love and beauty arose to the sight of gods and men in all the surpassing glory of her loveliness and "arrayed in all the panoply of her irresistible charms." Then, shaking her long, fair tresses, the water drops rolled down into the beautiful

---

[41] Others relate that Hebe was not relieved of her duties because of any malfeasance in office but because, when she married Heracles, she assumed a new full-time position.

[42] According to Euripides, at the battle which the Athenians fought with the Argives in defense of the Heraclids, two stars shone brightly on the chariot of Iolaus, and a diviner interpreted them as being Heracles and Hebe.

[43] In Crete, Aphrodite was identified with Ariadne, the daughter of Minos who assisted Theseus in his conquest of the Minotaur.

[44] In II Kings xxiii, 13 the Bible says that Solomon "builded for Ashtoreth . . . a mount of corruption."

[45] At Corinth (a principal crossroads of Greek and eastern commerce), Aphrodite was regarded as the patroness of the more than one-thousand courtesans who infested the city.

sea shell[46] in which she stood, and were transformed into glistening pearls. Wafted by soft breezes, she floated on to Cythera in the Aegean Sea and from there transported to the island of Cyprus.[47]

It was April when she arrived at Cyprus and as soon as her white feet touched the island-earth, grass and flowers sprang up and she was sweetly received by the three Graces.[48] These equally fair creatures bedecked her with golden ornaments and escorted her to the divine halls of Olympus, and "with her went Love and Desire (Himeros)—the whispering of maidens and Smiles and Deceits with sweet Delight and Graciousness."

Since the gods, as well as men, were susceptible to her supreme sway, the heavenly competition for the honor of possessing the love-goddess was indeed fierce, but, by the will of Zeus, Hephaestus became the unlucky winner—unlucky, because to him Aphrodite proved to be as faithless as she was beautiful. In addition to the *affaire du coeur* in which she was entrapped with Ares, she became the mother of love children by Hermes, Dionysus, Poseidon, and the mortal Achises.[49] At another time, stricken with the same passion which she so lightly created in others, she carried off Phaëthon—"a young boy in the tender flower of his glorious youth."[50] But the most celebrated recipient of her affection was Adonis, whom she loved so openly that jealous Ares finally gored him to death after assuming the form of a wild boar.

Aphrodite's love power was so great that lions, wolves, panthers, and tigers followed her like tame animals. On one occasion, Hera herself—in order to beguile her supreme consort—begged for the loan of her magic cestus, the golden girdle of the love-goddess which raised in gods and men a passion to possess its wearer. As one might suspect, such irresistible power was apt to be used for purposes not always benign. So it was, for in requiting slights to her divine honor, the vindictive beauty caused: Clytemnestra, Helen, and Timandra (the daughters of Tyndareus)[51] to make cuckolds of their husbands; Smyrna to lie with her own father, Cinyras; the husbands of the Lemnian women to desert their wives and bed with captive maids; Clio, the muse of history, to fall in love with Pierus and to bear a son, Hyacinthus, who died tragically;[52] Phaedra to kill herself because of her unrequited passion for her stepson Hippolytus; Ariadne to be deserted by her adored Theseus; Pasiphae to bear the monstrous Minotaur when stricken by lust for the Cretan bull; Circe to be cruelly spurned by Odysseus; Medeia to be successively and tragically enamoured of both Jason and Aegeus; and, the dawn-goddess Eos to be always heartsick as she ceaselessly cast off one lover for another.[53]

However, Aphrodite was not always portrayed in an unkindly role. For instance:

She dearly loved her son Aeneas and, when he was wounded at Troy, she threw her white arms around him and strove to draw him out of the turmoil of battle; but (it must be added) when

---

[46] At the Chicago World's Fair in 1934, one of the more daring exhibits among the peep shows was "Venus on the Half Shell."

[47] From this story, Aphrodite was often called Cytherea (the Cytherean), Cypris, or the Paphian (from Paphus, the principal city of the island of Cyprus). She was also called the Acidalian from the name of a well near Orchomenus in which she was accustomed to bathe.

[48] The Graces (also called the Charities) were daughters of Zeus and the Oceanid Eurynome, whose names were the personifications of bloom, brightness, and cheerfulness. Having first met Aphrodite, they were regarded as thereafter her perpetual attendants.

[49] The children of Aphrodite are later noted separately under our discussion of their various fathers, but their composite list follows: by Ares: Harmonia, Eros (Cupid), Anteros, Phobos, and Deimos; by Hermes: Hermaphroditus; by Dionysus: Priapus and Hymen; by Poseidon: Eryx (from whom Aphrodite was sometimes called Erycina); and by Anchises: Aeneas and Lyrus.

[50] Phaëthon, who was beloved by Aphrodite, was a son of the Trojan Tithonus and should not be confused with the son of Helios who perished in his attempt to drive the sun chariot.

[51] While Tyndareus was sacrificing to the gods, he forgot to include Aphrodite. Of his daughters: Clytemnestra dishonored Agamemnon for Aegisthus; Helen left Menelaus for Paris; and Timandra deserted Echemus for Phyleus.

[52] In reciting this instance of Aphrodite's vengeance, Apollodorus makes Clio the mother of Hyacinthus by Pierus; but later, in accord with the conventional story, he names Amyclas and Diomede as the youth's parents.

[53] Eos was a sister of Helios; Pasiphae and Circe were his daughters; and Phaedra and Ariadne were his granddaughters. The love misfortunes of these women were attributed to the vengeance of Aphrodite, wreaked on the Sun-god's family because he exposed her intrigue with Ares.

Diomedes slightly scratched her hand, she fled in tears and let Aeneas fall to the ground.

Beholden to Paris for awarding her the coveted golden apple, she broke the strap of his helmet, with which Menelaus was seeking to draw him prostrate from the field of Troy.

She was kind to the orphaned daughters of Pandareos, and tended them "with cheese, and sweet honey, and pleasant wine."

When Phaon of Mitylene graciously ferried her from Chios to Lesbos, without payment of fare, she bestowed upon him a magic philter, which caused him to become so handsome that he excited love in the hearts of all the women of Lesbos; and to him, legend says, Sappho addressed some of her tenderest and most beautiful songs.

She pitied love-stricken Hippomenes and gave him three golden apples which he used as a lure to win a footrace from Atalanta and thereby gained her hand in marriage.

She changed Pygmalion's beloved statue into the maiden Galateia, who became her creator's loving wife.

Sometimes, her well-intended efforts went astray, for even her great power could not overcome the inevitability inhering in the threads of Destiny, which were drawn off for every person by the grim Fates. Witness the tragic stories of Pyramus and Thisbe and Hero and Leander:

Pyramus and Thisbe were, respectively, the handsomest youth and the most beautiful maiden in the eastern kingdom of Semiramis, where their families lived in a single house which was divided by a sort of party wall. Thinking to perform an act of kindness, Aphrodite caused the young persons to fall in love, but their parents forbade their marriage and even tried to prevent them from speaking together. However, the lovers discovered a crack in the dividing wall and arranged a meeting in a nearby wood. Thisbe arrived at the appointed time, but Pyramus was late. As the maiden waited, a great lioness, whose jaws were dripping with the blood from a recent kill, approached to drink from a neighboring spring. Thisbe fled in terror; but dropped her veil, which the lioness tore into pieces and left smeared with blood. When Pyramus shortly arrived, he recognized the carmined veil as Thisbe's and, believing that she had been slain, he killed himself with his sword. The blood from his wound sank into the ground and, passing upward to the white berries of an overhanging mulberry tree, turned them to a deep red color. Thisbe now returned and, when she saw her torn veil and her lover's empty scabbard lying near his lifeless body, she realized what had happened—and why. Drawing the sword from his pierced heart, she plunged it

into her own and, mingling her blood with his, expired by his side. And for this reason, we know why mulberries are red.

Hero and Leander were, respectively, a beautiful maiden and a handsome youth; they lived on the Hellespont—she in Sestus and he in Abydus on the other side. And they knew very little about the kingdom of the great Queen Semiramis, because she had been dead for a long time. They, too, were made to fall in love by the kindly intentions of Aphrodite. Hero, however, had vowed to go through life as a maiden and at first permitted nothing more than an interchange of words with her lover. However, the power of the goddess was not to be resisted, and she finally consented that Leander should sometimes meet her at night, when she would signal him by torch to swim to her side from across the Hellespont. One night—just as she had given her usual signal—a violent tempest arose; but the love-sick Leander plunged into the waters with no thought of danger—and was drowned before he could reach the opposite shore. The stormy waves rolled his inert corpse in to the feet of waiting Hero, who tenderly clasped him, and then herself died of a broken heart.

The Roman counterpart of Aphrodite was Venus;[54] but the Roman worship seems to have been limited to the sensual character which impelled Plato to say, "Her we call common." Indeed, under the name of Cloacina, she sometimes was regarded in Rome as a sort of deity (as Purifier of Sewers). This was a far cry from the fay-like beauty who, emerging from the clean foam of the sea, was often called by the Greeks Urania and at whose sacrificial altar no offering was originally acceptable except the clear fire itself.

Hermes

Hermes was the son of Zeus and Maia—the eldest of the seven Pleiades, daughters of Atlas and Pleione. The Romans called him Mercury, and both Greeks and Romans sometimes called him Cyllenius (or the Cyllenian), because he was born in a cave of Mount Cyllene in Arcadia.[55]

---

[54] The statue known as the Venus de Milo was discovered on the island of Melos and brought to the Louvre in 1820—where it has become celebrated as among the most exquisite classical delineations of the female figure.

[55] In the Samothracian mysteries of the Cabeiri,

Like his half brother Apollo, he wasted no time in going into action. Born at dawn, the precocious infant almost immediately decided that he was hungry for roast beef. He leapt from his cradle to seek the cattle of Apollo, with divine intuition that their master was then absent (because he had been compelled by Zeus to tend the flocks of the Pheraean king, Admetus). As the child-god stepped over the cavern's threshold, he spied a tortoise waddling near the courtyard gate. Hilariously, he carried it within and, after scraping out its marrow, he converted the shell into a seven-stringed lyre.[56]

18. The Pedigree of Hermes

```
                        Gaea
                         ↓
                       Uranus
                         ↓
        _____
       Iapetus               Cronus
         and                   and
        Asia                  Rhea
     (d. Oceanus)              |
         ↓                     ↓
        Atlas                 Zeus
         and                   and
       Pleione                Maia
     (d. Oceanus)              |
         ↓                     ↓
        Maia                 Hermes
```

To the accompaniment of sweet music from his infant creation, he then sang about the comradeship in love of Zeus and "neat-shod" Maia. But his longing for meat persisted and, placing the lyre in his cradle, he again set forth for Pieria in Thrace where, at the birthplace of the Muses, "the divine cattle of the blessed gods . . . grazed the pleasant, unmown meadows."

When he arrived at Pieria, he selected fifty of the choicest cows and, placing sandals of boughs on his feet—so that no telltale tracks would appear, he drove them backwards to the river Alpheius at Pylus. As he was driving the herd in this manner, he came to an old man named Battus, who was tending his vineyard near the roadway. Hermes told his amazed spectator that he would have much wine when the vines should bear fruit, but only if he should never reveal the curious procession which he had seen.[57]

At the bank of the river Hermes kindled a fire[58] and, after roasting two of the cows, sacrificed their flesh to the twelve great gods; but he proudly overcame his physical longing to taste of their meat.[59] Then, he threw his leafy sandals into the river and, after spreading the hides of the slaughtered animals on a rock and hiding the rest of the herd in a nearby cave, he burned up the remaining fragments of his sacrifice and went back to Cyllene.

After returning to his birthplace, he passed through the keyhole and, walking softly, crept into his cradle. There, as he lay holding his lyre and playing with the bedcovers about his knees, his mother Maia let him know that she was fully aware of his bovine escapade. With a touch of maternal sorrow, she prophetically said: "Your father got you to be a great worry to mortal men and the deathless gods." She added that Apollo would soon arrive to administer a proper chastisement.[60] Defiantly, the young rogue boasted from his cradle that if the Delphian god should make such an attempt, he would soon find that his holy shrine would be

---

Hermes was worshipped as the fourth of the gods, under the name of Casmillus. In Egypt, he was identified with the dog-headed deity Anubis (attendant and messenger of Osiris) and also with Thoth—a deity, represented with the head of an ibis, who presided over landmarks.

[56] The apparent conflict between the story which makes Hermes the inventor of the lyre and the other which relates that his half brother Apollo—admittedly the older—demanded a lyre when he was born, is sought to be harmonized by alleging that Apollo's instrument had only three strings.

[57] Ovid relates that Hermes gave Battus a heifer in return for his promise not to reveal the theft. Later, returning in another form and with a changed voice, he asked the old man if he had seen the strange parade and offered him a cow and a bull for his truthful answer. Unable to turn down such a reward, Battus recited what he had seen; and, for the breach of his promise, was transformed into a black rock known as the touchstone.

[58] The Homeric hymn relates that the blaze was created by the friction of fire sticks, which Hermes invented on the spot. He is also said to have invented the alphabet, numbers, weights and measures, and the musical instruments known as the cithara and the syrinx.

[59] Since Hermes was himself one of the twelve great gods, he had to be mythologically content with the savor instead of the content of the sacrifice.

[60] Hermes was no sooner born but busy. Adding to his sportive theft of Apollo's cattle, later writers say that he also stole Apollo's quiver and bow, the tools of Hephaestus, the girdle of Aphrodite, the scepter of Zeus and, he would have made free with one of the supreme god's thunderbolts but that it proved too hot for his fingers.

plundered of its many treasures—including even the golden tripod upon which his Pythoness sat while delivering her mystic oracles. Meanwhile, Apollo had returned to Pieria and had discovered that fifty of his sacred herd were missing. In search of them, he encountered the aged Battus and inquired if he had seen any strayed cows. Battus told him about the strange sight which he had witnessed—an infant, shuffling along on leafy sandals and driving a herd of cattle backward. When the god came to Pylus, from where he had been directed, he saw the hides of the two slaughtered cows and (owing to his divinity) knew that Hermes was the culprit whom he sought.

Speedily, he traveled to the cavern at Mount Cyllene where he entered and found the little thief snuggled down in his cradle, wrapped in his swaddling clothes and pretending to be asleep. Apollo was not taken in by the pretense and, shaking the crib not too gently, asked the whereabouts of his stolen herd. Feigning innocence, the cunning infant seemed to awaken from his nap and guilefully replied:[61]

Am I a cattle-lifter, a stalwart person? This is no task for me; rather I care for other things; I care for sleep, and milk of my mother's breast, and wrappings 'round my shoulders, and warm baths. Let no one hear the cause of this dispute; for this would be a great marvel indeed among the deathless gods, that a child newly born should pass in through the forepart of the house with cattle of the field; herein you speak extravagantly. I was born yesterday, and my feet are soft and the ground beneath is rough; nevertheless, if you will have it so, I will swear a great oath by my father's head and vow that neither am I guilty myself, neither have I seen any man who stole your cows—whatever cows may be; for I know them only by hearsay.

Apollo, knowing the pretended innocence for the sham that it was, seized the youthful prevaricator and took him to Mount Olympus, where Zeus was holding a council of the gods. Here, he repeated the charge of theft and Hermes—again stoutly denying all knowledge of it—offered to buttress his lying words by giving his oath that he was not guilty. At the bald falsehood, Zeus could not help laughing out loud but, repressing his mirth, sternly ordered the young pilferer to show the place where the stolen cattle were secreted. The supreme god's will was not to be disregarded and Hermes dutifully led Apollo to Pylus, and pointed out the cavern wherein the remaining animals were penned. While they were being driven back to Pieria, the child-god struck the chords of his new-made lyre and the music so entranced his elder brother that he offered to give the cattle in exchange for the instrument. The offer was promptly accepted and, a reconciliation being thus effected, Hermes from then on became the god of herdsmen, while Apollo devoted himself even more enthusiastically to the art of music.

After returning to Mount Olympus, Apollo made his young brother swear by the river Styx that he would never steal his lyre or bow, nor invade his sanctuary at Delphi. This done, he gave him a golden wand called the caduceus, which was surmounted with wings; and told him that it possessed the power of uniting in love all beings divided by hate. At this instant, Hermes saw two snakes which were fighting nearby and threw the wand into their tangled coils—whereupon, the angry combatants clasped each other in a loving embrace and, curling around the staff, remained ever after permanently attached to it.

Zeus now added to Apollo's gift of the wand, by presenting Hermes with a winged silver cap, called the petasos, and silver wings (called talaria by the Romans) for attachment to the sandals of his feet. He then was appointed to be the herald of the gods and conductor of mortal shades to the realm of Hades.[62] Thus, accoutered and appointed, he was reformed to such an extent that he became a trustworthy ambassador whose wand gave him power, its twined serpents wisdom and his silver wings insuring dispatch.

In his role as messenger and general factotum

---

[61] Much of the account here given is taken from the Homeric "Hymn to Hermes" as translated in the Loeb Classical Series by H. G. Evelyn-White.

[62] Conformable to the chronology of their mythological deities, the rulers of the lower world were considered by the Greeks to have been successively Tartarus, Erebus, and Hades.

of the gods, Hermes performed a number of mythological chores, among which were the following:

1. He slew Argus Panoptes, the many-eyed creature set by Hera to guard Io—a maiden seduced by Zeus and changed by him into a cow, in a vain effort to deceive his jealous spouse.[63]

2. He stole the sinews of Zeus, which had been removed by the monster Typhon.

3. He rescued Ares from the brazen pot in which the gigantic Aloads had kept him prisoner for thirteen months.

4. He aided Athena in divinely pardoning the fifty daughters of Danaus for the murders of their husbands.[64]

5. He brought to Nephele the golden ram Chrysomallus which bore her children, Helle and Phrixus, away from their threatened sacrifice at the altar in Iolchus.

6. He guided Perseus (with Athena's assistance) to the Graeae, who told the hero where he might find the Gorgon Medusa; and gave Perseus the sickle which he used in cutting off her snaky head.

7. He restored to the Graeae the leathern wallet which they loaned to Perseus as a container for his gory trophy.

8. He gave Heracles an unneeded sword after that great hero had already conquered the attacking forces of Orchomenian Erginus.

9. He stayed the arm of Heracles, who was drawing the same sword against Medusa in the lower world, by explaining that her image was only a delusive shade.

10. He conveyed the infant Wine-god Dionysus away from the persecutions of Lycurgus.

11. He gave to Amphion a lyre, at whose music stones magically leapt into place to form the walls of Boeotian Thebes.

12. He bore a message from Zeus to Atreus, who was quarreling with Thyestes about the kingship of Mycenae, which permitted the former to gain the throne by prophesying that the Sun would go backwards.

13. He conducted Hera, Athena, and Aphrodite to Paris on Trojan Mount Ida, for his judgment as to which of them should receive the golden apple labeled "To the Fairest."

14. He brought back from the lower world the shade of Protesilaus and stood by while the dead man's ghost visited with his sorrowing wife.

15. He carried to Odysseus the root herb called "moly," which impregnated the returning hero against the magic potions of the witch Circe.

16. He communicated to Calypso the will of Zeus that Odysseus should be permitted to leave her island home.

17. He carried from Zeus to Deucalion and Pyrrha the message that they should throw over their shoulders "the bones of their mother," the stones of Earth which—so cast—turned into the race of mortals.

18. He escorted Orpheus to and from the realm of Hades on his fruitless journey to bring back his beloved wife, Eurydice.

19. He vainly warned Aegisthus against his intrigue with Agamemnon's wife, Clytemnestra.

20. He led Priam to Achilles to request the surrender of Hector's body for burial.

21. He secured Ixion to the revolving wheel in the lower world, as punishment for his attempted violation of Hera.

22. He acted as the auctioneer when Heracles was sold in slavery to the Lydian queen, Omphale, for having slain Iphitus.

23. He brought Pandora to Epimetheus, after she had been created by Hephaestus and endowed with guileful charms by the rest of the gods.

24. He bore to Pelops the divine scepter which, passing down to Agamemnon, was wielded by him as a symbol of his supreme authority over the Greeks in their war with the Trojans.

25. He escorted to the lower world the shades of the greedy suitors of Penelope who were slain upon the return of Odysseus.[65]

---

[63] From this exploit, Hermes gained the name of Argeiophontes (Argus-slayer) by which he was often called. When he was acquitted of the murder—on the plea that he was impelled to it by Zeus—some of the dissenting gods cast their voting pebbles at him.

[64] Although the daughters of Danaus were pardoned on earth for the murders of their husbands, they were punished in the afterworld by being forced to the vain task of carrying water in sieves.

[65] In honor of his role as official escorter of their departed souls to the lower world, the Greeks often placed images of Hermes on their graves.

Because of his diverse functions Hermes was regarded by the Greeks not only as a herald and messenger of the gods but, among mortals, as the protector of cattle and herds of all kinds, the divinity of serving-people, the patron of thieves[66] and the deity of gain—whether honest or dishonest. In his role as a peripatetic ambassador, he was worshipped by traveling salesmen and tradesmen, who did not hesitate to excuse their occasional overreachings or overstatements by pleading his divine example;[67] and, it is needless to say, his adherents quickly gained strength in both numbers and devotion.

Since he was the patron of travelers, the god's image was usually placed at crossroads, on doors and at the limits of boundaries. Similarly, it stood at the entrances to the stadia where the Greek national games were held. Since he was the protector of those who gathered from afar in the various inns of the world, he was considered the deity of sleep and dreams.[68]

Hestia

Hestia, whom the Romans called Vesta, was the goddess of the hearth. In the Greek legend, she was a virgin daughter of Cronus and Rhea, who was not accorded the same importance which the Romans gave to her counterpart. Being the first born of her mother, she was the first child swallowed by Cronus; and was the last to be delivered from her father's unnatural maw.

Although both Poseidon and Apollo sued for her hand, she swore by the head of Zeus to remain a maiden forever; and— maintaining her vow—she was universally worshipped as such, along with Athena and Artemis. In this character, it was appropriate that sacrifices made to her should be limited to heifers less than one year old.

19. The Pedigree of Hestia

Gaea
↓
Uranus
↓
Cronus
and
Rhea
↓
Hestia

Since the hearth of each house was regarded as the sacred center of its domestic life, Hestia was considered—almost equally with Hera—as the giver of all domestic happiness. And, she was considered to be the presiding deity, to whom first sacrifices were usually made.

In Greek myth, the functions of Hestia were, to a large extent, later assumed by Hera. The Romans, however, kept her worship apart and greatly extended it, to such a degree of importance that it is summarized below.[69]

---

[66] The ancients were accustomed to paint a likeness of Hermes on their doors to prevent the entrance of his light-fingered disciples; and, it was common mythological knowledge that he taught his own son Autolycus the allied arts of thievery and falsehood. Autolycus, in turn, is said to have taught Heracles how to wrestle—in the tricky style which was perhaps the forerunner of our present-day judo or jiu-jitsu.

[67] As the inspiration of eloquence (our euphemism), the tongues of animals were frequently placed as sacrifices on the god's altar.

[68] The last drink before retirement—our "stirrup cup"—was always dedicated to Hermes.

---

[69] Vesta was considered chief of the deities referred to by the Romans as their Lares and Penates. The town or city was thought of as an extended family and had its own sacred hearth, whose fire was always kept burning. If this fire of Hestia (Vesta) should go out, it was not allowed that it should be rekindled from another; and a new light had to be made by friction, or by drawing it from the sun with glasses. At Rome, the priestesses of Vesta—known as Vestal Virgins—presided over the sacred flame, which was alleged to have been first brought to Italy from Troy by Aeneas. These feminine attendants were six in number, chosen from girls of the noblest families who were between the ages of six and ten. Their chief duty was to protect the flame on the altar, because its extinction was regarded as almost certain to produce a national calamity. Their term of office was thirty years, divided with ten years in learning their duties, ten years in performing them, and ten years in instructing their successors. After their service was completed, they could go out into the world, could marry, and take more normal places in the community.

As a reward for their years of consecration, which included observance of vows of chastity, the Vestal Virgins were accorded great honors and privileges: the best seats were reserved for them at all public spectacles; great public dignitaries made room for them to pass; and they were granted the power to pardon any criminal whom they might encounter on his way to punishment. However, if any virgin violated her vow of chastity, the altar-flame flickered out and the guilty backslider was cruelly buried alive. It is related that, on one occasion, Tuccia—who was charged with breaking her vow—proved her innocence and escaped the dread punishment by carrying water in a sieve; another maiden, in like

Demeter

Demeter, the second child of Cronus and Rhea, was known by the Romans as Ceres. As goddess of the harvest, she had a number of other surnames, among which were: Deo, Chloë, and Mater Dolorosa; and she was identified with the fruitful Egyptian goddess Isis.

Like other Greek nature deities,[70] she was regarded as succeeding to the functions originally assigned to her elders, first Gaea[71] and then her own mother, Rhea. In her role as their successor, those who were favored by her were blessed with bountiful crops but, when she was displeased, blight and famine ensued.

20. The Pedigree of Demeter

By her brother Zeus, she became the mother of Persephone—called Proserpina by the Romans, and often referred to as Cora (or Kore) from the Greek word meaning the maid.[72] The attachment of the mother for her daughter was so deep and tender that she could find no happiness except while in her society; during their sweet companionship, all went well with the world.

However, without Demeter's knowledge,

Zeus betrothed Persephone to Hades, the ruler of the lower world.[73] One day, while the unsuspecting maiden was gathering flowers which Zeus had grown in order to tempt her, the earth suddenly opened and she was snatched below by her promised lover. Her anguished call for help was heard only by Hecate, but the abduction was seen by the Sun-god Helios. Although she heard only a faint echo of the call, Demeter had a divine intuition of what had occurred and immediately set out in search of her daughter. After wandering about for nine days without eating or bathing, she encountered Hecate who told her that she had heard Persephone's cries, but did not know what had caused them.[74] Both goddesses then went to Helios, who revealed that Hades had been the ravisher—and with the consent of Zeus.

Upon hearing what she had feared, Demeter angrily avoided Olympus and remained on earth among men, conferring blessings where she was kindly received and punishing those who failed to treat her with proper respect. She, however, sorrowfully wandered from place to place in the hope that she might somehow be reunited with her dear Persephone. One day, she came to Eleusis in Attica and sat down to rest near the well called Callichorus. There, she was approached by the youthful daughters of King Celeus, who had come to draw water. They spoke kindly to the tired wayfarer[75]—who told them that she had escaped from pirates and was looking for a home, in which she was willing to serve in any menial capacity. The maidens went to their mother, Metaneira, with this information, and soon came back to tell Demeter that a nurse was needed for their infant brother Demophoön. Returning with the maidens, the goddess was respectfully greeted by Metaneira —for she was enveloped in a radiant light which indicated her divinity. But she could not be induced to smile, or partake of any refreshment,

---

jeopardy, rekindled the sacred fire with a corner of her white garment—thus purging herself of the charge, but passing it on to one of her unlucky sisters.

[70] Thus, the Sun was successively Hyperion, Helios, and Apollo; the Moon was first Selene and then Artemis; the Sea was first Pontus and then Poseidon; and Hades was preceded by Erebus and Tartarus.

[71] When ancient Gaea lost (with Uranus) her position as a ruling divinity, her functions were taken over by Rhea as the wife of conquering Cronus. It is said, the primeval goddess retired into a subterranean cavern where she still remains, slumbering, moaning, and nodding forever.

[72] The generic surname of the maid was also applied to the virgin goddesses Athena and Artemis.

[73] A later version states that Hades was irresistibly impelled to love for Persephone by an arrow from Cupid's bow.

[74] Another story says that Hecate observed the abduction from a subterranean cave in which she was resting.

[75] According to a later legend, while Demeter was resting near the well she was mocked by Abas, a saucy son of Celeus, and resentfully turned him into a lizard.

until her cares were temporarily dispelled by the merry jests of a serving woman named Iambe.[76]

The young Demophoön was given over to the goddess as nurse and, wishing to make him immortal, she placed him in the fire by night in order to destroy his mortal parts, but Metaneira, ignorant of her object, screamed when she saw her babe in the flames and he was consumed to ashes. To make up for the loss, Demeter now founded a temple in her own honor at Eleusis and entrusted its keeping to Celeus as its first high priest.[77] She also conferred great honors on Triptolemus, who was an elder brother of the perished Demophoön, and he came to be worshipped as a minor agricultural deity.

Demeter's heart was still saddened by the loss of her daughter and the whole world felt the influence of her dejection. Because she no longer smiled, crops failed to grow, the earth was plagued with famine and the gods were threatened with the loss of their accustomed sacrifices. It became evident to Zeus that some measures must be adopted to appease the anger of the goddess. Accordingly, he dispatched Iris and many of the other deities to implore her to return to Olympus; but all of their supplications were in vain. Finally, Hermes was sent to the lower world to bring back Persephone. Upon his telling Hades that the supreme god had willed that he should resign his bride, Hades was forced to consent and Persephone joyfully prepared to follow her messenger-brother back up to the abode of life and light. But, before taking leave of his wife, Hades gave her several small seeds of a pomegranate, which she thoughtlessly swallowed. Hermes then proceeded to lead his charge up to Eleusis, where her mother was anxiously waiting in the temple; and there, they were joined by Hecate who thereafter remained as the maid's constant attendant and companion.[78]

The happiness of Demeter would now have been complete, had not Hades asserted his rights. These were that any mortal who had tasted food in his realms was bound to remain there forever. In order to prove his claim upon Persephone, he called Ascalaphus, son of the river-god Acheron, to bear witness that she had eaten the pomegranate seeds and, because he revealed the secret, Demeter cast a great rock on the tattler and eventually changed him into an owl.

To avoid a repetition of the world scourge, Zeus succeeded in effecting a compromise with Hades, whereby Persephone was allowed to spend a portion of each year with Demeter and the remainder with her grim lord below. Thus, the Greeks explained the annual change of seasons: for the goddess of the harvest was with her dear daughter on earth for the eight months which began with the sowing in the autumn (in Greece) until the harvest in May, and during this period she smiled upon the earth and blessed it. But, during the four months while the seed-grains were in the ground (in the custody of Hades), her daughter's periodic withdrawal to the lower world brought upon her fond parent a yearly dejection, from which all nature suffered.

---

[76] Iambe was said to have been a daughter of Pan and the garrulous nymph Echo; and her merry jests were made in the meter from which Iambic poetry is reputed to have derived its name.

[77] The Eleusinian Mysteries at first portrayed the sorrowing mother Demeter (Mater Dolorosa) in her search for Persephone. In later times, however, Hades (Pluto) as the maiden's ravisher and Dionysus (Bacchus) as a kindred god of fertility, were added as divine objects of the orgiastic worship. This does not appear to be true in the annual celebration known as the Thesmophoria, which was held in honor of Demeter not only at Eleusis but also at many other places throughout Greece. Akin to the orgiastic worship attending the Eleusinian Mysteries was that accorded—at Piraeus and other places—to the imported Thracian goddess Bendis whose cult had gained converts in Greece (during the life of Socrates).

---

[78] Persephone bore no children to Hades; but a curious tradition, of later times, related that she became the mother of a horned son, Zagreus, by her own father Zeus.

4

The Descendants of the Titans

THIS CHAPTER is largely concerned with a mere labeling of characters. Since many of them, however, play active parts in the manifold scenes which are to follow, they should be introduced now, rather than later, in order to avoid too much subsequent digression.

For convenience, it may be repeated here that Uranus and Gaea had numerous offspring, known as the Titans. They were: Oceanus, Coeus, Crius, Hyperion, Iapetus, Theia, Rhea, Themis, Mnemosyne, Phoebe, Tethys, and Cronus. Of these, the descendants of the first five and of the last (who were masculine divinities) will be discussed in some detail. Their goddess-sisters are given note in connection with their respective husbands.

Descendants of Oceanus

Oceanus, who stood apart in the War of the Titans, wedded his sister Tethys and by her begat a son, Caänthus, all of the Streams on earth, two-thousand nine hundred and ninety-nine daughters known as the Oceanides,[1] and numberless other fair daughters who were called Naiads or Naiades.

After his sister Melia was carried off by Apollo, Caänthus was sent to search for her, but he was unable to secure her release and was killed by an arrow of the Archer-god when he wrathfully set fire to one of his sacred groves.

---

[1] The River-goddess Styx made the number of the Oceanides an even three thousand.

21. Descendants of Oceanus

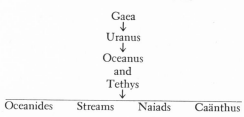

Of the Oceanides, we shall list only those who subsequently, either by marriage or other individual exploit, became parts of Greek mythology. Their names were:

Acaste	Doris	Meliboea	Plouto
Admete	Eidyia	Melobosis	Polydora
Aethra	Electra	Menestho	Prymno
Amphirho	Eudora	Metis	Rhode
Asia	Europa	Ocyrrhoë	Telesto
Callirrhoë	Eurynome	Pasithoë	Theia
Calypso	Galaxaura	Peitho	Thoë
Cerceïs	Hippo	Perseis	Torone
Chryseis	Ianeira	Petraea	Tyche
Clymene	Ianthe	Philyra	Urania
Clytie	Leucippe	Pleione	Xanthe
Daeira	Liriope	Plexaura	Zeuxo
Dione	Melia		

These, the eldest daughters of Oceanus and Tethys, were nymphs of the deep seas and "dispersed far and wide throughout the world, in every place alike served the earth and the deep waters."

The Naiads were likewise water nymphs, but, instead of the open sea, they haunted the streams and rivers flowing through mythological countries.[2] Those, of sufficient importance to be individually noted, were: Abarbarea, Arethusa, Bateia, Caliadne, Chariclo, Cleochareia, Creusa, Ephydateia, Helice, Iphianassa, Pasithea, Periboea, Polyxo, Rhodope, Salmacis, Syrinx, and Zeuxippe.

The Streams, and rivers, were personalized by the pretty conceit that each of them was presided over by a god of the same name, except in the case of the river Styx, whose guiding deity was the name-goddess classed among the Oceanides as "chiefest of them all." Since these offspring of the Greek "Father of Waters" included separate personifications of all the streams known to the ancients, they are fairly numerous. We shall content ourselves, however, with mentioning in detail only those figuring individually in our mythological potpourri.[3]

And, in the references which follow, no effort will be made to separate the name-gods from the Streams themselves.

Achelous and His Descendants

According to tradition, the greatest and oldest of all the Greek river-gods was Achelous, whose waters formed the boundary between Aetolia and Acarnania. His most celebrated performance was a wrestling match, in which he unsuccessfully contended with Heracles for the hand of the lovely Deianeira—an encounter which importantly affected the life of Zeus' heroic son.

By Perimede, daughter of Aeolus, the river-god was the father of Hippodamas and Orestes —two sons about whom nothing of interest is related. However, Hippodamas had a daughter, Euryte, who married Porthaon and became ancestress of a number of rather important people.[4]

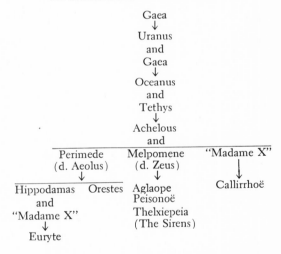

22. Achelous and His Descendants

Another daughter of Achelous—borne by an unnamed wife—was Callirrhoë, who married Alcmaeon and had some interesting marital experiences which are related later in connection with the magic necklace of Harmonia.

---

[2] The nymphs were inferior female divinities who inhabited the waters, woods, and mountains. They may be classified as: (1) water-nymphs—daughters of Oceanus, known as the Oceanides and the Naiads (Naiades); daughters of Nereus, known as the Nereids (Nereides); and daughters of individual streams, wells, and fountains who were also referred to as Naiads; (2) woodland-nymphs—daughters of Zeus and Gaea, called Dryads (Dryades) and Hamadryads (Hamadryades); distinguished because each Hamadryad was associated with a single tree and perished with it, whereas the Dryads, with roving commissions, were considered immortal; and, (3) mountain-nymphs—also daughters of Zeus and Gaea, called Oreads (Oreades), and usually attached to individual mountain localities.

[3] The honor accorded by the ancients to rivers and streams is expansively commented on by the editor of *Bell's New Pantheon*, published in London in 1790:

"Hesiod lays it down as a precept, that no person was to pass a river till he had first washed his hands. The Roman magistrates never crossed the little rivers of the Campus Martius till they had first consulted augurs. But the religious veneration of the ancients for rivers was yet carried much higher; Xerxes in his way to Greece, and before passing the Strymon, sacrificed horses to that river; and Tiridates one to the Euphrates, while Vitellius, who was with him, performed the taurobolic sacrifice in honor of the same river; for bulls were offered to rivers as well as to the ocean and the sea. This practice must have been very ancient, since Achilles says to Lycaon, 'The rapid river, the Xanthus, to which we offer so many bulls, will not protect you.' Indeed this superstition was carried so far, that the young virgins of Troy were obliged, the evening before their marriage, to go and offer their virginity to the river Scamander, in consequence of which we need not be told what sometimes happened. The Grecian youth, according to Pausanias, contented themselves with offering locks of their hair to the river Neda; and Homer informs us, that Peleus consecrated to Sperichius that of his son Achilles."

[4] Ovid relates that Achelous loved Perimele, daughter of another Hippodamas, who was changed into one of the islands of the Echinades group after her father hurled her from a cliff in anger at her acceptance of the river-god's advances.

By Melpomene, the muse of tragedy, he next had three daughters who were renowned in their own right. They were the Sirens,[5] who lived on the uncharted island of Anthemoessa, and whose sweet music enchanted, and fatally lured, all who heard them—until Odysseus avoided destruction by tying himself to the mast of his ship as his men rowed past, after their ears had been stuffed with wax. The individual names of the Sirens were usually stated as Peisonoe, who played the lyre; Aglaope, who sang; and Thelxiepeia, who played the flute. And, it is said that, when Odysseus failed to respond to their musical lure, they cast themselves into the sea from vexation and were drowned. However, a different version related that when Orpheus surpassed their harmonies, as the Argonauts sailed by, the Sirens threw themselves into the sea and were changed into rocks.

Acheron and His Descendants

Acheron was the god of the black river winding through Tartarus—placed in that dim residence because he had dared to refresh the Titans with cooling draughts during their war with Zeus. By the nymph Gorgyra (or Orphne), he was father of the first recorded tale-bearer, a son Ascalaphus, who bore witness against Persephone for having eaten the fatal pomegranate seeds. As previously related, by way of punishment for his tattling, Demeter buried the unfortunate lad under a stone and later turned him into a screech owl.

Alpheius and His Descendants

Alpheius, a river-god of the Peloponnesus, respectably married Telegone, a daughter of Phares, and had a son named Orsilochus. Diocles, the son of Orsilochus, in turn respectably married and had three children—two sons, Crethon and Orsilochus (who were honorably

slain by Aeneas in the Trojan War), and a daughter Anticleia, who became the lawfully wedded wife of Machaon, the eminent physician and surgeon of the Greek army. But there must

23. Alpheius and His Descendants

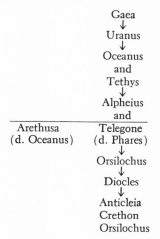

have been something of rakishness in the stream of old Alpheius because, late in life, he fell passionately in love with a young Naiad follower of Artemis, named Arethusa, and sought by force to embrace her. In terror, the nymph fled all the way from Greece to the island of Ortygia (later Syracuse) in Sicily, and there changed herself into a deep and beautiful well. The persistent, old river-god, however, speedily flowed under the sea and mingled his amorous waters with hers.[6]

Asopus and His Descendants

Asopus, another Peloponnesian river-god, was the father of two sons—Ismenus and Pelagon—and sixteen daughters, by Metope, who was a nymph-daughter of the river Ladon. The names of his daughters were: Aegina, Asopis, Chalcis, Cleone, Corcyra, Harpinna, Ismene,

---

[5] The ancient writers do not agree on the names, the numbers, or the parentage of the Sirens, who were collectively called the Acheloïdes or the Acheloïs. Names, differing from those given in the text, were Aglaopheme, Parthenope, Ligeia, and Leucosia. Plutarch says that Phorcys was their father and other writers variously name their mother as Sterope, Terpsichore, and Calliope. Later poets represent them as having wings, which they lost when they were defeated in a musical contest with the Muses.

[6] It was claimed that objects thrown into the river Alpheius reappeared in Arethusa's well. But the geographer Strabo gravely disproves the story, saying "Undoubtedly if before reaching the sea the Alpheius were to fall into some chasm, there would be a probability that it continued its course from thence to Sicily; but since the mouth of the river manifestly falls into the sea . . . it is altogether impossible; and this the water of Arethusa clearly proves, being perfectly fit for beverage."

Nemea, Ornia, Peirene, Plataea, Salamis, Sinope, Tanagra, Thebe, and Thespeia.

Nothing of interest is related about Ismenus or Pelagon, but several of the daughters were carried off by the greater gods, in glorious abductions which produced both stories and children of wide renown.[7]

Asterius and His Descendants

The god of the river Asterius, near Mycenae in Argolis, is mythologically remembered primarily because he was the father of three daughters—Acraea, Euboea, and Prosymna, who were said to have been nurses of the infant Hera.[8] Of these, it is related that Euboea later became the wife of the Argive king, Phorbas. Her sisters are not further mentioned.

Axius and His Descendants

Axius, a Macedonian river-god, was enamored of Periboea, who was the eldest daughter of the mortal Acessamenus. By her he begot Pelegon, who had a son named Asteropaeus—the tallest warrior to fight on either side in the Trojan War. But Asteropaeus had the misfortune to encounter Achilles and, although he was able to wound the greatest fighter among the Greeks, he was himself slain, was thrown into the river Scamander, and "then the eels and the fishes dealt, plucking the fat about his kidneys."

Cebren and His Descendants

By an unnamed mother, the god of the Mysian river Cebren fathered Asterope and Oenone—both of whom married sons of King Priam of Troy.

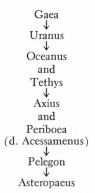

24. Axius and His Descendants

Gaea
↓
Uranus
↓
Oceanus
and
Tethys
↓
Axius
and
Periboea
(d. Acessamenus)
↓
Pelegon
↓
Asteropaeus

Asterope's husband was Aesacus, who was gifted with the power of interpreting dreams, but he grieved so deeply over his wife's premature death that the gods mercifully changed him into a bird.

Oenone was the first love of Paris and contentedly dwelt with him in the woodland fastness of Trojan Mount Ida. It was foretold by an oracle that she alone could save him, if he should ever be wounded. Later, after Paris had deserted her for Helen and was pierced by an arrow on the Trojan battlefield, he caused himself to be carried back to her in their mountain home, where he implored her by the memory of their past love to save his life. Mindful only of the terrible wrong which she had received, the nymph refused his plea and he was taken into the city of Troy to perish. Too late, Oenone repented her quick refusal and hastened within the walls, only to see the corpse of her dear husband as it was being consigned to the funeral fire. Remorsefully, she threw herself on his lifeless form and with it was consumed by the flames.

Cephisus and His Descendants

Cephisus, an Attic river-god,[9] embraced in his winding stream the Oceanid Liriope and by her had a daughter, Diogeneia, and a son, Narcissus.

Diogeneia mated with the mortal Phrasimus

---

[7] The stories are later related in connection with the husbands of the daughters of Asopus. When Zeus carried off Aegina, and Asopus had searched for her everywhere, he was told by Sisyphus that Zeus was her abductor. The indignant river-god overflowed his course and offered to fight with the supreme ruler, only to be struck back into his original bed by a thunderbolt. Pieces of charcoal, which were found in later times on the banks of the river, were supposed to have thus had their origin.

[8] According to Homer, Rhea delivered Hera to Tethys for her childhood education. The statement (of Pausanias) that the daughters of Asterius were her nurses is not necessarily in conflict, because they were the granddaughters of Tethys and might naturally be called upon to help her care for the infant.

---

[9] The Attic Cephisus was frequently confused with the Boeotian river of the same name, whose presiding god was sometimes named as the father of Diogeneia and Narcissus.

and her daughter Praxithea became queen of Athens, by her marriage to Erechtheus whose mythological importance will later appear.

When Narcissus was born, he was a handsome child—but was so delicately formed that his fond mother asked the seer Teiresias whether or not he would live to maturity. The seer's enigmatical reply was: "If he never know himself." The lad's beauty persisted through boyhood and remained when he attained maturity—remained to such an extent that he was sought in love by maidens and youths alike. To all overtures, however, his cold nature gave quick rejection. This included among his passionate victims the unfortunate nymph Echo, who had been reduced to her simple repetitive power of speech because of an earlier garrulity which had offended Hera. One day, while worn with the heat of the chase, Narcissus lay down to slake his thirst in the waters of a cool, clear spring. Seeing his own reflection for the first time, he fell in love with himself, but, being unable to satisfy his physical longing, he faded away—until merciful death proved true the prediction of Teiresias, which poor Liriope had thought to be a mere bundle of empty words.[10]

Eridanus and His Descendants

Eridanus, an Attic river-god, had a daughter Zeuxippe who married Teleon, son of Ion from whom the Ionians derived their name. Her son Butes is later mentioned as one of the more prominent among the Argonauts.[11]

Eurotas and His Descendants

Eurotas was a Laconian river-god, whose daughter Pitane became the mother of Evadne by the sea-god Poseidon.

Inachus and His Descendants

Inachus was the god of the greatest river of Argos (Argolis). In a dispute between Poseidon

and Hera about the possession of the country, he unwisely accepted appointment as one of the judges, who unanimously decided in favor of Hera. As a result, Poseidon—in an act of poor sportsmanship—deprived him of his waters, so that he became dry except in very rainy seasons.

25. Inachus and His Descendants

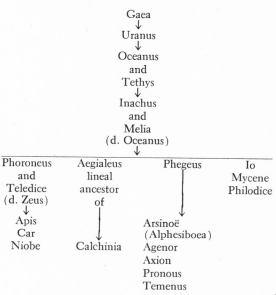

Inachus married Melia, one of the Oceanides, although some say that his wife was one of his own sisters named Argeia. He had three daughters—Io, Mycene, and Philodice—and three sons—Phoroneus, Aegialeus, and Phegeus.

Of his daughters: Philodice married Leucippus, son of Perieres, and had three daughters of such glamour as to attract godly attention; Io was ravished by Zeus and was forced by Hera's wrath to flee to Egypt, where her son, Epaphus, grew up to become worshipped as a divinity of that fertile country; and Mycene became the bride of Arestor and gave her name to the ancient Argive city of Mycenae.

By the nymph Teledice, Phoroneus had two sons, Apis and Car, and a daughter, Niobe. When his father died, Apis became ruler of the Peloponnesus and called the country Apia after himself, but he exercised his authority so harshly that he was assassinated. Car, being content with a smaller (and perhaps safer)

---

[10] Another version of the story relates that Narcissus was induced to the love of himself by Nemesis, who had been besought by Echo to revenge her unrequited love.

[11] Another Eridanus, identified with the Po in Italy, is said to have received the lifeless body of Phaëthon when he was knocked from the Sun-god's chariot by the thunderbolt of Zeus.

dominion, found the city later known as Megara, in Attica. There, he peacefully ruled until his death, meanwhile having erected a citadel called Caria and a temple to Demeter, which remained standing for many years as monuments to his memory. Although Niobe, the daughter of Phoroneus, was divinely descended, it was said that she was the first of many mortal women with whom Zeus consorted, and she bore to him two sons—Argus and Pelasgus—used as the dual justification for the inhabitants about the river Inachus to call their country Argos (or Argolis) and to call themselves Pelasgians.[12]

When the river-god Inachus left his kingdom to Phoroneus, his younger son Aegialeus went into the northern part of the Peloponnesus to the district later known as Achaea and gave his name to the land which was first known as Aegialeia. On the preceding chart, he is denominated as the lineal ancestor of Calchinia, who became one of Poseidon's more important wives.[13]

Phegeus, the third son of Inachus, became king of Phegia in the northwestern part of Arcadia, a city originally named Erymanthus, and taking its later name of Psophis from the mother of Echephron and Promachus (two of the many sons of Heracles). By an unidentified wife, he had four colorless sons—Agenor, Axion, Pronous, and Temenus—and a daughter named Arsinoe whom some of the ancient writers called Alphesiboea. She was wooed by Alcmaeon; and, as a wedding present, received the fatal necklace of Harmonia which is frequently mentioned in the chain of stories, later related in connection with the tragedies which beset the house of Cadmus—tragedies which also included the violent deaths of Phegeus and all his sons.

---

[12] There have been many scholarly books and treatises written about how, when, or where the Pelasgians originated, but it is beyond the scope of this compilation to attempt to resolve the discussion. It is merely noted that they mythologically took their name from the son of Zeus and Niobe.

[13] The chain from Calchinia back to Aegialeus is said, by Pausanias, to have been: Calchinia, daughter of Leucippus, son of Thurimachus, son of Aegyrus, son of Thelxion, son of Apis, son of Telchis, son of Europs, son of Aegialeus.

Ladon and His Descendants

By the nymph Stymphalis, the Arcadian river-god Ladon had three daughters named Metope, Telphusa, and Themis.

Of these, we have already mentioned Metope as the mother of the numerous progeny whom she bore to the river-god Asopus; Telphusa was the cunning nymph who talked Apollo out of building his temple beside her Arcadian spring, by suggesting that the noise of animals watering there might interfere with the devotions of the god's pilgrims; and Themis bore to Hermes a son, Evander, who is said to have led a band of Greek colonists into Italy sixty years before the Trojan War.

Maeander and His Descendants

Maeander, a river of Phrygia, was so distinguished for its many windings that its name has become proverbial. Its personalized god had two daughters, Samia and Cyanea. Samia married Ancaeus, a son of Poseidon who was king of the Leleges on the rugged island of Samos. Cyanea married Miletus, a son of Apollo, by whom she gave birth to Caunus and Byblis—a son and daughter born to unhappiness because their kinship forbade their love to be consummated.

Nilus and His Descendants

Nilus, god of the river Nile (Aegyptus) in Africa, fathered three daughters, whose unions with the descendants of Greek gods form connecting links with some of the myths of Africa —myths which later became so interwoven with those of purely Hellenic origin that the fact of their importation was sometimes overlooked.

One of his dusky daughters,[14] named Achiroë (or Anchinoë), married Belus, a son of Poseidon who traced his lineage back to Inachus; and her sons, Danaus and Aegyptus, returned to their ancestral homeland in Argos to assume the regal honors which were theirs by right of inheritance.

Another daughter, Memphis, had previously married Epaphus, the Egyptian-born son of Zeus and Io. Thus, she had early become tied

---

[14] In referring to the Egyptians, the ancient writers invariably mention the dark color of their skin.

26. Nilus and His Descendants

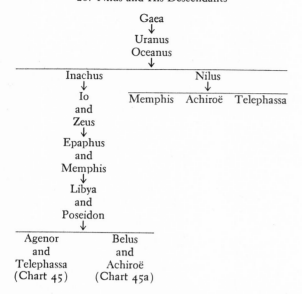

27. Peneius and His Descendants

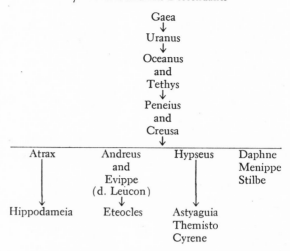

into the Greek pantheon. Similarly, her sister Telephassa[15] married Agenor, in the same line; and further commingled the blood and the histories of the families—both of whom traced back to a common ancestry.

Peneius and His Descendants

By the Oceanid Creusa, Peneius—god of the chief river of Thessaly—begat three sons named Atrax, Andreus, and Hypseus and three daughters named Daphne, Menippe, and Stilbe.

Menippe married Pelasgus, son of Zeus and Niobe; and Stilbe bore to Apollo a son Lapithes, who was the progenitor of a family which fought a famous battle with the curiously formed Centaurs.

About Daphne a story is told, that she was the first love of the god Apollo. As might be expected, mischievous little Eros (Cupid) was involved—for he pierced Apollo's heart with one of his deadly love arrows because the god had ridiculed him upon being too weak to draw the bowstring. At the same time, he loosed an arrow at Daphne, which had the effect of repelling love. The result was inevitable: Apollo

saw Daphne and yearned to take her into his arms, but she saw him and fled with her unbrushed tresses streaming after her in a tantalizing flutter which forced the god to give pursuit. As she was about to be overtaken, the despairing maiden prayed that her father might save her, and, just as Apollo sought her embrace, she was turned into a laurel tree. Despite his frustration, the god decreed that her leaves should always be green and, from her boughs, made himself a wreath which for all time since has been conceived, somewhat paradoxically, as the crowning glory of victory.[16]

Hypseus had three daughters, whose names were Astyaguia, Themisto, and Cyrene. Of these: Astyaguia wedded Periphas, a son of Lapithes; and Themisto became the third wife of Athamas—succeeding two others whose marital lives were wrapped deep in tragedy. The espousal of Cyrene by Apollo is vividly described by Pindar in his Ninth Nemean Ode, where the god is depicted as first seeing the maiden while she is wrestling with a monstrous lion—an action which mortal wooers might

---

[15] Our authority for considering Telephassa as a daughter of the ageless river-god Nilus is the statement of Theocritus that she was of "own blood with Libya," who was both his mother-in-law and his niece by marriage.

[16] Some writers call Daphne a daughter of the river-god Ladon. According to Pausanias, she was an Oread and a priestess of the Delphic oracle. Diodorus describes her as a daughter of Teiresias, better known as Manto. Another story relates that Leucippus, son of Oenomaus, approached her in the disguise of a maiden and was permitted to join her in the hunt, wherein he hoped to win her love. But Apollo's jealousy caused his discovery, while in the bath, and he was killed by the nymphs in Daphne's train.

consider as a dubious augury. However, strangely enough, the son Aristaeus whom she bore to her divine husband was not the powerful and destructive person that one would logically expect from such a union, but was a kindly soul. He was eventually worshipped as a protector of flocks, herds, bees, and olive trees.

Atrax became the father of Hippodameia whom he betrothed to Peirithous, a son of Ixion and half brother to the race of Centaurs—drunken guests at the wedding, which was almost disrupted when they sought to run off with the bride and her maids of honor.

According to the supposedly mythological tradition, Andreus and his son Eteocles ruled for a time the rich city of Orchomenus in Boeotia. When Eteocles died childless, the descendants of Aeolus[17] assumed the sovereignty of both Orchomenus and a strip of country on the coast of Asia Minor (known as Aeolia) which had been colonized by settlers under the rulership of Eteocles or his father. The mythological tradition has, in our generation, unexpectedly been proven as a fact of history. In the early years of the present century, a German scientific expedition uncovered the remains of an ancient city of the Hittites called Khatti (located near the river Halys in Asia Minor). Among other trophies, were unearthed a number of tablets, whose date is placed by archeologists at 1325 B.C. One of them recently has been deciphered as a treaty with a neighboring Syrian king in which the Hittite king, Mursil, calls Eteocles his "brother" and mentions his domain as having a power equal to that of his own.

Sangarius and His Descendants

Sangarius, the god of a fruitful, fishing river in Phrygia, married the Nereid Evagora, by whom he became the father of Hecuba—celebrated as the wife of Priam and the sorrowing mother of many Trojan heroes who were slain during the great war in which the Greeks finally gained victory.[18]

As the captive of Odysseus, Hecuba was taken to the Thracian coast, where she hoped to see her youngest son, Polydorus, whom she had sent to be reared by her daughter, Iliona, and her Thracian husband, Polymestor. When she learned that Polymestor had slain the boy for gold, or at the behest of the Greeks,[19] the furious mother tore out the murderer's eyes; whereupon, she was stoned by the Thracians, but escaped death upon turning into a dog.

Scamander and His Descendants

Scamander, the little stream which flowed through the plain of Troy, was by the gods called Xanthus.[20] The river's presiding deity married the nymph Idaea, who bore to him two daughters—Callirrhoë and Strymo—and a son named Teucer, from whom the country was

28. Scamander and His Descendants

Gaea
↓
Uranus
↓
Oceanus
and
Tethys
↓
Scamander
and
Idaea
↓

Teucer	Callirrhoë
↓	
Bateia	Strymo

---

des and Virgil call her a daughter of Cisseus. The mythographers Hyginus and Tzetzes leave it an open question, and Pherecydes says that she was a daughter of Dymas, or of Sangarius, by the Naiad Evagora. Hesiod names Evagora as a Nereid. Others name Hecuba's mother as Glaucippe, Eunoë, or Teleclia. Owing to conflicting accounts, it is reported that the emperor Tiberius loved to pose the grammarians of his time with the question, "Who was Hecuba's mother?" In this impasse, the text has (perhaps arbitrarily) named Evagora, a Nereid, as her mother and the river-god Sangarius as her father.

[19] Another version relates that Hecuba lured Polymestor to his mutilation with a promise that she was about to give him great treasures.

[20] Originally, Xanthus was a mighty stream into which Achilles was accustomed to cast the bleeding corpses of his Trojan victims. Indignant at this pollution of his waters, Xanthus leapt from his bed and pursued Achilles until the hero was forced to call upon the gods for help. In response, Hera sent Hephaestus who, with his fire, was about to dry up the flooding stream, but desisted while some small trickle still remained.

---

[17] Evippe, the mother of Eteocles, was a daughter of Leucon and a granddaughter of the Aeolid Athamas.

[18] According to Homer, Hecuba was a daughter of Dymas "who dwelt by the streams of Sangarius." Euripi-

anciently called Teucria and its inhabitants were called Teucrians.

Callirrhoë married Tros, and Strymo married Laomedon—both husbands being kings in the royal line of Troy. Teucer's daughter Bateia not only married into royalty, but started it. Her husband was Dardanus, the son of Zeus himself, who went from Greece into Phrygia and founded the town of Dardania, which preceded the establishment of Ilium (or Ilion)—as Troy was anciently called.

Simois and His Descendants

Simois was god of the river of that name, which had its source on Mount Ida, near Troy, and was a tributary of the Scamander. His two nymph-daughters also married into the Trojan line: Astyoche became the queen of Erichthonius, the son of Dardanus; and Hieromneme wedded Assaracus, who took over the rulership at Dardania when his elder brother Ilus decided to remain at his newly founded city of Ilium.

Spercheius and His Descendants

Spercheius, a river-god of southern Thessaly, was the father of Menesthius and Dryops, borne to him by Polydora, a daughter of Peleus, although the children were generally (and perhaps naturally) believed to be the sons of Borus —who was Polydora's husband.

Menesthius was one of the five captains under Achilles, who led the Myrmidons in the battle of Troy. The only thing of further interest related about him is that he wore a "flashing corslet."

Dryops had a daughter named Dryope who, it is said, was changed first into a snake and then into a bird. According to another story, she was approached by Apollo in the form of a tortoise and bore to him a son named Amphissus, who gained much renown for his great strength.

Strymon and His Descendants

Strymon, next to Axius the largest river of Macedonia, was not navigable in its upper part, because the exasperated Heracles filled its bed with stones as a punishment for help which he fancied the river-god had given in dispersing

the cows of Geryon—whose capture was one of the hero's Twelve Labors.

By Neaera, daughter of Pereus, the god of the river had a daughter named Evadne, who married Argus, the son of Zeus; and by Euterpe, the muse of Lyric Poetry, he had a son Rhesus, who in manhood became an ally of the Trojans in the great war. An oracle had foretold that Troy could not be taken if the horses of Rhesus were permitted to pasture on the plain outside the city. To prevent this happening, Odysseus and Diomedes went by stealth into his camp on the night of his arrival and the latter killed the unsuspecting newcomer as he lay sleeping— after which they drove off his horses to feed at a place where the fortunes of the Greeks would be mythologically undisturbed.[21]

Triton and His Descendants

The god of the river Triton in Libya[22] was noted chiefly in mythology for his connection with the goddess Athena who—born motherless —is said to have been placed in his care to be brought up with his daughter Pallas.[23]

One day, while the two girls were playing at war, Pallas was about to strike Athena when Zeus interposed his frightful shield called the aegis, whose sight no mortal could survive. Pallas immediately fell to the ground and expired, and the sorrowful Athena made an image in the likeness of her playmate, which she set up beside her great sire's throne on Mount Olympus.[24] Subsequently, either by accident or

---

[21] The arrival of Rhesus on the scene of battle, with his small bodyguard and snow-white horses "in speed like the winds," and his subsequent death by the sword of Diomedes, are the subject matter of an extant play of Euripides which tragically comes to a close with the appearance of the distraught Muse-mother—above stage and bearing her son's slain corpse in her arms.

[22] According to Herodotus, the Triton in Libya was a lake named Tritonis, in whose shallow waters the vessel of the Argonauts became temporarily grounded. Others connect the legend of Athena with the Triton which was a small river in Boeotia.

[23] Some here find the source of the double name— Pallas Athena—by which the goddess was often referred to.

[24] Athena not only honored the image herself but its protection was unsuccessfully supplicated by Electra, the daughter of Atlas, in attempting to escape the amorous advances of Zeus, by whom she later became the mother of Dardanus and Iasion.

tossed by Zeus in a fit of rage, the image fell into Athena's temple at Troy and, known as the Palladium, became its sacred preserver until it was stolen away by Odysseus and Diomedes during the course of the great war.[25]

The preceding comments have noted only those stream gods who became the fathers of children named by the various mythographers. Other stream gods (and streams) are mentioned throughout the text in connection with such activities as may appear to give them mythological importance. However, for convenience, the following supplemental list is here given:

Aesepus in the Troad; Anaurus in Magnesian Thessaly; Apidanus in Thessaly; Ardescus named by Hesiod without location; Caicus in Mysia; Callichorus in Paphlagonia; Caresus in the Troad; Cayster in Lydia; Cerynites in Arcadia; Cocytus in the lower world; Echedorus in Macedonia; Enipeus in Elis; Erymanthus in eastern Persia; Euphrates in Mesopotamia; Evenus in Aetolia; Granicus in the Troad; Haliacmon in Macedonia; Halys in Pontus; Heptaporus in the Troad; Hermus in Attica; Ilissus in Attica; Indus in India; Ismenus in Boeotia; Istrius (the Danube) in southern Europe; Lethe in the lower world; Meles in Ionia; Nessus in Thrace; Pactolus in Lydia; Parthenius in Paphlagonia; Peneius in Elis; Periphlegethon (Phlegethon) in the lower world; Phasis in Colchis; Phyllis in Bithynia; Practius in the Troad; Rhesus in the Troad; Rhodanus (the Rhone) in southern Europe; Rhodius in the Troad; Selleis in Elis; Thermodon in Pontus; Tiber in Italy; and Tigris in Mesopotamia.

Descendants of Coeus

Coeus, the second born of the Titans, by union with his sister Phoebe, had two daughters who were named Asteria and Leto (the latter being called Latona by the Romans). Although Asteria was already married to her cousin Perses, Zeus made amorous advances, which so frightened her that she turned herself into a quail and dived into the sea. She reappeared from the watery depths in the form of a floating island,

which in her honor was first called Asteria. It was sometimes called Ortygia from the Greek word for "quail."

29. Descendants of Coeus

Gaea
↓
Uranus
↓
Coeus
and
Phoebe
↓
Asteria
Leto

Zeus next turned his attentions to her sister, Leto, and was more successful, but the wretched girl could find no place for her accouchement, because jealous Hera sent a fearful dragon to pursue her—and all the world was afraid to give her entry, lest the well-known wrath of the goddess be incurred. In this unhappy condition, she came to the floating island of Asteria; and, at her touch, it suddenly anchored itself on four sturdy pillars. There, after nine days' labor and attended by all the heavenly goddesses—save only Hera—she gave birth to Apollo and Artemis, her glorious twins who grew up to become two of the brightest divinities in the Greek pantheon. The name of the island was changed to Delos, and it was honored ever after among the sacred places of the earth.

Descendants of Crius

Crius, third born of the Titans, was married to Eurybia, the daughter of Pontus and Gaea, who bore to him three sons named Astraeus, Pallas, and Perses. In connection with the War of the Titans, we have previously mentioned that Pallas, by the river-goddess Styx, fathered the powerful warriors Bia, Cratos, Nike, and Zelus.[26]

Before Asteria was transformed into the floating island, later known as Delos, she was married to Perses and became the mother of Hecate who, with her fiery torch, assisted Zeus

---

[25] Other versions of the story relate that the Palladium fell into Arcadia, from where it was later taken to Phrygia by Dardanus; or that it was sent down by Zeus to Ilus in response to a prayer that his new city should receive some manifestation of divine approval—after which it was housed in an appropriate temple.

---

[26] Of the four warriors, Bia (Force) and Nike (Victory) were represented as female divinities. Nike was called Victoria by the Romans, and her image as the goddess of Victory appears on many of their ancient works of art.

30. Descendants of Crius

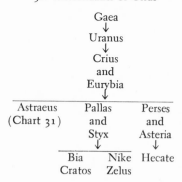

Gaea
↓
Uranus
↓
Crius
and
Eurybia
↓

Astraeus (Chart 31)	Pallas and Styx	Perses and Asteria
	↓	↓
	Bia Nike	Hecate
	Cratos Zelus	

in his war with the Giants. For her help, this mysterious maiden-deity was permitted to retain miraculous powers which she exercised throughout heaven, earth, and sea but especially in the regions of the dead. Her authority was so great that she could bestow on mortals wealth, victory, wisdom, and good luck. Conversely she could withhold such blessings from those whom she thought were undeserving.[27]

The family tree of Astraeus (chart 31) is rather complex, and is given separately.

In addition to their daughter Astraea, the dawn-goddess, Eos bore to Astraeus six sons whose names were Zephyrus (the West-wind), Boreas (the North-wind), Notus (the South-wind), Eurus (the East-wind), Hesperus (the Evening star), and Eosphorus (the Morning star).[28]

During the Golden Age, Astraea lived on earth—passing from country to country and bestowing her blessings upon all just mortals. With the coming of the cruel Brazen Age, when the gods returned to the heavens, she tarried longest among men, but finally withdrew and was placed among the stars as the constellation Virgo, the sixth sign of the zodiac.

Astraea's brother Zephyrus mated with Podarge, one of the foul Harpies, who produced two horses—Balius and Xanthus—which like Balaam's ass were gifted with the power of speech.[29] These semidivine animals (given by Poseidon as a wedding present to Peleus) were inherited by Achilles and, since they were as swift as their wind-father himself, they pulled the hero's battle chariot with a speed which did much toward making his reputation for invincibility.

Boreas, the second son of Astraeus and Eos, carried off Oreithyia, a daughter of Erechtheus, from a place near the river Ilissus which Plato chooses as the locale of his famous dialogue between Socrates and Phaedrus; and it is this incident which starts the old philosopher talking about his ideas on the current unquestioning belief in the whole train of Greek myths. Oreithyia gave birth to two daughters, Chione and Cleopatra, who were espoused by Poseidon and Phineus, respectively. She then bore Haemus and two winged sons named Calais and Zetes. When grown, these fleet warriors joined the Argonauts in their expedition to recover the Golden Fleece, and during their nautical journey, they encountered their brother-in-law, Phineus, whose food was continually being either stolen or loathsomely fouled by the Harpies. This punishment, together with that of blind-

[27] In the Homeric "Hymn to Demeter," Hecate is pictured as joining Demeter in her search for Persephone and, when the maid was found, she remained thereafter as her constant attendant and companion. She thus became identified as a deity of the lower world and was accorded honors at Samothrace, and other places, along with Cybele, Demeter, and Persephone. With her torch in hand, it was believed that she was accustomed to wander about at night accompanied by howling dogs and the souls of the dead. In this character, she was conceived as a three-headed ogress; and the Romans often placed her image at crossroads, where offerings were made to her in order to avert the evils which she controlled. Such offerings were usually dedicated to the goddess under her name as Brimo or Chthonia—appellatives which were likewise applied to Cybele, Demeter, and Persephone as divinities of the region of the dead. For the same reason both Hecate and Persephone were sometimes individually called the dark goddess.

[28] According to Hyginus, Astraea was a daughter of Zeus and Themis. The Roman names for the winds were Favonius (the West-wind), Aquilo (the Northeast-wind), Auster (the South-wind), and it was they who

added Eurus, as the East-wind. The Roman name for the Morning star was Lucifer or Phosphorus and Hesperus was unchanged (although often called Vesper). In later times, the planet Venus and others which, preceded the rising of the sun, were also variously referred to as the Morning star.

[29] The idea that the West-wind carried a curious sort of animal fertility is noted in one of Virgil's "Georgics," translated by John Dryden:
"The mares to cliffs of rugged rocks repair, and with wide nostrils snuff the Western air; when (wondrous to relate) the Parent-wind, without the stallion, propagates the kind."

31. Astraeus and His Descendants

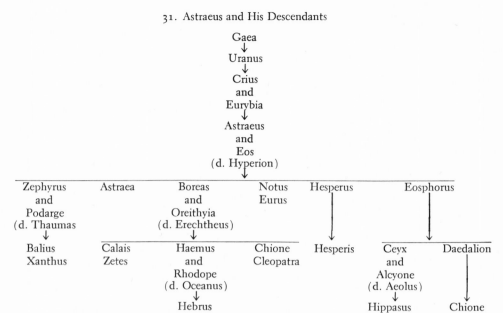

ness, was said to have been inflicted upon him by Zeus because he had foretold to mortals the happening of future events which the god wished not to be revealed.[30] With drawn swords, Calais and Zetes chased the Harpies away and, overtaking them in midair, were about to put an end their filthy lives, but Iris arrived with a message from Zeus that the clawed creatures should be spared and would cease to persecute their blind victim. Haemus, the other son of Boreas and Oreithyia, married the nymph Rhodope, who bore to him a son named Hebrus. The fond parents became so proud that they strutted about among their neighbors and were accustomed to refer to themselves as Zeus and Hera. For their presumption, they were changed into two mountain peaks and placed in the hilly chain which divided Thessaly and Macedonia.[31]

Notus, the south-wind son of Astraeus and Eos, is given but small notice by the mythographers, but they agreed that he was usually a bringer of rain, and it was he whom Zeus called upon to produce the downpour which flooded the earth in the deluge of Deucalion and wiped out the cruel men who were his contemporaries.[32] Eurus, the East-wind, is undistinguished in Greek mythology and was an importation of later writers to fill a manifest gap in the mythological family tree.

Eosphorus, the Morning star son of Astraeus,[33] had two sons named Daedalion and Ceyx. Daedalion gained a somewhat doubtful renown because of the illegitimate amours of his daughter Chione.[34] This beautiful and bold

---

[30] Another story relates that Phineus was punished by Helios for directing the sons of Phrixus about the course from Colchis to Greece. A third relates that he was punished for his cruel treatment of two sons who were borne to him by Cleopatra, sister of Calais and Zetes. Since the winged brothers were responsible for chasing off his tormenters, this last version appears inconsistent—even by the rather loose standards of some of the ancient writers.

[31] The metamorphoses of Haemus and Rhodope into stone peaks was one of the scenes which Athena

wove into her tapestry in the weaving contest which she had with the unfortunate Arachne. She was changed into a spider for challenging Athena to that contest. Respecting Hebrus, his inherited speed is compared (in the Aenid) with that of a Thracian maiden named Harpalyce who could run so fast that horses could not overtake her.

[32] The "south" continent of Australia takes its name from Auster, the Roman name for Notus.

[33] The name Lucifer, by which the Romans called Eosphorus, was sometimes given to Hesperus (the Evening star) because the two were early recognized as identical.

[34] According to Hyginus, the name of Daedalion's daughter was Philonis.

maiden was caressed by both Apollo and Hermes, and by them bore twin sons. With a rather brazen lack of modesty, she openly boasted of her affairs with the two gods, and even attributed the chastity of Artemis to her own want of personal attraction. Infuriated at the slur, the goddess shot an arrow through Chione's tongue, which not only silenced that wagging member but brought on the girl's death. Grieving at his disgrace, Daedalion threw himself from a high cliff but, en route to its rocky base, he was mercifully changed into a hawk and escaped destruction.

Ceyx was the king of Trachis, near the pass of Thermopylae, where the Spartans made their memorable stand against the overwhelming forces of the Persian king, Xerxes. He was a friend of the hero Heracles, but his friendship brought grief to him, because his son Hippasus was slain while aiding the great man in his war against Eurytus, the archer-king of Oechalia. In Ceyx's bereavement, he was sweetly comforted by his daughter Themistinoë, who was wedded to Ares' son, Cyenus, and by his loving wife, Alcyone, who was a daughter of the wind-god Aeolus. Soon after the death of Hippasus, however, the king learned of the tragic end which had come to his brother, Daedalion, and the double loss made him feel that the gods were hostile to him. He, therefore, thought that he should go to Delphi and consult the oracle of Apollo. When he told Alcyone of his intention, she intuitively sensed impending disaster and tried to persuade him to abandon the journey, but he set forth by sea and was drowned when a storm wrecked his vessel. Ignorant of her husband's death, but fearing for his safety, Alcyone prayed for him so incessantly that, in pity, Hera finally sent Iris to break the sad news. This she did, as a dream in the image of Ceyx, and the distraught woman leapt upon a pier head to throw herself into the sea. But, before she struck the water, she was changed into a kingfisher and, in similar form, the merciful gods permitted her lost husband to join her.[35]

Hesperus, the Evening star son of Astraeus, was worshipped with divine honors and was considered by the ancients to be the fairest star in the heavens. According to one legend (which made him a son of Atlas) he was distinguished above all others for his piety and love of mankind—for which he was carried by the winds and placed in the skies. His daughter Hesperis was one of the wives of Atlas, to whom she bore the three maidens known as the Hesperides—happy dwellers in a soft land on the banks of the great river Oceanus, where they presided as guardians of the tree of golden apples which Hera first received as a wedding present from Mother Gaea.

Descendants of Hyperion

Hyperion, next in order of the Titans, was the original god of the sun. He married his sister Theia, and their shining offspring were Helios (his successor as Sun-god), Selene (the Moon), and Eos (the Dawn).[36]

In keeping with his bright function, Helios was conceived as an all-powerful god, wearing a crown of rays and endowed with perpetual youth. Each morning, from the far eastern land of the "blameless Aethiopians," he left his resplendent palace and ascended the heavens in his blazing chariot drawn by four snow-white horses, whose names were Eoos, Aethiops, Bronte, and Sterope.[37] Sundown daily occurred when he descended to rest on the island of Trinacria (Thrinacria), which has been identified with the present Sicily. There, he kept seven flocks of sheep and seven herds of cattle, whose total number never increased and could

[35] Hesiod wrote a poem entitled the "Marriage of Ceyx," but the few fragments which remain do not disclose the name of his bride. The kingfisher—into whose form Alcyone and Ceyx were changed—was fabled to have the power of charming the waves and the winds

during its period of incubation (the seven days preceding December 21), so that the weather was then calm. From this belief, we derive our word "halcyon"—meaning calm or peaceful. The mythological basis for the story is that Alcyone was a daughter of the wind-god Aeolus, who might naturally be expected to extend such a favor to his own child. Another garbled version relates that the wife of Ceyx was a daughter of the first Aeolus (not the wind-god), and that the wedded pair were turned into birds for their presumption in referring to themselves as Zeus and Hera.

[36] The Roman names for Helios, Selene, and Eos were, respectively Sol, Luna, and Aurora. Hyperion, as the first god of the sun, was also sometimes called Sol.

[37] According to Ovid, the names of the horses of the sun were: Eoüs, Pyroïs, Aëthon, and Phlegon.

32. Descendants of Hyperion

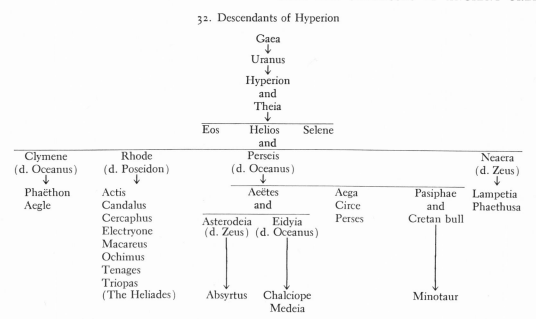

not be decreased without evoking the god's burning wrath. Each night, while he slept, the Sun-god (with his horses and chariot), was quietly placed in a golden boat and was miraculously carried along the river Oceanus, half-way around the earth, until he again reached the land of the Aethiopians—fully refreshed and ready to repeat his cycle.

Since his searching rays penetrated into every part of the earth and heavens, Helios saw everything and—on occasion—imparted to other deities knowledge about some rather odd happenings of which they were unaware. The god of the sun[38] was worshipped in many places, particularly by the inhabitants of the island of Rhodes, who erected a Colossus in his image more than one-hundred feet high and placed it astride the entrance to their principal harbor. (It was considered one of the Seven Wonders of the ancient world.) In Greece, it is said that he contested with Poseidon for the overlordship of Corinth, but was worsted in a decision given by the hundred-armed Briareus to whom the disputants submitted their respective claims.

Perseis, an Oceanid, was conventionally considered to be the wife of Helios. With divine liberty, however, he had children by three others, who were the nymph Neaera, Rhode, a daughter of Poseidon,[39] and the Oceanid Clymene, who was married to the Giant Merops.

The children borne by Perseis were three daughters—Aega, Circe, and Pasiphae, and two sons named Aeëtes and Perses. Aega was of such brightness that, when the Titans attacked Olympus, her rays so dazzled them that they prevailed upon Gaea to place her in a cave of Crete. There she was seduced by Zeus and gave birth to Aegipan, who later assisted Hermes in refitting to their supreme father the sinews of his hands and feet which had been cut out by Typhon.[40] Circe established herself on the mythical island of Aeaea, where she exercised the powers of sorcery—received from her sire—by turning into beasts those who had the misfortune to be shipwrecked upon her shores.[41] Pasiphae married Minos, the king of Crete, and bore to him several normal children, but her most renowned offspring was the Minotaur—a

[38] In Egypt, Helios was identified variously with Apis, Osiris, and Ra.

[39] Rhode was sometimes called Rhodos or Rhodeia.

[40] A foolish story, which ignores the leadership of fully grown Zeus against the Titans, relates that, in the Cretan cavern, Aega was one of his infant nurses and that it was her skin from which his "aegis" was fashioned. She is sometimes identified with the star Capella.

[41] Circe's connection with Odysseus and, later, with his son Telemachus are related in subsequent chapters.

fabulous creature, half man and half bull, who was eventually destroyed by the hero Theseus.[42]

Perses, the younger son of Helios and Perseis, was a mythological dud. Seemingly, he was born only to give his mother's name a somewhat labored perseverance. Not so with his elder brother Aeëtes, who was the king of Colchis, where the Golden Fleece of the ram Chrysomallus was closely guarded by a sleepless dragon. By the Oceanid Eidyia, he had two daughters named Medeia and Chalciope, and by the nymph Asterodeia, he had a son Absyrtus. These children, together with the activities of Aeëtes himself, figure largely in the story of the Argonautic quest and will be here mentioned only briefly.

Chalciope was given as wife to Phrixus, after his arrival at Colchis on the flying ram, and Medeia eloped with Jason when he came to recover its fabled golden fleece. But her lover was not too fortunate in his elopement, because she later killed the two sons borne to him and ran away to Athens, where she became mistress to King Aegeus.[43] Previously, when she and Jason left Colchis, they had taken Absyrtus with them, but, as they were about to be overtaken by Aeëtes, they tore the poor boy into pieces and cast his dismembered body into the sea. This frightful act accomplished its purpose: for the grief-stricken father tarried to gather the mangled remains, while the heartless objects of his pursuit rowed quickly out of sight and reach.[44]

So much—at present—for the descendants of Helios by Perseis. We shall next mention his children borne by Neaera, Rhode, and Clymene.

Neaera, like all nonwater nymphs, was conceived in myth as a daughter of Zeus and Gaea. By her, Helios had two daughters—Lampetia and Phaëthusa. It was their duty to guard the sacred sheep and cattle which he kept on the island of Trinacria or, according to another tradition, on the island of Erytheia, near Cadiz in Spain.

Rhode, a daughter of Poseidon and his queen, Amphitrite, mothered the children of Helios usually referred to as the Heliades,[45] whose names are individually given on the accompanying chart. Electryone, their only daughter, died while quite young and was canonized by the Rhodians. Their sons are remembered collectively because they instituted the practice of sacrificing to the gods on altars which were barren of fire.

Clymene was wedded to Merops, one of the Giants who is said to have been the original ruler of the island of Cos, but she was caressed by Helios and gave birth to a daughter, Aegle, and a son named Phaëthon. Piqued by a scoffing acquaintance who expressed doubt of his high paternity,[46] Phaëthon went to the court of his shining father to obtain proof.[47] Helios readily acknowledged his son and swore by the river Styx to grant any demand which he should see fit to make. When the youth asked permission

---

[42] Details of this incident are expanded in relating the Labors of Heracles and the exploits of Theseus.

[43] According to Apollonius Rhodius, Medeia was eventually given immortality and became the wife of Achilles in the Isles of the Blest.

[44] A different version calls the son of Aeëtes Apsyrtus and relates that he was slain from ambush by Jason on one of the Brygean isles, whence he had led an army of pursuers.

[45] Some writers loosely refer to all children of Helios as Heliades.

[46] The scoffing acquaintance is said to have been Epaphus, the son of Zeus and Io who was born in Egypt. The story itself is considered to have originated in Egypt, where the Sun was recognized as the supreme deity.

[47] As translated by Frank Justus Miller in the Loeb Classical Series, Ovid thus describes the sight which met Phaëthon's eyes when he arrived at his sire's palace:
"The palace of the Sun stood high on lofty columns, bright with glittering gold and bronze that shone like fire. Gleaming ivory crowned the gables above; the double folding-doors were radiant with burnished silver. And the workmanship was more beautiful than the material. For upon the doors Mulciber had carved in relief the waters that enfold the central earth, the circle of the lands and the sky that overhangs the lands. The sea holds the dark-hued gods: tuneful Triton, changeful Proteus, and Aegaeon, his strong arms thrown over a pair of huge whales; Doris and her daughters, some of whom are shown swimming through the water, some sitting on a rock drying their green hair, and some riding on fishes. . . . The land has men and cities, woods and beasts, rivers, nymphs, and other rural deities. Above these scenes was placed a representation of the shining sky, six signs of the zodiac on the right-hand doors, and six signs on the left. . . . The god of the Sun sat on his throne gleaming with brilliant emeralds. To right and left stood Day and Month and Year and Century, and the Hours set at equal distances. Young Spring was there, wreathed with a floral crown; Summer, lightly clad, with garland of ripe grain; Autumn was there, stained with the trodden grape, and icy Winter with white and grizzled locks."

to pilot the glowing sun-chariot in its travel through the heavens, the dumbfounded god almost tearfully besought withdrawal of the daring request and pointed out the tragic consequences likely to ensue from its concession.[48] But Phaëthon was obdurate and his sire's promise, because made in the name of Styx, was inviolable. So, the boy embarked on his perilous journey—only to discover almost immediately that his mortal strength could in no way control the winged steeds that drew his fiery vehicle. Plunging, first high into the heavens and then almost down to earth, he set them both ablaze. The waters of arctic rivers boiled and great deserts were made of lands which were formerly fertile with moist vegetation; even the cold stars were scorched, and many of the constellations fled in panic from the heat which surrounded their usual positions in the skies. At last, to save the whole world from destruction, Zeus knocked the foolish youth from his seat with a thunderbolt, and his lifeless form fell into the river Eridanus in Italy. On the banks of that stream his sisters (Aegle, Lampetia, and Phaëthusa) wept for him so ceaselessly that they were finally changed into poplar trees. And, in that form, they still weep for him—but their tears are amber.

Like their brother Helios, Selene and Eos were resplendent creatures bringing light to the heavens and earth. As goddess of the moon, Selene was conceived to be a beautiful woman with long wings and a golden crown, from which her soft light is shed. In later times, she was almost completely identified with Artemis, under her Roman name of Diana.[49] As with Helios, she was drawn by snow-white horses, but some of the more fanciful poets describe her as pulled by cows, from whose horns they symbolize the crescent moon. Although she mated with Zeus, her real love was Endymion, to

whom she bore fifty daughters and who was the object of her celestial caresses—bestowed while he lay in perpetual youth and sleep.

Eos, the rosy-fingered Dawn, was sometimes called Erigeneia. At the close of each night, she arose from the couch of her beloved Tithonus and in her golden chariot, drawn by the swift horses Lampus and Phaëthon, ascended to the heavens to proclaim the coming of her brother Helios. In this role, it is not strange that she was later identified almost completely with Hemera (Day), and was thought to accompany Helios in his passage from east to west. Not content with her heavenly mate Astraeus, she loved and carried off four handsome mortals.[50] Among them Tithonus was her adored; she loved and nursed him in old age until he was finally turned into a chirping cricket.[51]

Descendants of Iapetus

Iapetus was the last of the male Titans born before Cronus. By an unidentified wife he had a mysterious daughter Anchiale, who is said to have borne the unfathered Idaean Dactyls.[52] By the Oceanid Asia,[53] he had four sons whose names can be found in chart 33.

Both Atlas and Menoetius have been mentioned previously, as two of the unfortunate participants in the War of Titans who were punished by conquering Zeus—Menoetius being imprisoned in Tartarus, and Atlas being

---

[48] Among the dangers pointed out by Helios was the difficulty of managing the steeds "hot with those strong fires which they have within their breasts, which they breathe out from mouth and nostril." Another version of the story makes the golden chariot the repository of the heat, and relates that the horses of the Sun were protected by the insertion of an asbestos board between them and the fiery carriage which they drew.

[49] Selene is sometimes called Mene by the ancient poets.

[50] Apollodorus says that Aphrodite caused Eos to be perpetually in love because she had bedded with Ares. In addition to Tithonus, she carried off: Orion, the son of Hyrieus; Cleitus, the son of Mantius; and Cephalus, the son of Hermes. She also sought to corrupt Cephalus, the son of Deion. These undoubtedly acquiescent abductions are related in connection with the stories about the several men.

[51] When Eos carried away Tithonus, she begged Zeus to make him immortal, but she forgot to request him to add eternal youth. So long as he was young and beautiful, she lived happily with her mortal lover on the banks of Oceanus, at the ends of the earth. When he grew old, she nursed him until, at length, his voice disappeared and his body dried up. She then tenderly locked his withered form in her chamber and he was changed into a cricket.

[52] The Idaean Dactyls were also called Telchines. They are said to have resided on Mount Ida in Phrygia, where they were the first men to discover iron and adapt it to human use.

[53] The wife of Iapetus is also variously called Clymene, Tethys, Asopis, or Libya.

33. Descendants of Iapetus

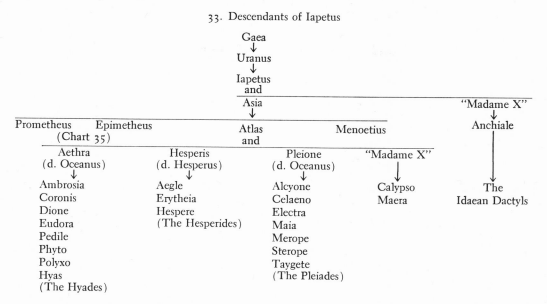

forced to share his fate with the added burden of forever upholding heaven and (perhaps) earth on his head and massive arms.

Menoetius is denied mythological progeny, but Atlas had four wives who bore to him a number of children. By an unnamed wife, he fathered two daughters named Calypso and Maera. Of these, Calypso was a beautiful nymph who lived on the mythical island of Ogygia, where she detained Odysseus for seven years, as he was seeking to return to Ithaca from the Trojan War. During his visit, she became so enamored of him that she offered to give him immortality if he would remain forever. Maera was married to Tegeates, one of the many sons of Lycaon; she is principally remembered because her shade, with those of other persons, appeared before Odysseus when he visited the regions of the dead.

The three other wives of Atlas were Pleione and Aethra (both Oceanids), and Hesperis, the daughter of the Evening star Hesperus. By them he had daughters who, in order, were called the Pleiades, the Hyades, and the Hesperides.

The Pleiades, seven in number, were quite successful in masculine society. Three of them —Electra, Maia, and Taygete—became mates of Zeus himself; Celaeno and Alcyone were lustfully espoused by Poseidon; Sterope was married to Oenomaus, son of Ares; and Merope became the wife of Sisyphus, a son of Aeolus. Notwith-standing their brilliant alliances, the Pleiades grieved so continuously for their father's cruel fate that Zeus mercifully changed them into stars and placed them in the constellation Taurus.[54] At times, one of the stars is invisible —believed by the ancients to be Electra, who has turned her face away while mourning over the fate of the Trojans, for she was the divine ancestress of that conquered race.[55]

Like the Pleiades, the "rainy Hyades" are considered a part of the constellation Taurus. Originally they were conceived as seven sisters who, with their brother Hyas, were children of Atlas and Aethra. Of the sisters, Dione was married to Tantalus, a son of Zeus, and became an ancestress of the commander-in-chief of the Greek forces in the Trojan War; Polyxo was one of several wives acquired by Danaus, an African grandson of Poseidon, but the others seem to have been mythological spinsters. Different versions are given of the reason for their astral translation. One relates that Zeus placed the Hyades among the stars in gratitude for their

---

[54] Pindar and Hyginus note that the Pleiades were virgin companions of Artemis who, together with their mother, were changed into doves and placed in the stars to avoid pursuit by the hunter Orion.

[55] Another story relates that Sterope sometimes became invisible from turning her head in shame that her conjugal mate was not of such divine blood as that of her sisters' husbands.

services in protecting his son Dionysus, either from the wrath of Hera[56] or the persecutions of Lycurgus;[57] and another relates that the action of the gods was taken out of pure compassion for the grief of the maidens at losing their brother Hyas, who had been devoured by a lion. No matter what the reason, the ancients were in agreement that the simultaneous rising of the Hyades and the Sun was a harbinger of rainy and stormy weather.

The names of the Hesperides were Aegle, Erytheia, and Hespere.[58] The classical poets describe them as possessed of the power of sweet song; but their chief mythological duty was to act as guardians of the golden apples[59] which Gaea gave as a wedding present to Hera. Perhaps because the dragon Ladon was assigned to assist them, the musical maidens appear to have taken their task not too seriously: for the golden apples sometimes mysteriously disappeared and, later turning up in the hands of gods or mortals, gave cause for great commotions in heaven and on earth.[60]

This completes the descendants of Iapetus, save only the families of Prometheus and Epimetheus—the two sons who cast their lots with victorious Zeus in the War of the Titans. For them, everlasting renown was in store, because it was ordained that they should be mythologically responsible for the preservation of the race of mortals. Their activities in that connection will be described in the next chapter.

Immediate Descendants of Cronus

The last born of the Titans was Cronus. By his sister Rhea, he had three daughters and three sons in order of birth who were named:

Hestia, Demeter, Hera, Hades, Poseidon, and Zeus.

34. Immediate Descendants of Cronus

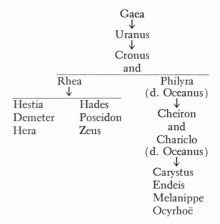

The three daughters, with their brother Zeus, were accounted among the twelve greater gods who dwelt on Mount Olympus and, as such, their functions and activities have previously been noticed in chapter 3.

Hades, the eldest son of Cronus and Rhea,[61] was the ruler of the lower world, who likewise has been referred to in chapter 3, as a principal actor in the story of Demeter and the abduction of her daughter Persephone. Since he was one of the sovereigns of the universe, he had the privilege of ascending Olympus. However, when he was in his own infernal realm, he was quite unaware of what was happening either in the heavens or on earth; only the oaths and curses of men reached his ears. In his travels through the land of the shades, and when he abducted Persephone from earth, his eerie chariot was drawn by four, immortal black horses of whom Abastor was the leader. Either in his own dark kingdom or on the island of Erytheia, he had herds of sacred oxen attended by his herdsman Menoetes, who faithfully performed his duties until Heracles broke his ribs in a wrestling match. The helmet of Hades, which rendered its wearer invisible, is said to have been given to him by Hephaestus, or by the Cyclopes after

---

[56] In their capacity as nurses of Dionysus, the Hyades were sometimes called the Nysaean nymphs.

[57] Hyginus relates that when Lycurgus threatened the safety of Dionysus, the Hyades fled with their infant charge to Thetis, or to Ino at Thebes.

[58] Others name the Hesperides: Aegle, Erytheia, Hestia (or Hesperethusa), and Arethusa.

[59] The place where the tree of golden apples grew was variously stated to be in the extreme west, in Libya or in the far northern land of the Hyperboreans.

[60] The golden apples dropped by Hippomenes in his footrace with Atalanta, and by Eris at the wedding of Peleus and Thetis, are said to have been stolen from the garden of the Hesperides; and, on one occasion, Heracles stole the entire crop.

---

[61] Hades was called Pluto by the Romans. He was regarded as the successor of Tartarus (and sometimes Erebus) in the government of the lower world; and had a number of surnames, which included Ades, Aides, Aidoneus, Apollyon, Chthonius, Dives, Dis, and Orcus.

their delivery from Tartarus to fight against the Titans. This dark cap was sometimes loaned to both gods and men for temporary, and usually laudable, purposes.[62] In keeping with his role, sacrifices made to Hades were supposed to be confined to black sheep; and those who sacrificed had to turn their faces away from his altar. Since he and Persephone had no children and, since the regions of the dead were somewhat removed from the activities which are mythology's primary subject matter, stories about the couple are pretty well limited to those growing out of the abduction already recounted.

Poseidon and Zeus, the last two sons of Cronus and Rhea—unlike their dread brother—were the progenitors of vast numbers of divine and semidivine beings; in the chapters which follow, they will appear and reappear many times.

Cheiron was the curiously formed son borne to Cronus by the Oceanid Philyra, after he consorted with her in the shape of a horse—a disguise adopted to conceal the god's illegitimate amour from his wife, Rhea. Owing to the manner of his conception, Cheiron's body was that of a horse; and, being neither man nor horse, he was called a Centaur.[63] With such mold, one would expect another cruel creature like Typhon or Medusa, but, perhaps because of his high parentage, he was fabled to be one of the wisest and gentlest of all beings. As a youth, he was instructed by Apollo and Artemis; in later life, was renowned for his skill in hunting, medicine, music, gymnastics, and the art of prophecy. These accomplishments he, in turn, transmitted to many distinguished heroes (who, in childhood, had become his pupils); even the great Achilles was proud to claim him not only as a teacher but also as an illustrious ancestor.

By the nymph Chariclo, Cheiron had four children who were named Carystus, Endeis, Melanippe, and Ocyrhoë; but nothing of interest is related about any of them except Endeis. She, however, became celebrated as the wife of Aeacus, a son of Zeus, and as the mother of Peleus and Telamon who, with their descendants, were outstanding actors in the leading events of the Heroic Age.

---

[62] Perseus used the invisible helmet to bring unsuspecting death to the Gorgon Medusa; Hermes concealed himself beneath its protection to slay the Giant Gration.

[63] The name Centaur was derived from the activities of the savage race of bull killers, with which Cheiron had the misfortune to be confused, because of his double form. This race was descended from Ixion, a grandson of the War-god Ares, and Cheiron was only a remote kinsman. Distinguished from them, he was apotheosized as a constellation in the southern hemisphere—called Centaurus—after surrendering his immortality in favor of Prometheus. He died from the painful effects of a wound caused by a poisoned arrow which Heracles had directed at one of the more violent creatures whom later writers considered his near-relative.

5

The Origin of Man

THE EARLIEST STORY of the origin of man considered him to be an autochthon—spontaneously sprung from the earth. But, even though the versions of origin differed, it was commonly agreed that the first age, called the Golden Age, was one of innocence and happiness. Without compulsion, truth and right prevailed; such things as swords, shields, and spears were unknown. The earth brought forth all provender necessary for human sustenance, without the burdensome necessity of sowing or plowing, and life was indeed "just a bowl of cherries." Even in death, a dulcet existence was encountered. After quietly falling into eternal sleep, those who had physically departed still mingled with their mortal brothers, as unseen and beneficent warders of their daily activities. But, with the accession of Zeus, the Golden Age came to its end, and the succeeding race of the Silver Age began to take on characteristics which brought wrath to the gods and misery to man.[1]

One of Zeus' first acts was to shorten the spring and to divide the year into seasons. Then, mankind first suffered the extremes of heat and cold, which forced them to burrow, animal-like, into the ground for protection from inclement nature. Crops no longer grew without planting and resentful men fell to slaying one another and neglected to give heavenly homage. In this state, the gods began to see the necessity of instituting fixed laws with regard to the sacrifices and worship due to them, as their meed for protecting the earth creatures in their miserable existence. Accordingly, an assembly was convened at Mecone (later known as Sicyon), and was attended by Prometheus as the champion of mortals. It was decided that he should slay an ox and divide it into two equal parts, and then the gods should select one part, which thereafter should always be dedicated and offered as a sacrifice to them. By trickery, Prometheus tried to save the better part of the token animal for man's future use: and, after slaying the ox, he wrapped its edible parts in the skin and covered them with uninviting entrails, but he garnished the bones with savory white fat. He then asked Zeus to make his choice of the two portions. The supreme god, pretending to be deceived, chose the bones and, using the insult as an excuse for punishing mankind, he deprived the race of fire. But Prometheus later regained the treasure, by climbing to the heavens and bringing it back to earth in a hollow tube which we know as the dog fennel.[2]

---

[1] Hesiod enumerates five separate Ages of the World: the Golden Age—when men were innocent, happy, god-loving, and free from toil; the Silver Age—peopled with sinful and impious simpletons; the Brazen Age—whose men were sprung from ash trees, died violently in battle, and were not vouchsafed immortality; the Heroic Age—celebrated by those who fought in the Trojan War and performed the great exploits of mythological story; and the Iron Age—which began after the great flood and still continues its unhappy course.

---

[2] Another version of the story makes Prometheus the creator of men, and represents him as originally stealing

Zeus, doubly enraged at the deceit attempted by Prometheus and at his recapture of fire for men, now planned to inflict a dire curse on the race championed by the bold son of Iapetus—a curse in the shape of woman.

It is somewhat of a mystery how mankind had persisted before this without woman; but that it had done so, with no slight degree of happiness, the experience of the Golden Age would seem to prove. However, the bewitching evil was fashioned in heaven by the great craftsman Hephaestus, and all of the gods and goddesses contributed to her perfection. Athena clothed her with silver garments and a seductive veil; Hephaestus added a golden crown to her ensemble; Aphrodite gave her maidenly beauty; Hermes endowed her with boldness and cunning; and each of the other Olympians gave her some power to sway the minds and hearts of men. With this makeup, she was aptly named Pandora: because she was "given" and had "everything."[3] "And wonder took hold of the deathless gods when they saw that she was sheer guile, not to be withstood by men."

Hermes brought the alluring creature as wife to Epimetheus, who promptly forgot the advice of Prometheus that he was not to accept any gift offered by revengeful Zeus. And the warning was not without good reason. Among the gifts from the gods was a jar which contained all ills "to plague men who eat bread"; and this unwelcome baggage she brought with her to the mansion of her bridegroom. Curious to learn what the jar held, Pandora raised its lid and eagerly looked within. Forthwith, there escaped a whole multitude of evils which have since laid their burden on mankind—Toil, Famine, Sorrow, Quarrel, and the whole tribe of physical and mental ailments.[4] Pandora hastened to close the lid, but all had escaped except Hope.

Having sent the beautiful scourge to impious mortals, Zeus now punished their champion by chaining Prometheus to a rock of Mount Caucasus in Asia; and there an eagle preyed upon his continuously regrowing liver until, thirteen generations later, the winged tormenter was slain by Heracles.[5]

The race of men now passed through the

35. Descendants of Iapetus and Asia

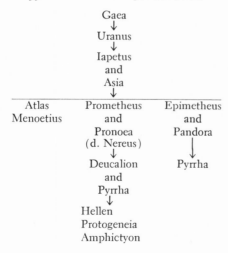

fire from the Sun-god Hyperion and bringing it to them to make their existence less miserable. Since this act was performed in contravention of the will of the gods, he was forced to suffer the same punishment hereinafter related.

[3] The popular conception that Pandora's name meant "a gift of all the gods" is erroneous.

[4] The story related in the text is that given by Hesiod. Other writers have tried to rationalize the myth by saying that the jar contained all of the blessings reserved by the gods for mankind and that, of these, only Hope was saved; or, that the jar contained human plagues and Hope, but that Pandora's frantic closing of the lid (after permitting the plagues to scatter throughout the world), had the doubly harmful effect of keeping that great panacea locked up from mortal use.

[5] The story of Prometheus (Forethought) and Epimetheus (Afterthought) is given in the text as the perhaps inconsistent account which is related by Hesiod. New features were added by Aeschylus in a dramatized trilogy—a part of whose story follows:

Prometheus (himself a god) was a friend of the human race. Although overcome by the superior power of Zeus, he refused to bend his inflexible will. When Zeus succeeded to the supremacy and wanted to extirpate all of mankind, Prometheus prevented execution of the scheme and saved them from destruction. In so doing, he deprived them of any knowledge of the future, but gave them Hope instead. He further taught them the use of fire and many useful arts which added to the comfort of earthly existence. But, as in these things, he acted contrary to the will of Zeus, the supreme god ordered Hephaestus to chain him to a rock in Scythia. There, he was visited and commiserated by Oceanus and he told the passing Io the final fate which was in store for her. Hermes then appeared and asked him to make known a great prophecy concerning Zeus: for Prometheus knew that the god was fated to have a son who would be greater than himself. But the chained Titan steadfastly refused to reveal the secret and Zeus knocked him down to Tartarus with a thunderbolt.

After a lapse of a long time, he was returned to the upper world to endure a fresh course of suffering—tor-

Brazen Age and became so wicked that fraud, violence, and slaughter occupied their waking hours. Truth and honor fled the earth and it was finally abandoned by the gods themselves— Astraea, the goddess of innocence and purity, being the last to leave.[6]

Zeus, burning with anger at the earthly wickedness, summoned the gods to Olympus and announced his intention to destroy the existing mortals and to replace them with others, who should be worthier of life and more reverent toward their deities. Intuitively, he reached for his thunderbolts but stayed his hand as he recalled how those powerful tools of destruction had almost ignited heaven itself when they had been hurled about in the War of the Titans. Accordingly, he decided to accomplish his purpose by the safer method of flooding the globe with waters whose crest would not reach Olym-

pus, but would suffice for a complete earthly inundation. Straightway, he called up Notus, the rain-bringing South-wind, and added to his torrents those of Poseidon and all the rivers in the world.

The ensuing flood engulfed the entire earth, except a small tip of Mount Parnassus, in Phocis near Delphi. There two persons (and only two), found refuge. They were Deucalion, son of Prometheus and the Nereid Pronoea, and his wife, Pyrrha, the daughter of Epimetheus and Pandora.[7] Because they were worshippers of the gods, Zeus permitted them to avoid destruction;[8] and, when the waters had subsided, they offered a sacrifice to him as "Helper of Fugitives."[9] Thereupon, Hermes appeared before them and stated that any wish which they might make would be granted; Deucalion asked that mankind should be restored. According to another tradition, Deucalion and Pyrrha went to the sanctuary of Themis[10] and prayed for the same thing. The goddess bade them cover their heads and to throw the bones of their mother behind them as they walked from the temple. After some doubts about the meaning of this command, they agreed in interpreting "the bones" of their mother to mean the stones of the earth—Mother Gaea. Accordingly, they threw stones behind them; and from those cast by Deucalion there sprang up men and those of Pyrrha produced women. Thus, say the ancients, the human race was mythologically brought into being.

Descendants of Deucalion and Pyrrha

Mere mortals, upsprung from stones, are not of divine blood and this outline is not con-

---

ment from the eagle on Mount Caucasus. According to the accepted version, his liver was renewed at night and eaten continuously during each day. This torment was destined to continue until some other immortal should take his place and descend to Tartarus as his substitute.

Prometheus is aware of his fate and, in a later chapter, we shall see that he was finally relieved of his cruel suffering, when the gentle Cheiron was permitted to substitute for his immortal spirit in the lower world.

[6] As translated by Frank Justus Miller in the Loeb Classical Series, Ovid describes the wickedness of the Age of Iron:

"Straightway all evil burst forth into this age of baser vein: modesty and truth and faith fled the earth, and in their place came tricks and plots and snares, violence and cursed love of gain. Men now spread sails to the winds, though the sailor as yet scarce knew them; and keels of pine which long had stood upon high mountain-sides, now insolently leaped over unknown waves. And the ground, which had hitherto been a common possession like the sunlight and the air, the careful surveyor now marked out with long-drawn boundary-line. Not only did men demand of the bounteous fields the crops and sustenance they owed, but they delved as well into the very bowels of the earth; and the wealth which the creator had hidden away and buried deep amidst the very stygian shades, was brought to light, wealth that pricks men on to crime. And now baneful iron had appeared, and gold more baneful still; war came, which fights with both, and brandished in its bloody hands the clashing arms. Men lived on plunder. Guest was not safe from host, nor father-in-law from son-in-law; even among brothers it was rare to find affection. The husband longed for the death of his wife, she of her husband; murderous step-mothers brewed deadly poisons, and sons inquired into their fathers' years before the time. Piety lay vanquished, and the maiden Astraea, last of the immortals, abandoned the blood-soaked earth."

[7] According to some, the wife of Prometheus was the Oceanid Clymene; and a tradition, ascribed to Hesiod, related that Pandora bore to Zeus a son Graecus, the patronymic of the Greeks.

[8] Another story attributes the deliverance of Deucalion and Pyrrha to Prometheus, who had warned them to build a boat and stock it with provisions—as was done by the biblical Noah.

[9] The surnames of Zeus (or Jupiter) were almost unlimited. Thus, as Jupiter Tonans he was the thunderer, as Jupiter Lucetius he was the bringer of light and, as Jupiter Pluvius he was the bearer of rain.

[10] Aeschylus makes Themis the mother of Prometheus. Her sanctuary in Phocis is said to have been the same as the one later erected—or appropriated—by Apollo and named Delphi.

36. Descendants of Deucalion and Pyrrha

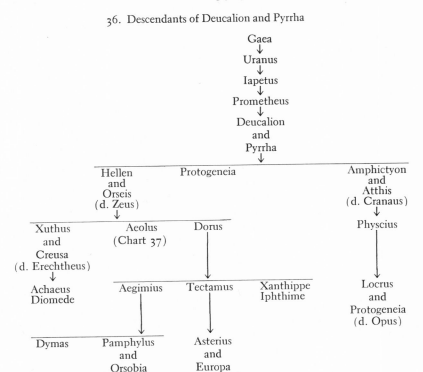

cerned with them, but Deucalion and Pyrrha had three children whose posterity traced their pedigrees back to primeval Gaea. They were Hellen, Protogeneia, and Amphictyon.

Protogeneia became one of the many wives of Zeus, by whom she had a son Aethlius—the mythical ancestor of both the Eleans and the Aetolians.

Amphictyon married Atthis, a daughter of the autochthonous Cranaus, and then proceeded to expel his father-in-law from the kingship of Attica—the district in which the city of Athens was later founded. But, after ruling for twelve years, he was himself expelled by Erichthonius, a curiously formed son of Gaea and Hephaestus—whose body was half man and half snake. Following his expulsion, he apparently went back to the northern mainland because his grandson Locrus was claimed as the eponymous ancestor of the Locrians.[11]

Hellen was considered, by later mythogra-

phers, as the mythical person from whom the Greeks derived their name of "Hellenes"— supplanting the Pelasgians of more ancient times. By the mountain-nymph Orseis, he had three sons named Aeolus, Xuthus, and Dorus.

Aeolus was the progenitor of those who, after his name, were called Aeolids. Their number and their mythological activities were so numerous that the chapters 6, 7, and 8 are devoted to them.

Xuthus followed the example of his uncle Amphictyon and went into the southern Peloponnesus, where he married Creusa, a daughter of the Athenian king, Erechtheus. By her, he had a son, Achaeus, from whom the Achaeans derived their name, and also a daughter, Diomede, who married the Aeolid Deion.[12]

Dorus was the mythological ancestor of the Dorians, who originally inhabited the region around Mount Parnassus, but later spread

[11] In a later chapter, we shall relate how Protogeneia, the wife of Locrus, conceived a son by Zeus from whom the Locrians claimed a more exalted descent.

[12] Ion—the eponymous ancestor of the Ionians—was sometimes called a son of Xuthus; but a story, immortalized by Euripides, relates that his father was the god Apollo.

throughout Greece.[13] He had a daughter Xanthippe, who married Pleuron—a king of the Aetolians, and another named Iphthime, who bore the goat-footed Silenus to Hermes. He also had sons named Tectamus and Aegimius. Of these, Tectamus led a Grecian colony to the island of Crete, where he assumed the government; his son, Asterius,[14] married Europa and brought up the three sons—Minos, Rhadamanthys, and Sarpedon—whom she had borne to supreme Zeus. Aegimius, having succeeded his father as king of the Dorians, became involved with the Lapith king, Coronus, about the boundary lines of their adjoining territories. In the war which ensued, Aegimius prevailed—but only with the help of Heracles, whom he repaid by thereafter holding a third-part of his dominions for later settlement by the descendants of the great hero. This action proved to be of great mythological (and perhaps historical) importance in the years following the Trojan War, when the Heracleidae were in need of a place to settle after they made an unsuccessful attempt to take over their ancestral lands in the Peloponnesus.[15]

Carrying on the alliance of their father, Pamphylus and Dymas—the sons of Aegimius —continued to fight as followers of Heracles; and both of them died while assisting his descendants in the Peloponnesian War. Neither of them left surviving children; but by his marriage to Orsobia, a daughter of the Heraclid Deiphontes, Pamphylus assured the connection between the families of Dorus and Heracles which brought equal luster to them both in the eventual victory over the forces of their enemies.

---

[13] The region lying between Mounts Parnassus and Oeta, which was the ancient home of the Dorians, was itself called Doris.

[14] The mother of Asterius is said to have been a daughter of Cretheus, but her name is not mentioned.

---

[15] The conquest of the Peloponnesus was historically known as the Dorian Invasion, but was mythologically called the return of the Heracleidae.

6

The Aeolids I

THE DEFICIENCY of mythological incident attending Xuthus and Dorus—the two sons of Hellen mentioned in the preceding chapter—is richly overcome when we turn to the activities of their brother Aeolus and his descendants. In his own right, the first Aeolus[1] was known as the first king of Thessaly and the eponymous ancestor of the Aeolians. The preservation of his memory, however, is largely from the interesting stories which were developed around the ten sons and four daughters borne to him by his wife Enarete. Their names are shown on the following chart.[2]

According to our plan, the daughters are later mentioned in some detail in connection with the stories about the children whom they had by their respective husbands—for the young ladies all married into mythology's high society. Suffice here to state that Calyce married Aethlius, a son of Zeus, Canace married Poseidon, Peisidice married Myrmidon (another son of

37. The Pedigree and Children of Aeolus

Gaea
↓
Uranus
↓
Iapetus
↓
Prometheus
↓
Deucalion
and
Pyrrha
↓
Hellen
and
Orseis
↓
Aeolus
and
Enarete
(d. Deimachus)
↓

Deion (Chart 38)	Calyce
Sisyphus (Chart 40)	Canace
Cercaphus (Chart 41)	Peisidice
Macareus	Perimede
Magnes	
Salmoneus	
Perieres (Chart 42)	
Mimas (Chart 43)	
Athamas (Chart 44)	
Cretheus (Chart 46)	

Zeus), and Perimede married the great river-god Achelous.

Deion and His Descendants

Deion reigned over the country later known as Phocis, and married Diomede—daughter of

---

[1] Aeolus, the Homeric god of the winds, was a son of Poseidon, but through his mother, was descended from the original of his name.

[2] The number and the names of the sons of Aeolus typify the manner of mythological development. The most ancient tradition recognized only four sons, namely, Sisyphus, Athamas, Cretheus, and Salmoneus. In the writings of Apollodorus (about 144 B.C.) the number increases to seven, by the addition of Deion, Perieres, and Magnes; Diodorus Siculus (about 60 B.C.) mentions Mimas; Ovid and Strabo (in the first century B.C.) add Cercaphus; and Hyginus (in the second century (A.D.) brings in Macareus.

38. Deion and His Descendants

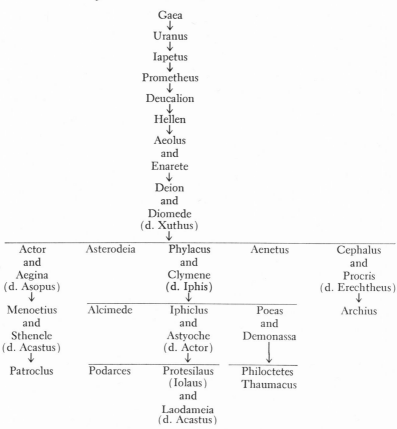

Gaea
↓
Uranus
↓
Iapetus
↓
Prometheus
↓
Deucalion
↓
Hellen
↓
Aeolus
and
Enarete
↓
Deion
and
Diomede
(d. Xuthus)
↓

Actor and Aegina (d. Asopus)	Asterodeia	Phylacus and Clymene (d. Iphis)	Aenetus	Cephalus and Procris (d. Erechtheus)
Menoetius and Sthenele (d. Acastus)	Alcimede	Iphiclus and Astyoche (d. Actor)	Poeas and Demonassa	Archius
Patroclus	Podarces	Protesilaus (Iolaus) and Laodameia (d. Acastus)	Philoctetes Thaumacus	

Xuthus—who bore to him a daughter, Asterodeia, and the four sons whose names are shown on the adjoining chart.

Asterodeia married Phocus, a son of Aeacus, while he was on a visit to her country;[3] but when she went to his home as his bride on the island of Aegina, it was only to become a widow, because her husband was slain by his jealous half brothers when he exceeded them in martial exercises.

Of the sons of Deion, nothing of interest is related about Aenetus, but Actor was doubly celebrated as the lawful husband of Aegina[4] and as the father of Menoetius, who was a member of the Argonautic expedition and a close friend of Heracles.[5] Menoetius married Sthenele, a daughter of Acastus, and they had a son named Patroclus; but the boy killed his playmate Clitonymus in a quarrel over a game of dice and his father was forced to take him from his home to the Centaur Cheiron on Mount Pelion. This normally unfortunate happening proved to be of great benefit to Patroclus, because it gave him the opportunity to become the companion of his kinsman Achilles who was being reared by the gentle Centaur. And when the Trojan War occurred, he went to the conflict as the charioteer and closest friend of the greatest of all the Greek warriors.

The kinship of Patroclus and Achilles is thus indicated:

----

[3] It was said that the visit by Phocus gave to that country the name of Phocis by which it was later known; but the conventional legend derived its name from Phocus, a son of Ornytion.

[4] Aegina was a daughter of the river-god Asopus who was carried off by Zeus.

[5] After the death of Heracles, Menoetius was one of the first to institute sacrifices in his honor.

39. Ancestors of Achilles and Patroclus

```
                  Aegina
                   and
        Actor              Zeus
          ↓                  ↓
       Menoetius           Aeacus
          ↓                  ↓
       Patroclus           Peleus
                             ↓
                          Achilles
```

Cephalus, the youngest son of Deion, married Procris, who was one of the daughters of the Athenian king, Erechtheus; they had a son Archius who is merely a name in the mythological record. Some time later, while Cephalus was hunting game in the forests, he was approached by Eos, the dawn-goddess, with amorous proposals[6] which he rejected because of his great love for his wife. The sly goddess, in apparent good humor, complimented him for his fidelity and bade him not to break his vow until Procris had broken hers. But then she urged him to test her faithfulness. When Cephalus agreed to the suggestion, Eos metamorphosed him into a stranger and gave him presents with which to tempt his unsuspecting wife—who unhesitatingly accepted both the presents and his advances. Thereupon, the angry husband revealed himself and Procris fled in anguish to the island of Crete, where she tearfully besought advice from Artemis. The goddess presented her unhappy supplicant with a dog named Laelaps and a magic spear, neither of which was fated to miss its object;[7] and, changing Procris into the form of a youth, sent her back to join her spouse as a hunting companion. When Cephalus perceived the unerring qualities of the dog and the spear, he offered to buy them, but Procris refused to part with them for any price save love. To this proposal he agreed and, after making herself known, the unhappy woman was able to effect a reconciliation. But tragedy ensued, for Procris was fearful that Eos would again win away her mate's affection and secretly followed him one day while he hunted. As she watched from a nearby thicket, she created a rustling which caused him to throw the never-missing spear at what he thought was a hidden animal. When he discovered that the slain quarry was his own wife, the grief-stricken man leapt into the sea and was drowned.

Phylacus succeeded his father, Deion, as king of Phocis but, for an unexplained reason, left the country and became the eponymous founder of Phylace in Thessaly. By Clymene, a daughter of Iphis, he fathered Alcimede, who later became the mother of Jason, the leader of the Argonauts. He also had two sons, named Iphiclus and Poeas,[8] who carved for themselves prominent niches in the Greek hall of fame.

In addition to an aristocratic position earned as a member of the Argonautic expedition, Iphiclus gained renown for his swiftness of foot by winning the prize for racing at the funeral games held in honor of Pelias. His sons, Podarces[9] and Iolaus, perpetuated their family's glory by valorously leading their fellow-Thessalians on the side of the Greeks at Troy. There, Iolaus gained the surname of Protesilaus by being the first to land upon the enemy's soil but it was not fated that he should hear for long the plaudits of his comrades, for he was the first Greek to be slain—falling victim to the well-aimed spear of Trojan Hector.[10] And, later in the war,

---

[6] Because Eos had an affair with Ares, the paramour of Aphrodite, the jealous goddess of love caused her rival to be perpetually infatuated with various semimortal men. Among them was another Cephalus—son of Hermes, who is often confused with the son of Deion.

[7] According to Apollodorus, the hound Laelaps was given to Procris by the Cretan king, Minos.

When Amphitryon asked the Theban king, Creon, to help him in a war against the Taphians, Creon promised to join the expedition if Amphitryon would first rid his domain of a ravaging vixen, known as the Teumessian fox. This creature was so swift that it was fated she could not be caught. Amphitryon induced Cephalus to lend him the hound Laelaps and, as one might surmise, a most interesting contest took place, because the dog was fated never to miss his quarry and the vixen was fated never to be caught. The apparent contradiction was resolved in true mythological fashion, when—in the midst of the chase—Zeus turned both of the animals into stone.

[8] A different story relates that the father of Poeas was Thaumacus.

[9] The birth of Podarces was mythologically brought about when childless Iphiclus followed the advice of the seer Melampus that he should drink a potion made from the rust of a knife.

[10] The strong affection which existed between Protesilaus and his wife Laodameia was proverbial in ancient story. Two versions have been preserved to us: According to Apollodorus, Laodameia loved her husband so

Podarces met a like fate at the hands of the Amazon Penthesileia.

Poeas, the other son of Phylacus, by a kind of happy (?) fortuity was walking along a path of Mount Oeta when Heracles was in the throes of death and, because he lighted the funeral pyre when requested by the dying man, he became the envied possessor of the great hero's bow and deadly arrows. These unerring implements of destruction were inherited by his son Philoctetes and eventually were largely instrumental in bringing to the Greeks the victorious end of their war with the Trojans.[11] Poeas had a second son, named Thaumacus; but he is remembered only as the eponymous founder of Thaumacia in Magnesian Thessaly, whence his brother Philoctetes led a group of warriors toward Troy.

Sisyphus and His Descendants

Sisyphus is said to have left his ancestral home in Thessaly and to have founded the isthmian town of Ephyra, which was later known as Corinth. According to another tradition,

however, he was given the rulership of the city by the sorceress Medeia, who had assumed it at the request of the inhabitants when their king, Corinthus, died childless.

During his rule, he found the body of his nephew Melicertes on the seacoast of the city and, after burying it, instituted the Isthmian games in the dead youth's honor. But this seems to have been one of the few decent acts in a life so filled with wickedness that, when Sisyphus died, he was punished in the lower world by being forced perpetually to roll a huge marble rock up a hill, from whose summit it always returned to the bottom.[12]

Sisyphus married Merope, a daughter of Atlas who was one of the Pleiades, and by her had four sons named Halmus, Ornytion, Thersander, and Glaucus.

Halmus migrated to Boeotia, where he was given part of the kingdom which his uncle Athamas had earlier received from Andreus, the ruler of the wealthy city later known as Orchomenus. In the new country, he had two daughters named Chryse and Chrysogeneia, who became wives of Phlegyas and Poseidon, respectively, and bore children to whom the rulership of the entire kingdom descended when Eteocles, the son of Andreus, died childless.[13]

Nothing of interest is related about Ornytion. Of his three sons, Thoas remained at

---

much that, after his death, she made an image of him and was accustomed to embrace it with such feeling that the gods took pity upon her and ordered Hermes to bring up the departed spirit from Hades. Laodameia joyfully greeted the phantom (believing it to be the flesh and blood of her spouse returned from Troy), but when it was returned below she was so desolate that she put an end to her own life.

According to Hyginus, when Laodameia heard of the death of her husband, she prayed to the infernal gods to be allowed to converse with him for the space of only three hours. The prayer having been granted, Hermes conducted Protesilaus to the upper world and, when the allotted time was up, Laodameia expired as her husband's shade was led back below.

[11] The actions of Philoctetes at Troy are later related in connection with the great war. However, it should here be noted that he did not enter the battle until a late date, because—initially—he was left behind by his comrades on the island of Lemnos when the stench from his wounded foot made his presence unbearable to them. The wound is said to have been caused from the bite of a serpent, or from an accidental piercing by one of his own arrows which had been dipped by Heracles into the blood of the poisonous Lernean Hydra. After suffering a miserable existence on the island, during the first ten years of the war, he was fetched to Troy by Odysseus and Diomedes. It had been foretold that the arrows of the great hero were a sine qua non of the Greek victory. And, according to legend, it was one of his arrows which brought death to Paris and an end to the conflict.

[12] The ancients were in agreement that Sisyphus was an evil man, but did not agree on any particular reason for his punishment in the lower world. Among the various reasons, it is related that: (1) he was fraudulent, avaricious, and a cheater in trade; (2) he betrayed to men the designs of the gods; (3) he attacked travelers and killed them with huge blocks of stone; (4) he tattled to the river-god Asopus that Zeus had carried off his daughter Aegina; (5) he lived in enmity with his brother Salmoneus, whose wife, Tyro, he seduced; and (6) he refused to return to the lower world when he was permitted to go up to earth for the purpose of punishing his wife for her failure to bury his corpse. His penetration and cunning were more than a match for the arch-thief, Autolycus, who derived from his father Hermes the power of changing the form of stolen goods so that they could not be recognized. By marking his sheep on the bottoms of their feet, Sisyphus was able to detect their theft by Autolycus and to enforce their return. For this, and other similar acts, Homer calls him "the craftiest of men" and, because of an equal cleverness, Odysseus was oftentimes said to have been his son.

[13] The successors were Minyas, the grandson of Chrysogeneia, and Ixion, the son of Chryse.

40. Sisyphus and His Descendants

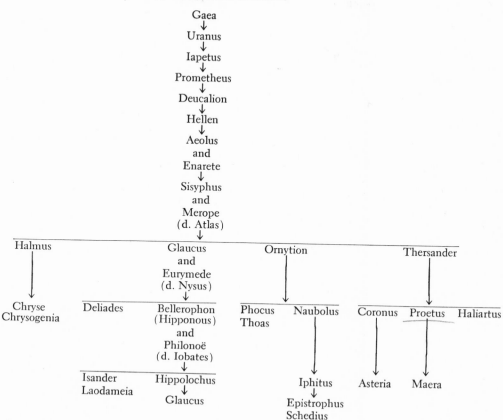

Corinth, where his descendants in the fourth generation were conquered by the forces which were led by the Heracleidae in the Dorian Invasion. Phocus and Naubolus, the brothers of Thoas, went to the district beyond Boeotia which had recently been quitted by their kinsman Phylacus[14] and changed its name to Phocis, when Phocus assumed the government. Later, he died without issue and was succeeded in order by Naubolus and his son Iphitus—the latter becoming famed as one of the Argonauts and also as father of Epistrophus and Schedius, who led their country's forces in the Trojan War. Epistrophus came safely through the conflict, but Schedius was slain by Hector and only his ashes were returned to his Phocian home.

Thersander had three sons, named Coronus, Haliartus, and Proetus. The first two were adopted by their great-uncle, Athamas, in the belief that he had slain (while mad) or had lost all of his own children.[15] Two of their names persevere in mythology as the eponymous founders of Coroneia and Haliartus—two ancient Boeotian towns which bore the same names as earlier localities in Thessaly. Coronus is remembered also as the father of Asteria who was espoused by Apollo. Proetus, the third son of Thersander, is remembered principally because he was the father of Maera, who is said to have been a companion of Artemis, slain by the goddess for having an affair with Zeus.[16]

[14] Phylacus was a son of Deion, who was a brother of Sisyphus.

[15] The adoption was prior to the marriage of Athamas with his third wife, Themisto, by whom he had five sons.

[16] According to some, it was the shade of Proetus' daughter which was seen in the lower world by Odysseus; but the conventional version relates that it was the shade of Maera, the daughter of Atlas, who was married to the Arcadian Tegeates.

Glaucus, who succeeded his father, Sisyphus, as king of Corinth, first ruled at Potniae in Boeotia, where he was noted as a lover of horse racing. Near the town was a magic well and, upon drinking its waters, his horses were stricken with madness.[17] As a result, they ran away while he was driving them in a celebration of the funeral games of Pelias; the chariot was overturned, and Glaucus was killed.[18]

By Eurymede, daughter of Nysus, Glaucus had two sons, named Deliades[19] and Hipponous. While the boys were out hunting, Hipponous accidentally killed his brother and, from the tragic circumstance, received the name of Bellerophon (or Bellerophontes) by which he was afterwards known.[20] According to custom (to avoid the dread Erinnyes), he fled to King Proetus at Tiryns in Argos, where he was kindly received and purified of his crime. During his visit, the king's wife, Anteia (sometimes called Stheneboea), conceived a passion for the youthful suppliant and sent to him proposals for a clandestine meeting. When her "proposals" were rejected, she revengefully told the king

that Bellerophon had made improper advances to her.

Proetus believed his wife and his first impulse was to slay his visitor, but the youth's manners had so endeared him to his host that he could not bring himself to commit the bloody act with his own hands. Accordingly, he sent Bellerophon to the court of King Iobates (his father-in-law) in Lycia, with a sealed letter which the boy assumed was one of introduction and commendation.[21] Actually, the message asked Iobates to bring about the bearer's destruction. Having read the letter, the Lycian king royally entertained his young guest for nine days, and then guilefully suggested that he could gain great honor by slaying the destructive Chimaera, which was pillaging the countryside and devouring its cattle.[22]

Bellerophon decided to accept the suggestion but, before starting out against the monster, he consulted his kinsman Polyidus, who was recognized as a great seer. Polyidus advised him to spend the night in the temple of Athena and—Bellerophon complying—the goddess brought him a bit and bridle and directed him to fasten them to the winged-horse Pegasus. This he easily did while the animal was quenching his thirst at the fountain of Peirene.[23]

Mounted on his swift and willing steed, Bellerophon soared into the skies and, when he saw the Chimaera below, he shot her down with his arrows and returned to the court of Iobates to announce the success of his mission. The amazed king pretended to be pleased, but was secretly chagrined at the ease with which the monster had been overcome; and he now sent the young hero successively against the Solymi, a fierce neighboring tribe, and against the warlike Amazons. But, carried on his winged horse

---

[17] A different legend relates that Glaucus did not permit his mares to breed lest it interfere with their racing speed; and that this so angered Aphrodite that it was she who caused the animals to upset his chariot and bring about his death. Strabo is not satisfied with such a mild end, and says that the king was torn to pieces by his maddened steeds. Others say that Glaucus fed the creatures on human flesh for the purpose of making them more spirited. In later years, when horses became frightened while racing in the Isthmian games, it was believed that their alarm was caused by the dead man's ghost.

[18] Glaucus of Potniae was often confused with Glaucus of Anthedon, who lived in another Boeotian town. One day, while the latter was angling, he threw several newly caught fish upon the bank and was amazed to see them nibble at the grass and then leap back into the water. He proceeded to gratify his natural curiosity by himself eating a few blades of the grass, and was irresistibly impelled to dive into the sea, where he was promptly immortalized as a deity. Like most marine gods, he was gifted with the power of prophecy, and there was a belief in Greece that once in each year he visited all of the coasts and islands, accompanied by a train of sea monsters, and foretold the future prospects of fishermen and sailors.

[19] According to Apollodorus, the son whom some called Deliades was also known as Peiren or Alcimenes.

[20] Since the last part of Bellerophontes means "slayer," some explain the name by saying that the person killed by Hipponous was his brother—or a stranger—called Bellerus.

[21] The message to Iobates seems to be the only evidence in the Homeric poems that the men of the Heroic Age were conversant with writing.

[22] The Chimaera—whom Homer mentions as "of divine stock"—was the offspring of Typhon and Echidna. She was reared by the Carian king, Amisodarus, whose sons, Atymnius and Maris, were slain at Troy by the sons of Nestor.

[23] The fact that the fountain of Peirene was located at Corinth, far removed from Lycia, seems to have offered no mythological hurdle.

and aided by the gods, Bellerophon continued to return victorious.[24] Realizing that the youthful warrior was not fated to be overcome, Iobates made him successor to the Lycian throne and gave him the princess Philonoë as his wife.

Elated by his earthly successes, Bellerophon now essayed a flight to the furthermost limits of the heavens, but, when he had reached a great height, Zeus sent a gadfly to sting Pegasus and the tortured animal threw his rider down to his death.[25]

Surviving him, Bellerophon left his wife, Philonoë, and the three children whom she had borne to him—a daughter, Laodameia, and two sons, named Isander and Hippolochus.[26] Laodameia was later espoused by Zeus, and her son, Sarpedon, took part in the Trojan War, where he was slain by Patroclus.[27] Isander died childless, but Hippolochus had a son Glaucus who challenged the indomitable Diomedes to single combat at Troy. As they were about to clash, however, Diomedes discovered that his adversary was a grandson of Bellerophon and embraced him, instead of fighting—because of an old friendship between their families.[28] But later in the war, Glaucus was slain by Ajax and his departed shade could take comfort only from the fact that his corpse was rescued by Aeneas as it was about to be mutilated by his conqueror.

Cercaphus and His Descendants

Cercaphus, son of Aeolus and Enarete, receives but small mention from the mythographers—except as the father of Ormenus, who was the eponymous founder and king of Ormenium in Thessaly.

41. Cercaphus and His Descendants

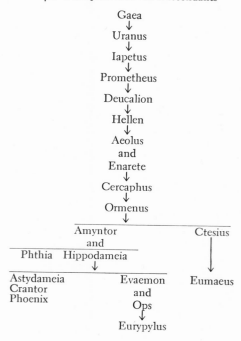

Ormenus was succeeded in the kingship by his son Amyntor, who owned a beautiful helmet that was stolen from him by Autolycus—the thieving son of Hermes.[29] The loss of this treasured possession seemingly set the pattern of an unhappy life, ending in Amyntor's death when he foolishly sought to oppose Heracles, who killed him and ravished his daughter Astydameia.[30]

Astydameia had been borne to Amyntor by his wife, Hippodameia, together with three brothers, whose names were Crantor, Phoenix, and Evaemon. When their father was defeated

---

[24] A different story relates that Bellerophon fixed lead to the point of his lance and thrust it into the Chimaera's throat, where her fiery breath melted the lead and caused her death. Homer adds that, as Bellerophon was returning from his victory over the Amazons, Iobates set a number of Lycian warriors in ambush against him, but the young hero killed them all.

[25] A different version of the story relates that Bellerophon was not killed by his fall but was lamed and made blind, and afterward he perished while miserably wandering about in a lonely field.

[26] According to a curiously inconsistent legend, Isander was slain by Ares as he fought against the Solymi beside his youthful father.

[27] Homer says that Laodameia was killed by the goddess Artemis; and later writers relate that she was thus punished for her assumption of haughty pride at having been wooed by Zeus. She was the wife of Evander—a son of the Sarpedon borne to Zeus by Europa, with whom her own son is often confused.

[28] In his heyday, Bellerophon was entertained for twenty days as a guest by Oeneus, the grandfather of Diomedes, with whom he exchanged presents to evidence their mutual admiration.

[29] Autolycus gave the helmet to Amphidamas; Amphidamas gave it to Molus; and Molus gave it to his son Meriones, who proudly wore it in the Trojan War.

[30] Ctesippus, the son of Heracles and Astydameia, was the great-grandfather of Deiphontes, who was one of the noblest mythological rulers of the Peloponnesus.

in battle by Peleus, king of the Myrmidons, Crantor was given to the conqueror as a hostage against any future breach of the peace treaty. He was assigned by Peleus to be his armor-bearer and later died, while bravely fighting at his master's side in the battle with the Centaurs.

Not content with his lawful wife, Amyntor acquired a mistress named Phthia. At the instigation of his jealous mother, Phoenix seduced the attractive interloper and Amyntor, learning of it, blinded his own son.[31] Phoenix then fled to Peleus, who took the suppliant to Cheiron, with whom his own son Achilles had been placed for rearing. The wise Centaur restored his sight and Peleus now made the refugee king of the Dolopians, a people of Thessaly who dwelt around the Pindus mountains. While at the house of Cheiron, Phoenix became greatly attached to the young Achilles and, when the Trojan War began, he faithfully followed him to the battlefield and continued to give the sage advice which had marked their early association. After the war, he lived for many useful years and, at his death, was tenderly buried at Trachis by Neoptolemus,[32] the worthy warrior-son of his erstwhile friend.

Evaemon, the third son of Amyntor, is remembered only as the father of Eurypylus, who is named by Homer as the leader of Troy of "those that held Ormenium."[33] Unlike some of the other suitors of Helen, Eurypylus fought furiously for her recovery. He was one of the Greek heroes who offered to meet Hector in single combat, but denied that honor he slew many a lesser Trojan. When he was himself wounded in the thigh by an arrow from the bow of Paris, he was nursed and healed by Patroclus, who had been one of his companions at the home of Cheiron. In the division of the Trojan spoils, he received a chest, containing an image of the wine-god Dionysus, which had been made by Hephaestus. Upon opening it, he was stricken with madness. He later recovered, but only after consulting the oracle at Delphi and going to Aroe in Achaea. There, he was received as a divinity and, at his death, was buried with great honors.[34]

Of the descendants of Cercaphus, it remains only to mention Eumaeus, the son of Ctesius and the grandson of Ormenus, who will be noted rather fully in a later chapter as the faithful swineherd of the Ithacan king Odysseus.

---

[31] According to Apollodorus, the accusation of seduction was false.

[32] It is said that Phoenix changed the name of Achilles' son from Pyrrhus to Neoptolemus, by which he later generally became known.

[33] Some writers relate that Eurypylus was a son of Hyperochus and was the father of Ormenus. Others call him a son of Poseidon and Celaeno; and, according to Tzetzes, he was married to Sterope (a daughter of Helios) and they had two sons named Lycaon and Leucippus.

[34] The story of this event in the later life of Eurypylus is thus related by Pausanias, in the Loeb translation of W. H. S. Jones:

"Between the temple of Laphria and the altar stands the tomb of Eurypylus. Who he was and for what reason he came to this land I shall set forth presently. The Ionians who lived in Aroe . . . had . . . a temple of Artemis named Triclaria, and in her honor . . . used to celebrate every year a festival and an all-night vigil. The priesthood of the goddess was held by a maiden until the time for her to be sent to a husband. Now the story is that once upon a time it happened that the priestess of the goddess was Comaetho, a most beautiful maiden, who had a lover called Melanippus. . . . When Melanippus had won the love of the maiden, he asked the father for his daughter's hand. It is somehow a characteristic of old age to oppose the young in most things, and especially is it insensible to the desires of lovers. So Melanippus found it; although both he and Comaetho were eager to wed, he met with nothing but harshness from both his own parents and from those of his lover. The history of Melanippus, like that of many others, proved that love is apt both to break the laws of men and to desecrate the worship of the gods, seeing that this pair had their fill of the passion of love in the sanctuary of Artemis. . . . Forthwith the wrath of Artemis began to destroy the inhabitants. . . . When they appealed to the oracle at Delphi the Pythian priestess accused Melanippus and Comaetho. The oracle ordered that they themselves should be sacrificed to Artemis, and that every year a sacrifice should be made to the goddess of the fairest youth and the fairest maiden. . . . The sacrifice to Artemis of human beings is said to have ceased in this way. An oracle had been given . . . to the effect that a strange king would come to the land, bringing with him a strange divinity, and this king would put an end to the sacrifice to Triclaria. When Troy was captured . . . Eurypylus the son of Evaemon got a chest . . . and, upon opening it, went mad. . . . In this condition he went to Delphi . . . and was told that where he should come across people offering a strange sacrifice, there . . . he should make his home. On landing near Aroe, he encountered a youth and a maiden who had been brought as sacrifices to the altar of Triclaria; and recognizing, and being recognized by the inhabitants, he assumed the throne and put an end to the abominable practice."

Macareus

Macareus, a son of Aeolus and Enarete, was also called Macar. He is remembered only as having committed incest with his sister Canace, and as a result Aeolus killed her.[35]

Magnes and His Descendants

The Aeolid Magnes is said to have given his name to the district of Magnesia in Thessaly.[36] By an unidentified Naiad-nymph, he had two sons, Dictys and Polydectes, who colonized the island of Seriphus, where the infant hero Perseus and his mother Danae were cast upon the shore after being consigned to the sea by the Argive king, Acrisius.

Dictys found the helpless strangers and took them to the court of his brother, who soon fell in love with Danae. Later, when his advances were rejected by her, he suspected that Perseus was responsible and sent the youth on his quest for the Gorgon Medusa, which is related in some detail in chapter 13.[37]

Salmoneus and His Descendants

Salmoneus was married to Alcidice, a daughter of the Arcadian king, Aleus, and by her had a daughter of surpassing beauty who was named Tyro. Leaving Thessaly, he became ruler of a city of Elis, which he called Salmone after himself. Shortly thereafter, Alcidice died, and Salmoneus took a second wife named Sidero, who treated Tyro so unkindly that the maiden was accustomed to leave her home and wander along the banks of the river Enipeus, where she tearfully complained of her step-mother's cruel actions.[38] During one of her visits, Poseidon assumed the likeness of the river-god and, when Tyro submitted to his embraces, she conceived twin sons, who were afterwards named Pelias and Neleus.

Owing to the continuance of Sidero's ill treatment of his daughter (and before the birth of Pelias and Neleus), Salmoneus sent Tyro back to Thessaly, where she became the ward of his brother Cretheus. But this kind act was not in harmony with his later life pattern, because, after Tyro's departure, Salmoneus became so increasingly arrogant that he presumed himself to be the equal of Zeus. In his presumption, he ordered his subjects to sacrifice to him as a god—even claiming that he had the power to produce thunder and lightning.[39] As might be expected, Zeus soon laid low such high pretensions by sending a thunderbolt which destroyed both the proud king and his city.

Meanwhile, in Thessaly, Tyro had secretly given birth to her twin sons and had developed into such a charming woman that she was taken as wife by her uncle Cretheus. When her boys grew into manhood and learned about the cruel conduct of Sidero to their mother, they determined to exact revenge and went to the place where she was living. The once-haughty queen fled in terror to a nearby temple of Athena for sanctuary, but Pelias cut her down even as she piteously knelt at the very altar of the goddess.[40]

Perieres and His Descendants

Perieres was called from Thessaly to become king of Messene, when its ruling family died out. By Gorgophone, the daughter of Perseus and Andromeda, he had two sons who were name Leucippus and Aphareus.[41]

The poet Ovid gives fame to Leucippus in his own right by counting him among the heroes who hunted the Calydonian boar; but he is remembered chiefly as the father of three daughters who were borne to him by Philodice, a

---

[35] Suetonius says that Nero was extremely fond of his own singing and included in his repertoire a number called "Canace in Labor."

[36] A legend reputed to Hesiod relates that Magnes and a brother Macedon were sons of Zeus and Thyia, a daughter of Deucalion.

[37] A variant of the story relates that Danae accepted the proposals of Polydectes and became his wife.

[38] Sophocles wrote two plays (not extant) about the romantic sorrows of Tyro and her love for the river-god Enipeus.

[39] Salmoneus built a bridge of bronze over which he drove his chariot at full speed, so that the rattling imitated thunder, while he had torches thrown into the air to represent lightning.

[40] This act of impiety was not forgiven by Athena and Pelias himself eventually came to a violent end—he was boiled to death by his own daughters.

[41] After Gorgophone was widowed by the death of Perieres, she married the Spartan king, Oebalus, and became the mother of Icarius, Tyndareus, and her own daughter-in-law Arene. The father of Oebalus was another Perieres. This fact, together with the double marriage, has naturally tended to confuse some of the mythological stories.

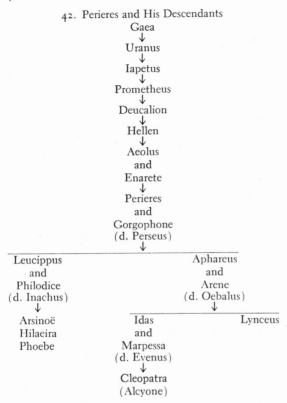

42. Perieres and His Descendants

Gaea
↓
Uranus
↓
Iapetus
↓
Prometheus
↓
Deucalion
↓
Hellen
↓
Aeolus
and
Enarete
↓
Perieres
and
Gorgophone
(d. Perseus)
↓

Leucippus   Aphareus
and   and
Philodice   Arene
(d. Inachus)   (d. Oebalus)
↓   ↓
Arsinoë   Idas   Lynceus
Hilaeira   and
Phoebe   Marpessa
           (d. Evenus)
            ↓
           Cleopatra
           (Alcyone)

daughter of the river-god Inachus. Their names were Arsinoë, Hilaeira, and Phoebe.

Arsinoë gained the somewhat doubtful renown of being considered as the mother of Asclepius by the god Apollo—doubtful, because most accounts credit Coronis as the mother of the man who was admittedly the first mythological physician to mortals. However, the love lives of Hilaeira and Phoebe were clouded in no such obscurity, for the ancient writers all agreed that they were chosen as wives by the Dioscuri —the glorious sons of Leda, whose devotion was so great that they mutually shared a divided immortality.[42]

Aphareus, the second son of Perieres and Gorgophone, wedded Arene, who was a daughter of his own mother and her second husband Oebalus. His sons, Idas and Lynceus, were re-

nowned for their fighting ability and were reputed members of both the Argonauts and the band who engaged in the hunt for the Calydonian boar. In addition, Lynceus was famed for his keen sight, which even permitted him to see things hidden underground or behind trees.[43]

In a winged chariot given to him by Poseidon, Idas carried off Marpessa, a beautiful daughter of Evenus for whose hand Apollo was also a suitor. Both Evenus and Apollo gave chase; but when Evenus was unable to catch up with his rival's vehicle, he slaughtered his own horses and threw himself into the river Lycormas, which was thereafter called Evenus. At Messene, however, Apollo overtook the fleeing pair and tried to take the maiden away from her abductor. At this juncture, Zeus interposed and told Marpessa that she could choose which of her suitors she should marry. After some thought, she decided in favor of Idas, because she feared that the divine Apollo might desert her in her old age—and the archer-god was forced to a humiliating withdrawal. In the course of time, Idas and Marpessa had a daughter, who was named Cleopatra[44] and matured to become the cherished bride of the Calydonian hero Meleager.

The most celebrated story about Idas and Lynceus is their fight with the Dioscuri (Castor and Pollux), with whom they had grown up from childhood. Once, so the legend goes, the four men jointly had stolen some herds of cattle from Arcadia, and Idas was named to allocate the booty. Dividing a bull into four parts, he declared that he who should eat his quarter first should get half of the cattle, and the one who should finish his portion next would be entitled to the remaining half. Idas himself not only devoured his own quarter but also that of his brother Lynceus, before the Dioscuri finished the amounts given to them, and he then drove all of the cattle, as his own, into the neighboring country of Messenia. The sons of Leda were not

---

[42] Although Castor and Pollux—known as the Dioscuri—were twins of Leda, Castor was the son of the mortal Tyndareus, and Pollux was the son of Zeus. When Castor was slain, during a cattle-stealing expedition, Pollux persuaded his supreme father to grant the brothers immortality on alternate days.

[43] From Lynceus, we receive our expression "lynx-eyed."

[44] Cleopatra was also called Alcyone, because Marpessa was once spirited away by jealous Apollo, and she lamented over the separation as Alcyone had earlier wept during the absence of her loved husband, Ceyx.

at all satisfied with such a procedure and, having retaken the herd while Idas and Lynceus slept, placed themselves in ambush in a hollow oak tree. When Idas and Lynceus awakened and discovered their loss, Lynceus went to the peak of a nearby mountain and his penetrating eyes located the place where their despoilers were hidden. Proceeding to the oak tree, they engaged the Dioscuri in a fight, and Idas killed Castor and Pollux ran Lynceus through with his spear. In return, Idas struck Pollux with a stone—so violently that he fell and fainted.[45] Whereupon, Zeus slew Idas with a flash of lightning and his shade was led by Hermes down to the lower world.

Mimas and His Descendants

Mimas, who is first mentioned as an Aeolid by Diodorus Siculus (a comparatively late mythographer), was seemingly brought into the mythological family tree for the purpose of giving a pedigree to Arne—the mother of Aeolus III, by the Sea-god Poseidon. Nothing of interest is related about Mimas himself, or about his descendants (shown on the following

43. Mimas and His Descendants

Gaea
↓
Uranus
↓
Iapetus
↓
Prometheus
↓
Deucalion
↓
Hellen
↓
Aeolus
and
Enarete
↓
Mimas
↓
Hippotes
and
Melanippe
↓
Aeolus II
↓
Arne

chart) except Arne, but, since she was the mother of the god of the winds, she was naturally a lady of degree not to be ignored.

Athamas and His Descendants

The Aeolid Athamas was king of the wealthy city later known as Orchomenus. He was first married to the cloud-nymph Nephele,[46] by whom he became the father of a son Phrixus and a daughter Helle. But he was secretly in love with Ino, a daughter of Cadmus, and had two children by her, who were named Learchus and Melicertes. When Nephele discovered that she had been replaced in her husband's affections, she angrily returned to her home in the skies and demanded of the gods that they should avenge her humiliation.

Multiplied misfortunes now fell on the house of Athamas. Ino hated the children borne by Nephele and vainly endeavored to destroy them; but finally, by inducing the women to roast their seed corn, she was able to create a famine so grave that Athamas sent messengers to the oracle at Delphi to inquire about the means of bringing it to an end. Ino bribed the messengers, and they returned to say that the oracle required the sacrifice of both Phrixus and Helle. Athamas spurned the ghastly suggestion, but his hungry people heard of the false answer and, believing it to be a true oracular pronouncement, demanded that he comply. Reluctantly, he acquiesced and was about to slay his own children on the sacrificial altar, when a wondrous thing occurred. From out of the heavens Hermes led a golden-fleeced ram, which took Phrixus and Helle upon its back and flew away towards the country of Colchis at the eastern end of the Black Sea, anciently known as the Euxine.[47] But, on the way, Helle fell into the strait dividing Abydus from Sestus and was drowned.[48] From this mishap, the waters into

---

[45] Pollux did not die because he was immortal. Lynceus was apotheosized as the six-star constellation, known as Lynx, which was placed in the heavens just north of the Gemini.

---

[46] Nephele's latinized name was Nebula and hence, our "nebulous."

[47] Colchis was considered coterminous with Armenia, before the borders of the latter were limited by the treaty of Versailles.

[48] According to Hyginus, Helle was embraced by Poseidon in the water's depths and bore to him a son named Paeon.

44. Athamas and His Descendants

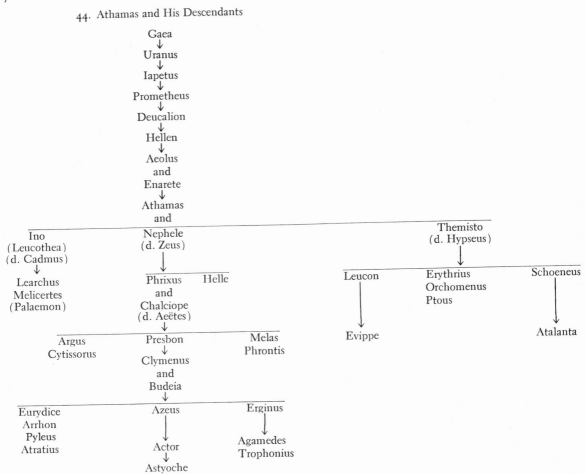

which she fell were anciently known as the Hellespont—now called the Dardanelles.

At Colchis, the golden ram[49] expired and the Colchian king, Aeëtes, hung its shining fleece upon an oak tree near his city, where he set a huge dragon to stand guard over it. Meanwhile, he hospitably received Phrixus and, after learning of his aristocratic lineage, gave the stranger his daughter Chalciope to wife. By her, Phrixus had five sons—the eldest named Presbon somehow contrived to make his way to the land of his forefathers in Greece. The four other sons remained with their parents at Colchis.

After the attempted sacrifice of Phrixus and

Helle, Athamas was seized with madness[50] and shot his son Learchus with an arrow. When this happened, Ino was so frightened that she threw herself, with her remaining son Melicertes, into the sea, and they were miraculously changed into sea-deities under the respective names of Leucothea and Palaemon.[51]

---

[49] The golden ram, gifted with the power of speech, is said to have been the offspring of Poseidon and Theophane and bore the descriptive name Chrysomallus.

[50] One version of the story relates that Athamas was driven mad by Hera because he and Ino had received the infant Dionysus (nephew of Ino) and had reared him as a girl in order to escape detection by the wrathful goddess.

[51] The Romans gave to the metamorphosed Ino the name of Matuta, as the goddess who ushers in the morning. They gave the name of Portumnus to Palaemon and painted him, with a key in his hand, as the guardian of harbors. According to Clement of Alexandria, when the corpse of Melicertes was cast ashore at Corinth, Sisyphus instituted the Isthmian games in his honor, but others say that the games were first introduced in honor of Poseidon, and later identified with the younger sea-deity.

As the murderer of his own son, Athamas was forced to flee his homeland[52] and the oracle, consulted at Delphi, told him that he should settle only where he might be hospitably entertained by wild beasts. Bereft of both wives and children, the crazed man wandered far and wide until, at last, he came to a place where wolves were devouring sheep. But, when he approached, the wolves ran away—leaving their prey behind. Realizing that he had reached the place designated by the oracle, he settled there and married Themisto, a daughter of Hypseus who, with mythological convenience, happened to be waiting for him. The five sons born of their marriage were Leucon, Erythrius, Ptous, Orchomenus, and Schoeneus. Of these, nothing of particular interest is related about Erythrius, Ptous, or Orchomenus.[53]

In the new country, Athamas was given part of the territory by its ruler, King Andreus and, in return, gave to the king as wife the daughter of Leucon[54]—who was the fugitive's granddaughter. As previously noted, this mutual exchange proved to be of both mythological and historical importance.[55]

Schoeneus, the last son of Athamas and Themisto, had a daughter named Atalanta. When she was born, her father was so disappointed that she was not a boy that he exposed her to the wild beasts of the forests. Under the care of Artemis, however, the infant girl was preserved from harm and, suckled by a she-bear, grew into a strong womanhood which enabled her to contest with pursuing Centaurs, to take part in the hunt for the Calydonian boar and to participate on even terms with the masculine heroes at the funeral games celebrated in honor of Pelias. Afterward, Schoeneus rather grudgingly recognized her as his daughter, but, when he desired her to marry, Atalanta made it a condition that all suitors must contend with her in a footrace. She further stipulated that her hand should be given to the first successful contestant, but that the penalty of death should be exacted of all whom she should conquer. Her reason for imposing such a harsh condition was that the Delphic oracle had warned her against marriage and she, who was known as the most swift-footed of mortals, thought that she might thus deter all possible wooers. But Hippomenes, the son of Megareus, took up the challenge, and, during his race with her, successively dropped three golden apples which the goddess Aphrodite had given to him. The maiden could not resist picking them up, and the time so lost permitted him to win both the race and her hand in marriage. Afterward, the wedded pair profaned a temple of Cybele by their embraces within its sacred enclosure and, it is said that, the angry goddess changed them into lions and yoked them to her chariot.[56]

We have mentioned in some detail all of the descendants of Athamas except those who traced their descent through the sons of Phrixus. As previously stated, his eldest son, Presbon, managed to leave Colchis and, arriving in Greece, settled at Orchomenus, a city ruled since its founding by members of his own family.[57] The younger brothers of Presbon were named Argus, Cytissorus, Melas, and Phrontis. Their mythological history is almost wholly connected with the story of the Argonauts, which is related in the following chapter.

After arriving in the land of his forefathers, Presbon asserted no claim; but, when Orchomenus died without issue, his son, Clymenus, inherited the government of the country. By

[52] As the husband of Ino, the daughter of Cadmus, Athamas was considered to be an early king of Boeotian Orchomenus near Thebes, but as a son of Aeolus the legends about him naturally tied in with those of Thessaly.

[53] Orchomenus, from whom the rich Boeotian city was said to have taken its name, was a son of Minyas (descended from Poseidon).

[54] The "new country" was a portion of Thessaly, called Athamantia. Pausanias is authority for the statement that Athamas gave Evippe (the daughter of Leucon) as wife to Andreus and that their son Eteocles succeeded his father in the Thessalian territory to which Athamas fled; he says that Leucon had previously died—and thus avoids a difficult hurdle of chronology.

[55] When Eteocles (the son of Andreus and Evippe, daughter of Leucon) died childless, the descendants of Athamas succeeded to the entire kingdom.

[56] The story given in the text is that which was related in Boeotia. The Arcadian version was generally the same; but the father of Atalanta was called Iasus, her lover was called Meilanion and the place profaned by their embraces was said to be a grove sacred to Zeus.

[57] The maternal ancestress of the Orchomenians (or Minyans, as they were sometimes called) was Chrysogeneia, a granddaughter of Sisyphus, who was a brother of Athamas.

a wife named Budeia, he had five sons, Erginus, Stratius, Arrhon, Pyleus, and Azeus—and also a daughter, Eurydice, who later married Nestor, king of the Pylians.

45. The Claim of Clymenus

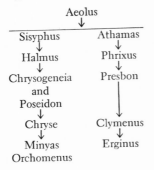

```
                    Aeolus
                      ↓
      ┌───────────────────────────────┐
   Sisyphus                       Athamas
      ↓                              ↓
   Halmus                         Phrixus
      ↓                              ↓
 Chrysogeneia                     Presbon
     and                            |
   Poseidon                         |
      ↓                             ↓
    Chryse                       Clymenus
      ↓                             ↓
    Minyas                        Erginus
 Orchomenus
```

When Clymenus was murdered at a feast of Poseidon by some men of Thebes (whom a trivial cause had thrown into a violent passion), his eldest son, Erginus, received the kingdom and, with his brothers, immediately attacked the neighboring city. Victorious in the battle, Erginus forced an agreement from the Thebans that they should pay him a specified tribute each year. But, when Heracles took over at Thebes, another battle was fought, in which the forces of Erginus were beaten; his brothers Arrhon, Stratius, and Pyleus were slain; his city was razed, and Erginus himself was forced to flee—leaving his youngest brother, Azeus, as the only hope of reviving the shattered Minyan kingdom. The kingdom was eventually revived, for Astyoche, the granddaughter of Azeus, became the mother of two mighty warrior-sons[58] who gloriously led the Orchomenians (Minyans) in the Trojan War.

The vanquished Erginus forlornly wandered

about[59] until he reached a wifeless and childless old age. He finally went to Delphi and inquired of the oracle how he might have some hope of posterity. The Pythia's reply was that he should take unto himself a young wife[60] and, when her advice was followed, the anonymous bride of his choice gave birth to twin sons who were named Trophonius and Agamedes. After the boys grew up, they proved clever at building sanctuaries for the gods and palaces for men, and so they obtained architectural commissions from both divine and mortal sources.[61] Among their works was a treasury which they built for King Hyrieus at his capital city of Hyria in Boeotia. In this construction, the builders inserted a stone which was removable from the outside and were accustomed to use their secret knowledge to pilfer from the treasury at will. Hyrieus was dumbfounded when he saw locks and seals untampered with, while his stored valuables continued to disappear with startling regularity. Accordingly, he placed over his more precious containers a number of traps to close upon anyone who should attempt to lay hands on the treasure. When the unsuspecting Agamedes next entered and was caught fast by one of the traps, Trophonius followed and cut off his head—lest his brother should be tortured and reveal that he himself was a partner in their crime. After this act was accomplished, the earth opened and swallowed up Trophonius at the place where his oracle later functioned.

---

[58] By Poseidon, Astyoche (daughter of Actor, son of Azeus) was the mother of Ascalaphus and Ialmenus.

[59] Pausanias says that Erginus gathered riches while he wandered.

[60] The literal reply of the oracle was that Erginus should "put a new tip to the old plough tree."

[61] At Lebadeia in Boeotia, there was an oracle of Trophonius which, according to Herodotus, was consulted by Croesus when he became afraid of the growing Persian power. Since he had his own oracle, it was sometimes said that Trophonius was a son of Apollo and the two brothers are reported to have assisted in the erection of the god's temple at Delphi.

7

The Aeolids II

Cretheus and His Descendants

THE AEOLID CRETHEUS was the reputed founder of Iolchus in Thessaly. When his brother Salmoneus was stricken dead by Zeus, because of his proud impiety, he left his orphaned daughter Tyro, whom Cretheus had theretofore adopted in order to protect her from the cruel abuses of her stepmother.

Although he was already happily married his ward grew into such an attractive woman that Cretheus made her his wife too.[1] Their marriage produced three sons (Aeson, Pheres, and Amythaon) and a daughter Astydameia, surnamed Hippolyte, who later became the wife of her kinsman, Acastus.

The House of Aeson

Before her marriage to Cretheus, Tyro—while wandering along the banks of the river Enipeus—had been ravished by Poseidon and had secretly given birth to twin sons, who were named Pelias and Neleus. When Cretheus died, Pelias (having learned that Tyro was his mother) came to Iolchus and, claiming the kingship, forced Aeson to flee the country. In his flight, Aeson took with him his young son Jason, whose care he entrusted to the Centaur Cheiron; but he left his wife, Alcimede, daughter of Phylacus,[2] at Iolchus, and she, shortly thereafter, bore another son to him who was called Promachus.

For ten years, Jason remained under the

46. Cretheus and His Descendants

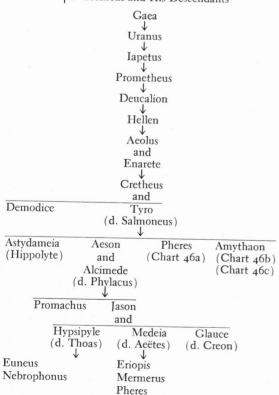

```
                    Gaea
                     ↓
                   Uranus
                     ↓
                   Iapetus
                     ↓
                 Prometheus
                     ↓
                  Deucalion
                     ↓
                   Hellen
                     ↓
                   Aeolus
                    and
                  Enarete
                     ↓
                  Cretheus
                    and
Demodice           Tyro
               (d. Salmoneus)
                     ↓
Astydameia    Aeson      Pheres       Amythaon
(Hippolyte)    and     (Chart 46a)  (Chart 46b)
             Alcimede                (Chart 46c)
           (d. Phylacus)
                 ↓
Promachus     Jason
               and
     Hypsipyle      Medeia        Glauce
     (d. Thoas)    (d. Aeëtes)   (d. Creon)
         ↓
Euneus           Eriopis
Nebrophonus      Mermerus
                 Pheres
```

---

[1] Another story related that the wife of Cretheus was Demodice, who loved Phrixus, the son of Athamas. When he rejected her advances, she went to Cretheus and accused him of improper conduct.

[2] Apollodorus says that the wife of Aeson was Polymede, a daughter of Autolycus; Diodorus Siculus says that her name was Amphinome.

Centaur's tutelage and, in the company of other noble youths, was instructed in all of the useful and warlike arts. But, upon attaining manhood, he was filled with an ambitious desire to return to Iolchus and reclaim the sovereignty which Pelias had stolen from his father. Taking leave of the gentle Cheiron, he set out on his journey and soon reached the river Anaurus.[3] On its banks, he encountered an old woman, who asked him to help her across the swift stream, and he obligingly lifted her in his arms and carried her to the opposite side. When he set the feet of his ancient passenger to the ground, he was astonished to see her change into a beautiful woman, around whose human form played subtle emanations which were the inevitable accompaniments of divinity. The goddess—for she was Hera—revealed her identity to the bewildered youth, and told him that from then on she would be his protectress. She then disappeared and Jason continued toward his destination.

In crossing the stream, Jason had lost one of his sandals, and he arrived at Iolchus shod on only one foot, at a time when Pelias was holding a public banquet in honor of his sea-god father Poseidon. With perhaps a guilty conscience, the usurper had previously consulted an oracle about his future, and had been told to beware of a stranger who should appear with only one sandal. As soon as he saw Jason, he recalled the warning, and sought by guile to avert the danger which it threatened. When Jason boldly announced his birth and the purpose of his entrance, Pelias treated him as a dear kinsman; after five days of feasting, said that he would willingly relinquish the rulership of Iolchus if Jason should first go to Colchis and bring back to Greece the fleece of the golden ram, which had miraculously borne Phrixus and Helle away from the altar whereon they had been placed for sacrifice. The seductive thought of such a glorious adventure so fired the young man's ambition that he readily agreed to his uncle's proposal. He did not, however, think of the perils which it involved, for the golden fleece was guarded by a formidable dragon and the pros-

pective journey to faraway Colchis would itself be an undertaking inevitably fraught with probable disaster.

The Argonauts

The report of Jason's intended expedition quickly gained wide currency, and a large number of his heroic contemporaries assembled at Iolchus to accompany him. As listed by Apollonius Rhodius, the more important personages who gathered were:

Acastus, son of Pelias[4]
Admetus, son of Pheres
Aethalides, son of Hermes
Amphidamas, son of Aleus
Amphion, son of Hyperasius
Ancaeus, son of Lycurgus
Ancaeus, son of Poseidon
Areius, son of Bias
Argus, son of Arestor[5]
Asterius, son of Cometes[6]
Asterius, son of Hyperasius
Augeias, son of Phorbas[7]
Butes, son of Teleon
Calais, son of Boreas
Canthus, son of Canethus
Castor, son of Tyndareus
Cepheus, son of Aleus
Clytius, son of Eurytus
Coronus, son of Caeneus
Echion, son of Hermes
Erginus, son of Poseidon
Eribotes, son of Teleon
Erytus, son of Hermes
Euphemus, son of Poseidon
Eurydamas, son of Irus[8]
Eurytion, son of Irus[9]
Heracles, son of Zeus
Hylas, son of Theidamas

[3] Others mention the river as the Evenus or the Enipeus.

[4] Even though it was the hope of Pelias that Jason and his band would be destroyed in the dangerous undertaking, he could not dissuade his own son from joining in it.

[5] Argus is sometimes called by his patronymic, Arestorides. Hyginus says that his father was Polybus; other writers confuse him with the son of Phrixus, who was later picked up on the way to Colchis.

[6] Asterius is often called Asterion.

[7] Augeias was often referred to as a son of Helios—the older deity who preceded Apollo as the Sun-god. Hyginus names his father as Eleius. Phorbas was a grandson of Apollo; and it may be conjectured that Augeias, as both king of Elis and a descendant of Apollo, was considered to be a son of Helios.

[8] Apollonius Rhodius says that the father of Eurydamas was Ctimenus.

[9] Apollodorus says that Eurytion was a son of Teleon.

Idas, son of Aphareus
Idmon, son of Apollo
Iphiclus, son of Phylacus
Iphiclus, son of Thestius
Iphitus, son of Eurytus[10]
Iphitus, son of Naubolus
Jason, son of Aeson
Laocoön, son of Porthaon
Laodocus, son of Bias[11]
Lynceus, son of Aphareus
Meleager, son of Oeneus
Menoetius, son of Actor
Mopsus, son of Amphycus
Nauplius, son of Clytoneus[12]
Oileus, son of Leodacus[13]
Orpheus, son of Oeagrus
Palaemon, son of Hephaestus
Peleus, son of Aeacus
Periclymenus, son of Neleus
Phalerus, son of Alcon
Phlias, son of Dionysus
Pollux, son of Zeus[14]
Polyphemus, son of Elatus
Talaus, son of Bias
Telamon, son of Aeacus
Tiphys, son of Phorbas[15]
Zetes, son of Boreas

Since the Argonautic expedition was an event of such importance in ancient mythology, it is but natural that later writers felt free to give honorary memberships to other heroic characters. Among these, Apollodorus includes:

Actor, son of Hippasus
Ascalaphus, son of Ares
Atalanta, daughter of Schoeneus
Autolycus, son of Hermes
Euryalus, son of Mecisteus
Ialmenus, son of Ares
Laertes, son of Arceisius
Leitus, son of Electryon
Peneleos, son of Hippalcimus
Phanus, son of Dionysus
Poeas, son of Phylacus[16]

Staphylus, son of Dionysus
Theseus, son of Aegeus

In order to make sure that nobody of mythological importance was left out, Hyginus added Peirithous, the son of Ixion, who accompanied Theseus in many of his celebrated adventures.

While the heroes were gathering, Argus—who was a master shipbuilder—constructed a fifty-oared vessel. It was a marvel of craftsmanship, and was endowed with divinity itself. For, under the supervision of Athena, its timbers included one that was gifted with the power of speech, because it had been cut from the famous oak of Dodona.[17] In honor of its builder, the boat was called the Argo, and the members of the expedition were called the Argonauts.[18]

When the vessel was completed, the collected heroes marched from Iolchus to the nearby beach of Pagasae, where the launching was to take place. As they left the city, Jason's mother Alcimede wept piteously but, with an outward show of confidence, he reassured her and went on his way. However, tears came to his eyes when an aged priestess of Artemis named Philias struggled feebly to his side and kissed his hand—an exertion itself full of meaning because she did not have strength left to speak the well-wishing words which were in her heart.

After arrival at the beach, Jason suggested that a leader of the expedition should be chosen, and the heroes automatically turned their eyes upon Heracles, who was admittedly the greatest of their number. He declined the honor and nominated Jason, as being the person responsible for their gathering. The nomination was acclaimed unanimously, and the proud young captain ordered that a proper sacrifice should be made to Apollo, as the god of embarkation.

The Argo was then launched, as the strong

---

[10] According to Diodorus Siculus, Iphitus was a son of Eurystheus and was slain at Colchis by king Aeëtes.
[11] Laodocus was often referred to as Leodocus.
[12] Hyginus confuses the son of Clytoneus with Nauplius, a son of Poseidon.
[13] The father of Oileus is said, by Eustathius, to have been called Hodoedocus.
[14] Pollux, or Polydeuces, the twin of Castor, was often referred to as a son of Tyndareus.
[15] Apollonius Rhodius and Apollodorus both say that the father of Tiphys was named Hagnias.
[16] According to Apollodorus, the father of Poeas was Thaumacus.

---

[17] This oak tree grew at the ancient oracle of Zeus at Dodona in Epeirus, and was supposed to speak to suppliants with the voice of the god.
[18] The Argonauts were often referred to as the Minyae, or Minyans, because many of them were descended from, or related to, Minyas, the grandson of Poseidon. The expedition itself is sometimes mistakenly referred to by some later writers as the "Argosy" —a word poetically descriptive of the rich merchant ships which plied between the Adriatic port of Ragusa and the eastern seas.

crew pushed her down the rollered ways.[19] In the assignment, the middle seats were given to Heracles and to Ancaeus, the strong son of Poseidon, because all agreed that those positions required the greatest power in rowing, and the role of helmsman was given to Tiphys, the clever son of Phorbas.[20] When the boat had been placed in the water, an altar was raised to Apollo and two steers were led forth by Jason's herdsmen. One was felled by a single blow from the great club of Heracles and Ancaeus killed the other with an axe—after which their carcasses were properly prepared and laid in the altar's flames. As the sacrificial smoke rose, the Argonauts rejoiced when Idmon, the seer-son of Apollo, told them that he saw omens which foretold their success. They grieved for him, however, when he added that the same omens also foretold his own death in their brave enterprise.

At dusk, they feasted and, while the wine cup was liberally passed about, began to tell tall stories about their past experiences and to boast of their anticipated exploits. As the merriment increased, Jason drew somewhat aside and, while brooding over the possible adverse fate of the expedition, was approached by Idas, who drunkenly ridiculed him upon being afraid. Idmon immediately took issue in Jason's behalf, and hot words followed, which were about to produce a fight, but Orpheus picked up his lyre and all angry passion was subdued by his sweet song and the music which flowed from the strings of his divine instrument. The quarrel was soon forgotten and, after a last libation in honor of Zeus, the heroes took to their blankets and slept.

At dawn, Tiphys awakened and aroused the rest with a cry that it was time to be up and away—a cry which was miraculously joined in by the speaking beam of the Argo herself.[21]

With each man in his allotted position, the vessel moved smoothly out of the harbor, as the oars flashed in the sunlight with perfect rhythm. That day, the gods from heaven looked down on the crew, which was composed of the bravest of men, while old Cheiron descended from the heights of Mount Pelion to cry "Good speed and a sorrowless home-return." And with him, came his wife Chariclo, the beautiful Naiad, who brought in her arms the infant Achilles to wave a farewell to his father Peleus.

When the open sea was reached, the sail was hoisted and a favorable wind arose, which rushed the sleek ship through the waters as her company rested luxuriously on their oars and listened to the inspired music of their minstrel Orpheus. At evening, they landed on the shores of Magnesia near the great barrow of Dolops,[22] in whose honor they made a reverent sacrifice of sheep. Owing to a huge swell of the sea, the journey was deferred for two days, but on the third morning the great vessel put out under full sail with a following breeze. For years afterward, men called the Magnesian beach the Aphetae of the Argo—meaning "the starting."

As evening came, the wind died down and a landing was made on the island of Lemnos. This was inhabited by women who had earlier killed the males of their race in a fit of jealousy caused by the actions of their husbands in consorting with captive maids. The queen of the Lemnian women was Hypsipyle; and her aged father, King Thoas, was the only man who had been spared in the general massacre—although even he had been put in a chest and pushed out to sea. When the Argonauts landed, the women thought at first that they were enemy Thracians and rushed down to their beach to engage in battle; Jason, however, sent his herald Aethalides to Hypsipyle, with a request for permission to make a peaceable entry into her city. She thereupon called a council of her women, who first agreed that the request should be denied, but, at the urging of their queen's wise old nurse

---

[19] A later legend relates that the Argo was persuaded to her lauching only by the seductive music of Orpheus and his divine lyre.

[20] As the great-grandson of the Sun-god Apollo, Tiphys may well have been chosen helmsman because of his inherited great sense of sight.

[21] The speaking timber was variously referred to as being in the prow of the Argo or as a beam running through the length of the vessel, and one version of the story said that it was the mast.

---

[22] Dolops is said to have been a son of Hermes, but the ancient literature assigns no reason why he should have been honored with such an imposing tomb.

Polyxo, it was finally decided that the strangers should be invited ashore.[23]

All of the heroes, except Heracles and a few of the younger men, disembarked and Jason went forward to meet Hypsipyle, wearing a purple mantle which Athena had given him when she first laid the keel of the Argo.[24] Marvelously woven into the garment were designs of blazing splendor: the Cyclopes forging a thunderbolt; Amphion and Zethus building the walls of Thebes; Aphrodite carrying the battleshield of Ares; the sons of Electryon fighting off the Taphian raiders; Pelops besting Oenomaus in the chariot race; Apollo shooting down gigantic Tityus; and, lastly, Phrixus in a pose as though listening to the words of his golden ram. In his right hand, Jason carried a "far-darting" spear, which Atalanta had given to him in the hope that she would be permitted to join the Argonauts in their glorious adventure—a request which the thoughtful leader had refused "for he feared bitter strife on account of her love."[25]

When Hypsipyle saw her visitor, as he came into her palace, she was stricken with such desire for him that she caused him to tarry for many days, and, even though the other heroes were not so gorgeously accoutered, each of them found a Lemnian woman in whom a like passion was aroused—and they, too, tarried. At this point, the quest for the golden fleece might well have foundered; but Heracles became tired of waiting on the Argo and went ashore to see what was going on. When he learned the reason for the delay, he chided his amorous comrades so roundly that, with shamed faces, they hastened back to their ship—followed by a host of loving Lemnians, who tearfully begged them not to leave. As Jason parted from Hypsipyle, he told her that, if she should bear him a son, she should send the boy to him at Iolchus. This injunction she later followed in good measure, for she sent him twin sons, who were afterward called Euneus and Nebrophonus.

On the evening of the day when the Argonauts left Lemnos, they landed on Samothrace, which was then called the island of Electra, because it was there that Electra, the daughter of Atlas, was said to have been espoused by Zeus.[26] The island was the seat of the mystic worship of Rhea (under her Phrygian name of Cybele) and the heroes were duly initiated into her secrets, through a ceremony whose rites the ancient mythographers thought it a sacrilege to reveal.

Leaving Samothrace, the expedition proceeded through the Hellespont to an island known as the Mount of Bears. The shores of the island were inhabited by a people known as the Doliones, whose king, Cyzicus, was a near-kinsman of Tiphys and Augeias.[27] He kindly greeted his visitors and invited them to fasten their ship's hawsers in the harbor of his city. This was done and, upon landing, they erected an altar to Apollo as the god of disembarcation. While Cyzicus was entertaining most of the crew ashore, Heracles, who had remained aboard ship, saw a crowd of earthborn monsters rushing down from the mountainside. As they hurled huge rocks at the vessel, he retaliated by slaying many of the savage attackers with his poisoned arrows; the noise of the conflict soon brought the other Argonauts to his assistance, so that the earthborn creatures were all killed and their heaped bodies were left rotting on the seashore to be preyed upon by birds and fishes.

Following this bloody incident, the heroes again took to the sea and sailed all day, but during the night, an adverse wind arose and blew them back from whence they had started. In the darkness, they did not realize where they were, and the Doliones did not know that the incoming men were their recent guests but thought

---

[23] Polyxo suggested that, if the Argonauts were permitted to land, the Lemnian women might have sons who would grow up to protect them against their enemies and to take over the burdensome task of tilling the fields.

[24] Athena is sometimes mentioned as the actual builder of the Argo; but the conventional story relates that Argus did the manual work under her divine supervision.

[25] Apollodorus, and other writers, name Atalanta as a member of the Argonauts, but the text follows the story related by Apollonius Rhodius, whose extant work contains the most detailed recital of the expedition.

---

[26] According to a different story, Dardanus and Iasion, the sons of Zeus and Electra, were born in Arcadia from which place Dardanus went to Phrygia, stopping en route at the island of Samothrace.

[27] Cyzicus was a half brother of Phorbas, who was the father of Augeas and Tiphys.

they were enemy Pelasgians. A furious battle followed, in which many of the Doliones were slain and Jason himself unwittingly killed their king, Cyzicus. At dawn, both sides perceived the fatal—and cureless—error, and the Argonauts were stricken with grief when they saw the lifeless bodies of their recent hosts. Cyzicus was tenderly buried and, for three days, the Argonauts joined with the Doliones in honoring him with funeral games. But no kind of atonement could assuage the sorrow of Cleite, the widowed wife of Cyzicus, and she hanged herself. And at her death, it is said that the nymphs of the groves about her palace wept so copiously that their tears made a fountain which, in her memory, was afterward called by her name.

As perhaps fitting punishment, the gods caused a tempest to arise, which continued for twelve days—during which the Argonauts were forced to remain ashore and feel sorry for both the Doliones and themselves. On the twelfth night, while Acastus and Mopsus were keeping watch over the sleeping heroes, a kingfisher flew from the skies and alighted upon the stern of their vessel. From its cries, Mopsus—who was gifted with the power to understand the speech of birds—learned that the tempest was about to cease, but the expedition should not proceed farther until after sacrifices had been made to Cybele on nearby Mount Dindymum. The indicated sacrifices were performed by Jason, who climbed the peak, accompanied by some of his younger comrades, and drove oxen, which were offered as propitiatory victims on the altar of the great mother-goddess. As a sign of her favor, she caused a stream to gush forth from the mountain top and, afterward, the dwellers around there called it the "spring of Jason." This done, an honorary feast was held on the neighboring Mount of Bears, and the Argonauts were gratified to see the storm die down.

In their joy at being permitted to resume their journey, they rowed all day long with vigorous strokes which sent the Argo through the sea with the speed of Poseidon's own steeds. But his comrades were eventually spent with their exertions and Heracles alone was left to propel the boat forward by his unaided power. In so doing, his oar snapped in the middle and the great man could only glare about him in dis-

gusted silence. However, the accident occurred just as a landing was made in the country of the Mysians, who welcomed the heroes hospitably and speedily produced food and wine for feasting.

Heracles was in no mood to join in the festivities and, accompanied by his young friend, Hylas, plunged into the forest in search of a tree from which to fashion another oar. He soon located a huge pine tree, which seemed fit for his purpose, and, with a single great effort, pulled it from the ground—roots and all. He then started to return to the beach. In the meanwhile, Hylas had gone farther into the wood in search of water for the evening meal. He approached a spring called Pegae and, as he leaned over it to fill his bronze pitcher, a Naiad-nymph named Ephydateia fell in love with his handsome form and pulled him to her bosom beneath the water's surface. Alone of his comrades, Polyphemus heard the boy's cry as he was drawn into the spring. Thinking that Hylas had been attacked by wild beasts or by men in ambush, he ran into the forest with drawn sword. There, he met Heracles as he was returning with the pine tree on his shoulders and told him of the cry which had come to his ears. Fearful for the safety of his youthful companion, he hastily threw down his burden and sped with Polyphemus toward the place from which the call had come.

After their night of entertainment by the Mysians, Tiphys urged the Argonauts to go aboard their vessel and to proceed on their voyage immediately, in order to avail themselves of a favorable wind which had sprung up. They eagerly followed his advice, without giving thought to the fact that Heracles, Polyphemus, and Hylas were missing. When they were well out to sea and it was discovered that their comrades had been left behind, a great quarrel arose. Telamon rushed in a rage upon Tiphys, and accused him of deliberately abandoning Heracles because of jealousy, but his attack was stayed by Calais and Zetes, who were in fact envious of the great man's exploits.[28] At this

---

[28] Heracles never forgave an enemy and, because Calais and Zetes had acquiesced in his abandonment, he later slew both of them as they were returning from the funeral games of Pelias.

juncture, the sea-god Glaucus came up from the depths and announced that Heracles was predestined to return to Argos and to continue the labors imposed upon him by Eurystheus; and that Polyphemus was predestined to remain among the Mysians for the purpose of founding a glorious city at the mouth of the Cius river.[29] He also told the Argonauts of the fate which had overtaken Hylas—and then plunged beneath the waters.[30] These divine revelations effectually put an end to the quarrel started by Telamon and, continuing on their way, the voyagers came at sunrise to the land of the Bebrycians (Bebryces).

When Heracles was unable to find Hylas, he threatened to lay waste the whole land of the Mysians; but they turned aside his wrath by swearing an oath that they would continue to search for the lost youth and gave as pledges some of their noblest sons. It is said that, for many years afterward, they persisted in their inquiries and that they often gave prayers for the safety of Trachis: because it was there, with his good friend Ceyx, that Heracles settled the Mysian hostages, and it was from there that he was himself later taken from earth to immortality.

The king of the Bebrycians was a proud son of Poseidon named Amycus, whose skill at boxing had never been matched by any man. On the arrival of the Argonauts, he went down to their ship and, in his insolence, scorned to ask them the occasion of their voyage or who they were. He bluntly announced that no stranger to his land was permitted to depart, unless he should first contend with its king in hand-to-hand battle without weapons. His challenge was promptly accepted by Pollux, the immortal son of Zeus; and Lycoreus, the Bebryx servant of Amycus, produced two pairs of gauntlets. In the match which followed, Castor and Talaus acted as seconds for Pollux, and Amycus was attended by two of his subjects named Aretus and Ornytus. However, seconds proved of little use in the one furious round of the contest: because Pollux, after skillfully evading the wild

swings of his gigantic adversary, struck him a terrific blow above the ear, which crushed in the bones of his skull and brought on quick death.

The enraged Bebrycians picked up their clubs and spears and charged in upon Pollux. The Argonauts leaped to his assistance and, in the fray which followed, many of the Bebrycians were slain and their whole body was so utterly worsted that they fled in dismay. In the fighting, Talaus, Iphitus, and some of the other Argonauts were wounded, but their injuries were soon mended, and the night of victory was spent in feasting and sacrifice to the immortals, while the glorious lyre of Orpheus mingled with his voice in songs of sweet harmony.

On the next morning, the Bebrycian shore was left and the expedition, passing through the Bosporus, landed the next day on the coast opposite the land of the Bithynians. At this place, the Argonauts encountered the blind seer, Phineus, a son of Agenor who—while king of the Thracians—had married Cleopatra, a sister of Calais and Zetes. For reasons previously related, he had been deprived of his sight and placed on the desolate coast, where the foul Harpies were accustomed to descend upon his table whenever he prepared to eat. When the Argonauts landed, they found the old man in a state of starvation. But Zeus had tempered the cruel punishment by having his oracle declare to the blind man that eventually he would be released from his misery by a band of great heroes.[31]

When Phineus heard the voices and footsteps of the approaching men, he intuitively knew that they were his destined deliverers. Feebly rising from his couch, he crept to the door of his dwelling and, as the Argonauts gathered around his emaciated form, he told them his pitiful story. In its telling, he revealed himself as the brother-in-law of Calais and Zetes and implored them, especially, to deliver him from the persecutions of the Harpies. Learning from him that such an act of mercy would not contravene the will of the gods, the winged sons of Boreas readily assented to assist their kins-

---

[29] The city was itself later known as Cius.
[30] According to another version, Glaucus revealed himself only to Jason.

[31] In chapter 4 an account is given of the reasons why Phineus was visited with his cruel punishment.

man, and a feast was prepared—which immediately drew the Harpies to their accustomed place of defilement.

When the famished old man attempted to transfer a morsel to his eager mouth, the foul creatures dived from above to snatch it from his trembling fingers—as had been their habit. But, this time, a surprise was in store for them, because, with swords in hand, the swift sons of the North-wind sprang from the ground on their own wings and the terrified Harpies were forced to flee through the air. Since Calais and Zetes were endowed with the speed of their windy sire, they soon overtook their quarry and were about to slay them in the clouds, but Iris, the messenger of the gods, suddenly appeared and proclaimed that, according to the will of Zeus, the filthy bird-women were to be spared and would never thereafter persecute the blind seer. When Calais and Zetes questioned her, and she told them that the promise of the supreme god had been buttressed by his oath made in the name of the river Styx, they sheathed their swords and returned to their comrades.

After this deliverance, Phineus feasted ravenously; and the Argonauts seized their opportunity to learn from his prophetic wisdom the future which was in store for them. He told them that the next danger which they were to encounter would be their passage between the Cyanean rocks, known as the Symplegades—accustomed to strike together so frequently and so forcibly that no vessel had been able to navigate the channel which intermittently separated them. He advised his hearers to approach the rocks carefully and then let loose a dove to essay the perilous journey—following which the Argo itself could be driven through the channel, if the rocks were caught on the rebound. On the hopeful assumption that this peril would be negotiated, he next told his visitors how to cope with others which would be met on their way to Colchis.[32]

After he ended his words of caution, he announced that he was ready to die, because he knew that in the afterworld he was destined to live in perfect bliss. But his neighbors now gathered around him and asked that he should remain in their midst, so that they might continue to have the benefit of his sage advice. Among them was Paraebius, who related a sad story of the atonement required of him for his father's reckless action in cutting down a tree and thus bringing death to its resident Hamadryad-nymph. Although the Argonauts sympathized with the youth, they secretly were irritated at the delay of their mission which was occasioned by having to listen to the long tale of woe. But it developed that no actual delay was thus caused, for the Etesian winds sprang up and, blowing from the north, effectually forestalled their departure for forty days.[33]

When the contrary winds finally abated, the heroes took their accustomed places in their vessel and—following the advice of Phineus—Euphemus carried on board a trembling dove, wherewith to test the passage between the clashing Cyanean rocks. Soon after the Argo was under way, it entered a narrow strait where the recurrent thud of the rocks could be plainly heard, and, as they rounded a bend of the strait, the Argonauts saw them. At the next rebound, Euphemus released the dove, which flew swiftly through the separating chasm and barely completed the passage as the huge rocks again rushed together and shored off part of her tail feathers. Speedily, they plied their oars and rowed with all their might through the channel which was again opened; and, with the unseen help of Athena who caused the rocks to pause in their motion, the Argo passed through safely. Thereupon, the rocks met and became fast rooted to each other—for this they were des-

---

[32] Phineus mentioned, in order, the prospective meetings of the Argonauts with: the rocks called Symplegades, the Bithynians, the Mariandyni, the Chalybes, the Tibareni, the Mossynoeci, the winged birds of Ares, the Philyres, the Macrones, the Becheiri, the Sapeires,

the Byzeres, and the Colchians (in whose land the Golden Fleece was guarded by a sleepless dragon).

[33] When the neighboring island of Ceos was parched with the heat of the Dog star (Sirius), Aristaeus—the pastoral son of Apollo and Cyrene—sacrificed to Zeus and prayed that the land might be relieved; and thereafter the north-winds, called Etesian, were permitted to blow through the region for forty days in each year and bring respite from the summer's heat.

tined to do whenever any ship should succeed in driving between them.[34]

Although Tiphys exultingly announced that their escape was certain proof of Athena's continuing protection, the margin of safety had been so slight that Jason—deeply feeling the responsibility of his leadership—declared that he had committed a great error when he allowed Pelias to persuade him to undertake the dangerous expedition. But his comrades shouted loudly with cheerful words which soon dispelled his distress and, pulling lustily on their oars, drove their vessel on into the mouth of the river Phyllis. Here they passed the shrine of Dipsacus, who had hospitably entertained Phrixus as he was flying to Colchis on the back of the golden ram. Not tarrying, they rowed on through the night until they came to an anchorage at the desert island of Thynias. When they mounted the shore, Apollo momentarily appeared in such divine splendor that the island quaked and waves surged high on the beach. Awed by the event, the Argonauts raised an altar upon which they sacrificed to the god as lord of the dawn; and, swearing to help each other ever after, they built a temple of Concord, which remained standing for many generations.

On the third morning, sail was raised and a fresh west wind bore the Argo past the mouth of the river Sangarius to the land of the Mariandyni, at a place where the river Acheron was said to burst forth from the lower world into the eastern sea. Here, Pollux and his comrades were welcomed by the natives and their king, Lycus, because they had heard of the destruction of Amycus and the rout of the Bebrycians, who were their long-time enemies. After Lycus had entertained them at a great feast, Jason told him in detail about the adventures already encountered, including the unwitting abandonment of Heracles in the land of the Mysians. Mention of the hero prompted Lycus to relate that, when

he was a youth, he had met Heracles in the halls of his father Daschylus, as the great man was returning to Greece with the girdle of the Amazonian queen, Hippolyte.[35] He further recalled that during his short (?) stay, Heracles had slain the champion Titias in boxing, had assisted Daschylus in subduing the Phrygians, had conquered the Bithynians, and had caused the Paphlagonians to yield. Now that the comrades of Heracles had again rid his people of neighboring enemies, Lycus gratefully asked them to let his son, Daschylus, join their expedition, as an assurance that they might receive a friendly reception from all those who would be encountered to the mouth of the river Thermodon. The offer was cheerfully accepted by Jason's band and, on the next morning, they left the halls of Lycus to continue their journey.

As they neared the Argo at its anchorage in the river, a white-tusked boar leapt from a reed bed on the bank and, rushing upon Idmon, cruelly gashed him in the thigh. Although Idas killed the beast with a thrust of his sharp spear,

---

[35] As might reasonably be expected when dealing with a mythological cycle, whose component stories have been supplied by different men living years apart, the chronology of the Labors of Heracles is not to be judged by a mathematical standard.

The generally accepted order of the Labors was: (1) the destruction of the Nemean lion; (2) the slaughter of the Lernaean Hydra; (3) the capture of the Hind of Artemis; (4) the capture of the Erymanthian boar; (5) the cleansing of the Stables of Augeias; (6) the destruction of the Stymphalian birds; (7) capture of the Cretan bull; (8) the capture of the Mares of Diomedes; (9) taking of the girdle of Hippolyte; (10) fetching the oxen of Geryon; (11) taking the golden apples of the Hesperides; and (12) bringing Cerberus up from the lower world.

According to Apollonius Rhodius, Heracles hastened to join the Argonauts when he heard of their impending expedition, as he returned to Mycenae with the Erymanthian boar. He then has Lycus remember that the hero long ago came through the land of the Mariandyni after taking the girdle of Hippolyte. Later, when the Argonauts land at the island of Ares, he has Amphidamas recall how Heracles had frightened the Stymphalian birds into the air. And, finally, he has the Argonauts arrive at the land of the Hesperides, just after Heracles has stolen their golden apples and has killed the dragon which was guarding them.

It is confusing but, nevertheless, interesting and should have been to Augeias, whose stables Heracles was supposed to be cleansing of their filth at a time when, some say, he and the great hero were comrades and shipmates on the Argo.

---

[34] According to a different version, the Symplegades stood motionless when they were charmed by the music from Orpheus' lyre. Contrary to the statement of Apollonius Rhodius given in the text, Homer relates that the rocks were again separated—and were recurrently clashing—when Odysseus encountered them on his return from the Trojan War.

the wound received by his comrade proved to be fatal—and he came to the death which he had foretold for himself before the expedition left the shores of Thessaly. The sorrowing Argonauts delayed for three days, while they lamented and buried Idmon in a tomb which long remained for men of later days to see. Before they could depart, however, tragedy struck again and their helmsman Tiphys fell sick and died.

With the burial of Tiphys, a feeling of deep foreboding descended upon the heroic band, and they would have stayed from going farther, had not Hera moved Ancaeus, the son of Poseidon, to announce that he was fully capable of taking over the post of steersman. Upon this statement, Erginus, Nauplius, and Euphemus— all likewise descended from the sea-god— quickly advanced their own qualifications;[36] but, by acclamation, the honor was given to Ancaeus. With a new hand at her rudder, the Argo sailed out through the river Acheron[37] on the dawn of the twelfth sad day. Aided by a strong breeze, it soon passed the outfall of the river Callichorus, where the wine-god Dionysus is said to have celebrated on the way back from his conquest of the Indians.

The voyaging band next came to the tomb of Sthenelus, whom the Amazons had killed in their battle with the forces of Heracles, and they were amazed to see his bloody ghost stare upon them from his crypt and then quickly vanish into nothingness. Upon the advice of the seer Mopsus,[38] they landed and offered libations to the dead man's departed spirit, and built an altar to Apollo upon which Orpheus dedicated his lyre.[39]

Pursuing their journey, the Argonauts passed by the mouth of the river Parthenius and, with a fair wind, arrived on the Assyrian (Paphlagonian) shore, where dwelt Sinope, a virgin daughter of the river-god Asopus.[40] Here, they picked up Autolycus, Deileon and Phlogius, the sons of Deimachus, who had gone astray and had become lost while they were accompanying Heracles in his quest for the girdle of Hippolyte.[41]

Rounding the headland where the Amazons dwelt about the mouth of the river Thermodon, some of the younger men wanted to go ashore and engage the warrior-women in battle, but cooler counsel prevailed and, driven by the northwest wind[42] the Argo proceeded on to the land of the Chalybes—a people who worked in iron, and exchanged their products with their agricultural neighbors in return for food.

The lands of two odd races were next passed. They were the Tibareni, whose men were accustomed to lie in bed and groan while their wives were in childbirth, and the Mossynoeci, who shamelessly had intercourse in public.

As the expedition neared the island of Ares, winged birds appeared and began shooting their tipped feathers at the Argonauts with the speed and accuracy of an arrow from a well-aimed bow.[43] But Phineus had told his deliverers that is was necessary for them to land on the island, and they pressed forward, while they protected themselves against the hail of feathered shafts

---

36 It seems logical that many of the sea-faring Argonauts should trace their descent back to Poseidon; and the same generalization might apply to the whole race of the Aeolids, whose ancestor (Deucalion) was the only man to ride out the great flood.

37 The limits of ancient geography were extremely flexible, but, according to the conventional legend, the river Acheron entered into the lower world from the Ionian Sea, on the west of Greece—far removed from the Argonautic orbit.

38 The Argonaut Mopsus was a son of Ampycus and should not be confused with the greater seer of the same name who was a son of Apollo.

39 Either from this dedication, or from the apotheosis of the sweet instrument at the death of its owner,

the lyre of Orpheus was considered by the ancients as Lyra—a constellation in the northern skies, sparked by the bright star Vega.

40 Sinope was a daughter of the Peloponnesian river-god Asopus. When Zeus desired her, he offered to grant any request which she might make, and she cunningly asked for her virginity. Later, Apollo carried her off to Asia Minor, and, according to Apollonius, her wish was respected. But a different legend relates that she bore to the Sun-god a son who was named Syrus.

41 The mythographers do not give a divine pedigree to Deimachus, although he is said to have been also the father of Enarete, the wife of the first Aeolus.

42 The directions, and the driving winds, are given in the text as related by Apollonius Rhodius; but all modern scholars are agreed that it is impossible to harmonize the (mythological) course of the Argonauts with anything except mythological geography.

43 The winged attackers on the island of Ares were often considered to have been the remainder—or descendants—of the Stymphalides, driven out of Greece by Heracles as one of his Twelve Labors.

by raising their shields as a roof over their vessel. A safe landing was made—notwithstanding great waves which sprang up with the sudden descent of the cold north winds. In the morning, the Argonauts realized why the blind prophet had insisted upon their making the stop: for they encountered the four sons of Phrixus, who had been miserably shipwrecked on the island during the furious storm of the night before. With gratitude, the sons of Phrixus identified themselves as Argus, Cytissorus, Melas, and Phrontis; and related that their disaster had occurred while they were fleeing from Colchis to Orchomenus, to assert their rights as successors of their grandfather Athamas. Jason quickly greeted the stranded brothers as his kinsmen,[44] and ordered that they be given dry clothing and food from the abundant stores of the Argo.

After appropriate sacrifices had been made to Ares as god of the island, the Argonautic leader explained the purpose of the expedition and invited the four men to return with him to Colchis as participants in the enterprise. The invitation was received with horror, as Argus explained that the Colchian king, Aeëtes, a son of the great god Helios, was a ruthless warrior with strength so fearful that he might prove to be a match for Ares himself. He went on to say that the numbers of the king's armed tribes were almost countless, and that the Golden Fleece was ceaselessly guarded by a sleepless dragon, which had sprung from the blood of monstrous Typhon. Upon hearing this, some of the Argonauts paled, but Peleus was quick to point out that they were themselves descended from the gods, and should stand in awe of neither men nor monsters. His cheering words dissipated the momentary fears raised by the recitals of Argus, and the wayfarers soon went to rest.

The next day's sail brought them, at nightfall, to the island of Philyra where, according to legend, the union of old Cronus and Philyra had produced the Centaur Cheiron "half like a horse and half like a god." From there, proceed-

ing past the lands of several tribes of no particular interest,[45] the travelers came within sight of Mount Caucasus, where Prometheus lay manacled to receive the perpetual punishment caused by his defiance of Zeus. High in the clouds above them, they saw the ravening eagle as it flew toward the mountain, with a whirr of its huge wings which caused the sails of their vessel to shiver. Soon after, they heard the bitter cry of Prometheus as his liver was being torn away, and the air continued to ring with his screams until, at dusk, they marked his flying tormenter rushing back from the mountain on its self-same track.

Guided by Argus through the night, the excusably nervous band entered the mouth of the river Phasis[46] in the Colchian land. Here, after letting down their sail, they rowed to a shady backwater and dropped anchor. And, when dawn came, they saw the palace of mighty Aeëtes in his city of Aea, behind the plain across the opposite shore.

With their joint charges having safely arrived at their destination, Hera and Athena now consulted on Mount Olympus to determine how best to overcome the threat of future perils. They agreed upon a plan to obtain, in Jason's behalf, the powerful assistance of Medeia, a daughter of King Aeëtes, whose knowledge of magic and sorcery—inherited from the great god of the sun—had been greatly increased by her visits at the shrine of infernal Hecate. In pursuance of their plan, they went to the adjacent palace of Aphrodite where they found her languidly brushing out her long tresses. They proposed to the powerful goddess of love that she should have her son Eros (Cupid) wing one of his golden shafts to Medeia's heart, so as to produce an irresistible passion for the young Argonautic leader. Flattered at the request of those who were her superiors in the Olympian council, she readily assented and went to the orchard of Zeus, where she found Eros tossing golden dice with Ganymedes. Brib-

[44] Jason's grandfather, Cretheus, was a brother of Athamas, who was the grandfather of the sons of Phirixus.

[45] The lands passed were those of the Macrones, Becheiri, Sapeires, and Byzeres.
[46] It is interesting to note that the pheasant is said to have come originally from the country of Colchis and to have taken its name from the river Phasis.

ing her prankish son with a round ball which had been a toy of the supreme god, she induced him to go to Colchis for his appointed purpose.

In the meanwhile, Jason—hoping to obtain the fleece amicably—left the Argo and was proceeding to the palace of Aeëtes, taking with him the four sons of Phrixus and his comrades, Augeias, and Telamon. As he passed through the intervening plain of Circe, he was surprised to see the corpses of many men hanging from the trees; but the sons of Phrixus explained that it was the Colchian custom to bury only their women. When the small group entered the city, Hera caused a heavy mist to descend, which effectually concealed them from the sight of the inhabitants; and they presently arrived at the palace, where the mist lifted and a glorious sight came into view. The palace itself was a marvel to see, with its high columns of stone and its gardens of foliage in full bloom; but, more remarkable, were the fountains—fashioned by Hephaestus—which flowed beneath the greenery, because one was gushing with milk, one with wine, another with fragrant oil, and the fourth with water, which grew warm at the setting of the Pleiades, but at their rising bubbled forth with the coldness of ice.

As Jason's company entered the palace, they were first seen by Medeia[47] who cried in delight when she recognized the sons of Phrixus, for they were her own blood nephews. At her call of welcome, her sister Chalciope rushed forward with her maids and joyfully embraced her sons, who had but recently left her for the ancestral land of their father Phrixus. King Aeëtes and his queen, Eidyia, hearing the commotion, soon came forth and the courtway was quickly filled with a throng of bustling retainers. In the confusion, Eros entered and shot his arrow of love into Medeia's heart, which caused her to gasp with sweet amazement as she looked upon Jason's form; "and the hue of her soft cheeks went and came, now pale, now red, in her soul's distraction." But little Eros—unseen and unheard—laughed loudly and, leaping through the high roof of the palace, returned to his game of dice on Mount Olympus.

At the banquet which followed, Aeëtes asked the sons of Phrixus to explain the reason for their unexpected return, and Argus related the incidents of their shipwreck on the island of Ares and their meeting with the Argonauts. His account naturally led into a statement that the purpose of the expedition was to fetch the Golden Fleece back to Greece—a statement whose impact he sought to soften by pointing out his own kinship with Jason and the divine descent of the Argonauts. But his words filled Aeëtes with rage, and he angrily accused Argus and his brothers of conspiring with the strangers to seize the rule of Colchis, and bade them all begone—saying, that if they had not first feasted at his table, he would have deprived them of their tongues and hands and—thus mangled—would have expelled them from his realm.

Jason's first impulse was to reply to the proud king's outburst with words of equally proud defiance, but he checked himself and, saying that he had been driven to the quest by inexorable fate, announced that the Argonauts entertained the most kindly intentions toward the Colchian people and their estimable ruler. He then offered, in exchange for the fleece, to have his heroic band fight for them against any, and all, enemies whom the irascible king might wish to bring under his sway.

Aeëtes pretended to be mollified by these flattering words but, in his heart, he desired the bold youth's destruction and devised a scheme which he thought would bring it about through his own immature rashness. He proceeded to relate that he was the owner of two fire-breathing bulls with brazen feet and that he (an old man) was accustomed to yoke the animals and drive them to the plow over an adjoining field of Ares—meanwhile sowing the furrows with teeth from the dragon killed at Thebes by Cadmus;[48] that the fruit of the horrid seed sprouted as armed men, whom he was accus-

---

[47] Hera had detained Medeia from going to her accustomed sacrifices at the shrine of Hecate, so that she should be present when Jason arrived at the palace.

[48] The dragon slain by Cadmus was a son of Ares and Gaea, and was descriptively called Draco. Half of its teeth were sown in Boeotia and produced an armed race of men known as the Sparti; and the other half were said to have been given by Athena to Aeëtes.

tomed to slay with his spear as they arose at once from all sides, and that, owing to his divinity as a son of Helios, he was used to perform the complete labor within the space of a single day. He finished his recital by telling Jason that, if he could accomplish the same task, his claim of divine descent would be substantiated, and he would be permitted to return to Greece with the fleece of the golden ram. After some pardonable hesitation, Jason accepted the dangerous proposal and—accompanied by Augeias, Telamon, and Argus—returned to his anchored vessel. Meanwhile, the other sons of Phrixus went with their mother, Chalciope, to her room in the castle, and Medeia, brooding over the calamity which threatened her loved stranger, entered her own apartment and fell into a deep slumber.

Without delay, Aeëtes called an assembly of his Colchians to meet at a place somewhat removed from his palace. There, plans were laid to destroy both the Argonauts and the sons of Phrixus, by an assault which was scheduled to take place as soon as Jason should be slain by the brazen-footed bulls: for it never occurred to Aeëtes that the young Greek might survive his foolish attempt.

When Jason reported to his comrades that he had agreed to the proposal of the Colchian king, Peleus offered to substitute for him in the dangerous undertaking. His offer was duplicated, in turn, by Telamon, Idas, Castor, Pollux, and Meleager (who was yet only a stripling). At this point, Argus interposed to say that his aunt Medeia was exceedingly gifted in the magic arts and that he thought he could persuade his mother to enlist her assistance. While he was talking, a trembling dove, chased by a hawk, fell onto Jason's lap and its winged pursuer was impaled on the stern-ornament of the Argo. The prophetic Mopsus saw in the incident an omen that the suggestion of Argus was good, but Idas jumped up and wrathfully declared that strong men should not look to women for help and should be content to rely upon their own arms and prowess. His impetuous words were greeted with silence; and, with the approval of the rest of the Argonauts, Argus was sent back to the palace to try out the success of his plan.

When he talked with his mother, he learned that his same idea had already occurred to her, because she wanted to save the lives of her sons, and knew that it was the purpose of Aeëtes to destroy them as fellow conspirators with the strangers. Meanwhile, in her sleep Medeia had a dream in which it appeared that Jason had come to Colchis not so much to win the Golden Fleece as to take her back as his wife to Greece. In her dream, she aided him to master the fire-breathing bulls with great ease and, when the wrath of Aeëtes put her to a decision, she preferred the young stranger to her own father. Upon awakening, she fell into an agony of doubt over the purpose of her vision, and wept so piteously that one of her handmaidens brought Chalciope into her chamber. When Medeia related her dream, Chalciope revealed that she and her sons had been debating the possibility of just such help as had been suggested to Medeia in her sleep. After further talk and mutual lamentation, the maiden-sorceress promised that she would go at dawn to the temple of Hecate to cast spells which would render the bulls and the earthborn warriors harmless to Jason. This promise Chalciope reported to her sons, and Argus sped back to the Argonauts to tell them of the success of his mission.

After a night of doubt and anxiety, Medeia set out at daybreak for the shrine of Hecate, accompanied by her twelve handmaidens. While the mules were being yoked to her chariot, she took from its casket a magic charm which had been made from the root juices of a flower that had sprung from the earth when the ravening eagle let fall a drop of blood from the tortured liver of Prometheus. By first bathing in seven different streams and then calling upon infernal Hecate seven times, she had previously created in the charm such powers that it could make both men and weapons invunerable to harm from bronze or fire. She arrived at her destination with the charm in her hand and now told her attendants of her promise to help Jason, and asked them to stand aside when he should appear to join her as a supplicant to the dark goddess.

As soon as Medeia left the palace, one of the sons of Phrixus had hastened to report her departure to Argus, and he soon proceeded to lead Jason over the plain to meet her. With them, went the seer Mopsus, who conceived it his prerogative to give counsel to those setting out on journeys—no matter how short; but he turned back, and also detained Argus, when he heard an old crow rather pointedly announce from a tree top that lovers did not relish the presence of third parties. Accordingly, Jason arrived alone at the temple to find Medeia so stricken with love for him that, at first, she was deprived of the power of speech; but soon, after an exchange of sweet nothings, she gave him the charm with instructions for its use. The instructions were that: (1) he should bathe in the river Phasis at midnight; (2) then should sacrifice a lamb to Hecate by burning it in a pit covered with a sauce of honey; and (3) at dawn, should steep the charm in water and anoint both his body and his weapons with the liquid. She further told him that, when the earthborn warriors should arise after the dragon's teeth were sown, he should throw among them a huge stone, which would make the creatures fall to slaying one another, so that their destruction would be expedited.[49]

After another exchange of tender words—in which Jason intimated that if Medeia should ever come to Greece he would make her his wife—the day drew to its close and she returned to the city with her twelve handmaidens, driving furiously in an ecstasy of love. Jason proceeded, somewhat more leisurely, to rejoin Argus and Mopsus; and, when they arrived back at the Argo, he told his assembled comrades of the advice which he had received and showed them the magic charm. Although Idas still sat apart, in wrath at what he considered the conduct of cowards, the rest of his band received the report of their leader with joy in their hearts, then peacefully took their rest.

On the next day, Telamon and Aethalides went to Aeëtes in his palace, where he readily gave them the teeth of the dragon, secretly exulting at the thought of the dread sport which

he thought the morrow would bring. At midnight, Jason faithfully followed the mystic instructions which he had received. Although he was greatly frightened upon the appearance of dark Hecate at the scene of his sacrifice—attended by horrible serpents, gleaming torches, and her hounds of Hell—he returned to the Argo with a feeling of security, which increased at dawn when he covered his body and his weapons with the liquid from the steeped charm. Nor was his assurance lessened when his anointed spear easily withstood the heavy sword thrusts of Idas and the mighty efforts of the other Argonauts, as they sought to test its invincible firmness.

After the rising of the sun, the heroes rowed with easy strokes to the plain of Ares, where they saw a great crowd of the Colchians gathered on the surrounding heights, but their king, Aeëtes, was stationed on the banks of the river, in order to be nearer the scene of the rash stranger's anticipated destruction. As soon as his comrades had made fast the hawsers of their vessel, Jason leapt ashore and came forward to the contest, carrying his shield, sword and spear, and a gleaming helmet which contained the teeth of the dragon.

Gazing over the field, he saw the bulls' yoke of bronze and, near it, the plow which was fashioned from a single piece of stone. Accompanied by Castor and Pollux, he walked to the yoke and, fixing his spear in the ground, placed against it his sword and the helmet. Then he advanced with the shield alone, as the bulls rushed forth from their stable beneath the ground and came toward him with their breaths emitting flaming fire. The Argonauts were unnerved at the sight, but their leader—standing with his shield before him and his feet wide apart—easily withstood the onset of the charging beasts. Grasping the horns of the bulls with his bare hands, he forced them beneath the yoke, which Castor and Pollux handed to him: meanwhile striding from side to side through the flames with an unconcern which caused the watching Aeëtes to regard him with warranted suspicion.

As Castor and Pollux left the field, Jason attached the yoked animals to the plow and placed his shield on his back. Then, after pick-

---

[49] By throwing stones among the Sparti, who sprang from the first sowing of the dragon's teeth at Thebes, Cadmus caused them to fight among themselves until all, save five, were slain.

ing up his spear and the helmet containing the teeth of the dragon, he pricked the bulls beneath their flanks and began to plow great furrows, in which he sowed the dragon's teeth as he went along. In the afternoon, his ploughing and sowing were completed and, unyoking his brazen-footed team, he so frightened them that they raced precipitately back to their subterranean barn. He then calmly sauntered down to his comrades on the Argo and took a drink from the river.

By now, the sown teeth of the dragon were bearing fruit and earthborn warriors were springing up all over the ploughed plain. Mindful of Medeia's advice, Jason seized a huge boulder and cast it into their midst, whereupon he was gratified to see the armed creatures immediately begin to battle among themselves. As they fought, he rushed back to the field and, with his charmed sword, cut them down one by one, until the last of the strange crop was felled and the newly ploughed furrows ran with blood. The amazed Aeëtes gathered his Colchian hordes and proceeded back to the city, realizing that his artful scheme had been somehow circumvented, but he was determined that the Argonauts should not accomplish their purpose.

Jason's comrades joyfully rowed their conquering leader to their shaded place of anchorage in the river, but Medeia fled to her chamber in the castle and was stricken with fear, lest her father should realize that her magic help had been the cause of his plan's failure. In desperation, she resolved to join Jason and go back with him to Greece, where he had said he would make her his wife. First, cutting off one of her tresses as a memento to leave with her mother Eidyia, she secretly left the palace and went to the bank of the river, across from the great fire in whose light the Argonauts and the sons of Phrixus were celebrating the day's success. When she called, Phrontis recognized her voice, and it was but a matter of minutes before the Argo crossed the stream and Jason leapt to her side.

She communicated to him the fears about her father's suspicion and, recalling to him his promise of marriage, said that if he would take her home as his bride she would charm the sleepless dragon so that the Golden Fleece could be easily taken and carried with them. Jason tenderly renewed his previous hesitant promise, and at his command his comrades speedily rowed their vessel to a place near the great oak tree in which the fleece was hanging. There, the lovers were set ashore. As they came by the pathway to the sacred grove of Ares, the dragon-guardian spied them and, stretching forth its long neck, hissed with a tremendous noise which resounded through the stretches of the river and was heard by Aeëtes and the rest of the Colchians at Aea.

Medeia approached the monster and, first invoking the protection of infernal Hecate, sprinkled its eyes with a mystic brew in which she had immersed a newly cut spray of juniper. Instantly, the dragon slumbered and its long coils were stretched motionless over the leaves of the forest. Jason now snatched the fleece from its resting place and, placing it over his shoulder, returned with Medeia to his waiting shipmates on the Argo. With Ancaeus at the helm, there was no delay in the start back to Iolchus, because the Argonauts all knew that the loud hiss of the dragon had penetrated to the ears of Aeëtes and that he would soon be in pursuit. And even as the Argo sped down the river, the Colchians were thronging to their own craft, under the leadership of Absyrtus, the son of Aeëtes who had been borne to him by the nymph Asterodeia.

Entering the open sea, Medeia declared that, to insure the successes already gained, the Argonauts should stop in the land of the Paphlagonians at the mouth of the river Halys and offer sacrifices to helpful Hecate. This they did, and another admonition from their mystic passenger now recalled to the voyagers a prophecy of Phineus that they were fated to return home by a course different from the one which they had followed on their outward journey—but they were at a loss to know in what direction to proceed. At this juncture, protecting Hera caused a trail of heavenly light to appear and, realizing that it was a signal to them, the Argonauts followed the channel to which it pointed, but, at his own request, they left Daschylus, the son of Lycus, in the land of the Paphlagonians.

The next stop was made at one of the (two)

Brygean islands of Artemis. Here, the returning heroes were dismayed to find that Absyrtus[50] and a large army of the Colchians had preceded them and were encamped on the nearby island, where the temple of the goddess was located. Since Aeëtes had promised that he would peaceably part with the fleece upon Jason's performance of his required task, some of the Argonauts believed that the Colchians had followed them only to retake Medeia; and they urged that she be delivered to her countrymen to avert a conflict in which the prospect of victory seemed doubtful. But Medeia convinced them that the Colchians would not engage in battle if they should be deprived of their leader, and proposed to lure Absyrtus into an ambush where he could be done away with. The Argonauts acquiesced in her suggestion and she sent presents to her half brother, with word that she had been unwillingly carried off by the sons of Phrixus and would meet him at night in the temple of the goddess. And, when Absyrtus unsuspectingly appeared at the place of meeting, she guilefully held him in conversation until Jason leaped from a spot where he had hidden and struck him down—after which he cut off the dead man's extremities and buried the remainder of his corpse.[51] Medeia then lighted a prearranged signal fire, and the Argonauts attacked the leaderless Colchians who were routed with a great shedding of blood. At the urging of Peleus, the victors took their seats in the Argo and rowed to the island of Electra (Samothrace), but the Colchians who survived the slaughter in the battle were afraid to return to face the wrath of their king and, being further restrained by lightnings sent by Hera, settled on the Brygean island where they had been conquered.

Faring from Samothrace, the Argonauts touched at the land of the Hylleans[52] where Jason left one of the two golden tripods given to him by Apollo, which had the power of protecting any country from the depredations of its enemies. The Hylleans were grateful for the gift and reluctantly bade their visitors a fair voyage when they put out to sea, but their good wishes were of small benefit, because a great storm arose and drove the Argonauts back to Samothrace. Here they were astonished and grieved to hear the sacred timber of their vessel speak out with human voice, to say that Zeus was greatly angered at the murder of Absyrtus and that they could be purged of the crime only by Circe, the witch-sister of Aeëtes.

After passing through the river Eridanus—which still smelled with the flesh of burning Phaëthon,[53] Jason and his band entered the river Rhodanus[54] and were about to sail into the stormy lakes beyond, where they would surely have been wrecked had not a sign from Hera caused them to turn back. Set aright on their proper course, they finally arrived at the harbor of Aeaea—the island of Circe, where the beautiful sorceress was herself seen as she was bathing her head, after a night of bad dreams which had foretold the arrival of her visitors. At her invitation, Jason and Medeia followed to her dwelling and she purged them from their slaying of Absyrtus—after which she sent them back to their vessel.

Hera knew of the dangers which her favorites were still to encounter, and sent Iris to summon the Nereid Thetis to Mount Olympus for the

---

[50] Absyrtus is sometimes referred to by mythographers as Apsyrtus.

[51] According to a later legend, when Medeia left Colchis she took her young half brother Absyrtus with her; and when Aeëtes was about to overtake the Argo, she cut the youth's body into pieces and threw his separated members into the sea. Thereupon, Aeëtes tarried to gather the mangled remains and the Argonauts were enabled to speed on without the danger of being pursued.

[52] According to Apollonius Rhodius, the mythical ancestor of the Hylleans was Hyllus, a son of Heracles and a Naiad named Melite; but the conventional legend relates that the mother of Hyllus was Deianeira, a daughter of Oeneus.

[53] It was generally agreed that Phaëthon fell into the Eridanus River, when Zeus knocked him from the sun-chariot with a thunderbolt; but the stream's location was a matter of great uncertainty—ranging all the way from the present-day Po in Italy to the Vistula in northern Europe. And, both Herodotus and Strabo gravely concluded that its existence was pure fiction.

[54] Rhodanus was the ancient name for the Rhone River, which Apollonius seemed to think was connected with both the Rhine and the Eridanus.

purpose of obtaining her powerful assistance.[55] On the same mission, Iris conveyed to Hephaestus Hera's will that he should let his sulphurous forges remain idle for a bit, and she told Aeolus, the god of the winds, that he was forbidden by the queen of the gods to loose any of his stormy blasts until further instructions. When Thetis dutifully presented herself, Hera asked her to see the Argonauts safely through the perilous channel where Scylla and Charybdis were accustomed to destroy rash mariners.[56] She buttressed her request by pointing out that Peleus (the mortal husband of Thetis) was one of the Argo's crew, and that Achilles (the son of Peleus and Thetis) was fated to be Medeia's husband in afterlife.[57]

Heeding Hera's request, Thetis returned to her sister-Nereids and told them to stand by in the Ausonian Sea.[58] Then, speeding to the island of Circe, she approached Peleus as he was watching his comrades in their contests of throwing the quoit and shooting arrows at a target. Invisible to all save her husband, she told him about the divine help in prospect, and urged him to have the Argo leave Aeaea at the dawn of the next day. When Peleus relayed this information to the rest, they quickly ceased their contests and, after sleeping through the night, set sail at daybreak.

Soon after leaving Aeaea, the island of Anthemoëssa was sighted and the Argonauts heard the voices of the Sirens, reaching their vessel with such sweet seduction that every member of its crew was seized with a longing to join the fair maidens ashore. But Orpheus—with remarkable prescience—began to strum on his divine lyre[59] and brought forth musical sounds which overcame the urge created by his opposition. But the urge was not overcome in Butes, the son of Teleon, because he leaped overboard and started to swim landward, until Aphrodite thoughtfully picked the smitten man from out of the sea and miraculously had him transported to a strange land.[60]

Although some of the Argonauts grieved for their lost comrade, they turned to their oars and rowed furiously past the shore of the Sirens— only to enter the meeting place of the Tyrrhenian and Ionian waters, where dread Scylla threatened on one side and roaring Charybdis on the other. Nearby were the wandering rocks, known as the Planctae, whose impact always caused shipwreck, and the fortunes of the heroes[61] seemed to be at their lowest ebb, when suddenly the fifty Nereids arose from the sea. With Thetis at the head, they lifted the Argo from the surface and carried the great vessel with its crew through the threatening perils—a remarkable feat of transportation, which caused Hera and Athena to approve with astonishment as they looked from above on its performance.

When the Nereids had carried their charges past the island of Trinacria, where the sacred cattle of Helios were feeding, they dived to their home beneath the waters and the unaided Argonauts resumed their journey. They next reached the island of the Phaeacians, which was then called Drepane[62] and were welcomed by King Alcinous, but their joy was dampened when they learned that another army of Col-

---

[55] Thetis was honored by Hera, and respected by Zeus, because she was one of the few women who had been able to resist the seductive advances of the supreme god.

[56] Scylla and Charybdis were supposed to have been stationed as the fearful guardians of the strait of Messina, which separates the island of Sicily from Italy.

[57] When Thetis refused Zeus, he decreed that she should marry the mortal Peleus. Another version of the legend relates that the supreme god forewent his amorous purpose when he learned from an oracle that her son would be greater than his father. Achilles, the son of Peleus and Thetis, became the mightiest warrior of his generation and, largely due to his prowess, the Greeks were able to win the Trojan War.

[58] Italy was anciently known as Ausonia.

[59] In the earlier dedication of his lyre, it would appear that Orpheus had parted with only its shadow.

[60] According to Apollonius, Butes was taken to the nearby heights of Lilybaeum, which some later writers erroneously identified as the site of Carthage.

[61] Owing to their similarity, the Planctae were often confused with the clashing rocks—previously passed by the Argonauts—which were known as the Symplegades.

[62] Drepane means the "Sickle island" a name given either because it was the place where Cronus mutilated his father Uranus with a sickle, or where Demeter is said to have stopped and taught the inhabitants to reap their crops with that useful instrument. In the Odyssey, the island of the Phaeacians is called Scheria, and it is said by present-day scholars to have been the same as Corcyra (Corfu), located off the coast of Epeirus.

chians had preceded them and was waiting to take Medeia back to her revengeful father.

At Medeia's urging, Alcinous' queen, Arete, pleaded with him to deny the Colchian demand, but he declared that the errant maiden must be handed over to her pursuers unless she had already become Jason's wife. Acting with queenly celerity, Arete speedily promoted the marriage of her suppliants, with a fanfare which included hymenal music from Orpheus as he sang to the accompaniment of his heavenly lyre in the presence of the gathering which included numberless beautiful nymphs.[63] When Alcinous was informed that the wedding had taken place, he refused to deliver Medeia to the Colchians, and, since they were afraid to return to their king empty handed they settled down among the Phaeacians and became good citizens.

After celebrating for seven days, the Argonauts reluctantly took leave of their hosts, taking with them twelve handmaidens whom Queen Arete had given to Medeia. Speeding onward, they ran into the shoals of the Libyan shore and the helmsman Ancaeus was at a loss as to whether to go forward or to set the vessel on a backward track. At this point the despairing heroes and their fair companions resigned themselves to death, but Athena sent to Jason three mysterious Warders of the land and told him to follow the car of Poseidon.[64] This enigmatic advice was clarified when a horse soon leaped from the sea and sped inland over the desert country. Upon the suggestion of Peleus, the Argo was placed on the shoulders of its crew and the footprints of the animal were followed for twelve days, whereupon, the shores of Lake Tritonis were reached and the tired men laid down their burden.

Incited by their thirst, the parched travelers went in search of fresh water and came upon the dragon Ladon as he lay dying, for he had but recently been overcome by their erstwhile comrade Heracles while capturing the golden apples

of the Hesperides. The Hesperides themselves were soon met as they shrilly lamented their ineffectual custodianship, and, when Orpheus addressed them, they turned into trees. But, as their maiden forms were being slowly covered with bark and foliage, they pointed out a fountain which Heracles had raised with his footstep—and the thirst of the Argonauts was quenched.[65]

A number of his old comrades now set out to look for Heracles, but their search was fruitless. Calais, Zetes, Euphemus, and Lynceus soon returned. Canthus was not so fortunate because he met Caphaurus, a grandson of Apollo, who was tending his sheep in the desert—and was slain by a stone cast when he tried to drive the flock away from their owner. Soon after, his comrades found his dead body and tenderly gave it burial. They retaliated by murdering Caphaurus and then feasting on mutton. On the same day, a poisonous serpent—said to have sprung from the blood of Medusa's head—bit Mopsus in the shin when he unwittingly stepped on its spine; and the Argonauts were sorrowfully forced to dig a grave for another member of their band.

When a south wind arose, the wanderers set sail through the lake in an effort to find its outlet to the sea. All day their vessel plowed aimlessly about the Tritonian shores without finding a channel of exit, until Orpheus suggested that the remaining tripod, which Apollo had given to Jason, should be offered to propitiate the gods of the land. As soon as his suggestion was followed and the tripod was set ashore, the god of the lake[66] appeared in the form of a youth and, as a token of friendship offered the strangers a piece of his country's earth. After disclosing his divinity, he announced that he would point the way out from the lake, and, when Euphemus questioned him further, he not only showed the outlet to the sea but also gave directions for the return voyage to Greece.

---

[63] Maeris, daughter of Aristaeus, who was the reputed discoverer of honey was also included.

[64] The so-called Warders were said to have been the nymph daughters of the god of the lake Tritonis, who had bathed Athena in the waters of the lake when she first leapt from the aching head of Zeus.

---

[65] Of the Hesperides: Aegle became a willow tree; Erytheia an elm; and Hespere was turned into a poplar.

[66] According to Apollonius, the god of the lake was Triton, a son of Poseidon; but others relate that (like other lake and river gods) he was one of the offspring of Oceanus and Tethys and, in this latter category, he was considered the father of the maiden Pallas.

The grateful Argonauts reentered their vessel and rowed for the indicated channel and Triton, shouldering the golden tripod, entered the waters behind them and disappeared beneath the surface. When Jason sacrificed a sheep to the kind deity, he reappeared from the depths of the lake—with the upper part of his body as a god and its lower parts shaped like the monsters of the sea—and, seizing the hollow keel of the Argo, guided the heroes to the junction of his lake with the outer sea, and then dove beneath his watery element.

With the aid of sail and oar, the island of Crete was later reached, and the Argonauts were about to fasten their ship's hawsers to the shore when they were driven off by the appearance of a huge creature made of bronze. He was Talos, fashioned by Hephaestus at the request of Zeus as a gift to King Minos of Crete; and, except for a single blooded vein near one ankle, he was invulnerable.[67] Retreating into the water beyond the reach of great stones which the bronze man was throwing at them, the Argo was anchored and Medeia called upon the spirits of the underworld for assistance. As she did so, Talos grazed his vulnerable ankle upon a sharp crag and the blood left his body. He toppled to the ground with a tremendous thud, and the Argonauts landed without further molestation.

After spending the night on the Cretan shore, where they raised a shrine to Athena, the voyagers continued homeward over the wide sea, which brought no sight of new land to them during daylight. As they rowed on after sundown, they encountered a night whose blackness was so deep that they became thoroughly afraid and, afterward, always referred to it as the Pall of Darkness. In reverent doubt, Jason raised his arms and prayed for help to Apollo, because neither the helmsman Ancaeus nor any of his comrades knew where their vessel was going. Quickly answering the prayer, the god flew down to a nearby island

peak and caused a great light to gleam, which showed the shores of Hippuris—one of the small Sporades—close at hand. Thus directed, the Argonauts rowed to a landing and gratefully sacrified to their deliverer with libations of water—which caused the Phaeacian handmaidens of Medeia to laugh, because they had never seen sacrifices offered except in the more substantial flesh of sheep or oxen.

On the third night out from Hippuris, Euphemus dreamed that the piece of earth given to him by Triton had turned into a maiden, who said that she was the water-god's daughter and asked that she be restored to the sea. When he imparted his dream, Jason told him that it must have been divinely sent and that the request of his vision should be honored. Accordingly, he dropped the soil into the surrounding waters and an island sprang up, which in later times was known as Calliste, and became a sanctuary for the descendants of Euphemus in generations to follow.

At the island of Aegina, the Argonauts stopped for water, which they fetched to their vessel in a race of friendly rivalry, whose course was periodically rerun in later times in memory of the event; and, proceeding thence without further adventures, they returned to the harbor at Pagasae—proudly bearing, for all to see, the prized fleece of the golden ram.

Shortly before the Argonauts returned, it was rumored in Iolchus that they had all perished drowning. Pelias heard the report and, believing himself to be safe from future vengeance, killed Aeson and Promachus, the aged father and the young brother of Jason.[68] When Alcimede, the bereft widow and mother, learned of the double crime, she hastened to the hearth of the king's palace and pronounced a curse that he might suffer the fate which his cruel actions had merited.[69] She then pierced

---

[67] According to another version of the story, Talos had a single vein running from his neck to his ankle, which was plugged by a bronze nail. Medeia, charming the giant into insensibility, pulled out the stopper and, when his blood had run out from his body, he fell over and died.

---

[68] Some say that Pelias forced Aeson to drink bull's blood and thereby cause his own death. According to Ovid, Aeson did not die, but was later rejuvenated by Medeia's powers of sorcery. Another story, related by Apollodorus, postpones the slaughter of Promachus until after the suicide of his mother.

[69] This placed a double curse on Pelias, who was already marked for destruction by Athena because he had slain Sidero at the altar of the goddess' sanctuary.

her own breast with a sword, and brought her sad life to an end.

It was on the night following the day of Alcimede's death that the Argonauts sailed into the harbor at Pagasae, near Iolchus but beyond the sight of the city's dwellers. Jason was soon told by one of the country folk about what had occurred and his triumphant joy was converted into a wrathful desire to attack Pelias immediately. His comrades stood ready to lend him their aid and to face any peril in his behalf, but they fell into dispute over how best to make the attack. Some urged that they should try to take the city at once, while they were not expected, but others advised that each of them should gather soldiers from his own birthplace and raise a general war—maintaining that it was impossible for their small band to overcome the large army controlled by Pelias. At the height of the debate, Medeia intervened with an offer to bring about the cruel king's death through her unaided cunning, and to deliver over the royal palace to the Argonauts without the necessity of their risking battle. Having previously seen the marvelous results of her magic powers on more than one occasion, the heroes voted to accept her offer and she revealed her plan to them.

The sorceress first fashioned a hollow image of Artemis, in which she secreted various kinds of mystic drugs. Next, she anointed herself with potent ointments, which turned her hair grey and filled her face and body so full of wrinkles that all who looked upon her thought that she was surely an old woman. In this disguise, and carrying the hollow statue, she entered the city the next morning; and, when the curious populace gathered around her, she told them that she had been sent by the goddess from the land of the Hyperboreans to bring good luck to Iolchus and its king. Followed by the crowd inspired by her words, she entered the palace of Pelias and related to the wondering king that Artemis, riding through the air in a chariot drawn by dragons, had chosen him as a pious ruler to whom she was sending her blessings. She then added that the goddess had commanded her to divest Pelias of his old age and had endowed her with powers by which she could make his body entirely young.

When the old king was skeptical of her crafty proposal, she announced that she would then and there prove her powers. She told one of the daughters of Pelias to bring pure water, and, when it was brought, she shut herself up in a small chamber, where she cleansed her body of the ointments which had given her the appearance of age. Being restored to her youthful form, she stepped back into the throne-room— amid the amazement of all who were there gathered. Also, by means of certain magical incantations, she caused dragons to appear, and declared that they had borne her, with the image of Artemis, to Iolchus from the land of the Hyperboreans. By these supernatural happenings, Pelias and his daughters were convinced, and agreed to do anything which Medeia might bid them.

When night came, and Pelias had fallen asleep, Medeia informed his daughters that they should dismember his body and place it in a boiling cauldron. The maidens demurred at her grim suggestion, whereupon, the sorceress cut up the body of an old ram which was kept at the palace and threw the pieces into the scalding water. When the image of a young lamb emerged from the cauldron, the natural fears of the king's daughters were dissipated and, cutting their sleeping parent into bits, they placed his dismembered body into the seething receptacle.[70] Pretending that she must be alone while she offered prayers to the goddess, Medeia now caused the maidens to ascend with lamps to the roof of the palace, and, thus, conveyed to the Argonauts by prearranged signal the success of her efforts. When the daughters of Pelias returned from the roof, they found Jason and his comrades assembled around the cauldron, in which the severed parts of their father's body were slowly disintegrating. In horror, they were about to make an end of their own lives, but the Argonautic leader, taking pity on their distress, restrained them by pointing out that they had been deceived and were blameless for the

---

[70] Alcestis, alone of the daughters of Pelias, refused to assist in laying hands upon her father.

gruesome act which they had committed only with the best of intentions.[71]

With a becoming nobility, Jason summoned the inhabitants of the city to an assembly where he magnanimously turned over the rulership to Acastus, the son of Pelias who had been his comrade on the Argo. He then made arrangements for the sisters of Acastus to marry various neighboring princes, and, with Medeia, went to Corinth where he dedicated his great vessel to Poseidon.[72] In his new home, he was given a great welcome by King Creon and lived in contentment for ten years—during which Medeia bore to him two sons, named Mermerus and Pheres, and a daughter Eriopis, who later became the mother of the Lesser Ajax.

In the meanwhile, Hypsipyle—from the island of Lemnos—sent her twin sons Euneus and Nebrophonus to their father at Corinth, and, attended by an apparently loving family, Jason was approaching a smug middle age as a devoted husband and father. But along came Glauce, the daughter of King Creon, and her fresher charms caused the greying adventurer to desert Medeia. With the king's consent, his daughter was married to the famed leader of the Argonauts, and the cast-off wife wrathfully prepared to leave. First invoking the gods, by whom Jason had sworn that he would be faithful to her, she made a beautiful robe and sent it to her successor as a wedding gift. As the unsuspecting bride donned the garment, it burst into fire and, in agony, she called for her royal father's help—only to have him perish with her in its flames.[73] Not satisfied with this revenge,

Medeia then murdered Mermerus and Pheres —her own young sons borne to Jason—and, mounting a winged car drawn by dragons, fled to Athens. To complete the tragedy, the furious Corinthians now seized Euneus and Nebrophonus—Jason's sons by Hypsipyle—and put them to death.[74] The desolate man wandered aimlessly about the city until he came to the altar of Poseidon where, ten years before, he had triumphantly dedicated the Argo. Lying beneath the great vessel's stern, he complained bitterly to the gods about his misfortunes, but, though Hera had earlier vouchsafed her protection, she was not to be appealed to by the prayers of a wayward husband, and did not seek to interfere when the Argo's after-deck fell upon the repentant suppliant and crushed out his life.[75]

At Athens, Medeia lost no time in gaining the affections of King Aegeus and by him had a son who was named Medus.[76] But, when Theseus, the son of Aegeus and Aethra, appeared at his father's palace, and she sought to have the king poison him as a stranger, she was forced to flee to Asia where, some say, her son Medus gave his name to the Median nation.[77]

According to the fate which was predestined for her, she was eventually given immortality and became the wife of Achilles in the Isles of the Blest.

---

[71] According to Apollodorus, Jason returned to Iolchus and delivered the golden fleece to Pelias who, at a later time, was dismembered and boiled by his daughters at Medeia's persuasion.

[72] Another version of the story relates that Acastus forcibly took over the government of Iolchus and, after celebrating funeral games in honor of his father, expelled Jason and Medeia from the city.

[73] According to another story, Medeia set the palace on fire before the wedding and Glauce was burnt up with Creon, but Jason escaped.

[74] In the Iliad, it is said that the Greek army at Troy received provisions sent from Lemnos by Euneus. Diodorus names Alcimenes, Thersander, and Thessalus as the sons of Jason and Medeia; and, to the children named in the text, Pausanias adds another son, Medus, who—according to Hesiod—was reared by Cheiron.

[75] Later writers represent Jason as having become reconciled with Medeia and returning with her to Colchis, where they received Aeëtes' blessing.

[76] Diodorus Siculus (who ignores the fact that Heracles was left by the Argonauts before they reached Colchis), says that Medeia first went from Corinth to Thebes to obtain the help which the great man had promised in her native country.

[77] According to Diodorus, the son of Medeia who gave his name to the Medes was borne by her to an unnamed Asiatic monarch.

8

The Aeolids III

Cretheus and His Descendants—
The House of Pheres

PHERES, the second son of Cretheus and Tyro, married Periclymene, a daughter of Minyas and became the king of Pherae in the portion of Thessaly west of Magnesia which was known as Pelasgiotis. They had three daughters, Antigone, Eidomene, and Periopis, and two sons, named Lycurgus and Admetus.

46a. Cretheus and His Descendants

	Pheres and Pericylmene (d. Minyas)	Amythaon (Chart 46b) (Chart 46c)
Lycurgus and Eurydice (d. Amphiaraus) ↓	Admetus and Alcestis (d. Pelias) ↓	Antigone Eidomene Periopis
Opheltes (Archemorus)	Eumelus and Iphthime (d. Icarius)	Perimele

Antigone married a mortal named Cometes. Their son Asterius was honored as one of the Argonauts; Eidomene married her uncle Amythaon and had children who are later mentioned in some detail. Periopis is remembered only because the mythographer Apollodorus names her as an alternate mother of Patroclus, the companion and charioteer of Achilles.

Lycurgus seems to have contributed nothing of importance to mythological legend, except to father Opheltes—who was killed while an infant from the bite of a snake, under circumstances later related in this chapter.[1]

Admetus was one of the Argonauts in his youth and is also said to have been among those who hunted the Calydonian boar, but he was not individually distinguished in either undertaking, and his mythological fame revolves chiefly about the devotion of his wife Alcestis, who was one of the daughters of Pelias. As background to the story, it may be helpful first to relate the activities of certain of the gods. Apollo's son, Asclepius, became such a successful physician to men that the mortal death rate was perceptibly lowered and Hades accused the doctor of poaching on his preserves. When the accusation was brought before Zeus, he killed Asclepius with a thunderbolt, whereupon, Apollo set about slaying the Cyclopes, who had forged the instrument of his son's destruction. For this presumption, the supreme deity would have hurled him into the depths of Tartarus, but—at the intercession of Leto—his wrath was tempered and he merely condemned Apollo to serve for a year as the servant of Admetus. The mortal king of Pherae proved to be such a kind taskmaster that his immortal servant became quite fond of him and caused his herds

---

[1] The wife of Lycurgus, and mother of Opheltes, was conventionally given as Eurydice, a daughter of Amphiaraus, but Apollodorus says that she was sometimes called Amphitheia.

to multiply rapidly.[2] And, during the year's service, he helped Admetus to gain Alcestis as his bride.[3] However, in offering sacrifices at his marriage, Admetus forgot to make an offering to Artemis, and she filled his bridal chamber with coiled snakes. Apollo again came to the help of his gentle master; the goddess was appeased; and the Fates were induced to announce that, when Admetus should be about to die, he might escape death if someone should volunteer to perish in his stead.

Years later, when he was on his deathbed, the promise of the Fates was recalled and it was suggested to Pheres and Periclymene—the aged father and mother—that either of them could ransom their son's life by volunteering to part with the short span left to them. Their paternal and maternal loves were overmatched by their desires to continue on earth—for no matter how brief a period—and they both refused; but Alcestis, although still a young woman, offered herself as her husband's substitute. Admetus immediately recovered, only to learn that his dear wife was now stricken in his stead, and her departure from earth was but a matter of minutes. He rushed into her chamber and, after a tender parting, she died and, soon after, was taken to her tomb.

While Admetus and the handmaidens of Alcestis were bewailing her unselfish sacrifice, a visitor arrived at the Pheraean palace. He was Heracles. After eating his fill at the table, he asked Admetus the reason for his manifest sorrow. Being told why, he went to the tomb of Alcestis, where he snatched her from the hands of Death (Thanatos) and returned her, fully restored to life, to the arms of her loving husband.[4]

Admetus and Alcestis had a daughter, Perimele, about whom nothing of interest is related, but their son Eumelus was one of the Greek captains at Troy. There he was distinguished for his excellent horses, trained by Apollo, and with which he would have won the racing prize at the funeral games of Patroclus if his chariot had not broken down. After the war, he returned to his home at Pherae and married Iphthime, a daughter of Icarius—and, presumably, they lived happily ever after.

The House of Amythaon

Amythaon is mentioned by Pindar as coming from his home in Messenia, with other members of the Aeolid family, to intercede with Pelias at Iolchus on behalf of Jason; and Pausanias says that one of the legends of Elis associated his name with the revival of the Olympic games.

By Eidomene, the daughter of his brother Pheres, he became the father of a daughter Aeolia and two sons, who were named Bias and Melampus.[5]

Aeolia is remembered only as the wife of the Aetolian prince, Calydon, and as the mother of the children whom she bore to him. Her two

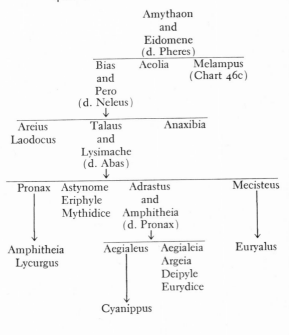

46b. Cretheus and His Descendants

[2] During the period of Apollo's service, the calves dropped by the cows of Admetus were all twins.

[3] Pelias had promised to give Alcestis in marriage only to the man who should come to his court in a chariot drawn by lions and boars, and, with the help of Apollo, Admetus was enabled to perform this condition.

[4] According to Apollodorus, Alcestis was sent back to Admetus by pitying Persephone after she had been taken by Death into the underworld.

[5] The mother of Amythaon's children was sometimes also named as Aglaea or Rhodope.

brothers, however, proved to be more interesting.

Melampus was considered by the ancients as the first mortal to be endowed with prophetic powers. He was also honored as the first to effect cures by drugs, and Herodotus ascribes to him the introduction into Greece (from Egypt) of the worship of the wine-god Dionysus. Upon reaching manhood, he moved into a house in the country, before which stood an oak tree containing a nest of snakes. His servants killed the old snakes and Melampus burned up their bodies, but raised the young ones to maturity. One day while he was sleeping, his curious pets came to his couch and, by licking his ears with their tongues, caused him to acquire the power to understand the speech of all creatures.

Shortly afterward, it happened that his younger brother Bias fell in love with Pero, a daughter of Neleus who had many other suitors. Her father had previously announced that he would give her hand only to the man who would bring him the cattle of Phylacus—a herd guarded by a ferocious dog that permitted no one to come near. Being unable to perform the ticklish task himself, Bias requested and received a promise of help from his brother, but Melampus prophesied that he would surely be detected in the act of stealing the cattle and that he would be imprisoned for a year before finally obtaining their possession. As he had foretold, he was apprehended when he tried to drive off the animals and the servants of Phylacus threw him into prison. After languishing there for a year, he heard the woodworms in the rafters of his cell say that the structure would soon fall down from decay. This information he communicated to his jailers who, though incredulous, let him out for a trial period. When the jailhouse soon collapsed, Phylacus realized that his captive was gifted with prophetic powers and asked him in what manner his son Iphiclus might become a father. Seizing the opportunity to drive a bargain, Melampus offered to give the answer in return for the cattle; and both Phylacus and Iphiclus agreed to his terms. The seer now summoned a vulture and learned that once, when Phylacus was gelding rams, he had laid down his bloody knife beside

his son and that, when the child became frightened and ran away, he had stuck the knife into a tree whose bark had later covered it. The vulture further said that, if the knife should be recovered and, if Iphiclus should drink a potion made from its rust, he would beget a son. Melampus repeated the advice of his feathered friend; it was duly followed; Iphiclus begot his son; and Melampus got the cattle, which—delivered to his brother Bias—brought into the family the beautiful Pero as a willing bride.[6]

The children of Bias and Pero were a daughter Anaxibia, who married her uncle Pelias, and three sons, Areius, Laodocus, and Talaus. All three of the sons were members of the Argonauts' band, and that distinction seems to have been enough to satisfy Areius and Laodocus, for nothing of further interest is related about them.

Talaus married Lysimache, a daughter of his cousin Abas[7] and their offspring were three daughters, namely, Astynome, who later married Hipponous; Eriphyle, who later married Amphiaraus; Mythidice, who later married Aristomachus; and three sons—named Mecisteus, Pronax, and Adrastus.

Of the sons of Talaus, Mecisteus, and Pronax are largely remembered only because of their own children—borne to them by unnamed wives. Mecisteus fathered Euryalus, who was one of the Epigoni—a group which later conquered Thebes;[8] and Pronax fathered a son Lycurgus,[9] and a daughter Amphitheia who married her uncle Adrastus. By him she became the mother of a son Aegialeus[10] who was later

---

[6] A legend preserved by Apollodorus relates that Pero was later seduced by Poseidon and became mother of the river-god Asopus.

[7] Hyginus says that the wife of Talaus was Eurynome and Pausanias calls her Lysianassa.

[8] Apollodorus names Euryalus as one of the Argonauts. He accompanied Diomedes to Troy, where he was thrown in wrestling by Epeius at the funeral games of Patroclus; but earlier at the Theban funeral games in honor of Oedipus, he is said to have conquered all competitors.

[9] Lycurgus is reported to have been among the number of men who were raised from the dead by the great physician Asclepius.

[10] In the attack on Thebes, Aegialeus was killed by Laodamas and left a son, Cyanippus, who later died childless. But, according to Apollodorus, Cyanippus was his brother.

one of the Epigoni, and four daughters: Aegialeia, who became the wife of Diomedes; Argeia,
who became the wife of Polyneices; Deipyle,
who became the wife of Tydeus; and Eurydice,
who became the wife of the Trojan king, Ilus.

The Seven Against Thebes

During a feud between the descendants of
Amythaon over the rulership of Argos, Talaus
was slain by his kinsman Amphiaraus and his
sons were forced to flee from the country. Afterward, however, Amphiaraus fell in love with
Talaus' daughter Eriphyle and her brothers
were permitted to return, under an agreement
that she should be given to Amphiaraus in marriage and that her brother Adrastus should become a joint ruler with her prospective husband.
As part of the bargain, Amphiaraus swore that
he would abide by her decision in any later
dispute which he might have with Adrastus.

One night, after Adrastus had been restored
to power, he was awakened by the noise of men
angrily fighting before the gates of his palace.
Appearing at the scene of the brawl, he parted
the combatants and discovered them to be two
young men, upon whose respective shields were
depicted the forepart of a lion and the forepart
of a boar.[11] The creators of the commotion were
Polyneices, son of Oedipus, and Tydeus, son of
Oeneus—one having been expelled by his
brother from the rulership of Thebes and the
other having been forced to flee from his kingdom at Calydon because of a murder which he
had committed. By mythological coincidence,
the two proud princes had arrived, almost simultaneously, at the palace of Adrastus for the
purpose of seeking his aid and, in the darkness,
each had assumed that the other was an enemy.
When Adrastus noticed the figures on their
shields, he was immediately reminded of an
oracular prediction that his daughters, Argeia
and Deipyle, should be given in marriage to a

lion and a boar. After inviting the strangers
within and learning of their noble birth, he
revealed the mysterious prophecy to them and
(presumably without any objection from the
maidens) bestowed Argeia upon Polyneices and
Deipyle upon Tydeus. Following the quick
double ceremony, Adrastus promised his newly
acquired sons-in-law that he would assist them
in regaining their lost thrones.

It was agreed that the first undertaking
would be to restore the government of Thebes
to Polyneices, and Adrastus set about gathering
a force of warriors for the purpose. The neighboring chieftains who were solicited readily responded to his call, save only Amphiaraus who
—being a seer—knew that the enterprise would
fail and that Adrastus alone would survive it,
and this foreknowledge he earnestly revealed.
But Adrastus, together with both Polyneices
and Tydeus, would not believe his prophecy and
insisted that he join their expedition. In disgust
and embarrassment at their obstinacy, he concealed himself in a hiding-place known only to
his wife Eriphyle, only to have it revealed when
Polyneices engaged her sympathy by giving to
the foolish woman the beautiful (and fatal)
necklace which the gods had presented as a
wedding present to his ancestress Harmonia,
when she married Cadmus—the founder of
Thebes. Thus bribed, Eriphyle directed Adrastus to her husband's place of concealment; and,
bound by his marriage oath to abide by her
decision, Amphiaraus reluctantly agreed to join
the attacking band. But, he enjoined his sons
to avenge his certain death upon their heartless
mother.

The army, which now gathered to assist Polyneices to recover his throne, was collectively
called the "Seven Against Thebes" because its
leaders were seven in number, usually considered to be: Adrastus, the son of Talaus; Polyneices, the son of Oedipus; Tydeus, the son of
Oeneus; Amphiaraus, the son of Oicles; Capaneus, the son of Hipponous; Parthenopaeus, the
son of Ares;[12] and, Hippomedon, the son of
Aristomachus.[13]

---

[11] A different version of the story is that the two
men were clothed in the skins of a lion and a boar,
respectively. The conventional interpretation is that the
lion on the shield of Polyneices depicted the lion-faced
Sphinx who had propounded her famous riddle outside
the Theban walls, and the boar on the shield of Tydeus
represented the Calydonian beast which had been
hunted by many heroes in the land of his birth.

[12] Other versions of the story relate that Parthenopaeus was a son of Meilanion or of Talaus.

[13] Aeschylus adds Eteoclus, the son of Iphis, thus
making Adrastus the leader of seven others; and, accord-

Proceeding toward Thebes along the road between Argos and Corinth, the invading princes halted for water near a plain of Nemea, which at the time was governed by Lycurgus, the son of Pheres. Here, they saw a beautiful woman seated on the trunk of a tree and nursing an infant. From her noble bearing, they concluded that she must be a goddess, but upon inquiry she revealed that she was the Lemnian queen, Hypsipyle, who had been carried off by pirates and sold as a slave to Lycurgus.[14] It further developed that she was nursing Opheltes, the small son of King Lycurgus and his wife, Eurydice—a daughter of Amphiaraus.[15] When the strangers mentioned their need of water, Hypsipyle laid her charge upon a patch of soft grass and graciously conducted them to a nearby spring, where their want was soon filled. But, upon returning, it was found to their grief that the child had died from the bite of a poisonous snake.

The reptile was quickly located and killed by the angry band, who then proceeded to bury the remains of the young victim with funeral honors in the adjoining plain. As a part of the funeral ritual, athletic contests were held and, for years afterward, were periodically celebrated as the Nemean games.[16] Among the victors were: Adrastus in racing horses; Eteoclus in footracing; Tydeus in boxing; Amphiaraus in leaping and throwing the discus; Laodocus in throwing the javelin; Polyneices in wrestling; and Parthenopaeus in archery.[17]

After the contests were over and prizes had

been awarded to the winners, the high-hearted heroes proceeded onward until they arrived at the walls of "seven-gated" Thebes in southern Boeotia.[18] Pausing there, Tydeus was sent forward to demand the city's surrender, in accordance with the pact which had been made earlier between Polyneices and his brother Eteocles.[19] When Tydeus returned to report that the demand had been refused, Adrastus divided his army into seven parts under the seven leaders and placed each division before one of the city's gates. Within the walls, Eteocles made a corresponding separation of his defending forces, but, before joining battle, he summoned the blind seer Teiresias and asked what the end of the conflict would be. Teiresias replied that a Theban victory was possible only if Menoeceus, the young son of Creon and a cousin of Eteocles, should offer himself freely as a sacrifice to Ares. When the seer's words were reported to the lad, he bravely mounted to one of the towers of his city's walls and, slashing his own throat, gloriously died before the eyes of the opposing armies.

The battle began and many acts of valor were performed on both sides. Capaneus tried to scale the walls with a ladder and boasted that even the fire of Zeus could not stay his progress, but the supreme god struck him with a thunderbolt and his corpse hurtled to the ground. Eteocles and Polyneices, the contesting sons of Oedipus, fought in single combat, in which they slew each other. In another sector, the sons of Theban Astacus, fighting furiously, killed Hippomedon, Eteoclus, and Parthenopaeus.[20] Am-

---

ing to Apollodorus, some legends included Mecisteus, brother of Adrastus, among the leaders.

[14] A variant tale recites that the Lemnian women themselves sold Hypsipyle into slavery when they discovered that she had saved her father, Thoas, from the universal slaughter of their men.

[15] Others name Amphitheia as the wife of Lycurgus or do not name Eurydice as the daughter of Amphiaraus —whose genealogical position was several generations later than that of Lycurgus.

[16] Some say that Heracles founded the games in celebration of his victory over the Nemean lion. The seer Amphiaraus saw no reason for the celebration by his comrades, because to him the death of the infant Opheltes appeared to be a bad omen; and he surnamed the slain child Archemorus, meaning "beginner of doom."

[17] The list of the victors given in the text is that of Apollodorus. Other legends name both different victors and competitive events.

---

[18] In addition to Boeotian Thebes, cities of the same name in Egypt ("hundred-gated") and in Mysia were mythologically important. The ancients were not agreed on the names of the seven gates of the Boeotian city. Nonnos says they were originally dedicated to the "seven-planets"—the western (Oncan) gate to Selene, and the others to Hermes, Electra, Helios, Ares, Aphrodite, Zeus, and Cronus. According to Apollodorus, their names were Homoloidian, Ogygian, Proetidian, Oncaidian, Hypsistan, Electran, and Crenidian; and Euripides substitutes Neistian for Hypsistan.

[19] The background of the pact between Polyneices and his brother Eteocles is related in the next chapter in connection with the story of Cadmus and his descendants.

[20] The sons of Astacus were Ismarus, Leades, and Amphidicus who, respectively, were victors over their foes in the order named in the text. Euripides says that

phiaraus fought as bravely as any man, even though he knew that he was not fated to survive, but was guilty of one act which seems rather questionable. It seems that he bore a special grudge against his companion Tydeus, because he suspected him of having instigated the foolish attack. During the battle, Tydeus was severely wounded by Melanippus[21] and Amphiaraus spied the goddess Athena as she hastened toward him with a divine medicine by which she intended to make him immortal. Perceiving her purpose, he cut off the head of Melanippus and gave the wounded man his brains to drink.[22] In horror at this ghastly performance, the goddess quickly turned away with her intended benefit and permitted Tydeus' life to expire.

As had been foretold, the invasion failed and the invaders were put to rout when they discovered that all of their leaders, except Amphiaraus and Adrastus, had been slain. Adrastus fled on his immortal steed Arion[23] and Amphiaraus, chased by Periclymenus, mounted his chariot and followed suit in the vain hope of escape: vain, because at the river Ismenus the earth was cleft with a thunderbolt by Zeus and, into its opening, disappeared not only Amphiaraus himself but also his chariot, horses, and charioteer.[24] Afterward, the vanished seer was worshipped as a divine hero throughout Greece and was honored with sanctuaries at Argos, Athens, Sparta, and other places. And not far from Thebes, on the road to Potniae, Pausanias saw the exact spot where he entered the earth—

for it was clearly marked off by a fence of pillars.

With Adrastus as the only survivor of the Seven Against Thebes, we turn now to consider the descendants of his great-uncle Melampus, who unselfishly suffered imprisonment in obtaining the cattle of Phylacus for his brother, Bias.

Sometime after Melampus returned from his imprisonment, the Argive king, Proetus, who knew of his prophetic powers, besought the famed seer to relieve his daughters from a madness, which had stricken them with such force that it was causing them to roam about his realm in a frantic state. Melampus agreed to undertake the task, on condition that, if he should be successful, Proetus should turn over to him and to his brother Bias equal shares of the kingdom of Argos, and that Melampus himself should receive the king's daughter, Iphianassa, as his wife.[25] When the offer was accepted, he proceeded to cure the mad women of their disease and (with Proetus and Bias) became a co-ruler of the Argive land with Iphianassa as his bride. In time, she bore to him three sons who were named Mantius, Antiphates, and Abas.[26]

By an unnamed wife, Mantius had two sons. One of them, named Cleitus, was loved for his beauty by the dawn-goddess Eos and she snatched him away from earth to live with her in the skies, where their daughter Eurymedusa was espoused by Zeus.[27] The other son, named Polypheides, went from Argos to Sicyon and there, under the guidance of Apollo, became such a famous seer that the infant boys Menelaus and Agamemnon were brought to him for rearing. In his new home,[28] he married an unidentified woman and had a son Theoclymenus, who inherited his father's great powers;

Parthenopaeus was slain by Periclymenus, a son of Poseidon; and another story relates that Hippomedon was overwhelmed by a cloud of Theban missiles.

[21] Melanippus was another son of Astacus who, by some, is said to have slain both Tydeus and Mecisteus.

[22] Apparently, Melanippus had just died of wounds previously inflicted by Tydeus in their hand-to-hand struggle. A different version of the story relates that, although Amphiaraus cut off the head, he merely handed it over to Tydeus, who himself split it open and drank the brains.

[23] Arion was the offspring of Demeter and Poseidon who was conceived when the god consorted with her in the shape of a horse, after she had changed herself into a mare to avoid his amorous advances.

[24] The name of the charioteer was Baton. It was believed that Amphiaraus, with his equippage, descended all the way to the lower world; and Sophocles mentions him as reigning there fully alive.

[25] Another version of the story places the madness of the Argive women in the reign of Anaxagoras, a grandson of Proetus, and relates that Melampus married his sister Iphianeira.

[26] Homer names only Mantius and Antiphates as the sons of Melampus, but Abas is added on the authority of Apollodorus. With his accustomed confusion, Diodorus Siculus says that the children of Melampus were Bias, Antiphates, Manto, and Pronoe.

[27] The son of Zeus and Eurymedusa was called Myrmidon.

[28] According to Homer, the place to which Polypheides repaired was called Hyperesia.

46c. Cretheus and His Descendants

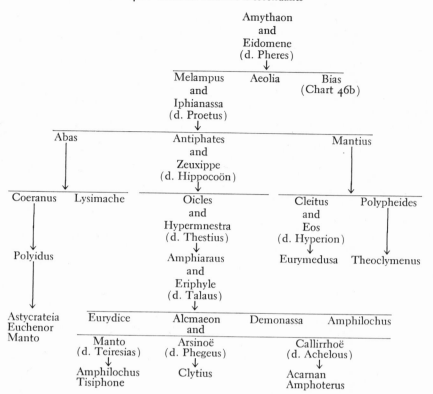

Amythaon
and
Eidomene
(d. Pheres)
↓

Melampus   Aeolia   Bias
and   (Chart 46b)
Iphianassa
(d. Proetus)
↓

Abas   Antiphates   Mantius
and
Zeuxippe
(d. Hippocoön)

Coeranus   Lysimache   Oicles   Cleitus   Polypheides
and   and
Hypermnestra   Eos
(d. Thestius)   (d. Hyperion)

Polyidus   Amphiaraus   Eurymedusa   Theoclymenus
and
Eriphyle
(d. Talaus)
↓

Astycrateia   Eurydice   Alcmaeon   Demonassa   Amphilochus
Euchenor   and
Manto

          Manto   Arsinoë   Callirrhoë
        (d. Teiresias) (d. Phegeus)   (d. Achelous)
           ↓   ↓   ↓
        Amphilochus   Clytius   Acarnan
        Tisiphone   Amphoterus

but, unfortunately, the lad accidentally killed one of his playmates and was forced to flee to Sparta, where he met Telemachus as he was searching for his lost father after the Trojan War.[29]

Abas' children were a daughter Lysimache, and a son, Coeranus, borne to him by a wife whose name is not given by the mythographers. Lysimache has previously been noted as the wife of Talaus and the mother of his three sons and three daughters. Coeranus is remembered chiefly becaue his son Polyidus inherited the prophetic powers of his ancestors to such a degree that he was invited to dwell at the court of the Cretan king, Minos. During his stay, the king's young son Glaucus, while chasing a mouse, fell into a jar of honey and was drowned. Upon his disappearance, Minos caused a great search to be made and was told by the Curetes that his child would be restored by the diviner who could best describe the color of a dappled cow among the royal herds. Polyidus compared the animal's markings to the fruit of a nearby shrub and was rewarded by finding the boy's body. Just as he did so, he saw a serpent approaching and killed it with a stone, only to see his victim revive when another serpent appeared and placed a herb on its head. Surprised and educated by this occurrence, Polyidus applied the same herb to the corpse of the child and was gratified to see Glaucus come back to life.[30]

As shown on chart 46c, Polyidus had two daughters, named Astycrateia and Manto, and a son named Euchenor. Nothing of interest is related about the daughters; but Euchenor went with the Greeks to Troy and was slain in the fighting by Paris.

Antiphates, the third charted son of Melampus and Iphianassa, married Zeuxippe, a daughter of the Spartan usurper Hippocoön. His son,

---

[29] The association of Theoclymenus and Telemachus is an integral part of the story of the Odyssey and is later mentioned in more detail.

[30] Hyginus says that when Alcathous murdered his own son Callipolis he was purified of his crime by Polyidus.

Oicles, accompanied Heracles on his expedition against Laomedon at Troy and was slain there.[31] Before his death he was married to Hypermnestra, one of the daughters of Thestius. By her he became the father of Amphiaraus whose exploits as one of the Seven Against Thebes already have been narrated.[32]

When Amphiaraus vanished into the earth outside the Theban walls, he left not only his greedy widow Eriphyle but also his daughters, Eurydice and Demonassa, and two sons who were named Amphilochus and Alcmaeon. It has been already related that Eurydice (by Lycurgus) was mother of the infant Opheltes, who was killed by the serpent's bite as the Seven Against Thebes sought water at the plain of Nemea. Her sister Demonassa later became the wife of Thersander, the son of Polyneices, and thus coupled herself with a family pursued by even more tragedy than that into which she had been born.

Amphilochus, the younger son of Amphiaraus and Eriphyle, was yet an infant when his father went against Thebes, but grew up to join his brother Alcmaeon in a later assault against the same city.[33]

The Epigoni

The name given to this second expedition— which is supposed to have occurred ten years after the defeat of the Seven Against Thebes— was the "Epigoni," because its members were the sons of the beaten attackers, who resolved to avenge the deaths of their fathers.

When the young heroes consulted the oracle, the god predicted their victory under the leadership of Alcmaeon. He was loath to leave Argos until he had punished his mother, Eriphyle, for having sent his father to a foretold doom,

but her artful tongue was able to persuade her sons, even as it had persuaded her husband.[34] They left with their comrades to attack the Theban citadel. As conventionally stated, the attacking forces are said to have been led by: Alcmaeon and Amphilochus, the sons of Amphiaraus; Aegialeus, the son of Adrastus; Diomedes, the son of Tydeus; Promachus, the son of Parthenopaeus; Sthenelus, the son of Capaneus; Thersander, the son of Polyneices; Euryalus, the son of Mecisteus; and Polydorus, the son of Hippomedon.

Outside the gates of the city, the Epigoni met an advancing army of their adversaries led by Laodamas, the son of Eteocles, and a furious battle was fought, in which he killed Aegialeus, but he was himself slain by Alcmaeon.[35] With the fall of their leader, the Thebans fled in dismay back within their protecting walls and appealed to their blind, old seer Teiresias who informed them that they could save their lives only by abandoning the city. Following this advice, a herald was sent to the attackers and, while he artfully protracted negotiations for surrender through the night, the Thebans evacuated their homeland. At morning, the Epigoni entered without meeting resistance and, after collecting the booty that remained, they tore down the city's walls and demolished its gates.[36]

The subsequent adventures of the fleeing Thebans, and the fortunes of their conquered city, are related in succeeding chapters.

When Alcmaeon returned to Argos, he learned that Eriphyle had received from Thersander the robe (peplus) of Harmonia to add, as another selfish gain, to the necklace with which she had been bribed to send Amphiaraus to his death. Remembering his father's injunction that she should not go unpunished, he now murdered her without the least feeling of com-

---

[31] According to another tradition, Oicles returned from the expedition with Heracles and settled in Arcadia where he was later visited by his grandson Alcmaeon.

[32] By some of the mythographers, Amphiaraus was accounted a member of the Argonauts, and it is said that, in the hunt for the Calydonian boar, he drew blood by shooting the beast in the eye with an arrow.

[33] Amphilochus is named as one of the suitors of Helen and as a participant in the Trojan War. Like many of his ancestors, he was considered to be a seer and, according to Strabo, he eventually lost his life in a combat fought with Mopsus, a son of Apollo.

---

[34] Adopting tactics similar to those used by his father, Thersander, the son of Polyneices, bribed Eriphyle with the divine robe of Harmonia to induce her sons to join in this second assault on Thebes.

[35] According to Herodotus, Laodamas did not fall in the battle, but, after his defeat, led a portion of the Thebans to the Illyrian tribe of the Encheleans, where his ancestors, Cadmus and Harmonia, had gained refuge.

[36] Apollodorus relates that part of the booty—which included Manto, the daughter of Teiresias—was sent to the oracle of Apollo at Delphi.

passion.[37] Then, taking with him the ill-fated necklace and robe, he abandoned Argos and went to Arcadia. But the dread Furies afflicted him with a madness which caused him to wander about aimlessly, until he came to Psophis, where King Phegeus purified him of his crime and gave him his daughter Arsinoë in marriage.[38] And, as bridal presents, Alcmaeon thoughtlessly gave her the necklace and robe of Harmonia, which had always brought unhappiness to their possessors.[39]

Although his madness had been removed, the curse which hung over Alcmaeon was transferred to the land of his adoption, and it soon became barren from a severe drought. Upon consulting the oracle at Delphi, the poor man was informed that any piece of earth which was in existence at the time when he murdered his mother would be cursed by the gods, and that the curse would be lifted only when he should settle at some place whose soil should have been later formed. Despairingly, he first went to Oeneus at Calydon in Aetolia and then to the country of the Thesprotians, from which he was driven away as a bringer of great pestilence.

Finally, he arrived at the banks of the mouth of the river Achelous where the down-flowing silt had created a delta, and there took up his abode. He was graciously received by the god of the river, whose daughter Callirrhoë he received as his wife—wholly unmindful of Arsinoë, and his young son, Clytius, whom he had left deserted at Psophis. But Callirrhoë knew of his previous marriage and, coveting the robe and necklace of Harmonia, said that she would not continue to live with her bigamous husband unless he should bring them to her. Faced with this ultimatum, Alcmaeon went back to Psophis and told his father-in-law, Phegeus, that he could be rid of his madness only if he should take the magic robe and necklace to Delphi and dedicate them to the oracle of Apollo.

Phegeus believed the story and directed Arsinoë to turn over the treasures, but, after Alcmaeon departed, a servant announced that he was really taking the divine gifts to his new wife. When he received this information, the indignant king had his sons waylay and kill Alcmaeon.[40] After they returned, bearing the robe and the necklace, Arsinoë learned of their bloody act and upbraided them so vociferously that they clapped her in a chest and carried her to Tegea and accused her of having murdered her own husband to King Agapenor.[41]

When she learned of what had happened, Callirrhoë prayed to Zeus that the infant sons, Acarnan and Amphoterus, whom she had borne to Alcmaeon, might quickly become full grown in order to avenge their father's slaughter. Her prayer was granted and, overnight, her boys matured into men, who took full vengeance by murdering Phegeus, his wife, and sons. But the warrior-subjects of Phegeus were enraged and Acarnan and Amphoterus were forced to flee, with the robe and necklace, to Tegea, where their pursuers were routed with the assistance of Agapenor, to whom they revealed the true state of affairs. Presumably, Arsinoë was released from detention and the boy-men, at the injunction of their river-god grandfather, finally made true the pretense of Alcmaeon by taking their sorrow-dealing booty to Delphi and dedicating it to the oracle.[42] Afterward they moved westward and, collecting settlers, colonized the country which was anciently called Acarnania.

---

[37] Apollodorus says that Eriphyle was murdered only after Alcmaeon had consulted the oracle of Apollo; and, according to a variant of the legend, Amphilochus assisted his brother in the crime.

[38] Euripides is cited by Apollodorus as relating that, in the time of his madness, Alcmaeon begot a son Amphilochus and a daughter Tisiphone by Manto, the daughter of Teiresias. Their father brought the babes to Creon, king of Corinth, to bring up; but when Tisiphone was nearing maturity she was sold by Creon's wife, who feared that her husband might be over-attracted by her extraordinary beauty. By chance, Alcmaeon bought her and kept her as a handmaiden—not knowing that she was his own daughter—and, later returning to Corinth, he recovered his son also.

[39] Some of the ancient tragedians referred to Arsinoë as Alphesiboea.

---

[40] According to Apollodorus, the sons of Phegeus were named Pronous and Agenor; but Pausanias calls them Temenus and Axion.

[41] When his uncles killed his father, Clytius could not bear to remain with his mother and, according to Pausanias, he left Psophis and fled into Elis.

[42] According to Pausanias, it was the sons of Phegeus, and not the sons of Alcmaeon, who dedicated the fatal necklace at Delphi; and there it was preserved until the fourth century B.C., when the temple was sacked by barbarian invaders.

9

Poseidon and His Descendants I

POSEIDON, son of Cronus and Rhea and the brother of Zeus, to whom was given the rulership of the seas, was often called the Earth-shaker because of his power to raise storms. He was not accounted among the greater gods on Mount Olympus,[1] but had a golden palace in the depths of the sea near Aegae in Euboea (or in Achaea) which, like the abodes of the other gods, was divinely wrought by Hephaestus. And there, subject only to the occasional overlordship of Zeus,[2] he ruled with full sway over the watery elements.[3]

In chapter 3, we have already related how the great sea-god was worsted in his attempt to have himself honored as the presiding deity of Athens.[4] And additional instances, mentioned throughout the text, state his connection with various other events of mythological renown.

Poseidon's conventionally acknowledged wife was the Nereid Amphitrite; but he had a host of other inamoratas—among whom Libya and her descendants will be discussed first, because she was the ancestress of some of the leading actors in the events which are narrated in the preceding chapter. Following her, the other wives (and their descendants) are mentioned in the alphabetical order of their names.

Descendants of Libya

In Egypt, Poseidon had three sons borne to him by Libya, who was the daughter of Epaphus. Their names were Agenor, Belus, and Lelex.

Agenor and Belus were twins, and, before coming to Lelex, we shall first discuss them and their descendants.

By a daughter of the god of the river Nilus, who was named Telephassa, Agenor had a daughter, Europa, and four sons, whose names are shown on the following chart. One of his sons—Phineus—was first married to Cleopatra, a daughter of the north-wind Boreas, and then to Idaea, a daughter of the Trojan king, Dardanus. Idaea became jealous of Pandion and Plexippus—her stepsons who had been borne by Cleopatra—and falsely accused them of trying to corrupt her virtue, whereupon, their father blinded both of them. As punishment

---

It is said that Poseidon was originally assigned a residence on Mount Olympus, but was expelled when he joined Hera and Athena in a conspiracy to put supreme Zeus in bonds. In addition to his expulsion, he was forced to serve the mortal Laomedon for a year and became a reluctant assistant in building the walls of Troy.

[2] At the bidding of Zeus, Poseidon was forced to pour his waters over the earth in the flood of Deucalion.

[3] As successor to the functions of their ancient progenitors, Poseidon was considered to be the ruler of the descendants of Pontus and Oceanus.

[4] Except for a few allusions to their king, Menestheus, and an occasional recognition of the Theseus myth, the older legends ignore the Athenians. Under the skillful hands of Aeschylus, Euripides, Sophocles and other resident composers, a fabulous genealogy was arranged which allowed them to tie themselves in as participants in most of the earlier heroic exploits.

47. Descendants of Poseidon and Libya

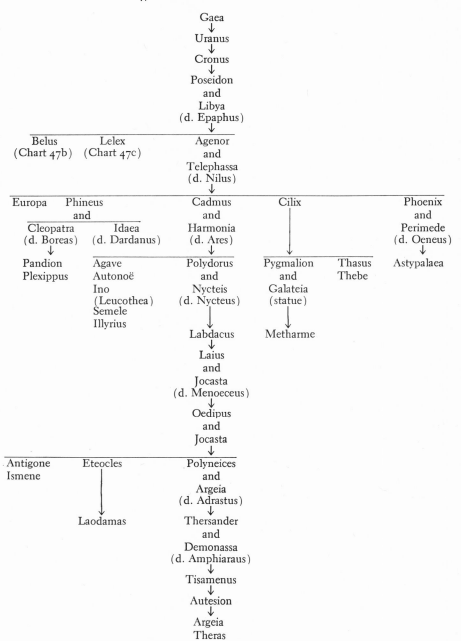

for his hasty act, Zeus blinded Phineus as previously related.[5]

Phoenix, another son of Agenor and Telephassa,[6] married Perimede, a daughter of Oeneus, and had a daughter, Astypalaea, who grew up to become one of the many wives of Poseidon and will again be referred to in that role. The legends about Phoenix himself are rather confused,[7] but they seem to agree on at least one point, namely, that in the search for his sister Europa he settled in the country which, from his name, was thereafter called Phoenicia.

Cilix, a third son of Agenor, is said to have given his name to the country of Cilicia, where the huge Typhon was born. He had a daughter named Thebe, who wedded the Cretan Corybas,[8] and two sons named Thasus and Pygmalion. Thasus is reputed to have gone in search of his lost aunt Europa and to have setled finally on an island off the Thracian coast, which took its name from him. His younger brother Pygmalion went to Cyprus and, becoming king of the island, earned a great reputation as a sculptor, and as a woman-hater. But he carved an ivory statue of a maiden with such beauty that he prayed Aphrodite to give life to his creation. Pitying his celibate state, the goddess granted his prayer and the statue, breathing life, became the lovely Galateia and the wife of her author, to whom she bore a daughter named Metharme.[9]

The House of Cadmus

Before proceeding to the story of Cadmus, the last of Agenor and Telephassa's sons,[10] it is necessary to mention that his sister, Europa, was enticed by Zeus, in the form of a gentle bull, to mount his back and take a ride to the island of Crete.[11] There, she gave birth to three sons of the supreme god who were among the most illustrious actors in the events of mythology.

When his daughter disappeared, Agenor sent in search of her not only his wife but also his sons Cilix, Phoenix, and Cadmus and his grandson Thasus. We have already noted that Cilix, Phoenix, and Thasus contributed their bits to the hunt by leaving it and getting places named after themselves. But Cadmus and his mother continued their search until she died in Thrace, where he tenderly buried her at some place which, presumably, already had a name.

Wondering what next to do, Cadmus went to the oracle at Delphi and made inquiry. The oracle's reply was that he should abandon his search for Europa and found a new city, at a place which would be indicated to him when and where a heifer should lie down. As he left the shrine,[12] he saw an animal meeting the oracle's description and, accompanied by his servants, followed her as she slowly ambled ahead. After proceeding into the country of Boeotia, the heifer halted and knelt down to rest in the long grass beside the roadway. Realizing that his long travels had come to an end, Cadmus decided to offer his pilot as a sacrifice to the gods and sent his servants to obtain water for the appropriate libation from a spring in the nearby forest. But, when his luckless men came to the spring, they found not only water but also a great dragon (the offspring

---

[5] Different stories about the reasons for the punishment of Phineus have been mentioned in chapter 7. According to Sophocles, Idaea herself blinded her stepsons by stabbing out their eyes with her knitting needles, and a story attributed to Hesiod, naming Thynus and Mariandynus as additional sons, relates that Phineus was punished for showing Phrixus the way to Colchis.

[6] Hyginus says that the wife of Agenor was named Argeiope.

[7] According to Homer, Phoenix was the father of Europa.

[8] Diodorus Siculus relates that Corybas married Thebe after the wedding of Cadmus and Harmonia, where those who followed his ecstatic antics gained the name of Corybantes.

[9] As might be suspected, the story of Pygmalion and Galateia is a pretty addition to the Greek mythology by later hands; but the story is so well-known in classical reference that it is given in the text. It should here be noted that Ovid says that the daughter of Galateia and Pygmalion was called Paphus, while others name Paphus as an additional child (son).

[10] The mythographers do not give the order of birth of the sons of Agenor and Telephassa; but we mention Cadmus last in an effort to present as consecutively as may be, a connected story of the full Greek epic.

[11] This journey from the ancient shores of civilization to an island in the direction of Greece was mythologically considered as the reason why the more northern continent was called Europe.

[12] According to Apollodorus, Cadmus left the oracular shrine and journeyed through Phocis before spotting the heifer among the herds of Pelagon. Both Pausanias and Hyginus relate that the animal had on each flank a white mark resembling the full moon.

of Ares and Gaea), which killed them all.[13]

After their failure to return promptly, Cadmus went to seek the cause and came upon their mangled bodies scattered about on the ground beneath the monster, whose golden crest reached almost to the skies as his triple tongues flickered out and in and his eyes emitted flames. Angered at the horrid sight, the courageous man drove his spear through the dragon's throat and pinned him to an oak tree, where he soon died. As Cadmus stood in quiet amazement at his easy victory, he heard a voice saying: "Thou too shall be a serpent for men to gaze upon"—and the voice (which was that of unseen Athena), then bade him to plow the earth and sow within the teeth of his dead victim.

He proceeded to follow the divine command, and was astonished to see a band of armed warriors spring up from the ground. Unknowingly inspired by Athena,[14] he threw a large rock into their midst and the strangely born men began to fight among themselves. They continued until only five of their number were left.[15] As ordained by the gods, those who survived— called Sparti from the Greek word meaning "sown"—made peace with each other and, under the leadership of Cadmus, became the first settlers in the city of Cadmeia, which was later known as Boeotian Thebes.[16]

Ares was furious at the slaying of his dragon-son and would have put an end to Cadmus' life, but Zeus intervened and forced the impetuous god of war to accept an "eternal" year's service[17] from his mortal victim as a temporary atonement.[18] At the expiration of this period, during which Cadmus humbly served, the great father of the gods decreed that he should be given Harmonia as his wife. She was the lovely daughter borne by Aphrodite to Ares.

The supreme will was not to be denied and, in due course, the marriage took place at a feast which was attended by all of the gods. There, Apollo played on his lyre, the Muses sang, old Demeter gushed with infatuation for young Iasion, Hermes gave the newlyweds a lyre, and Electra gave them the key to the sacred rites of Cybele; but, mythologically most important, Cadmus gave to his bride a wondrous robe and necklace wrought by the hands of Hephaestus.[19] There seems to be no extant description of the robe but, according to Nonnos, the necklace was made in the form of a two-headed serpent clasping an eagle between its double tongues. All of the ancients, however, were agreed that both the robe and the necklace brought nothing but bad-luck to their successive possessors.[20]

For many years, Cadmus and Harmonia ruled peacefully in the city which he had founded; and born to them were a son, Polydorus, and four daughters, named Agave, Autonoë, Semele, and Ino.

Of the daughters, Agave married Echion, one of the Sparti; Autonoë married Aristaeus, a son of Apollo; Semele was espoused by supreme Zeus; and Ino (Leucothea) became the secret love and second wife of Athamas, as related in the preceding chapter.

In later life, Cadmus was called upon by the Encheleans to deliver them from the attacking Illyrians and, being successful in his call, ruled for a time over the conquered people as their benevolent king. He became so fond of his new subjects that, in their honor, he named his last child (and second son) Illyrius.[21]

After old age came on, he turned over the

---

[13] The dragon is usually referred to by its generic Latin name of Draco, under which it was reputed to have been placed in the skies.

[14] Athena kept half of the dragon's teeth and gave them to King Aeëtes at Colchis, where (as narrated in chapter 7) Jason sowed them with similar result.

[15] The remaining five of the Sparti were named Echion, Chthonius, Hyperenor, Pelorus, and Udaeus.

[16] Some trace the name of Boeotia to the cow (Greek "bous" and our "bossy") which led Cadmus into the country.

[17] The "eternal" year was the equivalent of the eight normal years which were mythologically prescribed as the term of banishment for homicide.

[18] Ares never forgave Cadmus and placed a curse upon him which brought continuing tragedies to his family.

[19] The mythographers variously attribute the gift of the robe and necklace to Athena, Aphrodite, and Hephaestus himself.

[20] The tragedies brought on by possession of the robe and necklace are mentioned in the preceding chapter in connection with Eriphyle, the wife of Amphiaraus, and Arsinoe, the wife of Alcmaeon.

[21] The limits of Illyria—or Illyricum—were rather vaguely defined, but are supposed to have corresponded roughly to the land which, at the eastern shore of the Adriatic Sea, is now known as northern Albania and the southern part of Yugoslavia.

47a. Genealogy of the Sparti

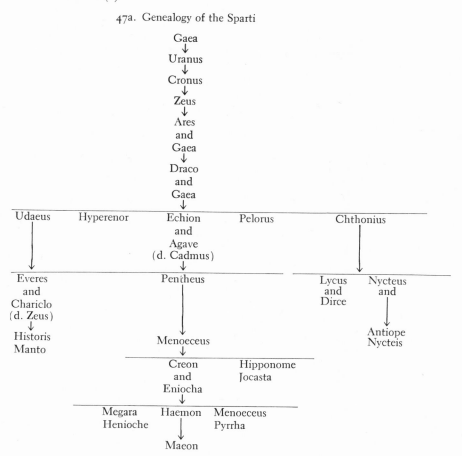

rulership of Thebes to Pentheus, the son of his eldest daughter, Agave, and her husband Echion, who was one of the Sparti.

Although the genealogy of the Sparti traces through Ares (and not Poseidon), it is given here, because it is such an integral part of the Cadmean story.

Meanwhile, Agave's sister, Semele, bore to Zeus a son named Dionysus, under marvelous circumstances which are related later. And, during the reign of Pentheus, he appeared at Thebes as the proclaimed wine-god, after first having wandered over Asia, India, and Thrace at the head of an excited troop of female followers, who were in the habit of celebrating their leader with frenzied rites which no man was permitted to observe.

The venerable Cadmus, together with his daughter Agave and the blind prophet Teiresias, promptly acknowledged the new divinity and began to worship him with all of the solemnities

which had been generated in his triumphal march through foreign lands. But Pentheus refused to be converted, forbade his subjects to participate in the orgiastic ceremonies and threw Dionysus himself into prison. Nor was his disbelief lessened when the prison doors flew open and the wine-god departed for nearby Mount Cithaeron to rejoin his feminine devotees, among whom were Agave and many other Theban women. Enraged at the disobedience to his command, the young ruler followed and climbed a tall pine tree overlooking the scene of the celebration, but he was quickly discovered by the mad worshippers, who pulled down the tree and tore him to pieces in an onslaught led by Agave. Still bereft of reason, she triumphantly carried back to the city the severed head of her own son.[22]

---

[22] A variant of the legend is that Acetes (or Acoëtes) a disciple of Dionysus, was imprisoned. In the "Bacchae"

Resignedly realizing that the curse of Ares was being perpetuated against his descendants and the place of his founding, aged Cadmus returned to the Illyrians, taking with him his wife and son, Harmonia and Illyrius. And there, after a full life, Zeus (in accordance with Athena's prophecy) changed the tired wanderer and his family into serpents and transported them to the sweet Elysian fields which were known as the Isles of the Blest.[23]

With the death of Pentheus, the government was assumed by Polydorus, the elder son of Cadmus. He chose as his queen Nycteis, a daughter of Nycteus and granddaughter of Chthonius who was one of the five Sparti.[24] Their son, Labdacus, succeeded to the throne, but did not rule for long, because he died while still young,[25] leaving a one-year-old boy named Laius.[26]

During his minority, the rulership was usurped[27] by Lycus, a brother of Nycteus who, through an earlier friendship with Pentheus, had already become commander of the city's armed forces. When he moved into the palace with his wife, Dirce, he also provided accommodations for his brother Nycteus and for Nycteus' unwed daughter Antiope who was accounted among the most beautiful of mortal women. Indeed, some doubting-Thomases averred that, in reality, her father was the god of the river Asopus. Zeus himself was attracted to the lovely

maiden, but, when she was with child by him, her father became so threatening that she ran away to Sicyon in the Peloponnesus, where King Epopeus married her. Despondent at his daughter's conduct, Nycteus killed himself—after first adjuring Lycus to punish both Antiope and Epopeus.[28]

Following his brother's dying directions, Lycus attacked Sicyon and, when the city capitulated, he slew Epopeus and led Antiope away as a captive. En route back to Thebes, she gave birth to twin sons whom she had conceived by Zeus, and left them to die by the roadside. But they were found and reared by a cowherd, who named them Amphion and Zethus. As the boys grew into manhood, Zethus directed his attentions to the breeding of cattle, agriculture, and other practical pursuits; Amphion was given a lyre by Hermes and, devoting himself to music, became so expert that the beasts of the forest, and even inanimate objects, were often swayed by his tuneful melodies.

Meanwhile, Lycus returned to Thebes and turned his captive over to his wife, who mistreated the unfortunate woman by placing her in chains and locking her up in a narrow cell. On one fine day, however, Antiope's bonds were miraculously loosed and, escaping from her detention, she wandered through the countryside until she came to the cottage where her sons were living. With mythological promptness, they recognized their mother, killed Lycus, and killed Dirce by tying her to the tail of a fast-moving bull[29] and threw her body into a spring, which was afterward called by her name. Taking over the government, they proceeded to send young Laius out of the country and to fortify the city by encircling it with a wall, whose stones were said to have rolled into place at the summons of Amphion's magic lyre.[30]

---

of Euripides, which relates the incident at length, Pentheus is hypnotized by the god so that he himself dons the Bacchanalian attire and is impelled to spy on the feminine celebrants.

[23] According to Hyginus, Cadmus and Harmonia were changed into serpents by Ares as punishment for the killing of his dragon-son.

[24] Although Apollodorus says that Nycteus and Lycus were sons of Chthonius, he later contradicts himself by relating that they were the sons of Hyrieus and the nymph Clonia.

[25] Apollodorus intimates that Labdacus, like Pentheus, was slain because he resisted the worship of Dionysus.

[26] The paucity of narrative about Polydorus and Labdacus—mere connecting links between Cadmus and Laius—is perhaps explained by the general statement of Grote that "The curious and imaginative Greek, whenever he does not find a recorded past ready to his hand, is uneasy until he has created one."

[27] According to Pausanias, Lycus was successively the duly appointed guardian of Labdacus and Laius during their respective minorities.

---

[28] According to Pausanias, Nycteus attacked Sicyon and suffered wounds from which he died and, although he was victorious, Epopeus also died later. He adds that Antiope was voluntarily sent back to Thebes by Lamedon who succeeded Epopeus as king of Sicyon.

[29] The episode has been preserved to us in the celebrated sculptured group known as the Farnese Bull—taking its name from the Italian family who were the owners of the work.

[30] The wall, with its seven-gated towers, was the same one which protected the city from the attack of the

The sovereignty of the twin brothers, however, was of short duration. Zethus married Aëdon, daughter of Pandareos, who unwittingly killed their son Itylus with a sword—a mishap which caused her husband to grieve himself to death. Amphion married Niobe, a daughter of Tantalus, and she proved to be the cause of his death: for, she boasted of the great number of children which he had given her, saying that she was superior to Leto, who had only two—a fatal boast, which Artemis and Apollo considered a slur on their mother and punished by sending their fatal arrows through the hearts of Niobe, all of her children, and that of Amphion too.[31]

When Laius was expelled from Thebes, he went to Pisa in Elis and was hospitably received by King Pelops. During his stay, he passed the time in teaching the king's son, Chrysippus, how to drive the chariot, and conceived such a passion for the youth that, when he was called back to his kingdom at Amphion's death, he took Chrysippus with him.[32]

Enraged at the loss of his son, Pelops laid a curse on Laius and his descendants—thus insuring continued miseries for the family which was already under the disfavor of Ares.[33]

After returning from Pisa, Laius married Jocasta,[34] daughter of Menoeceus, who was descended from Echion, one of the Sparti. At first, their marriage was not consummated because the Delphian oracle had prophesied that,

if they should have a son, he would slay his own father. But later, being flushed with wine, Laius retired to his wife's bed and, in due course, a son was born to them. Mindful of the oracular prediction, Laius pierced the babe's ankles with iron spikes and tied them together—after which he gave the child to a herdsman for exposure to the elements. And, following his instructions, the servant deposited his infant charge in the wilds of neighboring Mount Cithaeron, where he left it to perish.[35] However, some neatherds of the Corinthian king, Polybus, found the whimpering child and brought him to the king's wife, Periboea.[36] She and her husband adopted the small newcomer and called him Oedipus because of his swollen feet.[37]

Despite his crippled start, the boy grew in strength and soon so excelled his fellows in athletic exercises and games of skill that they jealously ridiculed him about his parentage. Stung by their taunts, he asked Periboea to tell him the truth, but she gave him an evasive answer which determined him to go in his chariot to Delphi, where he repeated his inquiry to the oracle. Here too, he failed to obtain a direct reply—being told only that if he should go to his native land he would kill his father and lie with his own mother.

Knowing of no land except Corinth which he could call "native," he left Delphi by the road leading eastwardly toward Boeotia, instead of returning to the kingdom of Polybus in the south. While he was driving along a narrow way in Phocis, he met another chariot,[38] occupied by an old man with two servants, one of whom roughly bade him to pull aside. Upon his failure to obey the rude command, the servant leapt from his vehicle and killed one of Oedipus'

Seven Against Thebes, as narrated in the preceding chapter. Since Homer names Amphion and Zethus as the founders of Thebes, Pausanias calls the earlier, and higher, part of the town the Cadmeia. According to Apollodorus, the new city gained its name from Thebe, a daughter of the River-god Asopus, whom he names as the wife of Zethus.

[31] Other versions of the legend relate that Amphion killed himself from grief at the loss of his children, or that he was slain by Apollo for making an assault on the god's temple at Delphi.

[32] According to Hyginus, Chrysippus was an illegitimate son of Pelops, who lived in disharmony with his stepmother Hippodameia; she induced her own sons, Atreus and Thyestes, to kill him. Another story relates that he killed himself from shame at having accepted the passionate proposals of Laius.

[33] Some writers add a different (or another) curse on the descendants of Cadmus, namely the curse of Hera, laid because Cadmus' daughter Ino gave sanctuary to the infant Dionysus when the wrathful goddess sought to destroy her faithless lord's latest son.

[34] In the Odyssey, the wife of Laius is called Epicaste.

---

[35] Another version of the legend says that, instead of obeying his master's order, the herdsman entrusted the crippled child to a shepherd who was tending the flocks of King Polybus, but, on returning to Thebes, informed Laius that his cruel command had been followed.

[36] According to Sophocles, the wife of Polybus was named Merope.

[37] Others say that the name Oedipus—meaning "swollen feet"—was given to the child by the neatherds of Polybus who rescued him from his exposure on the mountain.

[38] According to another version, the melee occurred when the other chariot overtook Oedipus and he was rudely pushed off the road.

horses—so enraging its owner that he retaliated by killing both the servant and his aged master,[39] and the second servant fled back in the direction from where he had come. Dismayed at the result of his unpremeditated action, Oedipus himself fled from the scene of the quarrel without learning that the old man whom he had slain was Laius, king of Thebes—and his own father.[40]

The surviving servant hastened back to Thebes and reported what had occurred. Fearing, however, that he would be accused of cowardice if it should be known that three men had been overcome by only one, he said that the murders had been committed by a large body of attackers.

With the death of Laius, Creon, the brother of Jocasta, succeeded to the Theban crown, again placing the rulership in a descendant of the curiously born Sparti. In his reign a great calamity fell upon the city. Hera—still wrathful over the birth and protection of Dionysus—sent the Sphinx to occupy a seat on Mount Phicium, overlooking the highway along which all had to pass in going to or coming from the city. This monster, the offspring of Typhon and Echidna, was molded with the head of a maiden, the breast and feet of a lion, the tail of a serpent, and the wings of a bat. Having learned a riddle from the Muses, she was accustomed to propound it to everyone approaching from either direction. The riddle was: "What walks on four legs in the morning, on two at noon and on three in the evening?" And all who failed to give the answer were immediately eaten by the fearsome creature.[41]

As time passed and the riddle remained unsolved, so many lives both of men and women were snuffed out that hardly a home remained in the stricken city which had not lost some member of its family. Finally, after an oracle had declared that the Sphinx would remain on her rocky perch until her riddle should be solved, and the suffering of the townspeople cruelly continued, Creon was obliged to offer both the crown and the hand of widowed Jocasta to any man who could achieve the city's salvation.

At this juncture Oedipus was seen approaching along the road where the hybrid monster lay in waiting. Although his walk was marked with a distinct limp, he carried himself with such a manly air that the watching Thebans felt truly sorry for the awful fate which appeared to them to be surely in store for him. They saw the creature order Oedipus to the top of her rock. They saw him make the steep climb and even marked the moving of the Sphinx' lips as she again put her accustomed question. They saw the young man's lips move in reply, and some of the more timid spectators involuntarily covered their eyes to avoid witnessing the death of one so noble and unsuspecting. But then an amazing thing happened. With a loud shriek that carried to the heavens, the Sphinx flung herself from the rock and was instantly killed, as she landed at its jagged base and miraculously disappeared. Her riddle had been solved by Oedipus, who answered it thus:

Man, as a baby, crawls on hands and knees and so really walks on four legs in the morning of his life; when he grows up and reaches the noon of life, he walks on his two legs; and, when he grows old and decrepit, in the evening of life, he uses a cane— which may be considered as giving him a third leg.

When Oedipus entered the city, he was acclaimed as its saviour and learned of the proclamation which Creon had made.[42] And, shortly afterward, he assumed the kingship with Jocasta as his queen, unaware that she was his own mother.

Peaceful years followed, during which the Theban rulers had four children: two sons, Eteocles and Polynices, and two daughters, named Antigone and Ismene. Suddenly, and without any apparent reason, a pestilence descended upon the land. Both men and beasts

---

[39] The name of the slain servant was Polyphontes.

[40] Apollodorus says that the corpse of Laius was buried by Damasistratus, the king of Plataea.

[41] Another version relates that whenever any traveler failed to answer her riddle, the Sphinx gobbled up a citizen of Thebes.

[42] Another version of the story relates that Oedipus somehow arrived at Thebes without encountering the Sphinx and that, when he heard of Creon's proclamation, he boldly offered to go out to contest with the sitting creature.

began to perish and the tilled earth refused to bear its annual harvest. In their distress, his subjects entreated the help of their king, who was thought to be a special favorite of the gods. Oedipus assured them of his sympathy and revealed that he had already sent Creon to the Delphian oracle to ask what should be done. Even as he spoke, Creon returned and announced the oracle's answer: the murderer of King Laius was still abroad in the city and the pestilence would not be abated until he should be apprehended and expelled.

Oedipus now invoked the gods to bring their curses upon the head of the unknown slayer and offered a reward to anyone who could furnish information about him, and he sent for the blind seer Teiresias and asked him to use his supernatural powers to assist in the search. As the old man appeared reluctant to speak, the king fell into a rage and even went so far as to accuse him of having been an accomplice in the crime. At this outburst, Teiresias blurted out that Oedipus was himself the murderer and intimated that he was guilty of an even greater shame. When he heard such an accusation, Oedipus lost all self-control and taunted the prophet by saying that he was afflicted with the same blindness in his art as in his eyes. Next, he furiously turned on Creon and charged him with having bribed the prophet to make the accusation in the hope of regaining the throne for himself. The heated quarrel ended only after Teiresias solemnly announced that a forthcoming doom would plunge Oedipus into the deepest abyss of miseries, after which the wrathful ruler ordered the blind man to be led away by force.

In proof of his statement, Teiresias now produced the old servant who had exposed Oedipus on Mount Cithaeron, the shepherd who had carried him to King Polybus and the servant who had fled from the scene where Laius and Polyphontes had been slain. When this latter witness retracted his story that a number of men had been the attackers, and described the place of the encounter, Oedipus realized his guilt and, frantic at the realization, put out his own eyes. Unable to survive the disgrace, Jocasta then hanged herself.

The furious Thebans now expelled their sightless king from the city, as commanded by the oracle, and, when he departed, his sons made no effort either to help or defend him. For this unfilial conduct, he called down another bitter curse upon them.[43] But, with his faithful daughter Antigone to lead him, he proceeded slowly to Colonus in Attica, where he became a suppliant at the shrine of the avenging spirits known as the Erinnyes or Eumenides. There, he was welcomed by King Theseus and was permitted to end his life quietly, attended by Antigone and by his other daughter Ismene who later joined the exiles.[44]

With their father's banishment, Eteocles and Polyneices made an agreement to rule the city in alternate years. By lot, Eteocles first assumed the throne; but, when his year was up, he refused to relinquish the sovereignty.[45] As a consequence, Polyneices was exiled and went to the court of King Adrastus in Argos, taking with him the robe and the necklace of Harmonia, which she had received as presents on her wedding to Cadmus. In the preceding chapter, it has been related how he enlisted the assistance of his host and other heroes in the attempt to obtain his throne which was known as the Seven Against Thebes. This was a vain attempt, because the attacking forces were routed and the contesting brothers slew each other in hand-to-hand combat. At the time of this occurrence, Antigone and Ismene had returned after their blinded father's death in Attica.

----

[43] At this stage, the unhappy sons of Oedipus rested under four separate curses, namely: (1) the curse of Ares placed upon them as descendants of Cadmus who had killed Draco; (2) the curse of Hera, arising from the connections of Semele and Ino with the birth and preservation of Dionysus; (3) the curse of Pelops, laid upon Laius and his descendants for the rape of Chrysippus; and (4) the curse of their own father.

[44] According to Sophocles, Ismene arrived at Colonus with word that Creon was on his way to take Oedipus back to Thebes, because the oracle had declared that he must be buried within its limits in order to confer safety upon the city over which Eteocles and Polyneices had quarreled. Soon after, Creon appears, but Oedipus is protected by Theseus and, after another meeting with Polyneices at which his curse is repeated, he goes off to die and be buried at a place known only to his protector.

[45] Another version relates that Polyneices ruled for the first year and, in accordance with his agreement, surrendered the throne to Eteocles—who, after his first year, refused to surrender the sovereignty.

Following the simultaneous deaths of Eteocles and Polyneices, Creon again assumed the Theban rule. His first official act was to decree that the body of Eteocles should be brought into the city and buried with appropriate honors, but that the body of Polyneices should lie where he had fallen—to become prey for dogs and birds of carrion. Antigone resolved to defy this inhuman decree, and asked her sister Ismene to help her in providing a decent burial for their slighted brother. When Ismene timidly demurred, Antigone stole from the city and undertook the task alone but was apprehended and brought before her uncle. Enraged at her disobedience, he ordered that the maiden should be immured alive in a closed tomb, notwithstanding the appeal of his own son, Haemon, to whom she was betrothed. As Antigone was led away, blind Teiresias appeared and made such dire predictions that Creon was forced to countermand both his order consigning her to the living grave and his earlier decree that Polyneices should remain unburied. But his action was too late—and the messenger with his countermanding orders returned to relate that Antigone was dead and that Haemon had slain himself by her side.[46] At this tragic moment, Creon's wife[47] appeared and, learning of what had happened, reentered the palace and stabbed herself before the altar.

Nor were Creon's troubles at an end, for, as related in the preceding chapter, the sons of the Seven Against Thebes—known as the Epigoni—made another attack on Thebes ten years after the unsuccessful effort of their fathers, which resulted in his being forced to flee from the city. In attempting to repulse the attack, Laodamas, the son of Eteocles, was slain—thus bringing to an end the line of Cadmus, with the exception of Thersander, the son whom Argeia had borne to Polyneices.[48]

Presumably, the various curses had now run their courses, because Thersander met an honorable death in Mysia, where he was slain by

Telephus; and his son, Tisamenus, borne by Demonassa—a daughter of Amphiaraus—came to a peaceful end. The avenging Furies, however, attacked his grandson Autesion and forced him to flee from the land of his ancestors to the country of the Dorians, where he had a son, Theras, and a daughter, Argeia, who seems to have paid all mythological debts by marrying Aristodemus, a descendant of the great Heracles.

The House of Belus

Following the example of his twin brother Agenor, Belus married one of the daughters of the river-god Nilus—named Achiroë, but sometimes called Anchinoe.

Before discussing the children whom she bore to him, we should mention Lamia who is said to have been his daughter by an unnamed woman. According to tradition, she was a maiden of such beauty that she was loved by Zeus, although she was happily married to a Libyan king. But jealous Hera robbed her of her children, which caused the bereft mother to go mad and steal the children of other women, whom she was accustomed to murder, from foolish motives of revenge. Through her indulgence in this horrid practice, she lost her beauty, and her face became so distorted that she was considered at last to be an ogress, to whom the gods had given the power of removing her eyes at will.

The son of Belus and Achiroë, who was named Cepheus, succeeded his father as king of Ethiopia and, by his wife Cassiopeia, had a daughter, Andromeda, who became the wife of the Greek hero Perseus. The circumstances will be related later. When Cepheus' brother Phineus, who was betrothed to Andromeda, objected to the wedding, Perseus changed him into stone by exhibiting before his frightened eyes the snaky head of the dead Gorgon Medusa.

After the births of Cepheus and Phineus, Achiroë bore to Belus twin sons, who were named Aegyptus and Danaus. Upon attaining manhood, they settled in Arabia and Libya, respectively, where they became rulers of their countries and gained great renown from the multitude of their progeny, because Aegyptus had fifty sons and Danaus had fifty daughters.

---

[46] According to Homer, Haemon had a son named Maeon, who was among the defenders against the attack of the Seven Against Thebes.

[47] Hesiod calls Eniocha the wife of Creon but, according to Sophocles, her name was Eurydice.

[48] Ismene also survived, but died childless.

47b. Descendants of Poseidon and Libya

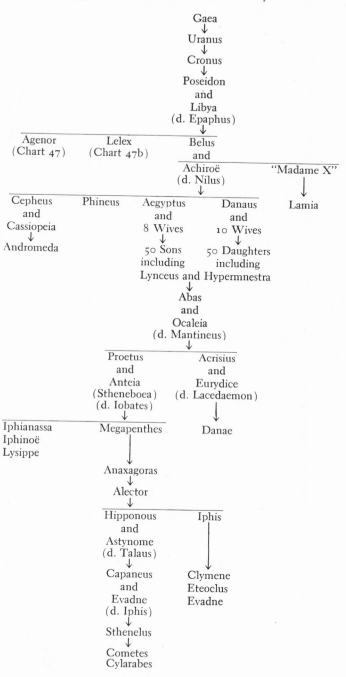

Gaea
↓
Uranus
↓
Cronus
↓
Poseidon
and
Libya
(d. Epaphus)
↓

Agenor (Chart 47)	Lelex (Chart 47b)	Belus and

Achiroë
(d. Nilus)
↓

Cepheus and Cassiopeia	Phineus	Aegyptus and 8 Wives	Danaus and 10 Wives	"Madame X"
Andromeda		↓ 50 Sons including	↓ 50 Daughters including	Lamia

Lynceus and Hypermnestra
↓
Abas
and
Ocaleia
(d. Mantineus)
↓

Proetus and Anteia (Stheneboea) (d. Iobates)	Acrisius and Eurydice (d. Lacedaemon)
↓	↓

Iphianassa Iphinoë Lysippe	Megapenthes	Danae

Anaxagoras
↓
Alector
↓

Hipponous and Astynome (d. Talaus)	Iphis
↓ Capaneus and Evadne (d. Iphis)	Clymene Eteoclus Evadne

↓
Sthenelus
↓
Cometes
Cylarabes

In a quarrel which developed between them, Danaus feared that his brother with his fifty sons would prove too powerful and, by the advice of Athena, he built a ship in which he sailed with his daughters to Argos in Greece.[49] When they arrived, the reigning King Gelanor surrendered the country to him[50] and, assuming the throne, he called the inhabitants Danaans, after his own name.

Shortly afterward, the sons of Aegyptus followed their uncle to Argos; and, exhorting him to lay aside his fears, asked to marry his daughters. Danaus distrusted their profession of friendship, as he still rankled from the exile which had been practically forced upon him; but, he saw that opportunity was now offered for revenge and consented to the proposed marriages, without disclosing the deadly scheme which his quick mind had conceived.

On the facing page are listed the names and the parentage of the fifty sons and daughters involved in the mass betrothal to which he agreed.

After the sons of Aegyptus had drawn their prospective brides by lot, Danaus gave daggers to all of his daughters and made them promise that they would slay their husbands on their wedding night. The girls dutifully obeyed, save only Hypermnestra, who spared Lynceus because he had respected her virginity. Her action, or lack of it, brought on the displeasure of her father who, at first, imprisoned her. Later he relented and permitted her to be reunited with her husband. The other daughters having been purified of their crimes by Athena and Hermes, were given in marriage to the victors in an athletic carnival which Danaus publicly proclaimed.[51]

When Danaus died, Lynceus became the king of Argos and was succeeded by his son Abas, whom Hypermnestra later bore to him. The reign of Abas was mythologically barren, except for the twin sons, Acrisius and Proetus, whom he had by his wife, Ocaleia, a daughter of Mantineus.[52] Like Esau and Jacob, the twins began to quarrel while still in their mother's womb and continued to quarrel after their birth. And, at their father's death, they both claimed the right of succession to his kingdom.[53] Acrisius was eventually victorious and drove Proetus out of the country, from where he went to the court of the Lycian king, Iobates. He met with a kind reception there, and married the king's daughter Anteia, who is referred to by the tragic poets as Stheneboea. With the help of the forces of his father-in-law, he returned to Argos (Argolis) and occupied the city of Tiryns, which the Cyclopes are said to have fortified for him.[54] This show of strength was enough to convince Acrisius and thereafter the twin brothers divided the Argive territory between themselves. Acrisius ruled at Argos, while Proetus made Tiryns his capital.

Before Acrisius expelled his brother from the country, he had married Eurydice, a daughter of his neighbor Lacedaemon, and their daughter Danae had grown into beautiful maturity. She later became the mother of the hero

---

[49] It is said that the ship of Danaus was the first to be built by man and that, on the voyage to Argos, he put in at the island of Rhodes and set up an image of his patroness Athena.

[50] According to another legend, Gelanor did not voluntarily surrender the government to Danaus and a dispute arose between them about which the citizens met to consider. After much discussion, the decision was deferred until the next day, at whose dawn a wolf rushed among the cattle and killed one of them. This was taken by the Argives as an omen to mean that Danaus should prevail and, accordingly, he was made their king.

The voyage of Danaus from Libya to Argos, and the friendly reception given him by the Argives, would seem rather peculiar to those who do not bear in mind the precedent genealogy, namely: the father of Danaus was Belus; the mother of Belus was Libya; the father of Libya was Epaphus; the mother of Epaphus was Io; the father of Io was the god of the river Inachus—the greatest river of Argos. Thus, Danaus was, in reality, returning to his ancestral home.

[51] Notwithstanding their purification, the Danaides were said to have been punished in the lower world by being forced to dip up water with vessels which were full of holes—a never-ending and useless task. Those so punished did not include Hypermnestra or Amymone, who had children by Lynceus and Poseidon; and, for this reason, some said that the punishment was inflicted by Hera, in her role as goddess of birth, because the punished women had purposely avoided motherhood.

[52] Ocaleia is sometimes called Aglaea.

[53] According to Apollodorus, the quarrel in life arose over the ill-conduct of Proetus toward Acrisius' daughter, Danae.

[54] In his excavations at Tiryns, Heinrich Schliemann unearthed portions of the wall—mythically said to have been raised by the Cyclopes—and found it to contain some stones which were ten-feet long and four-feet thick.

Sons' Mothers	Sons of Aegyptus	Daughters of Danaus	Daughters' Mothers
A Phoenician Woman	Aegius	Mnestra	An Ethiopian Woman
Gorgo	Aegyptus	Dioxippe	Pieria
A Phoenician Woman	Agaptolemus	Peirene	An Ethiopian Woman
An Arabian Woman	Agenor	Cleopatra	Atlantia or Phoebe
An Arabian Woman	Alces	Glauce	Atlantia or Phoebe
An Arabian Woman	Alcmenor	Hippomedusa	Atlantia or Phoebe
Hephaestine	Arbelus	Oeme	Crino
A Phoenician Woman	Archelaus	Anaxibia	An Ethiopian Woman
A Phoenician Woman	Argeius	Evippe	An Ethiopian Woman
Caliadne	Bromius	Erato	Polyxo
"Madame X"	Busiris	Automate	Europa
A Phoenician Woman	Cercetes	Dorium	An Ethiopian Woman
An Arabian Woman	Chaetus	Asteria	Atlantia or Phoebe
An Arabian Woman	Chalcodon	Rhodia	Atlantia or Phoebe
Tyria	Chrysippus	Chrysippe	Memphis
Caliadne	Chthonius	Bryce	Polyxo
Caliadne	Cisseus	Anthelia	Polyxo
Tyria	Cleitus	Cleite	Memphis
"Madame X"	Daïphron	Scaea	Europa
Hephaestine	Daïphron	Adiante	Herse
An Arabian Woman	Diocorystes	Philodameia	Atlantia or Phoebe
Caliadne	Dryas	Eurydice	Polyxo
"Madame X"	Enceladus	Amymone[55]	Europa
An Arabian Woman	Euchenor	Iphimedusa	Atlantia or Phoebe
A Phoenician Woman	Eurydamas	Phartis	An Ethiopian Woman
Caliadne	Eurylochus	Autonoë	Polyxo
Caliadne	Hermus	Cleopatra	Polyxo
Hephaestine	Hippocorystes	Hyperippe	Crino
An Arabian Woman	Hippolytus	Rhode	Atlantia or Phoebe
An Arabian Woman	Hippothous	Gorge	Atlantia or Phoebe
Hephaestine	Hyperbius	Celaeno	Crino
Hephaestine	Idas	Hippodice	Herse
Gorgo	Idmon	Pylarge	Pieria
Caliadne	Imbrus	Evippe	Polyxo
An Arabian Woman	Istrus	Hippodameia	Atlantia or Phoebe
Gorgo	Lampus	Ocypete	Pieria
Caliadne	Lixus	Cleodora	Polyxo
"Madame X"	Lycus	Agave	Europa
Gorgo	Menalces	Adite	Pieria
A Phoenician Woman	Menemachus	Nelo	An Ethiopian Woman
Gorgo	Oeneus	Podarce	Pieria
Hephaestine	Pandion	Callidice	Crino
Gorgo	Periphas	Actaea	Pieria
Caliadne	Peristhenes	Electra	Polyxo
Caliadne	Phantes	Theano	Polyxo
Caliadne	Polyctor	Stygne	Polyxo
Caliadne	Potamon	Glaucippe	Polyxo
Argyphia	Proteus	Gorgophone	Elephantis
Tyria	Sthenelus	Sthenele	Memphis
Argyphia	Lynceus	Hypermnestra	Elephantis

[55] Apollodorus says that, when Danaus arrived at Argos, he found the country waterless because Poseidon had dried up the springs from anger at Inachus for testifying that the sovereignty belonged to Hera. In search of water, Amymone threw a dart at a sleeping satyr, who started up and tried to force her but, Poseidon appeared, the satyr fled and, when Amymone embraced her saviour, he showed her the waters at Lerna.

Perseus, under circumstances which are related in our narrative of the wives of Zeus. Acrisius eventually met his death when he was accidentally struck by a quoit which was thrown by his illustrious son-in-law.

Anteia first bore to Proetus three daughters, whose names were Iphianassa, Iphinoë, and Lysippe. When they were grown, they were stricken with a madness, which was attributed to their failure to accept the rites of Dionysus or to their disparagement of the image of Hera. Whatever may have been its cause, their malady was so acute that all those dwelling in the Peloponnesus began to fear their approach.[56] Proetus appealed to Melampus (as related in the preceding chapter), and he made a proposal to undertake the cure upon condition that he and his brother Bias should receive a third part of his petitioner's kingdom. Proetus refused to accept these terms, and the madness of his daughters was communicated to other Argive women who abandoned their homes, murdered their own children, and flocked wildly into desert places. When the evil reached this high pitch, the king finally agreed to the stipulated proposal and Melampus went to work.[57] Taking with him a band of robust young men, he chased the women to Sicyon, with shouts and a sort of dance almost as frenzied as their own. During the chase, Iphinoë died, but, when the rest were corraled within the city's walls, Melampus completed his undertaking by driving out their madness, became a co-ruler with Proetus and Bias, and married Proetus' daughter, Iphianassa.

Some time afterward, Anteia bore to Proetus a son named Megapenthes, who succeeded to his father's part of the Argive kingship. When Perseus later accidentally killed his father-in-law, he was ashamed to claim the throne at Argos, where Acrisius had ruled. He, therefore, went to his kinsman and, effecting a bargain to exchange sovereignties, assumed the government at Tiryns while Megapenthes took over at Argos.

The Argive succession which followed for the next three generations appears to be nothing but a few names to fill in our genealogical charts, namely: Megapenthes was succeeded by his son Anaxagoras;[58] Anaxagoras was succeeded by his son Alector; and Alector was succeeded by his sons, Iphis and Hipponous.

Iphis had two daughters, Clymene and Evadne, and a son named Eteoclus. Of these: Clymene later became the wife of Phylacus, whose cattle Melampus obtained for his brother Bias, and Evadne married her cousin Capaneus, who lost his life in the attack of the Seven Against Thebes, when Zeus struck him down with a thunderbolt as he attempted to climb the city's wall. Later, his corpse was laid upon the funeral pyre and, as it was burning, Evadne heroically leapt into the flames where her body's ashes were mingled with those of her beloved husband.

According to some accounts, Eteoclus was numbered as one of the Seven Against Thebes and was the victor in the footrace at the Nemean games—instituted en route, after the infant Opheltes died from the bite of a serpent. His claim to be numbered among the band seems to be well grounded: because Pausanias says that his statue stood at Delphi, grouped with those of the other heroes, and Apollodorus says that he was slain in the attack by Leades, one of the sons of Theban Astacus.

Capaneus and Evadne were survived by their son, Sthenelus, who became a worthy successor to a portion of the Argive sovereignty when Iphis died. He was one of the Epigoni, who revenged the defeat of their fathers by conquering Thebes and, later, was one of the leaders of the Argive forces in the war against Troy, where he was the faithful companion of the mighty warrior Diomedes. According to Hyginus, he was one of the Greeks concealed in the Wooden Horse; and Pausanias says that, in the distribution of the Trojan booty, he received an image

---

[56] Pausanias places the madness of the Argive women in the reign of Anaxagoras, a grandson (or great-grandson) of Proetus. It may be conjectured that this was due to the fact that Proetus was not the king of the city of Argos, but was ruling at Tiryns, where he was succeeded by Megapenthes who later exchanged kingdoms with Perseus. However, the country known as Argolis was often referred to as Argos and contained both cities.

[57] A different version relates that Melampus raised his terms to require Proetus to part with two-thirds of his realm, so that he retained only one third with Melampus and Bias as his equal co-rulers.

[58] According to Pausanias, Megapenthes had a son named Argeius who was the father of Anaxagoras.

of a three-eyed Zeus which he brought back to Argos.

Of Sthenelus' two sons, nothing of interest is related about Cylarabes, but Cometes is said to have brought dishonor to his house by seducing Aegialeia, the wife of Diomedes, while his father was fighting at Troy beside the man thus made a cuckold.[59]

The House of Lelex

The generally accepted legend relates that Lelex came to Greece from Egypt and, settling at Megara in Attica, gave his name to the inhabitants, who were thereafter called Leleges. Another account, which names him as the first king of Laconia, says that he was an autochthon, sprung directly from Gaea.

47c. Descendants of Lelex

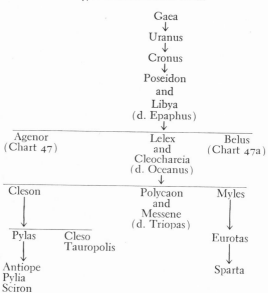

At Megara, he married the Naiad-nymph Cleochareia and by her had three sons named Cleson, Polycaon, and Myles. Cleson had a son Pylas (sometimes called Pylon) and two daughters, Cleso and Tauropolis, who are said to have found and buried the corpse of Ino—from which the Megarians were the first to offer sacrifices to the unfortunate wife and mother under her deified name of Leucothea.

Pylas also had two daughters, Antiope who married the Oechalian archer-king, Eurytus, and Pylia who became the queen of the Athenian king, Pandion.[60] Pausanias adds that he had a son Sciron, who married the daughter of Pandion and afterward disputed with his brother-in-law, Nisus, about the right to the Megarian rulership. Aeacus was called upon to settle the dispute and decreed that Nisus and his descendants should occupy the throne, but that Sciron and his descendants should be their city's leaders in war.[61]

Polycaon, the second son of Lelex, married Messene, who was a daughter of the Argive king, Triopas, and went into the southwestern part of the Peloponnesus, where he assumed the sovereignty and called the country Messenia after his wife's name.[62] According to Pausanias, the house of Polycaon continued to rule through five generations, after which Perieres, the son of Aeolus, was summoned to be king. Neither Pausanias, however, nor the other mythographers give the names of any of his children or lineal descendants.

In the Laconian myth, Lelex was succeeded in the rulership of that country by his son Myles and his grandson Eurotas, who is said to have created the river ruled by the god of his name when he dug a trench to the sea and led off the waters of the land, which had previously lain stagnant. At his death, he left only his daughter Sparta and the government was assumed by her husband Lacedaemon, a son of Zeus and Taygete. After him, the country was called Lacedaemonia and its inhabitants were called Lacedaemonians. The new king located his capital on the banks of the river Eurotas, where in his wife's honor he gave it the name of Sparta which, for all time since, has been esteemed among the greatest cities in both legend and recorded history.

---

[59] By some, Cylarabes and Cometes were considered as different names for the same person.

[60] This Pandion was the second of his name in the Athenian rulership.

[61] The story mentioned by Pausanias is at variance with the conventional account that Nisus was the leader of the Megarians when they were attacked by the Cretan king, Minos, and that the city's armed forces capitulated when he lost his life through the treachery of his daughter Scylla.

[62] According to Pausanias, the rites of Demeter were brought from Eleusis into Messenia and received by Messene while she ruled with Polycaon.

10

Poseidon and His Descendants II

HAVING COMPLETED the rather complex enumeration of the descendants of Poseidon from Libya, the daughter of Egyptian Epaphus, we shall proceed to mention the rest of his descendants in the alphabetical order of the names of their maternal ancestresses and will accompany the narrative with appropriate genealogical charts where needed.

Alcyone

There appears to be no detailed story about Poseidon's wooing of Alcyone, a daughter of Atlas. She was one of the Pleiades who bore to the sea-god a daughter named Aethusa and two sons, Hyperenor and Hyrieus.

48. Descendants of Poseidon and Alcyone

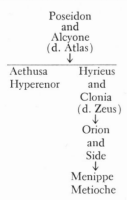

Of these, Aethusa was beloved by Apollo, and their son Eleuther (Eleutherus) is said to have been one of the first men to accept the

rites of Dionysus; but Hyperenor seems to have been only a name that Apollodorus wanted to get out of his system.

Hyrieus and his descendants were mythologically more noted. As previously related, he was king of the Boeotian town of Hyria and employed Agamedes and Trophonius to build his treasury, which they secretly looted until he put an end to their practice by catching Agamedes in a trap.[1] He married the nymph Clonia who bore a son to him named Orion—destined to be the tallest man on earth and its mightiest hunter.[2] Because of his gigantic stature, some traditions assert that he was an autochthonous son of Gaea, or of Poseidon by a daughter of King Minos of Crete.

Two daughters, named Metioche and Menippe, were borne to Orion by a mortal woman, Side, who was so beautiful that she was cast into the lower world by Hera from jealousy of her feminine charms. When this happened, Orion went to the island of Chios; but his grief must have been short-lived, because, almost immediately, he set about wooing Merope, a daughter of King Oenopion. In his ardor, he cleared the island of wild beasts and brought their pelts as

---

[1] Details of the incident are related in chapter 6.
[2] Apollodorus (contradicting another legend related by him) names Hyrieus as the father of Nycteus and Lycus, who were prominent actors in the story of Boeotian Thebes—perhaps because, at one time, they were said to have fled to Hyria after killing Phlegyas, a son of Ares.

presents to his beloved, and, although Merope seemed to be not unwilling, her royal father procrastinated in setting the wedding day. Exasperated at the delay, Orion finally attempted to force his way into the maiden's chamber—an alarming episode that caused the king to seek advice from his own father, the wine-god Dionysus. He was advised that he could easily handle the obstreperous giant if he should prevail upon him to become intoxicated; this he proceeded to do. Whereupon, he put out his eyes and cast him on the seashore in a state of drunken insensibility. As the blinded man regained consciousness, he was mysteriously informed that he could recover his sight by going toward the east and exposing his eyes to the rays of the rising Sun. Following the sound of the hammers of the Cyclopes,[3] he slowly waded through the sea to the island of Lemnos, where Hephaestus gave him a guide named Cedalion to lead him in the proper direction. Orion placed the man upon his broad shoulders and, under his pilotage, continued toward the home of the Sun until his sight was fully restored. He then returned to Chios to take vengeance. Oenopion, however, had learned of his coming and had already fled to a refuge which had been divinely prepared for him. After a futile search, Orion passed on to the island of Crete. There, the mighty hunter joined the goddess Artemis in her never-ending pursuit of game—an occupation in which only she excelled him. Indeed, he grew so proud that he boasted he would conquer every animal and clear the whole earth from wild beasts; the boast proved to be his undoing, because Gaea resented it and sent forth a huge scorpion from whose bite he perished.[4]

After his death, he was placed in the heavens as a constellation (opposite the chasing Scorpion)[5] which is still called by his name. His hound also was apotheosized as the dog-star Sirius. His orphaned daughters, Menippe and Metioche, grew up to beautiful womanhood, given to them by Aphrodite, and Athena taught them the art of weaving. Afterward, when their homeland of Boeotia was visited by a plague and the Delphian oracle ordered the inhabitants to propitiate the Erinnyes by the sacrifice of two maidens, they patriotically offered themselves and—committing suicide with their own knitting needles—brought the pestilence to an end.

Alope

The Attic robber Cercyon, who was later slain by Theseus, had a daughter named Alope endowed with such charms that Poseidon was attracted to her. As soon as her son was born, she left him in the woods in order to conceal her misstep from her father, but the child was suckled by a mare and was later discovered by some wandering shepherds, who got into a dispute between themselves as to the ownership of its fine clothes. Their dispute was brought before Cercyon and, when he recognized the garments which had brought on the dispute, he ordered that Alope should be put to death and that her child should be again exposed to the elements. However, after his second exposure, the boy was again found by the same shepherds, who named him Hippothoön—meaning "horse-fed." And Alope's dead body was changed by Poseidon into a well of pure water which was called by her name.

Amphitrite

The Nereid Amphitrite was the mythological queen and lawful wife of Poseidon, to whom she bore two daughters, Benthesicyme and Rhode, and a son named Triton.[6] When the

---

[3] Later stories place the forges of the Cyclopes in the west near Mount Aetna in Sicily.

[4] Other versions of Orion's death relate that: (1) Artemis fell in love with her giant retainer and Apollo, becoming indignant at his sister's affection, chided her upon being unable to hit with her arrow a distant point in the sea; taking up the challenge, she sent a deadly shaft to the distant point—which turned out to be Orion as he was taking his morning dip; (2) Artemis purposely slew her hunting companion when he attempted to violate her chastity; and (3) the dawn-goddess Eos became infatuated with the hunter's gargantuan beauty and carried him into the skies, where Artemis

---

sent one of her arrows through his heart because he had appeared to be a too-willing victim of his own abduction.

[5] The scorpion was said to have been translated to the heavens as Scorpius, or Scorpio, the eighth sign of the zodiac.

[6] Triton (not to be confused with the god of the river of his name), was sometimes considered as the generic singular for a group of creatures who, according

sea-god sued for her hand, she fled to Atlas for protection, but her lover sent a dolphin to plead with her, and he was successful in bringing about the marriage. In gratitude, Poseidon rewarded his services by placing him among the stars as the constellation Delphinus, which is sometimes peculiarly referred to as "Job's Coffin." But, after gaining his bride, the god was attracted by the maiden-charms of Scylla, a daughter of his fellow sea-deity Phorcys. Learning of his attachment, his jealous wife threw some herbs into the well where her rival was accustomed to bathe and changed her into a monster with six heads and twelve feet, who was later identified as a deadly menace to sailors in the strait of Messina which separates Sicily from the mainland of Italy.

Nothing of interest is related about Benthesicyme. Rhode, however, was one of the wives of the Sun-god Helios and bore to him eight children, who were collectively known as the Heliades.

Triton is supposed to have lived with his parents at their golden palace in the depths of the sea off the coast of Aegae, except while he was riding on his monstrous seahorse and blowing his long trumpet to quiet the waves at the bidding of his father Poseidon.[7]

Amymone

Amymone was one of the daughters of Danaus, who sailed with their father from Libya to Argos in order to escape the dangers which, they fancied, were threatened by Aegyptus and his fifty sons. And she was one of the daughters who slew her husband (Enceladus) on the night when she and her sisters had their mass wedding to their fifty cousins.

Prior to her wedding, she was sent by her father in search of water and, during her journey shot an arrow at a passing stag—but it missed

49. Descendants of Poseidon and Amymone

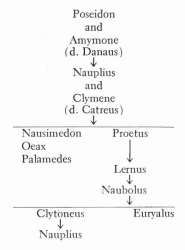

her target and hit a sleeping satyr, who awakened and pursued her. As she ran, Poseidon came to her rescue and, after gallantly (?) appropriating her to himself, he showed her the wells at Lerna.[8] The son whom she bore to the sea-god was said to have been the greatest sailor of his time and, by Clymene—a daughter of the Cretan prince, Cotreus—had four sons of his own, whose names were Nausimedon, Oeax, Palamedes, and Proetus. Of these, Nausimedon and Oeax fade into relative obscurity after being named. Palamedes, however, was a principal actor in some of the events leading up to the Trojan invasion, and more will be said about him when we come to consider that greatest of all mythological stories. Suffice here to say that, after reaching Troy, he was executed by his comrades for a supposed act of treachery. This sentence his father, Nauplius, considered unjust and so he shipwrecked many of the returning heroes by drawing them to a rocky promontory on the island of Euboea with lighted torches which he placed there. And to wreak further vengeance, it is said that he sent false messages to the wives of the Greeks who had gone to Troy, which had the effect of making them

---

to Pausanias, had green hair on their heads, very fine and hard scales, breathing organs below their ears, human noses, broad mouths, the teeth of animals, sea-green eyes, hands roughened like shells and, instead of feet, the tails of fishes.

[7] The palace of Poseidon is reputed to have been under the Gulf of Corinth near the town of Aegae in Achaea. Others identified it as near the Euboean city of the same name.

---

[8] A variant of the story relates that Amymone fell asleep while looking for water and was surprised by a satyr. She called upon Poseidon for help and, when he appeared, he threw his trident at the satyr, which missed but struck a rock from which a spring gushed forth, thereafter called the well of Amymone.

become unfaithful to their absent husbands.[9]

Proetus, the last charted son of Nauplius, together with his son, Lernus, and his grandson, Naubolus, seem to have been thoroughly undistinguished. But Naubolus had a son named Euryalus, who went to live at the court of the Phaeacian king, Alcinous, on the island of Scheria and, while Odysseus was staying there after being shipwrecked, he exceeded all others in wrestling. And his grandson Nauplius (the son of Clytoneus) is said by Apollonius Rhodius to have been one of the Argonauts.[10]

Aphrodite

Eryx, a son borne to Poseidon by Aphrodite, and from whose name the goddess was sometimes called Erycina, was the king of an island near Sicily to which one of the bulls from the herd of Geryon's cattle swam, while Heracles was driving them toward (?) Greece. When the king refused to return the bull unless he should be overcome in wrestling, Heracles pinned his shoulders to the ground three times and then killed him. His daughter, Psophis, bore twin sons to Heracles named Echephron and Promachus who migrated to Arcadia when they grew up.

Arne

Chart 50 illustrates how the identity of names of different persons has caused much of the confusion which attends our subject—in this case the name Aeolus.

Arne was the daughter of a second Aeolus, whose great-grandfather of the same name was

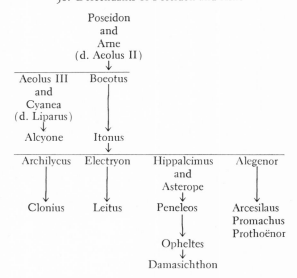

50. Descendants of Poseidon and Arne

the progenitor of the group known as the Aeolids. Her son—likewise called Aeolus—was the god of the winds, whose home is said to have been in the Liparian (Aeolian) islands, off the west coast of Italy. It was the daughter of this third Aeolus—named Alcyone—who became the wife of King Ceyx and was later changed into the kingfisher (which is accustomed to brood during the "halcyon days" when the seas are quiet). And it was the third Aeolus who kindly received wandering Odysseus and gave him a leathern bag in which all unruly winds were enclosed—winds which were afterward let loose with tragic results, when the curiosity of some of Odysseus' crew prompted them to open the container.

The second son of Arne and Poseidon was Boeotus who is said to have moved down from Thessaly and to have given his name to the country of Boeotia.[11] His son, Itonus and, his grandsons Archilycus, Electryon,[12] Hippalcimus,[13] and Alegenor did nothing of particular

[9] The rumor spread among the Greek wives by Nauplius was that their husbands were bedding with women who had been taken captive in the assault on Troy. Virgil seems to have been in ignorance of the story, for in the Aeneid he refers to Palamedes as a son of Belus.

[10] Although Nausimedon, Oeax, and Palamedes are conventionally stated to have been the sons of Nauplius, the son of Poseidon, Strabo would make them the sons of Nauplius, the son of Clytoneus, saying logically: "But the genealogy offends both against the mythology, and against chronology. For if we allow that he (Nauplius) was the son of Neptune, how could he be the son of Amymone, and be still living in Trojan times." As the reader may have noted, this apt observation is one which may be made with reference to a great many of the genealogies which are reported herein—largely due to the lack of surnames.

[11] A different legend relates that the country took its name from the cow followed by Cadmus and that Boeotus occupied only a small part of the land which had already received its title. But Pausanias gives Boeotus a more ancient pedigree, making him a grandson of Amphictyon, the son of Deucalion.

[12] Electryon is sometimes referred to as Alectryon or Alector.

[13] Hippalcimus is also called Hippalmus or Hippalcmus.

interest, and appear only as connecting links in the mythological chain which the ancient Greeks always sought to complete.

Clonius, the son of Archilycus, was one of the five leaders of the Boeotians in the Trojan War, where he was slain by Agenor. Electryon's son Leitus was numbered among the Argonauts by Apollodorus and was likewise a Boeotian leader at Troy. He seems to have been luckier than some of his kinsmen, because, although he was wounded by Hector, he lived to bring back home the bones of his cousin Arcesilaus.

By Asterope, whose antecedents are not given, Hippalcimus had a son named Peneleos, who was quite distinguished: for, according to Apollodorus, he was one of the Argonauts and was also numbered among the suitors of Helen; and, according to Homer, he was a co-leader of the Boeotians at Troy[14] where he slew Ilioneus and Lycon, and was himself slain by Polydamas. Nothing of interest is related about Peneleos' son, Opheltes. However, his grandson Damasichthon was chosen as the king of the Thebans when the line of Cadmus was extinguished by the departure of Autesion, who was driven from his homeland by the Furies pursuant to the multiple curses under which his unhappy family had suffered for many generations.

Arcesilaus and Prothoënor, the two elder sons of Alegenor,[15] went to Troy as Boeotian co-leaders and were accompanied by their younger brother Promachus. But the Fates took no account of rank and all three of them lost their lives in the fighting—Arcesilaus being slain by Hector, Prothoënor by Polydamas, and Promachus by Acamas, the son of Theseus.

Astypalaea

Ancaeus, the elder son of Poseidon and Astypalaea, the daughter of Phoenix, was king of the Leleges on the island of Samos.[16] He was one of the Argonauts, and became their helmsman when Tiphys died before the expedition reached Colchis. His activities as a member of the illustrious band have been related previously in chapter 7 and were followed by his safe return to his island-kingdom, where his wife Samia, a daughter of the river-god Maeander, bore to him four obscure sons (whose names are shown on the accompanying chart), and a daughter Parthenope, who became the mother of Lycomedes by Apollo.[17]

51. Descendants of Poseidon and Astypalaea

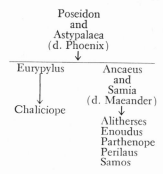

Eurypylus, the younger son of Poseidon and Astypalaea, had the misfortune to be king of the island of Cos at a time when Heracles decided to make a landing there, after he had been driven off his course by storms which jealous Hera had raised. When the Coans resisted his landing, the great man killed their king and—in accordance with his usual practice—appropriated his dead adversary's daughter Chalciope, who later bore to him a son named Thessalus.

Calchinia

The mother of Poseidon's son Peratus was Calchinia, daughter of Leucippus who was the king of Sicyon on the Gulf of Corinth. Realiz-

---

[14] According to Pausanias, Peneleos was chosen as the original commander of the Boeotians because Tisamenus, the lineal descendant of Cadmus, was not old enough to lead his countrymen. He also says that Peneleos was slain at Troy by Eurypylus, the grandson of Heracles.

[15] According to Hyginus, Arcesilaus was the son of Lycus and Theobula, and, in the Iliad, Areïlycus is named as the father of Prothoënor.

[16] It is interesting to note that Lelex, the eponymous ancestor of the Leleges, came from Egypt into Greece and that some of his descendants returned southward to settle in the Aegean island of Samos. From there, colonies were established northerly on the island of Samothrace and, west of Greece, on the island of the Ionian Sea which was known as Same.

[17] In one of the few instances not supported by ancient authority, we later consider this Lycomedes as the king of the island of Scyrus and the father of Deidameia, who was the wife of Achilles. This may be drawing something of a long bow, in view of the fact that Samos and Scyrus are about sixty-five miles apart.

ing the boy's divine paternity, Leucippus reared him as his own child and, when he died, Peratus succeeded to the rulership of the city.

52. Descendants of Poseidon and Calchinia

Poseidon
and
Calchinia
(d. Leucippus)
↓
Peratus
↓
Plemnaeus
↓
Orthopolis
↓
Chrysorthe

He was followed by his son Plemnaeus, who had several children by an unnamed wife, but each of them died the very first time that he wailed. At last, Demeter took pity on the unfortunate man and, coming to Sicyon in disguise as a mortal woman, she reared his next son Orthopolis to full manhood. Chrysorthe, the daughter of Orthopolis, was espoused by Apollo and bore to him a son named Coronus, who succeeded to the throne of his ancestors.[18]

Calyce

Cycnus, son of Poseidon and Calyce, ruled as king in Colonae—a city of the Troad.[19] By Procleia, a daughter of the Trojan prince, Clytius, he had two daughters, Glauce and Hemithea, and a son named Tenes (Tennes).

53. Descendants of Poseidon and Calyce

Poseidon
and
Calyce
(d. Hecaton)
↓
Cycnus
and

| Philonome (d. Cragasus) | Procleia (d. Clytius) ↓ Glauce Hemithea Tenes |

Procleia died after her children reached maturity and Cycnus took as his second wife, Philonome, a daughter of Cragasus, who fell in love with her stepson Tenes. The youth rejected her advances, and she wrathfully accused him to her husband of having been guilty of improper suggestions.[20] Believing the truth of the accusation, Cycnus placed Tenes, with his sister Hemithea, in a chest which he pushed out to sea. By good fortune, the chest rode out the waves and was carried to a nearby island which thereafter was called Tenedos.[21]

Some time afterward, when Cycnus learned of his mistaken belief in Philonome's accusation, he went to the island to right the wrong which he had inflicted upon his children. Tenes, however, angrily cut the mooring cables of his vessel and—with mythologically exact justice—set his father adrift on the same waters into which he had himself been launched.

After returning to the mainland, Cycnus was slain by the Greeks in one of the raids which they made upon the cities about Troy, and his daughter Glauce, being taken captive, became the slave-maiden of Telemonian Ajax.

Canace

Canace, a daughter of Aeolus, gained a somewhat doubtful renown by committing incest with her brother Marcareus, for which she was killed by her father. But, somewhere along the line, she bore five sons to Poseidon—who were named Aloeus, Hopleus, Nireus, Triopas, and Epopeus.

Aloeus married his niece, Iphimedeia, who bore to him a daughter named Pancratis. But his wife also had two sons, named Otus and Ephialtes, whose father was the sea-god Poseidon. Ignorant of their paternity, Aloeus reared them as his own children and they were known as the Aloads or the Aloadae. When Pancratis was carried off by a band of marauding Thra-

---

18 The paucity of narrative about Chrysorthe's ancestors leads one to suspect that they may have been invented to give a respectable pedigree to her son Coronus, as the son of a god and ruler of a powerful city.

19 Cycnus is described as a Thracian who emigrated to the Troad.

20 As the reader will note, the pattern of the story is often repeated—not only in the Greek mythology but also in later literature, a conspicuous example being the biblical accusation of Joseph by Potiphar's wife.

21 Tenedos was the island from where the Greeks returned to await the signal from their comrades whom they had left in the Wooden Horse outside the walls of Troy.

54. Descendants of Poseidon and Canace

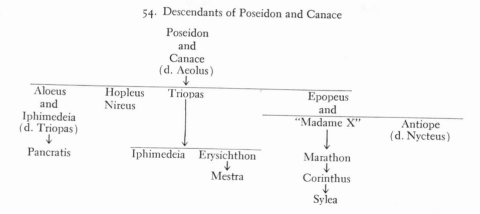

cians and was married to their King Agassamenus, Aloeus sent his supposed sons to recover their sister. And, with the unconquerable strength derived from their actually divine father, they easily overcame the despoilers. Pancratis, however, died before they were able to bring her back home.

Nothing of interest is related about either Hopleus or Nireus.

Triopas' daughter, Iphimedeia, was the wife of her uncle, Aloeus, as just mentioned. Her brother Erysichthon was punished by Demeter with an insatiable hunger, because he cut down the trees in a grove which was sacred to the goddess. In order to satisfy his appetite, he sold all of his possessions until—at last—he had nothing left except his daughter Mestra. Penniless, he sold even her, and used the purchase price for more food—which he soon devoured. As Mestra was being led away by the man who had bought her, she prayed Poseidon to save her from the impending slavery, and her features were miraculously changed into those of a fisherman, whom her new master did not recognize. She now returned to her father and, when he learned that she had acquired the power of self-metamorphosis, he sold her to many other purchasers, from whom she always escaped—variously in the form of a mare, a bird, a cow, and a deer. But finally, his malady became so serious that Erysichthon began to tear his own flesh with his greedy teeth—a practice which continued until he had consumed himself.

Epopeus is said to have come from Thessaly to Sicyon, where he was made king when Corax

died without issue. He is chiefly remembered as the protector (and husband) of Antiope, who fled to his court after she was expelled from Thebes by her father Nycteus for the affair with Zeus which resulted in the births of Amphion and Zethus. But by another wife, whose identity is not revealed, he had a son named Marathon who left Sicyon because of his father's violent temper and migrated to the seacoast of Attica, where he had a number of children, among whom only Corinthus (another son) is named by the mythographers. When Epopeus died, Marathon returned to the Peloponnesus and, establishing one of his sons on the throne at Sicyon, he made Corinthus the ruler at Ephyra, which was thereafter called Corinth.[22]

Celaeno

By Celaeno, a daughter of Atlas who was one of the Pleiades, Poseidon had a son named Lycus. According to Hyginus, he went to Thebes and threatened the lives of Megara and the children borne by her to Heracles, who was then traveling to the lower world to bring up the three-headed dog, Cerberus. As one might conjecture, Heracles returned unexpectedly

---

[22] Pausanias says that the Corinthians considered their city to have been first named Ephyra, from a daughter of Oceanus, and later called Corinth from Corinthus, a son of Zeus. He further says that Corinthus died childless and the inhabitants called Medeia from Colchis to assume the government. Another legend relates that Corinthus had a daughter named Sylea, who became by Poseidon mother of the robber Sinis—later slain by Theseus.

from his mission and, learning of Lycus' conduct, put a speedy end to his life.[23]

Chione

The legends about Eumolpus, the son of Poseidon and Chione, a daughter of Boreas, vary so greatly that some of the mythographers have sought to harmonize them by relating that there were several men who had the same name. According to Apollodorus, Chione threw her child into the sea in the hope of concealing her indiscretion from her wind-god father, but Poseidon carried his young son to Ethiopia and entrusted his rearing to his daughter Benthesicyme.

When Eumolpus was grown he married one of the daughters of Benthesicyme, by whom he had a son called Ismarus. Some time later, he tried to ravish his wife's sister and, as a result, he was banished from the country. Taking Ismarus with him, he went to live at the court of the Thracian king, Tegyrius. When the boy grew to manhood, he married one of the daughters of his father's royal host.

Despite this alliance and the kindness which had been extended to him over such a long period, Eumolpus was detected in a plot against Tegyrius and fled to the temple of Demeter at Eleusis, where he eventually became the chief priest of the goddess—an office which descended in his family (known as the Eumolpidae) for generations afterward.[24]

Chrysogeneia

According to Pausanias, the Boeotian territory which was anciently known as Phlegyantis received its name from Phlegyas, who was married to Chryse, one of the two daughters of Halmus. The second daughter, named Chrysogeneia, bore a son to Poseidon named Chryses and he succeeded to the government when the

55. Descendants of Poseidon and Chrysogeneia

Poseidon
and
Chrysogeneia
(d. Halmus)
↓
Chryses
↓
Minyas
and
Tritogeneia
↓
Alcathoë
Clymene
Elara
Leucippe
Orchomenus
Periclymene
Persephone

race of Phlegyas was destroyed by Zeus because of impiety.[25]

Chryses was followed in the rulership by his son Minyas, from whom the inhabitants were called Minyans.[26] The revenues received by him were so great that he is said to have been the first man to build a treasury for his riches, which were inherited with the crown by his son Orchomenus—after whom the principal city of the district took its name.

In addition to his son, Minyas' wife, Tritogeneia, bore six daughters to him.[27] Of these: Clymene became the wife of the Arcadian prince, Iasus; Periclymene married Pheres, king of Pherae in Thessaly; Persephone married her nephew Amphion, son of Iasus and Clymene; Elara bore to Zeus the giant Tityus;[28] but Alcathoë and Leucippe apparently stayed spinsters.

When Orchomenus died childless, the sovereignty was assumed by Clymenus, a great-grandson of the Aeolid Athamas—under the chain of kinship which has been previously detailed in chapter 6.

---

[23] According to another story, Lycus was not slain but was transported by his divine father to the Isles of the Blest.

[24] Apollodorus relates that the feud with Tegyrius was composed and that Eumolpus returned to Thrace and succeeded to his host's kingdom. Later, he was called back to Eleusis to help fight the Athenians and was slain. But, Pausanias says that he survived the battle, although Ismarus (Immaradus) and the Athenian leader Erechtheus lost their lives.

[25] A different legend relates that Phlegyas was survived by his son Ixion, who assumed the government of part of the country.

[26] Because many of the Argonauts were related to the descendants of Minyas, they were often collectively referred to as the Minyans or Minyae.

[27] According to other accounts, the wife of Minyas was named Clytodora or Phanosura.

[28] Apollodorus says that Elara was the daughter of Orchomenus, and others add that her mother was Phanosura, a daughter of Paeon.

Corcyra

Corcyra, a daughter of the god of the river Asopus, was carried off by Poseidon to an island west of the Greek mainland and there bore a son to him named Phaeax. After him the inhabitants were called Phaeacians and, in honor of his mother, the island itself was called Corcyra. However, in the Odyssey, the island is referred to as Scheria and on modern maps is designated as Corfu.

Demeter

In an endeavor to escape Poseidon's amorous advances, Demeter changed herself into a mare. He, however, deceived her by changing himself into a horse and she gave birth to Arion, an immortal steed which, after passing through several hands, came into the possession of Adrastus and bore him safely away from the carnage when the Seven Against Thebes were defeated. It is also said that Demeter bore a daughter to Poseidon, whose name was divulged only to those who were admitted to the secrets of the mysteries at Eleusis.

Europa

Europa, daughter of the huge Tityus, bore a son to Poseidon named Euphemus,[29] who was one of the hunters of the Calydonian boar and a member of the Argonautic expedition, during which he received a clod of earth from the water-god Triton. As previously related in chapter 7, when he later dropped the clod into the sea, the island of Calliste arose and, in the seventeenth generation following, was occupied by his lineal descendant Battus.

Eurycyda

Three of the four leaders of the Eleans (anciently called Epeians) at Troy were named Polyxeinus, Amphimachus, and Thalpius, whose descent from Zeus was conventionally related to have been as indicated on the adjoining chart. The legend, however, apparently did not satisfy some of the inhabitants, and they gained

a closer tie with the gods by tracing back to Eleius, who, they said, was the son of Poseidon by Endymion's daughter, Eurycyda—thus, also, explaining the name by which their country was later known.

56. Descendants of Poseidon and Eurycyda

```
                     Zeus
                      ↓
                   Aethlius
                      ↓
                   Endymion
                      ↓
   Aetolus          Epeius         Eurycyda
                      ↓               and
                   Hermina          Poseidon
                     and              ↓
                   Phorbas          Eleïus
                      ↓
   _____
   Augeias           Actor
      ↓                ↓
   Agasthenes      Cteatus          Eurytus
      ↓                ↓                ↓
   Polyxeinus      Amphimachus      Thalpius
```

In order to do no violence to the Homeric account, Augeias was named as a son of Eleius—without disturbing the genealogical positions of Agasthenes and Polyxeinus.

Euryte

Poseidon and the nymph Euryte had a son named Halirrhotius, who attempted to violate Alcippe, the wife of Evenus, but he was detected and slain by her father Ares. When Poseidon brought a criminal impeachment against the slayer, the twelve greater gods gave him a trial on the Athenian hill which was thereafter known as the Areopagus. The war-god was acquitted by a six to six tie vote, in which (being himself one of the twelve) he was presumably permitted to cast a ballot in his own favor.

Gaea

Poseidon and Gaea had a daughter named Charybdis and a son named Antaeus, both of whom had the misfortune to run afoul of Heracles.

Charybdis is said to have been a woman of such greedy appetite that she stole some of the hero's oxen and, as punishment, Zeus blasted her into the sea with a thunderbolt. She finally settled down beneath a fig tree on a great rock

---

[29] According to Apollonius Rhodius, Euphemus was gifted with the power to walk upon the sea without wetting his feet; Hesiod says that the name of his mother was Mecionice.

in the Strait of Messina—opposite the abode of Scylla—where thrice each day she swallowed and disgorged the waters of the sea with a cataclysmic voracity that often engulfed all nearby voyagers.

57. Descendants of Poseidon and Gaea

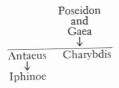

Antaeus was a mighty Giant in Libya, who could not be overcome while his body remained in contact with his mother (Earth). All strangers who came into his country were forced to wrestle with him and, when conquered, they were slain and their skulls were used in building a temple to his sea-god father. Everything went well until Heracles stopped by on his way to capture the cattle of Geryon. But he discovered the source of his adversary's strength and, lifting him from the ground, crushed him to death. Following his usual wont, the lusty hero took his dead opponent's daughter, Iphinoë, as a prize of victory. In due time, she bore to him a son who was called Palaemon.

Helle

Nothing of interest is related about Paeon, a son said to have been borne by Helle to Poseidon when she fell into his watery arms from the back of the golden ram Chrysomallus.

Hippothoë

Taphius was a son of Poseidon and Mestor's daughter, Hippothoë, who colonized an island near the coast of Acarnania which from his name was called Taphos.[30]

He had two sons, Teleboas and Pterelaus, from the former of whom the Taphians were sometimes referred to as Teleboans. Pterelaus had a golden hair in his head at birth, and the Fates had decreed that he would continue to live so long as it should remain. Thus, when his father died, he succeeded to the government

[30] Another story says that Taphius colonized a number of islands, which were collectively called Taphiae.

with the brightest of prospects for a long reign. But he was not content with his small island domain and sent all of his sons, except Ithacus,[31] to demand the kingdom of Mycenae from Electryon—claiming that its sovereignty was rightfully his by reason of his descent from Mestor, who was Electryon's older brother.

58. Descendants of Poseidon and Hippothoë

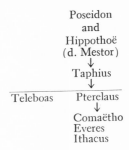

When the Taphians reached Mycenae and their demand was rejected, they drove off Electryon's cattle and a fight ensued in which all of his legitimate sons were slain[32] and, of the sons of Pterelaus, only Everes survived. Electryon hastily gathered his forces for a punitive expedition but, before he could start, he was accidentally killed by his nephew Amphitryon, who sorrowfully took over the command and proceeded with the army to Taphos. Although he won a few small engagements, he did not gain a complete victory over the Taphians until Pterelaus' daughter, Comaëtho, fell in love with him and plucked the golden hair from her father's head—bringing his life to its fated end. But, in abhorrence at a conquest gained by such means, Amphitryon caused the maiden to be slain and sailed home.

Historis

Historis was a daughter of the blind Theban seer Teiresias, by whom Poseidon had a son named Periclymenus. He fought with the defenders to ward off the attack of the Seven Against Thebes. According to one version, he

[31] Ithacus is said to have migrated to a neighboring island where he built a fountain and named the land Ithaca after himself.

[32] Electryon's illegitimate son, Licymnius, did not engage in the fight.

is said to have slain Parthenopaeus, the son of Ares and Atalanta. But he gained greater renown at the termination of the fighting, because it was he who was pursuing Amphiaraus when the fleeing prophet vanished into the earth with his horse-drawn chariot.

Iphimedeia

As earlier related, Iphimedeia was a daughter of Triopas who was married to Aloeus, son of Poseidon and Canace. Being both a granddaughter and a daughter-in-law of the sea-god, she was in the habit of walking along the shore and sprinkling her bosom with his briny waters. As a result, she gave birth to twin sons named Otus and Ephialtes, and commonly known as the Aloads or Aloadae. It is said that when the boys were only nine-years old their bodies were thirteen-feet wide and more than fifty-feet high,[33] and at this early age they essayed to attack the gods on Olympus by piling Mount Pelion on Mount Ossa. It is added that they would have been able to accomplish their purpose had they been permitted to continue their tremendous growth—but Apollo destroyed them before their beards began to appear.[34] As another childish exploit, it is related that they put the war-god Ares in a brazen jar, where he lay in chains for thirteen months and would have perished had not Hermes secretly effected his liberation.[35]

Medusa

When Perseus cut off the head of the Gorgon Medusa, Chrysaör and Pegasus sprang forth —two winged horses conceived by her when she had consorted with Poseidon "in a soft meadow among spring flowers."

59. Descendants of Poseidon and Medusa

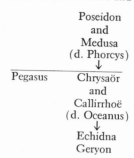

Chrysaör mated with Callirrhoë, one of the Oceanides, who bore two monstrosities named Geryon (or Geryones) and Echidna. Geryon had the body of three men grown together, but joined from the waist down. Echidna, born in a cave beneath the earth, was in form half a nymph with her lower body in the shape of a huge snake with speckled skin. So molded it was thoroughly in character for her to join with Typhon in producing the brood whom we have already numbered among the descendants of Tartarus.

Geryon was the owner of a herd of red cattle, which he pastured on the island of Erythia (identified as Cadiz in Spain), under the watchful eyes of a herdsman named Eurytion and a two-headed dog called Orthrus (or Orthus), which was one of Echidna's weird progeny. But Heracles drove away the cattle in the performance of one of his Twelve Labors and, when he was resisted, he killed Eurytion, Orthrus, and Geryon.

As soon as he was born, Pegasus flew to Mount Olympus and found a dwelling with Zeus, to whom he was accustomed to bring thunder and lightning.[36] His mythological prominence, however, is largely due to the fact that he was the steed of Bellerophon, while the

---

[33] The Iliad states that the Aloads were nine-cubits wide and nine-fathoms high; another story relates that each year they grew one cubit in breadth and three in height.

[34] According to Apollodorus, Ephialtes wooed Hera and Otus aspired to Artemis, who brought about their double death by leaping between them in the form of a deer—whereupon each threw his spear at the quarry and killed the other. We have earlier related (under Canace) how Aloeus sent his supposed sons to recover his daughter Pancratis from her Thracian abductors. Diodorus completes the story by saying that, after the Thracians were defeated, the Aloads fell into dispute and slew each other.

[35] In the Iliad, it is said that Hermes was summoned by the stepmother of the Aloads called Eriboea—a name which some of the mythographers give to Iphimedeia.

[36] Later writers make Pegasus the horse of the dawn-goddess Eos, and say that he was eventually placed among the stars as the square constellation bearing his name, which occupies a large space in the heavens, between Andromeda on the east and Cygnus on the west.

young hero was performing the feats of valor, at the behest of the Lycian king, Iobates (which have been previously detailed in chapter 6). Another, and later, story regarded him as the horse of the Muses. It relates that, when the maidens began to sing on Mount Helicon in Boeotia in their contest with the nine daughters of Pierus, the mountain was so filled with ecstasy that it rose toward the heavens, until Pegasus—at the command of Poseidon—stopped its upward progress with a kick of his hoof and thus created the Hippocrene spring, whose quaffed waters were afterward considered as an inspiration to music and poetry.

Melia

Melia was a nymph of Bithynia by whom Poseidon had two sons, named Mygdon and Amycus. While Heracles was traveling to the land of the Amazons to obtain the girdle of their queen, Hippolyte, he stopped at the court of the Mysian king, Lycus, and received hospitable entertainment. During his stay, Mygdon —who was king of the neighboring Bebrycians —made the mistake of attacking the domain of Lycus and the great man, politely assisting his host, killed him.

Amycus succeeded his brother as king of the Bebrycians and kept his realm free of all strangers by forcing them to box with him in contests wherein he was accustomed to end their lives. When the Argonauts landed on his shores, during their journey to Colchis, he went down to their vessel and, as usual, challenged the best man of the crew to contend with him in what he thought was his invincible art. Pollux accepted the challenge and, in the furious match which followed, he finally landed a blow above the ear of Amycus with such force that the bones of his head were crushed and he died.[37]

Peirene

Poseidon had two sons, Cenchrias and Leches, by Peirene, a daughter of Oebalus and the Oceanid Bateia. Pausanias, however, cites a Corinthian legend which said that she was a daughter of the river-god Achelous.

Cenchrias and Leches gave their names to the harbors of Corinth; and, when Cenchrias was accidentally slain by Artemis, it is said that Peirene wept for him so copiously that her tears were turned into a fountain which thereafter bore her name.

Periboea

Periboea must have been one of the earliest wives of Poseidon, because she was a daughter of the Giant Eurymedon, who was a son of Uranus and Gaea. Her son, Nausithous, originally ruled in the island of Trinacria, but, being continually harassed by the neighboring Cyclopes, he led his Phaeacian subjects to the island of Scheria. There, they became noted as great mariners, who were in the habit of ferrying shipwrecked persons back to their native homes.[38]

60. Descendants of Poseidon and Periboea

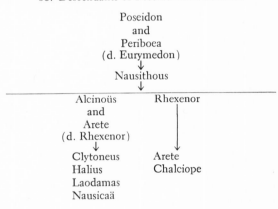

For some unexplained reason, Apollo slew Rhexenor, the elder son of Nausithous, while he was a young bridegroom, and so he did not live to see his daughters, Chalciope and Arete.[39] Chalciope became the second barren wife of the Athenian king, Aegeus; but Arete married her uncle, Alcinoüs, who succeeded to the govern-

---

[37] The account of the boxing match has been given in chapter 7.

[38] In telling Odysseus about Poseidon's displeasure over the safe carriage given to persons whom he had shipwrecked, Alcinoüs repeated a story, which had been told to him by Nausithous, that the sea-god would one day cut off the Phaeacians from his surrounding waters if they should persist in their hospitable practice.

[39] In the Odyssey, it is related that Arete was Rhexenor's only child. It is possible that Chalciope was the daughter of a different man of the same name.

ment when Nausithous died, and bore to him a daughter Nausicaa and three sons, named Clytoneus, Halius, and Laodamas.

Alcinoüs and Arete, with their children, are chiefly remembered for their kind treatment of Odysseus, when he was stranded on their island shore, and are later mentioned in more detail in the account of his wanderings as he was returning from Troy.

Pitane

Pitane was a daughter of the river-god Eurotas who conceived a child by Poseidon. When her daughter Evadne was born, she concealed her motherhood by sending the babe to the Arcadian king, Aepytus, for rearing.

After Evadne reached maturity, she too was embraced by a god—Apollo. She was unable, however, to keep her secret and Aeyptus went in wrath to Delphi to seek advice from the oracle. To his joy, he learned that his young ward's child had been begotten by the deity of the temple and was destined to be a seer with powers of soothsaying far beyond all mortals. While Aepytus was on his mission, Jamus (Iamus) was born and was abandoned by his fearful mother in a clump of rushes, but he was miraculously tended by two grey-eyed serpents and grew up to become the gifted person of the oracle's prophecy.[40]

Salamis

By Salamis, who was one of the many daughters of the river-god Asopus, Poseidon had a son named Cychreus. When the boy reached manhood, he went to an island—lying at the head of the Saronic Gulf between Attica and Megara—and killed a serpent which had been ravaging the land.[41] In gratitude, the inhabitants made him their king and, in his honor, called their island Cychreia, but it was later renamed Salamis for their ruler's mother.

Afterward, when Telamon was expelled from Aegina for the murder of his half brother Phocus, he went to the island and, marrying Cychreus' daughter, Glauce, succeeded to the kingship. And it was his son Ajax who gloriously led the Salaminian forces in the war against Troy.

Sylea

By Sylea, a daughter of Corinthus, Poseidon had a son named Sinis, who was a robber inhabiting the Isthmus of Corinth.[42] After stripping all who tried to pass, it was his custom to bend over two pine trees which, fastened to separate arms, were permitted to spring back and tear apart the bodies of his unfortunate victims. However, when the Attic hero Theseus came along, the tables were reversed, for he killed Sinis by giving him a dose of his own treatment.

Theophane

By Theophane, a daughter of Bisaltes, Poseidon fathered Chrysomallus—the speaking golden ram which carried Phrixus and Helle away from Iolchus, and whose fleece was brought back from Colchis by the Argonauts. When the ram died he was translated to the heavens, and fixed eternally as Aries, the first sign of the Zodiac.

Thoösa

Thoösa, a daughter of Phorcys and Ceto, is said to have borne to Poseidon the giant one-eyed, man-eating Polyphemus (Cyclops), who was slain by Odysseus under circumstances which are part of the narrative of the Odyssey.[43]

---

[40] Pindar relates that, when Jamus was grown, he went by night into the waters of the river Alpheius and called upon Poseidon and Apollo to reveal his fate. When Apollo answered the call, he followed the god's voice to Olympia in Elis and was told that, as soon as Heracles should have founded the Olympian games, he would receive the power to understand the talk of birds and to foretell the future from the sacrifices burning on the altar of Zeus.

[41] According to Strabo, Cychreus bred the serpent, which was ejected from the island of Eurylochus and found sanctuary in the temple of Demeter at Eleusis.

Pausanias cites a tradition that, while the battle of Salamis was in progress, a dragon appeared in one of the Athenian ships, which an oracle declared to be Cychreus bringing his assistance to their cause.

[42] Apollodorus names Polypemon and Sylea as the parents of Sinis.

[43] According to a story related by Ovid, Polyphemus was in love with the Nereid Galatea, but she preferred a handsome youth named Acis, whose head the jealous giant crushed with a stone.

Tyro

The circumstances under which Neleus and Pelias were conceived, and borne to Poseidon, by Tyro, the daughter of Salmoneus, have been rather fully related in chapter 6.

61. Descendants of Poseidon and Tyro

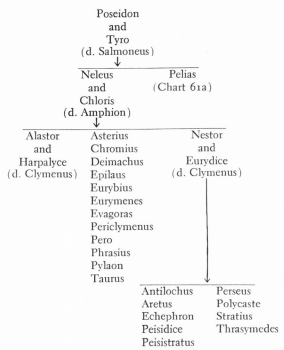

After the death of their stepfather, Cretheus, the two brothers quarreled about the succession to the throne of Iolchus, and Neleus, being worsted, went to Pylus on the west coast of the Peloponnesus, where his step-cousin Aphareus gave him the rulership. He took as his queen the daughter of the Orchomenian king, Amphion, who was named Chloris. By her he became father of the thirteen sons shown on chart 61 and a daughter Pero—whose hand Melampus won for his brother, Bias, as related in chapter 8.

Before proceeding with the story of Neleus, the unfortunate marriage of his son Alastor should be mentioned. He was betrothed to a maiden named Harpalyce, who was so beautiful that her own father, Clymenus, was overcome with a passion in which he was accustomed to indulge by secret intercourse with her. When the time arrived for her wedding to Alastor, Cly-

menus handed her over without hesitation and celebrated the event in magnificent style, but, after a short period, his passion induced him to change his mind. Hurrying after the newly wed couple, he seized Harpalyce and, bringing her back to Argos, lived with her openly as his wife. To avenge her humiliation, she slew her younger brother Therager and placed his flesh in a dish before her incestuous father on the occasion of a public festival which was being celebrated. When he learned that he had eaten the flesh of his own son, Clymenus hanged himself and—to end her miserable life—the gods mercifully changed Harpalyce into a bird. Shamed by the disgrace, Alastor returned to Pylus, where he was accepted back into the palace by his understanding father.

Some time later, Heracles came to Neleus to be purified of killing Iphitus, a son of Eurytus, whom he had thrown from the walls of Tiryns, but, because Neleus was a friend of Eurytus, he refused to honor the request. This so enraged the great man that he afterward returned to Pylus with an army and slew all of the sons of Neleus—except Nestor, who was being reared in the Messenian town of Gerenia. In the battle, Periclymenus—who had the power of changing his shape—metamorphosed himself into a lion, a snake, and a bee. In this last form, he was detected and killed.[44]

The weakened Neleus, deprived of the support of his sons, was now further dishonored by the Elean king, Augeias, who refused to return four prized racing steeds which the Pylians had sent to compete in the Olympic games. The old king angrily retaliated by seizing the herds of the Eleans, whereupon Augeias sent an invading force whose approach was heralded to Neleus by the goddess Athena. Meanwhile, Nestor had returned from his rearing at Gerenia, where he had become an expert horseman, and demanded that he be permitted to participate in the forthcoming battle, but his father, considering him still too young, refused his demand and hid his horses. The youth fought, however, on foot and, when the Eleans

---

[44] Other accounts relate that Periclymenus escaped Heracles in the form of an eagle and, flying away, lived to take part in the Argonautic expedition.

---

attacked, he killed Mulius, a son-in-law of Auge-ias, who was the leader of their cavalry. Upon this happening, the Eleans fled in a rout, during which many more of their number were slain, and Nestor was acclaimed the hero of the day by his victorious comrades.

The remaining stories about Nestor are an integral part of the Iliad and the Odyssey, and will be related in connection with them. He married Eurydice, a daughter of the Orchomenian king, Clymenus,[45] by whom he had two daughters, Peisidice and Polycaste, and seven sons, named Antilochus, Aretus, Echephron, Peisistratus, Perseus, Stratius, and Thrasymedes.

Nothing of interest is related about Peisidice, but Polycaste was later married to Telemachus, the son of Odysseus, and bore to him a daughter named Persepolis. Antilochus is characterized in the Iliad as one of the youngest,[46] handsomest, and bravest of the Greeks, with preeminence "in speed of foot." Accompanying his aged father to the Trojan War, he became a great favorite of Achilles. Upon his death at the hands of the Ethiopian prince, Memnon, his remains were buried beside those of his great friend, whom he continued to attend as a shade in the lower world.[47]

The other sons of Nestor—except Thrasymedes—apparently were either too young to fight at Troy or returned safely from the great war, because they are mentioned as being present at their father's palace in Pylus when Telemachus was seeking his father Odysseus.[48] However, Thrasymedes went along to battle with Nestor and Antilochus and was credited with slaying the Trojan Maris and performing other actions of valor—following which he returned home without mishap.

In connection with the story of Jason and the Argonauts, we have related in chapter 7 how Pelias forced Aeson from the rulership of Iolchus and the sad end which he met. In connection with the story of Salmoneus, we have related in chapter 6 how he and Neleus slew Sidero for ill-using their mother.[49]

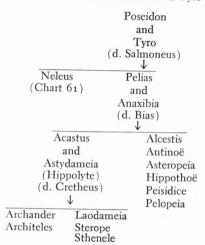

61a. Descendants of Poseidon and Tyro

The wife of Pelias was Anaxibia, a daughter of Bias, who bore to him a son, Acastus, and the six daughters whose names are shown on the accompanying chart. Of the daughters, Alcestis married Admetus, king of Pherae, for whom she would have given her life had not Heracles saved her from Death. The others, for the crime of killing their father, were forced to retire into Arcadia, where their names were saved from oblivion only by the persistence of the mounds which were heaped up over their graves.

When Acastus held funeral games in honor of his dead father, his wife, Astydameia (a daughter of Cretheus who was surnamed Hippolyte), fell in love with Peleus,[50] but he repulsed her and she accused him to her husband

---

[45] Apollodorus says that the wife of Nestor was Anaxibia, daughter of Cratieus.

[46] Notwithstanding his youth, Antilochus is said to have been among the suitors of Helen.

[47] According to a different legend, Achilles did not enter the lower world; but—with Medeia as his wife—was transported to the Isles of the Blest. However, in a colloquy between ghosts, which is described in the 24th book of the Odyssey, the shade of Antilochus is represented in the company of those of Achilles, Patroclus, and Ajax.

[48] It was on this visit that Telemachus met his future bride, Polycaste, and was escorted by Peisistratus to the court of Menelaus at Sparta.

[49] At birth, Neleus and Pelias were exposed by their mother in a forest, where Neleus was said to have been suckled by a she-dog, but they were found and reared by a shepherd, who gave Pelias his name because his face had been bruised by the hoof of a passing mare.

[50] According to Pausanias, Peleus and Jason wrestled to a draw at the funeral games of Pelias. A different legend relates that Peleus was conquered by the maiden Atalanta.

of having made improper advances. Acastus bided his time, until his guest fell asleep one day while they were hunting together on Mount Pelion, whereupon he took Peleus' sword from its sheath and, quietly departing, left him defenseless against the dangers of the wild country. Peleus, awakening to find himself the target of a host of savage Centaurs, vainly reached for his weapon to ward off his attackers, and he would have perished except that his old friend (and grandfather) Cheiron came to the rescue —but only after he had been cruelly wounded. When he had recovered, he returned to Iolchus and killed both Acastus and Astydameia. Later he was expelled from his kingdom of Phthia by their sons, Archander and Architeles.[51] Meanwhile, the vengeful Astydameia had sent word to Peleus' wife, Antigone, that he was about to marry her daughter Sterope and the credulous woman had hanged herself—so that, through no fault of his own, the aged king, who had once been honored with the bed of a goddess, found himself without either home or family.

Nothing further is related about Sterope. Of the other daughters of Acastus and Astydameia, Sthenele married Menoetius and became the mother of Patroclus, who was the dearest friend of Achilles; Laodameia, as related in chapter 6, became the wife of Protesilaus, the first Greek to die at Troy, and put an end to her own life after the gods permitted her to hold a conversation with her beloved husband's ghost.

As might be expected, the mythographers furnish us with but scant detail about the offspring borne to Poseidon by wives who were not important enough to be identified. We shall refer to them in the order indicated on chart 62.

Alebion[52] and Dercynus were sons of the sea-god, who were slain by Heracles in Liguria (now southern France) when they attempted to rob him of the cows of Geryon, which he was driving toward Greece.

Busiris[53] was known as a king of Egypt who was ruling after the country had been visited with a nine-year drought. A Cyprian seer, named Phrasius, came to his palace and informed him that the plague would cease if he should slaughter a stranger every year on the altar of Zeus. Busiris, accepting the advice, began by killing the seer himself and continued the practice until Heracles arrived. However, when the great man was seized and brought to the sacrificial altar, he burst from his bonds and slew not only the Egyptian king but also his son Amphidamas and his herald Chalbes.

Poseidon's daughter Cymopoleia is said to have been the wife of Briareus (Aegaeon)—one of the fifty-headed and hundred-armed Hecatoncheires, who was sometimes represented as a sea god. His son, Erginus, is mentioned only as being one of the Argonauts who vied for the position of steersman when Tiphys died.

Poltys, the brother of Erginus, entertained Heracles as the hero was returning to Greece with the girdle of Hippolyte, but Sarpedon, another brother of Poltys, was shot with an arrow because Heracles thought that he was "a lewd fellow."

We come now to Proteus, the "old man of the sea."[54] Although his home was in the sea, he is reputed to have arisen every day at noon to the island of Pharos near the Egyptian mainland, where he was accustomed to take a nap on the shore—accompanied by seals and other denizens of the deep. He was endowed with prophetic powers, but anyone wishing to have his fortune told was obliged to catch him while he slept. Even then, his inquisitors were not always successful, because he could change himself into various shapes and often used this trick to escape from answering objectionable questions.[55]

---

[51] Dictys Cretensis names the sons of Acastus as Menalippus and Pleisthenes, and says that they were slain by Neoptolemus in retaliation for their expulsion of his grandfather.

[52] A fanciful story identifies Alebion with Albion— the ancient poetic name for England.

[53] According to Apollodorus, the mother of Busiris was Lysianassa, a daughter of Epaphus.

[54] A late story makes Proteus the son of Poseidon and the Oceanid Phoenice. Nereus and Phorcys were also sometimes individually referred to as the "Old Man of the Sea."

[55] According to Diodorus, the Egyptian name for Proteus was Cetes. Apollodorus says that he hospitably received Dionysus upon a visit to Egypt—a visit which

62. Descendants of Poseidon and "Madame X"

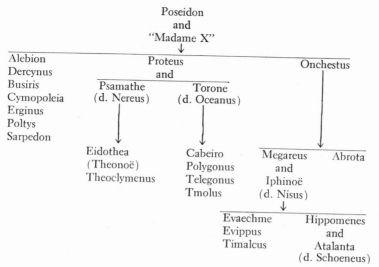

According to Euripides, Proteus was married to the Nereid Psamathe, after she became widowed at the death of Aeacus. Their children were a son, Theoclymenus, who succeeded his father as king of Egypt, and a daughter, Eidothea (who was also called Eido and Theonoë). When Menelaus became lost in Egypt, while returning from Troy, it is said that Eidothea fell in love with his helmsman Canobus and was induced to tell the wanderers in what manner they might seize her father and obtain instructions for their homeward journey.[56]

By another wife, usually said to be the Oceanid Torone, Proteus had a daughter, Cabeiro, who was wooed by Hephaestus, and three sons—Polygonus, Telegonus, and Tmolus—who were accustomed to conquer all strangers in wrestling. However, when Heracles was passing through Egypt, their victories, and their lives, were brought to an end because they had the temerity to challenge him, with the fatal result which always came to those with whom the great man contended.[57]

Onchestus, our last charted son of Poseidon,[58] is said to have founded an ancient town in Boeotia, which took its name from him. According to one legend, his daughter Abrota married Nisus, the king of Nisaea in Attica, who became involved in a war with the Cretan king, Minos, and called upon his brother-in-law, Megareus (brother of Abrota), for assistance. The latter responded to the call, but fell in battle, and the name of the city was changed to Megara in his honor.

A different story relates that Megareus was married to Nisus' daughter, Iphinoë and, succeeding his father-in-law as king, named the city Megara after himself. His elder son Timalcus was slain by Theseus, while on a campaign with the Dioscuri against Aphidnae to recover their young sister Helen, whom the Attic hero had abducted and hidden there. His younger son Evippus was destroyed by a lion, while he was

---

is said to have been invented for the purpose of explaining the close resemblance between the rites used in the worship of the wine-god and those of the Egyptian deity Osiris.

[56] Herodotus relates a story, amplified by Euripides, that Proteus took Helen away from Paris when he was driven upon the Egyptian shores on his way back to Troy, and that she safely remained in Egypt while only her wraith continued the journey. According to another legend, Proteus was originally an Egyptian, who went to Thrace and married Torone, but when his wrestling sons began to use such violence against strangers, he prayed to Poseidon for relief and the god opened a chasm in the earth, which he followed under the sea back to Pharos.

[57] A different version places the locale of the wrestling match at Torone in Macedonia.

[58] Hyginus names Oënope as the mother of Onchestus' son, Megareus.

walking about on Mount Cithaeron. In despair at his double loss, Megareus offered the hand of his daughter Evaechme to the man who should slay the lion. The task was successfully undertaken by Alcathous, a son of Pelops, who thus gained a wife and—at the death of Megareus—succeeded to the kingdom.

According to Ovid, Hippomenes was a third son of Megareus. He is remembered only for the stratagem of dropping the golden apples in the footrace by which he gained the fleet Atalanta as his bride. (See chapter 6.)

This concludes the descendants of Poseidon. Many of them will be repeatedly mentioned as actors in later scenes which primarily involve the descendants of his supreme brother Zeus.

11

The Descendants of Zeus I

In his scholarly "History of Greece," George Grote says:

"In the retrospective faith of a Greek, the ideas of worship and ancestry coalesced. Every association of men large or small, in whom there existed a feeling of present union, traced back that union to some common initial progenitor: that progenitor being either the common god whom they worshipped, or some semi-divine person closely allied to him. What the feelings of the community require is, a continuous pedigree to connect them with this respected source of existence, beyond which they do not think of looking back[1] .... The value of the genealogy consisted not in its length, but in its continuity; not (according to the feeling of modern aristocracy) in the power of setting out a prolonged series of human fathers and grandfathers, but in the sense of ancestral union with the primitive god."

Although Grote's statement is perhaps too general, it is peculiarly true of those localities which were able to trace the pedigrees of their leaders to a child of the supreme Zeus—a fact of which the god must have been aware, because he was most liberal in scattering his seed.

We here give, in alphabetical order, the names of the mothers of the children of Zeus, with an indication of the special localities which laid claim to divine filiation through his various offspring:

---

[1] The genealogical charts given herein suggest that once a "respected source" was reached, the Greeks were under no necessity of "looking back," because all such stemmed from primeval Gaea.

Aega: not localized
Aegina: Aegina and Salamis
Alcmena: Tiryns, Mycenae, and Thebes
Antiope: Thebes
Callisto: Arcadia
Danae: Tiryns, Mycenae, and Argos
Demeter: Eleusis
Dione: Cyprus and Corinth
Elara: not localized
Electra: Troy
Europa: Crete
Eurymedusa: Thessaly
Eurynome: not localized
Euryodia: Ithaca
Gaea: not localized
Hera: not localized
Io: Argolis
Laodameia: Lycia and Crete
Leda: Sparta and Mycenae
Leto: Delos and Delphi
Maia: Arcadia
Metis: Athens and Troy
Mnemosyne: not localized
Niobe: Argolis and Arcadia
Persephone: not localized
Plouto: Argolis and Attica
Protogeneia (No. 1): Elis and Aetolia
Protogeneia (No. 2): Locris
Selene: not localized
Semele: Thebes
Taygete: Sparta and Acarnania
Themis: not localized

This itemization is intended merely as a general indication of sources and should not be considered as restrictive, because many of the descendants of Zeus, and of the other deities, wandered far from their original homelands and, in their places of new settlement, identified the inhabitants with their divine ancestry.

For reasons, both of chronology and convenience, we shall not refer to the wives of Zeus in the alphabetical order given above, but shall consider them in what might appear to be an arbitrary sequence by those who fail to realize that, in the end, most of their descendants will have been intermarried, or tied in as common participants in the Trojan War and other heroic enterprises.

Metis—the Mother of Athena

Metis, one of the Oceanides, was the first love and wife of Zeus. It was she who assisted him in the scheme to induce his father Cronus to sip the emetic which caused him to expel the brothers and sisters of Zeus from his mighty maw.

When Metis was with child, Gaea informed Zeus that she would give birth to a daughter equal to himself in strength and understanding and would later bear a son, who would become king of both the gods and men. To avoid this happening, Zeus swallowed his wife[2] and, some time after, was stricken with such a headache that he asked Prometheus to strike his brow with an axe. Prometheus did as he was bidden, and a maiden leapt forth fully clad and fully armed. She was Athena, the goddess of wisdom. (See chapter 3 for the complete details.)

Taygete—the Mother of Lacedaemon

By Taygete, one of the Pleiades, Zeus had a son named Lacedaemon who married Sparta, the daughter of Eurotas, the ruler of the southeastern part of the Peloponnesus. When his father-in-law died, he succeeded to the kingdom and called it Lacedaemonia.

He named his capital city after his wife Sparta, who bore to him a son, Amyclas, and two daughters, Asine and Eurydice. Asine appears to have done nothing which was remem-

bered; Eurydice, however, married the neighboring Argive king, Acrisius, and became the mother of Danae, who was one of the later wives of Zeus.

When Amyclas succeeded to the throne, he founded the town of Amyclae on the seacoast and took as his queen a daughter of Lapithes (Lapithus), named Diomede, by whom he had the four sons and two daughters indicated on the accompanying chart. Of the daughters, nothing of interest is related about Leaneira, and Laodameia became the second wife of the Arcadian king, Arcas.[3]

Hyacinthus, the youngest son of Amyclas,[4] was a boy of such extraordinary beauty that he is said to have been the first to awaken passion in another male. Thamyris, a famous Thracian bard, fell in love with him and was followed by Apollo. Tragedy ensued however, for one day the god accidentally killed the youth by the cast of a quoit, and from his blood sprang a flower which was called Hyacinth.[5]

Harpalus migrated to Achaea and, when Amyclas died, the rulership of Lacedaemonia descended successively to his younger brothers Argalus and Cynortes, who appear to have governed quietly and without distinction. Cynortes was succeeded by his son, Perieres,[6] who was equally undistinguished. His younger son Borus wedded Polydora, the daughter of Peleus and Antigone, and reputedly had two sons, named

---

[2] According to Apollodorus, Metis had the power to metamorphose herself and changed into several forms in order to escape the embraces of Zeus. Another story relates that Zeus himself changed her into a bee in order to swallow her more easily.

[3] Another legend relates that Leaneira, and not Laodameia, was the wife of Arcas.

[4] According to another story, the parents of Hyacinthus were Pierus and the Muse Clio. He is sometimes confused with another Lacedaemonian of the same name, but not of divine descent, whose daughters (Aegleis, Antheis, Lytaea, and Orthaea) were slaughtered by the Athenians, pursuant to the advice of an oracle, when they were engaged in a war with the Cretan king, Minos.

[5] A different story relates that one of the wind-gods (Boreas or Zephyrus) was a rival for the affection of Hyacinthus; that he preferred Apollo; and that the jealous wind-god gained revenge by sending a blast which diverted the quoit so that it struck the youth on the head and killed him.

[6] Perieres, the son of Cynortes, is often confused with Perieres, the son of Aeolus because the Aeolid Perieres was married to Gorgophone, a daughter of Perseus; and, when her first husband died, she married Oebalus, a son of the Perieres descended from Cynortes. In relating the story, Pausanias adds that Gorgophone was reputed to have been the first widow to remarry.

63. Descendants of Zeus and Taygete

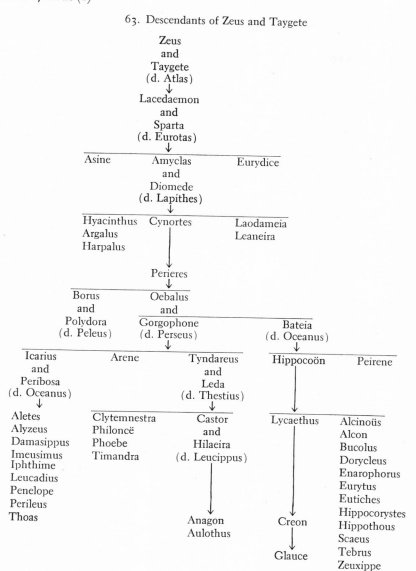

Dryops and Menesthius. In reality, however, their father was the river-god Sperchius. His elder son Oebalus married Gorgophone, a daughter of Perseus and the widow of the Aeolid Perieres, who bore to him a daughter Arene, and two sons, Icarius and Tyndareus. By the Naiad-nymph Bateia, he also begot a son, Hippocoön, and a daughter, Peirene. Arene became the wife of Aphareus, a son of the Aeolid Perieres, in a wedding which naturally tended to aggravate the confusion in the genealogy of her family, because her husband was also her half brother.

When Oebalus died, Hippocoön seized the government and expelled Icarius and Tyndareus from the country.[7] They went to the court of Thestius at Pleuron in Aetolia, where Tyndareus soon won the love of the king's daughter, Leda. Subsequently, Heracles killed Hippocoön, and Tydareus returned to his Lacedaemonian capital at Sparta. Icarius, however, went into Acarnania, where he became king and, marrying the Naiad Periboea, begot the seven sons and

---

[7] A different legend relates that Icarius assisted Hippocoön in expelling Tyndareus from Sparta.

two daughters whose names are shown on the accompanying chart.[8]

Nothing of interest is related about the sons of Icarius, except that Alyzeus is said to have succeeded his father as king of Acarnania. When his daughter Penelope reached maturity, Icarius promised her hand to that one of her many suitors who should be the victor in a foot-race, and she was won by Odysseus, who took her to his island kingdom of Ithaca. A different legend relates that Odysseus gained his bride through the intercession of Tyndareus. His other daughter, Iphthime, also left when she married the Thessalian prince, Eumelus, who was later renowned at Troy for his excellent horses, which had been trained by Apollo while he was serving Admetus at Pherae.

After Tyndareus returned to Sparta with Leda as his bride, she bore to him four daughters, Clytemnestra, Philonoë, Phoebe, and Timandra, and a son who was named Castor.[9]

Of the daughters, Clytemnestra became the queen of Agamemnon, the king of Mycenae; Philonoë, for some undisclosed reason, is said to have been given immortality by Artemis; Timandra married the Arcadian king, Echemus; but Phoebe appears only because Euripides has Agamemnon mention that she was Clytemnestra's sister.

Castor and his twin Pollux—who was reputedly a son of Zeus—were called the Dioscuri by the Greeks and the Gemini[10] by the Romans. They were so devoted to each other that, at Castor's death, Pollux prevailed upon his divine father to permit him to share his immortality with his brother—so that, on alternate days, they still moved among gods and men. In their lives, the parts which they played as members of the Argonautic band and their battle with Idas

and Lynceus, the sons of Aphareus, have already been related. A third noteworthy event, relating to their recovery of Helen after her abduction by Theseus, is detailed later when the exploits of that great Attic hero are discussed.

By Hilaeira, a daughter of Leucippus, Castor became the father of two sons named Anagon and Aulothus,[11] but nothing of interest is related about them.

The Dioscuri were anciently worshipped as the protectors of travelers; and it is said that Poseidon gave them the power to control wind and waves for the assistance of those who were shipwrecked. In later historical times, their symbolic representations as legendary kings of Lacedaemonia were carried by the Spartans whenever they entered the field of battle.[12] As has been stated previously an additional honor was that they were said to have been placed in the heavens as the twin stars which are numbered as the third sign of the zodiac (Gemini).

As previously stated, Oebalus' son, Hippocoön, was slain by Heracles after he had expelled Icarius and Tyndareus from Sparta. His sister, Peirene, has also been mentioned (in the preceding chapter) as the wife of Poseidon who was changed into a fountain outside Corinth, when she wept at the death of her son Cenchrias. His daughter Zeuxippe married Antiphates, who joined Heracles in his expedition against the Trojan king, Laomedon, unaware that his father-in-law was fated to be slain by his huge companion.

In the attack against him by Heracles, Hippocoön was assisted by his twelve sons whose names are given on the accompanying chart,[13] but they were all slain with their father, for the great man was never guilty of half measures. The reason for the attack was twofold: first, because Hippocoön, or one of his sons, had slain Oeonus, a kinsman of Heracles, when he threw

---

[8] According to Apollodorus, Icarius returned to Sparta with Tyndareus, and Pausanias says that Odysseus led Penelope (the daughter of Icarius) as his bride to Ithaca from Sparta. These stories, however, would set at naught the Acarnanian legend which considered Icarius and his son, Alyzeus, as ancient kings of that country.
[9] According to another tradition, both Castor and Pollux were the sons of Zeus and Leda, being born with their sister Helen from a single egg. Castor was renowned for his skill in the management of horses and Pollux for his ability as a boxer.
[10] The twins were often referred to as the Tyndaridae.

[11] Anagon is called Anaxus by some of the mythographers.
[12] It is related that, during the absence of Theseus, the Dioscuri raised Menestheus to the throne of Athens, their city's later rival.
[13] The number and the names of the sons of Hippocoön are variously given. Pausanias names only six and Diodorus names ten. The twelve listed in the chart are named by Apollodorus.

a stone in self-defense against their dog which was rushing at him; and second, because Hippocoön had assisted Neleus, when Heracles took vengeance upon him for refusing to purify the hero from the blood taint of killing Iphitus.

The only one of Hippocoön's sons to leave children was Lycaethus, who is said to have been the father of the Corinthian king, Creon, but it is not related how he gained that city's throne. Creon's daughter, Glauce, was the last love of Jason, but was prevented from consummating her marriage by jealous Medeia, who gave her the fatal robe in which she was burned to death. (See chapter 7.) And, in the conflagration started, it is related that Creon also perished.

After Tyndareus was restored to the government of Sparta, he was beset with a new trouble, for a swarm of suitors besieged his court to win the hand of Helen—the beautiful daughter borne by Leda when, on the same night, she was embraced by both her husband and supreme Zeus. Fearing that, if he should award the maiden to any one of them, the other suitors would be unmanageable, he asked the advice of Odysseus, who was reputed to be among the wisest of men. When he suggested that all of the suitors be put under oath to protect their successful competitor, and they acquiesced, Tyndareus rewarded the Ithacan king by having Icarius give him Penelope as his wife.[14] Menelaus, the son of Pleisthenes,[15] was chosen by Helen and afterward, when the Dioscuri had been received among the immortals, Tyndareus invited his son-in-law to Sparta and turned over the kingdom to him.

Selene—the Mother of Pandia

In the "Homeric Hymn to Selene," it is related that Zeus was joined with the Moon-goddess Selene in love, "and she conceived and bore a daughter Pandia, exceedingly lovely amongst the deathless gods."

---

[14] A different story, previously mentioned, relates that Odysseus won Penelope by besting her other suitors in a footrace.

[15] Menelaus and his brother Agamemnon were sons of Pleisthenes, the son of Atreus, but they were adopted by their grandfather when Pleisthenes died and he married their mother—his own daughter-in-law.

Gaea—the Mother of Nymphs

The nymphs were inferior female divinities who inhabited streams, woods, and mountains. Except those associated with the watery element, they were considered to be the daughters of Zeus and Gaea. The woodland nymphs were called Dryads (Dryades) and Hamadryads (Hamadryades)—distinguished by the fiction that each Hamadryad was associated with a single tree and perished with it, while the Dryads were considered to be immortal and, on occasion, even had the right of access to the great gods on Mount Olympus. The mountain nymphs were called Oreads (Oreades) and were associated with individual mountains or mountainous localities.

The list which follows—without classification—names those of the Dryads, Hamadryads, and Oreads about whom something of interest is related:

Arcadia, mother of Philonome by Nyctimus; Argeiope, mother of Thamyris by Philammon; Asterodeia, mother of Absyrtus by Aeëtes; Atlantia, mother of a number of children by Danaus; Bystonis, mother of Dryas and Tereus by Ares; Calybe, mother of Bucolion by Laomedon; Chariclo, mother of Teiresias by Everes; Chloris, mother of Mopsus by Ampycus; Clonia, mother of Orion by Hyrieus; Clymene, mother of Promachus by Parthenopaeus; Corycia, mother of Lycorus by Apollo; Cyllene, sometimes named as the mother of Callisto by Lycaon; Echo, lover of Narcissus and the mother of Iambe by Pan; Erato, mother of Apheidas, Azan, and Elatus by Arcas; Eurydice, mother of Musaeus and Dres by Orpheus; Euryte, mother of Hallirrhotius by Poseidon; Gorgyra, mother of Ascalaphus by the river-god Acheron; Idaea, mother of Teucer, Callirrhoë, and Strymo by the river-god Scamander; Lotis, changed into the lotus tree when she fled from the embraces of Priapus; Melissa, reputed to have been the discoverer of honey; Methone, mother of Oeagrus by Pierus; Neaera, mother of Evadne by the river-god Strymon and of Lampetia and Phaethusa by Helios; Nephele, mother of Phrixus and Helle by Athamas; Orseïs, mother of Aeolus, Dorus, and Xuthus by Hellen; Pareia, mother of Chryses, Eurymedon, Nephalion, and Philolaus by Minos; Pegasis, mother of Atymnius by Emathion; Phoebe, mother of a number of children by Danaus; Pyrene, mother of Cycnus by Ares; Rhene, mother of Medon by Oileus; Stymphalis, mother of Metope, Telphusa, and Themis by the river-god Ladon; and Teledice, mother of Apis, Car, and Niobe by Phoroneus.

Mnemosyne—the Mother of the Muses

The nine Muses, said to have been borne to Zeus by Mnemosyne (Memory), a daughter of Uranus and Gaea,[16] were conventionally considered to be: Clio (History), Euterpe (Lyric Poetry), Thaleia (Comedy), Melpomene (Tragedy), Terpsichore (Song and Dance), Erato (Love Poetry), Polymnia (Polyhymnia) (Hymnals), Urania (Astronomy), Calliope (Epic Poetry).

It was only natural that those gifted with the power to produce music or poetry should claim descent from the rhythmic sisters and, accordingly, it was said that Melpomene was the mother of the Sirens by the river-god Achelous; Euterpe was the mother of quick-moving Rhesus by the river-god Strymon; and Calliope was the mother of the musical Orpheus and of Marsyas by her husband, Oeagrus.[17]

The ancient home of the Muses was supposed to have been in Pieria, at the foot of Mount Olympus, but it was mythologically, and easily, removed to Mount Helicon in Boeotia, where the fountain of Hippocrene was created when the mountain rose toward the heavens in an ecstasy caused by the sweet singing of the maidens, and was kicked back into place by the hoof of the winged horse Pegasus at the bidding of his sire Poseidon. The famed Castalian Spring, held sacred to the Muses at Delphi, was reputed in later times to inspire all who washed in and drank its waters with music and poetry.

Eurynome—the Mother of the Graces

The three Graces (Charities or Charites) were Aglaea (sometimes called Pasithea), Euphrosyne, and Thaleia. Conventionally, they were considered to be the daughters of Zeus and the Oceanid Eurynome. Hera, Eunomia, Harmonia, and Lethe are all named as their mother, and both Apollo and Dionysus are named as their father.

The Homeric poems mention only one, Charis, described as the wife of Hephaestus. The three names given above, however, became generally accepted in classical literature at an early date. In the order named they were considered as the personifications of brilliance, joy, and bloom.

The Graces were conceived as the goddesses who enhanced the enjoyments of life by refinement and gentleness, and were companions of the Muses, with whom they lived at the foot of Mount Olympus. And as attendants of Hermes they assisted him, together with Peitho (Persuasion), in giving charm and eloquence to those who were favored by the gods.[18]

Themis—the Mother of the Hours

The Horae—known also as the Hours and the Seasons—were Eunomia, Dike, and Eirene, respectively considered the goddesses of order, justice, and peace.[19] Their parents were recognized as Zeus and Themis, the daughter of Uranus who was herself the personification of law and order.

In the Homeric poems, the Hours are named as the ministers of Zeus, who guard the divine palaces on Mount Olympus and promote the fertility of the earth by the various kinds of weather which they send down to mankind. They are also pictured as joining in the songs of the Muses and dancing to the music of Apollo's lyre, accompanied by the voices of the Graces, Hebe, Aphrodite, and Harmonia. Owing to the similarity of their functions, they were often confused with the Graces; according to some of the mythographers, it was they who adorned Aphrodite when she first rose from the sea.

---

[16] The parents of the Muses are also said to have been Uranus and Gaea, Zeus and Athena, or Aether and Gaea. Some legends name Pierus as their father (from which comes the Pierian Spring of the poets); Pausanias says that they were nursed by Eupheme.

[17] In the Iliad, the Muses dwell on Mount Olympus, where they are accustomed to regale the gods with their songs. Their accepted place of honor with the ancients is indicated by Herodotus, who called the nine books of the *History* by their names.

---

[18] Eustathius notes what appears to be the only incident in the lives of the Graces which was not of a general nature, saying that they contended in a beauty contest with Aphrodite and, when the seer Teiresias gave his decision to one of their number, the wrathful goddess changed the blind judge into an old woman.

[19] Pindar names Hesychia as the goddess of peace, and says that she was a daughter of Dike.

Elara— the Mother of Tityus

When Zeus debauched Elara, the daughter of Minyas and Tritogeneia,[20] he hid her in a cave beneath the island of Euboea to keep Hera from knowing of the affair. But, when she gave birth to her son, Tityus, Hera and all the world were let in on the secret—notwithstanding the god's pretension that his offspring was an autochthonous emanation of old Gaea. Nor was it to be wondered why the birth was no secret, because Tityus was of such monstrous proportions that Rhadamanthys came to Euboea all the way from the realm of Hades merely to look upon him.

At Hera's instigation, the great creature sought to seize Leto, as she was passing by on her way to visit her son's shrine at Delphi—a grievous mistake, because she called her archer-children to her assistance, and they made short work of the would-be ravisher with their fatal arrows. As punishment, he was pinned down to the floor of the lower world, where Odysseus later saw him stretched out over nine roods, while two vultures sat, one on either side, continually tearing out his liver, which ever renewed itself for more torture.[21]

---

[20] A different legend makes Elara a daughter of Orchomenus and, thus, the granddaughter of Minyas.

[21] As related in the preceding chapter, Tityus is said to have had a daughter Europa, who became the mother of Euphemus by Poseidon.

12

The Descendants of Zeus II

Leto—the Mother of Artemis and Apollo

THE CIRCUMSTANCES under which Leto gave birth to Artemis and Apollo and their individual characteristics have been fully related in chapter 3. Artemis persevered as the virgin goddess of the chase; but Apollo was not far behind his supreme father in the number of his amours and had a number of descendants who will be mentioned in the alphabetical order of the names of his wives.

Acacallis

In Crete, Acacallis (Acalle) bore to Apollo a son named Miletus, who was so attractive that her father Minos and her uncle Sarpedon quarreled over him—a quarrel which resulted in Sarpedon's fleeing with the boy to the country of Caria. There, Miletus remained and founded a city which he named for himself, but Sarpedon went farther eastward to Lycia.

By Cyanea, a daughter of the river-god Maeander, Miletus had a son, Caunus, and a daughter, Byblis, who fell in love with each other to such a degree that Caunus left his home for fear that he might commit incest with his sister, whereupon, Byblis hanged herself with her girdle and, from her sorrowing tears, a well was made, which was afterward called by her name.[1]

---

[1] According to Ovid, when Caunus left, Byblis followed him through Caria and Lycia until at last she was completely exhausted and, sinking to the earth, was changed into a well in the country of the Chimaera.

64. Descendants of Apollo and Acacallis

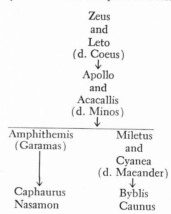

A second son of Apollo and Acacallis, named Amphithemis (known also as Garamas), somehow made his way to the country of Libya, where he became the father of Caphaurus and Nasamon, by a nymph-daughter of the water-god Triton. Nothing of interest is related about Nasamon, but Caphaurus slew the Argonaut Canthus as he was attempting to drive off his sheep and was, in turn, killed by the dead man's angered companions.

Aethusa

By Aethusa, a daughter of Poseidon and Alcyone, Apolo had two sons named Linus and Eleuther (Eleutherus).[2] Eleuther was re-

---

[2] Hesiod makes Aethusa the mother of Linus, but others name the Muse Calliope or Psamathe, a daughter of the Argive king, Crotopus.

garded as the founder of Eleutherae in Boeotia, where—according to Hyginus—he was the first to erect a temple in honor of Dionysus.[3]

65. Descendants of Apollo and Aethusa

		Zeus and Leto ↓ Apollo and Aethusa (d. Poseidon) ↓
Eleuther		Linus ↓ Pierus and
	Evippe ↓	Methone (d. Zeus) ↓
Acalanthis Chloris Colymbas Iyngx Pipo	Cenchris Cissa Dracontis Nessa	Oeagrus and Calliope (d. Zeus) ↓
Marsyas		Orpheus and Eurydice (d. Zeus) ↓
Musaeus		Dres ↓ Homer Hesiod

Linus, the ancient personification of the dirge, was a great musician, but his music was the cause of his death[4] because he was slain by Heracles with a blow from the lyre upon which he was attempting to teach the hero to play.[5]

Pierus, the son of Linus, apparently went to the birthplace of the Muses in Pieria at the foot of Mount Olympus, for it is said that there he married a woman named Evippe and became father of the nine maidens indicated on the accompanying chart.[6] Swollen with pride at their numbers and their honored birthplace, they wandered down through the country until they came to the Boeotian haunt of the Muses on Mount Helicon and proclaimed themselves as the greatest of singers. But, in the musical contest which followed, the victory was awarded to the Muses, and the humbled daughters of Pierus were changed into chattering magpies, although a similar version relates that they became doves.

As his second wife, Pierus married the nymph Methone and had a son, Oeagrus (Oeager), who is said to have become king of the Thracians. The musical blood of his ancestors was doubly fortified by his union with the Muse Calliope and their two sons, Orpheus and Marsyas, became two of its most renowned inheritors.

One day, while the goddess Athena was playing the flute on the banks of a Phrygian stream, she saw her reflection in the waters below and, observing how her features were distorted with the exercise, she threw the instrument away in disgust. When Marsyas later picked it up and blew upon it, ethereally beautiful strains issued forth—having been inspired by Athena's divine breath.[7] The foolish man was so elated at his success that he challenged Apollo to a musical contest, whose condition was that the victor might do as he pleased with his opponent, and the nine Muses were appointed to be the judges. After Apollo had played on the cithara (similar to our present-day zither) and Marsyas had played on his flute, the contest was declared a tie, but, when the god added his voice to the music of his instrument, he was awarded the victory and, as punishment for his presumption, bound Marsyas to a nearby tree and flayed him alive.

---

[3] Location of the temple in Boeotia is accounted for by the fact that Aethusa was a sister of Hyrieus, who was king of Hyria.

[4] According to Pausanias, Linus' mother, Psamathe, exposed him at birth and he was torn to pieces by dogs. Psamathe's grief betrayed her indiscretion to her father and he condemned her to death—a sentence which so aroused Apollo's indignation that he sent a plague upon the land, which ceased only when sacrifices were offered and dirges were sung in honor of his slain son.

[5] A tradition was current in Boeotia that Linus was slain when he ventured to contest in music with his father Apollo. Those who subscribed to the story of his death as an infant said that it was a second of the same name who was the slain tutor of Heracles.

[6] A different legend relates that Pierus was himself the father of the Muses, or that his nine daughters were originally called by the names of the Muses, which were changed to those shown on the chart when they were metamorphosed into magpies.

[7] The honor of inventing the flute is sometimes given to Olen—a semimythological person whose antecedents are not named. Another tradition, however, related that the inventor was Ardalus, a son of Hephaestus.

Even among a family of famous musicians, Orpheus, the son of Oeagrus, was acknowledged to have been pre-eminent. When still a youth, he was presented with a lyre by Apollo and became so proficient in performing upon it that rocks, trees and wild beasts were charmed and followed in his train. His valuable assistance as a member of the Argonautic expedition has been related in chapter 7. The best known story, however, of his musical powers is that which concerns his wife, the nymph Eurydice, who died from the bite of a serpent. His love for her was so great that he determined to brave the horrors of the lower world in order to implore her restoration. As he descended, armed only with his harp, his divine music arrested for a while the torments of the unhappy shades; the stone of Sisyphus remained motionless; Tantalus forgot his perpetual thirst and hunger; the wheel of Ixion ceased to revolve; and even the Furies shed tears. Hades and his queen, Persephone, were so sweetly affected that they consented to release Eurydice, on condition that Orpheus should not look upon her until they should have reached the upper world. Gladly promising to heed this injunction, he led the way upward, followed by Eurydice, but, at the very moment when they were about to pass the fatal boundary between life and death, the great musician was overcome by anxiety and, looking behind him, saw his dear wife being slowly drawn by invisible hands back into the realms of darkness. She was soon joined, however, by his spirit. For, in disgust at his constancy, the Thracian Maenads of Dionysus cruelly tore his body to pieces.[8]

The sons of Orpheus and Eurydice were Dres and Musaeus. Musaeus is said to have been in charge of the initiatory rites of Demeter at her temple in Eleusis,[9] but he is remembered primarily as the author of various poetic compositions, which were so well preserved that their author was often considered to have been a person of historical times. In the "Contest of Homer and Hesiod," a work composed either by Hesiod himself or by one of his admirers, it is stated that both of the ancient poets were descended from Dres, and the chain of their ancestry is so given as to make Hesiod the prior in point of time.[10]

By Asteria, a daughter of the Boeotian king, Coronus, Apollo had a son named Idmon to whom he taught the art of prophecy. As related in chapter 7, he joined the expedition of the Argonauts, although he knew beforehand that death awaited him; and he lost his life when he was attacked by a fierce boar in the country of the Mariandyni.

66. Descendants of Apollo and Asteria

Zeus
and
Leto
↓
Apollo
and
Asteria
(d. Coronus)
↓
Idmon
and
Laothoë
↓
Thestor
↓
Calchas
Leucippe
Theonoë

Thestor, the son of Idmon and his wife, Laothoë, had two daughters, Leucippe and Theonoë, and a son, Calchas.[11] Theonoë was carried off by pirates and sold to the Carian king, Icarus, who made her the mistress of his palace. When Thestor went in search of her, he was shipwrecked in Caria and was taken as a prisoner to the same palace, where he was set at

---

[8] Later legends connect Orpheus with the mysteries celebrated in honor of Dionysus and attribute to him the literature, known as the Orphic Theogony, which places at the inception of creation a double-sexed person called Phanes—shortly followed by the wine-god in the form of the horned Zagreus.

[9] The conventional legend related that the priest at Eleusis was Eumolpus, the son of Poseidon and Chione.

[10] The line of descent is continued from Dres through Eucles, Iadmonides, Philoterpes, Euphemus, Epiphrades, and Melanopus, who had sons named Dius and Apelles. Dius is said to have begotten Hesiod; Apelles begot Maeon, who was said to have been the father of Homer by a daughter of the river-god Meles, whence he received the name Melesigenes.

[11] Hyginus adds the seer Theoclymenus as a son of Thestor; but, in the Odyssey, it is related that he was a son of Polypheides, in the line of the Aeolid Cretheus.

menial labor outside the walls. After her father's failure to return from his search, Leucippe consulted the Delphic oracle and was directed to travel through all countries in the dress of a priest of Apollo. This she did and, when she finally came to the court at Caria, her own sister fell in love with her, believing that she was a man. But, as her love was not returned, Theonoë gave an order that the presumed priest should be slain—and Thestor was appointed to carry it into execution. As he was about to perform the royal command, he recognized his two daughters and Icarus (perhaps having tired of Leucippe), gave presents to all three and sent them back to their home in Corinth.[12]

Thestor's son, Calchas, was the chief soothsayer among the Greeks at Troy. His activities in that connection will be noted later, when we come to the narration of the greatest of all mythological wars.[13] While Calchas was still young, an oracle declared that his end would come when he should meet a seer wiser than himself. Returning from Troy in the company of Amphilochus, he met Mopsus, the son of Apollo and Manto, near the town of Colophon in Caria, and ventured to engage with him in the art of prophecy. But the combination of oracular blood which flowed in the veins of Mopsus[14] proved to be an overmatch for his challenger, who died of vexation when he was unable to state the number of fruits on a wild fig tree or the number of pigs which a sow was about to have—things which Mopsus was able to state with perfect accuracy.

Celaeno

According to Pausanias, a legend of Phocis related that Apollo's shrine at Delphi took its name from Delphus, who was borne to the god by Celaeno, a daughter of Hyamus, but the conventional story derives the name from the god himself as metamorphosed into a dolphin (Delphinus).

Chione

In chapter 4, we have related how Chione, the daughter of Daedalion, conceived twin sons by Poseidon and Apollo, and how she lost her life by boasting that she was personally more attractive than the goddess Artemis.

67. Descendants of Apollo and Chione

Zeus
and
Leto
↓
Apollo
and
Chione
(d. Daedalion)
↓
Philammon
and
Argiope
(d. Zeus)
↓
Thamyris
↓
Menippe

Philammon, the son whom she bore to Apollo, became closely associated with the worship of his father at Delphi, and, like his musical sire, is said to have become an outstanding performer on the cithara. As a composer of Delphian hymns, Pausanias relates that he was the victor in the second of the musical contests which were periodically held at the god's shrine in Phocis.

From the residence of his mother, Chione, at Trachis, Philammon was referred to as a Thracian bard. By the nymph Argiope he had a son Thamyris, who was equally celebrated as a musician and added a new touch to the family laurels (?) by falling in love with the boy Hyacinthus. Popular acclaim of his skill was so great that, in his conceit, he foolishly challenged the Muses to a singing contest—in which he was badly worsted and suffered the punishment of being blinded and also losing his power of song. He finally died of a broken heart, leaving a daughter, Menippe, who, according to one tradition, became the mother of Orpheus.[15]

---

[12] Asteria was descended through her father from the Aeolid Sisyphus, who was king of Corinth.

[13] Since the excavations of Heinrich Schliemann, made in 1873–76, many eminent scholars have conceded that the Trojan War was an actual event.

[14] Mopsus was said to have been the son of Apollo and Manto, the daughter of the Theban seer Teiresias.

---

[15] When he visited Mount Helicon, Pausanias saw a statue of Orpheus in the same group with that of Thamyris, who was represented as blind and with a broken lyre in his hand.

Chrysorthe

At Aegiale, on the Gulf of Corinth, Chrysorthe, the daughter of King Orthopolis, bore a son named Coronus to Apollo, who succeeded to the government when his grandfather died without male issue.

68. Descendants of Apollo and Chrysorthe

```
                  Zeus
                  and
                  Leto
                   ↓
                 Apollo
                  and
               Chrysorthe
              (d. Orthopolis)
                   ↓
                Coronus
                   ↓
       ┌──────────────────
     Corax        Lamedon
                  and
                  Pheno
               (d. Clytius)
                   ↓
                Zeuxippe
```

By an unnamed wife, Coronus had two sons, Corax and Lamedon. Corax was the elder and succeeded to the throne, but when he died childless it was seized by Epopeus, the son of Poseidon, to whom Antiope fled from Thebes—as we have related in chapter 9. After Epopeus was slain by Lycus, and Antiope was led away as a captive, Lamedon became king and married Pheno, the daughter of an Athenian named Clytius. In later years, when he was waging a war with Archander and Architeles, the sons of Acastus,[16] Lamedon procured the help of Sicyon, a prince of Attica, and gratefully bestowed upon him the hand of his daughter, Zeuxippe. And, when Lamedon died, his son-in-law became king and renamed the city Sicyon after himself.[17]

Coronis

When Coronis, the daughter of Phlegyas, was with child by Apollo, he set a raven to watch over her and was enraged upon receiving from his feathered watchman a report that the girl had become enamored of a handsome Arcadian youth named Ischys. At the god's request, his sister Artemis proceeded to destroy Coronis in her own house in Thessaly,[18] but, when the corpse was about to be burned, he saved his unborn child from the flames and carried him to the Centaur Cheiron for instruction in the arts of healing and hunting.[19]

69. Descendants of Apollo and Coronis

```
                  Zeus
                  and
                  Leto
                   ↓
                 Apollo
                  and
                 Coronis
              (d. Phlegyas)
                   ↓
                Asclepius
                  and
                 Epeione
                   ↓
       ┌──────────────────
   Podaleirius      Machaon
   Hygeia           and
   Panacea          Anticleia
                  (d. Diocles)
                   ↓
                 Alexanor
                 Gorgasus
                 Nicomachus
                 Polemocrates
```

The boy was named Asclepius[20] and, after he grew up, Athena gave him the blood from the veins on the right side of the Gorgon Medusa which, administered by him, possessed the power of curing all who were sick, and could even recall the dead.[21] But the power proved

---

[16] Pausanias says that Archander and Architeles were sons of Achaeus.

[17] The rather drab story related in the text is nevertheless interesting as an example of how the various parts of Greece were early brought in contact with each other: Aegiale is said to have been founded by Aegialeus, who came from Argolis; at the death of Corax, the kingdom was usurped by Epopeus, who came down from Thessaly, and married Antiope, a refugee from Thebes in Boeotia; and the city finally took its name from Sicyon, a man who was brought in from Attica.

[18] Another version relates that Apollo himself killed Coronis, who is sometimes called Arsinoë. The opportunity for her affair with Ischys is said to have been given while she was accompanying her father on an expedition into the Peloponnesus.

[19] According to Pausanias, the child was snatched from the flames by Hermes.

[20] The Roman name for Asclepius was Aesculapius.

[21] A different legend relates that Asclepius killed a serpent, which had twined itself around his staff, and that a second serpent appeared with a herb in its mouth which restored the life of its dead mate, and, it was this herb which gave Asclepius his power to restore the life of mortals.

fatal to Asclepius himself, for Hades complained to Zeus that the lower world was being deprived unjustly of its prospective inhabitants and the supreme god killed the great physician with a thunderbolt. At the request of Apollo, however, it is said that he was placed among the stars as the constellation Ophiuchus, and his entwined wand was apotheosized as the constellation known as the Serpent.

Some legends relate that, before his translation to the heavens, Asclepius participated in the hunt for the Calydonian boar and was also a member of the Argonautic expedition, but these honorary memberships were given out rather promiscuously, and no especial action of his is related in connection with either event. His wife was Epeione, who bore two sons, Podaleirius and Machaon, and two daughters, Hygeia and Panaceia, the respectively personifications of health and healing.

Asclepius was regarded as a semidivine person throughout all Greece, but his principal place of worship was at Epidaurus, where a local legend related that he was born and exposed by Coronis, while she was accompanying her father on an expedition into Laconia. There, his temple was surrounded by an extensive grove in which no one was permitted to die or give birth.

Like their father, Podaleirius and Machaon were skilled in the medical arts and were the physicians to the Greek army which attacked Troy. Podaleirius survived the conflict and is said to have settled, as a bachelor, among the Carians. His brother, Machaon, does not receive such summary mythological disposition. In addition to being joint leader with Podaleirius of the Oechalians at Troy, it is related that he was wounded by Paris and was carried from the battlefield by Nestor, only to be slain later, after he had cured Philoctetes of his gangrened foot.[22] At his death, he was survived by his wife, Anticleia, and the four sons named on the accompanying chart, who followed in the family footsteps by gaining renown as great physicians.

Corycia

A legend of Phocis, related by Pausanias, which gives the genealogy shown on the following chart, seems to have been invented only for the purpose of showing the descent of Celaeno, by whom Apollo is said to have sired Delphus.

70. Descendants of Apollo and Corycia

Zeus
and
Leto
↓
Apollo
and
Corycia
(d. Zeus)
↓
Lycorus
↓
Hyamus
↓
Celaeno

According to the legend, Apollo had a son, Lycorus, by a nymph named Corycia; from Lycorus, the Phocian town of Lycoreia took its name and, from his mother, a nearby fissure was called the Corycian cave. Lycorus had a son Hyamus; Hyamus had a daughter Celaeno; and the son of Celaeno and Apollo was Delphus— from whom (according to one legend) the place of the god's shrine was called Delphi.

Creusa

Although the ancient legends indicated that both Dorus and Ion (the eponymous ancestors of the Spartans and the Athenians) were grandsons of Deucalion, the Athenian dramatists tied their city more directly to a divine ancestor by claiming that Ion was actually a son of the god Apollo.[23] And, it was alleged that he marched with his army into Aegialeia (later Achaea), where the king, Selinus, gave him his daughter, Helice, as his wife, and surrendered the country which was thereafter, for a time, called Ionia.[24]

---

22 Perhaps ignorant of the legend which said that Machaon was killed at Troy by Eurypylus, the son of Telephus, both Ovid and Hyginus number him among the Greek heroes concealed in the Wooden Horse.

23 According to Euripides, Xuthus, the grandson of Deucalion, came from his home in Thessaly to assist the Athenians in a war with the Euboeans and was married to Creusa, a daughter of Erechtheus, who bore Ion to Apollo.

24 The Attic colonies along the Aegean coast of Asia Minor were collectively, and historically, called Ionia.

71. Descendants of Apollo and Creusa

Zeus
and
Leto
↓
Apollo
and
Creusa
(d. Erechtheus)
↓
Ion
and
Helice
(d. Selinus)
↓
Teleon
and
Zeuxippe
(d. Eridanus)
↓
Butes
Eribotes

Another legend relates that Ion rescued the Athenians from an attack of the Thracians under Eumolpus and, being made king of the country, divided the inhabitants into four tribes corresponding to their different modes of life, namely: soldiers, farmers, herdsmen, and artisans. The conventional story, however, is that the forces led by Eumolpus were those from neighboring Eleusis, and that the attack occurred in the reign of Erechtheus, who was Ion's maternal grandfather.

Ion's son, Teleon, is mentioned only as the father of Butes and Eribotes, who were two of the Argonauts. When the shoulder of Oileus was pierced by the dart-like feather of one of the birds of Ares, it was Eribotes who removed them and bound up the wound of his companion. Butes seems to have been more romantically inclined, for he was induced to leap from the Argo by the sweet sound of the Sirens' voices. Aphrodite, however, picked him up from the sea and carried him away to the heights of nearby Lilybaeum.[25]

Cyrene

Apollo saw Cyrene, a daughter of Hypseus, while she was wrestling with a lion on Mount Pelion in Thessaly, where her grandfather was god of the river Peneius. He carried the bold maiden to Libya and, there, she gave birth to her son Aristaeus—destined to be worshipped as a divinity because of his beneficent conduct on earth.

72. Descendants of Apollo and Cyrene

Zeus
and
Leto
↓
Apollo
and
Cyrene
(d. Hypseus)
↓
Aristaeus
and
Autonoë
(d. Cadmus)
↓
Actaeon
Macris
Nysa

While Aristaeus was still a child, his father took him to be reared by the Centaur Cheiron, and, when he grew up, the Muses gave to him as his bride, Autonoë, a daughter of Cadmus. With her, he quietly tended the flocks of the Muses as they grazed on the plains around Mount Olympus, until Apollo summoned him to the island of Ceos, which was being sorely parched from the heat of Sirius, the Dog star. There, he built a great altar and sacrificed to Zeus, with the result that the Etesian winds began to blow, which ever since, for forty days in each year, have relieved the region from the extreme heat of summer.

Within a short time, Autonoë had a son named Actaeon,[26] whom Aristaeus entrusted to Cheiron for training, as his own divine father had done with him. Under the tutelage of the gentle Centaur, the boy became a great hunter and proudly acquired a fifty-hound pack.[27] One

---

[25] One legend has it that Butes was the father of Aphrodite's son Eryx, but the conventional story relates that Poseidon was his father.

[26] Diodorus says that Aristaeus went into Libya, where his daughter Nysa acted as nursemaid to the infant Dionysus; and Apollonius says that another daughter, Macris, fed the wine-god honey on the island of Euboea.

[27] Ovid lists most of the pack, with names as follows: Melampus (Blackfoot); Ichnobates (Trail follower); Pamphagus (Voracious); Dorceus (Gazelle); Oribasus

day, however, he happened to come upon the goddess Artemis as she was bathing in the woods, and she was so infuriated that she changed him into a stag—in which form he was spotted and torn to pieces by his own dogs.[28]

Evadne

Jamus, the son of Apollo and Evadne, was born and preserved under the remarkable circumstances related in chapter 9, in connection with his grandmother, Pitane, as a wife of Poseidon. When he grew up, he went by night into the waters of the river Alpheius and prayed to be told what the future might have in store for him. The voice of Apollo was heard, commanding his son to follow where he led, and, when Jamus came to the hill of Cronus at Olympia in Elis, he was given the power to understand and explain the language of birds and to foretell events. These powers were transmitted to his descendants so that later they continued to be among the most honored families in all Greece.

Hecuba

Troilus is sometimes represented as the youngest son of Trojan Priam and his wife, Hecuba, but the conventional legend relates that Apollo was his father. Because an oracle had prophesied that Troy would never be taken if he should attain the age of twenty years, Achilles captured the youth and, in cold blood, either killed him or caused others to strangle him to death.[29]

Hyria

By Hyria, a daughter of Amphinomus, Apollo had a son named Cycnus who was considered the handsomest hunter in the country of Aetolia. Following the fashion which Thamyris first set, many suitors besought his love, but he repulsed all of them except Phyllius, who was so persistent that Cycnus tried to get rid of him by imposing three labors to be performed as the price for his affection. These were: (1) to kill a lion without weapons; (2) to catch alive and tame some wild birds, and (3) to bring in a wild bull. Phyllius completed all of the bidden tasks, but, when he hesitated to deliver the bull, Cycnus impetuously leapt from a cliff and was changed into a swan. In the belief that her son had been killed, Hyria melted away in tears and was metamorphosed into a lake, which was afterward called by her name.

Manto

As related in chapter 8, Manto, daughter of the blind seer Teiresias, was captured by the Epigoni after the fall of Thebes. Some time after being taken, she is reputed to have borne a son, Amphilocus, and a daughter, Tisiphone, to the crazed Alcmaeon and, being later dedicated with other captives to Apollo at Delphi, bore to the god a son who was named Mopsus.[30] Earlier, in this chapter, mention is made of the contest between Mopsus and Calchas, the son of Thestor, in which the former gained the victory by accurately naming the number of fruits on a wild fig tree and the number of pigs which a sow was about to farrow.

Although neither Mopsus nor Amphilochus is mentioned in the Iliad, Strabo notes a fable which said that they returned together from Troy and founded a town in Cilicia called Mallus. He adds, that Amphilochus proceeded on to Argos but returned to Mallus where, being excluded from a share in the government, he

---

(Mountain ranger); Nebrophonus (Faun killer); Theron (Hurricane); Laelaps (Hunter); Pterelas (Winged); Agre (Hunter); Hylaeus (Sylvan); Nape (Glen); Harpyia (Shepherd); Ladon (Seizer); Dromas (Catcher); Canace (Runner); Sticte (Gnasher); Tigris (Spot); Alce (Tigress); Leucon (Might); Asbolus (White); Lacon (Soot); Aello (Spartan); Thous (Whirlwind); Lycisce (Swift); Cyprius (Cyprian); Harpalos (Wolf); Melaneus (Grasper); Lachne (Black); Labros (Shag); Agriodos (Fury); Hylactor (White tooth); and others, whose translated names mean Barker, Black hair, Beast killer, and Mountaineer.

[28] Other traditions relate that Actaeon provoked the anger of Artemis by boasting that he excelled her in hunting, or that he was punished, at the command of Zeus, because he sued for the hand of his aunt Semele, upon whom the supreme god was casting covetous eyes.

[29] Although Troilus, and the names of other Trojans and Greeks at Troy, are used in the play of Shakespeare, entitled "Troilus and Cressida," the plot is wholly mediaeval.

[30] According to Pausanias, Manto and other Theban captives were sent by Apollo to found a colony in Asia Minor and came to Clarus, near Colophon in Caria, where they were overcome by some armed Cretans and taken before their leader, Rhacius. He married Manto and became the father of Mopsus, who assisted him in conquering the Carians and taking over their country.

engaged Mopsus in single combat in which both of them were slain.[31]

Melia

When old Oceanus sent out Caänthus to seek his sister, Melia, the boy found that she had been carried away by Apollo and threw fire into one of the god's sacred groves. As a result, he was slain by Apollo. In good time, Melia bore twin sons, named Ismenus and Tenerus. When they reached manhood, Tenerus became famed as a seer and gave his name to a plain of Boeotia, and Ismenus gave his name to the Boeotian river which had previously been called Ladon.[32]

Milesian Woman

The unnamed woman of Miletus, who bore Branchus to Apollo, dreamed during her delivery that the Sun was passing through her body—a dream which the seers agreed to be a favorable sign. And their prediction proved to be correct, because the god endowed his son with extraordinary powers of prophecy and appointed his descendants—the Branchidae—to preside as the priests of his renowned oracle, which was founded and greatly revered at Miletus for many years.

Parthenope

Parthenope, a daughter of the Argonaut Ancaeus, bore to Apollo a son Lycomedes on the island of Chios; but, when the boy grew up, he became king of the Dolopians on the nearby island of Scyrus.

He is remembered in mythology for two reasons. First, he hid Achilles among the maidens of his court,[33] in a futile attempt to prevent his

73. Descendants of Apollo and Parthenope

Zeus
and
Leto
↓
Apollo
and
Parthenope
(d. Ancaeus)
↓
Lycomedes
↓
Deidameia

conscription for the Trojan War—an attempt which, however, resulted in his obtaining the great hero as the husband of his daughter, Deidameia; and second, because when Theseus visited Scyrus to claim an estate which he had on the island, Lycomedes led him up to a mountaintop, on the pretext of showing him the lands from that point of vantage, and pushed him to his death over a precipice.

Phthia

The justification for this insertion in our composite genealogical chart is the statement of Apollodorus that Aetolus, after slaying Apis in Elis, fled to the country of the Curetes[34] and, there killed the sons of Apollo named Dorus, Laodocus, and Polypoetes—after which he took over the government and named the land Aetolia for himself.

74. Descendants of Apollo and Phthia

Zeus
and
Leto
↓
Apollo
and
Phthia
↓
Dorus
Laodocus
Polypoetes

---

[31] Amphilochus and Calchas traveled together from Troy to "Pamphylian and Cilician burgs"—according to Quintus Smyrnaeus, who does not mention the contest between Mopsus and Calchas.

[32] The Boeotian river, Ladon, should not be confused with the one of the same name which flowed through Arcadia.

[33] Pausanias relates that, at Chios, Apollo had a son Lycomedes by Parthenope, daughter of Ancaeus and granddaughter of Astypalaea, who was a daughter of Phoenix. According to Strabo, the Chians claimed that their original settlers came from Thessaly. Apollodorus says that, when Phoenix was blinded, Peleus brought him to Cheiron in Thessaly and made him king of the Dolopians. It is agreed that Lycomedes, the father of

Deidameia, was king of the Dolopians on the island of Scyrus, which is only about sixty-five miles distant from Chios. Under these circumstances, we take the liberty of inserting him in the genealogy above outlined.

[34] According to Strabo, the original inhabitants of Aetolia were called Curetes because of their long hair. When they were overcome, they retired to Acarnania, but, retaining their unusual hirsute custom, they were eventually confounded with the eccentric Curetes (Corybantes), who are said to have been the attendants of Zeus on the island of Crete.

The legend—insofar as it mentions Dorus as a son of Apollo—was advanced in later years by the Dorian inhabitants of Sparta to support their claim of direct descent from the archer-god—a claim used to offset the pretensions of the inhabitants of Athens that their eponymous ancestor, Ion, was of the same divine degree.

Rhoeo

When Staphylus, the father of Rhoeo, thought that she had been seduced by a mortal man, he shut her up in a chest and cast her into the sea. But the chest was carried by the waves onto the shores of the island of Delos, and Rhoeo gave birth to a son of Apollo, whom she named Anius. She laid the child on the altar of the temple and prayed to the god to save its life, if he should indeed be its father, and, with the dispatch peculiar to myth, the babe was mysteriously taken away, was reared in a place of concealment and reappeared as a man endowed with prophetic powers.

75. Descendants of Apollo and Rhoeo

Zeus
and
Leto
↓
Apollo
and
Rhoeo
(d. Staphylus)
↓
Anius
and
Dorippe
↓
Elaïs
Oeno
Spermo

By a wife named Dorippe, Anius had three daughters, Elaïs, Oeno, and Spermo, to whom Dionysus gave the faculty of producing at will any desired quantity of wine, corn, and oil.[35]

When the Greeks landed at Delos, on their way to Troy, Anius unsuccessfully tried to persuade them to remain with him for nine years, because it was foretold that Troy would not be taken until the tenth year. He promised, with the help of his three daughters, to provide them with all the nourishment which they might need during that long period. But his hospitable offer was refused, and the Greeks continued their voyage, after first loading their ships with supplies which the maidens deftly produced.[36]

Sinope

According to Diodorus Siculus, Apollo seized Sinope, a daughter of the river-god Asopus, and carried her from Greece to a place on the southern coast of the Euxine Sea, which was afterwards named for her. And there she gave birth to a son, Syrus, who was claimed as the eponymous ancestor of the Syrians.[37]

Stilbe

By Stilbe, a daughter of the river-god Peneius, Apollo had two sons who were named Lapithes and Aeneus.[38] Aeneus married Aenete, a daughter of Eusorus; their son Cyzicus became king of the Doliones in Mysia, near the home of the earthborn men, who were encountered by the Argonauts on their voyage to Colchis.[39]

---

[35] Dionysus was the father of Staphylus, the father of Rhoeo: this made the daughters of Anius his great-grandchildren. Each of the wine-growers, as they were collectively called, received the power of producing the thing from which she derived her name. Thus, Elaïs, whose name came from the Greek word for "olive" could produce olive oil; Oeno could produce wine; and Spermo, meaning "seed," could produce corn.

[36] Tzetzes says that, after the Greeks reached Troy, Agamemnon sent for the wine growers and peremptorily ordered them to feed his army, and they did so, but, according to Ovid, they were frightened and rushed away, with the Greeks in pursuit—whereupon, they prayed to Dionysus and he changed them into white doves.

[37] The geographer Strabo relates a different legend, saying that the Sinopians claimed that the founder of their city was Autolycus, who was an Argonautic companion of Heracles.

[38] Perhaps influenced by the association implicit in the battle of the Lapiths and the Centaurs at the wedding of Peirithous and Hippodameia, Diodorus adds Centaurus as a son of Apollo and Stilbe—making him the eponymous ancestor of the horse-men; but the generally accepted legend makes them the offspring of Ixion, a grandson of Ares.

[39] According to Apollonius Rhodius, the Doliones were descendants of Poseidon, who protected them from the inroads of their earthborn neighbors; but Strabo notes a legend that Dolion, their eponymous ancestor, was a son of Silenus and Melia.

76. Descendants of Apollo and Stilbe

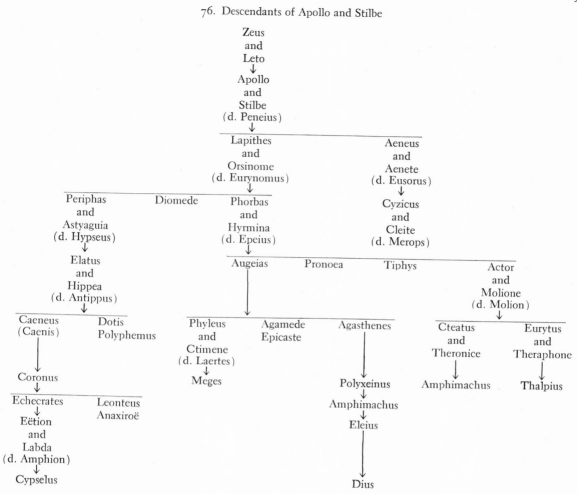

As related in chapter 7, Cyzicus and his fair wife, Cleite, kindly entertained the Argonauts with a banquet in their palace and, after giving them such information as they could about the remaining journey, saw their guests row off from the Mysian shores—only to be slain in battle with them when contrary winds drove the voyagers back in the night to the land which they unwittingly thought was held by hostile strangers.

By Orsinome, daughter of Eurynomus, Lapithes had two sons, Phorbas and Periphas, and a daughter Diomede, who became the wife of the Lacedaemonian king, Amyclas. After Lapithes died, his Thessalian kingdom was ruled jointly by his sons and its inhabitants were known thereafter as the Lapiths, or Lapithae. Periphas married Astyaguia, a daughter of

Hypseus,[40] and begot a son named Elatus, who is remembered as the father of three children, borne by Hippea, daughter of Antippus. They were a daughter Dotis, a son Polyphemus, and another child who turned out to be an odd combination of both genders.

Dotis became, by Ares, the maternal ancestress of the Centaurs, who were the offspring of her grandson Ixion, and Polyphemus, as related in chapter 7, was one of the Argonauts, who assisted Heracles in his search for the lost youth Hylas, and was left behind in the land of the Mysians, where he founded the city of Cius. The third child of Elatus and Hippea was a girl named Caenis, but, after she was seduced by

---

[40] Hypseus was a brother of Stilbe, who was the grandmother of Periphas.

Poseidon, the god granted her request that she be changed into an invulnerable man. Following the metamorphosis, he was called Caeneus; and, in the battle with the Centaurs, he was vanquished, although often wounded, only when he was driven into the earth like a pile by repeated blows which his assailants gave to him with fir trees. As he disappeared beneath the overwhelming heap, a bird with yellow wings was seen flying away from the place, and the seer Mopsus averred that it was the unconquerable man in a changed form.[41]

Coronus, the son of Caeneus, was one of the Argonauts. He returned from the expedition to become king of the Lapiths. But Heracles, seemingly, did not consider their past comradeship, because, when Coronus got into a war with his neighboring king, Aegimius, over their respective boundaries, the ubiquitous hero's assistance was enlisted by his adversary and he killed Coronus on the battlefield. Coronus was survived by his daughter, Anaxiroë, who married the Elean king, Epeius, and by him had two sons, Echecrates and Leonteus. The latter of these, with his kinsman Polypoetes, led the Lapiths from Gyrtone in forty ships to the Trojan War, where he killed a number of the enemy and contended in the funeral games of Patroclus.

Eëtion, the son of Echecrates, migrated to Corinth, which was then governed by an oligarchy in which a man named Amphion was a member. Amphion had a lame daughter named Labda, whom the newcomer married, but, as he had no children by her, he went to Delphi and received an answer which the Corinthian elders took to mean that he was destined to have a son who would overthrow their rule. Accordingly, they determined to destroy the child when it should be born and, upon the occurrence of its birth, they went to the home of Labda to carry out their purpose. The babe smiled so sweetly, however, that none of them could bring himself to commit the planned act, and they departed. As they closed the door of the house, they in-

dulged in mutual accusations over their soft-heartedness, and agreed to reenter to execute their original design, but Labda heard the conversation and hid her child in a chest where he could not be found. When he later grew up, he was named Cypselus and, following his father's example, consulted the oracle and was told to take possession of the city. This he did, and Corinth fell under the rulership of its first tyrant.[42]

According to one tradition, Phorbas—who succeeded to the government of the Lapiths jointly with his brother Periphas—left Thessaly, at the call of the Rhodians, and delivered their island from a plague of snakes, after which (according to one legend) he was placed in the heavens as the constellation Ophiuchus.[43] However, the conventional story relates that he went to Elis to assist its king, Epeius, in a war against Pelops, and wound up by receiving a share of the kingdom and the king's daughter, Hyrmina, as his bride.[44] By her, he had a daughter Pronoea, who married Aetolus,[45] and three sons, who were named Augeias,[46] Actor and Tiphys.[47]

In chapter 7, we have already related that Tiphys was the first helmsman of the Argo and that he died on the voyage to Colchis, when the Argonauts stopped at the land of the Mariandyni.

Actor (whose name was identical with at

---

41 According to another tradition, Caeneus set up his spear in the market place and ordered the Lapiths to swear their oaths by it as a divine symbol and, when he himself sacrificed to no other god, wrathful Zeus instigated the attack of the Centaurs against him.

42 The chest of Cypselus—made of cedar, ivory, and gold and richly adorned with figures in relief—remained in the possession of his descendants who dedicated it to Hera at her temple in Olympia, where it was seen by Pausanias about the end of the second century A.D.

43 The story of Hyginus, which considers the constellation Ophiuchus as the heavenly translation of Phorbas (instead of Asclepius), naturally follows from his extermination of serpents, which were the conventional insignia of physicians.

44 According to Apollodorus, the Elean king of Alector who married a daughter of Phorbas named Diogeneia and, in turn, gave his sister, Hyrmina, as a second wife to his ally.

45 The legends of Elis and of Aetolia, across the Gulf of Patras, are so intermingled that Pronoea's husband is said to have been her own great uncle, for her grandfather, Epeius, was her husband's brother.

46 Augeias was sometimes named as a son of Eleius, which being confused with Helios, resulted in his being called a son of Apollo, who succeeded to the functions of the older Sun-god.

47 Apollodorus and Apollonius Rhodius call Tiphys a son of Hagnias, a man whose antecedents are not given by them.

least five other mythological personages), is remembered chiefly because of the sons whom he had by Molione—two boys, named Cteatus and Eurytus, who were perhaps the first recorded Siamese twins.[48] But they surpassed all of their generation in strength and once, while Heracles was sick, forced him to retire before their double onslaught. As was the inevitable fate, however, of all who opposed the great hero, they were finally waylaid and slain by him—each leaving a widow and a son surviving. The widows were sisters, named Theronice and Theraphone, and their sons, Amphimachus and Thalpius, proved worthy of their ancestry by being among the foremost suitors of divine Helen and joint leaders of the Eleans in the expedition to bring her back from Troy.

The most renowned son of Phorbas and Hyrmina was Augeias who was one of the principal Argonauts;[49] but is better remembered as the king of Elis and the owner of many cattle whose filthy stables Heracles cleansed in one day. Ignorant of the fact that the hero was obliged to the task by the bidding of Eurystheus under a heavenly decree, Augeias promised to give a tenth part of his herds for the work's accomplishment. But, when Heracles led the rivers Alpheius and Peneius through the stables, and their combined current swept out the offal in less than the allotted time, the king reneged on his promise and the great man left—vowing a vengeance which he later took by returning and killing Augeias, after first defeating his army led by the Moliones.

Surviving Augeias were two daughters, Agamede and Epicaste, and two sons who were named Agasthenes and Phyleus. Agamede married Mulius, a man acquainted with the healing powers of plants and who was slain in battle by Nestor, as related in chapter 10. Epicaste was appropriated by Heracles, as a trophy of his victory over her father, and later bore a son to him who was called Thestalus. Agasthenes suc-

ceeded to the Elean kingdom and was followed by his son, Polyxeinus, who was one of the suitors of Helen and became a joint-leader with the sons of the Moliones in the Trojan War.[50]

Phyleus took the part of Heracles in the original dispute with Augeias and was forced by his father to flee to the island of Dulichium, off the coast of Acarnania. While there, he met and married Ctimene, daughter of Laertes, and sister of Odysseus who was the ruler of the nearby island of Ithaca. By her he had a son Meges, who was one of Helen's suitors and the leader of forty ships which were sailed to Troy by their crews from Dulichium and its surrounding islands.[51] Returning from the war, Meges was one of the unfortunate Greeks lured by the torches of Nauplius to the promontory of Caphareus, where he was shipwrecked and perished.

Thero

Pausanias relates that the ancient Boeotian town of Arne took its later name of Chaeroneia from Chaeron, a son of Apollo and Thero. She was a daughter of Phylas and Leipephilene.[52]

"Madame X"

It is said that Melaneus was considered to be a son of Apollo because he was a good archer. After the Aeolid Perieres was summoned from Thessaly to assume the throne at Messene (because there were no male survivors of the ruling house of Lelex), Melaneus followed him into his new country and was assigned a town for his habitation, which he called Oechalia after his wife.

---

[48] From their mother's name the strong youths were often referred to as the Moliones or the Molionides; from their father, they were sometimes called the Actorides. And, because of their strength, they were sometimes said to have been sons of the sea-god Poseidon.

[49] His activities as a member of the band are discussed in chapter 7.

[50] Apollodorus says that Polyxeinus returned safely from the war and begat a son Amphimachus (named for his kinsman, the son of Cteatus, who died at Troy). Carrying the genealogy farther, he says that Amphimachus had a son Eleius, who was king of Elis when the descendants of Heracles were preparing to invade the country, and Eleius had a son Dius, who surrendered his army to the victorious enemy.

[51] It is said that, after Heracles killed Augeias, he recalled Phyleus from Dulichium and placed him on the Elean throne. According to one of many contradictory legends, it was at this time that he instituted the Olympic games at Olympia in Elis, which—with interruptions—have continued to be held in every fourth year. However, in historical Greek chronology, the date of the first games was placed at 776 B.C.—long after the time of the great hero.

[52] Pausanias cites the "Great Eoeae" as relating that Thero had a twin-brother named Hippotes.

77. Descendants of Apollo and "Madame X"

Zeus
and
Leto
↓
Apollo
and
"Madame X"
↓
Melaneus
and

Oechalia   Stratonice
(d. Pleuron)
↓
Eurytus
and
Antiope
(d. Pylas)
↓

Clytius   Molion   Iole
Didaeon
Iphitus
Toxeus

Molione

When Oechalia died, he took as his second wife, Stratonice, a daughter of the Aetolian prince, Pleuron; by her had a son, Eurytus, who succeeded to the rulership of the city,[53] and became renowned as an archer of skill exceeding even that of his father. Eurytus solidified his political hold on his kingdom by marrying Antiope, a daughter of Pylas and great-grand-daughter of Lelex. By her, he begot a daughter, Iole, and five sons—named Clytius, Didaeon, Iphitus, Toxeus, and Molion—whom he taught to use the bow with accuracy almost equal to his own. His instruction was not wasted on Clytius and Iphitus in their expedition as members of the Argonauts. Certain of the family's invincibility, Eurytus now offered the hand of Iole as a prize to any man who should conquer his sons and himself in an archery contest. The challenge, however, proved to be too general, for along came Heracles, whom Eurytus had himself taught to use the bow in earlier

years. Stricken with a madness sent upon him by Hera, he had but recently killed his own children by Megara and, having left her matured charms, was in search of a younger wife. After one look at beautiful Iole, he took up the challenge and won—as he always did. But Eurytus and his sons (except Iphitus) refused to surrender the maiden for fear that he might again become mad and slay the children which she might bear to him.

Heracles went back to Thebes in anger and later, while he was away from home, some of the cattle of Eurytus were stolen by Autolycus, but the Oechalian king attributed the theft to him. However, Iphitus disbelieved the charge and, going to Thebes after the hero had returned, told him of the missing cattle, and received his promise to help in the search for them. Unfortunately, as they were about to set out, the old madness returned and Heracles killed his companion by throwing him from the walls of the city.

Years later, after many more adventures, the memory of Iole remained with Heracles and he attacked Oechalia, slew Eurytus and his remaining sons,[54] and took the maiden by force. But her marriage with the greatest of all heroes was prevented by his death, and she had to be content as the bride of his son Hyllus.

Since Apollo eventually came to be identified as the god of the sun, his worship was extended throughout the ancient world and the inhabitants of many places sought to trace their lineage back to him through other descendants, about whom nothing of particular interest is related.[55]

---

[53] Other cities named Oechalia, in both Thessaly and Boeotia, claimed to have been ruled by the archer-king, Eurytus.

[54] In the Odyssey, it is related that Eurytus was slain by Apollo for his temerity in challenging the god to an archery contest. As previously mentioned in the introduction, Molion was survived by his daughter Molione, who became mother of the Siamese twins, Cteatus and Eurytus.

[55] For example, Apollo and Dryope are said to have had a son named Amphissus, who was noted for his great strength, and is said to have founded the town of Oeta in Thessaly.

The Descendants of Zeus III

Niobe—the Mother of Pelasgus and Argus

NIOBE WAS a daughter of Phoroneus and was a granddaughter of the god of the river Inachus, the earliest name in the antiquity of Argos (Argolis). Notwithstanding her descent from a river-god, it is said that she was the first mortal woman with whom Zeus consorted, and she bore two sons named Pelasgus[1] and Argus to him.

By an unidentified wife, Pelasgus had a son, Temenus, who, according to a legend of Arcadia, dwelt at Stymphalus and there reared the goddess Hera. By another, he had a son, Haemon, from whom the country of Thessaly was anciently known as Haemonia—deriving its later name from Haemon's son Thessalus.[2] The best remembered son of Pelasgus, however, was Lycaon, who was borne to him by the Oceanid Meliboea. Unlike his half brothers, he despised the gods and, when he grew up, defied them by referring to himself as Zeus. Notwithstanding his presumption, the supreme god espoused his daughter Callisto—but with tragic results which are related in chapter 15.[3]

By various women, Lycaon had a daughter, Callisto (Helice), and a great number of sons, whose names are given on the following chart.[4] As inheritors of their father's impiety, they became known as the most savage and wicked of all mankind—a reputation which Zeus decided to investigate in person. Accordingly, he disguised himself as a mortal and appeared at their home as they were about to dine and, being invited to join in the meal, he was served with the flesh of a child whom they had slain. In complete disgust, the god overturned the dinner table and struck Lycaon and all of his sons dead with thunder, except Nyctimus.[5] And, according to tradition, it was this firsthand experience with men's wickedness which caused the supreme deity to send the flood from which only Deucalion and Pyrrha escaped.

---

[1] A different legend relates that Pelasgus was an autochthon, from whom the original inhabitants of Greece were sprung, and from whom they were known as Pelasgians.

[2] Others say that Thessaly took its name from Thessalus, the son of Heracles and Chalciope.

[3] The nymph Cyllene is sometimes called the mother of Callisto who, in afterlife, was often referred to as Helice.

---

[4] The names and numbers of Lycaon's sons are variously stated. The list given in the accompanying chart represents a composite of those named by Apollodorus and Pausanias. Lycaon is also said to have been a half brother of Phrastor, borne to Pelasgus by the Naiad-nymph Menippe, but nothing of interest is related about him.

[5] According to Pausanias, Lycaon and his sons were struck dead when they offered on the altar of Zeus a libation which consisted of the blood of a slain child. He adds that Lycaon was changed into a wolf. Nyctimus is said to have been Lycaon's youngest son (although Apollodorus calls him the eldest); and the multitude of his brothers is explained by the urge to create eponyms for various towns and localities. Thus, Macedonia for Macednus; Pallantium for Pallas; Orethasium for Orestheus; Phigalia for Phigalus; Trapezus for Trapezus; Thocnia for Thocnus; Acacesium for Acacus; and Tegea for Tegeates.

78. Descendants of Zeus and Niobe

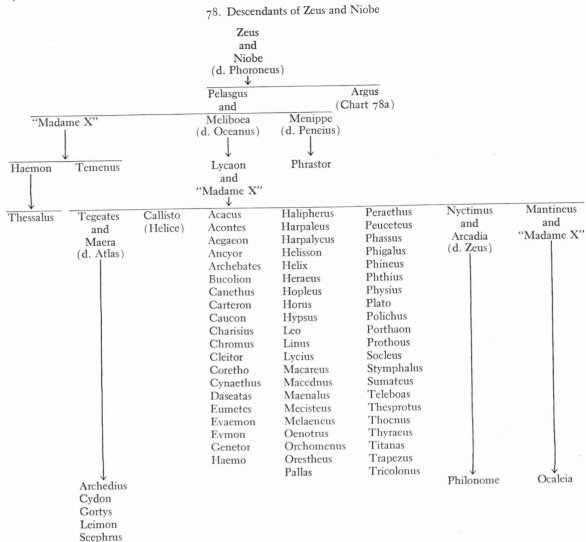

Nyctimus is said to have married the nymph Arcadia and to have begotten a daughter named Philonome, who became a companion to Artemis, but was later expelled from her huntress-train when she was seduced by Poseidon.

Of the other sons of Lycaon: Mantineus was survived by his daughter Ocaleia (sometimes called Aglaea), who became the mother of Proetus and Acrisius by the Argive king, Abas; Tegeates was survived by his wife, Maera (a daughter of Atlas), and his five sons whose names are given on the accompanying chart.[6]

The kingdom of Phoroneus (mentioned in chapter 4 as a son of the river-god Inachus) is said to have extended over the whole Peloponnesus. When he died, he left two sons—Apis and Car—of whom Apis took over the rulership

---

[6] Pausanias relates that Tegea was one of the places which refused admission to Leto when she was seeking a

place where she could give birth to Apollo and Artemis. After Apollo was born he came to the town and complained to Scephrus, in a private conversation which Leimon thought was aimed against him, whereupon, he rushed upon his brother and killed him. But immediate punishment overtook him in the form of a fatal arrow from Artemis. The three other sons of Tegeates, frightened at the event, migrated to the island of Crete, where they founded cities which were named after them, Cydonia, Gortyna, and Catreus (Archedius).

78a. Descendants of Zeus and Niobe

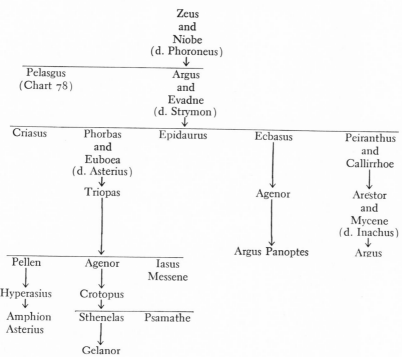

of the country, around the cities of Tiryns and Mycenae, which was first called Apia after his name. Car, however, went into Attica and founded the city which was later called Megara. Apis proved to be such a harsh ruler that he was assassinated by his subjects, and he was succeeded by Argus, the son of Zeus and his sister Niobe. After him, the kingdom of a portion of the country was given the name of Argos (or Argolis), and he erected his capital city at Argos about three miles from the coast of the Saronic Gulf. (The inhabitants became known as Argives.)

By his wife, Evadne, daughter of the river-god Strymon,[7] Argus had five sons, who were named Criasus,[8] Phorbas, Epidaurus, Ecbasus,[9]

and Peiranthus.[10] Of these, nothing of interest is related about Criasus; Epidaurus seems to have been created only for the purpose of giving an eponym to the city of that name located on the Argive coast. Phorbas married Euboea, a daughter of the river-god Asterius, who is said to have been one of the nurses of Hera when she was being reared at Stymphalus by Temenus. Their son, Triopas, succeeded to the kingdom when Phorbas died and, by an unnamed wife, had a daughter, Messene, and three sons, who were named Pellen, Agenor, and Iasus. Of these, Messene married Polycaon, a son of Lelex, and gave her name to his realm of Messenia (as well as his capital city of Messene); Pellen, migrating to Achaea, where the district of Pellene was named for him, gained an added, albeit vicarious, renown as the grandfather of the Argonauts Amphion and Asterius, sons of his son Hyperasius.

Agenor followed his father Triopas in the

---

[7] It is not explained how Argus, ruling in the Peloponnesus, happened to marry Evadne, who was a daughter of the god of the Macedonian river Strymon. Perhaps because of this geographical hurdle, others name the Oceanid Peitho as his wife.

[8] Criasus is called Crinus by Hyginus.

[9] Ecbasus is called Basus by Hyginus. A different legend, which ignores Phorbas, makes him the father of Agenor and grandfather of Argus Panoptes (as above indicated), but continues the genealogy by relating that

he was the great-grandfather of Iasus and the great-great-grandfather of Crotopus.

[10] Peiranthus is sometimes called Peiras or Piras.

rulership, but he soon died, leaving a young son Crotopus, during whose infancy Iasus acted as regent. When Crotopus reached his majority, he assumed the throne and was succeeded by his son, Sthenelas,[11] and his grandson, Gelanor a successive trinity of governments which seem to have been uneventful. In the reign of Gelanor, however, one of mythology's high spots appeared, for Danaus and his fifty daughters came to Argos from Egypt and, asserting a superior claim to the country, Gelanor was forced to abdicate.[12]

Ecbasus had a son, Agenor, who is barren of interest except as the father of Argus Panoptes. This man-creature was represented as having a hundred eyes which looked in all directions, and were never all closed by sleep at the same time. And it was he whom Hera set to act as guard over Io, a maiden ravished by amorous Zeus under circumstances narrated later in this chapter. In addition to his "all-seeing" powers, he was of superhuman strength and, prior to his custodianship of Io, was reputed to have slain a fierce bull which was ravaging Arcadia and also to have destroyed the assassins of Apis.[13]

Peiranthus, the last charted son of Argus and Evadne, married a woman of uncertain lineage named Callirrhoe, and their son, Arestor, married Mycene, a daughter of the river-god Inachus, who bore to him another Argus, famed as the builder of the ship Argo under the divine supervision of Hera.[14]

Aega—the Mother of Aegipan

Aega, a daughter of the ancient Sun-god Helios, was herself so dazzling that the Titans prevailed upon Gaea to place her in a Cretan cave, where she bore to Zeus a son who was called Aegipan. The story is a comparatively late fiction, which we have noticed here only because Apollodorus relates that Aegipan assisted Hermes in refitting to Zeus the tendons which had been taken from him by the giant Typhon.

Io—the Mother of Epaphus

On the island adjoining the Greek mainland, first known as Abantis, one of the priestesses of Hera was Io, a fair daughter of the river-god Inachus.[15] Attracted by her beauty, Zeus seduced her and, when Hera approached, he sought to hide his unfaithful action by changing the maiden into a white cow. From this circumstance, the island was thereafter called Euboea, from the Greek word meaning "fine cattle."

Knowing her spouse's natural bent for love-making, Hera was not taken in by his protestations of innocence[16] and, contriving to obtain possession of the animal, placed her under the care of Argus Panoptes, who tied her to an olive tree, where she continued to remain under the surveillance of his hundred eyes. At the bidding of his father, however, Hermes succeeded in putting all of the eyes to sleep through the soft music of his magic lyre and, in his helpless condition, slew the queer creature with the casting of a stone.[17] According to a later story, Hera gratefully rewarded Argus' services by placing his eyes in the tail of the peacock, which was known thereafter as her favorite bird.[18]

The vengeful goddess, now doubly wrathful, sent a gadfly to worry her unfortunate rival who, in the attempt to escape from her incessant

---

[11] Crotopus also had a daughter named Psamathe, who, according to Pausanias, was the mother of Linus.

[12] The claim of Danaus, although previously stated in chapter 9, is here repeated, as based on the following pedigree: Danaus was a son of Belus; Belus was a son of Poseidon and Libya; Libya was a daughter of Epaphus; Epaphus was a son of Zeus and Io; Io was a daughter of the god of the river Inachus, who was the aboriginal sovereign of the whole Peloponnesus.

[13] Even in a family whose relationships were much confused, Argus Panoptes appears as an extreme example. His father is variously named as Agenor, Arestor, Inachus, or Argus. Aeschylus in his "Prometheus Bound" has Io refer to her custodian as an autochthon.

[14] As the son of Arestor, the builder of the Argo is often referred to as Arestorides.

---

[15] Apollodorus says that the father of Io was Iasus, a son of Argus Panoptes and Ismene—thus making Argus the jailer of his own grandchild.

[16] From this incident, Hesiod says that "oaths touching the matter of love do not draw down anger from the gods"—perhaps the antecedent of our "all is fair in love or war."

[17] From this exploit, Hermes derived the surname of Argeiphontes, meaning "Argus-slayer."

[18] Schliemann's excavations at Mycenae unearthed a number of images of Hera herself, represented as a cow —conformably to her Homeric description as being "ox-eyed."

79. Descendants of Zeus and Io

Zeus
and
Io
(d. Inachus)
↓
Epaphus
and
Memphis
(d. Nilus)
↓
Libya

torment, wandered all over the ancient world[19] until, at last, she found freedom and rest on the banks of the river Nile in Egypt. There, she gave birth to a black son,[20] named Epaphus, who later became king of the country, and is said to have founded the city of Memphis, named in honor of his wife, a daughter of the god of the river where he was born.

In due time, Epaphus and Memphis had a daughter named Libya, who bore to Poseidon three sons—Agenor, Lelex, and Belus—previously mentioned in chapter 9 as connecting links in the dynasties and myths of Greece and Africa.[21]

Danae—the Mother of Perseus

Acrisius, a great-grandson of Danaus and a descendant of Io, was alarmed because he had no son to succeed him to his throne at Argos. But, when he consulted the oracle at Delphi, he was more alarmed upon being told that he would be slain by his own grandchild, if his daughter, Danae, should give birth to a son. To prevent such a happening, he returned to his palace and imprisoned his daughter in a subterranean apartment or, according to a different version of the legend, in a tower built of brass. But Zeus changed himself into a shower of gold and, coming down through a skylight in the roof, embraced the maiden, who thereafter became the mother of his son Perseus.

When Acrisius learned of the miraculous birth, he placed both mother and child in a chest which he put out to sea. Zeus, however, caused the chest to float onto the shore of the island of Seriphus—one of the Cyclades in the Aegean Sea—where it was found by Dictys, a son of the Aeolid Magnes, who carried its frail occupants to his brother, King Polydectes.

As the years passed by and young Perseus grew into manhood, the king courted Danae's favor, but his affection was not returned.[22] He thought of taking her by force and was restrained only by the fear that her strong son might intervene. He, therefore, sought to achieve his purpose by stratagem, and fired Perseus with an ambition to destroy the Gorgon Medusa—hoping that the attempt would fail, and that the youth would be turned into stone upon viewing the creature's snaky head.

Preparing for the adventure, Perseus first went to the island of Samos, where Athena showed him an image of the Gorgon and told him that he need not be concerned about her two immortal sisters, Sthenno and Euryale.[23] He then set out to equip himself, and was fortunate in obtaining divine assistance from several sources. The nymphs gave him winged sandals, a leathern pouch, and the helmet of Hades, which had the power of making its wearer invisible; Hermes gave him a sharp sword; and Athena gave him a shield, polished so brightly that it seemed like a mirror. Thus accoutered, he flew on his winged sandals to the home of the mysterious Graeae—the three grey-haired maidens who had only one eye and one tooth between them, and who were endowed with prophetic powers. Invisibly approaching, under the cover of his magic helmet, he seized their single tooth and eye, which he refused to restore until they told him how to reach the land of the Gorgons. Following their directions, he

---

[19] The ancient authorities are divided on the question of whether the Ionian Sea took its name from Io or from Ion, the son of Apollo and Creusa. But they seem to have agreed that the strait connecting the Propontis and the Euxine took its name of Bosporus—meaning "cow's ford"—from the metamorphosed maiden's unhappy passage.

[20] Since Epaphus was born in Egypt, he was considered to have had a dark skin—despite his purely Greek ancestry.

[21] Some writers name Lysianassa, Agenor's wife and the mother of Cadmus, as another daughter of Epaphus and Memphis.

---

[22] A different legend relates that Danae willingly married Polydectes.

[23] Athena was angry with Medusa because she had permitted herself to be violated by Poseidon in a temple sacred to the goddess.

80. Descendants of Zeus and Danae

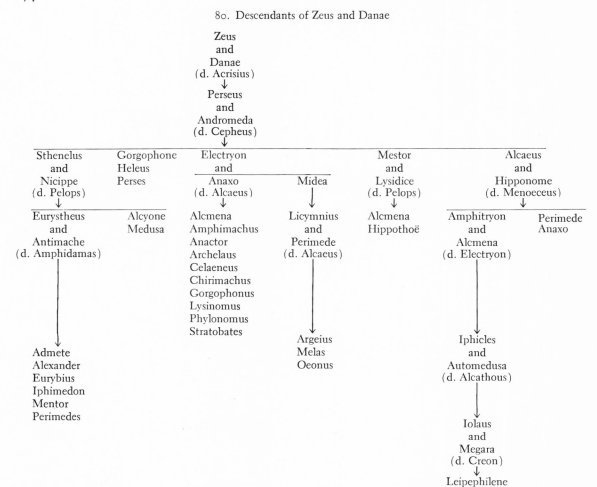

swiftly flew to Tartessus—a place on the edge of the river Oceanus[24]—and spied his prospective victim from afar, as she lay sleeping on a rock ledge with her two immortal sisters. He again put on the helmet of Hades and, guided by the mirror of his shield, came backward onto the ledge, where it was the work of but a moment to cut off Medusa's head and to thrust it, unseen except through the reflection of his shield, into the leathern pouch which the nymphs had given him.

As soon as the bloody act was committed, the winged horses Pegasus and Chrysaor sprang from the headless trunk, and the immortal Gor-

gons aroused from their slumber with the intent of avenging their sister's destruction. The helmet and the sandals were now invaluable to the young hero, for the former concealed him from the sight of his winged pursuers and the latter swiftly bore him over land and sea, far beyond the possibility of being overtaken. It is said that, in passing over the hot sands of of the Libyan desert, the drops of blood which oozed from Medusa's head fell to earth and produced a brood of parti-colored snakes—and, bitten by one of these, the Argonaut Mopsus later lost his life. It is also said that, when Perseus reached the African place where Atlas was upholding the heavens, he asked for rest and shelter, which were refused because Atlas feared that he would steal the golden apples, guarded in the vicinity by the Hesperides. So, Perseus produced the snaky head of Medusa and, holding it before the

---

[24] Tartessus is supposed to have been located in what is now the south of Spain, and is referred to in the Bible (at Ezekiel 27–12) as Tarshish, from where the Tyrians were accustomed to obtain their supplies of silver, iron, tin, and lead.

inhospitable giant, changed him into a mountain of stone—afterward called by his name.

Resuming the homeward journey, his winged sandals bore him over the African land until he stopped to refresh himself at the court of the Ethiopian king, Cepheus—only to find the country inundated with floods and signs of ruin everywhere about and, on a projecting cliff near the shore, he saw a beautiful maiden chained to a rock. She was Andromeda, the daughter of Cepheus and his queen, Cassiopeia, who had boasted that the girl's beauty exceeded that of the Nereids—a boast which so angered Amphitrite that she induced her sea-god husband to send both floods and a huge monster to ravage the Ethiopian kingdom. In their distress, the inhabitants had applied to the oracle of Zeus-Ammon, located in the Libyan desert, and had received a response that their land could be saved only by sacrificing Andromeda as an offering to the monster's maw. It was for this reason that she had been chained at a place near the sea from which the creature was accustomed to emerge.

Upon learning what had taken place, Perseus offered to save the maiden, on condition that she should become his bride, and her anxious parents willingly assented to the proposal. Once more donning the helmet of Hades, he mounted into the air on his winged sandals and hovered above Andromeda's head. Suffice to say that the sea monster soon appeared; Perseus changed it into a stone reef by exhibiting Medusa's snaky head before its eyes;[25] and, then, happily claimed his promised prize. Cepheus jubilantly ordered that a nuptial feast be prepared immediately, but Perseus was not to obtain his bride without further contest. For, during the banquet, Phineus—a brother of Cepheus to whom Andromeda had been previously betrothed—entered and claimed the maiden for himself. At this juncture, the Gorgon's head again proved its utility because, when Perseus held it up to the eyes of his objecting rival, he was quickly transformed into a stone statue.[26]

During his stay at the court of Cepheus, Andromeda bore to Perseus a son, whom they called Perses, and who was left in Ethiopia when they later went on to Seriphus, where Perseus was enraged to learn that his mother had been forced to seek refuge in the temple in order to avoid the embraces of Polydectes.[27] He angrily strode into the palace and, finding the king with a gay crowd of guests in his banquet hall, exhibited the head of Medusa to them, with the expected and inevitable result. He then presented the kingdom of the island to Dictys and, with Andromeda and Danae, proceeded to his ancestral home in Argos.[28]

But, before doing so, he restored the winged sandals, the leathern pouch and the helmet of Hades and gave the polished shield back to Athena, together with the Gorgon's head, which she placed in its middle with dire results to all those who thereafter sought to contest her will.[29]

When King Acrisius heard that his grandson was returning to Argos, he recalled the prophecy of the oracle and fled to the court of Teutemias at Larissa in Mysia. Anxious to appease the fears of the old man, Perseus followed him and begged him to return to his own kingdom. But, while at Larissa, the young hero competed in the funeral games which were being held in honor of Teutemias' father, and a quoit cast by him

---

Aconteus, one of his own retainers who accidentally happened to see the Gorgon's head.

[27] According to Hyginus, Polydectes married Danae soon after her arrival at Seriphus, and caused Perseus to be brought up in the temple of Athena. When Acrisius heard that his grandson had not been destroyed in the sea, he went to the island, and Polydectes made the boy promise that he would always treat his grandfather with the greatest respect. Acrisius, however, was detained at Seriphus by severe storms and, during his period of waiting, Polydectes died. During his funeral games, Perseus threw a quoit which killed Acrisius and, returning to Argos, assumed its government.

[28] In our attempt to coordinate the heroic genealogies, the marriage of Perseus and Andromeda is one of the higher hurdles, because Perseus is represented as a great-great-grandson of Danaus while the youthful maiden Andromeda is only his niece.

[29] In some legends the aegis (shield) of Athena is said to have been that of Zeus which, on occasion, was merely loaned to her but, according to the story related in the text, she was the sole proprietor of the one which contained the head of Medusa.

---

[25] The sea monster was apotheosized as the constellation Cetus, the Whale.

[26] Ovid makes a real battle out of this incident and has Perseus turn two-hundred men into stone—including

accidentally struck Acrisius and caused his death—as had long been foretold.

Perseus was loath to claim the throne of the man whom he had slain—even though by accident—and went to his kinsman Megapenthes at Tiryns,[30] with whom he made a deal to exchange sovereignties. For this reason, he and his descendants came to be identified with Tiryns, and with the new city of Mycenae, which he founded and built with the help of the Cyclopes.[31]

At their deaths, Perseus and Andromeda (together with Cepheus and Cassiopeia), were changed into constellations of the Milky Way, which still bear their names. Surviving them, were a daughter Gorgophone (who was successively the wife of the Aeolid Perieres and the Lacedaemonian Oébalus), and six sons, who were named Perses, Heleus, Sthenelus, Electryon, Mestor, and Alcaeus.

As previously mentioned, Perses remained in Ethiopia with his grandparents when Perseus returned to Greece. It is said that he grew up to become the first king of the nation which, after his name, was called Persia. Heleus assisted his nephew Amphitryon in a successful war against the Taphians and, in the distribution of spoils, shared with his ally Cephalus in taking over the rulership of the conquered islands of the enemy.

Sthenelus succeeded to the kingdom of Tiryns, and later added Mycenae to his realm, by expelling the sons of Electryon from their rightful heritage. He was married to Nicippe, a daughter of Pelops, who bore to him a son, Eurystheus, and two daughters named Alcyone and Medusa—seemingly inserted in the genealogy merely in order to give him a well-rounded

family to enjoy during his long life, for, according to Hyginus, he was eventually killed by Hyllus, who was his own grand-nephew.

The mythological birth and later activities of Eurystheus mainly revolve around his connection with Heracles who, by divine decree, was forced to become his servant, and more will be said about him in the following chapter. He followed his father Sthenelus as king at Tiryns and Mycenae, and by Antimache, a daughter of the Arcadian prince, Amphidamas, became the father of a daughter, Admete, for whose pleasure Heracles was forced to go in quest of the girdle of the Amazon queen, Hippolyte. Antimache also bore to him the five sons named on the accompanying chart—all of whom met death with their father when they later fought against the sons of Heracles.[32]

Electryon succeeded his father Perseus as king at Mycenae, and married his own niece Anaxo, by whom he had a daughter, Alcmena, and the nine sons whose names are shown on the accompanying chart. The names of the sons are not here repeated, because all of them were slain by the Taphians in an attack whose details are related in the next chapter; and they all expired without offspring or further mythological interest. Alcmena was embraced by Zeus and became the mother of Heracles—the greatest of all mythological heroes; and she, likewise, is the subject of later comment.

By a Phrygian slave-woman, named Midea, Electryon had a natural son Licymnius, who was honored with the friendship of Heracles. Despite his illegitimate descent, he married Perimede, the daughter of his paternal uncle, Alcaeus, and was treated as a respectable member of the family until he lost his life at the hands of Tlepolemus, the son of his great friend, by whom he was inadvertently struck by a stick with which a servant was being beaten. He was survived by his three sons, Argeius, Melas, and Oeonus. Of these, Oeonus is said to have been the first victor in the footrace at

---

[30] Megapenthes was a first cousin of Perseus' mother, Danae.

[31] Anciently, both Tiryns and Mycenae were supposed to have had their massive walls erected by the Cyclopes. In his excavations, Schliemann discovered stones of such size as to explain the reasons for the belief. In searching for the derivation of the name of the town of Mycenae, we are irresistibly led back to our genealogical charts and find that Mycene—the daughter of the god of the river Inachus—was a sister of Io and an ancient ancestress of Perseus: namely, Io was the mother of Epaphus; Epaphus was the father of Libya; Libya was the mother of Belus; Belus was the father of Acrisius; Acrisius was the father of Danae; and Danae was the mother of Perseus.

[32] In the battle, where the Heracleidae were aided by the Athenians, it is related that Hyllus cut off Eurystheus' head and gave it to Alcmena, who gouged out the eyes with her knitting needles. But, according to a different legend, Eurystheus was slain by Iolaus, who came up from the lower world to help his kinsmen in the conflict.

Olympia, but he was later slain by the sons of Hippocoön after he had accidentally killed one of their dogs—a foolish act of retaliation which so infuriated Heracles that he destroyed the whole Hippocoöntid family. The deaths of Argeius and Melas gave proof of their inherited affection for their father's great friend, because they lost their lives while fighting as members of his army in the attack on the Oechalian king, Eurytus, which has been mentioned in the preceding chapter.

In chapter 10, it was noted that Perseus' son Mestor was the ancestor from whom the Taphians claimed their right to the rulership of Mycenae: for, by Lysidice, a daughter of Pelops, he had a daughter, Hippothoë, who bore Taphius to Poseidon. His second daughter, Alcmena, married Pittheus, the king of Troezen, and their daughter, Aethra, grew up to become the mother of the famed Attic hero Theseus.

Alcaeus, the last charted son of Perseus and Andromeda, is not mentioned as having a kingly status, but he married Hipponome, a daughter of Theban Menoeceus. Apollodorus, however, says that his wife was Astydameia, a daughter of Pelops. By her he had the two daughters, Anaxo and Perimede, who have already been noted as the respective wives of Electryon and Licymnius. He also had a son, named Amphitryon, who became the mortal husband of Alcmena and begat Iphicles, born as a twin to Heracles.[33] Carrying on the genealogy, Iphicles married Automedusa, a daughter of Alcathous, and their son Iolaus became such a favorite of Heracles that the great man not only made him his charioteer but also gave him his cast-off wife, Megara.[34] By her, Iolaus had a daughter, named Leipephilene, who further cemented the Perseid family ties by marrying Phylas, one of the many descendants of the heroic blood which was already her inheritance.

[33] Laonome is sometimes mentioned as a sister of Heracles and, presumably, as a daughter of Amphitryon and Alcmena.

[34] According to Pindar, when Eurystheus demanded that the Athenians surrender the sons of Heracles, Iolaus was granted permission by the gods to return from the lower world to assist his former master's children. After slaying Eurystheus, he obediently departed from earth and resumed his ghostly status in the land of the dead. Pausanias adds that, after he won the victory with the horses of Heracles in the Olympic games, Iolaus was sent to Sardinia as the leader of the sons borne to the hero by the daughters of Thespius. Later, when the great man's remains could not be discovered, he was the first to sacrifice to him as a demi-god.

14

The Descendants of Zeus IV

Alcmena—the Mother of Heracles

WRITING IN THE century before the birth of Christ, Diodorus Siculus (of Sicily) prefaced his account of Heracles by remarking, "When the histories of myths are concerned, a man should by no means scrutinize the truth with so sharp an eye." This wise advice must be cheerfully heeded by anyone who attempts familiarity with the exploits of the greatest of the Greek demigods, because the inhabitants of many localities claimed him as their very own mighty neighbor or ancestor and, quite humanly, gave to his gargantuan activities those various, and often conflicting, shadings of truth which might reflect most glory upon themselves. Accordingly, the story which follows is offered only as an effort to realize a modicum of harmonized chronology in the hero's life and lays no claim to immunity from reasonable debate of its accuracy.[1] Since much of the story involves other descendants of Heracles' fabled ancestor Perseus, the preceding chart 78 is here repeated in part, with the addition of Heracles' own pedigree and the family which stemmed from his first wife, Megara.

During Electryon's reign at Mycenae, the sons of Pterelaus came with a band of their Taphian followers and claimed the kingdom of their maternal ancestor, Mestor.[2] When their presumptuous claim was refused, a fight followed in which all of Electryon's sons were slain, except Licymnius (who was borne to him by the slave-woman, Midea). And, likewise, all of the sons of Pterelaus, except Everes, lost their lives. The remaining Taphians, however, drove off Electryon's cattle and left them for safekeeping in the care of the Elean king, Polyxeinus, from whom they were later ransomed and returned to Mycenae by Electryon's nephew, Amphitryon.

Electryon swore to avenge the raid and gathered his forces for a punitive expedition, but first he turned over the affairs of state to Amphitryon and betrothed his daughter, Alcmena, to him with the understanding that the marriage could be celebrated only after Pterelaus should have been properly chastised. When this bargain was struck, Amphitryon proceeded to drive the cattle back into their native field but, unfortunately, he threw a club at one of the unruly beasts which accidentaly struck Electryon and killed him.[3] Sthenelus, the brother of Electryon who had succeeded to the kingdom

---

[1] Diodorus himself mentions an Egyptian, a Cretan, and a Greek as being three different persons—all of whom were called by the name of Heracles; Cicero counts six almost identical heroes of the same name; and Varro is said to have reckoned forty-four.

[2] Chronologically, this account of Apollodorus is one of mythology's longest bows, because the sons of Pterelaus were great-great-grandchildren of Electryon's brother, Mestor.

[3] According to Hesiod, the two men quarreled over the ownership of the cattle and Amphitryon killed Electryon in hot blood.

81. Descendants of Zeus and Alcmena

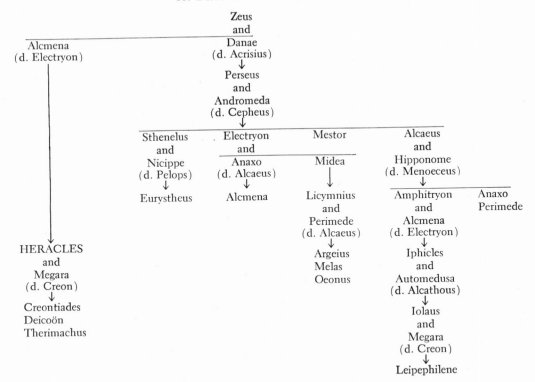

of Tiryns, seized upon the accident as a pretext to banish Amphitryon from all of Argos, and thus brought Mycenae also under his dominion.[4]

Accompanied by his sister Perimede, his kinsman Licymnius, and his betrothed Alcmena, the exiled man went to Thebes in Boeotia, where King Creon purified him from having shed the blood of a member of his own family. Amphitryon then gave Perimede to Licymnius and himself wedded Alcmena, but she conditioned consummation of the marriage upon his punishing the Taphians for having slain her brothers.

With the help of a well-equipped army which Creon furnished,[5] Amphitryon set sail

for the island of Taphos, near the coast of Acarnania, where Pterelaus had his palace. Although his forces were successful in a number of small engagements, he could not gain a decisive victory because, at birth, the Fates had given Pterelaus a golden hair in his head and had ordained that, so long as it remained, he would be invulnerable. However, the Taphian king had a daughter, named Comaetho, who knew the secret and, out of mad love for Amphitryon, she pulled out the hair while her father was ·sleeping. This unfilial act, which brought on both her fathers' death and her country's defeat, proved of no benefit to her, because Amphitryon was filled with contempt at the treason and ordered her to be slain.

Before the triumphant bridegroom reached Thebes with the news of his victory, Zeus assumed his likeness and, approaching Alcmena, told her that the deaths of her brothers had been avenged. Fulfilling her marriage vow, she

---

[4] Apollodorus relates that Sthenelus gave over a small portion of his sovereignty to Atreus and Thyestes, brothers of his wife, Nicippe.

[5] Creon conditioned his help upon Amphitryon's first freeing the Theban countryside from the ravages of a vixen known as the fox of Teumessus, destined never to be overtaken. Amphitryon accomplished this task by borrowing from Cephalus the never missing hound Laelaps. As the vixen was about to be overtaken, how-

ever, both she and the hound were turned into stone by Zeus.

lay with her supposed husband a night (which Zeus miraculously made three-fold), and, by him, became with child.[6] And, upon the return of Amphitryon in person, there were, perhaps, some interesting domestic discussions, ending only when the passage of time revealed the truth of what had occurred.

When Alcmena was at the point of being delivered, Zeus was led by Ate, the personification of ruin, to boast openly among the assembled gods that within the hour there would be born a male child of the blood of his son, Perseus, who would grow up to become the master of his race. Being derided by Hera, he made his boastful vow inviolable by repeating it in the name of the river Styx. Thereupon, Hera with her daughter, Eileithyia, the goddess of birth, darted from Olympus to Mycenae where Nicippe, the wife of Sthenelus, was seven months with child. Through exercise of their divine powers, the goddesses caused her to give immediate birth to Eurystheus and, at the same time, they retarded Alcmena's delivery.[7] Reascending to Olympus, Hera gloatingly announced to her thunder-stricken lord that his prophesied descendant had been born—Eurystheus, son of Sthenelus, son of Perseus, son of Zeus. Realizing that he had been tricked but was, nevertheless, bound by his oath, the supreme god wrathfully seized Ate by the hair and hurled her forever away from his presence.

Shortly thereafter, attended by her handmaiden Galanthis,[8] Alcmena gave birth to twin sons: Heracles, the son of Zeus, and Iphicles, the mortal and inferior son of Amphitryon. When Heracles was only eight-months old, Hera sent two great serpents to attack him in the apartment where he and Iphicles were quietly sleeping. Both infants fortunately awakened before they were harmed and Iphicles, upon seeing the creatures, fled from the house,

but Heracles calmly reached from his crib and, gripping one neck in each hand, strangled the huge snakes until they perished.[9]

In order to prevent his new son from becoming the continued victim of his queen's jealousy, Zeus finally prevailed upon Hera to promise that his thoughtless, but inviolable, oath would be fulfilled by having Heracles later enter the service of Eurystheus to perform twelve dangerous labors and that, if he should escape death in their performance, immortality would then be granted to him.

As the young boy grew up he was taught to drive the chariot by Amphitryon, to shoot with the bow by the Oechalian archer-king, Eurytus, to wrestle by Autolycus, the cunning son of Hermes, to fight with heavy armor by Castor, who (like Iphicles) was the mortal twin of a son of Zeus, and to sing and play on the lyre by Linus, the musical son of Apollo. Apparently, however, Heracles was fonder of muscle than music, because Linus one day punished him with a rod for his "sluggishness of soul"—whereupon, the pupil became violently angry and slew his teacher with a blow of the lyre. When he was tried for the murder, the precocious youth cited the law of Rhadamanthys which makes self-defense a proper plea of justification, and he was duly acquitted of crime. Amphitryon, however, feared that there might be a bad habit in the making, and sent his impetuous foster son away from Thebes to a cattle farm located in the neighboring mountain range known as Cithaeron. There he remained until grown, practicing daily with his bow and javelin and increasing in strength, skill, and stature.[10] Indeed, it is said that he quickly attained a height of more than seven feet.

At this early stage, Heracles began to exhibit two marked talents which regularly reappeared throughout his mortal existence: an infinite ca-

---

[6] It is said that the night was lengthened when Zeus ordered the Sun not to rise for three days.

[7] It is not explained why the goddesses had to be present physically at Mycenae to expedite the birth of Eurystheus while they simultaneously retarded Alcmena's accouchement at Thebes by apparent remote control.

[8] According to a different story, Alcmena's attendant was Historis, a daughter of the blind seer Teiresias.

[9] Another version of the story relates that the serpents were sent by Amphitryon in order to determine which of the twin boys was his son—information which was promptly revealed by the precipitate flight of Iphicles.

[10] In "The Choice of Heracles," composed by the poet Prodicus, the young hero is represented as deliberately electing to follow a life of strenuous accomplishment rather than one of indolent ease—a choice made by him after being solicited by two beautiful women respectively personifying Virtue and Happiness.

pacity for slaughter and an extreme fondness for female society. The story is succinctly told by Apollodorus, as translated in the Loeb Classical series by Sir J. G. Frazer:

While he was with the herds and had reached his eighteenth year, he slew the lion of Cithaeron, for that animal, sallying from Cithaeron, harried the king of Amphitryon and of Thespius. Now this Thespius was king of Thespiae, and Heracles went to him when he wished to catch the lion. The king entertained him for fifty days, and each night, as Heracles went forth to the hunt, Thespius bedded one of his daughters with him (fifty daughters having been borne to him by Megamede, daughter of Arnaeus); for he was anxious that all of them should have children by Heracles. Thus Heracles, though he thought that his bed-fellow was always the same, had connection with them all. And having vanquished the lion, he dressed himself in the skin and wore the scalp as a helmet.

The following list gives the names of the daughters of Thespius and the names of the children borne by them—all boys, for it was not fated that Zeus' favorite son should produce daughters any more than that he should learn to sing or play the lyre:

Alopius	by Antiope
Amestrius	by Eone
Antiades	by Aglaea
Antileon	by Procris
Antimachus	by Nicippe
Antiochus	by Antheia
Antiphus	by Laothoë
Archedicus	by Eurypyle
Archemachus	by Patro
Astyanax	by Epilais
Astybies	by Calametis
Atromus	by Stratonice
Bocolus	by Marse
Buleus	by Elachia
Capylus	by Hippo
Celeustanor	by Iphis
Cleolaus	by Argele
Creon	by "Madame X"
Dynastes	by Erato
Entelides	by Menippis
Erasippus	by Lysippe
Eumedes	by Lyse
Eurycapys	by Clytippe
Euryopes	by Terpsicrate
Eurypylus	by Eubote
Eurythras	by Exole
Halocrates	by Olympusa
Hippeus	by Procris
Hippodromus	by Anthippe
Hippozygus	by Hippocrate
Homolippus	by Xanthis
Iobes	by Certhe
Laomedon	by Meline
Laomenes	by Oreia
Leucippus	by Eurytele
Leucones	by Aeschreïs
Lycurgus	by Toxicrate
Lyncaeus	by Tiphyse
Mentor	by Asopis
Nephus	by Praxithea
Nicodromus	by Nice
Oestrobles	by Hesychia
Olympus	by Euboea
Onesippus	by Chryseis
Patroclus	by Pyrippe
Phalias	by Heliconis
Polylaus	by Eurybia
Teles	by Lysidice
Teleutagoras	by Eurycas
Threpsippas	by Panopeia
Tigasis	by Phyleïs

It will be noted that the preceding list shows the names of fifty-one sons—the reason being that by Procris, the eldest daughter, Heracles became the father of twins.

After destroying the lion of Cithaeron, the young hero started back to Thebes, and encountered an armed band of men, who were proceeding to the same destination. These were heralds of Erginus, king of Orchomenus, who arrogantly told him that they were sent from Creon to fetch the annual tribute of one hundred oxen, which the Thebans had promised to deliver as the agreed penalty for an earlier defeat which they had suffered at the hands of Erginus. Their statement so aroused the patriotic indignation of the proud youth that he cut off the ears, noses, and hands of the heralds, fastened the severed members with ropes around their necks and told them to carry that tribute home to their master. After the mutilated men returned to Orchomenus, their irate king demanded that Creon should yield up the guilty person, but Heracles miraculously received weapons from the goddess Athena, with which he armed a number of men of his own age, and set out to meet the approaching army of Erginus. By good generalship, he contrived to bring the forces together in a narrow pass, where the multitude of the enemy could not exert their full strength. In the battle which followed, he slew Erginus himself and practically all of the warriors who accompanied him.[11] Then, appearing unawares before the city of the Orchomenians and, slipping in through their unguarded gates, he burned the royal palace and razed the whole city to the ground.

The news of the great exploit was spread about through all Greece and, in appreciation, Creon gave to Heracles the hand of his eldest daughter, Megara, and entrusted him with the city affairs of Thebes as though he were his own son. The gods, too, showed their admiration of his valor, for he received a sword from Hermes, a bow and a quiver of arrows from Apollo, a golden shield from Hephaestus, a robe from Athena, and Poseidon gave him several swift horses.[12] But, as time passed, Eurytheus viewed the growing power of Heracles with alarm and summoned him to come to Mycenae and begin the service to which he was obliged by the heavenly agreement made between Zeus and Hera.[13]

According to Hesiod, the shield of Heracles was wrought by Hephaestus but was given to the hero as a present from Athena. The account of the mythological figures outlined on the shield is so graphically stated by the poet that his description is here given, as translated by Dr. H. G. Evelyn-White in the Loeb Classical series:

. . . his shield, all glittering: no one ever broke it with a blow or crushed it. And a wonder it was to see; for its whole orb shimmered with enamel and white ivory, and it glowed with shining gold; and there were concentric bands of deep blue color drawn upon it. In the center was Fear worked in adamant, unspeakable, staring backwards with eyes that glowed with fire. His mouth was full of teeth in a white row, fearful and daunting, and upon his grim brow hovered frightful Strife who arrays the

throng of men: pitiless she, for she took away the mind and senses of poor wretches who made war against the son of Zeus. Their souls passed beneath the earth and went down into the house of Hades; but their bones, when the skin is rotted about them, crumble away on the dark earth under parching Sirius.

Upon the shield Pursuit and Flight were wrought, and Tumult, and Panic, and Slaughter. Strife also, and Uproar were hurrying about, and deadly Fate was there holding one man newly-wounded, and another unwounded; and one, who was dead, she was dragging by the feet through the tumult. She had on her shoulders a garment red with the blood of men, and terribly she glared and gnashed her teeth.

And there were heads of snakes unspeakably frightful, twelve of them; and they always frightened the tribes of men on earth, whosoever made war against the son of Zeus; for they would clash their teeth when Amphitryon's son was fighting; and brightly shone these wonderful works. And there were spots upon the frightful snakes; and their backs were dark blue and their jaws were black.

Also there were upon the shield droves of boars and lions who glared at each other, being furious and eager; and rows of them moved on together, and neither side trembled but both bristled up their manes. For already a great lion lay between them and two boars, one on either side, bereft of life, and their dark blood was dripping down upon the ground. They lay with necks outstretched beneath the grim lions. And both sides were roused still more to fight because they were angry; the fierce boars and the bright-eyed lions.

And there was the strife of the Lapith spearmen gathered round the prince Caeneus and Dryas and Peirithous . . . and Theseus, the son of Aegeus, like unto the deathless gods. These were of silver, and had armor of gold upon their bodies. And the Centaurs were gathered against them on the other side, with Petraeus and Asbolus the diviner . . . these were of silver, and they had pine-trees of gold in their hands; and they were rushing together as though they were alive and striking at one another hand to hand with spears and with pines.

And on the shield stood the fleet-footed horses of Ares made of gold, and deadly Ares, the spoil-winner, himself. He held a spear in his hands and was urging on the footmen; he was red with blood as if he were slaying living men, and he stood in his chariot. Beside him stood Panic and Dread, eager to plunge amidst the fighting throng. There, too, was the daughter of Zeus, Tritogeneia, who drives the herds taken as spoil. She was arrayed as if for battle, with a spear in her hand, and a golden helmet, and the aegis about her shoulders. And she was going towards the awful strife.

And there was the holy company of the death-

---

[11] In this battle Amphitryon fell "fighting bravely." His widow Alcmena afterwards married Rhadamanthys, a son of Zeus who became one of the judges in hell.

[12] According to different legends, the horses given by Poseidon included Arion, borne by Demeter to Poseidon, and Balius and Xanthus borne by the Harpy Podarge to the west-wind Zephyrus.

[13] The seat of the government of Eurystheus is alternately given as both Mycenae and Tiryns; but, with the expulsion of Amphitryon by Sthenelus, both cities became parts of the same realm. From Heracles' identification with Tiryns, Virgil and others sometimes refer to him as the Tirynthian.

less gods; and in the midst, the son of Leto and Zeus played sweetly on the golden lyre. There also was the abode of the deathless gods, pure Olympus, and their assembly, and infinite riches were spread around the gathering. Also the goddesses, the Muses of Pieria, were beginning their clear-voiced song.

And on the shield was a harbor with a safe haven from the irresistible sea, made of refined tin wrought in a circle, and it seemed to heave with the waves. In the middle of it were many dolphins rushing this way and that, themselves fishing, for two dolphins of silver were spouting and devouring smaller fishes. And beneath them other fishes of bronze were trembling. And on the shore sat a fisherman watching; in his hands he held a casting net for fish, and seemed as if about to cast it forth.

There, too, was the son of rich-haired Danae, the horseman Perseus; his feet did not touch the shield and yet were not far from it—very marvellous to remark, since he was not supported anywhere; for so did the famous Lame One fashion him of gold with his hands. On his feet he had winged sandals and his black-sheathed sword was slung across his shoulders by a cross-belt of bronze. He was flying swift as thought. The head of a dreadful monster, the Gorgon, covered the broad of his back, and a bag of silver—a marvel to see—contained it; and from the bag bright tassels of gold hung down. Upon the head of the hero lay the dread cap of Hades which had the awful gloom of night. Perseus himself was at full stretch, like one who hurries and shudders with horror. And after him rushed the Gorgons, unapproachable and unspeakable, longing to seize him; as they trod upon the shield, it rang sharp and clear with a loud clanging. Two serpents hung down at their girdles with heads curved forward; their tongues were flickering, their teeth were gnashing with fury, and their eyes glared fiercely. And upon the awful heads of the Gorgons great Fear was quaking.

And beyond these there were men fighting in warlike harness, some defending their homes and parents, and others eager to destroy them; many lay dead, but the greater number still strove and fought. The women on well-built towers of bronze were crying shrilly and tearing their cheeks like living beings—the work of famous Hephaestus. And the men who were elders and on whom age had laid hold were all together outside the gates, and were holding up their hands to the blessed gods, fearing for their own sons. But these again were engaged in battle; and behind them the dusky Fates, gnashing their white fangs, lowering, grim, bloody, and unapproachable, struggled for those that were falling, for they all were longing to drink dark blood. As soon as they caught a man overthrown or falling newly wounded, one of them would clasp her great claws about him, and his soul would go down to Hades to chilly Tartarus. And

when they had satisfied their souls with human blood, they would cast that one behind them, and rush back again into the tumult and the fray. Clotho and Lachesis hovered over them and Atropos less tall than they, a goddess of no great frame, yet superior to the others and the eldest. And they all made a fierce fight over one poor wretch, glaring evilly at one another with furious eyes and fighting equally with claws and hands. By them stood Darkness of Death, mournful and fearful, pale, shrivelled, shrunk with hunger, swollen-kneed. Long nails tipped her hands, and she dribbled at the nose, and from her cheeks blood dripped down to the ground. She stood leering hideously, and much dust sodden with tears lay upon her shoulders.

Next, there was a city of men with goodly towers; and seven gates of gold, fitted to the lintels, guarded it. The men were making merry with festivities and dances; some were bringing home a bride to her husband on a well-wheeled car, while the bridal songs swelled high, and the glow of blazing torches held by handmaidens rolled in waves afar. And the maidens went before, delighting in the festival; and after them came frolicsome choirs, the youths singing soft-mouthed to the sound of shrill pipes, while the echo was shivered around them, and the girls led on the lovely dance to the sound of lyres. Then again on the other side was a rout of young men revelling, with flutes playing; some frolicking with dance and song, and others were going forward in time with a flute player and laughing. The whole town was filled with mirth and dance and festivity.

Others again were mounted on horseback and galloping outside the city. And there were ploughmen breaking up the good soil, clothed in tunics girt up. Also there was a wide corn land and some men were reaping with sharp hooks the stalks which bended with the weight of the ears—reaping Demeter's grain; others were binding the sheaves with bands and were spreading the threshing floor. And some held reaping hooks and were gathering the vintage, while others were taking from the reapers into baskets white and black clusters from the long rows of vines which were heavy with leaves and tendrils of silver. Others again were gathering them into baskets. Beside them was a row of vines in gold, the splendid work of cunning Hephaestus: it had shivering leaves and stakes of silver and was laden with grapes which had just turned ripe. And there were men boxing and wrestling, and huntsmen chasing swift hares with a leash of sharp-toothed dogs before them; they eager to catch the hares, and the hares eager to escape.

Next to them were horsemen hard set, and they contended and labored for a prize. The charioteers standing on their well-made cars, urged on their swift horses with loose rein; the jointed cars flew along clattering and the naves of the wheels shrieked loudly. So they were engaged in an unending toil, and the end with victory never came to them, and the contest was ever unwon. And there was set out for them within the course a great tripod of gold, the splendid work of cunning Hephaestus.

And round the rim Oceanus was flowing, with a full stream as it seemed, and enclosed all the cunning work of the shield. Over it swans were soaring and calling loudly, and many others were swimming upon the surface of the water; and near them were shoals of fish. A wonderful thing the great strong shield was to see. . . .

When Heracles ignored the summons, Zeus sent Hermes to say that it must be obeyed, but the still reluctant hero went to the oracle at Delphi and inquired where he should dwell. Here, for the first time, he was called Heracles—"one who has earned glory for himself"—because previously he had been called only Alcides, after his foster-grandfather Alcaeus.[14] His pleasure, however, at being so dubbed by the mystic Pythia was short-lived, for she answered his inquiry by revealing that he was inexorably fated to serve Eurystheus in Argolis until after he had completed the agreed Twelve Labors. Upon hearing this sentence, it was but small comfort to learn that his eventual lot would be immortality. Returning to Thebes, he fell into a despondency which, through the cunning of Hera, was turned into madness.

In his frenzy, he tried to kill Iolaus, the son of his half brother, Iphicles, but the lad luckily escaped by making quick use of his legs. He next spied the three young sons borne to him by Megara—Creontiades, Deicoön, and Therimachus—and, when his crazed brain conceived them as deadly enemies bent upon his destruction, he shot all three with arrows and shamelessly watched them expire.[15] Later recovering

from his disease and realizing what he had done, he dejectedly set out for the palace of Eurystheus and, upon arrival, submitted himself to his fated service.[16]

First Labor. The exulting king wasted no time in commanding his great thrall to slay a monstrous lion which had been ravaging the valley of Nemea, lying between Argos and Corinth. This beast was the offspring of huge Typhon and foul Echidna, and was of such toughness that no man had yet been able to wound him. On his way to the attack, Heracles arrived at the town of Cleonae and spent the night at the house of a day laborer named Molorchus. When his host was about to offer a sacrificial victim, Heracles told him to wait for thirty days and then, if he had returned safely from the hunt, to sacrifice to Zeus, but if he did not return, the sacrifice should be made to Heracles as a hero. Proceeding on to Nemea, the animal's huge tracks were seen and its quietly moving form was soon within bowshot, but after several arrows had fruitlessly found their mark, Heracles was determined to attack at close quarters with his great club, which he had fashioned while on Cithaeron. As he approached, the lion must have sensed that he was pursued by no ordinary man, and fled into a cave containing two mouths. Heracles, however, closed up one entrance with stones and, coming in through the other, put his arm around the beast's neck and choked him to death. He then picked up the huge carcass and carried it to Cleonae, where he found Molorchus, on the last of the thirty days, making ready to sacrifice to him as a dead man. But the plan was speedily revised, and the sacrifice was made—not to Heracles as a hero, but to Zeus as saviour.

When he returned to the palace of Tiryns with the dead lion over his shoulder, Eurystheus was so frightened at the sight that he fled from his throne and hid himself in a bronze jar beneath the ground; and he ordered that, from then on, all of his dealings with Heracles should be carried on through his herald Copreus, a son

---

[14] According to Diodorus, Alcmena—from fear of Hera—exposed her son in a field near Thebes, where he was found and suckled by the goddess; and, from the incident, he was given the name of Heracles, meaning "glorified by Hera." Other mythographers (explaining the same derivation) relate that Hermes carried the new-born child to Olympus, and put him to Hera's breast while she was asleep. Upon awakening, however, she pushed him away and her milk, spilled in the act, produced the heavenly galaxy known as the Milky Way.

[15] According to Apollodorus, the three children of Heracles, and also two children of Iphicles, were thrown into the fire.

[16] A different version of the legend relates that Heracles was stricken with madness before he went to the oracle at Delphi.

of Pelops. After flaying the lion, Heracles made its skin into a cloak, which he afterwards wore as an invaluable protection against many of the perils that were to follow. The lion was translated to the heavens as the constellation Leo, the fifth sign of the zodiac.

Second Labor. The second labor commanded by Eurystheus was the destruction of the Lernaean Hydra, another of the offspring of Typhon and Echidna, from whose single body sprang a hundred necks—each bearing a serpent's head. When one head was cut off, two others sprang forth from the wound—a marvelous occurrence which quite naturally gave rise to the belief that the creature was invincible. Periodically emerging from the swamps of Lerna, it was in the habit of laying waste the cattle and lands of the region, and its hundred poisoned tongues had brought quick death to many brave men in their attempts to stay its depredations.

In a chariot driven by his nephew Iolaus, Heracles proceeded to the place beside the springs of Amymone where the den of the Hydra was located. Pelting the great snake with fiery shafts, he forced it to come into the open, and they were soon locked together in a deadly grapple, as the Hydra wound itself about one of the hero's legs and clung to him. Nor could Heracles accomplish his release by smashing the creature's head with his club. For, as soon as one head was smashed, two others sprouted in its stead. Moreover, a huge crab came to the Hydra's assistance and viciously bit into Heracles' one free foot; but he crushed it with a blow of his club and, with the assistance of Iolaus, burned away the newly sprouting snake heads until the Hydra itself expired. He then slit up the monster's body and dipped his arrows in its poisoned gall.[17]

In some versions of the myth, wherein the fated labors of Heracles were limited to ten in number, it is related that Eurystheus refused to give credit for the slaying of the Hydra, on the quibbling ground that it could not have been accomplished without the help of Iolaus. It is also said that Hera was grateful to the giant crab for his attempted aid and that she translated him to the heavens, where he is still to be seen as Cancer, the fourth sign of the zodiac. The Hydra was apotheosized as a constellation under its own name.

Third Labor. Once while Taygete, a daughter of Atlas, was fleeing from the attempted embraces of Zeus, she prayed to the goddess Artemis, who brought salvation by changing the maiden into a cow. In gratitude, Taygete dedicated to her preserver a wonderful stag,[18] which had golden antlers and brazen feet and was accustomed to haunt the river Cerynites in Arcadia. As one might expect, the animal's swiftness was as remarkable as the beauty of its adornment. For his third labor, Heracles was ordered to capture this creature alive and to bring it to the court of Eurystheus.

First sighting his quarry at Oenoe in Argos,[19] he chased it for a whole year, until it became weary and took refuge on the mountain called Artemisium, and from there passed down to the river Ladon. There, Heracles wounded it with one of the arrows which had not been dipped in the Hydra's blood; and, putting the crippled animal over his shoulder, started back to Mycenae. On the way, he was met by Artemis and Apollo, who were furious with him for having outraged the dedicated creature, but he succeeded in soothing their anger by pleading that he was acting under the divine compulsion of their mutual father Zeus. So he was permitted to complete his journey and his third great labor.

Fourth Labor. The fourth command which Heracles received was to bring back alive a huge boar which, descending from its accustomed feeding grounds in the Erymanthus mountains, had lately been ravaging the country about Psophis in Arcadia. On his way to search for the beast, he stopped at the home of Pholus, the

---

[17] According to a different legend, the Hydra had nine heads, of which the middle one was immortal; and Heracles, after searing off the mortal heads, completed his task by chopping off the middle one and burying it under a heavy rock.

[18] A variant of the story relates that the animal was a hind.

[19] Pindar says that, in his chase, Heracles saw "the land at the back of the cold north wind," from which some commentators ingeniously deduce that the stag was a reindeer.

Centaur, who set roast meat before his guest but ate his own meat raw. When Heracles called for wine, his host opened a jar which was kept among the common stores of his tribe and, from afar, the other Centaurs, smelling the sweet odor, came rushing in, armed with rocks and uprooted fir trees. Upon their arrival, Pholus hid himself in fear, but Heracles—single-handed—withstood the attack. In doing so, he was forced to struggle with beings who were demigods on their mother's side,[20] who possessed the swiftness of horses, had the strength of two bodies and, in addition, enjoyed the experience and wisdom of men. Moreover, they were aided in their attack by Hera, who sent down a heavy rain—which made a slippery footing for the fighting man but failed to bother his four-footed assailants. Despite these handicaps, Heracles slew many of the Centaurs, and caused the rest to flee in a rout to the home of their illustrious fellow-being, Cheiron, who lived in the nearby district of Malea.[21]

The pursuing hero shot an arrow, which passed through the arm of Elatus and then stuck in Cheiron's knee. Owing to the venom of the Hydra, into whose blood the arrow had been dipped, Elatus immediately perished; but Cheiron—the son of great Cronus—was immortal and could not die, even though he earnestly desired that end as offering the only surcease from his cruel suffering. Misfortunes came also to the hospitable Pholus when, while burying some of his fallen kinsmen, he extracted an arrow from one of them and accidentally dropped it on his foot—resulting in his painful death as the poison of the Hydra entered his blood stream.[22]

After sorrowfully burying his host, Heracles

proceeded to chase the boar high up the slopes of Erymanthus, where it was caught in the deep snows and he was able to take it alive. And, when he returned to Mycenae with the ferocious beast, Eurystheus—having forgotten his previous experience and venturing in view—was so horrified at the sight that he took another nose dive into his brazen jar.

Fifth Labor. Augeias, the king of Elis, had so many cattle and flocks of goats that he was unable to till much of his land because of their accumulated dung. Naturally, his stables were in the same filthy condition, and Eurystheus gave to Heracles the humiliating task of cleansing them. The hero went to Elis and, without revealing that he had been ordered to the task, proposed to clear away the offal in one day, if Augeias would give him a tenth part of his herd. To this proposal the incredulous king readily agreed.

Taking along Augeias' son, Phyleus, as a witness, the great man broke down a large portion of the foundations of the stables and, through the breaches, diverted the united waters of the rivers Alpheius and Peneius, thus flushing the filth entirely away. The Elean king withheld the promised reward, however, on the ground that Heracles had acted by divine compulsion and not of his own free will, but he offered to submit the dispute to arbitration. When the arbitrators had taken their seats, Phyleus was called by Heracles and bore witness against his father—affirming both the promised reward and the accomplishment of the task in a single day. At this, Augeias flew into a great rage and, before the arbitrators had voted, ordered both Heracles and Phyleus to depart from Elis and never to return.

Unresisting, but with vengeance stored in his heart, Heracles went to the home of his friend Dexamenus at Olenus in Achaea, and Phyleus repaired to the island of Dulichium. It so happened that Heracles arrived at Olenus just after Dexamenus had been forced to betroth his daughter, Mnesimache, to the fierce Centaur Eurytion. Being asked for advice, he solved the problem in typical fashion by killing the Centaur when he came to claim his unwilling bride. He then returned to Eurystheus at Mycenae, but the contemptible king refused to give credit

---

[20] At variance with the story which makes all Centaurs—except Cheiron—descendants of Ixion and Nephele (a phantom of Hera), Apollodorus says that Pholus was the son of Silenus and an unnamed Median nymph.

[21] According to Apollodorus, Cheiron had been driven from his home on Mount Pelion in Thessaly by his Lapith enemies and was now living in Arcadia.

[22] Diodorus names the following as the most renowned of the Centaurs slain by Heracles, namely: Daphnis, Argeius, Amphion, Hippotion, Oreius, Isophles, Melanchaetes, Thereus, Doupon, and Phrixus. He says that Homadus, and all of the other Centaurs who escaped by flight, later received fitting punishments.

for the Augeian labor, on the technical ground that it had been performed for a promised reward.

Sixth Labor. Heracles next task was to clear the marshes of Arcadian Stymphalus of the man-eating birds which were congregated there, at a place whose uncertain footing and heavy undergrowth made it difficult for earth travelers to gain access. After he arrived at the marshes, he was at a loss how to drive out the pestilent creatures, but Athena gave him a pair of brazen castanets, made by Hephaestus, with which he created such a noise that the bird-women were frightened into the air. And, with his unerring poisoned arrows, he shot them down, one by one, and departed for Mycenae, where he announced to Eurystheus that his task had been performed.[23]

Seventh Labor. The seventh labor assigned to Heracles was to fetch from Crete a ferocious bull which Poseidon had sent up from the depths of the sea at the behest of King Minos. This animal had become sire of the monstrous Minotaur—by connection which vengeful Aphrodite had forced on Queen Pasiphae, a daughter of the Sun-god Helios.[24] When the great man arrived at Crete, he not only mastered the bull with his bare hands but forced it to carry him through the seas back to the Greek mainland. After first exhibiting his captive to Eurystheus, he set it free but, instead of remaining in Argos, the beast wandered all over the Peloponnesus, mangling men and women in its path, until it finally crossed over to the plain of Marathon in Attica. There, at a later time, Theseus put an end to its cruel existence.

Eighth Labor. Diomedes, a son of Ares, was king of a war-loving race known as the Bistones. In keeping with his cruel character, he acquired four man-eating horses, whose names were Podargus, Lampus, Xanthus, and Dinus.[25] Eurystheus ordered Heracles to bring these animals to Mycenae. Proceeding to Thrace, he overcame them and dragged them down to the seashore. At this point, however, the Bistones attacked and he turned the horses over to his young companion, Abderus, to guard. While Heracles was engaged in routing his assailants and capturing their king, the fierce creatures became unmanageable and tore their youthful custodian to pieces. On the great man's return, he tenderly buried the mangled remains at a place afterwards named Abdera and, characteristically, sated the hunger of the man-eating horses by throwing the body of their own master, Diomedes, to them. He then drove the wild herd to Mycenae and, after they were exhibited to Eurystheus, they were consecrated by him to Hera and set free. Some say that the liberated animals rushed off to the highlands and were harried to death by the beasts of the forest, but others solemnly state that, by Hera's protection, they remained unharmed and the breed continued down to the time of Alexander the Great.

Ninth Labor. King Eurystheus had a daughter named Admete, whose feminine desire specified the next labor assigned to Heracles. In a remote district of Asia Minor, near the Euxine Sea, dwelt the Amazons, warrior-women whose chief interest was in battle and only indirectly in motherhood. Of the children to whom they gave birth they reared only the females, and cut off their right breasts so as not to interfere with proper handling of the bow. Their queen was Hippolyte, a daughter of Ares, who had given to her a beautiful girdle in appreciation of her prowess in arms. It was this surrounding article of decorative apparel that Eurystheus commanded Heracles to obtain for his daughter.

Accompanied by a band of his comrades, the great man sailed to the island of Paros, where four sons of the Cretan king, Minos, lived whose names were Eurymedon, Chryses, Nephalion, and Philolaus. When two members of his crew landed and were slain by the hostile inhabitants, he retaliated by murdering all four of the sons of

---

[23] The Stymphalides were said to shoot out their feathered quills like arrows, and it is suggested by Apollonius Rhodius that they were identical with the Birds of Ares, encountered by the Argonauts. According to a different legend, they were not birds but were maidens—daughters of Stymphalus and Ornis—and by one of them, named Parthenope, Heracles had a son who was called Everes.

[24] Aphrodite, as related in chapter 2, revenged herself on many descendants of Helios because he revealed her intrigue with Ares.

[25] The animals of Diomedes are sometimes referred to as mares, although their names were masculine.

Minos, and besieged the island until envoys were sent to offer him two hostages to replace his lost men. The offer was accepted and he took on board two sons of Androgeus (grandsons of Minos), named Alcaeus and Sthenelus. Thereupon, he raised the siege and, sailing to Mysia, was royally entertained by King Daschylus. During his visit the Mysians were attacked by the Bebryces (Bebrycians), a fierce neighboring tribe, but, with the help of his mighty guest, the forces of Lycus routed the invaders and Heracles himself slew their king, Mygdon, who was a son of Poseidon.

Leaving the court of the Mysian king, the hero proceeded on to the harbor of Themiscyra at the mouth of the river Thermodon. When his ship had come to anchor, he received a visit from the Amazonian queen, who inquired what had brought him to her shores and, upon learning the reason, she readily promised to surrender her beautiful girdle. However, jealous Hera now turned up again and, in the likeness of an Amazon, went among the hosts of Hippolyte, saying that the strangers were about to carry off their queen. Thus incited, the warrior-women charged on horseback down to the ship's mooring, causing Heracles to believe that Hippolyte's promise had been guilefully given to mask an intended act of treachery. In this belief, he quickly slew her and removed her girdle. And, in the battle precipitated by his impulsive act, he killed many of the other Amazons and routed the rest.[26] Among those routed, and taken captive, were two of Hippolyte's sisters named Melanippe and Antiope. Of these, Melanippe ransomed herself by voluntarily surrendering her girdle to Heracles, but Antiope was carried away to Greece, and later was given as a slave to Theseus.

After leaving Themiscyra, the expedition set sail for home and, on the way, anchored at Troy where the voyagers were amazed to see a beautiful maiden chained to the rocks on the seashore. She was Hesione, a daughter of the Trojan king, Laomedon. In order to explain the reason for her cruel shackling, it is necessary to delve a bit into the chronicles of the Olympian deities, where a rather curious story follows:

Shortly after the Giants had been conquered and Zeus had assumed supremacy, the other gods on Olympus became jealous of his authority and formed a conspiracy to put him in bonds. Learning of the plot, the Nereid Thetis brought up from Tartarus the hundred-handed Briareus and stationed him at the side of Zeus, ready to give such assistance as might be needed. This so frightened the rebellious deities that they fled to earth and the conspiracy died a 'borning, but unforgiving Zeus punished Poseidon and Apollo, the ringleaders, by sentencing them to labor for Laomedon in building the walls of Troy.[27]

Thus impelled, the two gods approached Laomedon and made a bargain with him for their services, which were dutifully given for a full year.[28] However, when their work was completed, the faithless king not only dismissed them without paying their stipulated wage, but also threatened to lop off their ears and sell them into slavery unless they should promptly depart.

Being now insulted as well as robbed, Poseidon and Apollo retired with wrath and indignation in their hearts, but gained their revenge by sending a pestilence upon the land and a huge sea monster which snatched away the people of the Trojan plain. In despair, Laomedon consulted an oracle and was told that deliverance would come only if he should expose his daughter Hesione to be devoured by the great creature. It was in pursuance of this command that the maiden was exposed so as to be spied by Heracles, pitifully bound to the rocks and impotently awaiting her anticipated destruction.

The hero quickly landed and, learning why Hesione was chained, offered to save her on condition that Laomedon would deliver to him a pair of the divine horses which Zeus had given to Tros (grandfather of Laomedon) as compensation for having carried off his son, Ganymedes. Laomedon readily agreed to the pro-

---

[26] The names of some of the slain Amazons were: Aella, Celaeno, Asteria, Philippis, Eurybia, Marpe, Prothoë, Phoebe, Tecmessa, Eriboea, Alcippe, and Deianeira.

[27] The conspiracy is mentioned by Homer without naming Apollo as one of the conspirators.

[28] A variant of the legend relates that the walls of Troy were built by Poseidon alone, while Apollo served as a herdsman—tending the cattle of Laomedon in the glens of Mount Ida. Pindar adds that the two gods took with them the hero Aeacus to aid in the work of fortification, and a later scholiast, commenting on the poet's statement, explains that it was necessary for a mortal to assist in the construction, else the city (destined to fall to the Greeks) would have been forever impregnable.

posal, and Heracles killed the monster when it came up out of the sea.[29] Running true to form, however, the Trojan king again repudiated his promise and, without receiving the agreed reward, Heracles put to sea—vowing that he would one day return and obtain full revenge.

The voyagers next stopped at Aenus in Thrace and were graciously entertained by King Poltys, a son of Poseidon, but the king had a brother, named Sarpedon, who was such a "lewd fellow" that Heracles shot and killed him. After this diversionary episode, the expedition sailed on to Thasus, where the Thracian inhabitants were subjugated, and their island home was turned over to the rulership of Alcaeus and Sthenelus—the sons of Androgeus who had been taken as hostages from the island of Paros. Proceeding from there, anchorage was next made at Torone in Macedonia, a city governed by the sons of the Sea-god Proteus—Polygonus, Telegonus, and Tmolus—who prided themselves on their wrestling ability.[30] Challenged by them, Heracles used the grappling technique, which he had learned from Autolycus, with such deadly effect that they were successively crushed to death in his strong arms. He then returned to Mycenae and gave the belt of Hippolyte to Eurystheus for delivery to Admete.

Tenth Labor. On the island of Erytheia (generally understood as being near the present site of Cadiz in Spain), lived Geryon (Geryones), a son of the winged horse Chrysaor. He was a human monster with three bodies combined into one, and was known all over the ancient world as the owner of a herd of red cattle, which were guarded by Orthrus, the two-headed brother of the Hell-hound Cerberus. For a tenth labor, Eurystheus commanded Heracles to capture these cattle and to drive them to Mycenae.

Considering the island as a good place of departure upon a trip of such magnitude, the great man gathered his forces and brought them to Crete. He was magnificently received by the natives and acknowledged their reception by proceeding to clear the land of all wild animals —not only because of their acclaim, but also because Crete was the birthplace and early home of his supreme sire. After leaving the island, he proceeded to the mainland of Libya and, when his landing was resisted, he bested and killed the giant Antaeus in a wrestling match.[31] Because Gaea was his mother, the giant was invincible so long as his body maintained contact with the earth, but Heracles, knowing the secret of his adversary's strength, held him high in the air and squeezed out his life. He then appropriated the dead man's daughter, Iphinoë, and she later bore to him a son named Palaemon.

He next came to Egypt,[32] which for nine years had been uninterruptedly visited by scarcity until a soothsayer had predicted that the plague could be abated by each year sacrificing a foreigner to Zeus. This advice the king, Busiris, had been in the habit of following with good results. When the strangers arrived in the country, their leader was seized and carried to the sacrificial altar. But the mighty man burst his chains and slew Busiris himself—together with his son Amphidamas and his herald Chalbes.

Continuing to the Strait of Gibraltar, Heracles set up the two mountains—over against each other at the respective boundaries of Africa and Europe—which ever since have been called the "Pillars of Hercules."[33] After this muscular

---

[29] Tzetzes, a Greek writer living in the twelfth century A.D. (whom Andrew Lang calls "a master of nonsense"), relates that Heracles, in full armor, leaped into the jaws of the monster and was in its belly for three days, hacking and sawing at its vital parts—after which he emerged without any hair on his head.

[30] As previously indicated in chapter 10, the locale of the wrestling match (or matches) of Heracles with the sons of Proteus is sometimes assigned to Egypt, or the island of Pharos—where the "Old Man of the Sea" is said to have had his home.

---

[31] Antaeus was said to have roofed the temple of his sire, Poseidon, with the skulls of his victims.

[32] As elsewhere when dealing with mythological geography, one should not "scrutinize the truth with so sharp an eye" because, in the present instance, the procession from Libya to Egypt (from west to east) would appear to be quite a deviation in the course from Crete to Spain.

[33] The mythological names for the Pillars of Hercules were Calpe (in Europe) and Abyla (in Africa), but the ancients were not certain of their location. The usual opinion was that given in the text. Some relate, however, that the continents of Europe and Africa were originally joined by an isthmus, and that Heracles cut through it to create the Strait of Gibraltar. Others say that the strait

performance, the Sun-god Helios beat down upon him with such fierce heat that he shot an arrow at the head of the deity, who admired the foolish attempt so greatly that he gave the hero a golden boat with which to cross to the island of Erytheia.[34]

After having arrived at his goal, Heracles came upon the herd of Geryon's red cattle and, with his club he slew their herdsman, Eurytion, and the two-headed dog Orthrus, who were guarding them. Geryon, however, he could despatch only after shooting him with one of the arrows which had been dipped in the Hydra's poisoned gall. Gathering the herd into the golden boat, he sailed to the nearby mainland and returned his marvelous ferry to Helios.

After passing through the Iberian peninsula, now Spain and Portugal, the expedition was attacked by a multitude of hostile natives, led by Alebion and Dercynus—two sons of Poseidon who, in their attempt to steal the cattle, were slain by Heracles' deadly arrows. The number of the attackers was so great, however, that the supply of arrows was beginning to run short, and the hero prayed to his divine father for additional weapons. In answer to his prayer, Zeus rained down rocks from the sky, and these were used as missiles in turning the tide of the conflict, so that the attackers were wholly routed. The place where the battle occurred is said to have been a field located between Marseilles[35] and the Rhodanus (Rhone) River, and in olden days it was called the "Stony Plain" because of the vast quantity of large pebbles lying loose there.

The triumphant hero proceeded to lead his band through Liguria and down the west coast of Italy without further incident[36] until he came to the mouth of the river Tiber, where he was welcomed by Evander—a son of Hermes who had migrated to the country from his native home at Tegea in Arcadia. During the night, two bulls from the herd of Geryon were stolen by Cacus, a monstrous son of Hephaestus who dwelt in a nearby cave. By dragging the animals backward into his underground chamber, the cunning robber effectually concealed their whereabouts, and Heracles, although furious over his loss, was about to continue on his way. As he was leaving, however, he heard the hoarse lowing of the bulls within the cave, whose entrance Cacus had barricaded with great stones. With his accustomed vigor, the great man heaved aside the barrier, killed Cacus with his club and recovered his cattle—after which he sacrificed one of the bulls to Zeus and erected an altar to himself as "The Greatest."

Bidding farewell to Evander, Heracles now proceeded through the remaining length of Italy, meanwhile performing many actions of note and valor which have been preserved in that country as parts of localized tradition. At Rhegium, a bull broke loose and, swimming the strait to Sicily, mingled with the herds of King Eryx, a son of Poseidon. When he refused to surrender the animal unless Heracles should beat him in a wrestling match, the strong hero beat him thrice, killed him in the wrestling and celebrated the victory by lying with his dead adversary's daughter Psophis, who later bore to him twin sons named Echephron and Promachus.

According to Diodorus Siculus, Heracles now led his forces and his cattle back to Greece by going up the east coast of Italy and around the head of the Adriatic Sea by land, but other accounts relate that he sailed across the Ionian Sea and landed in Thrace.[37] There, it is said, many of the cattle were stung with a gadfly sent by Hera and fled into the mountains.[38] For some unexplained reason, Heracles blamed the river Strymon for this mishap and made its

---

was formerly wider and that he narrowed it, in order to prevent the monsters of the Atlantic from bursting into the Mediterranean.

[34] The golden boat appears to have been the same speedy vessel which nightly carried Helios from the western end of the earth back to his glorious palace in eastern Ethiopia. If this were so, the journey of Heracles from Africa to the island of Erytheia must have been but a matter of minutes.

[35] It is a settled historical fact that the city of Marseilles was colonized by Greek settlers.

[36] A composite of the many legends about the course taken by Heracles with the cattle would show that he traveled over practically the whole of southern Europe.

[37] A slight glance at the map suffices to show that this voyage was a roundabout course to Mycenae—even in mythological times.

[38] The story is supposed to account for the wild cattle roaming in the Thracian mountains in historical times.

upper part unnavigable by filling its bed with stones. With the remainder of the red herd, he then went on to Mycenae and delivered his troublesome charges to Eurystheus, who sacrificed them to Hera.

Eleventh Labor. The ten labors had taken in their performance eight years and one month; but the end was not yet, because Eurystheus (for reasons which have been stated previously) refused to give credit for the slaying of the Hydra or the cleansing of the stables of Augeias. Accordingly, two more tasks were assigned—the first being to bring to Mycenae the golden apples of the Hesperides. These had originally been given by Gaea to Hera as a wedding present, and their taking was a peculiarly difficult operation—not only because they were guarded by the Hesperides and the dragon Ladon, but also because their location was unknown to Heracles.[39]

Setting forth pretty much at random, he came to the river Echedorus in Macedonia where he encountered Cycnus, a son of Ares and Pyrene, and would have killed him in a challenged bout except for the intervention of a thunderbolt, which Zeus hurled between the struggling combatants.[40]

Passing on into the north of Europe,[41] Heracles came to a stream where he was told by some nymphs that only Nereus, the Sea-god son of Pontus, could reveal the location of the golden apples; and they told him how to reach the shoreland where the old god was accustomed to sun himself in the company of his fifty beautiful daughters.[42] Following his directions from the nymphs,[43] Heracles came upon Nereus, whom he found sleeping, and, although the god turned himself into many different shapes, the hero bound him and refused his release until the location of the garden of the Hesperides had been revealed.

Proceeding on the indicated way, he came to Mount Caucasus at the eastern end of the Euxine and, seeing the eagle that was devouring the liver of Prometheus, he indignantly shot the great bird with one of his poisoned arrows—after which he released from his chains the long-suffering benefactor who had brought fire to mankind.[44] Since it would have been a thwarting of the divine will to effect the release without offering someone as a substitute in eventual death, Heracles prevailed upon Zeus to permit Cheiron (whose wound was keeping him in continuous pain) to exchange his immortality with Prometheus and, by dying, to obtain relief from his earthly misery. The gods, however, perpetuated the memory of Cheiron's kindness by placing his image in the skies as the constellation Centaurus.

After this kind act, the great man traveled southward into Arabia and slew Emathion, a son of Tithonus and the dawn-goddess Eos, because he offered "unprovoked battle."[45] He then went westward along the African coast until he came to the place where he had been directed by Nereus, and found Atlas patiently upholding the heavens on his broad shoulders.[46] Upon advice previously given to him by Prometheus, Heracles asked the great Titan to fetch the golden apples and offered to relieve him of his galling burden while he accomplished the mission.[47] Grasping at this proffered respite,

---

[39] The location of the garden of the Hesperides is variously given as in the extreme west, in the northern land of the Hyperboreans, or near the Atlas Mountains in Africa.

[40] According to Eustathius, Cycnus was killed in the encounter and was reincarnated as a swan.

[41] Although the legends are conflicting, it has been conjectured that Heracles went to the banks of the Oder River where, seeing amber, he confused it with the Eridanus (Po) in Italy.

[42] Like Proteus, the son of Poseidon, Nereus was sometimes referred to as "the Old Man of the Sea."

[43] Apollodorus says that the nymphs were daughters of Zeus and Themis.

---

[44] The ancient writers differed about the period of time during which Prometheus was impaled on Mount Caucasus. Hyginus says that it was thirty years, but the grander Aeschylus makes it thirty thousand years.

[45] According to Apollodorus, Heracles stopped at the island of Rhodes and, notwithstanding the imprecations of the owner, loosed a bullock from the cart of a cowherd and sacrificed it to Zeus and, from that time on, the Rhodians were accustomed to sacrifice to the great hero with curses instead of blessings. The same writer also says that Antaeus and Busiris were slain during the journey to the Hesperides—instead of relating those adventures to the travels incident to the taking of Geryon's red herd.

[46] As earlier mentioned, much confusion existed about the place where Atlas is said to have had his footing.

[47] Atlas was presumed to know where the golden apples were located because they were guarded by the Hesperides, who were his daughters.

Atlas readily agreed and—transfer of the load having been lightly (?) effected—set out for the garden of the Hesperides. He soon returned with the apples but, unwilling to resume his thankless task, told Heracles that he would himself take them to Eurystheus at Mycenae. In this emergency, the great man's wit proved to be at one with his strength, for he seemingly acquiesced, and cunningly asked Atlas to reassume his old burden until he should procure a pad for his unpracticed head. The unsuspecting Titan fell into the trap and, again pinned down by the weight of the world, saw Heracles depart with the golden apples. However, after they were delivered to Eurystheus, they were returned into the custody of the Hesperides—for it was not destined that they should remain elsewhere.[48]

Twelfth Labor. As his last labor, Eurystheus ordered Heracles to go down to the world of the dead and bring up the hound Cerberus. This many-headed offspring of Typhon and Echidna had the tail of a dragon and a mane from which sprouted the hissing mouths of many serpents.[49]

Before departing from Greece, Heracles went to Eleusis and asked the presiding priest[50] to initiate him into the mysteries conducted at that place in honor of Demeter, whose daughter Persephone was the queen of the lower world. After first being cleansed of the slaughter of the Centaurs, he was duly initiated, and then proceeded to Taenarus in Laconia where he entered an opening in the ground, said to have been one of the mouths of the descent to the realm of Hades.

When he arrived at his destination, he encountered the shades of several persons whom he had known on earth,[51] and he drew his sword against the phantom of the Gorgon Medusa. However, he sheathed it after he was told by Hermes that he saw only a shadow. He released his kinsman Theseus from the imprisonment meted to him for assisting Peirithous in an attempted abduction of Persephone, but Peirithous was so firmly stuck in his dungeon seat that the whole region quaked at the great man's tugging and he was forced to discontinue his efforts at liberation.[52] He rolled away the stone which Demeter had cast upon Ascalaphus for having tattled that Persephone ate the fatal pomegranate seeds whereupon, the unforgiving goddess changed the contemptible talebearer into a screech owl. He next wrestled with Menoetes, the herdsman of Hades, until the unhappy fellow—with ribs already broken—was spared at the request of Persephone, and stood helplessly aside while one of his herd was slaughtered for the gratification of the gibbering shades.

Having given these exhibitions of his prowess, Heracles now asked Hades for his guardian hound and was given permission to take the monster if he could be mastered without the use of weapons. Heracles retraced his steps to the brazen gates and flung his arms around the brute's head. Although he was bitten many times by the serpents covering the scaly back, his strong grip was not released until Cerberus yielded and submitted to being led away. Returning to earth through an opening at Troezen in Argos, he triumphantly exhibited his trophy to the trembling Eurystheus, and then carried him back to the lower world.

Later Adventures

After completing his destined labors, Heracles returned to Thebes, where his first act was to hand over his wife, Megara, to his nephew Iolaus—a cold-blooded act which he defended on the ground that the madness which had caused him to slaughter their children had been sent by the gods to show their disapproval of his

---

[48] A different legend relates that Heracles himself obtained the apples after killing the dragon Ladon, but the story given in the text seems to be an equitable offset to the "sluggishness of soul" which was earlier claimed to blunt the great hero's musical appreciation.

[49] Cerberus is referred to in the text as "many-headed" because the classical writers vary in stating the number to be all the way from three to a hundred.

[50] The presiding priest is generally stated to have been Eumolpus, but Diodorus says that he was Musaeus, the son of Orpheus.

[51] Among the shades encountered was that of Meleager, who bade Heracles take his living sister, Deianeira, as his wife.

---

[52] Theseus was, also, so firmly stuck in his Stygian seat that, when he was pulled loose by Heracles, a portion of his posterior still remained—an incident which is gravely commented on by one mythographer as the reason why the Athenians were so thinly formed in that region.

union with her. But one may conjecture the actual reason to have been that he had become tired of matronly Megara, and wanted to replace her with someone else of fresher charms. Making some inquiries, he learned that the Oechalian king, Eurytus, who had been his boyhood instructor in archery, still claimed to be a past master in the art, and he was offering the hand of his beautiful young daughter, Iole, to any man who could outshoot himself and his sons. As previously related in chapter 12 (in connection with "Madame X" as one of the wives of Apollo), Heracles accepted the general challenge and won, but was refused his reward on the alleged ground that he might again be stricken with madness and slay the children whom Iole should bear to him.

Not long after, he visited the court of King Admetus at Pherae in Thessaly, and (under circumstances related in chapter 8) was instrumental in bringing back his friend's wife, Alcestis, who had volunteered to die in her husband's stead. During his absence, Autolycus—the thieving son of Hermes—stole some of Eurytus' cattle and the Oechalian king attributed their taking to Heracles, thinking it an act of revenge.[53] Iphitus did not share his father's suspicion, but went to Thebes after the great hero had returned from Pherae and asked his assistance in recovering the stolen herd. Although his aid was promised, Heracles was again stricken with his malady and killed the youth by throwing him down from the wall of the city.[54]

Wishing to be purified of the slaying, Heracles went to Neleus at Pylus, but his request was rejected in a decision wherein all of Neleus' sons joined—except Nestor. Although Neleus based his rejection plausibly on the score of friendship with Eurythus, Heracles was furious at his action, and departed only after vowing that he would some day return for the purpose of taking

revenge. He then went to Amyclae in Laconia[55] and obtained purification at the hands of Deiphobus, who is mentioned only as the son of an otherwise unidentified Hippolytus. But the ceremony had no mitigating effect on the hero's disease and he proceeded to Delphi, where he asked the Pythia for advice. When she refused to impart the healing wisdom of the oracle, he flew into a great rage and set about sacking the shrine itself. He even laid hold of the sacred tripod, upon which the Pythia was accustomed to sit, and vowed that he would establish an oracle of his own. At this juncture, however, Apollo appeared and resisted him with force in a struggle which might have ended disastrously had Zeus not parted his proud sons with a thunderbolt. The oracle then revealed to Heracles that he could obtain relief from his malady only by being sold into slavery, by paying to Eurytus the purchase price as compensation for his slain son, and following this, by serving three years in bondage. Acting as auctioneer, the mercenary Hermes sold the great man's services to the Lydian queen, Omphale, for three talents of silver (about thirty-five hundred dollars), but for some unexplained reason Eurytus refused the money when it was offered to him.[56] It does not appear, however, that the Lydian queen was overly cruel to her great slave, for during the period of his service, she bore two sons to him, who were named Agelaus and Maleus. On one occasion, she even playfully dressed the most masculine of all heroes in her dainty, feminine attire and herself paraded about in his huge lion skin.

With the gradual healing of his disease, Heracles returned to his accustomed activities, and we again find him meting fit punishment to all evildoers and performing exploits of renown. One day, while he was taking a nap by the roadside, two droll and thievish men, called the

---

[53] The gargantuan activities of Heracles were so numerous and so diversified that stories about him, necessarily concerning many others, are related throughout the text and, to a certain extent, much of this chapter may be repetitive.

[54] According to Homer, Iphitus himself had lost twelve mares and, after finding them, stopped at the house of Heracles, who murdered his guest and kept the animals.

[55] Amyclae, instead of Sparta, was considered by some as the seat of Tyndareus' government—a surmise which gains some confirmation from the fact that the compiler's scholarly friend, Theodore A. Buenger, found a beautiful, little leaden image of Helen while he was visiting the location.

[56] Omphale was a daughter of Iardanus and, according to one legend, was originally the wife of Tmolus, a Lydian mountain-god who decided the musical contest between Pan and Apollo.

Cercopes, robbed him of his weapons. Awakened by their chatter, he seized and bound them and, hanging them head-down over a timber, proceeded to carry them away for greater punishment, but they took their perilous situation in such good part that their pleasantries brought irrestible laughter to their captor and he set them free.[57]

Harsher treatment was accorded Syleus, a cruel man in Aulis who forced all passers-by to till his vineyards. When Heracles was ordered to dig, he uprooted all the vines, piled them together, placed Syleus and his daughter on top of the heap, and burned them to ashes.[58]

On another occasion, Heracles was walking along the shores of the island of Doliche, off the coast of Caria, and found the corpse of youthful Icarus who, in flying from Crete on wings attached to his body with wax, had soared so near the Sun that the wax melted and he fell into the sea. Seemingly out of character, the great hero tenderly administered the rites of burial, and announced that the island thereafter should be called Icaria and that its surrounding waters should be known as the Icarian Sea. Daedalus, the talented architect-father of Icarus, was grateful for this kind act, and made a statue of Heracles in a likeness so perfect that it deceived its impetuous original into throwing stones at what appeared to be his own living image.

During his period of bondage, the great man heard about the preparations being made by Jason and his comrades to recover the Golden Fleece and obtained Omphale's permission to join the expedition. With him, he took Hylas, a beautiful lad of whom he was exceedingly fond—because he had earlier slain Theiodamas, the boy's father! When he arrived at Iolchus, the assembled heroes tendered to him the leadership of their band; but he refused and nominated Jason for the honor, as having been the moving spirit in the enterprise. His subsequent

activities as one of the Argonauts, ending with the loss of Hylas, and his being left stranded on the shores of Mysia, have been related in chapter 7.[59] After giving up all hope of recovering Hylas, the great man sadly made his way back to Lydia and was informed by Omphale that the period of his service was completed and he was at liberty to leave her.

Heracles (perhaps reluctantly) returned to Greece and should have considered taking a small vacation. Instead, he set about raising a force to punish the Trojan king, Laomedon, for refusing to deliver the divine horses, which he had promised as the reward for saving Hesione from the sea monster. He soon mustered an army of noble volunteers, and sailed for Troy with a complement of eighteen ships, each manned by fifty oarsmen. After making port, he left the protection of the ships to a few men commanded by Oicles, and proceeded with the rest to attack the city. Meanwhile, advancing on the anchored ships by a roundabout way, Laomedon came upon the small guard and a sharp fight ensued, in which Oicles lost his life, but some of his companions were able to return to their vessels and put out to sea. Without attempting to follow, Laomedon quickly retraced his steps and returned to the city with his forces, just as Heracles was about to effect an entrance.

In the siege which followed, Telamon[60] was the first to breach the walls and enter the city. This act of precedence so infuriated Heracles that he drew his sword and rushed upon him. However, instead of drawing his own weapon, Telamon calmly began to collect a pile of stones —an act which prompted the great man to ask the reason. Telamon replied that he was intending to use the stones in building an altar to

---

[57] One story about the Cercopes relates that they were deceitful men, whom Zeus punished by turning them into apes. Another, attributed to Hesiod, relates that they were sons of Oceanus and Theia, named Acmon and Passalus.

[58] A later commentator, citing Pliny, says that Syleus was not necessarily cruel—but was in sore need of help lest his vines be not tended in time for their proper fruition.

---

[59] According to Apollonius Rhodius, Heracles hastened to join the Argonauts when he heard of their impending expedition, as he returned to Mycenae with the Erymanthian boar. Others state that, during his period of bondage to Omphale, he took part in the Calydonian boar hunt, but most recitals of that event do not include him among the participants. It seems obvious that if he had been present he would have killed the beast, but all accounts credit the accomplishment to Meleager.

[60] Telamon was a son of Aeacus, who is said to have assisted Poseidon and Apollo in building the Trojan walls.

"Heracles, the Glorious Victor," a clever answer which quieted the resentment of the vain hero, and undoubtedly saved Telamon from quick death.

Inside the broken walls, Heracles shot down Laomedon and his sons, Clytius, Hicetaon, and Lampus. He also captured Podarces, a son who had counseled Laomedon to deliver the divine horses after Hesione had been saved from the seamonster. Hesione was likewise captured and was bestowed on Telamon, as a prize for his forgiven gallant action. When she was allowed to select another captive to survive with herself, she chose her brother Podarces, but Heracles demanded that she give something in return, and she surrendered her veil. For this reason, Podarces was afterwards called Priam—a name derived from the Greek verb meaning "to buy."

As the victors were sailing away from the pillaged town, Hera caught Zeus napping and sent a violent storm which drove them to the island of Cos.[61] The inhabitants thought that the storm-driven squadron was approaching with intent of piracy and showered the vessels with stones. This reception so angered Heracles that he forced his way into their city by night and slew their king, Eurypylus, who was a son of Poseidon and Astypalaea. Then, according to his habit, he took the king's daughter Chalciope as his fair reward and, in due time, she bore to him a son named Thessalus.

In later fighting, Heracles was wounded by a Coan warrior named Chalcodon, but he was miraculously snatched away from the hand-to-hand conflict by Zeus before he received any greater harm or had the opportunity to chastise his impertinent adversary. The supreme god had other work for his son to do, for he was transported to the plain of Thessaly,[62] where he assisted the Olympian gods in their victorious battle with the Giants, which has been related in chapter 2.

The restless hero now remembered that, like Laomedon, King Augeias had failed to keep his pledged word—in that he had refused to deliver the promised tenth part of his cattle as compensation for cleaning his filthy stables. With the great man, to think was to act. So, assembling a host of volunteers from Arcadia, he marched into Elis, where he encountered the army of Augeias, which was jointly led by Eurytus and Cteatus. These were sons of Molione and Actor, who was a brother of Augeias,[63] and were two men joined into one, with a combined strength that surpassed all others of their generation. As the battle was about to begin, Heracles suddenly became ill and, without revealing the fact to the Moliones (as Eurytus and Cteatus were called), he made a truce with them. But, soon after, they learned of his illness and, in violation of the truce, attacked his army and slew many of his followers. Still stricken, he was forced to retreat in order to save the remainder of his force from defeat. Upon later recovering, he learned that the Eleans were sending the Moliones to take part in the Isthmian games which were periodically held near the city of Corinth. Heracles laid in wait at Cleonae, through which they had to pass, and there the double-formed warriors were killed with a single arrow from his mighty bow. And it is said that, as a result of this disaster, the Eleans ever after refrained from sending further representatives to the Isthmian games.[64]

With the Eleans deprived of their powerful leaders, Heracles marched to their city and, taking it by storm, killed Augeias and appropriated his daughter, Epicaste, who later gave birth to a son called Thestalus. The amorous warrior then recalled Phyleus from the island of Dulichium to take over the kingdom left by his faithless father. To celebrate his victory, he established the Olympic games, which have persisted to our times, and in the plain of Olympia near

---

[61] Upon awakening, Zeus was furious at Hera's presumption and, first tying two brazen anvils to her feet, suspended her from the heavens.

[62] A more exact statement places the locale of the battle with the Giants on the peninsula of Chalcidice called Pallene, and anciently known as Phlegra.

---

[63] The father of the Moliones (Molionides) was sometimes said to have been Poseidon.

[64] The Isthmian games, held every three (or five) years, were generally thought to have been instituted by Sisyphus in honor of his nephew Melicertes who, after a tragic, mortal death, was worshipped as the sea-deity Palaemon.

the town of Pisa, the great man himself won all of the contests.[65]

Another old score remained to be settled. It will be remembered that Neleus had refused to purify Heracles after his crazed slaying of Iphitus, and that his refusal had been approved by all of his sons except Nestor. Invading Pylus in Messenia, where Neleus ruled, the hero first encountered Periclymenus, one of the king's sons, who had been granted the power of changing his shape. And, when he was assaulted, he successively turned himself into a lion, a snake, and a bee—but, in the last form, he was smashed with a blow of Heracles' war club.[66] Thereafter, a great battle ensued, in which the Pylians were said to have been aided by Ares, Hera, and Hades, but despite their divine help, Neleus himself and all of his sons, save Nestor,[67] lost their lives in the fighting. Ares was wounded four times by the spear of Heracles, but was invisibly plucked from the ground before the hero could strip him of his arms; Hera also was wounded—by an arrow which pierced her breast; and Hades received a like barb in his shoulder, which brought such pain—even to an immortal—that the embarrassed ruler of the dead fled to Olympus, where the divine physician Paeon spread a healing salve over his aching wound. Although his aid proved ineffectual, the Pylians remembered his efforts in their cause and, thereafter, were one of the few peoples who were accustomed to offer sacrifices to the dark god.

Among others who had assisted the Pylians were the sons of Hippocoön—the illegitimate son of Oebalus, who had usurped the throne at Sparta after expelling Tyndareus and Icarius from the kingdom of Lacedaemon. Heracles was angry, not only at their assistance of the Pylians but also because they had previously slain his kinsman Oeonus,[68] when he threw a stone in self-defense against one of their dogs which was rushing upon him. While regrouping his army to punish the Hippocoöntids, the great man asked for reinforcements from Cepheus, the Arcadian king, but Cepheus refused, fearing that his capital city of Tegea might be attacked in his absence. His fear was overcome, however, when Heracles gave to his daughter Sterope a lock from the Gorgon's head, which he had received from Athena, and promised that any attackers would be turned to flight if the snaky tress should merely be held before them. With this assurance, the Arcadian king joined the expedition and brought along Aeropus and his nineteen other (unnamed) sons. During their absence, Tegea was not attacked but, in the battle with the Lacedaemonians, Cepheus and all of his sons, except Aeropus, were slain. It was a matter of little consolation to them that Heracles and his men killed Hippocoön and all of his sons. Nor was Heracles overjoyed with the victory because, in the same battle, he lost his beloved friend and half brother Iphicles. He spared, however, the conquered kingdom from pillage and returned its rule to Tyndareus, who returned from exile and is said, by some, to have established his capital at Amyclae instead of at Sparta.

Returning through Tegea, the great man celebrated his victory by debauching Auge, not knowing that she was the sister of his fallen ally Cepheus. When her aged father, Aleus, discovered her condition, he gave the girl to Nauplius, the son of Poseidon, and ordered him to drown her.[69] As she was being led away to the sea, she gave birth to her babe in a thicket near Mount Parthenium and left it there to perish and, soon rejoining Nauplius, proceeded to the

---

[65] Many others—including Clymenus, Endymion, Pelops, Theseus, and Zeus—are variously named as the founder of the Olympic games, which were held each fourth year. Historically, the date of the first celebration has been fixed as 776 B.C.

[66] According to a different legend, Periclymenus finally turned himself into an eagle and was shot with an arrow.

[67] It may be presumed that Nestor was spared because he had previously disapproved of his father's refusal to purify Heracles, but Apollodorus says that, at the time of the battle, Nestor was at Gerenia, where all accounts agree that he received his boyhood training.

[68] Oeonus was a son of Licymnius, who was a half brother of Heracles' mother, Alcmena.

[69] Unfettered by chronology, it is said that Nauplius was still living at the end of the Trojan War, and that he wrecked many of the returning Greeks on the island of Euboea, because they had executed his son Palamedes for an alleged act of treachery.

harbor of Nauplia in Argolis. But, instead of drowning his charge, Nauplius sold her to some Carian sailors who were about to set sail for Mysia in Asia Minor. After arriving at their destination, the sailors gave their fair purchase to Teuthras, the king of the country, and—soon after—he made her his wife.[70]

In the meanwhile, Auge's son was nursed by a doe until he was found by some shepherds, who named him Telephus from the Greek words meaning "doe's dug." The shepherds took their find to King Corythus, who was so pleased with the infant's appearance that he raised him as his own child. But, when Telephus reached manhood, he was told the truth about his discovery and went to the oracle at Delphi for advice. Suffice to say that he was directed, without further explanation, to go to the court of King Teuthras in Mysia; in so doing, he was reunited with his mother Auge; and he eventually married Astyoche, a daughter of the Trojan king, Laomedon. Upon the death of Teuthras, he succeeded to the kingdom of Mysia.[71]

When Heracles went to the lower world to bring up the hound Cerberus, among the shades whom he encountered was that of Meleager, who had died in a tragic episode growing out of the Calydonian boar hunt. In this strange conversation with the dead, Heracles proposed to marry Meleager's sister, Deianeira, although, at the time, he was still lawfully wedded to Megara. Having heartlessly given Megara to his nephew Iolaus, and having slain his only legitimate children, he now remembered his Stygian promise and went to Calydon in Aetolia to sue for the maiden's hand. Upon his arrival, he found that the river-god Achelous was also seeking her love; and the rival suitors forthwith engaged in a tremendous wrestling match, during which the river-god changed himself into a bull and Heracles broke off one of his horns. This was confused by some of the ancient writers with the horn of plenty, which Zeus took

from the goat Amaltheia, and the same, or similar, stories are often told about it. At any rate, Achelous sorely needed the severed portion of his anatomy and, when Heracles returned it, the river-god abandoned his amorous claims, and Deianeira became the great man's second wife.

Now being a member of their royal family, Heracles proceeded to join the Calydonians in a conquest of the Thesprotians, who dwelt about Ephyra in Epeirus. Having vanquished the Thesprotian king, Phylas, the invincible bridegroom—unshackled by mortal convention—had connection with his daughter Astyoche, who later bore to him a son named Tlepolemus.

Victoriously returning to Calydon, and to Deianeira, he remained as a guest of his father-in-law, Oeneus, for three years. During this period, he thought of the sons who, in his early youth, had been borne to him by the fifty daughters of Thespius. So, he sent word to Thespius to keep seven of them at Thespiae, to send three to Thebes, and to dispatch the remainder to plant a colony on the island of Sardinia.[72]

One day, while he was dining with Oeneus and was being waited on by a young servant named Eunomus, the lad made some slip which caused Heracles to strike him with his knuckles—a blow which unintentionally resulted in death. Although he was forgiven by Eunomus' father, the law required that the careless act must be followed by the penalty of exile. Taking Deianeira with him, the great man departed for the court of King Ceyx at Trachis in Thessaly. Upon arrival at the river Evenus, they were met by the Centaur Nessus, who was accustomed to ferry on his back all travelers desiring to cross the stream. Heracles disdained his assistance and crossed alone, but left Deianeira to be carried over by the obliging creature—only to hear her cry out in midstream as her biformed porter attempted a rude intimacy. Swiftly turning, the hero sent one of his poisoned arrows through the Centaur's heart and he crawled up on the bank to die. Unseen by Heracles, he called pitying Deianeira to his side and, giving her a mix-

---

[70] The western part of Mysia, ruled by Teuthras, was sometimes called Teuthrania.

[71] Another version of the story relates that Auge and her child were both carried by the Carian sailors to King Teuthras.

---

[72] It is said that the town of Olbia, in the northeastern part of Sardinia, thus had its beginning.

ture of his oozing blood, promised her that it would serve as a love charm to revive her husband's affection, if it should ever wane.

After leaving the dead Nessus, they entered the country of the Dryopians and, when none would give them food, Heracles was forced to seize a bullock which was being driven in harness. This he killed and ate, vowing that the inhabitants should soon be punished for their inhospitality.

Proceeding on to Trachis, the great man and his new wife were graciously received by King Ceyx and his queen, Alcyone, who was the fairest daughter of the wind-god Aeolus. Soon after their arrival, it was learned that the neighboring Dryopian king, Phylas,[73] had impiously feasted at a shrine of Apollo which was located inside the realms of Ceyx. Still rankling because of the ill-usage accorded to him while passing through that monarch's country, this news was a sufficient excuse to set Heracles again on the warpath, and he speedily attacked the Dryopians, killed their king and his sons, and scattered the rest of the tribe so widely that some of its members fled all the way to Asine in Argos. He then started back to Trachis but tarried long enough to lie with the dead king's daughter, Meda. In due time, she bore to him a son called Antiochus.

Some time afterward, while still visiting with Ceyx, Heracles was called to the assistance of Aegimius, king of the Dorians, who was engaged in a dispute with the Lapith king, Coronus, about the boundaries of their respective domains. With his powerful help, the Dorian king was victorious in a battle, wherein Coronus was slain and his Lapith warriors were utterly routed. Before enlisting the hero's aid, Aegimius had promised to give him a third part of his territory if he were delivered from his enemy, and after the victory he offered to carry out the bargain. But Heracles asked him to keep the land in trust for his sons who, some day after his death, might be in need of a place of refuge.

While he was riding back to Trachis, in his chariot driven by Iolaus, he spied the war-god Ares and his son Cycnus[74] at Itonus, in a grove which was sacred to Apollo. Ares was also accompanied by his two sons, Deimos and Phobos, who were always present whenever the bloodthirsty deity essayed battle.[75] Heracles, however, was unafraid because at Pylus, he had previously encountered the brash war-god and had proved more than his match at arms. Cycnus first charged, but found his opponent's shield invulnerable to all thrusts, and lost his own life, when Heracles' great spear entered an opening in his armor and pierced cleanly through his neck. Furious at his son's defeat, Ares now attacked and was forced to the ground by a spear thrust which tore deeply into his thigh. Upon this happening, Phobos and Deimos speedily drove up on the god's chariot and, lifting their stricken sire into the carriage, "lashed the horses and came to high Olympus." The mightiest son of Zeus had again shown his prowess.

Continuing toward Trachis, Heracles came to Ormenium, a small town at the foot of Mount Pelion. Here King Amyntor, the son of Ormenus, took arms and forbade him to pass. Whereupon, the great man killed him and—according to custom and usage—lay with his daughter, Astydameia, who subsequently gave birth to a son named Ctesippus.

When he finally arrived back at Trachis, the hero was joyfully greeted by Deianeira and the four sons who were the fruit of their union, Hyllus, Ctesippus, Glenus, and Onites.[76] For a few days, he relaxed and enjoyed the comfort of his family and the abundant hospitality of Ceyx and Alcyone, but relaxation was not for his nervous blood, and he began to gather a new army to punish the Oechalian king, Eurytus, for having refused to deliver Iole, whom he had fairly won—years before—in the archery contest. At his call, his band of faithful Arcadians

---

[73] According to Apollodorus, the Dryopian king was named Laogoras.

[74] The mother of Cycnus was Pelopeia, a daughter of Pelias. Ares had another son of the same name by Pyrene, one of the nymphs.

[75] The practically interchangeable names of Deimos and Phobos were each personified variously as Fear, Fright, Terror, Dismay, or Panic.

[76] Apollonius Rhodius says that the mother of Hyllus was the water-nymph Melite.

were joined by a number of men from Trachis, and also by a company of Locrians from the east coast of Greece. He led them to Oechalia where a sharp battle took place, in which the forces of Eurytus were overcome—resulting in the death of the archer-king and all of his remaining sons.[77] Heracles first paused to bury those who had fallen on his side, and was grieved to learn that among them were Hippasus, the son of his friend Ceyx, and Argeius and Melas, the last two sons of his kinsman Licymnius.[78] He then proceeded to pillage the conquered city quite thoroughly, led Iole away as his captive, and built an altar in honor of his supreme father Zeus.

Wishing to perform his sacrifice properly, he sent his servant Lichas to Deianeira at Trachis to ask for the tunic which he customarily wore in such celebrations. When she heard that Iole was being brought back as a captive, she feared that the maiden was about to steal her husband's affections and, remembering the advice of the dying centaur, smeared the tunic with the blood mixture which the biformed creature had told her would act as an irresistible love philter.

In due time, Lichas delivered the tunic, but as soon as Heracles put it about his body, the poison of the Hydra—carried by his arrow into the Centaur's blood—began to corrode his skin and, lifting his guiltless servant by the feet, he hurled him over a cliff to destruction. Desperately, he tried to tear off the tunic, only to find that it clung ever closer, and those of its pieces which he was able to pull loose bore with them great bands of his raw flesh. In this sad condition, he was carried on a stretcher to Trachis where Deianeira, in anguish at her precipitate action, hanged herself.

The great man knew that his mortal end was approaching, and ordered that he should be taken to Mount Oeta—first charging his eldest son, Hyllus, to marry Iole when he should become of age. After arriving at the mountain, he

laboriously built a funeral pyre of wooden boughs and, lying down upon it, instructed his retainers to set it on fire. None of them would obey the heart-breaking command, but Poeas (the son of Phylacus) who happened to be passing by in search of a lost sheep, was prevailed upon to apply a torch to the heaped boughs and Heracles gratefully gave him his great bow and the remaining arrows which had been dipped in the Hydra's poison. While the pyre was burning, a cloud passed under the dying man and, accompanied by a peal of thunder, miraculously wafted him up to the heavens. Pursuant to his divine destiny, he was given immortality;[79] and, becoming at last reconciled with Hera, was wedded on Olympus to her daughter Hebe, by whom he had two sons named Alexiares and Anicetus.

It is appropriate at this point to recapitulate the sons of Heracles and to name their descendants who are more than casually mentioned by the ancient writers. To clarify comment, the following chart is given, showing the various wives in the order previously mentioned in the text.

The Fifty Daughters of Thespius, and the fifty-one sons whom they bore to Heracles, have been enumerated in the text. According to Diodorus Siculus, when the Thespiadae (as the sons were known) attained manhood, seven of them continued to dwell at Thespiae and two others moved to the capital city of Thebes. The rest were led by their father's friend and kinsman, Iolaus, to the island of Sardinia, where they founded the town of Olbia which became celebrated for the imposing public buildings erected by the architect Daedalus, who was brought up from Sicily by Iolaus.[80]

Megara after being divorced by Heracles (following his murder of their three sons) was

---

[77] Iphitus had previously died when Heracles threw him from the walls of Tiryns. His remaining brothers were named Clytius, Molion, Toxeus, and Didaeon.

[78] As previously related, Oeonus, the son of Licymnius, was murdered by the Hippocoöntids.

---

[79] Heracles was immortalized as the constellation bearing his name (the Great Cluster of Heracles), which is surrounded by others known as Ophiuchus, Corona, Boötes, Draco, Lyra, and Aquila.

[80] It would appear that the number of the sons mentioned on the accompanying chart should have been large enough to satisfy even the most worshipful of Heracles' admirers, but Hyginus lists six more (Leucites, Leucippus, Ophites, Deucalion, Evenus, and Lydus), and the Jewish historian Josephus even brings the great hero into the Biblical line—saying that he had a son, Didorus, by a daughter of Aphra, a son of Abraham.

82. Descendants of Heracles

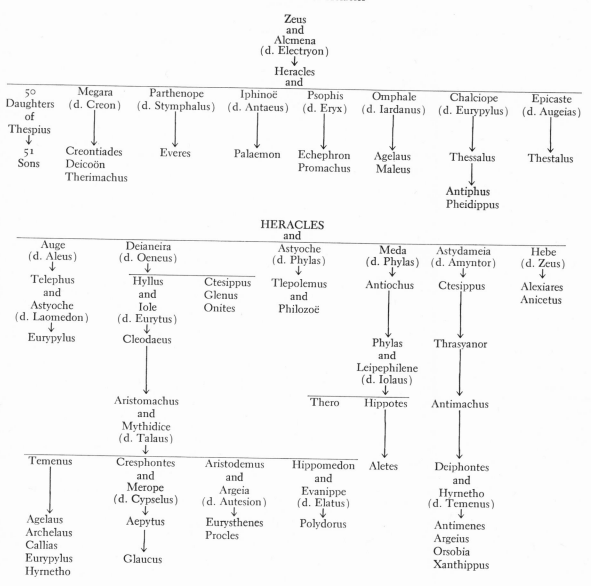

handed over to Iolaus and presented her second husband with a daughter named Leipephilene, who became the wife of Phylas.

Parthenope—as previously related—was one of the Stymphalides, whose extermination constituted the sixth labor of Heracles. Presumably, she did not fall a victim to his poisoned arrows, for it is said that she bore to him a son named Everes, about whom nothing further is mentioned.

Iphinoë, daughter of the giant Antaeus, whom Heracles bested in wrestling, is noted by the mythographers only as having borne a son Palaemon to her father's conqueror.

Psophis, the daughter of Eryx, bore Echephron and Promachus to Heracles in Sicily. But, when her sons were grown, they migrated to Phegia in Arcadia (earlier known as Erymanthus) and changed the name of the town to Psophis in their mother's honor.

Omphale, daughter of Iardanus, under whom Heracles served a period of bondage for his murder of Iphitus, bore to him two sons named Agelaus and Maleus, of whom the former was claimed as an ancestor by the wealthy Lydian king, Croesus.

Chalciope, daughter of Eurypylus, bore a son to Heracles named Thessalus, remembered primarily because he was the father of Antiphus and Pheidippus, who led the Coans in the Trojan War. Another legend, however, relates that it was he (and not Thessalus, the son of Haemon) who gave his name to the country called Thessaly.

Epicaste, daughter of Augeias, bore to the great man a son named Thestalus, mentioned by Apollodorus without ascribing to him any action of note.

Auge, daughter of Aleus, brings a refreshing oasis to our desert of "begat": for the interesting circumstances of her accouchement, previously related, were followed by the exploits of her son Telephus, which were in line with those of his mighty father. When the Greeks first set out for Troy and attempted to land on his Mysian shores, Telephus furiously opposed them and would have driven their forces away; but Dionysus caused him to stumble over a vine and he was wounded by Achilles as he lay defenseless on the ground. It was then discovered that he was a son of Heracles and the Greeks urged him to join their expedition, a request which he refused, on the plea that his wife, Astyoche, was a daughter of Laomedon, a deceased king of the Trojans.[81] Later, when his wound failed to heal, it was miraculously cured by the rust from the sword of Achilles which had been its cause. In gratitude, he led the invading Greek army to its Trojan objective. His son Eurypylus, however, was induced by presents from Priam to fight for his mother's family, and it is related that he slew the Greek leech Machaon, and was subsequently himself destroyed by Achilles' son Neoptolemus.

Deianeira, the daughter of Oeneus, who became the second lawful wife of Heracles, following his lower world conversation with the shade of her brother Meleager, bore four sons to the hero. Nothing of interest is related about Ctesippus, Glenus, and Onites; but Hyllus (the eldest son) carries on in story. After his father was translated to the heavens from his funeral pyre on Mount Oeta, Hyllus obeyed his dying command, and married the maiden Iole, who soon bore a son, Cleodaeus, to perpetuate the line of his mighty ancestor.

For a time, Hyllus remained with his family, and with many of the other sons of Heracles, at the court of their friend Ceyx, the king of Trachis. Finally, however, they became restless, because an oracle had foretold it to be the will of Zeus that the Heracleidae (as they were collectively known) should reoccupy the Peloponnesus.[82] Eurystheus heard of their growing aspirations and, when he threatened war, the unorganized brothers—feeling as yet unable to resist his seasoned forces—fled from Trachis to Athens, and asked their kinsman Theseus for protection.

83. Ancestors of Heracles and Theseus

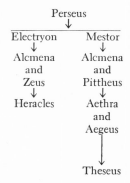

Shortly after their arrival, Eurystheus came with his army and demanded that the Athenians surrender their suppliants. Led, however, by Iolaus,[83] and with the assistance of the Athenians, the Hericleidae boldly attacked and

[81] Another version of the story relates that Astyoche was a daughter of Priam, the son of Laomedon who was ruling at Troy during the Great War.

[82] Argos was claimed as the hereditary kingdom of Heracles; Sparta was claimed, from his overthrow of the Hippocoontids; Messenia, from his victory over the forces of Neleus at Pylus; and Elis, from his victory over the forces of Augeias.

[83] According to Euripides, the Heracleidae made their petition to Demophon, the son of Theseus, and one version of the legend relates that Iolaus was brought back from the dead to assist the sons of his great master.

routed their attacking enemies, in a battle wherein Eurystheus and his sons were slain.

After the battle, the Heracleidae entered the Peloponnesus without meeting further resistance and took over the rulership of the whole country, but at the end of a year a plague fell upon the land and, upon inquiry, an oracle declared that it was due to the fact that they had returned before their predestined time. Accordingly, they quitted the peninsula and retired to the plain of Marathon in Attica. Hyllus, not being completely satisfied with the oracular pronouncement, made inquiry at Delphi—where the greatest of all oracles was located. The answer of the Pythia was that the Heracleidae should await the "third crop" before assuming their ancestral lands. Hyllus supposed that her reply meant three years and, having waited for that period, gathered his army and proceeded back to Argos.

Following the death of Eurystheus, Atreus had now taken over the kingship at Mycenae and Tiryns,[84] and his forces met the invaders on the isthmus of Corinth. When the opposing lines of battle were drawn up, Hyllus proposed that he would meet any one of the enemy in a single combat, whose issue should be accepted by both sides as decisive. His proposal was accepted and it was agreed that, if he should conquer his opponent, the Heracleidae should receive the kingdom formerly ruled by Eurystheus, but if he should be defeated, his kinsmen would not return to the Peloponnesus for another fifty years.[85]

Allied with the forces of Atreus were some Arcadians from Tegea, whose leader was Echemus, the son of Aeropus. It may be remembered that, in the war against the Hippocoöntids, the Tegean king, Cepheus, had reluctantly joined Heracles, and had taken into the battle his twenty sons. Of these, Aeropus alone survived the fighting. It was his son, Echemus, who now offered to meet Hyllus in the proposed single combat. In the duel which followed, Hyllus was slain and, pursuant to the agreement, the Heracleidae gave up their effort to enter the Peloponnesus. Some few of their number were admitted to citizenship and remained in Argos, but the greater part went to the Dorian king, Aegimius, at Doris near Mount Oeta and received from him the third part of his lands, which he was faithfully holding in trust for them—as his promised reward for the help which Heracles had earlier given to him in the war against the Lapiths.[86]

Cleodaeus, the son of Hyllus, seems to have realized that the "third crop" of the oracle meant the third generation from his great ancestor, and kept the bargain which had been made on the Corinthian isthmus, but his son Aristomachus was slain in another vain attempt to take the Peloponnesus before the fated time. When he died, he left four sons—who had been borne to him by his wife Mythidice, a daughter of Talaus. As shown on the preceding chart, their names were Temenus, Cresphontes, Aristodemus, and Hippomedon. We have previously related, in chapter 8, that Hippomedon was slain in the attack of the Seven Against Thebes, and that his son Polydorus followed as one of the victorious Epigoni—circumstances which (perhaps for reasons of chronology) seem to have eliminated them from the mythological events narrated next.

At the expiration of the agreed period, when Atreus' lineal descendant Tisamenus had come into the rulership of the Peloponnesus, the Heracleidae gathered to claim their promised country. The surviving sons of Aristomachus joined their half brothers, accompanied by Eurysthenes and Procles—two sons of Aristodemus who had been borne to him by Argeia, a daughter of the Theban king, Autesion. The invading forces were reinforced by an army of Dorians[87] under the leadership of Dymas and Pamphylus, the sons of Heracles' erstwhile

---

[84] Atreus was a brother of Nicippe, the mother of Eurystheus.

[85] Both Herodotus and Thucydides name the period of the proposed truce as one hundred years.

[86] Another version of the legend relates that the Heracleidae returned from their defeat on the isthmus to Tricorythus in Attica, and later went on to Doris where King Aegimius adopted Hyllus as his own son.

[87] Because the Heracleidae were assisted by the Dorians, or from having themselves become part rulers of the country of Aegimius, the entry into the Peloponnesus was variously referred to as the "Return of the Heracleidae" or the "Dorian Invasion."

friend Aegimius—a reinforcement which proved of great assistance in the campaign which followed.

When the expedition was about to set out, Aristodemus was struck and killed by a flash of lightning which is said to have been an arrow from Apollo, sent in anger because his Delphian oracle had not previously been consulted. Calamity also befell the army, assembled at Naupactus in Ozolian Locris, for there appeared to them an Acarnanian soothsayer, named Carnus, who they thought was a magician sent by Tisamenus, and Hippotes, the son of Phylas, killed him with a javelin. Consequently, the naval force was hit by a great storm and the land army was stricken by a famine. Temenus, who had been appointed leader of the Heracleidae, speedily inquired at Delphi concerning these dual evils, and was told that they had been brought on by the murder of the soothsayer. Continuing, the oracle said that further disaster could be avoided only by banishing Hippotes and taking the "three-eyed one" as a guide.

Pursuant to the oracular injunction, Hippotes was thrust from the camp, and a search was instituted for the guide thus peculiarly designated. When the search had continued but a little while, Oxylus—a son of the Aetolian king, Haemon[88]—arrived on a one-eyed horse. The Heracleidae, rightly guessing the intent of the oracle's answer, induced him to become their guide—upon the promise that they would make him king of Elis if their invasion should prove successful. Under his direction, the gulf of Patras was crossed and a landing was made on the coast of Achaea, whence a march was made through Arcadia into Argos.[89] There, the army of Tisamenus was thoroughly defeated and, in the fighting, he was himself slain—bringing to an end the tragic dynasty which had always suffered under a curse laid upon its original ancestor Tantalus (for having served his son Pelops as food to the gods). On the side of the

Heracleidae, it may be presumed that a number of warriors were slain, but the only ones whom the mythographers mention as being lost were Dymas and Pamphylus, the sons of the Dorian king, Aegimius.

Being complete masters of the whole Peloponnesus, the victors now proceeded to distribute the territory among themselves. In accordance with their previous stipulation, the fertile land of Elis was reserved for Oxylus, in recompense for his services as guide. Since the Arcadians were the long-time allies of the Heracleidae, the succession to the government of their country was not disturbed, but it was agreed that lots should be drawn by Temenus and Cresphontes and, jointly by Procles and Eurysthenes (sons of deceased Aristodemus), for the rulership of Argos, Laconia, and Messenia. Cresphontes wished to have Messenia assigned to him and, when he saw that the lots were to be drawn from a pitcher of water, he cast in a clod of earth, whereas the others threw in stones. As the clod was dissolved, it naturally happened that the stones were drawn first. Thus, Temenus received Argos, the sons of Aristodemus received Laconia (also known as Lacedaemonia and Sparta), and Cresphontes received his desired Messenia.

Almost as soon as Temenus assumed the Argive rulership, his sons began to quarrel about which of them should succeed to the kingdom. By concerted action, Agelaus, Callias, and Eurypylus expelled their brother Archelaus and he went from Argos to Macedonia. There, King Cisseus promised to give him the hand of his daughter and the succession to his throne, if the fugitive prince should help him in a war against some neighboring enemies; but when Archelaus aided in the victory, and asked for his reward, the false king dug a hole in the earth, filled it with burning coals and covered it with branches —planning that Archelaus should fall into it and be destroyed. Fortunately for the intended victim, the plan was discovered and, with exact mythological justice, he threw Cisseus into his own burning trap and brought an end to his life. In later times, the story of his bold act so captivated the imagination of Alexander the Great that he boastfully traced his own descent back to the ingenious Argive hero.

---

[88] According to Apollodorus, Oxylus was a son of Andraemon and was returning to Aetolia from Elis, where he had spent a year's banishment for an accidental manslaughter.

[89] It is said that Oxylus deliberately avoided leading the invading army through Elis, because he wished to preserve inviolate the country which had been promised to him.

In disgust at the unfilial wrangling of his sons, Temenus announced that, on his death, the sovereignty of his realm should descend to his daughter Hyrnetho and her husband Deiphontes, who was the great-great-grandson of Heracles and Astydameia. To circumvent their father's design, Agelaus, Callias, and Eurypylus hired assassins who murdered him. Upon learning, however, of the will of their dead king, the Argive army decided that it should be carried out, and placed Hyrnetho and Deiphontes upon the throne.[90]

When Cresphontes assumed the Messenian throne, he married Merope, a daughter of the Arcadian king, Cypselus, who bore to him a son named Aepytus. Since the time of Neleus, the seat of the kingdom had been at Pylus, but Cresphontes built his palace at Stenyclerus, where he began to dispense justice so evenly that a group of his resentful nobles procured his murder. Thereupon, Polyphontes, another descendant of Heracles, usurped the throne and —against her will—married the widowed Merope. Aepytus, at the time being only a young boy, was spared by the conspirators and was taken to Arcadia, where he was reared by his grandfather Cypselus. When he reached manhood, he returned to Messenia and, after slaying Polyphontes, punished the murderers of his father, together with all who were accessories to their crime. Warned by his father's fate, however, he treated the rich and the noble with deference and made lavish gifts to the poor— thereby attaining such honor among his subjects that his descendants were given the name of Aepytidae and were no longer referred to as Heracleidae. His son, Glaucus, was content to imitate his life-saving example in all other matters but attained a greater reputation for piety by establishing regular sacrifices to some of the gods not previously so honored, and as a result was fortunate enough to come to a natural death after a peaceful rule.

According to Herodotus, the Spartans, ig- noring the tradition that Aristodemus was killed before the Heracleidae recovered the Peloponnesus, claimed that he was the first of the Dorian invaders to rule their country. But, they alleged that he died immediately after his sons, Eurysthenes and Procles, were born and did not have time to decide which of them should succeed to the kingdom. Faced with this dilemma, the citizenry applied to the oracle at Delphi and were told to make both of the boys their kings, but to give the greater honor to the elder of them. When their mother, Argeia, professed her inability to name the one who was born first, it was decided to resolve the difficulty by watching to see which of the twins she first washed and fed. It proved to be Eurysthenes and, accordingly, the first rank was given to him and ever after was retained by his descendants. This story is supposed to account for the dual kingship which was an early institution in Lacedaemonia (Laconia), the country which sent forth the famed Spartan warriors who defended the pass at Thermopylae against the onslaught of the invading Persians until their last man was slain.[91]

Astyoche, a daughter of the Thesprotian king, Phylas, bore to Heracles a son named Tlepolemus. During the year when the Heracleidae first occupied the Peloponnesus, after their victory over Eurystheus, he became angered at a servant and was beating him with a stick when Licymnius, the kinsman of Heracles, ran in between and was slain. According to some other accounts, however, the homicide was not accidental but was committed in hot blood. No matter how the deed occurred, it was mythologically necessary for Tlepolemus to exile himself; and he went to the island of Rhodes with a body of his retainers. "There his people settled in three divisions by tribes and were loved of Zeus that is king among gods and men; and upon them was wondrous wealth poured by the son of Cronus."

At the outbreak of the Trojan War, Tlepole-

---

[90] The territory originally allotted to Temenus included only the city of Argos and its immediate neighborhood. But from there Troezen, Epidaurus, Sicyon, Aegina, Philius, and other places were successively occupied by Deiphontes and his descendants.

[91] Whether or not any Spartan escaped, the ancient legend related that all of the defenders were buried at Thermopylae and that their joint tombstone recited: "Stranger, go tell Lacedaemon that we lie here in obedience to her laws."

mus was named as the leader of the Rhodians, and brought nine ships manned by his "lordly" islanders to the assistance of the Greeks. Although his was the winning side, he lost his life at Troy, when he was speared through the neck by Sarpedon, a son of Zeus and Laodameia, whom he had challenged to engage in single combat. In commemoration of his death, funeral games were instituted by his wife, Philozoë. According to the commentator Tzetzes, they were regularly celebrated by the Rhodians for many succeeding years.

Meda, the daughter of the Dryopian king, Phylas, bore to her father's conqueror a son, Antiochus, whose statue was later placed in a prominent spot at Athens, because one of the tribes of that city was named in his honor. Antiochus' son, Phylas, named for his maternal grandfather, married Leipephilene—a daughter of Heracles' kinsman Iolaus—and had a son, Hippotes, who was banished from the army at Naupactus for slaying the soothsayer Carnus. He also had a daughter, Thero, who became one of the many wives of Apollo. When Hippotes died, he left a son named Aletes, who waged a successful war against Corinth and, according to Pausanias, the conquered city continued under his rule and that of his descendants for five generations.

Astydameia, the daughter of Amyntor, bore a son to Heracles named Ctesippus, whose mythological inconspicuity equalled that of the great man's other son of the same name who was borne to him by Deianeira. He filled an important gap in the family tree, however, for his son, Thrasyanor, and his grandson, Antimachus, were the lineal ancestors of Deiphontes, to whom Temenus left the throne of Argos. By Hyrnetho, the daughter of Temenus, Deiphontes had three sons—Antimenes, Argeius, and Xanthippus—who greatly extended the Argive kingdom; and his daughter, Orsobia, is remembered as the loving bride of Pamphylus, who was changed into a sorrowing widow when her husband lost his life when he bravely fought on the side of the Heracleidae against the forces of Tisamenus.

Hebe, the eternally youthful daughter of Zeus and Hera, was given to Heracles as his wife in immortality, but nothing of interest is related about Alexiares and Anicetus—the two sons mentioned by Apollodorus as having been borne by her to the apotheosized greatest of all mortal heroes.

The reputation of Heracles was so spread through the ancient world and his exploits were so many that Cicero, in his "De Deorum Natura," felt constrained to explain his universality by saying that there were at least six different persons of the same name. As translated by Richard Baker (in an English edition printed at London in 1683), he says:

Nay, I would fain be satisfied too, which of the Hercules it is, that we are to worship: For, that search into the more recondite, and hidden Mysteries deliver, that there have been several of them. The Ancientest, is that he was gotten by Jupiter; (by the Elder Jupiter I mean for, in the old Greek Histories, we find many Jupiters also:) Of Lisyto and Him, then, came that Hercules, who is said to have contended with Apollo about the Tripos. The second is reported to have been an Aegyptian, got by Nilus; and he (they say) invented the Phrygian Character. The Third came from the Idaei Dactyli, who Sacrifice to him: The Fourth, was the son of Jupiter and Astraea; (Latona's sister) and him the Tyrians more particularly Worship, and tell that Carthago was his daughter. The Fifth is worship'd in India and there call'd Belus: The Sixth, he that was got on Alcmena by Jupiter.

As will be noticed from the text, among the great numbers of the children of Heracles, there were no daughters. Nor is there, in the ancient legends, even a slight hint of such a possibility. However, what seemingly appeared to him as a mythological deficiency was remedied by Euripides in his play "The Children of Heracles," in which it is stated that a daughter of the great hero, named Macaria, sacrificed herself at Athens—after an oracle had declared that the army of Eurystheus would be victorious unless a highborn maiden should freely die for the city. Thus, the patriotic dramatist created for his homeland a slight claim to filiation with the favorite son of Zeus, who probably never even heard of the place or its inhabitants.

15

The Decendants of Zeus V

Callisto—the Mother of Arcas

CALLISTO, the daughter of the impious Pelasgian king, Lycaon,[1] was a huntress-companion of the goddess Artemis. Although she had vowed a life of chastity, Zeus persuaded her to his embraces[2] and, in order to conceal his illicit amour from Hera, changed her into a she-bear.[3] But this precaution was in vain because, by the contrivance of Hera, Artemis was led during the chase to slay the metamorphosed girl without being aware of her identity. As she lay dying, Zeus snatched her unborn babe and gave it to Maia to rear in the land known as Pelasgia. Pityingly, he then caused Callisto to be carried on high and placed her in the heavens as the constellation which has been known ever since as the Great Bear—often referred to by the Latin name of Ursa Major.[4]

The boy was called Arcas, from the Greek word meaning "bear" and, upon attaining manhood, succeeded his maternal uncle Nyctimus in the rulership of the country, which was thereafter known as Arcadia.[5] By an unnamed woman, he had a son Autolaus, who is said to have brought up the infant Asclepius and, by Laodameia—daughter of Amyclas—he had a son, Triphylus, who gave the name of Triphylia to the coastal portion of Elis lying around the river Alpheius.[6]

After his two early amours, Arcas settled down at his capital city of Tegea and married the nymph Erato, who bore to him three sons, Apheidas, Elatus,[7] and Azan. When they had attained manhood, he divided his kingdom into three parts—allotting Azania to Azan, Tegea to Apheidas, and the country around Mount Cyllene to Elatus. This done, it is said that he was carried to the heavens and placed as the constellation Ursa Minor (the Little Bear) alongside the apotheosized form of his mother and, with her, is still fancifully chased by Arcturus, the brightest star in the constellation Boötes. Pausanias, however, relates that, by command

---

[1] Callisto is sometimes referred to as a nymph, or as a daughter of Nycteus, and it is intimated that her mother was the nymph Cyllene.

[2] Apollodorus says that Zeus forced Callisto against her will.

[3] Variations of the legend of Callisto relate that: (1) Artemis herself caused her to be turned into a bear, when she discovered her pregnancy in the bath; (2) it was Hera who caused the metamorphosis; (3) when Arcas was on the point of killing his mother in the chase, Zeus translated both of them to the skies as the Great and Little Bears; and, (4) that Callisto was known as Helice in afterlife.

[4] Seven of the stars in the large constellation of Ursa Major are commonly known as the Big Dipper.

[5] Nyctimus was the only one of Lycaon's sons to escape death from the lightning flash with which Zeus destroyed his father and his brothers because of their wickedness.

[6] Triphylus seems to have been otherwise undistinguished, although, according to Pausanias, statues of him and of his son, Erasus, were seen for many years at Delphi, where they had been dedicated to the oracular shrine by the citizens of Tegea.

[7] According to Apollodorus, the wife of Elatus was known as Leaneira or Meganeira.

84. Descendants of Zeus and Callisto

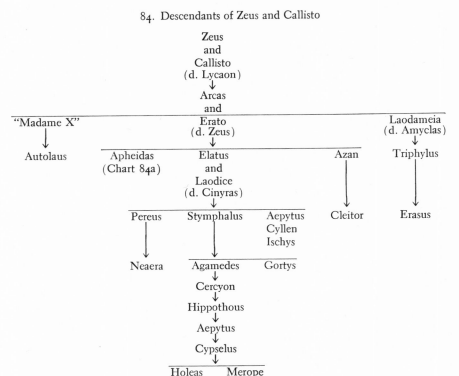

of the Delphic oracle, his remains were buried in the city of Mantineia. At the death of Azan, funeral games were instituted in his honor which are said to have been the first celebrated in all Greece. His kingdom was taken over by his son, Cleitor, who seems to have ruled without distinction and died childless.

By his wife, Laodice, Elatus had five sons named Aepytus, Cyllen, Ischys, Pereus, and Stymphalus. During his reign, he was called upon to protect the Delphian oracle of Apollo from an assault by the Phrygians. Responding to the call, he drove off the invaders and settled in Phocis at the place which, in his honor, was afterwards called Elateia. His abandoned kingdom around Mount Cyllene was taken over by his eldest son, Aepytus, who also assumed the rulership of Azania when Cleitor died without issue. He was killed, however, from the bite of a serpent while out hunting. And since he was childless, the double sovereignty went to Aleus —a son of Apheidas, who will be further mentioned in connection with chart 84a.

Concerning the other sons of Elatus: it was related in chapter 12 how Ischys had the temer-

ity to poach on that part of Apollo's preserves represented by the maiden Coronis—a presumptuous act for which he was slain by the goddess Artemis with an arrow; Cyllen is remembered only as having given his name to Mount Cyllene—famous as the birthplace of the god Hermes; Pereus, who appears to have been the youngest son, is noted primarily as the father of Neaera—the Arcadian queen of her kinsman Aleus;[8] and Stymphalus seems to have died early, because Pausanias says that Aleus succeeded Aepytus, who was one generation nearer to Arcas than were Agamedes and Gortys, Stymphalus' sons.

Although Gortys is mentioned as having founded a city which was named after him, nothing is related about Agamedes except that he was the father of Cercyon and was the grandfather of Hippothous, who assumed the Arcadian rulership when Agapenor failed to return from Troy.[9] The only noteworthy act attributed

[8] According to Pausanias, Neaera married Autolycus, a son of Hermes.

[9] Agapenor was the great-grandson of Aleus and the last of his line.

to Hippothous is that he moved the capital of his kingdom from Tegea to Trapezus, where he died and was succeeded by his son (a second) Aepytus. In the latter's reign, it is said that Orestes, the son of Agamemnon, came into Arcadia from his home at Mycenae. The move, however, does not appear to have been hostile because, when Aepytus was stricken with blindness, and died after entering a forbidden sanctuary of Poseidon, he was peacefully followed in the Arcadian rulership by his son, Cypselus.

It was at this time that the Heracleidae and their allies returned to the Peloponnesus in the Dorian Invasion. When Cypselus learned of their coming, he made his own country doubly safe by marrying his daughter Merope to Cresphontes, who later gained neighboring Messenia as his own kingdom.[10] As related in the preceding chapter, however, the Messenian throne was usurped by Polyphontes after Cresphontes was assassinated[11]—leaving his young son (a third) Aepytus. Upon the death of Cypselus in adjacent Arcadia, his son, Holeas, came to the throne and one of his first acts was to assist his nephew, Aepytus, in throwing out the usurper and assuming his rightful sovereignty.[12]

When Apheidas died, he was succeeded at Tegea by his son, Aleus, who also assumed the sovereignty of Azania upon the childless death of his cousin Aepytus. In his own honor Aleus founded the small town of Alea, which later became noted for its temples erected in honor of Artemis, Athena, and Dionysus. He retained Tegea as his capital, however, and it was there—and not at Alea—that he built the celebrated sanctuary of Athena Alea.

The children borne to Aleus by his wife, Neaera, a daughter of his cousin Pereus, were three sons, Lycurgus, Amphidamas, and Ce-

pheus, and two daughters named Alcidice and Auge. The marriage of Alcidice to the Aeolid Salmoneus, and the birth of her beautiful daughter, Tyro, have been related in chapter 6; the circumstances under which Auge bore her son Telephus to Heracles are discussed in chapter 14.

Aleus was followed in the sovereignty of his augmented kingdom by his eldest son Lycurgus, who is primarily remembered for the ingenuity which he exercised in slaying Areithous, a king of the Boeotian town of Arne, who was known as the Club-bearer. For, when the two men fought a duel, Lycurgus drove his opponent back into a narrow pass, where he could not effectively swing his weapon, and pierced him through with a lance. He then appropriated the ownerless club and afterward used it with telling effect until, as death approached, he bequeathed it to his slave Ereuthalion.

By Cleophyle, whose antecedents are not stated, Lycurgus had three sons—Ancaeus, Epochus, and Iasus—all of whom predeceased him. Of these, Ancaeus returned safely from the Argonautic expedition, but was later killed by the Calydonian boar—leaving a son, Agapenor, who had been borne by his wife, Iotis. Agapenor grew up to become one of the suitors of Helen, and was the leader of the Arcadian forces against Troy. He did not return, however, to his Tegean throne because, after leaving the scene of the great war, a storm arose and drove his fleet to the island of Cyprus, where he remained and founded the town of Paphus, in which he built a beautiful sanctuary to Aphrodite. Concerning the other two sons of Lycurgus, nothing is related about Epochus except that he became ill and died; Iasus does not appear to have been of particular importance, except as the husband of Clymene, a daughter of Minyas, and as the father of Amphion who—by virtue of his mother's descent—became king of Orchomenus.[13] Amphion cemented his claim to the Orchomenian kingdom by marrying his maternal aunt, Peresephone, and it is said by some that their daughter Chloris grew up to

---

[10] The stratagem by which Cresphontes gained the rulership of Messenia is related in the preceding chapter.

[11] It should be borne in mind that Polyphontes not only usurped the kingdom of Cresphontes but also forcibly married his widow Merope—the daughter of Cypselus and the sister of Holeas.

[12] The accession of Holeas carries the line of Elatus through the mythological period sought to be covered here. Pausanias proceeds on to historical times by naming Bucolion as the son of Holeas, Phialus as the son of Bucolion, Simus as the son of Phialus, Pompus as the son of Simus, Aeginetes as the son of Pompus, and Polymestor as the son of Aeginetes.

[13] Pausanias says that the winner of the prize in the horse race at the first Olympic games was Iasus, an Arcadian, but he does not name him as the son of Lycurgus.

84a. Descendants of Zeus and Callisto

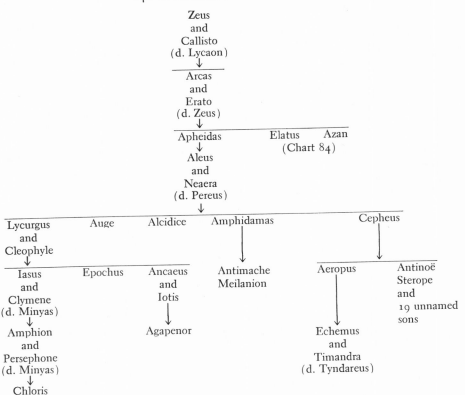

become the wife of Neleus and mother of the renowned Nestor.[14]

Returning to the sons of Aleus, Amphidamas was one of the Argonauts, but seems to have added little of interest to the success of the expedition. His daughter, Antimache, married the Argive king, Eurystheus, who imposed on Heracles the Twelve Labors. According to the Arcadian version of the story, it was his son Meilanion who became the successful suitor of the swift-footed maiden Atalanta.[15] Cepheus is also named among the Argonauts—and rivaled his brother Amphidamas in the barrenness of his remembered activities in connection with the bold enterprise. After his return, he became king at Tegea[16] and, by an unnamed wife, had two daughters—Antinoë and Sterope—and twenty sons, of whom only Aeropus is identified by name. According to Pausanias, Antinoë was told by an oracle that she should lead the inhabitants of the old town of Mantineia[17] from the place of its original founding to the location of its later eminence, and this she did by following a snake (or dragon) which miraculously appeared to act as her pilot.

[14] The wife of Neleus, and mother of Nestor, is uniformly referred to as Chloris, a daughter of Amphion, but her mother is nowhere named. As will be seen from the accompanying chart, Chloris—the daughter of Amphion and Persephone—was one generation later than her kinsman Agapenor, who led the Arcadians at Troy. This would make Nestor two generations younger, although he was admittedly so old and experienced at the time of the conflict that his name has become a figure of our speech with that meaning. In recognition of the paradox, it would seem better to accept the version of other mythographers, which relates that the wife of Neleus was a daughter of Amphion of Thebes and Niobe—originally known as Meliboea, but later as Chloris when she turned white at the slaughter of her brothers and sisters.

[15] The Boeotian version of the story, which makes Hippomenes the suitor of Atalanta and makes Schoeneus her father, has been related in chapter 6.

[16] At this point, the Arcadian rulership was divided between Cepheus, who ruled at Tegea, and Hippothous, who had set up another capital at Trapezus.

[17] The original Mantineia is said by Pausanias to have been founded by Mantineus, one of the many sons of Lycaon.

When Heracles was preparing to march against the Hippocoöntids, he was accompanied by Cepheus and all of his sons, under the circumstances related in the preceding chapter.[18] After they were all slain in the fighting, the only male survivor of the house was Echemus, the son of Aeropus, and it was he who slew Hyllus in the single combat on the isthmus of Corinth which repulsed the Heracleidae when they first tried to return to the Peloponnesus. From this exploit, one might expect to hear that Echemus performed other feats of valor; but, seemingly, he was content to settle down to a quiet rulership at Tegea with his wife, Timandra, who was a daughter of the Spartan king, Tyndareus.[19]

In the eastern country later known as Phoenicia, Zeus changed his form into that of a white bull, and mingled with a herd of cattle grazing near a place on the seashore where the maiden Europa, a daughter of King Agenor,[20] was playing with her companions. When he trotted quietly up to the young princess, she was taken with his gentleness and mistakenly seated herself on his back—mistakenly, because the creature bounded away and swam over the sea to the island of Crete. And there, his lovely burden bore to the "father of gods and men" three sons who were named Minos, Rhadamanthys, and Sarpedon. Their supreme father's bull form now left him, but it was wafted to the skies and became the constellation Taurus, the second sign of the zodiac.

On the disappearance of Europa, Agenor sent out his sons and his wife, Telephassa, to search for her, with the fruitless but interesting results which have been related in chapter 9.

Asterius, a Cretan prince whose Dorian father, Tectamus, had migrated to the island from Greece,[21] became attracted to the young mother and, marrying her, brought up her children to manhood. But when they were grown, they quarreled over a young boy, Miletus, who was a son of Apollo and Acacallis, a daughter of Minos.[22] As a result, Sarpedon and Miletus quitted their island home and went to the mainland of Asia Minor, where Sarpedon became king of the Lycians,[23] and Miletus founded a city in Caria which was called by his name. In Lycia, Sarpedon had a son named Evander, who later married Laodameia, a daughter of the hero Bellerophon.

Because of his just dealing, Rhadamanthys became the law giver among many of the Aegean islands,[24] earning a reputation which possibly made Minos jealous. For a dispute arose between them, and Rhadamanthys was forced to flee to Boeotia where he was graciously received and later married Alcmena, after the death of her husband, Amphitryon. Because of his justice throughout his life on earth, he was made one of the immortal judges in the lower world and, with Alcmena, was permitted to dwell in the Isles of the Blest—thus becoming perhaps the first commuter, for the place of his abode was conceived by some as being in the far western part of the upper world.

When Asterius died, Minos assumed that the Cretan rulership would fall to him, since both of his brothers had left the country, but his accession to the throne was opposed by some of the islanders. Thereupon he claimed that the gods willed he should become king, and offered to prove his claim by performing a miracle. As the sceptical islanders looked on, he sacrificed to Poseidon and prayed aloud that a bull might

---

[18] Suffice to repeat, that Cepheus was persuaded to leave Tegea undefended only after Heracles had given to his daughter Sterope a snaky lock from the head of the Gorgon Medusa with assurance that it would serve as a protection against all possible invaders.

[19] The tomb of Echemus at Tegea was adorned with a representation of his combat with Hyllus.

[20] This is one of the few instances where our text does not follow the genealogies of Homer, who names Phoenix as Europa's father—the reason for the deviation being that, in classical literature, wider currency has been given to the paternity of Agenor.

[21] A different genealogy makes Asterius a son of Cres, the eponym of the island.

[22] Apollodorus says that the mother of Miletus was Aria, a daughter of Cleochus; he mentions an alternate story that the boy over whom the quarrel arose was Atymnius, a son of Zeus and Cassiopeia.

[23] The mythographers frequently confuse Sarpedon, the son of Minos, with the son of Zeus and Laodameia (Sarpedon's daughter-in-law), who fought in the Trojan War, because some add that the gods gave him the privilege of living for three generations.

[24] In the preceding chapter, it has been related how Heracles avoided punishment for the killing of Linus by citing the law of Rhadamanthys that one who defends himself against an aggressor shall be acquitted.

85. Descendants of Zeus and Europa

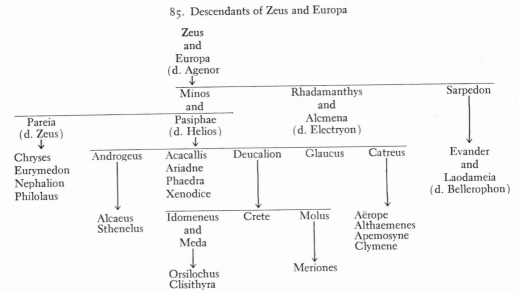

appear from the depths of the sea—vowing in advance to sacrifice the animal to the great earthshaker.[25] The bull duly appeared, and Minos obtained his desired kingdom, but he sent the creature to his herds and sacrificed another on the god's altar.

Minos had previously married Pasiphae, a daughter of the Sun-god Helios, who had borne him several children. She now gave birth to a monstrosity, for Poseidon, angry at the sacrificial substitution and aided by the goddess Aphrodite, caused Pasiphae to have connection with the animal brought up from beneath the sea—resulting in an ugly offspring called the Minotaur, which had the body of a man and the head of a bull.[26] At the command of Minos, his architect, Daedalus,[27] constructed an intricate labyrinth in which the creature was stabled and remained prisoner until a later time, when it was finally destroyed by the Athenian hero Theseus.

Perhaps in retaliation for his wife's gross infidelity, Minos embraced the nymph Pareia,

who bore to him four sons named Chryses, Eurymedon, Nephalion, and Philolaus.[28] Nothing of interest is related about them except that all four were killed by Heracles on the island of Paros after they had slain two of the great man's crew who had made a landing there, on their way to procure the girdle of Hippolyte.

The children borne to Minos by Pasiphae were four daughters—Acacallis (sometimes called Acalle), Ariadne, Phaedra, and Xenodice—and four sons named Glaucus, Androgeus, Catreus, and Deucalion. Of the daughters: Acacallis bore two sons, Amphithemis and Miletus to Apollo, as related in chapter 12; Ariadne became successively the beloved of Theseus and of the wine-god Dionysus; Phaedra became not only the beloved of Theseus but his second wife also—only to destroy herself from shame brought on by her own wrongdoing; Xenodice seemingly is mentioned by Apollodorus merely as another name to clutter our mythological index.[29]

---

[25] Another version of the story names Zeus as the god to whom Minos prayed.

[26] Since Pasiphae was a daughter of Helios, who had revealed the amour between Aphrodite and Ares, it is said that her attraction to the Cretan bull was inspired by the vengeful goddess of love.

[27] It is related that Pasiphae seduced the Cretan bull by placing herself in a wooden cow which Daedalus built at her direction.

[28] Apollodorus says that Minos had another son, Euxanthius, by a woman named Dexithea.

[29] According to later writers, the first Minos married Itone, by whom he had a son named Lycastus; and Lycastus married Ida, a daughter of Corybas, by whom he became the father of a second Minos—father of the children mentioned in the text. The story is undoubtedly an attempt to rationalize the Minoan genealogy with the acknowledged mythological legend that the original Minos appeared in such remote times that he was ac-

A remarkable story is told about Glaucus. While still an infant, he fell into a jar of honey as he was chasing a mouse, and was drowned, but he was brought back to life by the seer Polyidus,[30] under the circumstance previously related in chapter 8.[31] And, although Minos had now recovered his son, he would not permit Polyidus to return to his home in Argos until he had taught his young son the secrets of divination. Under this compulsion the seer did as he was commanded but, as he was about to depart from Crete, he bade his pupil spit in his mouth and, when Glaucus complied, he immediately lost the prophetic art which he had just been taught.[32]

Some time afterward, Minos' son Androgeus went to Athens to compete in the games at the festival of Panathenaea and conquered all of his opponents in the contests which he entered. He then set out for Thebes to take part in similar games which were periodically held in honor of Laius but, on the way, was attacked from ambush by some of the jealous men whom he had bested at Athens and, in resisting their assault, he lost his life.[33] Upon learning of his son's death, Minos sailed from Crete with an army to punish the Athenians, but met with such stout resistance that he was unable to enter the city. Resorting to other means, he prayed to Zeus that his loss might be avenged; in answer to his son's prayer, the supreme god visited the Athenians with a famine and pestilence which continued with such severity that they consulted an oracle to learn how they might be relieved. The reply of the oracle was that they should give to Minos whatever satisfaction he might choose to exact.[34] Accordingly, they made overtures to him and were obliged to accept harsh terms which required that in every ninth year they should send seven of their youths and the same number of girls as fodder for the Minotaur.

At the time when Heracles slew the four sons of Minos (by the nymph Pareia) on the Island of Paros, he took with him the two sons of Androgeus, Alcaeus and Sthenelus, as hostages. But, after obtaining the girdle of Hippolyte, the great man seemingly felt that his prisoners had been sufficiently humiliated—for he put in at the island of Thasus and, first subjugating the native Thracians, gave the country to Alcaeus and Sthenelus as a place for their future habitation.

Catreus, another son of Minos and Pasiphae, had three daughters, Aërope, Clymene, and Apemosyne and also a son named Althaemenes. When he inquired of an oracle how his life would end, he was told that one of his own children was fated to kill him. He did not publicly reveal the oracle's answer, but Althaemenes heard of it and, fearing lest he should be his father's murderer, left Crete with his sister, Apemosyne, and settled on the island of Rhodes. There Apemosyne was ravished by Hermes[35] and tearfully reported her plight to her brother who, refusing to believe that she had been forced by a god, kicked the poor girl to death.

Meanwhile, to eliminate the possibility of being killed by them, Catreus gave his remaining two daughters to the Euboean king, Nauplius, to sell into foreign lands. This cruel action, however, proved fortunate for the maidens, because Aërope became the wife of the Argive prince, Pleisthenes, and mother of the famous

---

customed to converse with supreme Zeus about the affairs of state, which he directed from his ancient capital city of Cnossus (Gnossus).

[30] Polyidus, a descendant of Melampus, had been invited to Crete by Minos because of his great reputation as a diviner.

[31] A different version of the story relates that Glaucus was raised from the dead by Asclepius.

[32] When Priam's daughter, Cassandra, refused to grant her favors to Apollo, in return for the gift of prophecy which he had bestowed upon her, he spat into her mouth and, by so doing, prevented her from convincing others that her predictions would come true.

[33] According to an alternate version related by Apollodorus, Androgeus lost his life when the Athenian king, Aegeus, sent him against the bull of Marathon—the same animal that came from the depths of the sea in response to the prayer of Minos and was later brought to Greece by Heracles as one of his Twelve Labors.

---

[34] An oracle, previously consulted by the Athenians, had bidden them to slaughter the four daughters of a Lacedaemonian named Hyacinthus who happened to be visiting at Athens; but the performance of this cruel act had brought no relief. In the same war, Minos already had conquered Nisus, king of Megara.

[35] After Apemosyne fled from Hermes and he was unable to overtake her, the god spread fresh hides along the path over which she had to return and, when she slipped, he was able to accomplish his purpose.

kings, Menelaus and Agamemnon,[36] while Clymene was wedded to Nauplius and became the mother of the hero Palamedes and his brothers, Oeax and Nausimedon. Afterward, in old age, Catreus went to Rhodes for the purpose of transmitting his possessions to Althaemenes and, having landed at a deserted place on the island, was chased by some cowherds who suspected him as a pirate. He was captured and tried to explain his identity, but they could not hear him for the barking of their dogs and began to pelt him with stones. At this juncture, Althaemenes arrived and, thinking that his men were contesting with an enemy, thrust his javelin through the old king's body—thus bringing about the death which years before had been prophesied by the oracle.

According to some of the ancient writers, Deucalion—the son who succeeded Minos in the Cretan kingship—was a member of the Argonautic expedition and was also among the heroes who hunted the Calydonian boar. By his unnamed wife he had a son, Idomeneus, and a daughter named Crete and, by an unnamed mistress, he had a son, Molus. Nothing further is mentioned about Crete, and it appears probable that she was included as a daughter of Minos in order to bring the name of the island into the genealogy of its greatest ruler.[37]

Idomeneus was a man of handsome appearance and is listed among the suitors of Helen, but he had to content himself with a wife of lesser degree and married Meda (or Batis), a woman of unknown lineage who bore to him a son, Orsilochus, and a daughter, Clisithyra.[38] Together with Meriones, the son of his half brother Molus, he led the Cretans in eighty ships against Troy, where he proved to be one of the bravest heroes among the Greeks, notwithstanding the fact that he was past the prime of life. He offered to fight in single combat against Hector, and especially distinguished himself in the battle about the Greek ships—a desperate clashing of arms. As he was returning home after the fall of Troy, a great storm arose which endangered his ship's safety and Idomeneus prayed to Poseidon to calm the high-running waters—promising to sacrifice to the god whatever living thing he should first meet on his landing. Unfortunately, the first living thing proved to be his own son Orsilochus but, bound by his oath, the grief-stricken father was forced to murder him and to offer the bloody corpse on the sacrificial altar.[39] Nor was this the end of Idomeneus' domestic misfortunes, for upon his arrival at Crete, he learned that his wife and daughter, Meda and Clisithyre, had both been murdered by a man named Leucus who had been accepted by Meda as a paramour while her husband was detained at Troy.[40] Although he drove the intruder from the island, the heartbroken warrior could not himself remain at the scene of his earlier felicity and migrated first to Italy and, later, to Colophon in Asia Minor, where it is said that he died at an advanced age and was buried with great honors.

An odd legend of Crete related that Idomeneus's brother, Molus, attempted to violate a nymph and was thereafter found without a head. But his indiscretion brought no mythological ill effects to his son Meriones who, as before stated, was a co-leader with Idomeneus at Troy. Among other acts of bravery attributed to him in the great conflict, it is related that he also offered to fight with Hector and sought to accompany Diomedes on his expedition to explore the Trojan city but, when Diomedes chose Odysseus as his companion, Meriones ungrudgingly gave to the latter a bow, a quiver, a sword, and a helmet. The helmet had originally been stolen by the arch-thief Autoclycus and, transmitted through various hands, had come into

---

[36] The conventional story that Atreus was the father of Menelaus and Agamemnon is explained by the statement that Pleisthenes died leaving Aërope and her two young sons, who were adopted and raised as his own by Atreus when he married his widowed daughter-in-law.

[37] Apollodorus says that some persons named Crete, instead of Pasiphae, as the lawful wife of Minos.

[38] In one of his fictitious stories, Odysseus told Athena (not knowing her to be the goddess) that he had slain Orsilochus when the latter had tried to steal booty brought from Troy.

[39] A similar story occurs in the Bible at Judges 11:31, where it is related that Jephthah slew his daughter in performance of a vow made as he was about to engage in battle with the Ammonites.

[40] Meda's infidelity, like that of other Greek wives, was attributed to the machinations of Nauplius who was enraged because his son Palamedes had been put to death at Troy on a charge of treason.

the possession of Molus, who bequeathed it to Meriones. Owing to its mythological significance, its appearance is described in detail in the Iliad.

Further stories about Meriones relate that he fought beside Ajax the Greater in protecting the body of Patroclus after he had been slain by Hector and, at the funeral games for the dead man, he won first prize in shooting with the bow, second prize in throwing the javelin, and fourth prize in the chariot race. According to a later tradition, he was shipwrecked on the coast of Sicily while returning from Troy and was joyfully received by a band of Cretans who had settled there. Another version, however, relates that he returned safely to Crete where, at death, he was buried with great honors and was thereafter worshipped as a hero.

This concludes recital of the descendants of Minos, who himself is said to have become one of the judges in the lower world after being killed by King Cocalus in Sicily, whither he had gone in pursuit of his escaped artisan Daedalus.[41]

Eurymedusa—the Mother of Myrmidon

When Eurymedusa, daughter of Cleitus, bore a son to Zeus he was called Myrmidon, because the god had seduced her in the form of an ant—"myrmex" in the Greek language. By Peisidice, who was a daughter of the original Aeolus, Myrmidon had two sons, Antiphus and Actor, and a daughter, Eupolemeia. Neither the father nor his two sons did anything of note,[42]

86. Descendants of Zeus and Eurymedusa

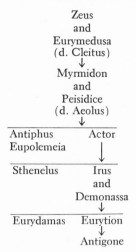

but Eupolemeia bore a son to Hermes, named Aethalides, who was distinguished as the herald of the Argonauts.

Irus, the elder son of Actor, is seemingly inserted in the family tree in order to give a name to the father of the Argonauts, Eurydamas and Eurytion, who were borne to him by Demonassa —a lady named by Hyginus without comment on her lineage.[43] Sthenelus, the second son of Actor, does not meet such short treatment, because he was a companion of Heracles in the expedition to obtain the girdle of Hippolyte. He did not return, however, for he was struck by an arrow and died on the beach of the Amazons, where the Argonauts later beheld his grave, with his bloody shade hovering above.

Neither Eurydamas or Eurytion performed any noteworthy act with the Argonauts, but Eurytion returned to become king of Phthia, and later purified Peleus of the killing of his half brother Phocus.[44] Afterward, he gave his daughter, Antigone, as wife to his guest and then took him along on the hunt for the Calydonian boar—only to meet death when he was

---

[41] Variants of the legend as to how Minos met his death are related in connection with the story of Daedalus.

It is beyond the scope of this book to discuss the Minoan civilization, which archeological discoveries have placed as definitely preceding that of the Greek mainland by more than two thousand years. It may be noted, however, that the biblical Philistines, who had already learned to fashion their arms from iron while the forces of Saul were yet fighting with primitive weapons, were a Cretan race who had migrated to the coastal country of Asia Minor which, from their name, is known as Palestine.

[42] Myrmidon was regarded as the ancestor of the Myrmidons in Thessaly. According to a later story, however, their name came from an Attic maiden named Myrmex who was changed into an ant by Athena for boasting that she had invented the plow, which was discovered by the goddess herself. A third legend is later

---

related in connection with the genealogy and the exploits of Aeacus and his descendants.

[43] Apollodorus names Ctimenus as the father of Eurydamas, and names Teleon as the father of Eurytion.

[44] According to Diodorus, Peleus was purified by Actor who, dying childless, left the Myrmidon rulership to his guest. Others name Eurytion as a son of Actor, or say that Peleus succeeded to the kingdom by marrying a daughter of Actor named Polymela.

struck by a dart which his newly acquired son-in-law had thrown at the animal.

Antiope—the Mother of Amphion and Zethus

In chapter 9, as an integral part of the Theban story, it has been related: (1) how Antiope bore to Zeus her twin sons, Amphion and Zethus; (2) how they avenged the ill-treatment of their mother at the hands of Lycus and his wife, Dirce; (3) how they took over the government of Thebes and encircled the city with a stone wall; (4) how Zethus married Aëdon, daughter of Pandareos, who unwittingly killed their son, Itylus, with a sword, and thereby caused Zethus to die of grief;[45] (5) how Amphion married Niobe, daughter of Tantalus, who was slain with all her children for boasting herself to be superior to Leto; and (6) how Amphion also came to his death.

87. Descendants of Zeus and Antiope

Zeus
and
Antiope
(d. Nycteus)
↓

Amphion and Niobe (d. Tantalus) ↓		Zethus and Aëdon (d. Pandareos) ↓
Agenor	Ismenus	Itylus
Amyclas	Meliboea	
Astycrateia	("Chloris")	
Astyoche	Ogygia	
Cleodoxa	Pelopeia	
Damasichthon	Phaedimus	
Ethodaea	Phthia	
Eupinytus	Sipylus	
	Tantalus	

Great diversity of opinion prevailed among the ancients as to the number of the children of

Amphion and Niobe. Apollodorus said that they were fourteen but named the sixteen which are mentioned in the accompanying chart. Homer placed the number at twelve, and Hesiod expanded it to twenty.

Chloris, as a surname for Meliboea, is said to have been given to the maiden because she turned perfectly white from terror at seeing the destruction of her brothers and sisters as they were shot down by the arrows of Apollo and Artemis.[46]

Regarding Niobe, a later legend related that she was not slain in the general holocaust, but left Thebes and went to her father on Mount Sipylus in Lydia where, on praying to Zeus, she was transformed into a stone fountain, whose dripping waters continued as her tears of grief.

Semele—the Mother of Dionysus

While Zeus was flying through the skies in the form of an eagle, he spied Semele, a daughter of Cadmus, as she lay naked on the bank of a river in which she had been bathing. Being desirous of her love, he solicited her in mortal form; but later revealed his divine identity and she willingly accepted his embraces.[47]

Upon learning of her great lord's new love, Hera flew into her customary rage and, assuming the figure of Semele's old nurse Beroë, insinuated doubts in the girl's mind that her seducer was really Zeus—suggesting that the truth could be proven only if he should appear before her in his full godly splendor. Accordingly, on the occasion of his next visit, Semele asked her lover to grant her a favor but did not name it; unthinkingly, he swore by the river Styx that whatever she wished would be granted. Thereupon she made her request which, because of his inviolable vow, Zeus was forced to honor. But, when he appeared with the thunder and lightnings, which were the concomitants of his Olympian

---

[45] Aëdon's jealousy at the number of Niobe's children resolved her to kill the eldest of her nephews, who was accustomed to sleep in the same bed with her own single son. On the day chosen for commission of her intended crime, she instructed Itylus to sleep elsewhere that night, but the boy forgot her instructions and was slain by the sword thrust which was planned to pierce his bedfellow. Aëdon grieved so greatly at her loss that the gods mercifully changed her into a nightingale and, in that form, it is said that she still sings her mournful dirge.

[46] Apollodorus cites another story-that Chloris and her brother, Amyclas, survived, and several of the ancient writers say that it was she (instead of Chloris, the daughter of Arcadian Amphion) who became the wife of Neleus and the mother of his fourteen sons.

[47] According to Nonnos, Semele first dreamed that she was embraced by Zeus, and afterward he appeared at her couch as a bull, who changed his form successively into that of a lion, a panther, and a snake.

88. Descendants of Zeus and Semele

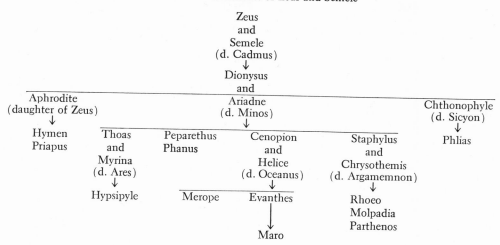

presence, Semele's mortal frame could not withstand the shock and she burst into flame. As she dissolved into ashes, the god snatched from her womb his unborn child and, to preserve its life, sewed it into his own thigh.[48]

After Semele's death, the report was spread that her lover had been a mortal, and that she had been punished by Zeus for claiming his paternity of her child. When the proper time for birth arrived, however, Zeus went to the island of Naxos[49] and, opening his thigh, drew forth his son who was called Dionysus.[50]

The motherless boy was entrusted to Hermes, who took him to Orchomenus to be raised as a girl by Semele's sister, Ino. Implacable in her desire for vengeance, Hera now caused Athamas —Ino's husband—to become mad and caused Ino to commit suicide. After these tragic occurrences, Zeus instructed Hermes to carry his young son to the nymphs who inhabited the region around Mount Nysa in Thrace.[51] There,

the boy grew rapidly into manhood and, one day discovering some wild grapes as he roamed through the woods, learned how to change their juices into the exhilarating beverage which was afterward called wine.[52] The results of his discovery were quickly transmitted to others, who were so agreeably affected that they followed in his train and honored the youth as a true son of Zeus.

Still enraged—more so because of the swelling numbers of devotees who were beginning to worship the charming, young wine-god—Hera now threw him into a state of madness which caused him to wander through many foreign places. Finally coming into Phrygia, he was cured of his malady by the goddess Cybele (Rhea), and she taught him the mysteries which were accustomed to be celebrated in her honor on the island of Samothrace as well as elsewhere.[53] This new knowledge proved an added attraction, and the number of the god's followers (known as Bacchantes, Bassarids, or Maenads) grew, so that he soon found himself

---

[48] In a subsequent chapter, a curious story—from the so-called Orphic literature—is related, which considered Semele's child as the rebirth of Zagreus whom Persephone had previously borne to Zeus.

[49] Other traditions placed the birth of Dionysus in India, Libya, Crete, or Thebes.

[50] The name Dionysus is said to have been given to the child because he was "twice born." By the Romans he was called Bachus and Liber, and by both Greeks and Romans he was sometimes called by the surname Lyaeus. Appearing through the fire of his birth, he was often referred to as Bromius.

[51] Some derive the name of Dionysus from that of the mountain where he was reared. Besides the nymphs

---

on Mount Nysa, others were said to have assisted as his nurses, namely: the Muses, the nymphs on the island of Naxos, and a daughter of Aristaeus, who was named Nysa. Macris, another daughter of Aristaeus, is said to have fed the infant with honey.

[52] Dionysus taught the use of wine in moderation, and the stories which depict him as being attended by drunken followers are said to be later inventions.

[53] After his initiation by Cybele, Dionysus was himself honored in the celebration of the mysteries.

at the head of a large army of men, women, and satyrs.[54]

With the return of his reason, Dionysus consciously resumed his travels, seated in a chariot drawn by panthers and accompanied by thousands who clashed their cymbals, shrieked loudly their mystic cry, "evoe," and waved aloft the thyrsus—a curious sort of staff entwined with vine leaves which concealed a sharp blade at its end. According to legend, the joyful host first went into Egypt, where they were cordially welcomed by King Proteus, a son of Poseidon. From there, they went to Syria and, when its king, Damascus, opposed introduction of the vine, he was flayed alive. Many other places were visited, and there were only few who failed to accept Dionysus as a god and to join in his adoration. Nor did Zeus neglect to shed added glory on his son. For, when he had crossed the river Euphrates over a bridge and was approaching the Tigris, the supreme father sent a tiger to ferry him across the stream.

The triumphal march continued through the land of the Amazons, who were overcome when they sought to resist its progress, and it extended even to India where, although conquered, the inhabitants were won over to the wine-god's worship. After, they remembered him as the founder of towns in which he established a more civilized and sociable mode of life. Sometimes uncomfortable incidents occurred, however, which temporarily interfered with the plans of the advancing Maenads. On one occasion, their leader was taken captive by some Tyrrhenian pirates, who carried him aboard their vessel and placed him in chains, with the purpose of selling him as a slave in some distant land. But, at sea, the fetters miraculously dropped from his limbs and the pilot Acoetes, perceiving him to be a god, urged his shipmates to restore their captive to the place where he had been taken—suggesting that otherwise their voyage would result in disaster. When they refused to heed his warning, the vessel suddenly became motionless, and clustering vines covered its mast and sails, to the accompaniment of heavenly strains of music,

which proceeded from an invisible source. The terrified, and now repentant, crew gathered around Acoetes for protection and entreated him to steer back to shore. Their repentance was too late, however, because Dionysus assumed the form of a lion and, joined by a bear, rushed upon the captain and tore him to pieces. Upon this happening, the other sailors leaped overboard and were changed into dolphins. The discreet and pious steersman was unharmed and, being ordered by the god, who had reassumed his original form, sailed the vessel to the island of Naxos. Upon landing there, Dionysus found Ariadne, the beautiful daughter of the King Minos whom Theseus had cruelly abandoned and, after he had revealed his divine pedigree and had dispelled her grief, she consented to become his wife. As a wedding present he gave her a beautiful tiara, which at her death, was placed among the stars. It is still known as Corona, the Crown of Ariadne.

Returning to Greece, he and his Maenad host landed at Argos, but Perseus, who was then ruling, was sceptical of his half brother's claims that he was entitled to be worshipped as a god, and drove him from the country.[55] Proceeding onward to Thebes, they met a similar reception from King Pentheus, who caused Acoetes (or Dionysus) to be cast into prison and himself spied on the secret Bacchanalian rites, with tragic consequences which have been related in chapter 9. From Thebes, the merry horde pushed northeastward into Thrace and, there too, encountered an unbeliever—Lycurgus, the fierce king of the Edones, who forced Dionysus to jump into the sea and seek haven with the goddess Thetis. In retaliation, however, the wine-god caused the Thracian king to be stricken with a madness which, as elsewhere related, caused him to kill the members of his own family and to destroy himself.[56]

---

[54] The satyrs were considered to be the offspring of the god's old steward Silenus, son of Hermes and Iphthime, and were sometimes called the Sileni.

[55] Perseus and Dionysus were later reconciled, and the wine-god was received and worshipped in Argos as elsewhere.

[56] The order of travel, and of the incidents connected with it, is differently given by the various mythographers. Some say that Dionysus first landed in Thrace, after his expedition to India, and from there proceeded southward; others give last place to his capture by the Tyrrhenian pirates, ignoring the generally accepted story

All setbacks proved to be only minor, however, and the divine nature of the wine-god was eventually established and recognized throughout the ancient world. He was especially honored on the island of Naxos, and many pilgrims brought sacrificial victims to his oracle in Thrace—among which the ram was considered most acceptable.[57] As a final proof of his godhead, he went down to the lower world and brought back his mother Semele, whom he raised with himself to Olympus, where she too was honored as a deity under the name of Thyone.[58] And, at the home of the gods, it is said that the beautiful and faithless Aphrodite bore to him two sons, named Hymen and Priapus, who were afterward recognized respectively as the deities of marriage and vegetation.[59]

Meanwhile, he had an affair with Chthonophyle, a daughter of Sicyon, who bore to him a son Phlias (Phlius), from whom the Peloponnesian town of his name was called after he had served as one of the less distinguished of the Argonauts.

The five sons borne to Dionysus by Ariadne, following her desertion by Theseus, were Peparethus, Phanus, Thoas, Oenopion, and Staphylus. Of these, nothing of interest is related about Peparethus, and Phanus is mentioned only as one of the Argonauts—without, however, ascribing to him any specific action in the great adventure upon which they embarked.[60] Thoas

went to the land of the Amazons and married their queen, Myrina, a daughter of Ares. Afterward, having been given the rulership of the island of Lemnos by Rhadamanthys, he took her there and she bore a daughter to him who was named Hypsipyle. At a later time, the women of the island grew negligent in offering sacrifices to Aphrodite, and the enraged goddess visited their bodies with smells which were so noisome that their husbands sought the beds of captive maids from a neighboring country. Smarting at such dishonor, the Lemnian women murdered both their husbands and their fathers, but Hypsipyle saved Thoas from destruction by concealing his whereabouts. His hiding place, however, was later discovered and he was put to death, and as punishment for her filial attempt, Hypsipyle was sold into slavery.[61]

Oenopion received from Rhadamanthys the sovereignty of the island of Chios, and took as his queen the Naiad Helice, who bore to him a son, Evanthes, and a daughter, Merope. Evanthes is only a mythological connecting link to his son, Maro (Maron), who gave Odysseus a bottle of wine used in befuddling the Cyclops Polyphemus, but Merope had a somewhat more exciting experience. She was wooed by the giant hunter Orion, who proved so importunate that he attempted to break into her bed chamber. Upon this happening Oenopion gave Orion wine until he was intoxicated, and then blinded him. The injured giant later recovered his sight, under the circumstances previously related in chapter 10, and returned to seek revenge; but Thoas was hidden by his friends (or by the god Poseidon) and, after a futile search, Orion went on to the island of Crete.

Staphylus was also a recipient of Rhadamanthys' favor—receiving from him a kingdom on the island of Peparethus, which lay off the

that their steersman Acoetes, having become a convert, was imprisoned by Pentheus.

[57] Some report that human sacrifices were offered at the god's Thracian oracle, and Pausanias says that, at his oracle in Phocis, the diseases of supplicants were cured by the application of remedies which were revealed in their dreams.

[58] It seems to be conceded that Dionysus was a foreign importation into the Greek pantheon, although he is mentioned in the Iliad as the son of Semele, and notice is given there to his persecution by Lycurgus.

[59] Hymen—or Hymenaeus—is sometimes said to have been a son of Apollo and one of the Muses, and is reported to have been among those raised from the dead by Asclepius. There are several fanciful stories about his earthly activities, but they were composed by later writers whose works are beyond the scope of this compilation. It is also said that Hera disapproved of Aphrodite's promiscuity, and caused Priapus to be born as an ugly child with extremely large genitals.

[60] Apollodorus appears to be alone in naming Peparethus as a son of Dionysus and Ariadne, and it may be

that he derived the person by confusion with the Aegean island known as Peparethus and ruled by his brother Staphylus.

[61] A different legend relates that Hypsipyle was captured by pirates and sold as a slave to Lycurgus. Her attachment to Jason, to whom she bore two sons, and her service as nurse of the infant Opheltes, whom the Seven Against Thebes buried at Nemea, have been related in chapters 7 and 8.

coast of Thessaly.[62] By Chrysothemis, daughter of Agamemnon, he had three daughters named Rhoeo, Molpadia, and Parthenos. Rhoeo became with child by Apollo, and when her father did not believe that her lover was a god, he locked her up in a chest, which he threw into the sea. The chest, however, was washed up on to the shores of the island of Delos, and her son Anius was safely born. Her sisters, likewise, incurred their father's anger because, when they

---

[62] Plutarch makes Theseus the father of Staphylus, and Apollodorus names him as one of the Argonauts.

were set to guard his wine, they went to sleep and permitted it to be spoiled by his pigs. Upon awakening, and discovering the result of their negligence, they were in such fear of parental punishment that they threw themselves over a cliff but, for love of their sister, Rhoeo, Apollo saved their lives and transported them to distant lands, where Staphylus was unable to find them.

Demeter—the Mother of Persephone

The myth concerning Demeter, daughter of Chronus and Rhea, who bore a daughter Persephone to her brother Zeus, has been rather fully related in chapter 3.

16

The Decendants of Zeus VI

Hera—the Mother of Eileithyia, Hebe, and Ares

THE BIRTHS, and a general account of the activities, of Hebe and Ares have been related in chapter 3. Eileithyia, the second daughter of Zeus and Hera, was the goddess of birth, who had the power of easing, accelerating, or protracting the labors of women. Her functions were sometimes conceived as exercised by an abstract plurality of divinities, who were collectively called the Eleithyiae.[1] On occasion they were completely assumed by Hera herself, or by Artemis under her Roman name of Diana (of which Lucina was a surname).

The war-god Ares had many children by various mothers. Their number is too great for inclusion in a single chart and, together with their descendants, they will be noted separately, by reference to their respective mothers.

Agraulos

By Agraulos, a daughter of the Attic autochthon Cecrops, Ares had a daughter named Alcippe, who became the wife of her half brother Evenus. But, notwithstanding her marriage, Halirrhotius, a son of Poseidon, attempted to violate her and was slain by Ares.[2] When Posei-

don preferred a charge of murder, the war-god was brought to trial before the twelve Olympian gods and was acquitted by a tie vote. Since Ares was himself one of the twelve judges (or jurors), it may be presumed that he was permitted to cast a ballot in his own favor. From this incident, the place of the trial, on a hill of Athens, was thereafter called the Areopagus.

Aphrodite

Although Aphrodite was mythologically the lawful wife of the fire-god Hephaestus, she was unfaithful to her lame spouse, and had affairs with others, of whom Ares was perhaps the most prominent. To him she bore the children whose names are shown on the adjoining chart.

89. Descendants of Ares and Aphrodite

Zeus
and
Hera
↓
Ares
and
Aphrodite
(d. Zeus)
↓
Harmonia
Eros (Cupid)
Anteros
Deimos
Phobos

Their fair daughter, Harmonia, was married to Cadmus, the son of Agenor, in a ceremony which was attended by all of the heavenly

---

[1] The most celebrated mythological event, involving the exercise of Eileithyia's powers, was her retardation of the birth of Heracles so that he might be subject to the dominion of Eurystheus, whose birth was accelerated in order to make him the senior.

[2] According to Pausanias, Halirrhotius was successful in his attempted ravishment, which occurred beside a spring in the sanctuary of Asclepius at Athens.

deities and, among the wedding presents were a magic necklace and robe which brought tragic consequences to their immediate and subsequent possessors, as related in chapter 9.

Eros, perhaps the most celebrated of the children of Ares and Aphrodite, was the capricious creator of sensual love whom the Romans called Cupid. He was usually depicted as an infant equipped with wings, a bow, and a quiver filled with love darts, which never missed their mark and always took effect, whether aimed at god, man, or beast.[3] His brother Anteros was conceived as the punisher of those who failed to return the love of others.

The other two children of Ares and Aphrodite took their characters from their violent

father, for they were warrior sons, named Deimos and Phobos—personifying terror and dismay or panic and fear, who were usually considered to be the attendants of the war-god whenever and wherever he was engaged in furthering or creating the carnage of battle.

Astyoche

Astyoche, daughter of Actor and a descendant of the Aeolid Athamas, bore to Ares two sons who were named Ascalaphus and Ialmenus. They were numbered by Apollodorus as among the Argonauts and the suitors of Helen, and it was generally agreed that they were the joint leaders of the Minyans from Orchomenus in the Trojan War, where Ascalaphus was slain by Priam's son, Deiphobus. Ialmenus came through the conflict safely but, for some obscure reason, did not return home, because Strabo relates that he wandered about the country of Pontus with a band of his men and founded a number of new colonies there.

Atalanta

Parthenopaeus, the son of Ares and Atalanta, the swift-footed daughter of Schoeneus,[4] was among the adherents to the cause of Polyneices (who were known as the Seven Against Thebes). At the funeral games, held in honor of the infant Opheltes, and afterward conducted as the Nemean games, he won the first prize in archery. But his skill with the bow

90. Descendants of Ares and Atalanta

Zeus
and
Hera
↓
Ares
and
Atalanta
(d. Schoeneus)
↓
Parthenopaeus
and
Clymene
(d. Zeus)
↓
Promachus

---

[3] In Virgil's "Aeneid," it is related that Cupid inspired the Carthaginian queen, Dido, to love Aeneas by letting his head rest upon her breast, as she fondled him in the belief that he was Aeneas' son Ascanius, whose form he had assumed.

The story of the love of Cupid for Psyche (the personification of the human soul) is thus succinctly related in the Encyclopaedia Britannica, 11th ed., 1911, 22:543–44. "In this connection Psyche was represented in Greek and Graeco-Roman art as a tender maiden, with bird's or butterfly's wings, or simply as a butterfly. Sometimes she is pursued and tormented by Eros, sometimes she revenges herself upon him, sometimes she embraces him in fondest affection. The tale of Cupid and Psyche, in the 'Metamorphoses' of Apuleius, has nothing in common with this conception but the name. In it Psyche, the youngest daughter of a king, arouses the jealousy of Venus, who orders Cupid to inspire her with love for the most despicable of men. Cupid, however, falls in love with her himself, and carries her off to a secluded spot, where he visits her by night, unseen and unrecognized by her. Persuaded by her sisters that her companion is a hideous monster, and forgetful of his warning, she lights a lamp to look upon him while he is asleep; in her ecstasy at his beauty she lets fall a drop of burning oil upon the face of Cupid, who awakes and disappears. Wandering over the earth in search of him, Psyche falls into the hands of Venus, who forces her to undertake the most difficult tasks. The last and most dangerous of these is to fetch from the world below the box containing the ointment of beauty. She secures the box, but on her way back opens it and is stupefied by the vapour. She is only restored to her senses by contact with the arrow of Cupid, at whose entreaty Jupiter makes her immortal and bestows her in marriage upon her lover. The meaning of the allegory is obvious. Psyche, as the personification of the soul, is only permitted to enjoy her happiness so long as she abstains from ill-advised curiosity. The desire to pry into its nature brings suffering upon her; but in the end, purified by what she has undergone, she is restored to her former condition of bliss by the mighty power of love."

[4] According to other legends, Parthenopaeus was a son of Meilanion and Atalanta, Meleager and Atalanta, or Talaus and Lysimache.

proved to be of little value when the attack was made on the Theban citadel, because he was slain by Amphidicus, a son of Astacus.

Promachus, the son of Parthenopaeus by the nymph Clymene, followed in the footsteps of his illustrious father and was one of the Epigoni, who later made another—and successful—assault on Thebes. The mythographers mention no special deed of valor performed by him, but his statue—together with those of his comrades—was seen at Delphi by Pausanias during his ramblings in the second century A.D.

Bystonis

By the nymph Bystonis, Ares had two sons named Dryas and Tereus. Dryas was noted chiefly as one of the hunters of the Calydonian boar. His brother Tereus was told by an oracle that his infant son would be slain by a close relative and, believing that Dryas was the person so designated, murdered him to avert fulfillment of the prediction.

91. Descendants of Ares and Bystonis

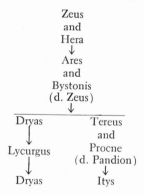

Dryas left a surviving son named Lycurgus, who became king of the Edones in Thrace. During his rule, the wine-god Dionysus arrived with a great throng of followers, and so incurred his anger that he furiously assaulted the deity and caused him to flee from the kingdom. According to the Iliad, Dionysus plunged into the sea and was received by the goddess Thetis, but another version of the legend relates that he was taken to Ino and Athamas at Orchomenus. As a result of his impiety, either Zeus or Dionysus himself caused Lycurgus to become

mad and he killed his own son, in the belief that he was cutting down a vine. By way of additional punishment, the gods made his country barren,[5] and the Edones were informed by an oracle that it would remain in that condition so long as Lycurgus continued to live. On receiving this report, his countrymen led their mad king to a nearby mountain, where he was bound and was later destroyed by wild horses.

Tereus, who killed his brother Dryas, was the king of that part of Thrace which was afterward known as Phocis. The Attic king, Pandion, called in his assistance against an enemy and, as a reward for his services, gave him his daughter, Procne (Progne), in marriage. By her, he became the father of a young son, named Itys. Being wearied of his wife, however, he plucked out her tongue by the roots and sent her into the country. Then, pretending that she was dead, he married her sister Philomela. Procne wove her pitiful story into a piece of embroidery, and was thereby enabled to inform Philomela of the cruelty which Tereus had inflicted upon her. In retaliation, the sisters killed Itys and served up his flesh as food to his father. Thereupon, the indignant gods changed Philomela into a swallow, Procne into a nightingale, forever bemoaning her murdered son,[6] and Tereus was changed into a hawk, who was symbolized as perpetually pursuing the two sisters.[7]

Cyrene

By Cyrene, whose lineage is not given, Ares had a son named Diomedes, a king of the Thracian tribe known as the Bistones, who was

---

[5] According to Hyginus, Dionysus caused Lycurgus to become intoxicated with wine, under whose influence he first attempted to do violence to his own mother and to destroy all of the vines in the country. He was then visited with madness and, after killing both his wife and his son, cut off his own legs in the belief that they were vines.

[6] The similarity of the stories—whereby both Procne and Aedon (the wife of Zethus) were changed into nightingales—has often caused their children (Itys and Itylus) to be confused with each other.

[7] Ovid reverses the story: saying that Tereus ravished Philomela, while he was bringing her to visit his wife (and her sister) Procne, adding that it was Philomela whose tongue he pulled out with pincers, and who revealed to her sister the horrible truth which she had woven into her tapestry.

noted as the owner of four man-eating mares.[8] As the eighth of his twelve labors, Heracles was ordered by Eurystheus to bring these fierce animals to Mycenae. He did so; in performing the task, he met with resistance from the Bistones which was effectually ended when he tossed their king, Diomedes, to his own hungry herd, by whom he was greedily devoured.[9]

Demonice

By Demonice, daughter of Agenor, Ares had four sons named Evenus, Molus, Pylus, and Thestius.[10] Nothing of interest is related about either Molus or Pylus. Evenus married his half sister Alcippe,[11] and their beautiful daughter Marpessa was wooed both by the god Apollo and by Idas, son of Aphareus, under circumstances previously related in chapter 6.

92. Descendants of Ares and Demonice

Ares
and
Demonice
(d. Agenor)
↓

Thestius and Laophonte (d. Pleuron) ↓	Molus Pylus	Evenus and Alcippe (d. Ares) ↓
Althaea	Iphiclus	Marpessa
Leda	Plexippus	
Hypermnestra	Prothous	
	Cometes	
	Eurypylus	
	Evippus	

Thestius married Laophonte, a daughter of the Aetolian king, Pleuron. Some say, however, that the name of his wife was Leucippe or Eurythemis. His children were the three daughters and the six sons whose names are given on the accompanying chart.

Of the sons, Iphiclus was one of the Argonauts and engaged in the hunt for the Caly-

donian boar, but his brothers appear to have been undistinguished by any named personal achievement, and are mentioned only as having been slain by their nephew, Meleager, in a quarrel for possession of the dead boar's hide.[12]

The daughters of Thestius were more noted. Althaea was married to Oeneus, king of Calydon, and became the mother of several children, including Meleager, who was the leader in the famed boar hunt.[13] She killed herself under tragic circumstances, which are later narrated in connection with that adventure. Hypermnestra married Oicles, who had inherited a third part of the kingdom of Argos, which his grandfather Melampus had exacted from Proetus. Leda married the Spartan king, Tyndareus, by whom she had several children. She is chiefly renowned as the beloved of Zeus to whom she bore the beautiful and immortal Helen.[14]

Dotis

By Dotis, a daughter of the Lapith king, Elatus, Ares had a son, Gyrton, from whom the Thessalian town of Gyrtone took its name, and another son, Phlegyas, who succeeded to the Lapith throne when his maternal grandfather died. After him, his subjects were sometimes referred to as the Phlegyes.[15] He added to his domain the country around Orchomenus in Boeotia by marrying Chryse, a daughter of Halmus.[16]

Phlegyas and Chryse had a son Ixion and a daughter named Coronis, who became with child by Apollo—an incident which so enraged Phlegyas that he set fire to the temple of the god at Delphi. For his impiety, he was slain with an arrow by Apollo, and was condemned to perpetual punishment in the lower world.[17]

---

[8] Hyginus says that the animals were horses and gives their names as Podargus, Lampus, Xanthus, and Deinus.

[9] According to Apollodorus, Diomedes was slain by Heracles.

[10] Pausanias says that Thestius was a son of Agenor and was a grandson of the Aetolian king, Pleuron.

[11] The attempted ravishment of Alcippe by Halirrhotius, a son of Poseidon, has been mentioned earlier in this chapter.

[12] Pausanias says that, at Tegea in Arcadia, he saw the statues of Cometes and Prothous.

[13] A variant of the legend is that Althaea bore Meleager to the war-god Ares.

[14] Pollux is conventionally considered to have been a twin of Helen.

[15] It is said that Phlegra, the ancient name for the peninsula of Pallene where the forces of Zeus fought the giants, was so called for Phlegyas.

[16] Halmus left no male heirs, and Phlegyas succeeded to the kingdom as his son-in-law.

[17] According to Apollodorus, Phlegyas was killed by Lycus and Nycteus, the sons of Chthonius.

93. Descendants of Ares and Dotis

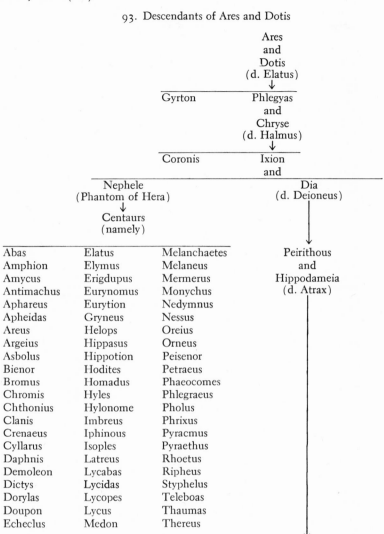

Ares
and
Dotis
(d. Elatus)
↓

Gyrton   Phlegyas
and
Chryse
(d. Halmus)
↓

Coronis   Ixion
and

Nephele   Dia
(Phantom of Hera)   (d. Deioneus)
↓
Centaurs
(namely)

Abas	Elatus	Melanchaetes	Peirithous
Amphion	Elymus	Melaneus	and
Amycus	Erigdupus	Mermerus	Hippodameia
Antimachus	Eurynomus	Monychus	(d. Atrax)
Aphareus	Eurytion	Nedymnus	
Apheidas	Gryneus	Nessus	
Areus	Helops	Oreius	
Argeius	Hippasus	Orneus	
Asbolus	Hippotion	Peisenor	
Bienor	Hodites	Petraeus	
Bromus	Homadus	Phaeocomes	
Chromis	Hyles	Phlegraeus	
Chthonius	Hylonome	Pholus	
Clanis	Imbreus	Phrixus	
Crenaeus	Iphinous	Pyracmus	
Cyllarus	Isoples	Pyraethus	
Daphnis	Latreus	Rhoetus	
Demoleon	Lycabas	Ripheus	
Dictys	Lycidas	Styphelus	
Dorylas	Lycopes	Teleboas	
Doupon	Lycus	Thaumas	
Echeclus	Medon	Thereus	

Polypoetes

Ixion followed his father as king of the Lapiths (Phlegyes), and married Dia, the daughter of Deioneus. When his father-in-law demanded bridal gifts which had been promised, Ixion invited him to a pretended banquet and caused him to fall into a pit filled with fire. The gods were indignant at this act of treachery and would permit no one to purify him of the murder. Zeus, however, finally taking pity on his wretched state, performed the requisite act of purification, and also invited Ixion to his table. Instead of showing gratitude, the foolish man requited his divine benefactor by attempting to win the love of Hera. Enraged (or per-haps amused) at his guest's audacity, the su-preme god made a cloud phantom of his queen, which Ixion embraced in the belief that he was accomplishing his desire. But he was soon disillusioned, when forthwith out of the cloud (Nephele) sprang the race of Centaurs.[18] And,

[18] Another version of the legend related that a single creature, named Centaurus, issued from the cloud phantom and, afterward, having connection with the wild mares of Magnesian Thessaly, became the sire of the race of Centaurs—or Hippocentaurs, as they were sometimes called. The ending of the name, from the Latin "taurus," meaning bull, is supposed to have signi-fied that the Centaurs were bull killers.

as punishment for his impudence, when he died he was led by Hermes into the lower world and chained to a fiery wheel, which perpetually turned as the impaled victim was scourged and compelled to repeat that "benefactors should be honored."

Peirithous, the son borne to Ixion by his wife, Dia,[19] was one of the hunters of the Calydonian boar. His next exploit was to drive away the cattle of Theseus from the plain of Marathon— an act prompted by a desire to make a test of the great strength and courage which the Attic hero was reputed to possess. When Theseus pursued, Peirithous turned and faced him, whereupon, the two men were immediately affected by a reciprocal admiration, and Peirithous, holding out his hand in friendship, bade Theseus himself to assess the damages of the cattle raid, saying that he would willingly submit to whatever penalty might be suggested. Theseus replied that he had already forgotten the quarrel, and invited Peirithous to become his comrade. The invitation was promptly accepted, and the newly made compact of friendship was ratified by their mutual oaths.

Some time later, when Peirithous was about to marry Hippodameia, the daughter of Atrax, he invited his friend to the wedding.[20] Theseus was pleased to accept the invitation and, arriving at the Thessalian site of the ceremony, was entertained magnificently by Peirithous and his Lapith kinsmen. Because of his relationship to them, Peirithous had also invited the Centaurs; and these curious creatures proceeded to enjoy themselves thoroughly with the wine which the bridegroom set out in plentiful quantity. As a result, one of them (named Eurytion) imbibed so freely that, when the bride appeared, he seized her by the hair and violently dragged her away. The other Centaurs, drunkenly taking this for a signal, followed suit—each of them attacking a Lapith woman, and the scene is described by Ovid as "like the sacking of a town." Peirithous and the Lapiths leapt to arms and,

with the mighty help of Theseus, and other Greek heroes who were present, fought a bloody battle which finally ended when the biformed guests were either slain or driven back to their home in the mountains.[21] In the fray, many feats of valor were performed, not only by Theseus and Peirithous but by others of the Lapiths —among whom Caeneus, Exadius, and Polyphemus were particularly distinguished.[22]

---

[21] The legendary home of the Centaurs was on Mount Pelion in Thessaly.

[22] As related by Ovid, in the Loeb translation of Frank Justus Miller, the following were the highlights of the battle between the Lapiths and the Centaurs:

"The Centaur Amycus crushed Celadon's head with a chandelier snatched from a shrine; Pelates killed Amycus with a table leg; the Centaur Gryneus smashed down Broteas and Orios with an altar on which the first was still burning; Exadius pierced Gryneus' eyeballs with the antlers of a stag; the Centaur Rhoetus killed Charaxus with a blazing brand of plum-wood, snatched from the altar fire; the dying Charaxus threw a huge stone at his assailant, but his cast was weak and his own friend Cometes was crushed by the missile; Rhoetus, using his same charred stake, killed young Evagrus by thrusting it down his throat; Dryas pierced Rhoetus with his own weapon and the Centaur fled, trailing blood; the Centaurs—Abas, Orneus, Lycabas, Thaumas, Peisenor, Pholus, Melaneus, Medon, Mermerus, and Asbolus all fled—Medon and Mermerus with wounds, and Asbolus after having tried in vain to dissuade the other Centaurs from the battle; Nessus also fled, although Asbolus (augur of the Centaurs) told him that he was fated to be killed later by the arrow of Heracles; Dryas killed the Centaurs Eurynomus, Lycidas, Areus, and Imbreus; the Centaur Crenaeus was slain when struck by a javelin; Phorbas killed the Centaur Pheidas as he lay in drunken sleep; Peirithous killed the Centaurs Petraeus, Lycus, and Chromis; Helops was slain by an unidentified Lapith javelin; Dictys, fleeing from Peirithous, fell over a precipice and was impaled on an ash tree; Theseus killed Aphareus with an oaken club; and, springing on Bienor's back, beat him to death with the same weapon; with like effect, he used it against Nedymnus, Lycopes, Hippasus, Ripheus, and Thereus; the Centaur Demoleon wrenched up a pine tree which, in falling, killed Crantor; Peleus killed the Centaurs Demoleon, Phlegraeus, Hyles, Iphinous, Clanis, and Dorylas; the Centaur Cyllarus, loved by Hylonome, was slain by a javelin from an unknown hand and, when she saw that her lover was dead, the female Centaur threw herself on the same javelin and expired; Nestor killed the Centaurs Chthonius and Teleboas with his sword; the Centaur Pyraethus was overcome by Periphas; Ampycus thrust a pointless shaft through the body of the Centaur Echeclus; Macareus hurled a crow-bar at the Centaur Erigdupus and laid him low; before fleeing, the Centaur Nessus buried a hunting spear in the groin of Cymelus; the seer Mopsus, son of Ampycus, slew Hodites with a javelin which pinned his tongue to his cheek and his cheek to his throat; Caeneus, with his

---

[19] A different tradition, preserved in the Iliad, makes Peirithous the son of Zeus and Dia.

[20] According to Diodorus Siculus, the father of Hippodameia was Butes, and Plutarch names the wife of Peirithous as Deidameia.

With the passage of time, Hippodameia bore a son to Peirithous, who was named Polypoetes. He inherited the warlike spirit and courage of his father and, with Leonteus, led the Lapiths in forty ships to the Trojan War. There he fought bravely, slaying the Trojans Astyalus, Damasus, Pylon, and Ormenus, but he is chiefly remembered for making the farthest cast in the shot-put at the funeral games held in honor of Patroclus. At the war's end, he went into Pamphylia on the south coast of Asia Minor where, in conjunction with his kinsman Leonteus, he founded a new colony named Aspendus.

When Theseus was fifty years old, Peirithous joined him, and the two friends went to Sparta where they kidnapped young Helen, whom they took to Aphidnae in Attica and left in the custody of Theseus' mother, Aethra. During the journey, they made a compact that whoever should win the maiden by lot was to have her as his wife, but must help the other to an equally desirable marriage. Upon casting lots on this understanding, Theseus won. Because of Helen's immaturity, however, he could only look forward with pleasurable anticipation to the day when their union could be consummated. Peirithous now daringly proposed that they should abduct Persephone, the queen of Hades for his wife. When Theseus assented, the two friends descended into the lower world to effect their plan, but were apprehended by the furious god of darkness, and were placed in seats to which their posteriors became unyieldingly fixed. And there they remained, until later when Heracles rescued Theseus, but Peirithous was so firmly fastened that even the strongest of all men was unable to pull him loose.[23]

Gaea

By Gaea, Ares had a dragon-son, generically called Draco, who lived in a spring of Boeotia near the river Ismenus.[24] The incidents relating to Draco's slaughter by Cadmus and the subsequent sowing of his teeth, from which grown men upsprang, have been related in chapter 9—dealing with the foundation of Thebes.

The names of the so-called Sparti are shown on the following chart. Of the men who bore them, Hyperenor and Pelorus receive only slight mythological notice; but Chthonius, Udaeus, and Echion became the progenitors of a number of v.i.p.'s.

Nycteus and Lycus, the sons of Chthonius, together with Nycteus' daughters—Antiope and Nycteis—and Lycus' wife, Dirce, have already been mentioned in connection with the Theban story, and nothing further need be related about them.

Udaeus had a son, Everes, who is remembered only as the father of Teiresias—borne to him by Chariclo, a nymph daughter of Zeus and Gaea. Teiresias became renowned as a great soothsayer. He was blind from his seventh year —having been afflicted when Athena sprinkled water on his eyes as he gazed upon her while she was bathing. His mother prayed to the goddess to restore her son's sight, but she was unable to do so and, in lieu of the prayed restoration, conferred upon the lad the power to understand the language of birds. She also gave him a magic staff, by whose help he could walk about as safely and as surely as though guided by his eyesight. Another tradition relates that, while still a youth, he was on Mount Cithaeron one day and saw a male and female serpent together. He struck at them with a stick and killed the female whereupon, he was transformed into a

---

battle axe, put to death the Centaurs Styphelus, Bromus, Antimachus, Elymus, and Pyracmus; the Centaur Latreus slew Halesus; the Centaur Phaeocomes hurled a log which crushed in the head of Tectaphus; Caeneus drove his sword to the hilt in Latreus' side and twisted the buried weapon until the Centaur expired; the Centaurs attacked Caeneus in a throng but, when he proved invulnerable to their weapons, he was buried beneath a pile of tree trunks which his assailants gathered at the command of Monychus; from the middle of the pile, a bird with golden wings was seen to fly, and the seer Mopsus hailed it as the invincible son of Elatus, who had been born as a maiden named Caenis."

23 According to Plutarch, Theseus and Peirithous went to Epeirus to obtain the daughter of the Molossian

king, Aidoneus, who called his wife Persephone, his daughter Kore, and his dog Cerberus. All of his daughter's suitors were bidden by him to fight his dog, and the victor was to receive her hand. As he suspected that Theseus and Peirithous had come, not as wooers but as ravishers, he cast them into prison. He put an end to Peirithous at once and set his dog to guard Theseus, who thus remained until he was later liberated by Heracles.

24 Other legends name Ares and Aphrodite as the parents of Draco, or relate that he was sacred to Ares, without identifying either his father or his mother.

94. Descendants of Ares and Gaea

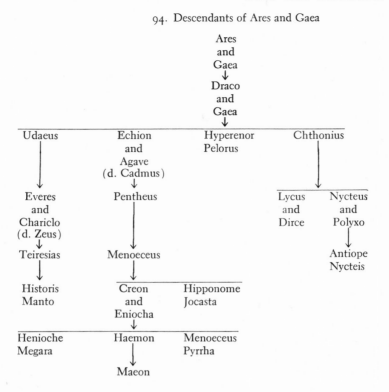

maiden himself. Seven years later, he (or she) again saw two serpents together and this time, killing the male, was returned to his original sex. Shortly thereafter, Zeus and Hera disputed as to whether a man or a woman received the greater carnal enjoyment and, being unable to settle their difference, referred the question to Teiresias, who presumably had experienced the sensations of both sexes. When he declared, in favor of Zeus, that men received the greater enjoyment, indignant Hera blinded him, but Zeus gave him the power of prophecy and granted that he should live for seven generations.[25]

By an unnamed wife (or wives) Teiresias had two daughters, who were named Historis and Manto. Historis is said to have assisted Alcmena in her labors when Heracles was born;[26] and by Poseidon, she became mother of a son, Periclymenus, who slew Parthenopaeus, and chased Amphiaraus beneath the earth (in the attack of the Seven Against Thebes). Manto was taken captive by Alcmaeon, one of the Epigoni, and bore to him a son and a daughter respectively named Amphilochus and Tisiphone. Afterward, she was taken by the Epigoni to Delphi and dedicated to Apollo, by whom she became the mother of Mopsus—the greatest seer in all mythology.[27]

Owing to his long life, Teiresias was connected with practically all of the mythological events of early Thebes. It was he who revealed to Oedipus that he had killed his father, Laius, and had married his own mother, Jocasta. In the war of the Seven Against Thebes, he prophesied that the city would be saved if Creon's son, Menoeceus, should sacrifice himself, and, during the assault of the Epigoni, he advised the Thebans to commence negotiations for peace

[25] A third tradition related that Teiresias was blinded because he revealed to men the secrets of the gods.

[26] Another version names Galanthis as the attendant of Alcmena.

[27] According to Pausanias, Manto was herself a prophetess by inheritance from her father. She is said to have served in that role first, at the temple of Apollo in Thebes, next at his temple in Delphi, and finally, at his shrine located in the Carian town of Clarus. At Clarus, Pausanias says that she met and married a Cretan named Rhacius, who by her became the father of Mopsus, the seer.

and to take flight during the armistice thus afforded. When the city was evacuated, he fled with his townsmen but, on the way, drank from the spring near Haliartus called Tilphussa and, expiring, was buried beside it.[28] Even in the lower world, he retained his reason and his gift as a soothsayer: although the departed souls of all others were accustomed to flit aimlessly about as gibbering shades.

The Sparti Echion married Agave, one of the daughters of Cadmus, who bore to him a son named Pentheus—doomed to suffer from the curse laid on the line of Cadmus for the slaughter of Draco. When Cadmus became old, his son, Polydorus, was still too young to administer the government of Thebes, and Pentheus was appointed to the throne. During his rule, the wine-god Dionysus came to the city, attended by his frenzied Bacchantes, and began to enlist additional followers from the Theban women. Despite a previous warning from Teiresias that he should accept the god's rites, Pentheus ordered his servants to take Dionysus by force and bring him to the royal court. The servants returned and reported that they were unable to find him, but they delivered up one of his devotees named Acoetes, who told Pentheus a wonderful story which was intended to prove that Dionysus was really a gifted son of divine Zeus. The unbelieving king angrily ordered that the captive should be thrown into prison and tortured; but, as his servants were complying with his order, the chains fell from the arms of Acoëtes, and his prison doors flew open of their own accord.[29] Notwithstanding this miraculous happening, Pentheus stood fixed in his purpose, and his rage was increased when he learned that his own mother, Agave, and his aged father-in-law, Cadmus, had accepted the divinity of the wine-god. Thereupon, he went to Mount Cithaeron and spied on the mystic ceremonies—and was torn to pieces under the circumstances which have been previously related in chapter 9.

With the death of Pentheus, Polydorus—now grown—succeeded to the kingdom of Thebes, but the descendants of Pentheus continued to play an active part in the city's affairs. Nothing of importance is related about his son, Menoeceus,[30] except that he became the father of Hipponome, Jocasta, and Creon. As previously related in chapter 14, Hipponome married Alcaeus, a son of the hero Perseus, and became the mother of Amphitryon—the stepfather of Heracles. And, in chapter 9, we have detailed the tragic life of Jocasta, which ended with her suicide upon learning that she had unwittingly married her own son, Oedipus.

When Eteocles and Polyneices, the sons of Oedipus and Jocasta, died in their duel during the attack of the Seven Against Thebes, their uncle Creon again assumed rulership of the city.[31] His refusal to permit the corpse of Polyneices to be buried, and his cruel treatment of Antigone, when she disobeyed his royal decree, have been detailed at some length in chapter 9. In the same chapter, we have related how his son Menoeceus sacrificed himself, pursuant to the suggestion of the seer Teiresias, and how Haemon, his son, died by a self-inflicted wound at the side of his beloved Antigone.[32]

After fleeing from Thebes when it was attacked by the Epigoni, Creon was permitted to return, and was again ruling when Amphitryon was expelled from Argos by his uncle Sthenelus. Amphitryon came to Thebes; was purified by Creon; enlisted his assistance against the Taphians; married Alcmena; Heracles was born and, upon attaining manhood, defeated the forces of Creon's enemy Erginus; and, for his efforts, was rewarded by marriage to Creon's daughter, Megara—incidents which have been mentioned in more detail in chapter 14.

Nothing is said by the mythographers about how Creon came to die. It is only necessary to

---

[28] A different legend relates that Teiresias was captured by the Epigoni and taken to the temple of Apollo at Delphi.

[29] As noted in chapter 9, a different legend related that Dionysus was himself the captive of Pentheus, for whom the prison doors miraculously opened.

---

[30] The Scholiast on Euripides says that Menoeceus was a grandson of Pentheus, but does not name his father.

[31] Creon had previously been the ruler of Thebes between the death of Laius and the assumption of the kingship by Oedipus.

[32] According to Apollodorus, Haemon was the last victim of the Sphinx, before Oedipus solved her fatal riddle.

mention that, by his wife, Eniocha, he had two other daughters named Henioche and Pyrrha, who are preserved in mythological lore only as names. Maeon, a son earlier borne to Haemon by an unnamed woman, is mentioned as having fought to protect his city when it was attacked by the Seven Against Thebes, and was a survivor of the battle,[33] but, with Heracles as a member of his family, one could not reasonably suppose that he would succeed to the kingship—nor did he.

Harpinna

By Harpinna, daughter of the river-god Asopus, Ares had a son named Oenomaus, who became the king of Pisa in Elis.[34] He married Sterope, a Pleiad daughter of Atlas, and she bore to him a daughter, Hippodameia, and a son, Leucippus.

95. Descendants of Ares and Harpinna

Ares
and
Harpinna
(d. Asopus)
↓
Oenomaus
and
Sterope
(d. Atlas)
↓
Hippodameia
Leucippus

Leucippus fell in love with the nymph Daphne, a daughter of the river-god Peneius who was beloved by Apollo but, as she avoided all men, he despaired of winning her by open courtship, and resorted to trickery. He first let his hair grow long, and braided it as though he were a maiden. Then, putting on female garments, he went to her and said that he was a daughter of Oenomaus and would like to share her hunting. The supposed maiden soon surpassed all of Daphne's other companions in the chase and, being quite constant in his atten-

tions, drew the nymph into a great friendship, which he hoped would soon bring about fulfillment of his desire. Apollo, however, became jealous of his mortal rival and, when Daphne and her companions were about to swim in the river Ladon, he caused them to strip Leucippus of his clothes in order to join them. After he was disrobed and they discovered his imposture, they became so indignant that they killed the exposed youth with their javelins and hunting knives.

An oracle had declared that Oenomaus was fated to die upon the marriage of his daughter. In order to discourage all suitors, he made it a condition that Hippodameia should be wed only to the man who should conquer him in a chariot race from Pisa to the isthmus of Corinth —further specifying that all those whom he bested should be put to death. One after another, twelve suitors appeared[35] and entered the contest, but all of them lost their races—and their lives—because Oenomaus not only had swifter horses but also was aided by his divine father Ares. Moreover, he cautiously sacrificed to Zeus before every race, and his charioteer Myrtilus was a son of the god Hermes. Finally, a new contestant appeared, in the person of Pelops, son of the wealthy Lydian king, Tantalus. He secretly bribed Myrtilus to draw out a linch pin from one of the wheels of Oenomaus' chariot, which caused the wheel to fall off during the race and the chariot to overturn— killing Oenomaus in its crash.[36] Having thus become victor, he married Hippodameia and, with her as his queen, succeeded to the kingdom of Pisa.[37]

---

[33] With Polyphontes, Maeon attacked the forces of Tydeus from ambush. Polyphontes was slain but Maeon was spared and, in gratitude, afterward buried Tydeus when he lost his life in the assault.

[34] Other traditions related that Oenomaus was a son of Ares and Sterope, or of Alxion (or Hyperochus) and Sterope.

[35] Pindar says that the number of suitors preceding Pelops was thirteen. Pausanias says that they were all buried in one tomb and names eighteen, namely: Marmax, Alcathous, Euryalus, Eurymachus, Crotalus, Acrias, Capetus, Lycurgus, Lasius, Chalcodon, Tricolonus, Aristomachus, Prias, Pelagon, Aeolius, Cronius, Erythras, and Eioneus.

[36] When, instead of paying off his promised bribe, Pelops threw Myrtilus into the sea, the drowning youth prayed for still another curse on the house of Tantalus.

[37] According to Pindar, Pelops fairly won the race in a golden chariot and with steeds "unwearied of wing" which were given to him by the god Poseidon. Still another version relates that Oenomaus survived his wreck, but killed himself when he realized that he could not hope to win the race.

Otrera

By Otrera, whose antecedents are not given, Ares is said to have been the father of the Amazons, a race of warrior women who lived at Themiscyra in Pontus around the mouth of the river Thermodon.[38] According to legend, all of them had their right breasts seared off at infancy, in order not to interfere with drawing the bow or throwing the javelin.

Among their more important exploits, it is related that the Amazons: (1) invaded Lycia in the reign of Iobates, only to be defeated by Bellerophon, who was then staying at the king's court; (2) attacked Phrygia while Priam was still a youth; (3) fought a battle with the forces of Heracles when he came in quest of the girdle of their Queen Hippolyte; (4) invaded Attica during the rule of Theseus; and, (5) fought on the side of the Trojans in the war with the Greeks.

The principal mythological stories about the Amazons concern Antiope, Hippolyte, Melanippe, Myrina, and Penthesileia.[39] Of these: Antiope was captured by Heracles and, being taken by him to Greece, became the first wife of Theseus; Hippolyte was slain by Heracles when her forces attacked his men, after she had already promised to surrender her beautiful girdle;[40] Melanippe would have suffered a like fate but, after she was captured, surrendered her girdle and was set free; Myrina married Lem-nian King Thoas and, at death, was buried on the plain before Troy which was thereafter called by her name; and, Penthesilea was slain by Achilles in the Trojan War.

Pelopeia

By Pelopeia, a daughter of Pelias, Ares had a ruffian son named Cycnus,[41] who lived at Itonus in Thessaly, where he was accustomed to cut off the heads of passing strangers—intending, with his gory trophies, to build a temple in honor of his war-god father. But the temple was never completed because, as Heracles was traveling through the country, on his way to visit King Ceyx at Trachis, the foolish man challenged him to single combat. And, although Cycnus was aided in the fight by Ares, Heracles quickly killed him, and wounded his immortal sire so seriously that he had to be lifted into his battle chariot and driven away by his sons Deimos and Phobos.

Philonome

By Philonome, daughter of Nyctimus[42] and of the nymph Arcadia, Ares had twin sons, who were named Lycastus and Parrhasius. When the boys were born, Philonome feared that her father would not believe their divine paternity, and threw them into the river Erymanthus in eastern Persia. The god of the river took pity on the infants, and carried them to a hollow oak tree, where they were suckled by a she-wolf until they were found by a shepherd named Tyliphus, who took them safely back to their mother.

Protogeneia

By Protogeneia, daughter of the Aetolian king, Calydon, Ares had a son who was named Oxylus. Nothing of interest is related about him except that, when grown, he became the father of Andraemon. Andraemon's wife, Gorge, was

---

[38] According to the geographer Strabo, a mountain separated the Amazons from a race to the north of them who were known as the Gargareans. During two months in the spring, both races were accustomed to ascend the mountain, where promiscuous mating took place between the Gargarean men and the Amazonian women. The female children were retained by the Amazons, but the males were either destroyed or sent back to their fathers.

[39] The names of other Amazons, as given by various ancient writers, were: Aella, Alcibia, Antandra, Antibrota, Asteria, Bremusa, Celaeno, Clonia, Deianeira, Derimacheia, Derinoë, Eriboea, Eurybia, Gyandra, Harmothoë, Hippothoë, Marpe, Philippis, Phoebe, Polemusa, Prothoë, Tecmessa, and Thermodosa.

[40] The conventional story is that Hippolyte was slain by Heracles, after which Melanippe assumed command and continued to fight until she and Antiope were taken as prisoners. Another version, however, says that Hippolyte survived and later led an expedition into Attica to recover Antiope, who had been given to Theseus by Heracles. A third legend describes Theseus himself as Antiope's captor.

[41] According to Hesiod, Cycnus was the husband of Themistinoë, the daughter of Ceyx—the great friend of Heracles, to whose court the hero was proceeding when his progress was challenged.

[42] As related in chapter 13, Nyctimus was the only son of Lycaon who was not slain by the thunderbolt of Zeus—hurled by the god in disgust at having been served human flesh.

a daughter of Oeneus—the king who had succeeded to the rulership of all Aetolia. By her, he had a son, Thoas, who later led the Aetolians with forty ships to the Trojan War. This honor was his by inheritance from his father, who had assumed the kingship (by virtue of his marriage to Gorge), when Oeneus became old.[43]

96. Descendants of Ares and Protogeneia

Ares
and
Protogeneia
(d. Calydon)
↓
Oxylus
↓
Andraemon
and
Gorge
(d. Oeneus)
↓
Thoas
↓
Haemon
↓
Oxylus
and
Pieria
↓
Aetolus
Laias

At Troy, Thoas took a leading part among his comrades, as one whose advice was often asked. His reputation for wisdom was so great that Poseidon assumed his voice when he sought to arouse the Greeks, after an engagement in which the Trojans had been victorious. Nor was Thoas lacking in courage, for he offered to meet Hector in single combat, and slew the Thracian warrior Peirous, who was one of the two leaders of his countrymen on the side of the Trojans. Unlike some of the other victors, he returned safely from the war to die a natural death among his own people, and was followed in the Aetolian government by his son, Haemon.[44]

Haemon had a son who, after his early an-

cestor of divine descent, was named Oxylus. When the Heracleidae were gathered at Naupactus, preparatory to invading the Peloponnesus, they were told to accept as their guide "the three-eyed one." It was Oxylus who met this description and thereby gained the rulership of Elis—as narrated in chapter 14.[45] Although the Heracleidae kept their promise to give the Elean domain to him, they left it to Oxylus to take possession of it by his own efforts. When he approached with his army, the incumbent King Dius refused to give way. Anxious to avoid a pitched battle, Oxylus proposed to him that the issue should be decided by an engagement between single champions from each of their followers. The proposal was accepted and the champions chosen were the Elean Degmenus, who was an archer, and the Aetolian Pyraechmes, who was a slinger. In the contest which followed, Pyraechmes won the victory—and Oxylus obtained his kingdom. He proved to be a beneficent ruler, allowing the old inhabitants (who were still called Epeians), to keep their possessions but brought in additional colonists from Aetolia, and gave them shares in the land. He permitted Dius to retain many of his royal privileges, and kept up the worship of the Elean heroes—especially continuing the honors paid to Augeias. And, under his government, Elis became a more populous and prosperous country.

The wife of Oxylus was named Pieria but, beyond this, nothing of interest is related about her. Of his two sons, Aetolus predeceased both of his parents, and was buried in a tomb which they had built at the gate opening to the sacred grove where the Olympian games were held and, when Oxylus died, his surviving son, Laias, succeeded to the kingdom—but did nothing of interest (and the sovereignty passed on to others who are outside our mythological pale).

Pyrene

By the nymph Pyrene, Ares had a second son named Cycnus. Like his half brother of the

---

[43] According to Apollodorus, Andraemon was placed on the Aetolian throne by Diomedes, who had either slain or driven from the country all of the sons of Agrius—next in the line of succession. His tomb and that of his wife were pointed out to Pausanias, when he visited Amphissa in the second century A.D.

[44] Some name the son of Thoas as Andraemon, and relate that he was married to Dryope, who bore Amphissus to Apollo.

[45] According to Pausanias, Oxylus happened to pass through the camp of the Heracleidae upon his return to Aetolia after a year's exile, following his unintentional slaying of his brother Thermius (or Alcidocus, son of Scopius), with a discus.

same name (the son of Ares and Pelopeia), he challenged Heracles to single combat, when the ubiquitous hero came to the Macedonian river Echedorus, on his journey to the land of the Hesperides. And, as he had come to the aid of Pelopeia's son, so Ares gave his assistance to the son of Pyrene. The outcome, however, was indecisive, because Zeus hurled a thunderbolt between the combatants, and forced them to drop their weapons.

This story is given by Apollodorus. According to Hyginus, Cycnus was killed by Heracles; Eustathius relates that, at his death, Cycnus was changed into a swan by Ares and, according to some of the ancient mythographers, it was he who was transported to the heavens and changed into the constellation which bears his name. The conventional version, however, is that the constellation was supposed to depict Zeus in the swan form assumed by him when he approached Leda.

Rhea Silvia

As stated in the first chapter of this compilation, the Roman mythology is not intended to be covered herein but, since it is—with few exceptions—almost identical with that of the Greeks, the accompanying chart is inserted, as illustrative of the tie-in.

97. Descendants of Ares and Rhea Silvia

Ares
and
Rhea Silvia
(d. Numitor)
↓
Romulus
Remus

Under his Latin name of Mars, the Greek war-god Ares became the father of twin sons, Romulus and Remus, who were borne to him by Rhea Silvia, a daughter of Numitor.[46] Together with their mother, the boys were thrown into the river Anio, upon orders of their great-uncle Amulius, who had seized the throne of Alba Longa from their grandfather Numitor.[47] But, instead of drowning, the children were carried in their cradle into the river Tiber, and were stranded on its banks at the foot of the hill which was afterward called Palatine. Here, according to Roman legend, they were miraculously suckled by a she-wolf (Lupa) and were fed by a woodpecker (a bird sacred to Mars), until they were found by a shepherd named Faustulus, and taken to his home for rearing by his wife, Acca Laurentia.

The twin boys grew up with the twelve sons of their foster-parents, and soon they became distinguished from their playmates by their beauty and bravery, so that they were accepted as the acknowledged leaders of the youth of the countryside around the Palatine hill. When a quarrel arose between their band and the herdsmen of Numitor, Remus was taken by stratagem during the absence of Romulus and was carried off to Alba Longa. His age and noble bearing made Numitor think of his grandsons, and the old man's suspicion was changed to certainty when Romulus later appeared with Faustulus, and related the marvelous circumstances of their nurture and preservation.

Upon learning of their grandfather's continuing humiliation, and their own royal descent from him, Romulus and Remus resolved to avenge their family's ill-treatment and, with the help of their comrades, who had flocked to their rescue at Alba Longa, they slew Amulius and restored Numitor to the city's throne. However, they loved their old abode, and so they returned to found a city of their own on the Tiber. As they possessed equal authority and power, an argument arose as to where the city should be raised and what should be its name. Romulus was in favor of the Palatine hill as a site, but Remus preferred the nearby Aventine. At this impasse, it was agreed that the question should be decided by augury, and each of the dispu-

---

[46] Numitor is said to have been a descendant from Aeneas in the fourteenth generation, but the legend is unsettled as to whether he was descended from Aeneas' Greek son, Ascanius (called Iulus by the Romans), or from his Latin son, Silvius.

[47] When Amulius dethroned his brother Numitor, he forced Rhea Silvia to become a Vestal virgin, so that she might not have heirs to disturb him in his usurpation, but she was overpowered by Mars in a cave whence she had fled to escape from a wolf. After she was thrown into the river Anio, it is said that she changed her earthly life into that of a goddess and became the wife of the god of the stream.

tants took a station on the top of his chosen elevation. As the dawn broke, Remus saw six vultures, but later, Romulus saw twelve flying past the Palatine. When each claimed the augury to be in his own favor, the matter was put to a vote of the gathered shepherds, and they decided in favor of Romulus, who proceeded to lay out his city, with a wall which separated it from the adjacent country. And thus, Rome is said to have been founded on the twenty-first day of April, which was afterwards celebrated annually as the festival of Pales—the divinity of shepherds.[48]

---

[48] According to legend, Remus resentfully leaped over the wall, and was killed by Romulus, but the latter was seized by remorse and afterward set up by his side an empty throne, with a scepter and crown, in token that the city should be considered as jointly ruled by himself and his slain brother.

The Decendants of Zeus VII

Hera—the Mother of Hephaestus

THE BIRTH of Hephaestus, and a description of his life and functions as the god of fire, have been noted rather fully in chapter 3. He had children by a number of wives and they, with their descendants, will be mentioned in the alphabetical order of the names of their mothers.

Aglaea

Aglaea, the youngest of the Graces, is called Charis in the Iliad.[1] By her, it is said that Hephaestus became the father of Aethiops, from whom the country of Ethiopia took its name.

Anticleia

By Anticleia, Hephaestus had a son named Periphetes. He dwelt near Epidaurus in Argos and, being a cripple, carried an iron club. The club, however, was not always used as a crutch, for Periphetes was accustomed to use it also as a weapon and, with it, killed many of those who were passing by. This practice continued until Theseus came along and, after being attacked, wrested the weapon from the hands of its owner and crushed in Periphetes' skull with it.[2]

Aphrodite

As related in chapter 3, Aphrodite, the goddess of love and beauty, was the lawfully wedded wife of Hephaestus on Mount Olympus. But she was not overly fond of her lame husband, and bore him no children.

Cabeiro

By Cabeiro, a daughter of the sea-god Proteus and the Oceanid Torone, Hephaestus had two sons, named Alcon and Eurymedon, who came from the island of Lemnos to accompany Dionysus on his victorious expedition to India.

Gaea

Although much of the ancient Greek mythology has been preserved for us by Aeschylus, Sophocles, Euripides, Aristophanes, and the other great dramatists who made Athens their headquarters in the Golden Age of Pericles, the Athenians themselves were conscious of the fact that their city was new and that neither it, nor its inhabitants, could claim the intimate connection with the gods which was the pride of older Thebes, Mycenae, Tiryns, and Cnossus.[3]

They were especially embarrassed because their titular divinity was Athena—a maiden

---

[1] Since Homer recognized Aphrodite as the lawful wife of Hephaestus, some consider that Charis was her surname.

[2] Theseus kept the club, and afterward used it as his own weapon against other adversaries.

[3] The Athenians receive but scanty mention in the Iliad, and their leader Menestheus is assigned no divine ancestor, as was Homer's custom when mentioning other peoples. This fact, and other persuasive evidence in both the Iliad and the Odyssey, caused the scholarly Andrew Lang to suggest that the references to their inhabitants in the Homeric poems were interpolated by the Athenians themselves, long after the time of the original composition of the poems.

98. Descendants of Hephaestus and Gaea

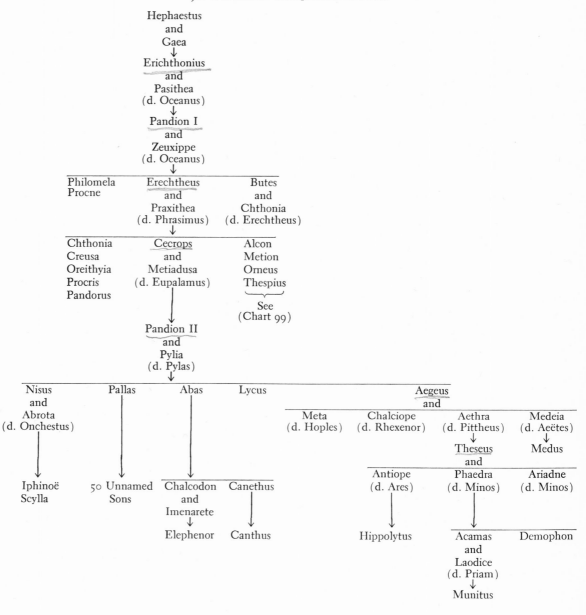

goddess, from whom it was impossible to trace any line of descent without sullying her chaste reputation. Being put to it to invent a divine pedigree for themselves, they accomplished the task by means of a most ingenious story. Since the fire-god Hephaestus was relatively unappropriated, they chose him as the conduit from Olympus to Athens, and said that their ancestor

Erichthonius was sprung from his seed when he attempted to embrace Athena.[4]

Prior to the birth of Erichthonius, the country of Attica (where Athens was located), is said

---

[4] The text describes Hephaestus as relatively unappropriated because earlier he was considered as associated only with the island of Lemnos.

to have been ruled by autochthonous kings;[5] and, perhaps for this reason, Erichthonius was himself conceived as half man and half serpent. In order to give their government a mythological continuity, the Athenians announced that he was reared by Athena, and was concealed in a chest, which she delivered to the daughters of King Cecrops, with instructions that it should remain unopened. The command of the goddess, however was disobeyed and, when the maidens looked upon their serpentine charge, they were stricken with madness and committed suicide. Erichthonius escaped from his confinement into Athena's shield and later, after expelling the ruling king, Amphictyon, took over the rulership of the country.

As king, it is said that he introduced the worship of Athena among his people, and instituted in her honor the festival known as the Panathenaea.[6] Also, he was credited with having decided the dispute between Athena and Poseidon which resulted in the appointment of the goddess as the divine protectress of the city. According to legend, he built a temple for her worship on the Acropolis.[7] At his death, he was himself honored with a temple called the Erechtheum, where he was for years worshipped as a divinity.

By Pasithea, a Naiad daughter of Oceanus,[8]

Erichthonius had a son who is usually referred to as Pandion I, to distinguish him from his great-grandson of the same name. When he succeeded his deceased father as king of Attica, he married Zeuxippe—his mother's sister (and thus, his aunt as well as his wife). By her, he had twin sons, Erechtheus[9] and Butes, and also, two daughters—Procne and Philomela, whose tragic story has been related in the preceding chapter, in connection with Tereus, the son of Ares and Bystonis.

At Pandion's death, Erechtheus became king and took Praxithea as his wife. She was a daughter of Phrasimus (otherwise unmentioned) and Diogeneia.[10] She bore four daughters and six sons to him whose names are given in the accompanying chart. All of the daughters married husbands of illustrious lineage: Chthonia married her own uncle Butes; Creusa married Xuthus, son of Hellen, and was also espoused by the god Apollo; Oreithyia was carried off by the wind-god Boreas; and Procris was preferred by Cephalus, son of the Aeolid Deion, over the dawn-goddess Eos.[11]

According to one tradition, Erechtheus fought a successful war against the Eleusinians, in which the latter were assisted by the Thracian Eumolpus. And in the war, it is said that he killed both Eumolpus and his son, Ismarus. A different version, however, relates that he was defeated by the enemy and lost his own life in

---

[5] The first ruler is said to have been Actaeus, an autochthon, from whose name the country was first called Acte. Cecrops, a second autochthon, married a daughter of Actaeus (Agraulos) and succeeded his father-in-law in the kingdom, whose name was then changed to Cecropia. He was followed by his son Erysichthon, who died childless. Cranaus, a third autochthon then came to the throne, and changed the name of the country to Attica, in honor of his daughter Atthis. Cranaus was expelled by Amphictyon, a son of Deucalion who had married Atthis and, as related in the text, Amphictyon was ousted by Erichthonius.

[6] The festival was originally named only the Athenaea, and received the name of Panathenaea at the time when Theseus united the Attic inhabitants into one body. The so-called Lesser Panathenaea was celebrated every year and the Greater Panathenaea was held every fifth year.

[7] The early temple to Athena built by Erichthonius should not be confused with the later—and lasting—architectural masterpiece raised in the time of Pericles and called the Parthenon.

[8] According to Apollodorus, the wife of Erichthonius was called Praxithea. Others relate that she was a Naiad

daughter of the god of the Attic river Eridanus—a stream bearing the same name as the Italian resting place of Phaethon's corpse.

[9] Owing to the similarity of names, Erichthonius is sometimes called Erechtheus I and Pandion's son is referred to as Erechtheus II. As may be imagined, much has been written (with the expected varying conclusions), discussing the question as to whether or not the original myth concerned one or two individuals. Similar conjectures have been made in learned circles with respect to Pandion I and Pandion II, and also with respect to Cecrops, the son of Erechtheus, and the autochthon of the same name.

[10] Diogeneia was a daughter of the god of the river Cephisus. The more renowned stream bearing the name was in Boeotia, but a smaller one was in Attica.

[11] It is related that, when Erechtheus was warring with the Eleusinians, his daughters sacrificed themselves, after an oracle had declared that one of them should voluntarily die to insure their father's victory.

the fighting.[12] When Erechtheus succeeded Pandion as king, his twin brother, Butes, assumed the office of priest of Athena, and is said to have gained added renown as a ploughman, shepherd, and warrior.[13] At his death, an altar was dedicated to him in the Erechtheum, and his descendants, known as the Butadae, long continued to be honored among the first families of Athens.

Nothing of interest is related about Pandorus, son of Erechtheus and Praxithea, but his brothers—Cecrops, Alcon, Metion, Orneus, and Thespius, who, with their descendants, will next be remarked upon in order.

As previously mentioned, Cecrops is often confused with the autochthonous king of the country who was among the rulers preceding Erichthonius[14] but, considered as a son of Erechtheus, he is remembered only as the father of Pandion II, by Metiadusa, a daughter of his own nephew Eupalamus.

After Pandion II succeeded his father Cecrops as king, he was expelled by his uncle Metion's sons and fled to Megara on the Saronic gulf. There, he married Pylia, daughter of the king Pylas, who bore to him five sons—Aegeus, Lycus, Pallas, Nisus, and Abas.[15] At a later time, Pylas was forced to leave Megara because he had slain one of his kinsmen, and he turned the government of the city over to Pandion.[16] At his death, Pandion was not immediately succeeded in the rulership by any of his sons, as they preferred to live at Athens.[17] Accordingly, they raised a force and marched against that city, where they successfully overcame the sons of Metion, who had previously been responsible for the dethronement of their father. Victorious, they proceeded to divide the government among themselves in four parts, but gave to Aegeus the supreme power.[18]

Aegeus, eldest of the sons of Pandion II and Pylia,[19] first married Meta, a daughter of Hoples, and then Chalciope, daughter of Rhexenor;[20] but, as both wives failed to bear him children, he went to the oracle at Delphi to inquire what he should do to supply the deficiency. The answer given to him was: "The bulging mouth of the wineskin, O best of men, loose not until thou hast reached the height of Athens." Not knowing what to make of this, the baffled man now set out on the return to his home. Journeying by way of Troezen,[21] he lodged with Pittheus, a son of Pelops, and related to his host the oracle's ambiguous words. Pittheus understood their meaning and, after making his guest drunk with wine, caused him to lie with his daughter Aethra. And it is said that, in the same night, Poseidon also had connection with her. When Aegeus left Troezen, he charged Aethra that, if she should have a son, she should rear him without revealing to anyone the name of his father. And he placed a sword and a pair of sandals under a large rock,

---

[12] According to Diodorus Siculus, Erechtheus was an Egyptian who brought corn to Athens during a famine, and was himself the founder of the Mysteries, which were celebrated at nearby Eleusis in honor of Demeter.

[13] Those who give Butes a reputation as a warrior perhaps confuse him with Butes, the son of Teleon, who was one of the Argonauts.

[14] Erichthonius was sometimes considered the same with the autochthonous Cecrops (see chart 4)— both being half serpent; and Cecrops, not Erichthonius, is often mentioned as the judge who decided the dispute between Athena and Poseidon for the overlordship of Athens.

[15] It is said that, during Pandion's reign at Athens, Demeter and Dionysus came into Attica but, since their entry resulted in the founding of the Mysteries which brought Eleusis into being, the reference is seemingly to the first Pandion, who was the son of Erichthonius. The entry of Dionysus into Attica was welcomed by a citizen named Acrisius, whom the god taught to make wine. When some shepherds, however, drank without diluting it, they thought that they had been bewitched and killed him. His dog Maera discovered the dead body and led Erigone, Acrisius' daughter, to it. She then hanged herself.

[16] According to a different version of the legend, Pandion's sons restored him to the kingship at Athens.

[17] Some say that Pandion was married to Pylia before he was expelled by the sons of Metion, and that his children were born and reared in Athens.

[18] Nisus either remained in, or subsequently returned to, Megara and became king of the city.

[19] Some said that Aegeus was a son of Scyrius, and that he was adopted by Pandion.

[20] The lineage of Hoples is not mentioned, nor is that of Rhexenor with respect to his paternity of Chalciope. Since, however, it offends neither the chronology nor geographical limitations, Chalciope has been placed in chart 58 as a daughter of Rhexenor, the Phaeacian, who is the only (other) person bearing the name assigned to her father.

[21] The journey from Delphi to Athens, by way of Troezen in southern Argos, was manifestly a bit roundabout.

saying that when the boy should become strong enough to roll away the rock, Aethra should send him to Athens.

Returning to Attica, Aegeus married Medeia, who had fled from Corinth after murdering the children whom she had borne to Jason, and by her he had a son named Medus. Some time later, in the games held at the festival of Panathenaea, the Cretan prince, Androgeus, vanquished all of his opponents and was subsequently slain by them—bringing on the war between Athens and Crete (related in chapter 15) which resulted in a treaty under which the Athenians were obligated periodically to send seven boys and seven of their maidens to be devoured by the Minotaur.

Meanwhile, Aethra gave birth at Troezen to a son who was called Theseus. When he was grown, his mother told him the circumstances of his conception, and pointed out the rock under which Aegeus had placed the sword and sandals. With scarcely an effort, the strong youth picked up the rock and secured the articles which it covered. Then, following Aethra's injunction, he set out on the road to the court of his father at Athens.

Emulating the performance of his kinsman Heracles,[22] Theseus decided to clear the way of the many perils which were reputed to infest it. First, at Epidaurus, he killed the robber Periphetes and—as previously related in this chapter—appropriated his iron club for an additional weapon for his own future use. At the southern end of the isthmus of Corinth, he encountered Sinis, a son of Poseidon and Sylea known as the Pine bender, and slew him (as related in chapter 10) by the same device which the ruffian was accustomed to use with others.[23] When he came to Crommyon on the isthmus, he heard of a wild sow named Phaea, that had been ravaging the near countryside. And this animal he turned out of his way to destroy, so that people might not think that his exploits were performed only to save himself.[24] Approaching the outskirts of

Megara, he slew the robber Sciron, by kicking him down a precipice into the sea, where a turtle devoured him.[25]

At Eleusis, Theseus was challenged by Cercyon, a son of Hephaestus,[26] and broke his bones to pieces in a wrestling match. Journeying a little farther, he came upon Damastes—a robber who was surnamed the Stretcher (Procrustes), because he compelled all who approached to lie in his bed. If they were too short, he stretched them to its full length; but, if they were too tall, he cut off their hands and legs so as to make a perfect (though bloody) fit. Presumably, the robber was accustomed to sleep with plenty of head room, for Theseus stretched him to the length of his own couch and, in so doing, caused him to suffer the same cruel death which he had been in the habit of bringing to others.[27]

When the bold youth finally arrived at Athens, he proceeded to the court of Aegeus and, through the gift of her magic power, was immediately recognized by Medeia. The king had now become an old man and, fearing everyone as his enemy, was persuaded by her to test the claims of the young stranger by sending him against the bull of Marathon.[28] Happy at this opportunity to demonstrate his prowess to his father, Theseus went to the plain where the bull was feeding, and quickly put an end to its life with his sword.[29] He then returned to Athens, and sent word to Aegeus that his mission had

---

[22] See footnote 84 in chapter 14 for the relationship between Theseus and Heracles.

[23] According to a legend preserved by Plutarch, Sinis had a daughter named Perigoune who bore a son to Theseus.

[24] Some said that Phaea was a murderous and licentious woman, who was called a sow because of her filthy habits and, with a similar thought, others numbered her among the loathsome offspring of Typhon and Echidna.

[25] The story is related in more detail in chapter 10. Plutarch, confusing Sciron with the centaur Cheiron, calls him the grandfather of Peleus and Telamon and the great-grandfather of Achilles.

[26] According to Apollodorus, Cercyon was a son of Branchus and the nymph Argeiope.

[27] Damastes or Procrustes was also caled Polypemon. According to both Apollodorus and Hyginus, he had two beds: one of which was short and the other long. Thus, his tall victims had their legs sawed off to fit the short bed and his short victims were beaten out with a hammer to fit the long bed.

[28] The bull of Marathon—originally known as the Cretan bull—was brought to Greece by Heracles as one of his Twelve Labors.

[29] A different legend relates that Theseus captured the bull after he was recognized by his father, and that he drove it alive through the streets of Athens.

been performed but, under Medeia's influence, the old king continued to believe him an enemy. At her suggestion, he was invited to a feast in the palace, where she proposed that he should be poisoned. After preparing a cup, which she gave to Aegeus for presentation to his unrecognized son, the young hero came to his father's table and drew his sword to cut meat. Thereupon, Aegeus at once recognized the same weapon which he had placed beneath the rock at Troezen and, realizing that his son was before him, overset the cup of poison and made public acknowledgment of his paternity. According to legend, the wicked Medeia, whose design was now exposed, did not tarry but fled with her son Medus to Asia Minor where, in later days, the country in which they came to rest was itself called Medeia—and its inhabitants became known as Medes.

The fifty, unnamed sons of Pallas, brother of Aegeus, seized on the incident to declare war—in the hope of taking over the government.[30] They divided into two forces, one of which marched openly into the city, while the other lay in ambush. But one of their number betrayed their strategy to Theseus, and he suddenly attacked those who had concealed themselves and killed them all. Upon hearing of his success, the remaining brothers, who had been led into the city by their father, were thoroughly frightened, and their forces were quickly dispersed.

Shortly afterward, the time arrived for the Athenians to send their customary tribute of fourteen youths and maidens as food for the Minotaur of the island of Crete. Some of his subjects began to revile Aegeus, complaining that he took no share in their affliction, but permitted their legitimate children to be destroyed while he made a bastard foreigner the heir to his kingdom. When these mutterings were heard by Theseus, he came forward and offered himself as one of the prospective victims. Although Aegeus tried to dissuade him, he persisted in his resolution, so that only the remain-

ing thirteen were chosen by lot.[31] It had been the habit of the Athenians to send their doomed children to Crete in a ship with a black sail, but Theseus boasted that he would overcome the Minotaur, and so encouraged his father that a second sail—a white one—was given to the steersman with instructions that it should be hoisted on the return voyage if the creature should have been destroyed.

Upon the arrival of the black-sailed vessel at Crete, Ariadne—a daughter of King Minos—was so stricken with love for Theseus that she offered to help him, on condition that he should take her back to Athens and make her his wife. In his desperation (and perhaps himself amorously disposed), he readily agreed to her proposal, and Ariadne besought Daedalus, who had built the labyrinth in which the Minotaur was housed, to disclose the secret of its winding passages. At his suggestion, she gave Theseus a spool of thread, the end of which he fastened to the door as he entered, and thereafter fed out the line as he proceeded to the innermost chamber where the bull-man awaited the coming of his victims. As they approached the monster, the Athenian children drew back in horror, but Theseus boldly attacked and slew him with his bare fists. Then, following his thread, they all regained the entrance and hastily embarked on their vessel—joined by Ariadne who hopefully looked forward to her union with the heroic Grecian youth. On the return journey, however, a stop was made at the island of Naxos and Theseus, having already become tired of his promised bride, left her there—but she was soon found and loved by the wine-god Dionysus.[32]

As they approached the shores of Attica, the delight at their successful return caused both Theseus and his steersman to forget to raise the white sail which was to be the signal of their victory. And Aegeus, seeing the black sail still hoisted, threw himself from a high cliff and

---

30 According to Plutarch, the sons of Pallas were enraged at the appearance of Theseus, because they expected to inherit the kingdom on the death of Aegeus without issue.

---

31 A variant of the legend relates that Minos was accustomed to select the Athenian children and that, on this occasion, he chose Theseus first.

32 Other legends relate that Ariadne killed herself or was slain with an arrow from the bow of Artemis. Although Homer mentions her as having been carried off by Theseus, he says nothing about the incident of the Minotaur.

drowned in the sea below. Thereafter, it was called the Aegean after him. With his father's death, Theseus was accepted by the thankful Athenians as their lawful king, and—for many years—ruled with such benevolence that his name and memory became honored as greatest in the city's history. He instituted many reforms in the government which heightened his popularity, but still found time to engage in other heroic exploits which added to his reputation for valor.

One of his most renowned adventures was his expedition against the Amazons, whom he is said to have assailed before they had fully recovered from an earlier attack by Heracles. After conquering them, he carried their queen, Antiope, back to Athens and made her his wife;[33] and, in due time, she bore to him a son who was named Hippolytus. Subsequently, when the Amazons had sufficiently regained strength, they attacked Athens for the purpose of releasing their erstwhile queen, believing that she was being treated as a captive slave, and not knowing of the real affection which she had come to have for Theseus as her husband and as the father of her child. And, in the battle which ensued, Antiope fought with him against her own people—only to meet the death of a heroine by his side.

While Theseus was in Crete, he had met not only Ariadne but also her sister Phaedra, whom —in his lonely state—he now remembered as possessed of a desirable charm. Accordingly, he went again to the ancient island[34] and brought her back to Athens as his second wife. At first, all went well, but Aphrodite caused Phaedra to fall in love with her stepson Hippolytus, and she solicited his advances. The thunderstruck youth repulsed her suggestion, whereupon she fell into a passion and told Theseus that it was he who had made improper proposals to her.[35] In the belief that she was telling the truth, Theseus now proceeded to lay a curse upon his son and prayed to Poseidon that he might be destroyed.[36] As a result, while Hippolytus was driving his chariot along the shore of the sea, the god sent a bull up from the waters, which frightened his horses and caused them to overturn the chariot, in a wreck causing the youth's death. When Theseus afterward learned of his son's innocence and revealed his knowledge to Phaedra, she was so filled with shame that she killed herself.[37]

At her death, Phaedra left two sons whom she had borne to Theseus, named Acamas and Demophon. Theseus, however, was not content to stay at home and attend to their rearing, for his restless nature demanded action and adventure. It is said that he was one of the hunters of the Calydonian boar, and that he aided Adrastus in recovering the bodies of the attackers who were slain in the attempt of the Seven Against Thebes.[38] And the enthusiastic inventor of one story named him as a member of the Argonautic expedition—overlooking the manifest anachronism implicit in Medeia's attempt to poison him.

In chapter 16, we have already given an account of his friendship with Peirithous, whom he assisted in the battle with the Centaurs, and have related how the two men abducted Helen, and tried to abduct Persephone—only to be apprehended and firmly fixed to seats in the lower world. When Theseus was released from below by Heracles,[39] he returned to Athens to find that his kinsman Menestheus had incited his

---

[33] As related in chapter 14, another story relates that Heracles captured Antiope and gave her to Theseus.

[34] The discoveries of modern archeologists have revealed that the civilization on the island of Crete was almost as early as that of Egypt and Babylon.

[35] As Phaedra was a granddaughter of Helios, who had disclosed Aphrodite's intrigue with Ares, she was a victim of the wrath of the goddess. The story of her passion for her young stepson—reminiscent of that of Potiphar's wife for Joseph—is the subject matter of an extant tragedy of Euripides called "Hippolytus."

[36] Because Poseidon was reputed to have had connection with Aethra at Troezen on the same night when Theseus was conceived, the god was sometimes considered to be his father.

[37] Hippolytus is said to have been among those whom Asclepius raised from the dead, and he was later adopted and worshipped as a Latin deity. Phaedra's suicide was conventionally related as by hanging, but there are variant versions both of her death and of the events which brought it about.

[38] In chapter 9, it has been related how Antigone brought her blinded father Oedipus to Theseus at Colonus and was kindly received by him.

[39] According to Virgil, Theseus was immovably fixed in his Stygian seat and was seen there by Aeneas during his visit to the lower world.

subjects against him. Heartbroken at his reception and wearied with age, he retired to the island of Scyrus, where earlier he had acquired an estate. There, he hoped to spend his last days in peace; but King Lycomedes, inspired by Menestheus, took him onto a mountain under pretense of showing him a far view of his properties and, while the old man peered into the distance, shoved him over a precipice to his death.

Acamas and Demophon, the sons of Theseus and Phaedra, were said to have accompanied the Greeks to Troy.[40] During his stay there, Acamas won the affection of Laodice, a daughter of Priam, and begot by her a son, Munitus, who was reared by Aethra—the mother of Theseus taken to Troy as a servant of Helen.[41] The only other mention of Munitus is that, in later life, he died on the island of Cyprus when he fell from a horse onto his own sword.

Demophon seems to have gained no renown as a fighter at Troy but, while there, is said to have liberated Aethra from her captivity as Helen's slave. On his return from the great war, he was loved by Phyllis, daughter of a Thracian king, and consented to marry her. But he first went to Athens to put his affairs in order and tarried so long that the maiden—believing herself to be forgotten—put an end to her life. When he returned to Thrace, and learned what had happened, Demophon was shown a tree into which his betrothed had been transformed and, as he embraced it, buds and leaves immediately covered its previously barren limbs. Afterward, when Diomedes began to ravage the coast of Attica (in the belief that it was a foreign country), Demophon marched out against the invaders, but he had the misfortune to kill one of his Athenian townsmen in the fighting. For this mishap, it is said that he was tried as the first man before a court—newly set up in the

city to hear cases of involuntary homicide—but whether or not he was acquitted, we do not know, for nothing further is said about him. Thus, the mythological story of Aegeus and his descendants comes to its end. We turn now to consideration of his brothers, Lycus, Abas, Pallas, and Nisus.

For some reason which is not mentioned by the mythographers, Lycus was expelled from Athens. A legend of Messenia, related by Pausanias, relates that he was gifted with the powers of a seer, and introduced into that land the mysteries of Demeter as they were celebrated at Eleusis in Attica. It is also said that he later took refuge with Minos' son, Sarpedon, in Asia Minor, and that the country which received him was thereafter called Lycia in honor of his name.

Abas went from Attica to the near island of Euboea (known sometimes as Negropont) and, either by reason of his royal blood or individual valor, took over the rulership of the natives to such an extent that they became known as Abantes.[42] His sons, Chalcodon and Canethus, appear to have been merely connecting links to his grandsons, Elephenor and Canthus—who are respectively named as leader of the Abantes at Troy and as one of the Argonauts. As related in chapter 7, the latter was slain in Libya by Caphaurus, whose flocks he was trying to steal.[43]

Pallas and his fifty, unnamed sons have already been mentioned as having attempted unsuccessfully to capture the government of Athens, after Aegeus publicly announced his recognition of Theseus as heir to the throne, and nothing of importance is further related about him or them.

Nisus, the last charted son of Pandion II and Pylia,[44] succeeded his father as king of Megara, and was ruling there when Minos attacked the

---

[40] The Iliad does not mention Demophon as being at Troy, and does not name Acamas as a son of Theseus. These omissions are pointed out by some scholars as additional evidence that the Athenians were unknown to Homer, and that the references made to them in his poems were later interpolations of their own writers.

[41] Plutarch relates that Aethra was taken captive by the Dioscuri when they recovered their sister Helen from her custody at Aphidnae, whither the maiden had been taken by Theseus and Peirithous

---

[42] The mythographers are at variance as to whether Abas migrated to Euboea himself, or was placed in that island by reason of the earlier migration of his grandfather Cecrops. And it seems probable that his name was invented to account for the appellation of Abantes, by which Homer calls the island's inhabitants.

[43] The legend that Canthus, an Argonaut, and Elephenor, a participant in the Trojan War, were brothers casts some doubt upon the validity of their genealogies.

[44] Variants of the legend make Nisus the son of Deion or of Ares.

Greeks in retaliation for the murder of his son, Androgeus. Among other towns, the Cretan king beleaguered Megara but, under the leadership of Nisus, his forces were held at bay. During the period of the siege, Minos was seen by Scylla, a daughter borne to Nisus by his wife Abrota and, when she saw the handsome son of Zeus, the maiden promptly fell in love with him. Pondering how to satisfy her mad longing, she remembered that an oracle had prophesied death for her father whenever he should lose a single purple lock which grew among the hairs of his head.[45] As Nisus slept, she pulled out the fatal purple and saw his life expire. Then, anticipating the consummation of her love, she took the extracted hair to Minos, and proudly related what she had done for his benefit. But he was horrified at her unnatural action, and caused the foolish girl to be drowned in the waters of the Saronic gulf.[46]

With the loss of their king, the Megarians were unable to continue the defense of their city, and it was sacked by the forces of Minos in a furious fight where, among others, Megareus was slain. He was a son of Onchestus who had married Iphinoë, another daughter of Nisus and Abrota. And, from him, the town which was before called Nisaea is said to have taken its name of Megara.

Thespius, one of the brothers of Cecrops, was the king of Thespiae in Boeotia. By his wife Megamede he had fifty daughters. When Heracles was engaged in his hunt for the Nemean lion, he was entertained by Thespius for fifty days and, each night, took a different daughter as his bed mate, for the king was desirous that all of them should have children by the illustrious son of Zeus.[47] As a result, Procris had twin sons, and her sisters each had single sons, whose names have been previously given in chapter 14.

Alcon, brother of Cecrops and Thespius, was such a skillful archer that once, when a serpent entwined itself around his son Phalerus, he slew it with a well-aimed arrow, avoiding any harm to the boy. When grown, Phalerus became a member of the Argonautic expedition and, in honor of his participation in the fabled adventure, it is said that the Athenian harbor of Phalerum received its name.

Metion, another son of Erechtheus and Praxithea, had two sons named Eupalamus and Sicyon, who (as previously related) expelled their cousin Pandion II from the Athenian throne and forced him to flee to Megara. But they were themselves overcome by the sons of Pandion, who returned to Athens and raised Aegeus to the kingship.

By his wife, Alcippe, Eupalamus had two daughters, Metiadusa and Perdix, and a son named Daedalus. Metiadusa married her uncle Cecrops and became the ancestress of Theseus and other descendants who have been mentioned earlier in this chapter. Perdix is remembered primarily because she was the mother of Talos, who was such a gifted inventor that his envious uncle, Daedalus, threw him from a rock of the Acropolis and caused his death.[48] Daedalus was tried for his crime in the court known as Areopagus and, being condemned to death, fled to the island of Crete. There, his established reputation for skill and ingenuity obtained for him a welcome reception from King Minos.[49] His first act, however, seems to have been a rather poor requital of the king's hospitality, because he built a wooden cow in which Queen Pasiphae concealed herself and had intercourse with the Cretan bull. When the Minotaur was born, Minos forced Daedalus to build the labyrinth in which the monster was housed, and then, for his part in the horrid amour, the clever architect was imprisoned, together with his son Icarus, borne to him by a slave named Naucrate.

---

[45] Ovid says that the other hairs of Nisus were grey, but Pausanias says that they were red.

[46] According to Ovid, Scylla leaped into the sea where she was spied by Nisus, who had been turned into an eagle and, when he swooped down upon her, she was herself transformed into a bird.

[47] According to Apollodorus, Thespius substituted a different daughter in the bed of Heracles each night, but his great guest thought that his companion was always the same. Diodorus relates an even more remarkable story, saying that the fifty daughters were all sent in to Heracles—one by one—in a single night.

---

[48] Talos does not appear on our genealogical chart because the name of his father is not given anywhere by the mythographers.

[49] Daedalus had been the instructor of Talos, who was about to exceed him in the inventive art when he was murdered.

99. Descendants of Hephaestus and Gaea

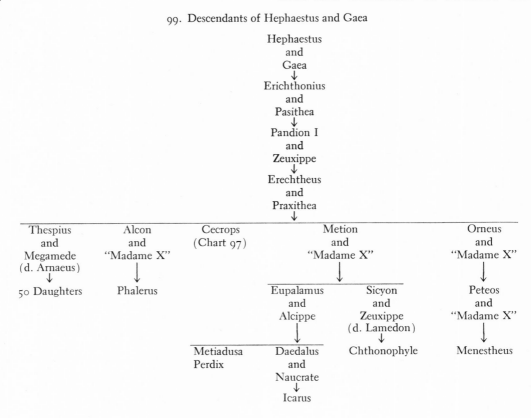

Sometime later, they were stealthily released by Pasiphae, and sought a vessel in which to flee from the island; but Minos had learned of their escape and had seized all of the ships on his coast. Daedalus thereupon constructed wings for himself and his son—made of wood and fastened to their bodies with wax; using them they flew over the Aegean Sea. However, as they approached the island of Samos, Icarus soared so high that the heat of the sun melted the wax, so that his wings became loose and, falling into the sea, he drowned. His corpse was washed to the island's shore, where it was later found and buried by Heracles. And, after his name, the waters into which he had fallen were later called the Icarian Sea.

Daedalus continued on his flight until he reached Camicus on the island of Sicily, where he became court architect to King Cocalus. During his stay, he was approached by Iolaus, who had led the sons of Heracles (borne by the daughters of Thespius) to found a colony on the island of Sardinia. Upon request, he accom-

panied his distant kinsman[50] to the new settlement, which he proceeded to modernize by the erection of various public works. Returning to Sicily, he heard that Minos had arrived in search of him—for the furious Cretan king had sworn that his escape should not go unpunished. He concealed himself with the connivance of Cocalus, who promised to deny all knowledge of his whereabouts. When Minos, however, produced a conch shell and wagered that no one could pass a thread through it, Cocalus accepted the challenge and took the shell to the ingenious architect, who solved the problem by tying the thread to an ant, which drew it through the winding passages. Thereupon, Minos—knowing that only Daedalus could have devised the plan—charged Cocalus with his deceit, and the shamed king promised to surrender his guest. But, before receiving his

---

[50] Iolaus was the son of Iphicles, half brother of Heracles, and the fifty daughters of Thespius were first cousins of Eupalamus, the father of Daedalus.

prisoner, Minos was drenched in a bath with boiling water by the daughters of Cocalus and died.[51]

Sicyon, the second son of Metion and uncle of Daedalus,[52] was the eponym of the Peloponnesian town originally known as Mecone, but later called by his name when he became its ruler. This he did as the successor of Lamedon, whose daughter, Zeuxippe, he married.[53] By her, he had a daughter named Chthonophyle, who was endowed with such charm that she attracted the attentions of the gods Hermes and Dionysus, and bore sons to both of them.

Orneus, the last charted son of Erechtheus and Praxithea, is remembered only as the father of Peteos, who was expelled from Athens by Aegeus. According to legend, Peteos fled to Phocis where, by an unnamed mother, his son Menestheus was borne. When the boy reached manhood, and learned that Theseus was being held prisoner by Hades in the lower world, he went to Athens and usurped the government. Returning as an old man, Theseus was unable to recover his throne and, proceeding on to Scyrus, left the usurper with a free hand.[54] As leader of the Athenians at Troy, Menestheus was accounted the equal of ancient Nestor in the arrangement of chariots and warriors for battle, but he was slain by an unnamed Trojan

and, dying childless, the rule of Athens reverted to the descendants of Theseus.[55]

By an unnamed wife, or wives, Hephaestus had four sons, who were named Ardalus, Cercyon, Palaemon, and Cacus. Of these, Ardalus is said to have been the first man to play on the flute, and Palaemon is mentioned as having served without special distinction as one of the Argonauts.[56]

100. Descendants of Hephaestus and "Madame X"

Hephaestus
and
"Madame X"
↓
Ardalus   Cercyon   Palaemon   Cacus
↓
Alope

Cercyon had a daughter named Alope, who was afraid to have her father learn that she was with child by Poseidon. The story of her attempted concealment, and her father's discovery of his grandson Hippothoön, has been related in chapter 10. And, in connection with the adventures of Theseus, reference has been made to how Cercyon met his death in a wrestling match with the great Attic hero. Similarly, in chapter 9, we have related the circumstances under which Heracles destroyed the Italian robber Cacus, who had the temerity to steal one of the herd of Geryon's cattle as the great man was driving them back to Mycenae in performance of his tenth labor.

---

[51] According to another account, Daedalus persuaded the daughters of Cocalus to lead a pipe through the roof, which poured a stream of boiling water (or pitch) upon Minos as he was bathing.

[52] Others name Marathon, Erechtheus, or Pelops as the father of Sicyon.

[53] Pausanias intimates that Sicyon succeeded his father, Marathon, as king.

[54] Plutarch says that Menestheus was aided in resisting Theseus by the Dioscuri, who were still wrathful because he had carried off their sister Helen.

---

[55] Plutarch is the authority for the statement that Menestheus died at Troy—an incident not mentioned in the Iliad.

[56] Palaemon was perhaps considered as descended from Hephaestus because he was lame, but Apollonius Rhodius says that his father was Lernus.

18

The Descendants of Zeus VIII

Dione—the Mother of Aphrodite

THE CIRCUMSTANCES attending the birth of Aphrodite, the goddess of love borne to Zeus by the Oceanid Dione, have been related in chapter 3. Although she was mythologically wedded to Hephaestus, and was supposed to live with him on Mount Olympus, she bore him no children. The uninhibited beauty, however, had a number of offspring by others, namely: Harmonia, Eros (Cupid), Anteros, Deimos and Phobos by Ares; Hermaphroditus by Hermes; Hymen and Priapus by Dionysus; Eryx by Poseidon; and Aeneas and Lyrus by the mortal Anchises.

Persephone—the Mother of Zagreus

According to the Orphic theogony, Persephone bore to her own father Zeus a horned child named Zagreus, who was predestined—if he should reach maturity—to succeed to supreme dominion. Jealous at the favor with which her great spouse looked upon this oddest of his offspring, Hera incited the Titans to cut up his body and boil it in a cauldron, but the heart was saved by Athena and later, being swallowed by Semele, was reborn from her in the form of the wine-god Dionysus.[1]

Leda—the Mother of Pollux and Helen

Leda, a daughter of Thestius and Laophonte, was the wife of the Spartan king, Tyndareus. In the form of a swan, Zeus consorted with her one day, and when night followed, she also had connection with her husband. As a result, she produced two eggs: from one of which issued Pollux and Helen, the children of Zeus, and from the other were born Clytemnestra and Castor, whose father was Tyndareus.[2]

101. Descendants of Zeus and Leda

```
                  Zeus
                  and
                  Leda
              (d. Thestius)
                   ↓
         ┌─────────────────────┐
       Pollux              Helen
        and
       Phoebe
    (d. Leucippus)
         ↓
     Mnesileus
```

Helen quickly grew into a maiden of such surpassing beauty that she attracted the atten-

---

[1] Among the Hymns of Orpheus, translated from the original Greek and "printed for the Author" in London in 1792, appears one which is dedicated to Melinoë—described as a daughter of Zeus and Persephone whose limbs were "partly black and partly white."

[2] According to Homer, both Castor and Pollux were sons of Tyndareus, and they were often jointly referred to as the Tyndaridae. Another version of the legend relates that Castor, Pollux, Helen, and Clytemnestra were all produced from a single egg, but gives their paternity as stated in the text. Athenaeus cites a story that Helen was reared on an upper floor, which was called by the Greek word meaning "egg"—thus giving rise to the report of her odd birth.

tion of Theseus as she danced in a temple while still a young child, although at the time he was himself said to have been fifty-years old. He determined to seize her and keep her in custody until she reached an age when she could become his wife, and lost no time in carrying out the first part of his plan. In the abduction, he was assisted by his friend Peirithous, as related in chapter 16; but as Helen was not yet ripe for marriage, she was taken to Aphidnae, where she was left for safekeeping with Theseus' mother, Aethra. The elderly kidnappers then departed for the lower world to obtain Persephone for Peirithous—only to be apprehended and imprisoned by her husband Hades. Meanwhile, Castor and Pollux came to Attica in search of their sister and, with the help of a native named Academus, she was liberated and taken back to Sparta, with Aethra as her captive maid.

Within a few years, Helen grew into a beautiful woman, and princely suitors for her hand appeared from all parts of Greece.[3] Seeing their large number, Tyndareus became fearful that, if he should prefer any one of them, the others would be affronted. In this dilemma, he sought the advice of the Ithacan king, Odysseus, who —himself numbered among the suitors—was considered to be the wisest of all men. It so happened that, although he greatly admired Helen, he was really in love with Penelope, a daughter of Icarius and niece of Tyndareus; and he agreed to suggest a way to eliminate the possibility of all hard feelings among the suitors, on condition that Tyndareus would help him to win Penelope's hand. When this proposal gained quick assent, he told the Spartan king to exact a prior oath from all of the suitors that they would defend the favored bridegroom against any wrong which might ever be done him respecting his marriage to Helen. To this suggestion, all acceded—each man hoping that he would have the good fortune to be chosen, and the oaths were duly taken. Thereupon, Tyndareus chose Menelaus, son of Pleisthenes and adopted son of Atreus, to be his son-in-law and, in performance of his promise, successfully solicited Icarius to bestow Penelope on Odysseus.

The subsequent events in the life of Helen are an integral part of the story of the Trojan War (which was fought by the Greeks to recover her from the court of King Priam), after she was taken there by his son Paris—and will be fully related later.

Pollux (often called Polydeuces) and his half brother Castor were so inseparable on earth that even in death they were permitted to share equally in the immortality vouchsafed to Pollux alone as the son of Zeus. By the Greeks they were jointly known as the Dioscuri, and, as the Gemini, the Romans considered them to have been translated to the skies as the fifth sign of the zodiac.[4]

The first great event in the lives of the Dioscuri was their recovery of Helen after her abduction by Theseus. The incident has been related in the preceding chapter but, it should here be added that, in the performance of their mission, they found it necessary to ravage the Attic country around Aphidnae, and availed themselves of the opportunity to become initiated into the Mysteries at Eleusis. Their next adventure occurred when they participated as members of the Argonautic band, and during the voyage Pollux exhibited his prowess in boxing by killing the giant Bebrycian king, Amycus.[5] Even in marriage, the brothers acted in concert —both being wedded to daughters of Leucippus, son of the Aeolid Perieres. As a result of

---

[3] Apollodorus names the following as the suitors of Helen: Odysseus, son of Laertes; Diomedes, son of Tydeus; Antilochus, son of Nestor; Agapenor, son of Ancaeus; Sthenelus, son of Capaneus; Amphimachus, son of Cteatus; Thalpius, son of Eurytus; Meges, son of Phyleus; Amphilochus, son of Amphiaraus; Menetheus, son of Peteos; Schedius and Epistrophus, sons of Iphitus; Polyxeinus, son of Agasthenes; Peneleos, son of Hippalcimus; Leitus, son of Alector (Electryon); Ajax, son of Oileus; Ascalaphus and Ialmenus, sons of Ares; Elephenor, son of Chalcodon; Eumelus, son of Admetus; Polypoetes, son of Peirithous; Leonteus, son of Coronus; Podaleirius and Machaon, sons of Asclepius; Philoctetes, son of Poeas; Eurypylus, son of Evaemon; Protesilaus, son of Iphiclus; Menelaus, son of Atreus; Ajax and Teucer, sons of Telamon; and Patroclus, son of Menoetius.

[4] The Gemini were worshipped as the protectors of travelers—especially by mariners and others who traveled by sea, and it is conjectured that it is from prayers to them we have our expression "by jiminiy!"

[5] As Pollux was skilled in boxing, so Castor is said to have been expert at taming and managing horses.

this connection, they became friends with Idas and Lynceus, the sons of Aphareus who were first cousins of their wives, but their friendship was terminated (as was the mortal life of Castor) in the quarrel over stolen cattle which has been stated in chapters 6 and 7. And it was following this tragic event that the half brothers were permitted by the gods to share an equal fate—residing, alternately, one day in the lower world and on the next at the abode of the celestials on Mount Olympus.

According to Apollodorus, Pollux' wife, Phoebe, bore a son to him who was named Mnesileus, but nothing further is said about him.

Laodameia—the Mother of Sarpedon

Although she was married to Evander, the son of Sarpedon and a grandson of Zeus, Laodameia, a daughter of Bellerophon and Philonoë, herself bore a son to the supreme god. He too was named Sarpedon and, when grown, became king of the Lycians, whom he led to Troy as allies against the assault of the Greeks.[6] In the fighting, he acquitted himself with distinction and killed Tlepolemus, a son of Heracles, in single combat from which he emerged with a serious wound. But later, he was slain by the spear of Patroclus, and the Greeks strove furiously to strip the armor from the body of one of their mightest foes.[7] This indignity, however, Zeus could not permit so at his command, Apollo took up the corpse, which he cleansed of the dust and anointed with ambrosia. It was then miraculously wafted back to Lycia and given an honorable burial.[8]

Protogeneia—the Mother of Aethlius

The Eleans and the Aetolians boasted one of the most complete and ancient pedigrees in mythological Greece, for they claimed that their common ancestor was Aethlius, a son borne to Zeus by Protogeneia, whose parents—Deucalion and Pyrrha—were the only survivors of the great deluge.

Although Deucalion's home was considered to have been in eastern Locris, Protogeneia's son was said to have migrated to the Peloponnesus, where he became the first king of Elis.[9] There, his wife Calyce, a daughter of Aeolus and Enarete, gave birth to a beautiful son named Endymion, who later succeeded his father as ruler of the country.[10] The handsome, young king took as his queen the nymph Iphianassa, by whom he had a daughter, Eurycyda (who was wooed by Poseidon), and three sons, Paeon, Aetolus, and Epeius.[11]

After he became old, Endymion still retained the beautiful form of his youth, but he must have been very tired, because, when the Moongoddess Selene solicited his love, he agreed to her proposal only on condition that Zeus would grant him immortality and perpetual sleep.[12] His terms were accepted by the lady, and he was supernaturally transported to the heavens where, after begetting fifty, unnamed daughters by her, he was placed on a soft couch—to remain ever after in ageless and deathless repose.[13]

Before leaving the earth, Endymion chose

---

[6] For evident reason, Sarpedon, the son of Zeus and Laodameia, was often confused with Sarpedon, the son of Zeus and Europa. It is said that, when Isander and Hippolochus, the sons of Bellerophon, were disputing about the kingdom of Lycia, it was proposed that they should shoot arrows through a ring fixed upon the breast of a child. When others hesitated, Laodameia, sister of the rivals, offered her own son for the purpose, and his admiring uncles solved their quarrel by appointing him as king.

[7] Although Sarpedon was a son of Zeus, the supreme ruler was persuaded by Hera not to save his life, lest others of the gods should take similar action with reference to their own sons who were engaged in the conflict.

[8] A more detailed account of Sarpedon's activities in the fighting will be given in narrating the events at Troy.

[9] A different tradition related that the father of Aethlius was actually Aeolus, who boastfully called himself Zeus, and a third considered that Eleius, son of Poseidon and Eurycyda, was the first king of Elis.

[10] A variant of the story, making Endymion, a son of Zeus and Calyce, related that he colonized the country of Elis with Aeolian settlers brought in from Thessaly, after forcibly taking over the government from Clymenus —a Cretan who had come to the Greek mainland fifty years after the great flood of Deucalion.

[11] Cromia, daughter of Itonus, and Hyperippe, daughter of Arcas, are also mentioned as the wife of Endymion and the other of his children.

[12] Other legends relate that Zeus threw Endymion into perpetual sleep as punishment for his presumptuous attentions to Hera, or that Selene herself brought about his unconscious condition so that she could kiss him at will without being observed.

[13] According to the usual version, the couch of Endymion was on Mount Latmus in Caria—from which he was sometimes called the Latmian.

102. Descendants of Zeus and Protogeneia (daughter of Deucalion)

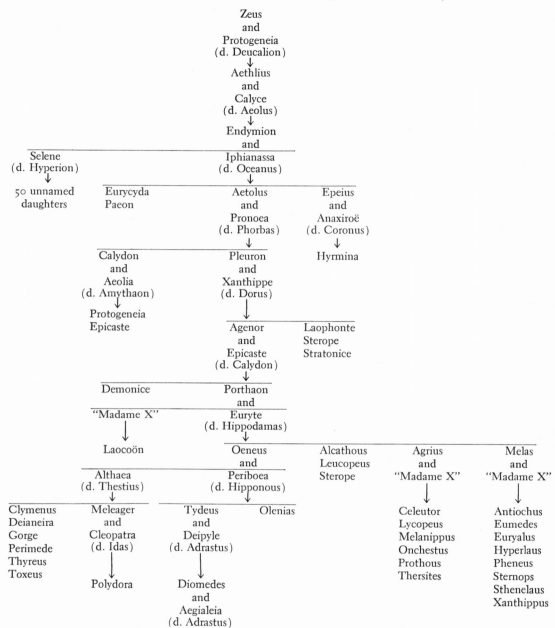

his successor to the kingdom of Elis by having his sons run a race at the grove of Olympia.[14] Epeius, being the victor, assumed the throne and, in his honor, the inhabitants of the country called themselves Epeians for many years after. In his reign, it is said that Pelops conquered Oenomaus in the chariot race for the hand of Hippodameia, and took over the government of Pisa—bringing in new settlers who were thereafter distinguished from the Epeians.[15] By his wife Anaxiroë, Epeius had a daughter Hyrmina, who married the Lapith prince, Phorbas, but he had no male issue and, upon his death, his brother, Aetolus succeeded to the kingdom.

Meanwhile, his brother, Paeon—disgusted at having lost the race at Olympia—went to Macedonia and settled in the country around the river Axius, which in his honor was afterward called Paeonia.

While Aetolus was king of the Epeians, he went to Arcadia to participate in the funeral games for Azan, and had the misfortune to run his chariot over a man named Apis. When death resulted from the accident, Aetolus was driven from his throne by the sons of his victim, and crossed the gulf of Patras to the country which was inhabited by the Curetes.[16] His entrance was resisted by Laodocus, Dorus, and Polypoetes—three sons of Apollo and Phthia, but he slew them all and, taking over the government, called the land Aetolia after his own name. Some time later, he married Pronoea, a daughter of Phorbas and his niece Hyrmina, and begot two sons, Pleuron and Calydon. And, at their father's death, they divided the kingdom, and ruled the country from the two towns which were called by their names.[17]

The early mythological history of Aetolia is largely uninteresting; but it is necessary to give the genealogy of its royal house in order to provide the connecting links with stories which are undoubted high spots of our subject.

Calydon married Aeolia, a daughter of the Messenian king, Amythaon, who bore to him two daughters named Epicaste and Protogenia.[18] Pleuron married Xanthippe, daughter of Dorus, and had a son Agenor and three daughters named Laophonte, Sterope, and Stratonice.[19] Epicaste became the wife of her cousin Agenor, and Protogeneia had a son Oxylus by the god Poseidon. Of the daughters of Pleuron, Laophonte had a number of children by Ares; Stratonice married Melaneus, a son of Apollo; but Sterope appeared to have been content with a quiet spinsterhood.

Upon the deaths of Pleuron and Calydon (the latter leaving no male issue), Agenor became king of all Aetolia, but nothing of consequence is related about him except that his cousin Epicaste, bore to him a son, Porthaon, and a daughter, Demonice—who later was perhaps a willing mistress of Ares.

Porthaon—sometimes called Portheus—raised his family's rather dim luster by his marriage to Euryte, a daughter of Hippodamas, lineally descended from the great river-god Achelous.[20] By her, he had five sons—Alcathous, Leucopeus, Agrius, Melas, and Oeneus—and also a daughter Sterope who, according to one legend, became the mother of the Sirens.[21] And, by an unnamed servant, he had a son Laocoön.

Oeneus, being the eldest son, succeeded to the kingdom when Porthaon died. It is said that he was the first man to be instructed in the planting of vines and the making of wine.

---

[14] Olympia was the seat of the renowned Olympian games.

[15] Pelops was the son of the wealthy oriental king, Tantalus, and was naturally considered a foreigner at the time when he assumed the government of Pisa.

[16] The early inhabitants of the country later known as Aetolia are not to be confused with the Curetes who are said to have drowned out the cries of the infant Zeus with the noise of their brazen cymbals.

[17] Aetolus was succeeded as king of the Epeians by Eleius, the son of his sister Eurycyda and the god Poseidon. From him the country gained its name of Elis, although for some time its inhabitants were still referred to as Epeians. For a different version, see footnote 9 of this chapter.

---

[18] Amythaon, a son of the Aeolid Cretheus, went with Neleus into Messenia after being expelled from Iolchus in Thessaly.

[19] Previously in the text, Xanthippe has been referred to as the daughter of Dorus, the son of Hellen. Since the name of her grandfather is nowhere stated, it may be that she was a daughter of Dorus, the son of Apollo, who was slain by Aetolus upon first arriving in the new country.

[20] The river Achelous formed the boundary between Aetolia and Acarnania.

[21] The more generally accepted story recited that Melpomene, or one of the other Muses, was the mother of the Sirens.

It also may be added that he was often in need of a drink to drown the sorrows which later beset him. He first married Althaea, a daughter of Thestius and his great-aunt Laophonte, who bore to him three daughters and four sons. Of the daughters, Deianeira married Heracles, after being won by him in a wrestling match with the river-god Achelous; Gorge married Andraemon, who succeeded her father as king of Aetolia; and Perimede married Phoenix, a son of Agenor and brother of Cadmus.

Except for mention of their birth, the legend is silent about Clymenus and Thyreus, two of the sons of Oeneus and Althaea, but a third son, named Toxeus, is said to have been slain by his father's own hand when he leaped over a ditch which he had been forbidden to cross.

We come now to the fourth son, Meleager. When he was seven days old, the Fates came to his mother, and declared that her son was destined to die when a brand then burning on the hearth should be consumed. Hearing this awful prediction, Althaea hastened to snatch up the brand, and—after extinguishing the flame—placed it in a secret chest. The boy grew up to become a gallant and invulnerable man and, among other exploits, distinguished himself as a member of the Argonauts—in company with his uncle Laocoön, who went along on the expedition as his elder protector.

When he returned safely to Calydon, which had become recognized as the capital city of Aetolia, he married Cleopatra, the beautiful daughter of Idas and Marpessa. In due time, she bore a daughter named Polydora. In his pride at becoming a grandfather, Oeneus offered thankful sacrifices to the gods but, through carelessness, forgot to include the goddess Artemis. Enraged at the slight,[22] she sent into the country a wild boar of extraordinary size and strength, which ravaged the fields and cattle and destroyed many persons who attempted to bring an end to its depredations.

As time passed, and famine threatened the land—for the boar's continued incursions prevented the Aetolians from planting their crops

—and Meleager called together all the bravest warriors of Greece, promising that he who should slay the beast would receive its hide as a glorious prize. His call was quickly heeded by many among whom were: Dryas, son of Ares, who was also dwelling at Calydon; Idas and Lynceus, the sons of Aphareus, who came from Messenia; Castor and Pollux, the sons of Tyndareus, from Lacedaemon (Sparta); Theseus, the son of Aegeus, who came from Athens; Admetus, the son of Pheres, who came from Pherae in Thessaly; Ancaeus and Cepheus, respectively, the sons of Lycurgus and Aleus, who came from Arcadia; Jason, the son of Aeson, who came from Iolchus in Thessaly; Iphicles, the son of Amphitryon and half brother of Heracles, who came from Thebes; Peirithous, the son of Ixion, who came from Larissa in Thessaly; Peleus, the son of Aeacus, who came from his home at Phthia; Telamon, the son of Aeacus and brother of Peleus, who came from the island of Salamis; Eurytion, the son of Irus, who came from Phthia with his son-in-law Peleus; Amphiaraus, the seer-son of Oicles, who came from Argos; and last Atalanta, the swift daughter of Schoeneus, who came from Boeotia.[23]

Meleager entertained his illustrious guests with a nine-day feast, during which Ancaeus and Cepheus, and some of the others, voiced doubts about the advisability of taking a woman on the dangerous hunt; but Meleager had fallen in love with Atalanta, despite the fact that he already had a wife and child, and eloquently argued away their forebodings of calamity. At last setting out for the boar's lair, the assembled host were joined by Eurypylus, Evippus, Iphiclus, Plexippus, and Prothous—the uncles of Meleager and brothers of his mother Althaea.

The approach to the boar's place of concealment was made with an assurance which proved to be careless overconfidence, because the beast, not waiting for his attackers, rushed into their midst—goring Ancaeus and a retainer named

---

22 The oversight of Oeneus was doubly culpable, because Artemis was considered almost equally with Eileithyia to be the goddess of birth.

---

23 The Boeotian legend names Schoeneus as the father of Atalanta, while the Arcadian legend relates that she was the daughter of Iasus. Apollodorus compromises the difficulty by saying that she was the daughter of Schoeneus who came to Calydon from Arcadia.

Hyleus so seriously that they died from their wounds. Upon this happening, Peleus cast his javelin, but his aim was poor and, instead of the quarry, he killed his own father-in-law Eurytion. Almost simultaneously, the rest of the brave throng attacked, and the maiden Atalanta drew first blood, by an arrow which pierced the boar's back. Amphiaraus next shot it in the eye, but Meleager made the kill by a stab in the flank, and was unanimously voted as winner of the dead beast's skin. Hoping to gain Atalanta's favor, he gave the prize to her—saying that she had rightly earned it, because she had inflicted the first wound. At this, the brothers of Althaea (the sons of Thestius) snatched the skin from her, claiming that it belonged to them by right of their kinship as uncles of Meleager—if he did not choose to keep it for himself. Meleager now flew into a great rage and slew all five of his brash relatives but, by so doing, brought on his own death. For, when Althaea learned of what had happened, she withdrew the fatal brand from the chest wherein she had placed it years before, and again set fire to it. As it was finally consumed by the flames, her gallant son's life expired, and his shade was led by Hermes down to the land of the dead; there, at a later time in converse with Heracles, directed the great man to marry Deidameia upon his return to earth.[24]

The story now ends because Althaea and Cleopatra hanged themselves: one from shame at destroying her own son, and the other from grief at the loss of her husband—unmindful of what the future might hold in store for her innocent and orphaned daughter Polydora.[25]

After observing a respectable period of mourning, the widowed Oeneus took Periboea as his second wife. She was a daughter of an Achaean king named Hipponous who ruled at Olenus. By her, he had two sons named Tydeus and Olenias.[26] When they were grown, the sons and their uncle Melas conspired to seize the Aetolian throne, but Tydeus put an end to the conspiracy by killing all eight of them.[27] In the fighting, however, he accidentally killed his own brother Olenias also, and was forced to leave the country.[28] As related in chapter 8, he fled to Argos, where he married Deipyle, a daughter of King Adrastus, who afterward bore to him a son named Diomedes. But Tydeus never saw his son because, before he was born, the assault of the Seven Against Thebes occurred and, as one of the attacking party, he lost his life at the hands of Melanippus.

Adrastus, alone of the seven, survived the conflict. Returning to Argos, however, he reared his grandson with almost daily exhortations that Thebes must be humbled—so that the death of the boy's father might be avenged. Upon attaining manhood,[29] Diomedes proved himself worthy of the task for which he had been trained and, as one of the Epigoni, was responsible for the destruction of many Thebans who, years before, had successfully repelled the fathers of their young conquerors. Returning triumphantly to Argos, he married Aegialeia, the youngest daughter of Adrastus, and went with her on to the homeland of his father in Aetolia. Upon arriving there, he found that the sons of Agrius had wrested the kingdom from his aged grandfather Oeneus, and had imprisoned him in a place where he was subjected to continuous torture.[30] With the help of Alcmaeon—one of the Epigoni who had accompanied him—he put all of the usurpers to death, except Onchestus and Thersites, and gave the rulership of the country to Andraemon, who had married Oeneus' daughter Gorge. Meanwhile, word came that Adrastus had died at Argos, leaving Diomedes as the successor to his throne. Informed of this event, the new sov-

---

[24] According to Homer, Meleager slew the sons of Thestius in a battle which was being fought between the Calydonians and the Curetes; and it is said that the Calydonian women who mourned Meleager's passing were turned into guinea fowls—known as Meleagrides.

[25] Pausanias cites a story that Polydora became the wife of Protesilaus (Iolaus), but the conventional legend gives the role to Laodameia, a daughter of Acastus.

[26] A later story makes Tydeus a son of Oeneus by his own daughter Gorge.

[27] The sons of Melas are named on the accompanying chart.

[28] A different version relates that Tydeus was forced into exile for killing his uncle Alcathous.

[29] Since the attack of the Epigoni against Thebes is said to have occurred ten years after the defeat of their fathers, it is manifest that Diomedes was indeed remarkable, even by mythological standards—for at the age of ten he appears to have been an indomitable warrior.

[30] The six sons of Agrius are named on the accompanying chart.

ereign journeyed back to the land where he had been reared—taking with him his wife Aegialeia, his friend Alcmaeon, and also his old grandfather Oeneus. On the way (while his attentions were perhaps centered on his delayed honeymoon), Onchestus and Thersites attacked his company and killed Oeneus, whose corpse however was rescued and carried on to Argos for decent burial.[31]

When the Trojan War began, Diomedes joined the Greeks as leader of eighty shiploads of warriors from Argos and Tiryns. In the great conflict, he was one of the preeminent actors whose exploits of valor will be fully detailed later; but it may here be noted that, in addition to his many victories over his mortal enemies, it is related that he inflicted wounds upon the immortals Ares and Aphrodite. However, upon his return from Troy, he found that Aegialeia was living in a state of adultery with Cometes, the son of his great friend Sthenelus, and the heartbroken warrior migrated to Italy, where he died at an advanced age.

Protogeneia—the Mother of Opus

Not content with the pedigree which traced their descent back to Deucalion, through his great-grandson Locrus, the Locrians claimed another ancestry stemming more directly from Zeus.[32] Since Protogeneia, the daughter of Deucalion, had already been appropriated by the Eleans and the Aetolians as the mother of their common forefather Aethlius, the Locrians seem to have invented a second Protogeneia, as a daughter of Opus. And they claimed that, although she was married to Locrus, she was likewise favored by the supreme god—and bore to

him a son, who was named Opus in honor of his maternal grandfather.

103. Descendants of Zeus and Protogeneia (daughter of Opus)

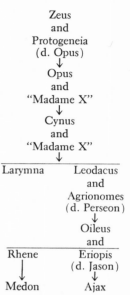

This second Opus had a son Cynus, who became the father of a daughter Larymna and a son Leodacus.[33] Nothing further is related about Larymna, except that she gave her name to the Boeotian town of Lary. Leodacus is said to have married Agrionomes, the daughter of an otherwise unidentified man named Perseon. By her he had a son Oileus—who finally added something more than a mere name to the family tree. He became a member of the Argonautic expedition, and is mentioned as having been struck by one of the barbed feathers loosed by the birds of Ares. And, returning safely, he was rewarded with the hand of Eriopis, a daughter borne to his leader Jason by the sorceress Medeia. By her, he had a son—later called Ajax the Lesser, to distinguish him from the more formidable Ajax, who was the son of Telamon. He

---

[31] Onchestus is not mentioned further, but Thersites reappears in connection with the Trojan War.

[32] The Locrians were divided into eastern and western settlements, separated by the country of Phocis, and respectively called Opuntian and Ozolian. The western settlement was colonized by inhabitants from the eastern and, accordingly, claimed the same pedigree. The Opuntian Locrians took their name from Opus, but those called Ozolian were said to have been so named from the Greek word meaning "smell"—because their land was filled with the scent of the asphodel or, as others related, with the nauseous emanations from the rotting corpse of the Centaur Nessus, who had been slain by Heracles at the nearby river Evenus.

---

[33] Another version relates that the son of Cynus was named Hodoedocus, and that he was married to Laonome, a half sister of Heracles. Not mentioning her marriage to Hodoedocus, Pausanias says that Laonome was a daughter of Gouneus and the mother of Amphitryon, who reared Heracles.

also had a son Medon by Rhene, a woman of obscure family.[34]

Medon had the misfortune to cause the accidental death of a kinsman of Eriopis, and was forced to flee from Opuntian Locris to Phylace in Thessaly. He obtained a position of importance in his new community and took over the command of the neighboring Olizonians at Troy, when their leader Philoctetes was bitten by a snake and left behind by the Greeks. But it was not destined that he should return either to Thessaly or to Locris, and he was slain on the Trojan battlefield by Aeneas.

Ajax was one of the most renowned warriors at Troy, to which place he led the Locrians in forty ships. Although he was small in stature, he was especially skilled in throwing the javelin and, next to Achilles, was the swiftest among the Greeks. His many valorous exploits will be noted later when we come to the detailed story of the great war. He would have returned to his people in Locris but, by the machinations of Nauplius, was wrecked on the Euboean promontory of Caphareus and crawled safely onto a rock—only to be blasted by Poseidon when he boasted that he had been preserved despite the will of Athena.[35]

---

[34] A variant of the legend relates that Rhene was a nymph.

[35] Ajax is said to have incurred the wrath of Athena for his violation of Cassandra at the Trojan shrine of the goddess, to which the maiden had fled when the city fell to the Greeks.

19

The Descendants of Zeus IX

Aegina—the Mother of Aeacus

WHEN ZEUS carried off Aegina (daughter of the river-god Asopus) from the Peloponnesus to the nearby island of Oenone, her father searched for her everywhere, and was at last told the name of her abductor by King Sisyphus of Corinth. Ignoring the supreme god's power, the wrathful father offered to fight with him— arising from the bed of his stream to give battle, but Zeus struck him back with a thunderbolt, which is said to account for the pieces of charcoal that were in later times found around the banks of the river.

At Oenone, Aegina gave birth to a son, who was named Aeacus, and in her honor the island thereafter was called Aegina. When Aeacus reached manhood, his mother returned to the Peloponnesus and, the land being uninhabited, Zeus changed the ants of the island into men over whom his son afterward ruled as king.[1] His reign proved to be so just that he gained a reputation for fairness among the neighboring islands and throughout all Greece, and he was often called upon as sole arbiter of disputes in which others were involved.[2] It is also said that he was summoned by Poseidon and Apollo to assist them in building the walls of Troy.[3]

By Endeïs, daughter of the centaur Cheiron and his nymph wife, Chariclo, Aeacus had two sons, who were named Peleus and Telamon, and by the Nereid Psamathe, he had a third son named Phocus, who became his favorite. The manifest preference of their father for their half brother excited in Peleus and Telamon a jealousy which was heightened because he was accustomed to excel them in athletic games. Accordingly, they plotted to take his life and, after drawing lots, Telamon killed Phocus with a quoit and the two of them hid his body in a nearby forest.[4] When the murder was detected by Aeacus, he expelled both of his sons from Aegina, whereupon Telamon went to the court of King Cychreus on the island of Salamis, and Peleus went to the court of King Eurytion at Phthia in Thessaly.[5] Soon after, Aeacus died and, because of his exemplary life on earth, it is said that he was made one of the judges of the dead in the lower world.[6]

At Salamis, Telamon married the king's

---

[1] A different tradition related that Hera's jealousy depopulated the island, and that Zeus created new subjects for his son by changing its ants into men called Myrmidons.

[2] Among others, Aeacus arbitrated the dispute between Sciron and Nisus over the rulership of Megara.

[3] Since it was fated that Troy should fall, it was mythologically necessary that a mortal should have assisted in erecting its walls, which would have been invulnerable if raised only by godly hands.

[4] Another legend related that Telamon stunned Phocus with a quoit, and that Peleus completed the kill with the stroke of an axe.

[5] The judgment of Aeacus against his own sons was considered as additional proof of his integrity.

[6] According to Plato, Aeacus sat in judgment of the shades of Europeans.

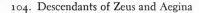

104. Descendants of Zeus and Aegina

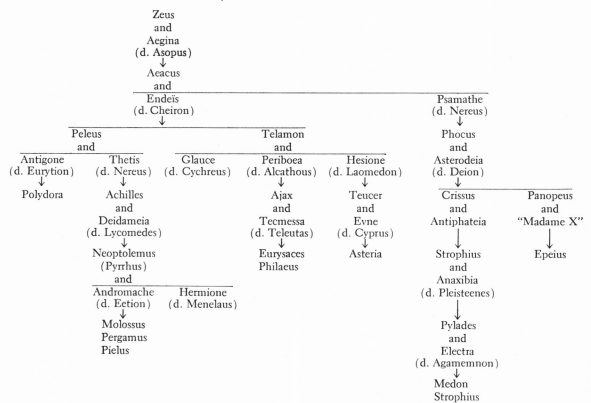

daughter, Glauce, and succeeded to the throne when Cychreus died. When Glauce proved barren, however, he discarded her in favor of Periboea, a daughter of Alcathous and granddaughter of Pelops, who bore a son to him named Ajax (Aias)—destined to become one of the greatest warriors at Troy.[7] Because of his reputation for bravery, Telamon was numbered among the Argonauts and the hunters of the Calydonian boar, and Heracles enlisted his assistance in his expeditions against the Amazons and against the Trojan king, Laomedon. For his valiant services in the last of these adventures, he was given Laomedon's daughter, Hesione, as a prize and she bore to him a son, Teucer, who also took an important part in the Trojan War.

At Phthia, King Eurytion purified Peleus of

the murder of Phocus, and gave him his daughter, Antigone, in marriage—together with the rulership of a third part of his realm. Presumably after a short honeymoon, Peleus now (or later) joined the Argonautic expedition and, as related in chapter 7, distinguished himself as one of the more important actors. Upon his return, he went on the Calydonian boar hunt, and had the misfortune to slay his father-in-law with a javelin which he had thrown at the beast. Because of this mishap, it was mythologically necessary for him to suffer exile from Phthia, and he proceeded to Iolchus, where he was hospitably received and purified of the bloodshed by Acastus, the son of Pelias who had been one of his companions in the Argo. His arrival was but a few days after Pelias had been boiled to death by his own daughters at the instigation of Medeia, and while funeral games were being held by Acastus in the old man's honor. In the games, Peleus became a competitor in the wrestling and drew as his opponent the swift-footed

---

[7] Ajax, known as the Greater to distinguish him from Ajax, the son of Oileus, led the Salaminians to Troy in twelve ships. His great exploits in the war are noted later. The two men were jointly referred to as the Aiantes.

maiden Atalanta, and was greatly chagrined when she overpowered him. Notwithstanding this humiliation, he now received a proposal of intimacy from Astydameia, the wife of Acastus —known also as Hippolyte. When he refused the offer, the scorned woman maliciously sent a messenger to Phthia to tell his wife that Peleus had fallen in love with the maiden Sterope—a daughter of Acastus and Astydameia. Antigone believed the false report and, tenderly bidding farewell to her daughter Polydora,[8] forthwith hanged herself.

Not content with this single act of vengeance, Astydameia now told her husband that Peleus had tried to seduce her. Acastus was quite naturally incensed but, since he could not summarily kill the man whom he had purified, he devised a plan to accomplish the same result in a manner which would not offend mythological convention. Conformably, he took Peleus out to hunt on nearby Mount Pelion and, when his guest fell asleep from the exhaustion of the chase, he deprived him of his sword and left him to become the prey of the wild animals which infested the region.[9] Upon awakening, and while still looking for his sword, Peleus was attacked by some of the cruel centaurs who were the offspring of Ixion, but the gentle centaur Cheiron, who was the son of Cronus (and who was Peleus' own grandfather), rescued him and gave him his sword which he had found in an adjacent thicket where Acastus had hidden it.

Learning from Cheiron of Antigone's suicide, the widowed man went with his biformed relative to dwell at his mountain home.[10] Some time later, he was informed how he could improve his lonely state by gaining as his wife the Nereid Thetis, who had spurned the advances of Zeus.[11] And, although the sea-goddess had

the power of transforming herself into different shapes, she did not discourage his approach, but readily consented to become his wife. Their wedding was celebrated by the attendance of all the gods. In due time, she bore to him a son named Achilles, whose activities are an inseparable part of the Trojan story—in that connection they will be recounted later. Peleus himself is said to have gone back to Phthia, where he lived to a great age, and finally came to a peaceful death.[12]

Because Achilles, Ajax, and Teucer played such important roles in the war against Troy, further discussion of them, and of their descendants, is postponed until the later chapters where that great mythological conflict is narrated.[13] However, it is here appropriate to mention briefly the descendants of Phocus, the half brother who was slain by Peleus and Telamon. Before his death, he married Asterodeia, a daughter of the Aeolid Deion, and left surviving him two sons, named Panopeus and Crissus—twins who quarreled while still in their mother's womb.[14] Panopeus is said to have been one of

---

[8] As related in chapter 9, Polydora, the daughter of Peleus and Antigone, married the Spartan prince Borus —but bore children to the god of the river Spercheius.

[9] Contesting in the hunt, Peleus cut out and put in his pouch the tongues of the animals slain by him. When Acastus derided him as if he had taken nothing, he produced the tongues and complacently laid himself down to sleep.

[10] A variant story relates that Peleus proceeded back to Iolchus and slew both Acastus and Astydameia.

[11] When Thetis refused the advances of Zeus, he decreed that she should become the wife of a mortal.

According to one legend, Peleus captured her after she had changed herself into many shapes, but another relates that she sent a marine deity to him on Mount Pelion, where he was dwelling with Cheiron, and herself solicited his love.

[12] The various legends about Peleus are studded with more than their expected share of anachronisms. His visit for purification of the murder of Eurytion is said to have been made to Acastus at Iolchus immediately after the return of the Argonauts; and, as a member of the band, Peleus is mentioned as talking with his wife, Thetis, on the homeward journey. However, his marriage to her is conventionally related as taking place after he was left in the mountains by Acastus. Respecting the feud between the two men: it is related that Acastus— or his sons Archander and Architeles—began it by expelling Peleus from the kingdom of Phthia.

[13] The archaeological excavations of Schliemann and Dorpfeld together with other proofs have convinced scholars that the Trojan War was an historical event which took place around the hill in Asia Minor known now as Hissarlik.

[14] Although the country of Phocis is said to have derived its name from Phocus, the son of Ornytion, its boundaries (according to a legend given by Pausanias) were extended by Phocus, the son of Aeacus, during a visit which he made shortly before his death. Another legend, noted by both Tzetzes and by Antoninus Liberalis, related that Psamathe afterward took vengeance for the murder of her son by sending a wolf to ravage the flocks of Peleus, but that she was prevailed upon by Thetis to turn the animal into stone.

the hunters of the Calydonian boar, and afterward joined Amphitryon—the stepfather of Heracles—in his expedition against the Taphians, who had sought to take over Argos. During his participation in the successful counterattack, however, he broke his vow that he would appropriate no part of the booty and, as a result, his son Epeius was born and grew up to be effeminate. Notwithstanding this, it is also related that it was he who built the Wooden Horse.

Crissus married Antiphateia, and their son Strophius became the father of Pylades by Anaxibia, the daughter of Pleisthenes. The story of Pylades and of his friendship for his cousin Orestes is among the highlights of the Greek mythology subsequent to the fall of Troy—and is narrated later in some detail.

Maia—the Mother of Hermes

The birth and a general outline of the activities of Hermes, the son borne to Zues by Maia, a daughter of Atlas and Pleione, have been related in chapter 3. Like many of the other major deities, he had a number of children and, for convenience, they will be mentioned with their descendants in the alphabetical order of the names of their mothers.

Antianeira

By Antianeira, a daughter of Menetes, Hermes had twin sons named Echion and Erytus, who were members of the Argonautic expedition. They are also mentioned as among those who hunted the Calydonian boar, but they do not appear to have performed any act worth noting in connection with either adventure.

Aphrodite

When Hermaphroditus, a son of Hermes and Aphrodite, was fifteen years old, he wandered into the country of Caria and went swimming in a clear pool which was the dwelling place of the nymph Salmacis. She had previously seen the handsome youth as he walked about in the adjacent woods and, falling in love with him, now seized the opportunity to embrace him with both arms and legs. Concurrently, she prayed that they might never be separated, and their entwined bodies miraculously merged into

a single form which combined both of their sexes into one.

Chione

On the same day, both Hermes and Apollo embraced Chione, a daughter of Daedalion. Prideful of her affairs with the two gods, she rashly boasted that the goddess Artemis retained her chastity only because of her own lack of personal attraction. Enraged at this foolish and impious slur, the goddess shot her through the tongue with an arrow which proved fatal. Before she died, Chione gave birth to twin sons Autolycus and Philammon, fathered by Hermes and Apollo, respectively.

105. Descendants of Hermes and Chione

Hermes
and
Chione
(d. Daedalion)
↓
Autolycus
and
Amphitheia
↓

Several unnamed sons	Anticleia

Autolycus grew up to become a true son of his parents, inheriting the boldness of his mother coupled with the cunning of his father. He is said to have lived on Mount Parnassus in Thessaly, where he gained a great reputation for thievery,[15] and his innate cleverness was supplemented by the power which he had to change both himself and his stolen goods into other forms which made detection almost impossible. On one occasion, however, he met his match in the Corinthian king, Sisyphus, who marked his sheep on the bottoms of their feet and was thus able to identify them among a large flock with which they had been mingled by the crafty robber.[16]

_____

[15] Apollodorus says that Autolycus was one of the Argonauts, and that he instructed young Heracles in the art of wrestling. His most notable action at Parnassus was the theft of Amyntor's helmet which, through various hands, finally came into the possession of Odysseus.

[16] It is related that Sisyphus discovered his sheep while on a friendly visit to the house of Autolycus. On the same visit, it is said that he seduced Anticleia, daughter of his host, who later married Laertes and gave

By a woman named Amphitheia (whom Pausanias calls Neaera), Autolycus begot several unnamed sons and a daughter Anticleia, who became by Laertes the mother of Odysseus. As a young boy, he received his name—meaning "man of wrath"—from an incident which occurred when he went to visit his grandfather Autolycus and his unnamed uncles on Mount Parnassus. To initiate the lad in manly pursuits, they took him with them on a boar hunt, and were amazed to see him kill the first beast which they flushed from its hiding place; but, in the encounter, Odysseus received a flesh wound above his knee, inflicted by the boar's tusk. The resulting scar afterward proved to be of great mythological importance as a means of his identification.

Chthonophyle

By Chthonophyle, a daughter of Sicyon and Zeuxippe, Hermes had a son named Polybus, who is said to have been king of Corinth at the time when Laius was king of Thebes. It was he, with his wife Periboea who reared young Oedipus after his herdsmen found the mutilated infant in the mountainous region where he had been exposed to die.[17]

Cleobula

Myrtilus, a son of Hermes and Cleobula, was the charioteer of King Oenomaus at Pisa in Elis. Having learned from an oracle that he was destined to die when his daughter Hippodameia should wed, Oenomaus decreed that no suitor might gain her hand except by conquering him in a chariot race from Pisa to the isthmus of Corinth; he made it a further (and deterrent) condition that all who lost should forfeit their lives. As a result, many ambitious youths came to their ends and gained the rather doubtful distinction of having their skulls become ornaments upon the walls of the king's hallway.

Pelops, son of the wealthy, Lydian king, Tantalus, finally entered the contest, which he won through bribing Myrtilus to cause the chariot of Oenomaus to break down. But, when Myrtilus asked for his promised reward, Pelops threw him into the Aegean Sea near the island of Euboea, and he was drowned. With his expiring breath the youth breathed a curse on the house of his corrupter which—added to other curses—brought on some of the greatest tragedies in mythology. Owing to the intercession of his divine father, it is said that Myrtilus was translated to the skies as the constellation which we call Auriga—or the Charioteer.[18]

Daeira

Eleusis, son of Hermes and the Oceanid Daeira, was seemingly given his mythological birth to create an eponym for the town of his name where Demeter is said to have rested in Attica during her worldwide search for her stolen daughter Persephone.

106. Descendants of Hermes and Daeira

Hermes
and
Daeira
(d. Oceanus)
↓
Eleusis
and
Cothonea
↓
Dysaules   Celeus
and
Metaneira
↓
Abas
Callidice
Callithoë
Cleisidice
Demo
Demophoön
Triptolemus

By a woman, identified only as Cothonea, he had sons named Dysaules and Celeus, who were in local residence at the time of the goddess' arrival. When she sat down dejectedly near the well called Callichorus, she was mocked by Abas, the eldest son of Celeus and his wife, Metaneira, and wrathfully changed him into a lizard. Some time later, his sisters—Callidice,

---

birth to Odysseus, and this story was often repeated to prove that he was the actual father of the cunning warrior.

[17] According to Pausanias, Polybus was king of Sicyon and had a daughter named Lysianassa who became the wife of the Argive king, Talaus.

---

[18] A variant story considered the constellation as the apotheosis of Erichthonius, son of Hephaestus and Gaea.

262

Callithoë, Cleisidice, and Demo—came along and, after kindly slaking the thirst of the goddess, took her back with them to become the nurse of their youngest brother, Demophoön.

Without revealing her identity,[19] Demeter fed her small charge on heavenly ambrosia, and sought to make him immortal by placing him in the fire by night. However, once during the process, Metaneira shrieked loudly when she saw what was happening, and the alarmed goddess dropped the babe into the flames where he perished. As part compensation, she now disclosed her divinity and bade Celeus and Metaneira to build a temple in her honor over which they should preside as caretakers. And she took over the rearing of their remaining son Triptolemus, to whom she imparted all of the secrets of husbandry to such a degree that he himself was later recognized as a minor deity. In later days, the temple was given into the custody of Celeus and Metaneira and became the seat of the Eleusinian Mysteries. The secret rites, in adoration of the goddess, were said to have been carried by Dysaules to Phlios where he died (and was buried).

Eupolemeia

By Eupolemeia, a daughter of Myrmidon and Peisidice, Hermes begot a son Aethalides, who (as related in chapter 7) grew up to become the herald of the Argonauts. From his father, he is said to have received the faculty of remembering everything—something which persisted even after death, for his soul, transmigrated to various living persons, was said to have retained recollections connected with its precedent possessors.

Herse

By Herse, a daughter of the Attic autochthon Cecrops, Hermes had a son named Cephalus who was carried off by the dawn-goddess Eos.[20] From their union were successively descended

Tithonus, Phaëthon, Astynous, and Sandocus—who serve only as ancestral names to precede the birth of the Paphian king, Cinyras, said to have been a son of Sandocus and his wife, Pharnace.[21]

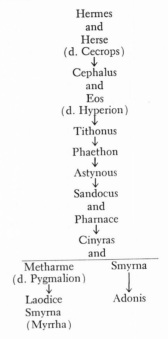

107. Descendants of Hermes and Herse

Hermes
and
Herse
(d. Cecrops)
↓
Cephalus
and
Eos
(d. Hyperion)
↓
Tithonus
↓
Phaethon
↓
Astynous
↓
Sandocus
and
Pharnace
↓
Cinyras
and

Metharme   Smyrna
(d. Pygmalion)
↓   ↓
Laodice   Adonis
Smyrna
(Myrrha)

Cinyras was reputed to have been a Syrian who migrated to Cilicia, and from there came to the island of Cyprus, where he founded its principal city of Paphus. There, he married Metharme, a daughter of the Cyprian king, Pygmalion, by whom he had several daughters—including Laodice[22] and Smyrna. The latter, who was known also as Myrrha, neglected the worship of Aphrodite and as punishment was stricken with an unnatural love for her own father. With the assistance of her nurse, she contrived to share his bed without his knowledge for twelve nights. When Cinyras discovered his unwitting union, he drew his sword and pursued his deceptive daughter with intent to kill her; but, she prayed to the gods to be made

---

[19] A variant of the story related that Demeter's divinity was immediately perceived by Metaneira because of her attendant halo.

[20] Cephalus, the son of Hermes, should not be confused with the man of the same name who was a son of Deion, and who was likewise loved by the dawn-goddess.

---

[21] Pindar suggests that Cinyras was a son of Apollo by his own priest Paphus.

[22] Without explaining the geographical circumstances of their meeting, Apollodorus says that Laodice grew up to become the wife of the Arcadian king, Elatus.

invisible and they turned her into a tree which was called "myrrha."[23] Ten months later, the tree burst open and beautiful Adonis was born.[24]

Aphrodite was so charmed with the fruit of her machination that she concealed the infant in a chest, which she entrusted to Persephone for temporary safekeeping. But Persephone became likewise attached to her fair charge and refused to give him up. The dispute was brought before Zeus, who ordained that Adonis should stay by himself during four months of each year and that, thereafter, Persephone and Aphrodite should successively have his custody for four months each.[25] Adonis, however, made over his own share of the year to Aphrodite in addition to her annual period, but he was eventually killed by a wild boar and was changed into a flower.[26]

A different legend related that, at his death, Adonis was compelled like other mortals to descend as a shade into the lower world. Owing, however, to Aphrodite's great love for him, he was permitted to return to earth for six months out of each year, which he spent in her company. In eastern countries, where the goddess of love was considered as the fructifying principle of nature, this annual departure and return was identified with the beginning and end of their growing seasons.[26]

Iphthime

By Iphthime, a daughter of Dorus, Hermes was said to have been the father of Silenus—the steward and inseparable companion of the wine-god Dionysus, whom he usually accompanied riding on an ass, because he was depicted as being too jovially intoxicated to walk. He was reputed to have been gifted with the power of prophesy which, when he was drunk and asleep, mortals could force him to exercise by surrounding his recumbent form with chains of flowers.

108. Descendants of Hermes and Iphthime

Hermes
and
Iphthime
(d. Dorus)
↓
Silenus
↓
The Sileni
(Satyrs)

His sons, the Sileni—known also as Satyrs—are described by later poets as minor deities of woods and fields, who delighted in prankish merriment and, at times, in lasciviousness. They were reputed to be bearded creatures, with the ears and feet of a goat and the tail of a horse.[27]

[23] The drops of gum which oozed from the myrrh tree were thought to be the tears shed by the transformed Myrrha for her sad fate.

[24] Other legends related that Adonis was a son of Phoenix and Alphesiboea, or of the Assyrian king, Thias, and his daughter Smyrna. In Babylonia he was identified with a deity named Tammuz.

[25] According to another version of the story, when the dispute was referred to Zeus, he appointed the Muse Calliope to act as arbitrator. She decided that Adonis should spend six months of the year with each of the contesting goddesses, but Aphrodite was so enraged at the decision that she instigated the Thracian women to rend in pieces Calliope's son, the musician Orpheus.

[26] The boar is said to have been the god Ares, who transformed himself and killed the youth from jealousy at Aphrodite's affection for him.

[26] That the myth of Adonis should be identified with the forces of nature seems obvious, but many writers have so far stretched the principle of allegory that G. K. Chesterton (in *The Everlasting Man*) has been led to object, saying:

"The true origin of all the myths has been discovered much too often. There are too many keys to mythology, as there are too many cryptograms in Shakespeare. Every-

thing is phallic; everything is totemistic; everything is seed-time and harvest; everything is ghosts and grave-offerings; everything is the golden bough of sacrifice; everything is the sun and moon; everything is everything. Every folk-lore student who knew a little more than his own monomania, every man of wider reading and critical culture like Andrew Lang, has practically confessed that the bewilderment of these things left his brain spinning. Yet the whole trouble comes from a man trying to look at these stories from the outside, as if they were scientific objects. He has only to look at them from the inside, and ask himself how he would begin a story. A story may start with anything and go anywhere. It may start with a bird without the bird being a totem; it may start with the sun without being a solar myth. Set ten thousand children talking at once, and telling tarra-diddles about what they did in the wood, and it will not be hard to find parallels suggesting sun-worship or animal-worship. Some of the stories may be pretty and some silly and some perhaps dirty; but they can only be judged as stories. In the modern dialect, they can only be judged aesthetically . . . We may be fanciful about everything except fairy-tales."

[27] Others relate that the Satyrs were sons of Pan, or that they sprang from Gaea. Nonnos gives some of their names as follows: Poimenius, Thiasus, Hypsicerus, Orestes, Phlegraeus, Napaius, Gemon, Lycon, Phereus, Petraeus, Lamis, Lenobius, Scirtus, Oistrus, Pherespondus, Lycus, and Promomus.

Penelope

When Hermes visited Penelope, the daughter of Icarius and faithful wife of Odysseus, he took the form of a ram, by whom she unwittingly conceived and gave birth to Pan—destined to become the Greek god of flocks and shepherds.[28] When he was born fully grown—with horns, beard, tail, and the feet of a goat—his frightened mother ran away from him; but he was brought up by woodland nymphs, and Hermes later carried him to Olympus, where the great gods were delighted with his quaint form and manners.[29]

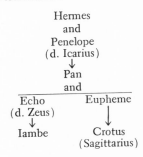

109. Descendants of Hermes and Penelope

Hermes
and
Penelope
(d. Icarius)
↓
Pan
and
───────────────────
Echo　　　　Eupheme
(d. Zeus)　　　　↓
↓　　　　Crotus
Iambe　　　(Sagittarius)

By the chattering nymph Echo, Pan is said to have been the father of the serving-woman Iambe, whose remarks were able to bring a smile to the face of sorrowing Demeter when she came in search of Persephone to the home of Celeus and Metaneira at Eleusis. She is believed to have been the original cause of the hilarious rites which lightened the otherwise serious proceedings of the Eleusinian Mysteries, and from her the poetry known as iambic—or satirical—derived its name. But, owing to the hurt which was often caused by her cutting words, in self-imposed retribution she finally hanged herself.

By Eupheme, the nurse of the Muses, Pan begot a son named Crotus who was such a skillful archer on earth that, when he died, he was translated to the heavens under the name of Sagittarius, where he is still said to remain as the ninth sign of the zodiac.[30] According to a later story, Pan pursued the naiad-nymph Syrinx until she ran into a river in Arcadia and was changed into a reed, and from this Pan made himself a flute.

Philodameia

Hermes had a son named Phares by Philodameia, a daughter of Danaus and Atlantia, who had murdered her previous husband, Diocorystes, on his wedding night.

110. Descendants of Hermes and Philodameia

Hermes
and
Philodameia
(d. Danaus)
↓
Phares
and
"Madame X"
↓
Telegone

In his own right, Phares is remembered only as the founder of Pharae in Messenia, where no fish were permitted to be caught because they were considered as sacred to his divine father. He gained additional recognition, however, as the father of Telegone, his daughter who bore a son named Orsilochus to the god of the great river Alpheius.

Polymela

A son named Eudorus was borne to Hermes by Polymela, a daughter of the Phthian Phylas. At first, the father was angry at his daughter's indiscretion but, when he learned that her se-

---

28 Pan is also called the son of Hermes by Callisto, or by a daughter of Dryops, and one odd story relates that Penelope bore him to all of her suitors in common. In the Orphic theogony, he is considered as the demiurge—or subordinate deity—from whom the physical world took its being. His fearsome appearance is said to have caused "panic" to those who first saw him.

29 In a musical contest between Pan and Apollo, the rich, Lydian king Midas disagreed with the judgment of Tmolus that Apollo was the victor, and was punished by having his ears turned into those of an ass. Unable to keep his master's disfigurement a secret, one of the unhappy man's slaves dug a hole in the ground into which he whispered the story, but a thick growth of reeds sprang up and repeated his buried words, so that all the world knew and laughed.

30 Hyginus relates that Pan was also the father of Aegipan by Aega, a daughter of the Sun-god Helios, but in view of the conventional story that he was a son of Hermes and Penelope, this tale draws our chronological bow a bit too taut—for Aegipan is said to have assisted Hermes in recovering the sinews of Zeus from the giant Typhon at the very dawn of Olympian supremacy.

ducer was a god, his anger changed to pride and he reared the boy as though he had been his own son. Eudorus grew up to become swift of foot, and was so outstanding in the use of arms that he was appointed by Achilles to be one of the captains of the Myrmidons at Troy.

Themis

By Themis, a daughter of the god of the Arcadian river Ladon, Hermes had a son, Evander, who forms one of the connecting links between the mythologies of Greece and Rome.[31] Because of an accidental manslaughter, he was forced to flee in exile from his native city of Tegea in Arcadia and went to Italy, where he was hospitably received by King Turnus on the banks of the Tiber at a place which afterward became the site of Rome. Either by conquest or by gift from Turnus, he came to be ruler over a portion of the country, and is said to have taught his subjects various social amenities, such as music and writing—the latter having been communicated to him by Heracles.[32] According to Virgil, he was still living in Italy when Aeneas arrived there after the fall of Troy, and joined him in subduing the Latins. Virgil also mentions a son and two daughters, who were borne to Evander after his move to Italy, but their names are not noted here because they are a part of the Roman mythology which is beyond the scope of this compilation.

"Madame X"

Perhaps because he was the messenger of the gods, and was the ubiquitous patron of merchants and traveling men throughout the earth,

the later poets mention a large number of children as begotten by Hermes with unnamed women—and at various places. Nothing of particular interest, however, is related about most of them, and only Daphnis and Dolops will be discussed.

The locale of the story of Daphnis is said to have been the island of Sicily. There, the son of Hermes grew up to become a handsome shepherd, who was a companion of Artemis and greatly admired as a skilled piper. He was beloved by the nymph Chloë, who sought to retain his affections by threatening that he would lose his sight if he should ever prove unfaithful to her —which he did, and was immediately blinded.[33]

Dolops, another son of Hermes by an unnamed woman, is remembered only because it is related that the Argonauts, while passing the shore of Magnesian Thessaly, saw a sepulchral barrow which had been erected in his honor (for some reason which is not explained). But he must have been a person of consequence, because Apollonius Rhodius says that the voyagers put ashore and offered sacrifices to his shade.[34]

---

[31] A different legend relates that Evander was the son of Echemus and Timandra, and Virgil say that his mother was a nymph named Carmentis.

[32] As related in chapter 14, Heracles spent the night with Evander during his progress through Italy with the herd of Geryon.

---

[33] The story noted in the text is that related by Parthenius. Longus, another late writer whose nativity is uncertain, authored the love adventures of Daphnis and Chloë which were supposed to have taken place near Mytilene on the island of Lesbos. He relates that they were both discovered as infants, who had been suckled at birth, respectively, by a she-goat and an ewe, and that, being raised by neighboring peasant families, they grew up to consummate the love which first arose when they were reared together as children.

[34] It may be appropriate here to notice the story related by Ovid of the visit which Hermes made with Zeus to the earth, where they were graciously received and humbly feted by a poor Phrygian couple whose names were Baucis and Philemon. When the wine bowl miraculously replenished itself during the course of the meal, the divinity of the travelers was recognized and—for their hospitality—the two gods established Baucis and Philemon as guardians of their temple and permitted them to escape death by simultaneously being changed into trees.

20

The Descendants of Zeus X

THE LATER DESCENDANTS of Zeus from Euryodia, Plouto, and Electra—whose names are shown on the genealogical charts given in this chapter —were primarily actors in the Trojan War, or in subsequent events, and will be brought into our story at their appropriate places for entrance; but, for reasons of convenience and continuity, they are included in their composite family pedigrees without being commented upon presently.

Euryodia—the Mother of Arceisius

The paucity of detail given about Euryodia, Arceisius, and Chalcodemusa (perhaps Chalcomedusa)—the ancestors of the hero Odysseus who are shown on the following chart—is undoubtedly one of the causes from which arose the widespread story that he was actually a son of cunning Sisyphus.

With reference to Laertes, the father of Odysseus, it is not related how he happened to acquire the rulership of the island of Ithaca. In the Odyssey, however, the old man states that during his youth when he was lord of the Cephallenians, he took the fortified town of Nericus, which was on the neighboring island of Leucas. Perhaps in order to give him an added respectability, Apollodorus names Laertes as one of the Argonauts, and Hyginus lists him among the hunters of the Calydonian boar; but in connection with neither adventure does his role appear to have been occupied with any special distinction. In addition to his great son Odysseus,

Laertes' wife Anticleia, bore to him a daughter named Ctimene, who became by Phyleus mother of Meges, the leader of the Echinaeans at Troy.[1]

Plouto—the Mother of Tantalus

By the Oceanid Plouto, Zeus had a son named Tantalus who became renowned as a wealthy king of Lydia—ruling the country around Mount Sipylus. He was particularly celebrated in ancient legend because of the severe punishment inflicted upon him in the lower world after his death. It is said that he was placed in the middle of a lake, whose waters always withdrew when he would slake his thirst, and that branches laden with fruit extended over his head, but always sprang away when he would appease his hunger. And from this depiction, we obtained our word "tantalize."[2]

There are several accounts of the reason why Tantalus was so cruelly punished. Firstly, it is said that he divulged to men certain divine secrets which Zeus had entrusted to him while they were dining together; secondly, he is sup-

---

[1] As related in chapter 14, Phyleus was expelled from Elis when he testified on behalf of Heracles against his father Augeias, and went to the island of Dulichium —one of the Echinades in the same group with the island of Samos (Same). This latter was also known as Cephallenia, and was quite near Ithaca, where Ctimene went to be wedded.

[2] According to another legend, a huge rock was suspended over the head of Tantalus, ever threatening to crush him.

111. Descendants of Zeus and Euryodia

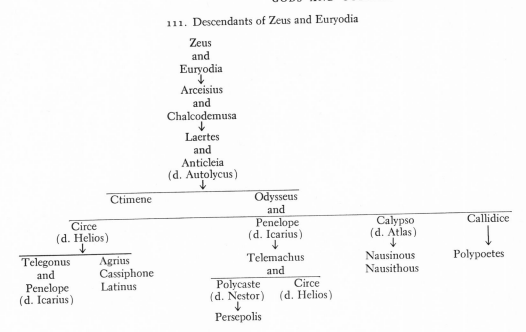

posed to have stolen ambrosia and nectar from the tables of the gods; thirdly, he lied to Zeus about having possession of a golden dog which had guarded the supreme deity while still an infant in Crete;[3] and fourthly, he served his own son, Pelops, as edible meat to the gods. With reference to the last episode, however, it should be noted that—in the course of mastication—the feasting deities miraculously (?) discovered what they were eating, and restored the boy to life. But, it is added, they were forced to equip him with one shoulder of ivory to replace that portion of his anatomy which Demeter had absent-mindedly consumed.

In addition to Pelops, the wife of Tantalus—conventionally said to have been Dione, a daughter of Atlas and Aethra[4]—bore a son to him named Broteas and a daughter Niobe. They too were doomed to suffer for the wickedness of their father, for as noted in chapter 15,

Niobe was turned into a stone fountain, and it is related that Broteas went mad and burned himself to death.[5]

In chapter 16, it has been related how Pelops came into Greece and gained Hippodameia for his bride by conquering her father Oenomaus in the chariot race from Pisa to the isthmus of Corinth.[6] Concurrently, with the death of Oenomaus, he became king of Pisa, and soon so extended his sway that the whole of the southern Greek peninsula is said to have taken its name of Peloponnesus from him. The names and the number of the children borne to him by Hippodameia are variously given, but those listed in the preceding family chart appear to have been conventionally accepted. His favorite child, however, was his son, Chrysippus, whose mother is said to have been a woman of uncertain name and lineage.[7] His favoritism became

---

[3] The story ran that the animal was stolen by a Milesian named Pandareus who entrusted it to Tantalus for safekeeping, and that when Zeus sent Hermes to reclaim his property, Tantalus denied on oath that he knew anything about it. For this act of perjury, it is said that he was buried under Mount Sipylus, and Apollodorus relates that his tomb was shown there in ancient times.

[4] According to Ovid, the wife of Tantalus was one of the Pleiades, whereas Dione was one of the Hyades.

[5] As additional reasons for their misfortunes, it is interesting to note that both Niobe and Broteas incurred the displeasure of the goddess Artemis—Niobe by boasting herself to be more blessed in her children than Leto, and Broteas by refusing to honor her divinity.

[6] Pelops is said to have come into Greece from Mount Sipylus when he was expelled by Ilus and was permitted to bring with him the great wealth which he had inherited from his rich father Tantalus.

[7] The mother of Chrysippus is said to have been named either Axioche or Danais. As with Pelops' other

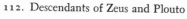

112. Descendants of Zeus and Plouto

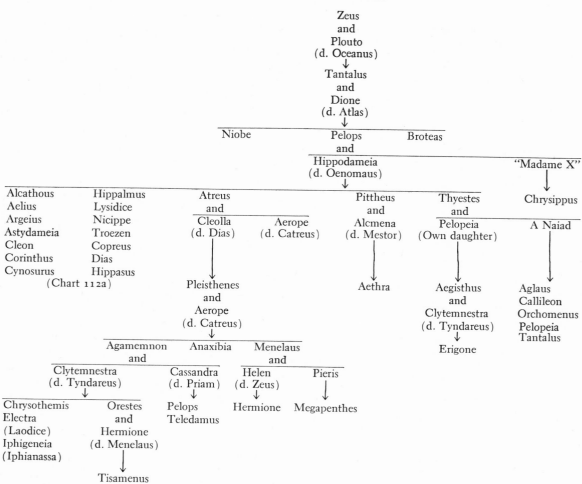

so marked that it aroused the jealousy of the sons of Hippodameia and, with the connivance of their mother, they prevailed upon Atreus and Thyestes—the two eldest of their number—to murder their half brother and throw his body into a well.[8] According to the common tradition, when Pelops learned of the crime, he expelled all of his sons and they scattered all over the Peloponnesus. Hippodameia, dreading the anger of her husband, fled to Argolis, from where her remains were afterward returned to

Elis and buried at Olympia. Some time later, Pelops himself died and was buried at the same place, where he continued for many years to be honored above all the great heroes who gained victories in the famous Olympian games.[9]

After being expelled from Elis with the rest of his brothers, Pittheus settled in Argolis, where he later married Alcmena, daughter of

---

children, Chrysippus was sometimes referred to as a Pelopid.

[8] As related in chapter 9, a different story related that Chrysippus killed himself from shame at the unnatural relations which he had indulged in with the Theban king, Laius.

[9] Pausanias relates that a shoulder bone of Pelops (whether ivory or not, he does not mention) was taken to Troy after an oracle had prophesied that the city could not be taken without its presence. Afterward, it was returned to Elis, following a period in the depths of the sea where it fell overboard on the return journey. But, he adds, that it had disappeared when he visited Elis in the second century A.D. "because, I suppose, it had been hidden in the depths so long, and besides its age it was greatly decayed through the salt water"!

Mestor, and became king of Troezen. He is said to have taught the art of speaking, and even to have written a book upon the subject, but he is chiefly remembered as the father of Aethra, who became the mother of Theseus. (The circumstances have been related in chapter 17.)

Sharing in the common exile, Atreus and Thyestes went to the court of the Argive king, Sthenelus, who was the husband of their sister Nicippe, and he gave to them the town of Midea for a small realm and place of residence. Prior to leaving Elis, Atreus had married Cleolla, a daughter of his brother Dias, who had given birth to a son named Pleisthenes. Apparently, however, she died in the childbirth, because she is not mentioned in connection with the later tragic events which occurred in Argos.

As related in chapter 15, Pleisthenes married Aerope, a daughter of the Cretan king, Catreus, who had been sent from her home in the mistaken belief that she was destined to bring about her father's death. By her, he had a daughter, Anaxibia, and two sons, Agamemnon and Menelaus.[10] But Pleisthenes died while they were still young children, and they were adopted by their grandfather Atreus, who concurrently married his widowed daughter-in-law Aerope.[11] Owing, however, to the continuing curse on the house of Tantalus, she preferred Thyestes and secretly became his paramour.

After Eurystheus, the son of Sthenelus, was slain in resisting the first attempt to take over the Peloponnesus by the sons of Heracles, both Atreus and Thyestes claimed the right to succeed to his throne at Mycenae, for the people had received an oracle which bade them choose a Pelopid for their king. When a public discussion took place, it was agreed that he who could produce the greatest portent from the gods should take office. It so happened that, prior to this time, Atreus had vowed to sacrifice to Artemis the finest of his flocks, but when a golden lamb appeared among them, he neglected to perform his vow and, choking the animal to death, had deposited it in a box which, unknown to him, Aerope had given to her lover Thyestes. Atreus now sought his remarkable treasure—intending to produce it as divine proof of his claim but, instead, Thyestes brought it forth and was awarded the crown. With the assistance of Zeus, however, Atreus was able to exhibit a still greater portent—for, at his bidding, the sun retraced its course in the heavens and came to rest below the eastern horizon. Upon this happening, the verdict of the people was reversed, Atreus was made king and Thyestes was sent into exile, leaving behind the four sons and one daughter noted on the preceding family chart, who had been borne to him by an unnamed naiad.

Some time later, Atreus learned of his wife's adultery, and sent a herald to Thyestes with a proposal to make up their differences. Lured by this pretence of friendship, Thyestes came to the palace for dinner and ate heartily of the meat which was served—only to learn, when Atreus exhibited their extremities, that he had feasted on the bodies of his own sons, which had been cut up and boiled.[12] Struck with horror at the sight, Thyestes rushed from the table and, it is said that, even the Sun-god Helios turned away his face from the frightful scene.[13]

Seeking vengeance, the bereft and infuriated man asked the oracle how it could be obtained, and received answer that, if he should have a son by his own daughter Pelopeia, his aim would be accomplished. Accordingly, he did so and, when his son Aegisthus attained manhood, he murdered Atreus and turned over the rulership to his father.[14] According to Pausanias, the

---

[10] Since the statement that Agamemnon and Menelaus were the sons of Atreus is so generally accepted, it may be proper to deviate from the plan of this compilation and give exact references to the sources which relate that they were actually the sons of Pleisthenes, namely: Hesiod, "Catalogues of Women," 69; Aeschylus, "Agamemnon," 1581; Apollodorus, "Library," 3-2-2.

[11] According to Hyginus, Atreus killed Pleisthenes under circumstances inconsistent with his having been Aerope's first husband and the father of her children.

[12] According to Apollodorus, the sons of Thyestes whose bodies were served as food to their father were named Aglaus, Callileon and Orchomenus. Pausanias relates that his fourth son, Tantalus, was the first husband of Clytemnestra, who afterward became the wife of Agamemnon, by whom he was slain.

[13] At the same time when he murdered the sons of Thyestes, it is said that Atreus drowned Aerope in the sea.

[14] According to Hyginus, Aegisthus was so named because he was exposed by his mother at birth and was

dead king was buried at Mycenae, where his tomb was still pointed out in the second century A.D.; and in 1876, Heinrich Schliemann uncovered a great chamber which contains features identifying it with those mythologically assigned to the rich treasury of Atreus. Subsequent excavation and research have cast doubt about its assumed identity. The later life of Aegisthus, and his seduction of Clytemnestra, Agamemnon's wife, are later related in connection with the events which followed the fall of Troy.

With reference to the children of Pleisthenes, who were adopted and raised as his own by Atreus—Anaxibia married the Phocian king, Strophius, and became the mother of Pylades; Agamemnon succeeded Thyestes as king of Mycenae[15] and, marrying Clytemnestra, daughter of Tyndareus, begot the three daughters and one son whose names are shown on the preceding family chart; and, as related in chapter 18, Menelaus became the successful suitor of beautiful Helen.

We turn now to brief comment upon the less important children of Pelops and Hippodameia, together with their descendants.

The first wife of Alcathous was a woman named Pyrgo about whom nothing of interest is related. Presumably she died, and Alcathous went to Megara—in the general exodus from Pisa of the sons of Pelops which followed the murder of their half brother Chrysippus. At this time, Megareus, the king of the city, was without male heirs. He lost his sons, Timalcus and Evippus, under the circumstances which have been related in chapter 10. As noted, Evippus had been destroyed by a lion, and Megareus now offered the hand of his daughter, Evaechme, and the succession of his kingdom to the man who should slay the fierce animal, which was still ravaging the countryside. Alcathous suc-

cessfully undertook the task and, when he came to the throne, is said to have built a temple to Artemis and Apollo, in whose construction the Delian god himself gave assistance.[16]

Of the children borne to Alcathous by Evaechme: Automedusa married Iphicles, the half brother of Heracles, and became the mother of Iolaus; Periboea married Telamon, and became the mother of the Greater Ajax; but Iphinoë died a virgin, to whom the women of Megara were accustomed to dedicate locks of their hair on the eves of their weddings. Callipolis and Ischepolis, the sons of Alcathous and Evaechme, are said to have joined in the hunt for the Calydonian boar, during which the latter lost his life. Callipolis hastened to carry the sad tidings back to his father, whom he found engaged in offering a sacrifice to Apollo. Thinking it an unfit time to offer sacrifices, the youth snatched away the wood which had been placed on the altar, whereupon Alcathous killed him on the spot for what he considered to be wanton sacrilege.

Some of the sons of Pelops and Hippodameia who are listed on the following chart appear to have nothing of importance related about them; and, in this category Aelius, Argeius, Corinthus, Cynosurus, and Hippalmus may be placed. Of the others: Cleon was the eponym of the small town of Cleonae, where Heracles stopped in his pursuit of the Nemean lion and near the place where the great man is said to have slain the Siamese twins, Cteatus and Eurytus; Troezen was the eponym for the town of his name where Pittheus was ruling when Aegeus came by and spent the night with Aethra; Copreus was the steward of Eurystheus and had a son named Periphetes who was slain at Troy by Hector; Dias was the father of Cleolla, who bore Pleisthenes to her uncle Atreus; and Hippasus is named by Apollodorus as the father of the Argonaut Actor.

In addition to their many sons, Pelops and Hippodameia had three daughters named Astydameia, Lysidice, and Nicippe. Astydameia is

---

suckled by a goat—"aega." A later mythographer relates that the incest resulting in his birth was committed at Sicyon during the night and that Pelopeia did not recognize the identity of her ravisher until she identified the sword which she had wrested from him as belonging to her own father whereupon, she stabbed herself to death.

[15] Homer intimates that Agamemnon peaceably succeeded Thyestes, but, according to Aeschylus, he usurped the throne and again sent Thyestes into exile.

[16] Pausanias relates that, in later times, the stone upon which Apollo placed his lyre while at work was said to give forth the ringing sound of that instrument when struck.

112a. Descendants of Zeus and Plouto

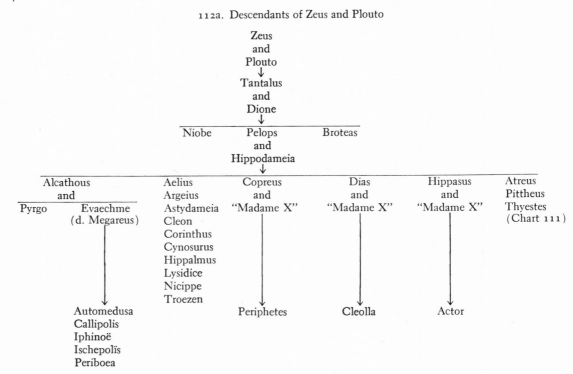

said by Apollodorus to have been the wife of Alcaeus and the mother of his children, but the conventional account gives that role to Hipponome, a daughter of the Theban Menoeceus who was descended from one of the original Sparti. Lysidice was married to Mestor to whom she bore two daughters named Hippothoë and Alcmena—previously mentioned in connection with the legends respecting Heracles and Theseus.[17] And Nicippe, as related earlier, became the wife of Sthenelus and was the connecting link which resulted in the Pelopid ascendency to the rulership of Argos.

Electra—the Mother of Dardanus and Iasion

It is of significant mythological importance that the royal line of the Trojans stemmed from the same roots as those of the Greeks. Tracing back to Zeus as their divine ancestor, they claimed that he had two sons—Dardanus and Iasion—who were borne to him by Electra, a Pleiad daughter of Atlas, whose six sisters all became mothers of illustrious Greek heroes. Nor should it be overlooked that the birthplace of

Electra's twin sons was reputed to have been in Arcadia, the very heart of the Greek Poloponnesus.[18]

At the wedding of Cadmus and Harmonia, the goddess Demeter fell in love with Iasion and, lying with him "in a thrice-ploughed field," in due time became the mother of twin sons named Plutus and Philomelus.[19] When they were born, Zeus was so angered at Iasion's presumption in mating with an immortal that he struck him dead with a flash of lightning.[20]

---

[17] According to Pausanias, Lysidice was the wife of Alcaeus and the mother of Amphitryon.

[18] Virgil names Ausonia (the ancient name of Italy) as the birthplace of Dardanus and Iasion, and says that their father was Corythus, an Italian hero reputed to be a son of Jupiter (Zeus). Diodorus Siculus, with more than his accustomed confusion, names the island of Samothrace as the place of Electra's accouchement and relates that she was also the mother of Harmonia. Still another legend placed the blessed event in Crete, with King Minos as the sire.

[19] Hesiod located the "thrice-ploughed field" in the island of Crete, but the wedding of Cadmus and Harmonia was conventionally reputed to have been celebrated at Boeotian Thebes.

[20] Variants of the legend related that Iasion was killed by Dardanus, or by his own horses, and another represented him as living to an old age, and traveling about through the world as a teacher of the mysteries of Demeter.

113. Descendants of Zeus and Electra

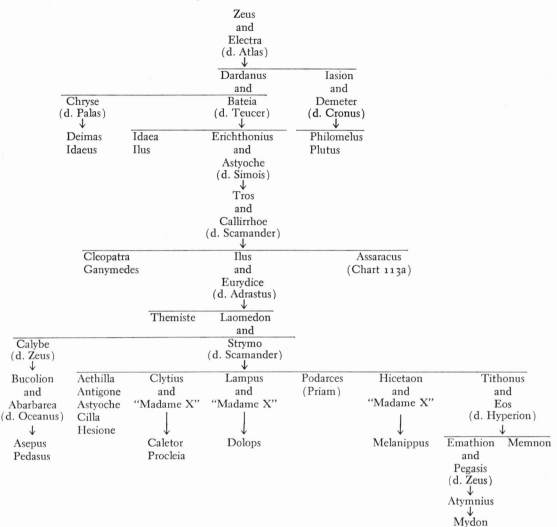

Plutus (sometimes called Pluton) was considered as the personification of wealth—naturally attaching to him as a son of the goddess of the harvest. In this role, he was represented as a young boy (but sometimes as an old man) carrying a cornucopia from which he blindly dispensed earthly blessings—having been deprived of his eyesight by Zeus so that his gifts would be received without regard to the merit of his beneficiaries. Philomelus, however, was not a recipient of his brother's bounty and, being obliged to earn his living, is said to have become a renowned agriculturist. To ease his labor in removing his harvests from the fields, it is re-

puted that he invented the wagon—whereupon his admiring mother caused him to be translated to the heavens as the constellation known as "Bootes," which starts at the end of the handle of the Big Dipper.

When Dardanus reached manhood, he assumed the government of the Arcadian realm which is said to have been subject to his grandfather Atlas. He married Chryse, daughter of Palas,[21] who bore to him two sons named

---

[21] It may be conjectured that Chryse was a daughter of Pallas (son of Lycaon—one of the earliest names in Arcadian legend).

Deimas and Idaeus. Some years later when the boys had grown up, a great flood so damaged the country that Dardanus surrendered its rulership to Deimas and, accompanied by Chryse and Idaeus, migrated to the island of Samothrace. Among his belongings, he took to the new land an image of the goddess Athena, known as the Palladium, which had been received as a part of his wife's dowry. It is said that he introduced in Samothrace the worship of this image, and of the other Greek gods, without, however, revealing their names. After bringing this bit of *Kultur* to the barbarians,[22] he moved on to the Phrygian mainland and established a city, which he called Dardania.[23] Some time thereafter, Chryse died, but Dardanus did not remain a widower long and, marrying Bateia, a daughter of the neighboring King Teucer, had a daughter Idaea and two sons named Erichthonius and Ilus.

Idaea became the second wife of Phineus and, according to one legend, was so cruelly treated by her stepsons that she caused her husband to punish them—as a result he was himself blinded and subjected to the plague of the Harpies (which has been mentioned in chapters 7 and 9). Upon the death of Dardanus, Erichthonius succeeded to the rulership—his brother Ilus had died earlier without issue. The realm taken over by him included the whole country previously ruled by his grandfather Teucer, who had bequeathed it to Dardanus. From then on it was now known as Dardania—equally with the original city of that name.[24]

Erichthonius married Astyoche, a daughter of the river-god Simois, and begat Tros—a son who succeeded to the kingdom when his father died and changed its name to Troy, or Troad, after himself. Following the example of his fa-

ther, he also took as his wife the daughter of a local river-god. She was Callirrhoë, daughter of the god of the river Scamander,[25] and by her he had three sons named Ganymedes, Ilus, and Assaracus and a daughter named Cleopatra about whom nothing of interest is related.

Ganymedes was a youth of such beauty that he was beloved by Zeus, who had an eagle convey him from earth to Olympus, where he was given immortality and displaced Hebe as cupbearer to the deities who dwelt there.[26] Tros grieved so greatly for the loss of his son that, by way of partial assuagement, Zeus had Hermes lead down to him a number of divine horses, whose speed outstripped the winds.[27]

Tros' eldest son, Ilus, while visiting a neighboring Phrygian king, contested in games, which were being celebrated for some undisclosed reason, and was the victor in wrestling. As a prize, he received fifty youths and the same number of maidens and, in obedience to the command of an oracle, the king gave him also a dappled cow and bade him found a city at the place where the animal should first lie down. When she came to rest at the bottom of a Phrygian hill called Ate, Ilus built the afterward renowned city which he called Ilium from his own name. As was the custom, he prayed to Zeus for a sign of divine approval, and was pleased the next morning to find outside his tent the image of Athena known as the Palladium.[28] This he

---

[22] The Greeks considered all who did not speak their language barbarians.

[23] Because of Dardanus' visit, the island of Samothrace was sometimes called Dardania and, from his mother, was known also as the island of Electra. According to Strabo, the city of Dardania founded on the mainland was located somewhat north and east of the site of the later Ilium or Troy.

[24] In the Italian legend, it is related that Dardanus (the son of Corythus) migrated to Phrygia and that Iasion went to Samothrace—after first dividing between themselves their family gods, known as Penates.

[25] The river Scamander was called Xanthus by the gods.

[26] According to Ovid, Zeus transformed himself into an eagle and abducted Ganymedes. The youth is said to have been apotheosized as Aquarius, the eleventh sign of the zodiac. The eagle which carried him was identified with the northern constellation known as Aquila.

[27] The Iliad relates that the divine horses of Tros were twelve fillies begotten by the north-wind Boreas on the mares of Erichthonius, who is described as the richest of mortal men and the owner of three thousand steeds.

[28] A different version relates that the Palladium at Ilium was the same image which Dardanus had brought from Arcadia. The circumstances of its creation and its fall to earth are given in chapter 4, in connection with Pallas as a daughter of the river-god Triton. It may be added here that, when Zeus cast down the Palladium, he is said to have done so because Electra was seeking sanctuary at the image from his amorous embraces and, with it, he flung out from above the ruinous goddess Ate, from whom the hill beneath which the cow of Ilus rested is said to have received its name.

housed in a temple erected in honor of the goddess, where it continued inviolate until Ulysses and Diomedes carried it off by stealth during the Trojan War.[29]

When Tros died, Ilus took possession of the divine horses which Zeus had bestowed as recompense for the rape of Ganymedes but, notwithstanding his senior right of succession, he preferred to stay at Ilium and permitted his younger brother Assaracus to assume the government of Dardania. As queen of his new founded city, he brought into his palace a daughter of the Grecian king, Adrastus, who was named Eurydice. In due time, she bore to him a daughter, Themiste, and a son named Laomedon.[30] Although his city was unprotected by fortifications, it remained under the rule of Ilus until his death—whereupon his body was placed in an imposing tomb by his son Laomedon, who succeeded to the government.[31] Meanwhile, Themiste went from Ilium to Dardania and married her cousin Capys, son of Assaracus.

Laomedon took as his wife a daughter of the river-god Scamander who was named Strymo, although some of the mythographers call her Rhoeo, Thoösa, Zeuxippe, or Leucippe. By her, he had a number of children, including a daughter, Hesione, and a son, Podarces. Feeling that his city needed additional protection against possible attack, he conceived the plan of surrounding it with a strong wall. It so happened that, at this time, Zeus discovered the gods Poseidon and Apollo in a conspiracy against his rule and, as punishment, decreed that they should serve for a year as Laomedon's slaves.

In obedience to the supreme will, they presented themselves at Ilium and offered to perform whatever tasks might be given them. Delighted at their proffered help, and not knowing that it had been decreed by Zeus, Laomedon set the two deities to work at building his planned fortifications, and promised to give them an ample reward when their work should be completed.[32]

After the celestial slaves had labored steadily for a full year, the great walls were in place—broken only by strong gates, of which the westernmost was called Scaean and the easternmost Dardanian.[33] His divine servants now asked for the reward which had been promised them, but Laomedon refused to make payment and haughtily bade them leave his city—threatening that if they did not do so he would lop off their ears, would bind their hands and feet, and would sell them as slaves in distant lands. Furious at this treatment, the two gods departed, but Poseidon soon gained revenge by sending a terrible sea monster to attack the country's cattle, crops, and its human inhabitants. The creature's depredations became so severe that Laomedon was forced to consult an oracle about the possible means of deliverance—and learned that the general calamity could be overcome only by the daily delivery of a virgin to the monster's maw.

Having no other choice, Laomedon complied with the oracle's command, and the wholesale devastation ceased; but every day the Ilian air was rent with the lamentations of the relatives of some unfortunate maiden who had been chosen as a poor victim for the cruel sacrifice. At length, the lot fell to Laomedon's own daughter Hesione and, like her predecessors, she was led to the shore of the sea and was chained to await the monster's coming. Here, as related in chapter 14, she was rescued by Heracles, on

---

[29] The Palladium was undisturbed in a war said to have been waged by Ilus to drive Tantalus from neighboring Lydia (or Paphlagonia), after the latter was condemned by the gods for his arrogant impiety. A legend noted by Plutarch relates that once, when the temple of Athena was consumed by fire, Ilus rescued the divine image from the flames and was blinded, because no mortal was permitted to look upon it, but afterward propitiating the goddess, it is said that his sight was restored.

[30] The Iliad does not mention the name of Laomedon's mother, and Apollodorus, followed in the text, gives no hint of the circumstances under which the Asiatic king, Ilus, happened to obtain his bride from Argos in Greece.

[31] According to tradition, the Palladium was destined to prove an invulnerable protection to the land of its location.

[32] Since the walls were later razed by the Greeks, it was related that Aeacus assisted in their erection—thus accounting for a vulnerability not compatible with the concept that their construction was wholly by divine hands. According to a variation of the legend, Apollo did not assist in the construction, but spent his year's bondage in tending Laomedon's flocks and herds.

[33] The excavations of Schliemann, supplemented by those of Wilhelm Dorpfeld, have disclosed a number of other gates in the walls of Troy, whose names are not mentioned by the ancient mythographers.

his return to Mycenae with the girdle of Hippolyte. Before performing the rescue, however, he had bargained with Laomedon that he should receive as a reward two of the divine horses which Tros had been given by Zeus but, after the monster was slain and Hesione was thus saved, the faithless king repudiated his promise and sent the great hero away empty handed. Yet, his perfidy did not go unpunished because, when Heracles had completed his Twelve Labors, he returned to Ilium with an army of Greeks, and shot down Laomedon and all of his sons who were present except Podarces. He was taken as the only male captive, but was ransomed by his sister, Hesione, and thereby gained the name of Priam—by which he was afterward known.[34] Hesione was taken as a prisoner herself and, being given to Telamon, was taken back by him to the island of Salamis, where she became the mother of his son Teucer.[35]

In addition to Hesione, Laomedon left four daughters surviving him, who were named Aethilla, Antigone, Astyoche, and Cilla. Of these, Aethilla is said to have been made captive at the fall of Troy by Protesilaus (Iolaus) and taken by him to Thrace, where she was so taken with the country that she burned up his ship and remained.[36] Antigone boasted that she excelled Hera in the beauty of her hair and, for her presumption, was changed into a stork. Astyoche was married to Telephus, the son of Heracles and Auge who was reared by King Teuthras[37] and, despite his descent from the greatest of the legendary Greeks, her son, Eurypylus, was induced to fight on the side of his mother's kinsmen in the Trojan War. Cilla was married to one of the Trojan elders named Thymoetes, and gave birth to a son Menippus on the same night when Paris was born to Priam and Hecuba. When the seer Aesacus (or the seeress Cassandra) declared that both the

mother and her new-born child should be destroyed in order to avert a great calamity, Priam referred the prediction to Cilla and her son, and they were put to death.[38]

The sons of Laomedon and Strymo, not mentioned before by name, were Clytius, Lampus, Hicetaon, and Tithonus.

While he was still a youth, Tithonus was carried off by Eos, the goddess of the dawn who bore to him two sons named Memnon and Emathion. It is said that the goddess so loved her husband that, at her request, Zeus granted to him immortality, but she did not think to ask that he should be freed from the infirmities of old age and, eventually, he became so feeble that he could stir neither hand nor foot, and his voice changed into a meaningless lisp. When this happened, his body was changed into that of a cricket, which Eos locked up in a chamber and left there to babble forever. Memnon grew up to become king of the Ethiopians,[39] and led an army against the Greek forces in the Trojan War—in this connection he is later mentioned in more detail. Emathion had the misfortune to provoke Heracles, as he was passing through Ethiopia in quest of the golden apples of the Hesperides and, like all the unfortunates who incurred the great man's anger, came to a violent and speedy end. He was survived by Atymnius, a son borne to him by the nymph Pegasis, but he too lost his life when he was slain at Troy by Odysseus. Nor was the family of Tithonus fated to survive, for Atymnius' son Mydon, serving in the great war as charioteer of the Paphlagonian leader Pylaemenes, was slain by Nestor's son Antilochus, who also killed Melanippus, the son of Hicetaon.

Lampus is said to have had several sons, of whom only Dolops is mentioned as being the bravest. But his bravery did not save him at Troy, and he came to death from the spear of Menelaus while he was fighting furiously with the Elean king, Meges.

Clytius is described in the Iliad as one of the

---

[34] Loosely translated—Priam in the Greek may be converted into "that which has been sold."

[35] A more detailed account of Heracles' attack on Laomedon is given in chapter 14.

[36] The story that Protesilaus was the captor of Aethilla is at variance with the conventional legend that he was the first of the Greeks to be slain in the Trojan War.

[37] A different legend relates that Astyoche was a daughter of Priam.

---

[38] According to Virgil, Thymoetes later obtained a doubtful revenge by advising the Trojans to bring the Wooden Horse within their walls.

[39] The country of the Ethiopians was conceived as being in the easternmost part of the earth, where the dawn-goddess had her palace.

113a. Descendants of Zeus and Electra

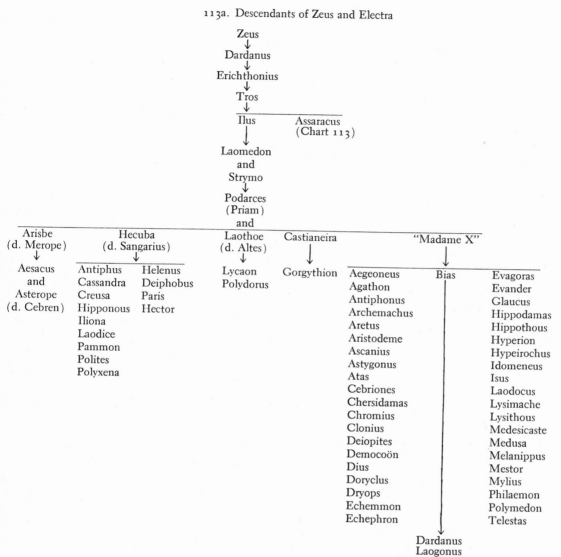

Zeus
↓
Dardanus
↓
Erichthonius
↓
Tros
↓
Ilus — Assaracus (Chart 113)
↓
Laomedon and Strymo
↓
Podarces (Priam) and

Arisbe (d. Merope)	Hecuba (d. Sangarius)		Laothoe (d. Altes)	Castianeira	"Madame X"		
↓	↓		↓	↓	↓		
Aesacus and Asterope (d. Cebren)	Antiphus Cassandra Creusa Hipponous Iliona Laodice Pammon Polites Polyxena	Helenus Deiphobus Paris Hector	Lycaon Polydorus	Gorgythion	Aegeoneus Agathon Antiphonus Archemachus Aretus Aristodeme Ascanius Astygonus Atas Cebriones Chersidamas Chromius Clonius Deiopites Democoön Dius Doryclus Dryops Echemmon Echephron	Bias	Evagoras Evander Glaucus Hippodamas Hippothous Hyperion Hypeirochus Idomeneus Isus Laodocus Lysimache Lysithous Medesicaste Medusa Melanippus Mestor Mylius Philaemon Polymedon Telestas

Dardanus
Laogonus

more respected of the Trojan elders.[40] His daughter, Procleia, was married to the Thracian king, Cycnus, who was one of the many sons of Poseidon. By him, she had two daughters, Hemitheia and Glauce, and a son named Tenes, but she died while still young and was spared from sharing in the tragedies of her family, which have been related in chapter 10. Clytius also had a son named Caletor, who was killed at Troy by Ajax the

Greater, under circumstances narrated later.[41]

This concludes recital of the descendants of Laomedon and Strymo, except for the family of Podarces—better known as Priam—who was king of both Trojans and Dardanians during the ten-year assault of the Greeks which is the subject matter of later chapters.

In addition to his legitimate children, Laomedon had a son named Bucolion, borne to him by the nymph Calybe. Nothing of interest

---

[40] Clytius is named as a Trojan elder in the Iliad, where no reference is made to the attack of Heracles in which legend says that Laomedon was slain with all of his sons except Priam.

[41] It is worth noting briefly the fate of many of the participants at Troy in connection with their respective family charts, even at risk of sometimes inevitable duplication in the later narrative of the war.

113b. Descendants of Zeus and Electra

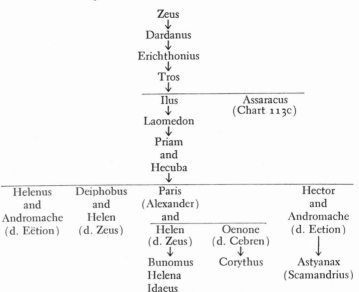

Zeus
↓
Dardanus
↓
Erichthonius
↓
Tros
↓
Ilus   Assaracus
↓   (Chart 113c)
Laomedon
↓
Priam
and
Hecuba
↓

Helenus and Andromache (d. Eëtion)	Deiphobus and Helen (d. Zeus)	Paris (Alexander) and		Hector and Andromache (d. Eetion)
		Helen (d. Zeus) ↓ Bunomus Helena Idaeus	Oenone (d. Cebren) ↓ Corythus	Astyanax (Scamandrius)

is related about Bucolion himself, but he had two sons, Aesepus and Pedasus, by the fountain nymph Abarbarea, who were slain in the Trojan War by Euryalus, the son of Mecisteus—earlier renowned as one of the Epigoni and captor of Thebes.

According to some of the later writers, Laomedon was buried in a tomb which was near the western—Scaean—gate of Troy. At his death, Priam succeeded to the rulership, and took as his first wife, Arisbe, a daughter of the Percotian king, Merops. After she had borne a son named Aesacus to him, he surrendered her to his friend Hyrtacus, by whom she had two sons named Asius and Nisus—destined to gain much renown in defending their country against the attack of the Greeks. By his grandfather Merops, who was a famous seer, Aesacus was taught the art of interpreting dreams. He did not exercise his skill for long however, because his wife Asterope, a daughter of the god of the river Cebren, died while she was still quite young, and he grieved so greatly at her passing that the gods mercifully changed him into a bird.[42]

As his second wife, Priam married Hecuba, a daughter of the god of the river Sangarius. By her, and by three (or more) other women, he became the father of the great number of children shown on the preceding chart, who were either of no mythological importance or will be later noted in connection with the events of the Trojan War.

The preceding chart is inserted here without further comment, because those who are named were, likewise, actors in the Trojan War, or in subsequent events, and will be referred to again. As previously related, the rulership of Dardania was taken over by Assaracus when his brother Ilus elected to remain in his newly founded city of Ilium. His sons, and their descendants whose names are given on the preceding chart, are mentioned in some detail in connection with the Trojan War.[43]

[42] According to Ovid, Aesacus was the son of a daughter of the god of the river Granicus who lived in a mountain retreat and, while pursuing Hesperia, a daughter of the god of the river Cebren, she was stung by a viper and died. Thereupon, Aesacus threw himself into the sea, and was changed by Thetis into an aquatic bird.

[43] There is no express statement of ancient authority that Aesyetes was a son of Assaracus. However: (1) his barrow occupied a prominent place on the field outside the Trojan walls; (2) his son Antenor, as a Trojan elder, is given dignity comparable to that accorded Priam himself; (3) Archelochus and Acamas, his grandsons, were captains of the Dardanians in the war; (4) his grandson Helicaon was married to Priam's daughter, Laodice; (5) his son Alcathous was married to Anchises' daughter Hippodameia; and (6) the Italian mythology claims his son Antenor as founder of their city of Padua. These considerations appear to be manifest indications of the assigned royalty.

113c. Descdenants of Zeus and Electra

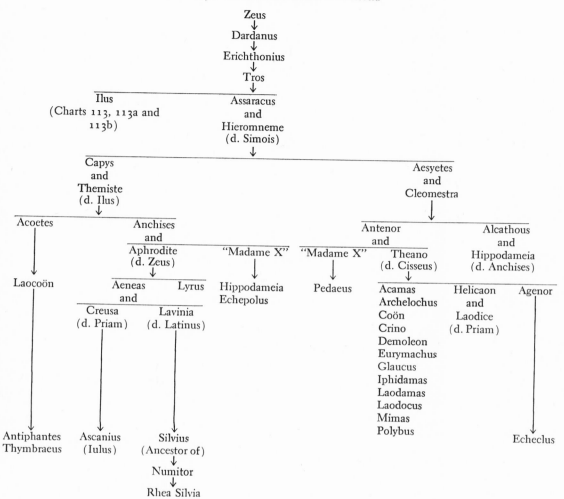

Zeus
↓
Dardanus
↓
Erichthonius
↓
Tros
↓

Ilus
(Charts 113, 113a and 113b)

Assaracus
and
Hieromneme
(d. Simois)
↓

Capys
and
Themiste
(d. Ilus)
↓

Aesyetes
and
Cleomestra
↓

Acoetes

Anchises
and
Aphrodite
(d. Zeus)
↓

"Madame X"
↓

"Madame X"
↓

Antenor
and
Theano
(d. Cisseus)
↓

Alcathous
and
Hippodameia
(d. Anchises)

Laocoön

Aeneas
and
Creusa
(d. Priam)

Lyrus

Lavinia
(d. Latinus)

Hippodameia
Echepolus

Pedaeus

Acamas
Archelochus
Coön
Crino
Demoleon
Eurymachus
Glaucus
Iphidamas
Laodamas
Laodocus
Mimas
Polybus

Helicaon
and
Laodice
(d. Priam)

Agenor

Antiphantes
Thymbraeus

Ascanius
(Iulus)

Silvius
(Ancestor of)
↓
Numitor
↓
Rhea Silvia

Echeclus

21

The Trojan War I

THE COMPLETE story of the Trojan War is not found in any ancient writing, but is pieced together by a succession of narratives, whose accepted order is as follows: (1) "The Cypria," whose authorship is attributed to Stasinus of Cyprus;[1] (2) The Iliad, whose authorship is attributed to Homer of Chios;[2] (3) "The Aethiopis," whose authorship is attributed to Arctinus of Miletus; (4) "The Little Iliad," whose authorship is attributed to Lesches of Pyrrha;[3] (5) "The Sack of Ilium," whose authorship is attributed to Arctinus of Miletus; (6) "The Returns," whose authorship is attributed to Hegias of Troezen; (7) "The Odyssey," also by Homer; and (8) "The Telegonia," whose authorship is attributed to Eugammon of Cyrene.

Beginning, perhaps, with Proclus,[4] these compositions (excluding the Iliad and the Odyssey) were referred to as the Epic Cycle, but they are known only from fragments mentioned by writers who were not the original authors or compilers.[5] In view of the many discrepancies in the stories, coupled with some rather remarkable and (sometimes foolish) dove-tailing, it cannot be doubted that a multitude of later hands assisted in creating the mythological congeries which is our fascinating heritage.

The Cypria

In coherently describing the events which brought on the Trojan War, we must go far beyond the abridgement of the Cypria preserved to us, because it consists of less than a hundred lines. Accordingly, the account which follows is a considerable amplification.

In order to please Hera, the Nereid Thetis avoided union with Zeus[6] whereupon, he became enraged and swore that she should become the wife of a mortal. Through the Centaur Cheiron, the supreme god's decree was conveyed to Peleus, the son of Aeacus, together with instructions as to how he might take the beautiful sea-nymph, who was gifted with the power of changing her shape as she wished. While she was slumbering in a grove near a bay of Thessaly, she was seized by Peleus, who did

---

[1] Anciently, all of the separate narratives were attributed to Homer; but the consensus of modern criticism seems to support the divisions indicated in the text.

[2] In addition to Chios, other cities claimed the honor of having been Homer's birthplace, namely: Smyrna, Colophon, Salamis, Rhodos, Argos, and Athens.

[3] According to a different story, Lesches was a native of Mytilene.

[4] Proclus was one of the tutors of the Roman emperor Marcus Aurelius Antoninus (121–180 A.D.). His abridgement of the "Cycle" has been preserved to us by Photius, who wrote about the middle of the ninth century A.D.

[5] The "Eoiae" and the "Great Eoiae"—two poems ascribed to Hesiod—are sometimes considered as parts of the Epic Cycle, but their disconnected subject matter places them outside the conventional pale.

[6] According to another version of the legend, Zeus discontinued his advances when Themis foretold that the son of Thetis would grow up to become a greater man than his father.

not release his grasp even though she successively changed herself into fire, water, wind, a tree, a tiger, a lion, a serpent, and a cuttle fish. Realizing that the will of Zeus was not to be flouted, she now consented to become the wife of her mortal wooer, and set the date for their wedding celebration.[7]

Meanwhile, old mother Gaea had complained to Zeus that "the countless tribes of men, though wide-dispersed," were unduly oppressing the surface of her deep bosom, and had asked him to do something about it. He consulted his wise aunt Themis, and she advised him to bring about a great war for the purpose of reducing the overpopulation. The supreme god was agreeable to her suggestion, and it was decided that the forthcoming wedding of Peleus and Thetis would offer a perfect time and place for sowing the seed which would grow into the proposed conflict.

Owing to the divinity of Thetis,[8] it was only natural that all of the gods and goddesses should be invited to her nuptials and, owing to the plan of Zeus, it was only natural that all of the invitees should attend. And attend they did—bringing all manner of beautiful and marvelous presents for the bride and others, perhaps more utilitarian, for the groom.[9] As the splendid throng sang and feasted on ambrosia and nectar, a golden apple fell into their midst—an apple whereupon were inscribed the words: "To the fairest." This unexpected gift had been dropped by Eris, the goddess of strife and discord, who (due to the divine design) had been overlooked when the wedding invitations were sent out. And so, a quarrel began, which effectively ended the festivities—for each of the attendant goddesses was certain in her own mind that it was she for whom the golden offering was intended.

Because they were mythologically the most powerful of the squabbling ladies, the beauty contest eventually narrowed down to only three contestants: Hera, Athena, and Aphrodite. The assembled deities were afraid to cast their votes against any member of such a mighty trio, lest the feminine wrath of the losers should result in a cataclysm which would shake both heaven and earth. Accordingly, it was decided to leave the decision to an unsuspecting mortal. By common consent, youthful Paris, who was a son of King Priam of Troy, was selected as sole arbiter, and the three contesting goddesses (each feeling that she would be the certain winner) agreed to accept his judgment.

At the command of Zeus, they were conducted by Hermes to the hill of Callicolone on Mount Ida in Phrygia, where Paris was living in pastoral simplicity with his wife Oenone, a nymph-daughter of the god of the river Cebren.[10] When Hermes stated the purpose of the divine visit, Paris was flattered beyond measure, and readily consented to act. Oenone, however, was stricken with an intuitive apprehension and pleaded with him to reject the proffered judgment role, but Zeus willed otherwise and, when Paris made light of her misgiving, his wife fled in tears down the mountainside.

Hera now proceeded to take the young man aside, and sought to purchase his decision by offering to make him the master of a great empire. Athena followed, with like intent, by offer-

---

[7] Quintus Smyrnaeus relates that, as a reward for her consent to mary Peleus, Zeus promised Thetis that her son should be the most glorious among men.

[8] Although Peleus was considered a mortal, he was himself of divine blood, for his father, Aeacus, was a son of Zeus, and his mother, Endeïs, was a granddaughter of Cronus.

[9] Cheiron gave Peleus a spear with an ashen shaft polished by Athena and a blade fashioned by Hephaestus; Poseidon gave him the immortal horses, Balius and Xanthus; and the gods, jointly, gave him a wondrous suit of armor—also made by the fire-god.

[10] Paris followed Hector, as the second son of Priam and Hecuba. Before he was born Hecuba dreamed that she had given birth to a firebrand whose flames enveloped the whole city. Her dream was interpreted by Aesacus, or Cassandra, to mean that she would bear a son who was fated to bring about the destruction of Troy and—to avoid fulfillment of the prediction—her new-born child was entrusted to a shepherd named Agelaus for exposure on Mount Ida. After the lapse of five days, the shepherd returned to find that the babe had been suckled by a she-bear and, taking it to his home, he raised him as his own son and named him Paris. When the boy grew up, he so distinguished himself as a defender of both flocks and shepherds that he was given the surname of Alexander, meaning protector of men. Later engaging in funeral games at Troy which (unknown to him) were being held in his own honor, he overcame his own brothers in the various contests, and his identity was revealed by his prophetic sister, Cassandra. Life in the city, however, did not appeal to him and, returning to the mountains where he had been reared, he married the nymph Oenone.

ing to give him wisdom. Lastly, Aphrodite turned on all her charm and, as her bribe, offered to make him the husband of the most beautiful woman in the world. Seduced by her promise (and strangely forgetful of his dear Oenone), Paris awarded the golden apple to the irresistible goddess of love, and his heavenly visitors whisked themselves from Ida to their palaces on Mount Olympus.[11]

In due time, Thetis bore to Peleus a son who was first named Ligyron. Wishing to make him immortal, the sea-goddess (unknown to Peleus) placed her babe in the fire by night, in order to destroy the mortal element inherited from its father and, by day, she anointed him with divine ambrosia. But, one night, Peleus happened to enter and, seeing the child lying in the fire, cried out in alarm and snatched him from the purifying flames, which as yet had consumed only an ankle bone.[12] Thus she was prevented from accomplishing her purpose, and departed to rejoin her sister nereids in the depths of the sea—leaving Peleus and her infant son to the makeshifts of mortality. Nor was her deserted husband lacking in ingenuity for, to replace the missing portion of his child's anatomy, he dug up the skeleton of Damysus—the fleetest of all the giants—and, extracting from it the ankle bone, fitted it neatly and applied drugs which caused the new, or rather old, bone to coalesce perfectly with those of his young son's leg.

He now took his remodeled offspring to Mount Pelion in Thessaly, and entrusted his rearing to the centaur Cheiron, who fed his charge on the flesh and marrows of wild beasts, in order to give him strength, courage, and swiftness of foot. It is said that, he was renamed Achilles because he had not put his lips to the breast. This hardy diet proved so efficacious that, at the early age of nine, the boy had attained such skill and muscular development that he was able to best grown men in feats of exercise and arms. Among those with whom he was accustomed to contend were his kinsman Patroclus[13] and Phoenix, the son of Amyntor—both having been given refuge by the kind centaur after they were forced to leave their own homes. Nor did the fact that Achilles was accustomed to exceed them at play cause any rancor or ill-feeling—for, in the turbulent later years, Patroclus and Phoenix were his most devoted companions and trusty guardians.

While Achilles was growing up at the home of Cheiron, a son named Corythus was born to Paris and Oenone, and with him they continued to live at their quiet home on Mount Ida. But, one night, Aphrodite appeared, and bade Paris build ships to sail in quest of the beautiful woman who had been promised to him—revealing that she was Helen, the daughter of Zeus and Leda, who was the wife of King Menelaus of Sparta. The fact that Helen was already married did not seem to bother Paris at all, but Oenone was overwhelmed at her impending desertion and again fled tearfully into her mountain forests. With the help of a Trojan named Phereclus, the ships suggested by Aphrodite were built and, in due course, Paris sailed for Greece with a crew of whom Aeneas, a son of Aphrodite and Anchises, was a leading member. His departure, however, was not made with the complete approval of his family; for Oenone vowed that she would be avenged,[14] and Helenus and Cassandra—his prophetic brother and sister—both foretold that nothing but evil would come of his voyage.

After an uneventful crossing, a landing was made at Laconia in Greece, where the expedition was hospitably entertained by Castor and Pollux (the twin brothers of Helen). Proceeding from the coast, Paris went inland to Sparta and, upon arriving at the palace of Menelaus, received a warm welcome from the unsuspecting king. Helen was soon presented to the visitor, and graciously received his gifts—with an immediate heart flutter which has always

---

[11] According to a different legend, the place on Mount Ida where Paris gave his judgment was the promontory of Gargarus instead of the hill of Callicolone.

[12] A later—and better known—story relates that Thetis tried to make her son immortal by dipping him in the river Styx, and succeeded except as to the ankle (or ankles) by which she held him in the process.

[13] Aegina, daughter of the god of the river Asopus, was the grandmother of Patroclus and the great-grandmother of Achilles.

[14] Oenone was gifted with the power to heal wounds, which she now vowed never to exercise for the benefit of Paris if he should be in need of her assistance.

been understood as the concomitant of love at first sight. And, as ordained by the gods, Paris was heavily stricken with a similar emotion, but he guilefully concealed it until a few days later, when Menelaus foolishly left for the island of Crete to visit his friend King Idomeneus. However, when he left, no time was lost by Paris and Helen because, as soon as they were left alone, their mutual love was declared and consummated and, packing up the most precious and portable treasures of the palace, they set out for Troy.

The return trip was naturally more exciting to Paris. Nor was it made less so when Hera, still smarting from his decision in favor of Aphrodite, sent a storm which drove his ships off their course and carried them to Sidon on the coast of Asia Minor.[15] When the inhabitants of the country showed signs of hostility, Paris grasped the opportunity to exhibit his prowess to Helen and, with the help of his men, proceeded to rout the opposing forces and to sack their city. Laden with Phoenician booty, his ships sailed on to Troy, where he and his beautiful woman were formally and fatefully wedded.

Meanwhile, Castor and Pollux had gone to Messene, and had driven off the cattle of Idas and Lynceus, with the disastrous results which have been narrated in chapter 6—a story, breaking the thread of the Cypria, which is manifestly inserted to explain why the Dioscuri were not participants in the conflict at Troy.

After Paris and Helen had landed, Zeus sent his messenger Iris to Crete to tell Menelaus what had taken place during his absence from Sparta. Thereupon, the thunderstruck king hastened back to Greece and consulted, first, with his brother Agamemnon at Mycenae and then with ancient Nestor at Pylus. His visit to Nestor was rather trying, because the garrulous old man insisted upon telling stories about the "good old days." These included the destruction of Epopeus, the tragic saga of the house of Oed-

ipus, the madness of Heracles, the exploits of Theseus, and other heroic events of earlier times. His discourse, however, was eventually completed and, getting down to the matter at hand, Nestor agreed with Agamemnon that a call should be sent throughout all Hellas, summoning the original suitors of Helen to respect their vows by mustering their forces at Aulis, in Boeotia, as the starting point for a punitive expedition against Paris and his Trojan kinsmen.

Response to the call was enthusiastically made by all who were summoned except Odysseus, who was, nevertheless, brought in after attempting to feign a madness which was detected by Palamedes.[16] And, chief of those who responded, was Achilles, the son of Peleus and Thetis, who, though still young, was acknowledged to be the greatest of all warriors.[17]

The Cyprian fragment preserved by Proclus merely mentions the catalogue of the Greek invaders, but in the second book of the Iliad a complete list is given as follows:

---

[15] In the "Helen" of Euripides, it is related that the beautiful daughter of Zeus was left with King Proteus in Egypt, and only her phantom was taken on to Troy by Paris to become the prize for which the great war was fought.

[16] Odysseus learned about the impending expedition before the Greek messengers came to him on his island home at Ithaca. When they arrived—led by Palamedes the son of Naplius—he pretended to be insensible to their words, but Palamedes, seeing through the pretense, snatched Telemachus (the young son of Odysseus) from his mother's bosom, and drew his sword as though to kill the child. In his anxiety, Odysseus quickly confessed the sham and agreed to heed the call to war. According to another version, he supported his pretense of insanity by yoking an ox and a horse to his plow and sowing salt in the furrows, and while he was busy in this fashion, the envoys arrived. Palamedes, however, realizing the intended deception, laid the infant Telemachus in front of the plow and, admitting his sanity, Odysseus brought his team to a stop.

[17] When the Greeks first gathered at Aulis, their seer Calchas declared that Troy could not be taken without the aid of Achilles. Thetis foresaw that it was fated her son should perish if he went to the war and, disguising him in female garb, sent him to the court of King Lycomedes on the island of Scyrus where, under the name of Pyrrha, he was intermingled with a group of maidens. In the process of intermingling, it may be noted that he had an intrigue with Deidameia, daughter of Lycomedes, who bore to him a son first named Pyrrhus and afterward called Neoptolemus. When Odysseus was sent to apprehend him, the crafty emissary disguised himself as a peddler and was permitted to enter with his baskets, which were overlaid with feminine apparel and also contained arms of war. While the real maidens pounced eagerly on the trifles which appealed to them, Achilles snatched up the weapons and thus revealed his identity.

Peneleos, Leitus, Arcesilaus, Prothoenor, and Clonius, with fifty ships, leading the Boeotians

Ialmenus and Ascalaphus, with thirty ships, leading the Minyans of Orchomenus

Epistrophus and Schedius, with forty ships, leading the Phocians

Ajax the Lesser, with forty ships, leading the Locrians

Elephenor, with forty ships, leading the Abantes

Menestheus, with fifty ships, leading the Athenians

Ajax the Greater, with twelve ships, leading the Salaminians

Diomedes, Sthenelus, and Euryalus, with eighty ships, leading the forces from Argos and Tiryns

Agamemnon, with one hundred ships, leading the Mycenaeans

Menelaus, with sixty ships, leading the Lacedaemonians

Nestor, with ninety ships, leading the Messenians

Agapenor, with sixty ships, leading the Arcadians

Amphimachus, Thalpius, Diores, and Polyxeinus with forty ships, leading the Eleans

Meges, with forty ships, leading the Echinaeans

Odysseus, with twelve ships, leading the Cephallenians

Thoas, with forty ships, leading the Aetolians

Idomeneus and Meriones, with eighty ships, leading the Cretans

Tlepolemus, with nine ships, leading the Rhodians

Nireus, with three ships, leading the Symeans

Antiphus and Pheidippus, with thirty ships, leading the Coans

Achilles, with fifty ships, leading the Myrmidons

Podarces and Iolaus (Protesilaus), with forty ships, leading the Phylaceans

Eumelus, with eleven ships, leading the Pheraeans

Philoctetes and Medon, with seven ships, leading the Thaumacians

Podaleirius and Machaon, with thirty ships, leading the Oechalians

Eurypylus, with forty ships, leading the Ormenians

Polypoëtes and Leonteus, with forty ships, leading the Gyrtonians

Gouneus, with twenty-two ships, leading the Enienes

Prothous, with forty ships, leading the Magnesians

When these great forces had all been assembled at the promontory of Aulis, their leaders offered sacrifices to the gods for the success of their venture. While the ceremonies were taking place, a serpent appeared in their midst and devoured eight young birds from their nest and, lastly, ate up the mother of the brood. The incident was interpreted by the seer Calchas as an omen that the forthcoming war would swallow up nine full years and, although many of the gathered heroes were dismayed at his prediction, Agamemnon (who had been chosen as commander-in-chief) ordered the expedition to put out to sea.[18]

After an unnamed period of sailing, a landing was made on the part of the Mysian shore which was known as Teuthrania and, in the mistaken belief that they had reached the Trojan coast, the Greeks began to ravage the country.[19] At the time, Telephus, the son of Heracles and Auge, had become king of the Mysians and, resisting the pillage of his realm, he assembled his warriors and chased the invaders back to their ships—meanwhile, himself slaying many of them, including Thersander, the son of Theban Polyneices. But, when Achilles rushed upon him, he fled until he was entangled among some vines, where he was overtaken and wounded in the thigh by the spear of his pursuer.[20] Realizing that they had steered the wrong course, the Greeks again put out to sea—only to encounter a storm of such terrific intensity that the fleet was widely scattered and the voyagers were forced to return to their various homelands by different passages.[21]

After the lapse of eight years,[22] the Greek forces again gathered at Aulis, but were still without a pilot to direct the way to Troy. While waiting for the full assembly, Agamemnon took a day off for hunting and, when he shot a stag, he boasted that his marksmanship was even better than that of the archer-goddess Artemis. As disclosed by later events, this boasting proved to be a great indiscretion. However, one diffi-

---

[18] According to legend, Achilles was chosen to be the admiral of the fleet, although he was only fifteen years old at the time of embarkation from Aulis.

[19] As related in chapter 14, Teuthrania took its name from Teuthras, who wedded Auge and reared her son Telephus.

[20] The spear was the same one which Achilles' father Peleus had received as a wedding present from Cheiron.

[21] According to Proclus, it was on this return voyage that Achilles landed at the island of Scyrus and married his youthful love, Deidameia.

[22] In the Homeric story, Helen states—after the fall of Troy—that it had been twenty years since she left Sparta. Since the great war lasted ten years, the author of the Cypria (seeking to harmonize her statement) says that it took two years for the first muster at Aulis and eight years for the second.

culty disappeared rather miraculously. It seems that the wound which Telephus received in Mysia from the spear of Achilles had never healed, notwithstanding the long passage of time. The poor man had continued to suffer such agony from it that finally he had gone to the oracle at Delphi, where he was told that he could be cured only when the one who had wounded him should turn physician. Following this enigmatic answer, he came from Mysia to Aulis, clad in rags, and begged the help of Achilles—promising that if his wound should be healed, he would show the Greeks how to steer their course to Troy. Promptly accepting the proposal, Achilles scraped the rust from the blade of his spear into the festered wound; Telephus was immediately cured; and the Greeks had a pilot!

But now, Artemis' feelings had been quite hurt by Agamemnon's boast,[23] and she sent strong winds to blow from the east which, day after day, prevented the expedition from sailing. When the seer Calchas was consulted, he divined the cause and reported that the wrath of the goddess could be appeased only by the sacrifice of Iphigeneia,[24] the fairest of Agamemnon's daughters. Upon receiving this ghastly advice, the Greek chieftain sent his herald Talthybius and Odysseus to Mycenae, with instructions to direct Clytemnestra, his wife, to send the maiden to the camp to become the bride of Achilles.

Dazzled by the prospect of such a brilliant alliance, the unsuspecting mother entrusted her daughter to the messengers, who brought her back with them to Aulis. There, Agamemnon led her to an altar which had been erected for her consecration and was about to perform the required sacrificial slaughter but, it is related, Artemis relented and, substituting a stag on her altar, wafted the maiden across the seas to Tauris—the peninsula on the north side of the Black Sea (Euxine) known now as the Crimea.[25]

Propitiated by the attempted sacrifice, the goddess directed the adverse winds to subside and, setting sail from Aulis, the expedition made an early anchorage at the island of Tenedos. When the landing was resisted by the natives, Achilles slew their King Tenes, a son of Cycnus and a descendant of Poseidon.[26] Having routed the leaderless opposition, the Greeks feasted and offered a sacrifice to Apollo but, during the performance of the rites, a watersnake emerged from the altar and bit Philoctetes' foot. He was the son of Poeas who was the leader of the Olizonians. Later on the voyage, the sore caused by the bite brought on such a stench that his comrades put the unlucky man ashore on the island of Lemnos, and left him there to be protected only by the famous bow and arrows of Heracles, which he had inherited from his father.[27]

From Lemnos, the Greeks sailed on until they stood off the coast of Troy.[28] Before beaching their ships, they sent Odysseus and Menelaus ashore as emissaries to demand the restoration of Helen and the treasures which she and Paris had taken with them in their departure from the palace of Menelaus. But the Trojans, having met in assembly, refused the demand and even threatened to kill the impertinent envoys. They, however, heeded the counsel of Antenor—one of their elder statesmen—and Odysseus and Menelaus were permitted to return to the Greek fleet, where they reported the rejection of their demand and the insolent treatment which they had received.

The invading forces now moved in, and were met by the warriors of Troy, who threw stones at the ships to resist their landing. But Iolaus, son of Iphiclus and the leader of the Phylaca-

---

[23] Another version of the story relates that the anger of Artemis was incurred when the Greeks omitted to include her among the deities to whom they offered sacrifices for the success of their underaking.

[24] In the Iliad, no mention is made of Iphigeneia, but it is conjectured that the daughter of Agamemnon and Clytemnestra who is there referred to as Iphianassa was the same maiden concerned in the tragedies of Euripides which are styled "Iphigeneia at Aulis" and "Iphigeneia in Tauris."

[25] At Tauris (Taurica), Iphigeneia became the priestess of Artemis, and, according to Proclus, she was made immortal.

[26] According to Apollodorus, Tenes was a grandson of Apollo (who also had a son named Cycnus) and Thetis had forewarned Achilles not to kill him, lest he should later lose his own life at the hands of his victim's divine ancestor.

[27] As related in chapter 14, Heracles gave his bow and arrows to Poeas as a reward for lighting his funeral pyre.

[28] The mythological story takes no account of the geographical fact that the island of Lemnos lies west of Tenedos.

eans, leapt to the shore and killed many of the Trojans until he was himself slain by Hector.[29] And, as a result of his being the first to set foot on the enemy's territory, he was afterward known and honored under the name of Protesilaus.

Following the death of his comrade,[30] Achilles landed with his force of Myrmidons, and drew the first foreign blood in killing Cycnus, a son of Poseidon (or of Apollo), by throwing a stone at his head.[31] When the Trojans saw him fall, they fled back within their city's walls, in a rout which permitted the invaders to slay many of their straggling members. After this preliminary trial of strength, the Greek ships were drawn up on shore by their sterns and placed in positions to afford ready entrance and egress, but a camp was set up farther inland as a base for future besieging operations.

Before Agamemnon's army had set forth from Aulis, they had obtained a supply of corn, wine, and other provisions from the Delian king, Anius, and his three remarkable daughters who could produce such things by merely touching the ground.[32] Their larder, however, now was beginning to be exhausted, and the invaders set about ravaging the fields and the towns near the walled city from which, at first, the Trojans did not dare to venture. In the course of their pillaging, Achilles waylaid and slaughtered young Troilus, who was reputed to be a son of Apollo and Priam's wife, Hecuba.[33] He also killed Mestor, a son of Priam, captured another son of his named Lycaon,[34] slew Mynes and Epistrophus (sons of Evenus), and drove off the cattle of Aeneas, the son borne to Dardanian Anchises by Aphrodite. But a more important event occurred in connection with the sack of the Mysian city of Thebes because, from its spoils Achilles received, among his share, a beautiful woman named Briseis, and acquired a fondness for her that almost changed the course of the great war.[35]

Meanwhile, Odysseus revenged himself on Palamedes (who had detected the feigned madness by which the Ithacan prince had sought to evade service in the war) by drowning him, as he was peacefully fishing—a crime in which he was assisted by his friend Diomedes.[36] When Nauplius, the father of Palamedes, learned of his son's death he sailed to Troy from his kingdom on the island of Euboea and demanded satisfaction, but his demand was not met and he returned home, vowing that retribution would eventually overtake the entire Greek army.[37]

The "Cypria" here ends with a catalogue of the defending forces, which had been mustered during the period covered by the events previously related. The Cyprian list has not been preserved to us but, as given in the Iliad, the Trojans and their leaders, will be referred to in the following chapter.

---

[29] The tragic reunion of Iolaus (Protesilaus) with his wife, Laodameia, has been related in chapter 6.

[30] Achilles seems to have been as smart as he was strong because, according to Apollodorus, Thetis had told him that the first Greek to land at Troy would be the first to die.

[31] The accounts of the mythographers are quite consistent in their confusion of Cycnus, the son of Apollo, with Cycnus, the son of Poseidon and vice versa. According to Ovid, the Cycnus who opposed the Greek landing was said to be invulnerable. Hence, neither the spear nor the sword of Achilles could bring about his death; and the Greek champion throttled him with the thongs of his own helmet—whereupon, the body of the dead man was changed into that of a swan.

[32] The powers of food production given to the daughters of Anius are related in chapter 12, under Rhoeo as a daughter of Apollo.

[33] There was a prophecy that Troy could not be taken if Troilus should live to the age of twenty, and this is given as the excuse why Achilles slew the lad in cold blood.

[34] After capturing Lycaon, Achilles sold him into slavery on the island of Lemnos, but he was ransomed and, returning to Troy, again met his captor—this time on the field of battle—and was slain by him.

[35] In capturing Briseis, Achilles first had to slay her husband, and in the same foray he took from the Theban king, Eetion, the horse Pedasus that the hero teamed to his battle chariot with the immortal steeds, Balius and Xanthus. They had been given to his father Peleus as a wedding present from Poseidon.

[36] Apollodorus relates that Odysseus, having taken a Phrygian prisoner, compelled him to write a letter of treasonable import, ostensibly sent by Priam to Palamedes, and having buried gold in the latter's quarters, dropped the letter in the Greek camp. There, it was read by Agamemnon, who found the concealed gold and delivered up Palamedes to the army to be stoned as a traitor.

[37] Nauplius sailed back down the western coast and induced a number of the wives of the Greeks to become unfaithful to their absent husbands. Later, he lighted fires on the Euboean promontory of Caphareus which attracted some of the returning warriors to their destruction.

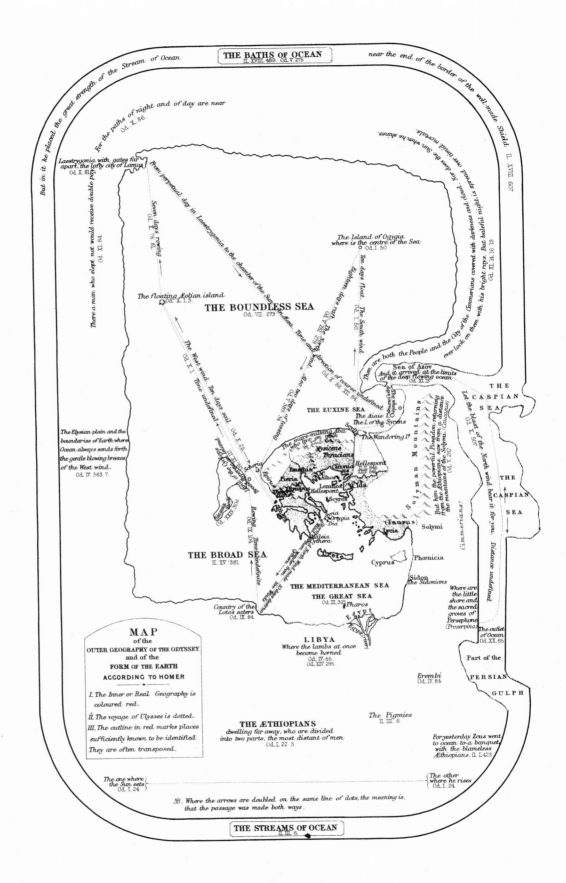

THE BATHS OF OCEAN
Il. XVIII. 489. Od. V. 275.

near the end of the border of the well-made Shield. Il. XVIII. 607

But in it he placed the great strength of the Stream of Ocean

For the paths of night and of day are near Od. X. 86.

Nor does the Sun, when he arises, ever look on them with his bright rays. But bright night is spread over these unhappy mortals.

There are both the People and the City of the Cimmerians covered with darkness and cloud. Od. XI. 14. 16. 19

Laestrygonia with gates far apart, the lofty city of Lamos Od. X. 81.

There a man who slept not would receive double pay Od. XI. 84.

From perpetual day in Laestrygonia to the chamber of the Sun join Aiaie

Seven days rowing Od. X. 78. 81.

The Island of Ogygia where is the centre of the Sea Od. I. 50

Ten days float. The South wind. Od. I. 80

THE BOUNDLESS SEA
Od. VII. 273.

The floating Æolian island Od. X. 1. 3.

The West wind. Ten days sail. Od. X. 1. Time undefined.

The Elysian plain and the boundaries of Earth where Ocean always sends forth the gentle blowing breezes of the West wind. Od. IV. 563. 7.

Sea of Azov And it arrived at the limits of the deep flowing ocean Od. XI. 13

THE CASPIAN SEA

Let the blast of the North wind bear it for you. Od. X. 507.

THE CASPIAN SEA

THE EUXINE SEA
The Aiaie I.O
The I. of the Syrens

Solyman Mountains

The Wandering I.

Mysicene
Thracians
Cicones
Hellespont Il. II. 845
Il. II. 848

Emathia
Pieria
Olympus
Lemnos
Scyros
Hellespont
Ida

Scheria

Syria
Ortygia
Dia

(Taurus) Lycia

Solymi

Maleia
Cythera

Cyprus
Phœnicia

THE BROAD SEA
Il. XV. 381.

But him the powerful Poseidon, returning from the Ethiopians, saw from a distance from the mountains of the Solymi. Od. V. 282.

(Cimmerians?)

Sidon
The Sidonians

Where are the little shore and the sacred groves of Persephone (Proserpina) Od. XX. 65

The outlet of Ocean Od. XX. 65

THE MEDITERRANEAN SEA
THE GREAT SEA
Od. III. 321

Country of the Lotos eaters Od. IX. 84.

Pharos

Egypt
(Egyptians)

LIBYA
Where the lambs at once become horned Od. IV. 85. Od. XIV. 295.

Erembi Od. IV. 84.

Part of the PERSIAN GULPH

MAP
of the
OUTER GEOGRAPHY OF THE ODYSSEY
and of the
FORM OF THE EARTH
ACCORDING TO HOMER
·
I. The Inner or Real Geography is coloured red.
II. The voyage of Ulysses is dotted.
III. The outline in red marks places sufficiently known to be identified
They are often transposed.

THE ÆTHIOPIANS
dwelling far away, who are divided into two parts, the most distant of men Od. I. 22. 3.

The Pigmies Il. III. 6.

For yesterday Zeus went to ocean to a banquet with the blameless Æthiopians. Il. I. 423.

The one where the Sun sets Od. I. 24

The other where he rises Od. I. 24

N.B. Where the arrows are doubled on the same line of dots, the meaning is that the passage was made both ways.

THE STREAMS OF OCEAN
Il. III. 6.

22

The Trojan War II

The Relationships of the Forces Involved
The Greeks

NOWHERE IN THE Homeric poems are the Greeks referred to by that name.[1] Instead, they are variously designated—without apparent distinction—as the Danaans, the Argives, or the Achaeans. These "three great appellatives," as Gladstone calls them, are said to have been derived, respectively, from Danaus, Argus, and Achaeus.[2]

Although it is, to a great degree, repetitive of much which is dealt with in preceding chapters, it seems appropriate to attempt at this point a correlation of the relationships of those who fought in the Trojan War, in order to bring attention to their common ties of blood and legend. For convenience, the discussion will follow the order given in the catalogue of the Iliad.

The Boeotians are described as coming from Hyria, Aulis, Schoenus, Scolus, Eteonus, Thespeia, Graea, Mycalessus, Harma, Eilesium, Ery-thrae, Eleon, Hyle, Peteon, Ocalea, Medeon, Copae, Euthresis, Thisbe, Coroneia, Haliartus, Plataea, Glisas, Thebes, Onchestus, Arne, Mideia, Nisa, and Anthedon. They were led to Troy in fifty ships by Peneleos, Leitus, Arcesilaus, Prothoënor, and Clonius.

The capital city of the localities named in the Iliad was Thebes, and the legends of its origin and subsequent history were the common property of all Greece. At the outset, we must turn to Argos (Argolis) in the Peloponnesus, where Io—a daughter of the river-god Inachus —became with child by Zeus, and was driven from her homeland by jealous Hera's gadfly. Fleeing to Egypt, she gave birth in that hot country to her dark son Epaphus, whose daughter, Libya, bore to Poseidon three sons named Agenor, Belus, and Lelex.

When Zeus, in the form of a bull, carried off Agenor's daughter, Europa, the bereft father sent his son Cadmus in search of her and, after much wandering, it was he who founded Thebes on the mainland of Greece in the district known as Boeotia. From him, the city's rulership extended successively through his lineal descendants—Polydorus, Labdacus, Laius, Oedipus, Eteocles and Polyneices, and Polyneices' son, Thersander. But there was an interregnum during the minority of Laius, when the government was taken over for a short period by Amphion and Zethus. Another occurred when Creon ruled, after the deaths of Eteocles and Polyneices, while Thersander was too young to rule.

---

[1] According to a later story, the Greeks and their country both took their names from Graecus, a son of Zeus and Pandora; and, similarly with Sicily and the southerly part of Italy, which were anciently known as Magna Graecia.

[2] In his book *Juventus Mundi*, Gladstone discusses the "three great appellatives" at length, and concludes that Homer used them as interchangeable and synonomous. The author proceeds to point out distinctions between the three titles, in a scholarly argument—not here repeated, because it is beyond the scope of this compilation.

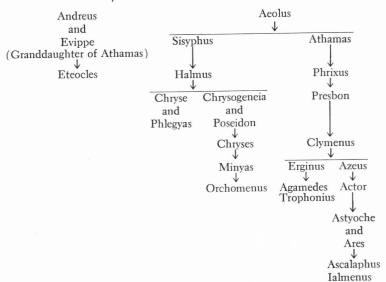

114. Successions of Andreus and Aeolus

The multiple curses placed by the gods on the line of Cadmus persisted and the avenging Furies forced his descendants to flee their city. Thereupon, Boeotus—a son of Poseidon and the Aeolid Arne—moved in from Thessaly and, taking over the country, named it Boeotia after himself.[3] And, the five leaders named in the Iliad were his lineal descendants.

The Minyans are described as coming from Aspledon and Orchomenus, which were two of the more prominent cities of Boeotia. They were led, in thirty ships, by Ascalaphus and Ialmenus, the sons of Ares and Astyoche, the daughter of Actor.

The first ruler of the district, whose capital city was Orchomenus, was Andreus, a son of the Thessalian river-god Peneius. He assigned part of his realm to the Aeolid Athamas, who adopted two of the grandsons of his brother, Sisyphus, and they gave their names to the Boeotian towns of Haliartus and Coroneia. In the remaining part of his kingdom, Andreus was succeeded by his son Eteocles, who sent out colonists to found the territory in Asia Minor later known as Aeolia, and was recognized as a powerful monarch of the "Achaeans" by the

Hittite emperor, Mursil II (Murshilish), reigning at Khatti about 1340 B.C. When Eteocles died childless, his crown was given to Halmus, a son of the Aeolid Sisyphus who had earlier come to Orchomenus, either from Thessaly or from Corinth. At his death, Halmus was succeeded by Phlegyas, the son of Ares who had married his daughter Chryse.[4] He named the country Phlegyantis after himself, but he ruled with such cruelty that he was driven from the throne and fled into the adjacent territory which was later known as Phocis. Upon this happening, the government was assumed by Chryses, a son borne to Poseidon by Chrysogeneia—a second daughter of Halmus.

Chryses was followed, successively, by his own son Minyas, from whom the inhabitants were thereafter called Minyans, and by his grandson Orchomenus, who gave his name to the capital city. When Orchomenus died without issue, the entire country became ruled by Clymenus, the great-grandson of Athamas, who was already ruling in that part which was his direct inheritance. Clymenus was slain at Onchestus by a stone, which was thrown by a charioteer of the Theban noble Menoeceus, and was

---

[3] As related in chapter 9, a different legend related that the country took its name from the cow which Cadmus followed prior to the founding of Thebes.

[4] A different version of the legend relates that Chryse was the mother of Phlegyas—borne by her to Ares.

succeeded by his eldest son Erginus, who avenged his father's death by conquering Thebes and forcing its citizens to pay him an annual tribute—continued until Heracles came upon the mythological scene and killed him in battle, under the circumstances narrated in chapter 14.

Since Agamedes and Trophonius—the sons of Erginus—predeceased their father (as related in chapter 6), the rulership of the Minyans descended to Ascalaphus and Ialmenus, the sons of Ares and Astyoche—a niece of Erginus; and they became the leaders of their countrymen in the Trojan War.

The rather complicated succession, just related, is shown by the grouped family charts: 114, 115, and 116.

The Phocians are described as coming from Cyparissus, Pytho (Delphi), Crisa, Daulis, Panopeus, Anemoreia, Hyampolis, and Lilaea (by the springs of the river Cephisus). They were led in forty ships by Schedius and Epistrophus.

The first ruler of the country, chiefly noted as the location of Apollo's oracular shrine at Delphi, was the Aeolid Deion. He was followed in the government by his son Phylacus who, however, migrated to his ancestral Thessaly and founded the town of Phylace. Upon his departure, the kingdom was taken over by his kinsman Phocus, from whom the land is reputed to have taken its name.[5] When Phocus died without leaving children, his younger brother Naubolus succeeded him in the government and was followed, in turn by his son, Iphitus, and his grandsons, Schedius and Epistrophus. The related succession is shown by the following chart:

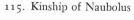

115. Kinship of Naubolus

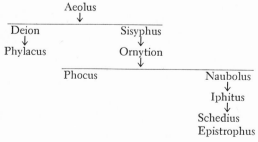

The Locrians are described as coming from Cynus, Opus, Calliarus, Bessa, Scarphe, Augeiae, Tarphe, and Thronium (about the streams of Boagrius). They were led in forty ships by the son of Oileus known as Ajax the Lesser. The following charts may be of assistance in explaining the Locrian succession.[6]

116. The Locrian Succession

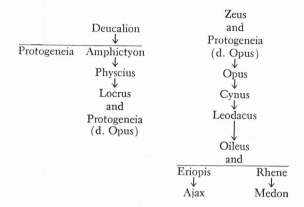

The country was originally ruled by Deucalion, after his survival in the great flood and its inhabitants[7] were said to have been the descendants of the men and women who sprang from the stones which he and his wife, Pyrrha, cast over their shoulders.

Locrus, the great-grandson of Deucalion, gave his name to the land. When it appeared that he was destined to die without an heir, Zeus gave Protogeneia to him as his wife. She was the daughter of Opus who was already with child by the god himself. Her son Opus—named for his maternal grandfather—succeeded to the kingdom upon the death of Locrus and it was his lineal descendant, Ajax, who led the Locrian warriors in war.

The Abantes are described as coming from the towns on the island of Euboea which were

---

[5] Because Phocus, the son of Aeacus, visited the country, he was sometimes credited as its eponym.

[6] Homer mentions only the eastern, or Opuntian, Locrians. The western, or Ozolian, inhabitants were said to have been their kinsmen, but they claimed their descent from Protogeneia, a daughter of Deucalion, who was also the reputed ancestress of the Aetolians.

[7] Although some later writers relate that the Locrians were descended from Lelex—an Egyptian son of Poseidon and Libya who came to be intermingled with the legends of Laconia—it should be noted that, in the Iliad, the Leleges are described as allies of the Trojans.

known as Chalcis, Eretria, Histaea, Cerinthus, Dios, Carystus, and Styra. They were led in forty ships by Elephenor.

The island was first colonized by Attic inhabitants, who crossed over from the mainland of Greece with their king, Cecrops—the second of that name.[8] And, it was from him that Elephenor gained his right as ruler and as leader of his people in the Trojan War. As suggested by the following chart, the designation of the islanders as "Abantes" was taken from Abas, an intermediate king in the line of succession:

117. Kinship of Abas

Cecrops
↓
Pandion II
↓
Abas
↓
Chalcodon
↓
Elephenor

The Athenians are described as coming from the "well-built citadel" of Athens. They were led by Menestheus in fifty ships.

As previously mentioned, some scholars believe that the Athenians were either unknown to Homer or were a relatively unimportant people at the time of the Trojan War, and the slight references to them in the Iliad and the Odyssey were later interpolations. In support of this view, it may be noted that Menestheus appears to be of a generation too early to have participated in the heroic undertaking with his grand-nephew Elephenor, who led the Abantes from Euboea. The apparent paradox was recognized by some of the later mythographers and,

118. Kinship of the Athenians

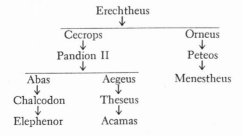

instead of Menestheus, they named Acamas, a son of Theseus, as the principal Athenian engaged in the conflict.

The Salaminians were led to Troy in twelve ships from the island of Salamis by Ajax, son of Telamon. As related in chapter 19, Telamon and his brother, Peleus, were born on the island of Aegina, from where they were expelled for killing their half brother Phocus. Peleus went to Phthia in Thessaly, but Telamon went to the nearby island of Salamis and, marrying the king's daughter (Glauce), succeeded to the government when he died. It was his son, Ajax—by a second wife—who led the Salaminians at Troy, and his second son Teucer, by a third wife, was also a member of the expedition. He gained renown as the best archer among all the invading forces.

119. Kinship of the Salaminians

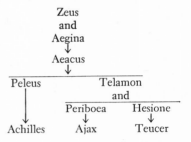

The Argives are described as coming from Argos, Tiryns, Hermione, Asine, Troezen, Eionae, Epidaurus, Aegina, and Mases. They were led in eighty ships by Diomedes, Sthenelus, and Euryalus.

The earliest legends relate that the first ruler of the country, afterward known as Argos (or Argolis), was the god of its great river Inachus. Indeed, it is said that his youngest son, Aegialeus, founded the city of Mecone (later Sicyon) before ancient Uranus made his appearance in Greece, and it was here that Prometheus, incurred the wrath of Zeus which brought on the great flood of Deucalion. Inachus was succeeded by his eldest son, Phoroneus; Apis, the elder son of Phoroneus followed in the rulership, which he extended to include all of the Pelaponnessus. His younger brother, Car, went into the northern mainland, and founded the city afterward known as Megara. During these activities,

---

[8] A different legend relates that Euboea was settled by a Thracian people who came down from the north.

Niobe—sister of Apis and Car—bore to Zeus her two sons, Argus and Pelasgus. When Apis was assassinated and left no children, Argus became king. For him, the city of his birth was thereafter known as Argos, and the adjacent country was called both Argos and Argolis. Argus was followed on the throne—now called Argive—by his lineal descendants, Phorbas, Triopas, Agenor, Crotopus, Sthenalas, and Gelanor.

At this point, we must revert to Inachus and note his daughter Io, who was driven by Hera's gadfly to Egypt, where she gave birth to her dark son Epaphus whose father was Zeus. He grew up to have a daughter Libya, who bore Agenor, Lelex, and Belus to the sea-god Poseidon. Subsequently, and still in Egypt, the wife of Belus presented him with the twin sons, Aegyptus and Danaus, respectively, who became fathers of the fifty sons and daughters named in chapter 9. In fear of his brother and of his fifty nephews, Danaus built the first recorded sailing vessel and, accompanied by his fifty daughters, sailed to Argos, where Gelanor is said to have surrendered the throne to him without contest.

Danaus now gave to the inhabitants the name of Danaans (Danoi) which, by the time of Homer, was extended to include all of the Greeks.

Soon after, Aegyptus and his fifty sons followed from Egypt and, in a mass ceremony, became the husbands of Danaus' daughters but, by a concerted plan, all of them except Lynceus were murdered by their brides on their wedding night. Since Danaus had only daughters, Lynceus succeeded to the kingdom when his father-in-law died.

Lynceus was followed in order by his son Abas and by his grandsons Acrisius and Proëtus, who shared the rule equally after settling an enmity which had begun while they were still in their mother's womb. Pursuant to their final agreement, Acrisius governed at Argos and Proëtus ruled his share of the country from Tiryns.

During the reign of Proëtus, his daughters were stricken with madness and were cured by the seer Melampus, who had previously stipulated that he and his brother, Bias, should each receive a third part of the realm if his efforts should be successful. The legends of the northern mainland thereby became integral with those of Argos, for the new rulers were descendants of the early Thessalian king, Aeolus.[9]

The portion of the domain taken by Melampus was abandoned, in favor of his kinsman Adrastus, by Melampus' great-grandson Polyidus, who migrated to Megara in Attica. The country, however, continued under the rulership of those in the three lines of descent from Proëtus, Acrisius, and Bias—thus indicated:

120. Lines of Proëtus, Acrisius, and Bias

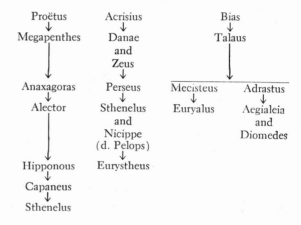

The line of Eurystheus (as related in chapter 14) was extinguished when he and all of his sons were killed in battle by the Heracleidae. When Perseus succeeded his grandfather Acrisius, he exchanged the sovereignty of Argos for that of Tiryns, which was then held by Megapenthes, the son of Proëtus—not wishing to govern the land formerly ruled by one whose death he had caused. It was owing to this exchange that his descendant Heracles considered Tiryns as his ancestral home, but the great man died before the Trojan War was fought, and the Argives were led at Troy by the warriors previously mentioned.

---

[9] As already noted, the leaders of the Boeotians were descended from the Aeolid Arne; those of the Orchomenians (Minyans) were descended from the Aeolid Athamas; those of the Phocians were descended from the Aeolid Sisyphus; the Locrians were descended from Amphictyon, who was an uncle of Aeolus; and the Aetolians were descended from Protogeneia, who was an aunt of Aeolus.

The Mycenaeans are described as coming from Mycenae, Corinth, Cleonae, Orneiae, Araethyrea, Sicyon, Hyperesia, Gonoessa, Pellene, Aegium, Helice, and throughout Aegialeia (the ancient name for the northern part of the Pelopponesus). They were led in a hundred ships by Agamemnon.

The capital city of the district, Mycenae, is said to have been founded by Perseus after he became king of Tiryns.[10] According to legend, its walls were built by the Cyclopes. Its sovereignty continued from Perseus through his son Sthenelus,[11] and into the hands of his grandson Eurystheus, but the latter was slain in battle by Hyllus, the son of Heracles, and his throne was assumed by Atreus, son of Pelops—whose sister Nicippe was the mother of Eurystheus. Atreus was followed by his grandson Agamemnon—the Greek commander-in-chief at Troy—whom he adopted in infancy and reared as his own child. It may be of interest to note that Agamemnon (a descendant of Lydian Tantalus) was accompanied to the war by Sthenelus (a descendant of Egyptian Epaphus), by Euryalus (a descendant of Thessalian Aeolus), and Diomedes (a descendant of the founder of Aetolia), and they all now ruled in the country of Argos, or Argolis, and thus were called Argives.

The Lacedaemonians are described as coming from Pharis, Sparta, Messe, Bryseiae, Augeiae, Amyclae, Helus, Laas, and Oetylus. They were led in sixty ships by Agamemnon's brother Menelaus.

The capital city of Lacedaemonia (called also Laconia) was Sparta, whose name was taken from the wife of Lacedaemon—the eponymous ruler in the intermediate line of succession shown on chart 121. Prior to him, the original ruler of the land is said to have been Lelex, a brother of Agenor and uncle of the Theban founder Cadmus.[12] Lelex was succeeded in order by his son Myles and by his grandson Eurotas, the latter having given his name to the

principal river of the country.[13] From his daughter Sparta and her husband, Lacedaemon, the throne was successively occupied by Amyclas, Cynortes, Perieres, and Oebalus.

121. The Succession of Lacedaemon

When Oebalus died, he left the two sons, Icarius and Tyndareus, and also a third son named Hippocoön, borne to him by the nymph Bateia, who drove his half brothers from the country. After, however, the usurper was later slain by Heracles, Tyndareus returned and assumed the throne. When his wife, Leda, bore Helen to Zeus, the child was accepted as his own by the Spartan king and, after she married Menelaus, the aged ruler gave over the kingdom to his son-in-law.[14]

The Messenians are described as coming from Pylus,[15] Arene, Thryum, the ford of Alpheius, Aepy, Cyparisseis, Amphigeneia, Pteleos, Helus,

---

[10] Schliemann measured the distance from Argos to Mycenae and found it to be only 5.8 miles.

[11] According to Apollodorus, Sthenelus also seized the throne at Tiryns, but he was later expelled by Heracles.

[12] A different legend relates that Lelex was an autochthon.

---

[13] Another river—the Tanaus—divided Laconia and Argolis.

[14] Euripides represents Tyndareus as still living (at least twenty years later) after Orestes slew Aegisthus and Clytemnestra.

[15] The Messenians are not called by name in the Iliad, and this omission permitted the inhabitants of Pylus in Elis to claim that it was their city which was named by the poet.

and Dorium, where the bard Thamyris was beaten by the Muses in a musical contest. They were led in ninety ships by Nestor.

The first rulers of the country were Polycaon, a younger son of Lelex, and his wife, Messene—a descendant of Argus who gave her name to the kingdom. According to Pausanias, the descendants of Polycaon ruled through five generations, but the line died out and the Aeolid Perieres was summoned to take over the throne.

Perieres was followed by his sons, Aphareus and Leucippus—the former of whom received into his palace his cousin, Neleus, when he was driven from Thessalian Iolchus by Pelias. The exiled man was given the rulership of the maritime part of the country and founded the seat of his government at Pylus. Leucippus died, leaving only daughters and, when Idas and Lynceus, the sons of Aphareus, were slain in their fight with the Dioscuri the entire kingdom passed to Nestor, the son of Neleus.

Thus a Laconian, of Egyptian descent, and married to an Argive woman was succeeded in the government of Messenia by a line of rulers descended from the first king of Thessaly.

The Arcadians came from the mountain of Cyllene, from Pheneus, Orchomenus, Rhipe, Stratia, Enispe, Tegea, Mantineia, Stymphalus, and Parrhasia. They were led in sixty ships by Agapenor. As shown by the adjoining chart, Agapenor's line of descent traces back doubly to Zeus—first as the father of Pelasgus and second, as the father of Arcas, from whom the country took its name.

In addition to the close tie with Argos—through Argus, the brother of Pelasgus—it should be remembered that Agapenor's father, Ancaeus, was one of the Argonauts and, as such, was associated with other heroes who came from Thrace, Macedonia, Thessaly, Attica, Euboea, Aegina, Messenia, Boeotia, Laconia, Elis, Phocis, and other localities. Similarly, he was among those who engaged in the hunt for the Calydonian boar and, there too, his comrades were gathered from various parts of Hellas.

In these, almost national, undertakings which preceded the war with Troy, opportunity was given (and inevitably taken) to exchange

122. Line of Agapenor

Zeus
and
Niobe
(d. Phoroneus)
↓
Pelasgus
↓
Lycaon
↓
Callisto
and
Zeus
↓
Arcas
↓
Apheidas
↓
Aleus
↓
Lycurgus
↓
Ancaeus
↓
Agapenor

boasts of local and family prowess so that, in no great period of time, the myths of each section became blended into a connected series of legends, which became the common property of all Greeks.

The Eleans[16] are described as coming from Buprasium, Elis, and "all that part thereof that Hyrmine and Myrsinus on the seaboard and the rock of Olen and Alesium enclose between them." They were led by Amphimachus, Thalpius, Diores, and Polyxeinus in forty ships.

According to Pausanias, the first to rule the country which was later known as Elis was Aethlius, the son of Zeus and Protogeneia, the daughter of Deucalion. He was followed in the government by his beautiful son, Endymion—the beloved of the Moon-goddess Selene—who settled the claims of his own sons to the succession by having them run a footrace at Olympia.

Winning the contest, Epeius took over the throne and gave his name to the inhabitants but, during his reign, Pelops came into the country and assumed the overlordship at Pisa. The encroachments of the newcomer upon his dominions caused Epeius to summon the assistance of Phorbas, a prince of the Lapiths, to

---

[16] The Eleans were earlier called Epeians from Epeius, son of Endymion.

whom he gave his daughter, Hyrmina, in marriage.[17]

123. Kinship of Epeius

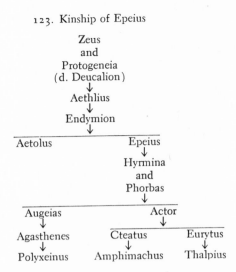

When he died, Epeius was temporarily succeeded by his brother Aetolus who—under circumstances related in chapter 18—later crossed over to the northern mainland, and Phorbas came to the throne by virtue of his alliance with the deceased king's daughter. He, and his descendants (shown on the adjoining chart) continued to rule until the Trojan War, and his great-grandsons were three of the four leaders of their country men at Troy. The fourth leader, Diores, was the son of a Thessalian named Amarynceus whom Augeias had called in to assist in defending his kingdom against the attack of Heracles, and also to whom a portion of the rulership had been given for his services.

The Echenaeans are described as coming from Dulichium and the Echinades, a group of small islands lying off the coast of Acarnania. They were led in forty ships by Meges, the son of Phyleus.

Phyleus was the son of Augeias who had earlier been driven from Elis when he supported the claim of Heracles that the hero was entitled to the promised payment for his services in cleaning out his father's filthy stables.

The Cephallenians are described as coming from Ithaca, Neritum, Crocyleia, Aegilips, Za-

cynthus, Samos, and the mainland shores adjacent to those islands.[18] They were led in twelve ships by Odysseus. Although Odysseus, because of his cunning, was often referred to as a son of the Aeolid Sisyphus, his Homeric genealogy follows that which is shown by the adjoining chart.

124. Genealogy of Odysseus

Zeus
and
Euryodia
↓
Arceisius
↓
Laertes
↓
Odysseus

It appears surprising that one of the greatest of the heroes in the Trojan War, and in those adventures which later followed, was represented as the leader of such a comparatively small group of retainers,[19] but it is conjectured that the poet minimized their numbers to accentuate the individual worth and exploits of their chieftain.

The Aetolians are described as coming from Pleuron, Olenus, Pylene, Chalcis, and Calydon. They were led in forty ships by Thoas. It will be seen from observation of the adjoining chart that Zeus and Protogeneia, daughter of Deucalion, were the common ancestors of both the Aetolians and the Eleans, who traced their descent through Epeius.

According to Apollodorus, Aethlius was originally king only in Elis, and neither he nor his descendants ruled in the northern mainland until his grandson, Aetolus, crossed over the gulf of Patras and conquered the land to which he gave his name. A statement of Pausanias, however, that Elis was colonized by settlers

---

[17] A different story relates that the Elean (or Epeian) king who called in Phorbas was name Alector.

[18] The island of Dulichium, whose inhabitants were led by Meges, is sometimes said to have been considered within the group governed by Odysseus.

[19] According to Thucydides, the ships of the Boeotians were the largest of the Greek fleet and carried one hundred and twenty men each; while those led by Philoctetes (from Magnesian Thessaly) carried only fifty warriors. By assuming an average of eighty-five men to a ship, it has been estimated that the total of the Greek forces numbered approximately one hundred and two thousand.

125. Ancestors of the Aetolians

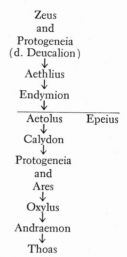

Zeus
and
Protogeneia
(d. Deucalion)
↓
Aethlius
↓
Endymion
↓
_____
Aetolus   Epeius
↓
Calydon
↓
Protogeneia
and
Ares
↓
Oxylus
↓
Andraemon
↓
Thoas

from Aetolia, seems to be more logical when we consider that Deucalion—and, ergo, his daughter Protogeneia—is generally conceded by the mythographers (including Apollodorus) to have been identified with the country around Mount Parnassus, where they found refuge from the great flood.

The Cretans are described as coming from Cnossus (Gnossus), Gortys, Miletus, Lycastus, Phaestus, and Rhytium. They were in eighty ships led by Idomeneus and Meriones.

126. Ancestors of the Cretans

Zeus
and
Europa
↓
Minos
↓
Deucalion
↓
_____
Idomeneus   Molus
↓
Meriones

Chart 126 shows the line of descent as recognized by Homer and Hesiod. Another tradition relates that Minos, the son of Zeus, was the grandfather of another of his name, who was Deucalion's father.

The Rhodians are said to have come from Lindos, Ialysus, and Cameirus. They were led in nine ships by Tlepolemus, a son of Heracles and Astyoche. She was the daughter of the Thesprotian king, Phylas. The presence of

Tlepolemus on the island of Rhodes is accounted for by the fact that he fled there from the Peloponnesus after inadvertently killing his kinsman Licymnius—a half brother of his grandmother Alcmena.

The Symeans came from Syme, an island off the coast of Caria. They were led in three ships by Nireus. Nireus was the son of King Charops and his wife, Aglaea, to neither of whom was assigned a divine pedigree but, partially atoning for the deficiency, legend related their son was the "comeliest man" of all the Greeks, save only Achilles.

The Coans are described as coming from Nisyrus, Crapathus, Casus, Cos, and the Calydnian islands, all lying off the Carian coast. They were led in thirty ships by Pheidippus and Antiphus, who were grandsons of Heracles (see the adjoining chart).

127. Ancestors of the Coans

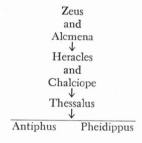

Zeus
and
Alcmena
↓
Heracles
and
Chalciope
↓
Thessalus
↓
_____
Antiphus   Pheidippus

Their appearance as leaders of the islanders is due to the temporary stay of their illustrious ancestor when he was driven to Cos by adverse winds which Hera sent as he was returning from the pillage of Laomedon's kingdom at Troy for, during his sojourn, he slew their ruler, King Eurypylus, and then thoughtfully provided the vacant throne with an heir, who was later borne by the king's daughter Chalciope and named Thessalus.

The Myrmidons are described as coming from Pelasgian Argos,[20] Alos, Alope, Trachis, Phthia, and Hellas.[21] They were led in fifty

---

[20] "Pelasgian Argos" was a poetic name for Thessaly.

[21] Gladstone, with a modicum of caution, indicates that in Homer's time the Greek mainland was called Hellas, but the name is used only four times in the Iliad, and in each instance seems to be restricted to the neighborhood of the Myrmidons at Phthia.

ships by Achilles. Phthia happened to be the home of Achilles because his father Peleus had fled there, after having been expelled from the island of Aegina with his brother Telamon for the murder of their half brother Phocus.

128. Ancestors of the Myrmidons

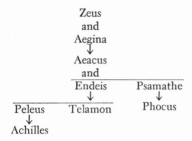

In the Iliad, the forces led by Achilles "were called Myrmidons and Hellenes, and Achaeans." The Myrmidons were a race said to have sprung from ants on Aegina—changed into men by Zeus in order to give Aeacus subjects over whom he might rule. Presumably, they—or some of them—followed Peleus to Phthia when he was exiled from the island.

The Phylaceans came from Phylace, Pyrasus, Iton, Antron, and Pteleos.[22] They were led in forty ships by Protesilaus (Iolaus) and Podarces, whose descent is shown on the adjoining chart. Their grandfather Phylacus was the founder of Phylace, having come into the country from Phocis where his father, Deion, was king. As mentioned in a previous chapter, Protesilaus was the first of the Greeks to meet death at Troy, so that Podarces ended up as sole leader of his men in the later fighting.

129. Ancestors of the Phylaceans

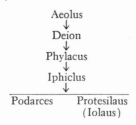

---

[22] The towns mentioned were located in the southern part of Thessaly called Phthiotis, which is said to have been the original homeland of the Achaeans.

The Pheraeans[23] are described as coming from Pherae, Boebe, Glaphyrae, and Iolchus, all towns of Magnesian Thessaly located in the neighborhood of Mount Pelion. They were led in eleven ships by Eumelus.

When Aeolus, the first king of Thessaly, died, his son, Magnes, gave the name of Magnesia to the southeastern part of the kingdom, which lay on the seacoast about Mount Pelion and Mount Ossa. Dictys and Polydectes, the sons of Magnes, emigrated to Seriphus—one of the islands in the group called the Cyclades; and Cretheus, one of the brothers of Magnes, assumed the government at the principal city of Iolchus.

130. Ancestors of the Pheraeans

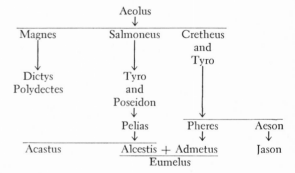

By his niece Tyro, indicated as a daughter of Salmoneus on the adjoining chart, Cretheus had sons named Aeson and Pheres. Upon their father's death, Pheres founded the city of Pherae, and his elder brother Aeson inherited the throne of Iolchus. The latter, however, was expelled by Pelias—his half brother whom Tyro had secretly borne to Poseidon. It was this incident which gave rise to the expedition of the Argonauts, led by Aeson's son Jason.

After the expedition proved successful, Pelias was boiled to death through the machinations of Medeia, Jason's wife; but Jason harbored no ill-will against Acastus, the son of Pelias who had been one of his comrades in the great adventure, and permitted him to succeed his father in the usurped government of the city. Some time later, Acastus was himself dethroned by the forces of Peleus, whom he had earlier

---

[23] The Pheraeans are not called by that name in the Iliad and could perhaps better be referred to as Aeolids.

wronged, and Iolchus became a part of the realm of Admetus, which had originally been confined to the country around Pherae. The sovereignty of Admetus was doubly strengthened by his marriage to Alcestis, one of the daughters of Pelias, and their son Eumelus thus led a unified force into the war with Troy.

The Thaumacians are described as coming from Methone, Thaumacia, Meliboea, and Olizon, which were towns of upper Magnesia around Mount Ossa. Initially, they were led in seven ships by Philoctetes, whose brother Thaumacus had founded the city of Thaumacia; but he was dropped off by his comrades on the island of Lemnos when his wound, previously received from the bite of a serpent on Tenedos, failed to heal.

131. Ancestors of the Thaumacians

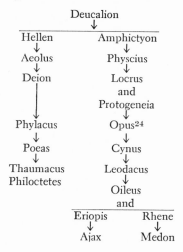

He was succeeded as leader by Medon, the son of Oileus, who had been forced to flee into Thessaly from his Locrian home because he had slain a kinsman of his stepmother Eriopis. Years later, when it had been foretold that the Greek cause could not prevail without the assistance of Philoctetes, he was fetched from Lemnos to Troy by Odysseus and Diomedes. Reassuming his command, it was one of his poisoned arrows

—given to his father Poeas by Heracles—that caused the death of Paris.

The Oechalians are described as coming from Tricca, Ithome and Oechalia. They were led in thirty ships by Podaleirius and Machaon.

132. Ancestors of the Oechalians

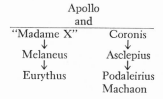

The district from which the Oechalians came is a matter of considerable dispute, among both mythographers and geographers. In the Iliad, however, they are identified with the country of Messenia.[25]

The Ormenians are described as coming from Ormenius, the fountain of Hypereia, Asterium, and "the white crests of Titanus," localities in the central plain of Thessaly around the confluence of the rivers Apidanus and Enipeus. They were led in forty ships by Eurypylus.

133. Ancestors of the Ormenians

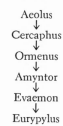

As suggested by the adjoining chart, they derived their own name and that of their principal city from Ormenus, the grandson of Aeolus.

---

[24] As previously mentioned, in connection with the descent of Locrian Ajax, Opus is said to have been a son whom Protogeneia conceived by Zeus before she became the wife of Locrus.

[25] Tricca, Ithome, and Oechalia were closely connected towns of the portion of Thessaly known as Histiaeotis, which was adjacent to Mount Olympus. This fact, plus the weight of a well-known legend that Coronis gave birth to Asclepius in a town of the plain of Dotis near Mount Ossa, would normally be determinative. However, the authority of Homer was so great that, as Pausanias says, the Messenians called a desolate spot in their land by the name of Tricca and—admittedly having towns called Oechalia and Ithome—gave buttress to the poet's statement.

The Gyrtonians (Lapiths) are described as coming from Argissa, Gyrtone, Orthe, Elone, and the "white city of Oloösson"—towns of a part of Thessaly which adjoined the district of Magnesia and known as Pelasgiotis. They were led in forty ships by Polypoëtes and Leonteus, whose descent is shown on the adjoining chart.

134. Ancestors of the Gyrtonians

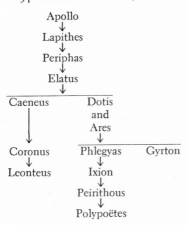

The apparent incongruity which separates the Gyrtonian leaders by two generations is not commented on by the ancient mythographers and, seemingly, was passed over by them as one of the excusable vagaries of the Greek imagination.

The Enienes and the Peraebi (Perrhaebi) are described as coming from Cyphus, Dodona, and the country around the river Titaressus—located in Thessaly (or Thessalian) Pelasgiotis adjacent to those occupied by the Gyrtonians. They were led in twenty-two ships by Gouneus, whose antecedents are not given.

The Magnetes (known also as the Magnesians) are described as living "about Peneius and Pelion, covered with waving forests." They were led to Troy in forty ships by Prothous, son of Tenthredon—neither of whom is further mentioned by the poet.

The Trojans and their Allies

Before proceeding, one fact should be stressed again which is vital to a proper understanding of the Homeric poems and the relationships, in other mythological encounters, between the Greeks and the Trojans, namely:

the two peoples not only worshipped the same gods but were themselves of blood kin.

Dardanus, the mythical ancestor of the Trojans, was born in Arcadia whence he emigrated to Phrygia, leaving his son, Deimas, in Greece. Electra, the daughter of Atlas who bore Dardanus to Zeus, was one of the Seven Pleiades. Of her six sisters: Alcyone's son, Hyrieus, founded the town of Hyria in Boeotia; Celaeno's son, Lycus, was transferred to the Isles of the Blest (westward); Maia's son, Hermes, was born in a cave of Mount Cyllene in Arcadia; Merope married the Aeolid Sisyphus, who was king of Corinth;[26] Sterope married Oenomaus, king of Pisa in Elis; and Taygete's son, Lacedaemon, gave his name to the Peloponnesian kingdom which later had its focus at Sparta. Nor was the original blood tie the last for Ilus, the paternal grandfather of Priam, went to Argos and brought back Eurydice, the daughter of Adrastus, as queen of his Trojan domain.

Because, in most instances, their ancestry is nowhere related by the mythographers, consideration of the leaders of the Trojan allies is largely limited to geographical, rather than genealogical comment.

The Trojans, in the strict sense of their appellation, were those who lived in and nearby the walled city of Troy, which was also called Ilium or Ilios. They were led by Hector, whose line of ascent is shown on the adjoining chart.

Ilus, the brother of Erichthonius, died childless. During the lifetime of his father Tros, the

135. Ancestors of the Trojans

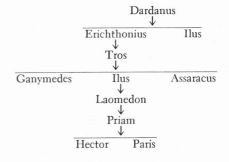

---

26 Through Merope's son Halmus, the Minyans were cousins to the Trojans; through her son Ornytion, the Phocians stood in an equal relation; and the hero Bellerophon, who married the Lycian Philonoë, was her grandson.

second Ilus left his home (Dardania) and founded the city about which the great war centered. When Tros died he permitted his younger brother Assaracus to succeed to the Dardanian throne, although he drove to his new home the divine horses which Zeus had given to Tros in requital for the abduction of Ganymedes.

The Dardanians came from the town or district of Dardania which was founded, and named for himself, by Dardanus when he came to Asia Minor from Greece. They were led by Aeneas: with his cousins Acamas and Archelochus, sons of Antenor, as his lieutenants.

136. Ancestors of the Dardanians

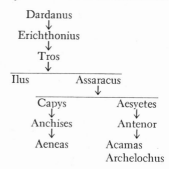

The location of Dardania is a matter of dispute among both ancient and modern writers, but there seems to be general agreement that it was located to the east of Troy, and perhaps northward, along the foot of the mountain chain known as Ida. With some disregard to chronology, its location is variously said to have been in Phrygia, Mysia, or the Troad. But, whatever may have been the geographical homeland of the Dardanians, or wherever they may have lived, they were close blood relatives of the Trojans and were their most intimate allies.

After Tros succeeded to the Dardanian throne, the town seems to have retained its name, but the neighboring territory was called Troy or the Troad. As previously mentioned, the city which we know as Troy was founded by Ilus and was known to Homer and the other ancients as Ilium. The rulership of Dardania was assumed by Assaracus, younger brother of Ilus who, as shown on the adjoining chart, was the great-grandfather of those who led their country's warriors at Troy.

The other Trojan allies were:

1. The Troes, led by Pandarus, the son of Lycaon, from Zeleia "beneath the nethermost foot of Ida";

2. The Percotians, led by Adrastus and Amphius, the sons of Merops, from Adrasteia, Apaesus, Pityeia and the mount of Tereia;

3. The Hellespontians,[27] led by Asius, the son of Hyrtacus, from Percote, Practius, Sestus, Abydus, and Arisbe;

4. The Pelasgians (Pelasgi), led by Hippothous and Pylaeus, the sons of Lethus, from Larisa, said by Strabo to have been a town of Mysia in the district known as Ocolis;

5. The Thracians, led by Acamas and Peirous from their country across the Hellespont;

6. The Ciconians (Cicones), led by Euphemus from their Thracian homeland;

7. The Paeonians, led by Pyraechmes from Amydon in Macedonia;

8. The Paphlagonians, led by Pylaemenes from Cytorus, Sesamon, Cromna, Aegialus, Erythini, and the land of the Eniti;[28]

9. The Halizones, led by Odius and Epistrophus from Alybe in Pontus;[29]

10. The Mysians, led by Chromis and by Ennomus, "the augur";

11. The Phrygians, led by Phorcys and Ascanius from Ascania;

12. The Maeonians, led from their homeland beneath Mount Tmolus in Lydia by Methles and Antiphus, the sons of Talaemenes;

13. The Carians, described as "uncouth of speech," were led by Nastes and Amphimachus, the sons of Nomion, from Miletus, the mountains of Phthires and Mycale and from the river Maeander; and

14. The Lycians were led by Sarpedon and Glaucus. They tie into the line of the Greeks and their Cretan allies, as shown by the following:

---

[27] The poet does not use the appellative Hellespontians; but those led by Asius all came from towns located on the Hellespont.

[28] The land of the Eniti is described as the habitat of a race of wild "she-mules."

[29] Alybe is called the "birthplace of silver." Strabo places it in the country of Pontus, after noting that others invented a town in the Troad to fit the poet's description.

137. Ancestors of the Lycians

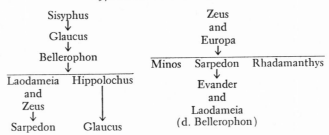

This completes the listing of the Trojan allies described in the Catalogue which appears in the second book of the Iliad. In Book X, additional warriors are said to have come from Thrace under the leadership of Rhesus,[30] who was slain while sleeping by Diomedes. According to the later legends, other allies were brought in toward the conclusion of the ten-year war, among whom the more noted were the Amazon Penthesileia and the Ethiopian Memnon.[31]

---

[30] Rhesus was said by Euripides to have been a son of the Macedonian river-god Strymon and the Muse Euterpe but, in the Iliad, his father is named as Eioneus.

[31] Because of the shifting dominion of various conquering peoples, the names of localities in Asia Minor were changed in the course of time—thus causing some confusion in nomenclature which has always been a perplexing problem of geography. In the fifteenth century B.C., all of the area between the Hellespont (now the Dardanelles), the Propontis (now the Sea of Marmara), the Bosporus and the Euxine (now the Black Sea), lying to the north—and the Mediterranean, lying to the south—was controlled by the Hittites. Under

their rule, only the eastern portion—Cilicia—was called by a separate name. In the seventh century B.C.—when the Assyrians succeeded them as the dominant power—the same region was known as Phrygia, except that part around Sardis on the coast, which was known as Lydia (anciently Maeonia). In the sixth century B.C., the Lydians pushed the Phrygians northward to the Euxine, and the Medes—encroaching from the east—gave the name of Cappadocia to the territory north of Cilicia. In the fifth century B.C., the northeastern part of Phrygia was occupied by the Paphlagonians, and the Mysians wedged in above the Lydians to the south. Here it was that the Troad was situated and, at the hill called Hissarlik, Schliemann discovered the ruins of Troy. It should be borne in mind, however, that the ancients often refer to the Trojan site as in Phrygia, and modern archeology has buttressed their accounts by dating the rulership of Priam at different times which extend back from the seventh all the way to the thirteenth century.

The limits of the extensive country anciently known as Pontus were not clearly defined, but its northern boundary is generally acknowledged to have extended along the southern coast of the Euxine. The locations of Caria, Lycia, and Pamphylia on the southern coast of Asia Minor and of Phoenicia, above Palestine, are better known from the accounts of later writers which have permitted them to be shown on maps appropriate to the times of their existence as political entities. The whole of the country is now a part of Asiatic Turkey.

23

The Trojan War III

The Iliad

Book I. In a raid upon Chrysa, a town near Troy, Agamemnon had taken for his captive tent mate the maiden Chryseis (Astynome), daughter of Chryses, a priest of Apollo. The Iliad opens, after a poetic invocation to the Muses, with a visit to Agamemnon by the old priest, who pleads for the return of his daughter. But, although the Greeks "in shouts their joint assent declare," their haughty leader spurns the request and insolently commands his suppliant to depart. Thereupon, the anguished father returns to his shrine and, when he prays to Apollo for vengeance, the god obliges by sending a pestilence, which first strikes the mules and dogs of the Greeks and then fixes itself upon their assembled warriors.[1]

On the tenth day of the affliction, Achilles called the army into council and demanded that Calchas (their attendant seer) should explore and explain the reason for the calamity. When the prophet appeared, he was reluctant to answer—saying that his words might imperil his life, but Achilles bade him speak the truth, and promised to defend him against any and all who might take umbrage. Thus assured, Calchas explained that the pestilential arrows were

sent because Apollo was angry at the abduction of Chryseis, and that, to bring an end to the plague, she must be returned to her father, with the sacrifice of a hecatomb to the god himself.[2]

With rage in his heart and eyes ablaze, Agamemnon arose and denounced Calchas as a prophet of evil, but he ended his denunciation by saying that he would send back the damsel if the army would give him another "prize of honor." Achilles now spoke and, accusing his titular leader of being covetous, said that he would be properly recompensed for his loss when a Trojan city should be taken. Thereupon, Agamemnon replied that he would restore Chryseis forthwith, but darkly threatened that he would concurrently replace her by seizing from the tent of Achilles the beautiful Briseis, who had been taken by him as a captive in the sack of Mysian Thebes. In furious retort, Achilles announced that, if the threat were carried out, he would return with his Myrmidons to his home at Phthia in Thessaly. When this statement was publicly made, Agamemnon heatedly said that he would take Briseis and, after boasting that he had other men in his command who were the peers of Achilles, piously declared that, in addition, he had the strong, right arm of Zeus to aid him. His words so infuriated Achilles that he was about to draw his sword, but Hera sent the goddess

---

[1] The animals and men who fell were supposed to have been pierced with the arrows of Apollo who is called Smintheus—said to have been the Phrygian name for "mouse"—and applied to the god because he put an end to a plague of mice which had harassed the country about Troy.

[2] Hecatomb: a hundred cattle or other animals offered for sacrifice.

Athena from Olympus to restrain his impetuous action, and she took her stand behind him, and caught him by his golden hair. The colloquy which followed ended by a demand of the goddess that Achilles should sheathe his sword, coupled with her promise that—at a later time — he should receive a three-fold atonement for Agamemnon's insult. Reluctantly, the young warrior put his sword back and, turning to Agamemnon, called him "dog-face with the heart of a deer," and declared openly that the Greeks would sorely miss his arm, which was being withdrawn from their assistance solely because of their leader's insolence.

As the angry disputants stood glaring at each other, ancient Nestor arose to soothe their pride —and seized the occasion to bring into his dissertation some remarks about the heroes of older days, when men who were men harkened to his advice.[3] But, even though he talked with a tongue flowing speech sweeter than honey, his effort to appease was fruitless and the assembly broke up. Odysseus left to take Chryseis back to her father while Agamemnon sent his heralds, Talthybius and Eurybates, to fetch Briseis from the tent of Achilles, who—scoring to offer resistance—ordered his comrade Patroclus to deliver his captive to them. He repeated, however, his prophecy that ruin would fall upon the Greeks, now deprived of his sword. As his beloved tent mate was unwillingly led away, however, the great warrior withdrew to the seashore, where he burst into tears. Sitting there, he called for his mother, and from the water's depths, the seagoddess Thetis answered his call and quietly seated herself beside him. When she inquired the cause of his tears, he related (in the epic manner) the whole story of the dishonor to which he had been subjected by Agamemnon, and bade her go to Zeus and beseech him to succour the Trojans until the Greeks should be slaughtered at the sterns of their ships, which were drawn up on Trojan soil. Meanwhile he reminded his divine mother of the obligation

owed by Zeus to her for assisting him on a previous occasion, when Hera, Poseidon, and Athena had conspired to put the supreme god in bonds.[4] The goddess wept, with her son, when she heard of the base treatment accorded him, for whom a short life was already fated, and promised to seek the intercession of Zeus in his behalf but, she added, that he had presently gone with all the other gods to feast with the "blameless Ethiopians," and that she would have to await his return on the twelfth day following. "So saying, she went away and left him where he was, wroth at heart for the fair-girdled woman's sake."

Meanwhile, Odysseus arrived at Chrysa with Chryseis and, after sacrificing the required hecatomb to Apollo, delivered his fair charge to her joyful father—who receipted for the precious package by praying to the archer-god that the plague on the Greeks should cease—and it did.

After Thetis had left the Trojan shore, Achilles went back to his tent, and sulked there for twelve days. When that time had elapsed, Zeus returned to his home on Mount Olympus where Thetis, rising up from the sea, found him meditating. But she lost no time in asking him to honor her son by granting victory to the Trojans. Zeus throught about her request for some time and then, with some hesitation, said that, if he should grant it, he might have trouble with Hera because she was a partisan of the Greeks. He promised, however, to think the matter over and attested his words with a nod, which Thetis took as a favorable sign. Her audience ended, the goddess now returned to her watery element, and Zeus went into his Olympian palace where, as the other deities respectfully stood, he sat down upon his throne.

As soon as Zeus thought he was in a position to relax, Hera—who had spotted the departing Thetis—began to taunt him about the promise which she suspected him of having given, a promise that he would do honor to Achilles by bringing harm to the Greeks. "If it be so," said

---

[3] Nestor had seen two generations of men pass away and was now a king among the third. The earlier heroes named by him as his contemporaries in the war with the Centaurs were Peirithous, Dryas, Caeneus, Exadius, Polyphemus, and Theseus.

[4] When Zeus asked her aid in overcoming the conspiracy against him, Thetis brought up from Tartarus the powerful hundred-handed monster "whom the gods calle Briareus, but all men Aegaeon," and the rebellious deities fled in terror.

Zeus, "then such must my good pleasure be." At this rebuke, Hera and all of the other assembled gods maintained a trembling silence, until lame Hephaestus piped up to tell of the time when his great sire had caught him by the foot and had hurled him down to earth. His ludicrous recital broke the heavenly tension and, amid the laughter of the company, he walked haltingly through the palace and poured wine for all. The rest of the day was spent by the gods in feasting and listening to Apollo's lyre accompanying the sweet voices of the Muses. But, when night came and others slept, Zeus lay awake—planning how he should bring honor to Achilles.

Book II. Zeus decided to send a deceitful dream to Agamemnon—a vision which, in the form of Nestor, told the sleeping leader that all of the Olympian gods had been won over to the side of the Greeks by Hera's supplications, and that the armed invaders might now easily rout the Trojans and take over their city.

When he arose in the morning, Agamemnon ordered the heralds to summon the whole army to a place of gathering and, at a smaller council held beside the ship of Nestor, he related his dream to the leaders of the various forces under his supreme command. He added that—before the rank and file were informed of the purpose of the dream—he thought it well to make trial of their feelings by suggesting that the expedition should be abandoned and all should return home. After Nestor acquiesced to the suggestion, the leaders proceeded to the place of general assembly, and Agamemnon stood up to speak, bearing in his hands his ancestral scepter of authority.[5] Instead of relating the dream as it had actually come to him he said that he had been bidden by Zeus to renounce all hope of taking the walled city, which was defended not only by the strong-hearted Trojans[6] but also by their allies from other cities. Saying this, he bade his host to break up the assembly and return to their native lands.

Nor did his words go unheeded, for the Greek warriors rushed toward their ships, and from beneath their feet the dust rose up. At this critical moment, Hera sent Athena to bid Odysseus hearten the fleeing army, and he went to the tent of Agamemnon, who—learning the purpose of his visit—turned over willingly the scepter (which had descended to him from Pelops). With it, as an additional badge of authority, Odysseus went into the milling throng and, wherever he encountered one of the leaders who had been in the council at Nestor's tent, he reminded him that Agamemnon's speech was only a ruse to try the temper of his men but, wherever he encountered one of the lesser men, he smote him with his staff and chided him for being a coward.

These measures had their intended effect, and all finally returned to the place of gathering, coming from the ships and huts where they had been making preparations for their departure. While the others quietly sat down, a certain evil-favored Greek named Thersites[7] began to revile Agamemnon, accusing him of keeping his men at Troy only for the purpose of stocking his own tent with women and other prizes which they were forced to bring to him. Upon this happening, Odysseus angrily ordered him to cease his tirade and, threatening even greater punishment, beat him about the back and shoulders until bloody welts appeared, which caused the cowered man to become quiet amid the jeering laughter of his comrades.

Odysseus now turned to address the seated host, and by his side the goddess Athena, in the likeness of a herald, bade all remain silent. As the wise man spoke, he recalled to his comrades that, before they set out from Aulis, Calchas, their seer, had prophesied that Troy would be taken in the tenth year after their departure. Pointing out that nine years had already elapsed, he brought such cheer to their hearts

---

[5] The scepter was originally fashioned by Hephaestus and given to Zeus. From him, it passed successively to Hermes, Pelops, Atreus, and Thyestes—the latter having "left it to Agamemnon to bear, so that he might be lord of many isles and of all Argos."

[6] The expression "like true Trojans" seems to have been first used by Samuel Butler in his "Hudibras," published in 1663, and it may be conjectured that this is the source of the later phrases "as brave as a Trojan" and "work like a Trojan."

---

[7] As related in chapter 18, Thersites was a son of Agrius and a kinsman of Diomedes, but in the Iliad he is described as bandy-legged and lame in one foot, with rounded shoulders and a warpen head on which his hair grew as a scant stubble.

that they raised loud shouts in his praise.[8] Nestor followed, echoing the sentiments expressed by Odysseus, and suggested to Agamemnon that each of the assembled tribes should be led in battle only by its own captains—so that the glory of success (or the stigma of cowardice) to his own group would be an incentive for each man to do his best. On this note, and the opinions of all now being solidified into a single will to stay and fight, Agamemnon directed that his men should proceed to put their arms in order for the fierce battle which he promised to wage incessantly.[9] He ended his discourse by suggesting that it was time to eat.

After the warriors had scattered to their different ships and huts, the Greek chieftain called to his own table six of his principal leaders, Nestor, Idomeneus, Ajax the Greater, Ajax the Lesser, Diomedes, and Odysseus. And, when a fat bull had been slain as a sacrifice to Zeus, the party was joined by Menelaus, who stood in silence with the rest, as Agamemnon prayed aloud that the Sun should not be permitted to set until after the Trojans were conquered and their city burned to the ground.[10] The sacrifice was then completed by ceremoniously placing the thigh pieces of the bull upon the altar, where they were consumed by the flames. Afterward, the chieftains feasted upon the remainder of the animal's flesh. Then, at the suggestion of Nestor, Agamemnon directed the heralds to summon the Greeks for battle. When they had

gathered, the goddess Athena sped throughout the ranks into which they had been marshaled by their respective leaders.

At this point in the poem, the Muses are called upon to name the captains of the Greeks (Danaans) and the Catalogue of their forces is inserted, as described in the preceding chapter. Following the Catalogue, it is related that of horses, the mares of Eumelus which had been reared by Apollo,[11] were the best, and of warriors, Telamonian Ajax was preeminent. But, with reference to the latter, it is added that his was the honor only because Achilles—far the mightiest—lay sulking in his tent in wrath against Agamemnon for depriving him of Briseis, while his men stood idle or roamed through the camp and refused to take any part in the fighting.

When the Greek army started across the Trojan plain—although unaccompanied by Achilles and his Myrmidons—the earth is said to have groaned beneath their tread, just as when Zeus scourged the land about the giant Typhon in the country of the Arimi with his thunderbolts. As they approached the city's great walls, Zeus sent his messenger Iris to give warning to the Trojans, who were holding assembly at Priam's gate. After assuming the likeness of Polites, a son of Priam who was accustomed to sit as a sentinel on the topmost part of the barrow of Aesyetes,[12] the deity related that she had seen the invaders oncoming in numbers like the leaves or the sands, and that—with Hector, Priam's son, as supreme commander—the lesser captains of the Trojans and of their allies (who spoke different languages) should marshal all their forces and go to meet the attack. Recognizing the divinity of the messenger, Hector speedily broke up the gathering and all rushed in arms through the gates of the city to a mound far out in the plain, where the leaders proceeded

---

[8] At Aulis, a serpent—gliding from beneath the altar —had darted to a plane tree, upon whose topmost bough a sparrow cowered with her eight fledglings. When the serpent ate all nine of them and was miraculously turned into stone, Calchas interpreted the happening as an omen that Troy would not be taken until the tenth year.

[9] The words of Agamemnon may have been prophetic of the historic speech of Winston Churchill, made after the rout at Dunkirk, in which he promised the English people under his leadership "blood, sweat, and tears." In similar vein, Agamemnon is described as saying: "For of respite shall there intervene, no, not a whit, until night at its coming shall part the fury of warriors. Wet with sweat about the breast of many a man shall be the baldric of his sheltering shield, and about the spear shall his hand grow weary, and wet with sweat shall a man's horse be, as he tugs at the polished car."

[10] It is mentioned here in the Iliad that, although Zeus accepted Agamemnon's sacrifice, the god was not yet minded to grant fulfillment of his prayer.

---

[11] The mares of Eumelus were considered the best only because Balius and Xanthus—the immortal steeds of Achilles—took no part in the initial fighting.

[12] Aesyetes (equally with his brother Capys) is said to have been a son of Assaracus by Hieromneme, a daughter of the god of the river Simois. Thus, he was of the Dardanian line and was not technically a Trojan— a term sometimes strictly used as a connotation of residence at Troy.

to separate their companies.[13] At this point in the poem, the Catalogue of the Trojans and their allies is inserted in the detail which has been rather fully given in the preceding chapter.

Book III. The marshaled Trojan forces came toward the enemy with a clamor like the cry of birds, but the Greeks advanced in silence, albeit breathing fury.[14] When the two armies approached each other, Paris leapt forward and, brandishing two spears, challenged the bravest of the Argives to face him. But, when Menelaus came out to meet him, the great lover faded back into the throng of his comrades, where he was roundly chided for being a coward by his brother Hector. Stung by the scornful words, Paris now offered to engage Menelaus in single combat, provided all the other warriors on both sides would stand aside—a proposition which the Greeks accepted when it was shouted to them by Hector. In preparation for the duel, the two hosts now stepped forth from their ranks and laid their arms in heaps near together. At the same time, Hector sent heralds to the city to get Priam and to bring lambs for sacrifice, while Agamemnon sent his herald Talthybius to bring a lamb from the Greek camp for the same purpose.

During these activities, Iris went to the hall where Helen was weaving and, assuming the likeness of Laodice—the comeliest of the daughters of Priam[15]—bade her go to the wall above the Scaean gates to witness the impending spectacle, in which the principal actors were to be her erstwhile husband and her present lover. First veiling herself in a linen gown, she proceeded as directed, accompanied by her handmaid, Clymene, and by Aethra, the daughter of Pittheus. Arriving above the gates, they saw Priam seated below amid a group of his elder statesmen, which included Panthous, Thymoetes, Lampus, and Clytius,[16] Hicetaon, Ucalegon, and Antenor.[17] As the old men marveled at her beauty, Priam called upon Helen to come down and point out the various heroes among the Greeks, and she obligingly designated by name Agamemnon,[18] Odysseus,[19] Telemonian Ajax, and Idomeneus, but she specifically noted the absence of her brothers Castor and Pollux.[20] After she concluded, the herald Idaeus approached and, at his summons, Priam and Antenor mounted a chariot and drove over the plain into the midst of the Trojans and Achaeans, where they went through the ceremony of having their hands washed.[21] Following this, Agamemnon cut hair from the heads of the lambs, which the heralds portioned out to the leaders of the Trojans and Achaeans alike; he prayed to Zeus and Helios that the loser should respect the agreement as to the duel. This was that Helen and her treasure should be returned if Menelaus won and that the Greeks should depart if Paris won. Thereupon, the lambs' throats were cut and Priam, having seen enough of blood, mounted his chariot and went with Antenor back to the city.

When Hector and Odysseus had laid out the battle area and had drawn lots as to which of

---

[13] Although men called the mound Bateia, the immortals called it the barrow of Myrina—presumably the Amazonian mother of the Lesbian queen Hypsipyle.

[14] The cries of the advancing Trojans were likened to those of the cranes which, according to legend, were accustomed to war with the Pigmy men of the country around the mouth of the river Nile.

[15] Laodice was wed to Helicaon, who was one of the many sons of Antenor.

[16] The presence of Lampus and Clytius at the Trojan War is at variance with the legend related by Apollodorus that all of the sons of Laomedon, except Priam, were slain by Heracles when he sacked Ilium earlier.

[17] Antenor was the son of Aesyetes, whose barrow was located on the Trojan plain.

[18] Upon Helen's mention of Agamemnon as a son of Atreus, Priam was reminded of a visit, made in his younger days, to the people of Otreus (and "godlike Mygdon") when the Phrygians fought with the Amazons.

[19] Odysseus' name recalled to Antenor that it was he and Menelaus who were first sent as ambassadors to demand that the Trojans should return Helen; and the old man recalled that, although Menelaus spoke fluently, the words of Odysseus fell "like snowflakes on a winter's day"—notwithstanding his cunning attempt to give the impression that he had no great intellectual ability.

[20] Apparently Helen had not heard of the deaths of the Dioscuri which came in their fight with the sons of Aphareus after she had departed from Sparta with Paris.

[21] Upon their arrival, Priam and Antenor were greeted by Agamemnon and Menelaus, who were in the midst of offering their sacrifice, and it may be that they—and not their Trojan enemies—were those whose hands were washed with water from the bowls of the heralds.

the combatants should first throw his spear, Menelaus and Paris faced each other, the latter wearing, among other armor, the corselet of his brother Lycaon.[22] So, Paris cast his spear, whose point was turned by his opponent's shield, but Menelaus' return weapon pierced through the shield of Paris all the way to his tunic, and would have proved fatal had he not bent aside. Nor was the Greek king more successful with his sword, which shattered as it struck the horn of the Trojan's helmet—a happening which so infuriated Menelaus that he seized Paris by his crest and dragged him on the ground so that he was about to choke from the strap of his helmet which was drawn tight beneath his chin. Aphrodite, however, came to the aid of the unhappy man and—breaking the thong so that the empty helmet came away in Menelaus' strong hand—she shrouded him in a thick mist and set him down in his own bed chamber at Troy, and then she went to summon Helen. In the likeness of an old dame who had served at Sparta, the goddess bade the most beautiful of women to go in to her miraculously rescued lord and, after an interchange of recriminations which ended as sweet nothings, they went to their couch. Meanwhile, Menelaus ranged through the host of the warriors like a wild beast in vain search of his hated opponent who had been taken away unseen. Nor could any of the Trojans produce him to continue the contest, though they would have done so—because he was detested as the man who had brought the cruel war to their people. Finally, Agamemnon announced that the victory belonged to the Greeks, and called upon the Trojans and their allies to make good their promise of returning Helen and the treasures which had been taken from the Spartan palace when she had deserted Menelaus.

Book IV. The scene of the story now changes to a meeting of the gods on Olympus where Zeus, for the mere pleasure of teasing Hera, asks whether the fighting should continue or peace should come. Hera answers that, if peace should come on the conditions agreed to, the Trojans would remain unpunished in contravention of her fixed determination that they should be utterly destroyed. Upon hearing this, Zeus fiercely replied that she should have her pleasure, but added that he might some day lay waste to one of the cities as dear to his strange queen as that of Ilium was to him. Retorting, Hera suggested that he might do as he wished with her favorite cities of Argos, Sparta, and Mycenae and, regally bringing the argument to an end, concluded by asking him to send Athena down to contrive how the Trojans should break their oaths.

Reluctantly, Zeus gave the requested order and the maiden goddess leapt down to the Trojan plain where, in the guise of Antenor's son Laodocus, she incited Pandarus to let an arrow fly at Menelaus but, though his aim was sure, Athena contrived that the speed of the shaft should be lessened by passing through the belt and corselet of Menelaus before reaching his skin, which was not entered deeply enough to cause a serious wound—although his blood flowed freely. Agamemnon saw at once that the cause of Troy was lost by this act of perfidy, and prophesied that the day was not far off when Zeus would shake his dark aegis and permit the city to be laid low. Thereupon, at his bidding, the herald Talthybius fetched the leech Machaon, who sucked out the blood from the wound and covered it with soothing simples which the centaur Cheiron had, years before, given to his father, Asclepius.

Meanwhile, the ranks of the Trojans approached and Agamemnon, leaving his chariot and horses in the custody of his squire Eurymedon, ranged on foot through the army—encouraging his men, and rebuking those who were slow in going into action. Among the first, he came to the Cretans and was glad to see them being led in the van by his friend Idomeneus, while Meriones was speeding on the hindmost battalions. Passing on, he came to the two Aiäntes whose dark legions bristled with spears and shields and moved like a cloud which brings on the whirlwind. Next coming to the Pylians, he found Nestor arraying his comrades and urging them to fight; and around him were his trusted warriors Pelagon, Alastor, Chromius, Haemon, and Bias. At sight of the old man, Agamemnon praised his spirit—to which Nestor replied that, even though he was not as

---

[22] Lycaon's mother was not Hecuba, but Laothoë, hence he was a half brother of Paris.

strong as when he had slain Ereuthalion,[23] he would still accompany his men and give them the benefit of his counsel. Passing by the Athenians under the leadership of Menestheus, the commander-in-chief reached an adjacent place where—like the Athenians—the Cephallenians under Odysseus were standing and waiting for other battalions to begin the attack. These he ridiculed on their laziness, but when Odysseus indignantly retorted that he would soon be seen among the foremost fighters, Agamemnon smiled—because his words had taken their intended effect—and moved on to where he found Diomedes and his comrade Sthenelus also late in getting their forces into the line of battle. These, too, he rebuked upon being unworthy sons of braver fathers and, although Sthenelus fiercely denied the charge, he was quieted by Diomedes, and again Agamemnon was gratified at his ruse, which sent the two warriors rushing forward to fight with heightened fury.[24]

The battle now began, with Ares encouraging the Trojans and Athena the Greeks. Antilochus was the first to slay a warrior of the Trojans—driving his spear through the forehead of Echepolus; and, as he fell, Elephenor sought to strip him of his armor, only to be himself slain by Agenor (a son of Antenor). Next, Telemonian Ajax slew a young Trojan, named Simoeisius because his mother had borne him beside the banks of the river Simois. In retaliation, Priam's son Antiphus cast his spear but—missing Ajax—killed Leucus, a comrade of Odysseus, whose death was avenged when his great leader threw his spear through the temple of Priam's bastard son, Democoön. Upon this happening, Hector and the other foremost Trojans gave ground,

but were encouraged to stand fast by the god Apollo, looking down from Pergamus.[25] Offsetting his divine aid, however, was the urging which Tritogeneia (Athena) continued to give to the Greeks (Achaeans). A second Greek leader now fell,[26] as Diores—one of the captains of the Eleans—was knocked to the ground with a jagged stone by Peirous leader of the Thracians. While he lay gasping, his enemy thrust a spear through his navel and he died. Thereupon, as the Thracian sprang back, the warrior Thoas from Aetolia stabbed him with a spear in the breast, and completed the kill with his sword.

Book V. In another part of the conflict, Diomedes, emboldened by Pallas Athena—and perhaps still smarting from the rebuke of Agamemnon—started a field-day all of his own, for, in addition to killing many Trojan warriors, he wounded the war god Ares, the semidivine Aeneas, and the goddess Aphrodite. The first of his victims was Phegeus, a son of Hephaestus' priest Dares, and he would also have slain his brother Idaeus had not the god made him invisible, so that his aged priest might not himself die from grief.

At this point in the Iliad Ares and Athena retired from direction of the fighting and seated themselves on the sandy banks of the river Scamander. The Trojans now turned in flight as one of their men was slain by each of the Greek captains. Sepecifically mentioned are: Agamemnon, who drove his spear through the back of Odius, leader of the Halizones; Idomeneus, who slew the Maeonian warrior Phaestus; Menelaus, who brought down Scamandrius—taught in youth to hunt by the goddess Artemis; Meriones, who slew Phereclus—described as "skilled in all manner of curious work" and as the builder of the ships of Paris;[27] Meges, who

---

[23] In an attack on Pylus, Eureuthalion was slain by Nestor even though he was armed with the club of Areïthous, the fierce king of Arne.

[24] In referring to the might of Tydeus, the father of Diomedes, Agamemnon recalled how he had come to Mycenae to gather recruits for the attack of the Seven Against Thebes, but had been refused aid because Zeus sent unfavorable omens; how, later when he had been sent into the city of Thebes as an advance ambassador to demand its surrender, he had bested all of the sons of Cadmus in feats of strength; and how, when he was ambushed by fifty men upon leaving the city, he slew all of them save only Maeon, whom he let return home after receiving a divine portent that the youth's life should be spared.

[25] Behind the city of Ilium, on the southeast, rose a hill forming a peak of Mount Ida, surmounted by an acropolis called the Pergamus, whereon were located the temples of the gods and the palaces of Priam, Hector, and Paris.

[26] The first of the Greek leaders to fall was Elephenor, who was the son of Chalcodon and captain of the Abantes from the island of Euboea.

[27] Despite the role of Phereclus, the Iliad relates that Pallas Athena loved him above all men—a fanciful hyperbole dictated by the belief that she was goddess of handicraft as well as of wisdom.

smote down Pedaeus—a bastard son of Antenor but raised by his wife Theano as her own; and Eurypylus, who killed Hypsenor by lopping off his arm and causing him to bleed to death.[28]

Nothwithstanding the valor of his comrades, it was still Diomedes who created the greatest havoc among the enemy, for he stormed through both armies with such fury that it was hard to tell whether he was allied on the Greek or the Trojan side. And, even when an arrow from the bow of Pandarus[29] lodged in his right shoulder, he paused only long enough to have Capaneus pull it out, while he prayed to Athena for renewed strength. Nor did the goddess fail to hear him, for, drawing near, she whispered that he was destined to fight with the heart of his great father Tydeus. She warned, however, that he should engage with none of the immortals, save only Aphrodite. Thus encouraged he proceeded with his carnage and successively slaughtered the Trojans Astynous, Hypeiron, Abas, Polyidus, Xanthus, Thoön, Echemmon, and Chromius—the last two being sons of Priam.

When Aeneas, the son of Anchises and Aphrodite, saw how the raging Greek was bringing such great destruction to the Trojan forces, he sought out Pandarus and proposed that the two of them should join to put an end to his rampage, but Pandarus related how he had already wounded Diomedes and intimated that he might be a god in disguise, because of his quick recovery.[30] After a colloquy, however, in which Aeneas asserted that his swift horses—descended from those which Zeus had given to Tros—would insure their safety, Pandarus agreed to make another attempt to bring the life of the seemingly invulnerable man to an end. As they neared the place where Diomedes was momentarily paused, his companion Sthenelus saw them approaching and suggested that it might be the better part of valor to give ground before the chariot of two such warriors—one a peerless bowman and the other the son of a goddess. But Diomedes indignantly refused to recognize their superiority, and urged upon Sthenelus the great renown which would be gained by overcoming those who were themselves so preeminent, and moreover privileged to be drawn by horses of divine descent.[31]

Accordingly, they stood fast until their enemies approached and Pandarus, alighting from the chariot of Aeneas, vauntingly declared that his spear would now bring on the downfall which his arrow had been unable to accomplish. So, he hurled it through the shield of Diomedes and gloried in the thought that it had pierced his body, but the shaft was stopped by the corselet and, with the divine assistance of Athena, the counter-spear of his adversary passed through the mouth of the proud Lycian and his spirit departed to the lower world. Upon this, Aeneas leapt from his chariot to protect the corpse, but he was struck in the hip by a stone which Diomedes threw, and would have perished had not Aphrodite flung her white arms about him and drawn him away under the shelter of her bright garment.

While the goddess was bearing Aeneas from the battlefield, Sthenelus took the opportunity to drive off the horses of the unconscious man and, leading them into the Greek ranks, turned

---

[28] Hypsenor's father Dolopion was a priest of Scamander, one of the river-gods of the Trojan plain.

[29] The father of Pandarus was a Lycian named Lycaon—not to be confused with Priam's son of the same name.

[30] As shown by chart 113c in chapter 20, Aeneas was descended from Zeus through Assaracus, Capys, and Anchises in the line of those identified with earlier Dardania instead of Ilium (Troy). Together with his brother Lyrus (about whom nothing of interest is mentioned), it is said that he was borne to Anchises by the goddess Aphrodite on Mount Ida. He was reared from infancy in the home of Alcathous, the husband of his half sister Hippodameia and, since he was part of the Dardanian branch, was not involved in the beginning of the great war. Indeed, later in the Iliad, the poet intimates that there existed some ill-feeling between Priam and him—which perhaps arose from the decree of destiny that his descendants were to be the perpetuators of the Trojan race (in Italy) after the house of

---

Priam should be extinguished by the Greeks. Prior to the actual conflict (and while the Greeks were ravaging the country about Troy), Aeneas was attacked by Achilles while on Mount Ida tending his flocks, which the great warrior took as he put their owner to flight. However, this incident—plus the admonition of Apollo —so aroused his spirit that he was induced to lead his Dardanians against the Greeks as allies of his Trojan kinsmen; and, in the later stages of the conflict, he was considered as second only to Hector among the city's defenders.

[31] Diomedes related to Sthenelus that Anchises stole the horses given to Tros by Zeus, as recompense for the rape of Ganymedes, and bred them to his own mares, from which the horses of Aeneas were descended.

them over to his comrade, Deipylus. He then mounted his own chariot and went in search of Diomedes, but his relentless comrade meanwhile had pursued the goddess and—wounding the surface of her delicate hand[32]—bade her keep from war and fighting. As she departed in panic, she was led by Iris to another part of the plain where her brother Ares was abiding with his two-horse chariot. At her entreaty, she rode with Iris in the war-god equipage to Olympus and complained to her mother, Dione, that she had been wounded by a mortal. Soothingly, Dione bade her be of good heart and recalled that many of the immortals had previously suffered at the hands of men.[33] While this was going on, Athena and Hera ridiculed the goddess upon her tenderness, and Zeus, smiling, bade her limit her future activities to the works of marriage, and to engage no further in the works of war.

Back on the Trojan battlefield, Diomedes leapt upon the prostrate Aeneas but was prevented from taking him by Apollo and, mindful of Athena's warning, the Greek chieftain gave ground.[34] Thereupon, the god wafted the stricken son of Aphrodite to his temple on the Pergamus (Pergamum), where he was tenderly healed of his wound by Leto and Artemis. When this was done, Apollo bade Ares enter the battle and avenge both the wound which had been given by Diomedes to Aphrodite and also the affront given to himself while he was assisting Aeneas from the place where he had fallen. Eagerly complying, the war-god entered the ranks of the Trojans and, in the likeness of their Thracian ally Acamas, urged them to save their kinsman Aeneas—not mentioning that he had already been miraculously taken from the battlefield and healed. His words prompted Sarpedon[35] to rebuke Hector for his inactivity so

that the latter sprang into his chariot, and rallied the Trojans. In his effort, he was aided by the presence of Aeneas who—now healed of the wound caused by Diomedes—came down from Pergamus and stood by his side.

But, notwithstanding this double Trojan leadership, the Aiäntes, Odysseus, and raging Diomedes urged on the Danaans to fight relentlessly, and their chieftain Agamemnon slew Deicoön with his spear, a warrior whom the Trojans honored as greatly as they did the sons of Priam. In turn, Aeneas laid low Crethon and Orsilochus, the sons of Diocles, whose bodies were rescued and dragged back into the Grecian lines by Antilochus and Menelaus. These two then attacked the Paphlagonian leader, Phylaemenes, whom Menelaus pierced with his spear, and Antilochus slew his charioteer Mydon with the casting of a stone. Marking their action, Hector rushed upon them with his forces—in whose van were Ares and Enyo.[36] And the great Trojan leader made short shrift of Menethes and Anchialus, who were in one car. But, as they fell, Telamonian Ajax retaliated by killing Amphius and was about to strip the armor from his corpse until the spears of the Trojans caused him to draw back.

In another part of the battlefield, Tlepolemus, the son of Heracles, met Zeus' son, Sarpedon, and ridiculed him upon being born later than his own great father, who had previously sacked Troy with a small force borne in only six ships. This chip-on-the-shoulder remark set the two men to fighting, and Tlepolemus was killed, but only after he had wounded Sarpedon seriously with his spear. Upon this happening, Odysseus pondered briefly whether he should pursue Sarpedon, but Athena so swayed his mind that he attacked others of the Lycians and slew Coeranus, Alastor, Chromius, Alcandrus, Halius, Noemon, and Prytanis. And he would have slain more of them had not Hector come to their relief, and to that of their leader Sarpedon—from whom his comrade Pelagon was now given the opportunity to draw the

---

[32] No blood poured from the wound, because the veins of the gods flowed with immortal "ichor."

[33] Dione recalled: how Otus and Ephialtes had kept Ares bound in a brazen jar for thirteen months; how Heracles had smitten Hera on her right breast with a three-barbed arrow; and how the same great hero had wounded Hades in the shoulder during his attack on the Pylians.

[34] Apollo's championship of the Trojan cause is generally related back to Agamemnon's rape of Chryse—notwithstanding the atonement made for that at the expense of Achilles.

[35] As related in chapter 18, Sarpedon was the son of Zeus and Laodameia, wife of Evander and daughter of Bellerophon.

[36] As related in chapter 16, Enyo was the goddess of war whom the Romans adopted under the name of Bellona.

spear wherewith he had been wounded by Tlepolemus.

The efforts of Ares on behalf of the Trojans now began to be felt[37] and, under the leadership of Hector, they forced the Greeks to give ground. Nor did the Trojan leader rely solely on those who served under him—for, with his own weapons, he destroyed the Greek warriors (otherwise undistinguished) Teuthras, Orestes, Trechus, Oenomaus, Helenus, and Oresbius.[38]

At this turn of events, Hera and Athena hastened to Olympus and appealed to Zeus[39]— claiming that, in breach of his promise, Ares was actively aiding the Trojan cause. Conceding the justness of their claim, the supreme god consented that his war-loving son should receive a proper chastisement, and the two goddesses (both partial to the Greeks) did not delay, but immediately drove their chariot to the place on the plain where the Simois and the Scamander joined their streams. There, they dismounted[40] and, going to where the Greek forces were grouped about Diomedes, Hera assumed the likeness of Stentor, whose voice was like that of fifty men,[41] and tauntingly shouted that the Trojans would not dare to pass even their Dardanian gate if Achilles should oppose them.[42] Nor did her barb go astray, but had the intended effect of rousing the army's spirit to fight.

Meanwhile, Athena approached Diomedes and inquired why he had so suddenly lessened his furious efforts. To which he replied that she had previously forbade him to fight with any deity except Aphrodite, and that he now perceived the Trojans to be led by Ares. Revealing that the prohibition was now withdrawn, the goddess displaced Sthenelus as charioteer and, with Diomedes as her passenger, drove speedily upon the war-god as he was stripping the armor from the corpse of the huge Aetolian Periphas. She put on her head the cap of Hades, however, so that she was rendered invisible to her bloodthirsty brother.

When Ares saw the approaching chariot— seemingly occupied by Diomedes alone—he left off his pillaging and threw his spear at the oncoming warrior, but Athena caught the weapon in her hand, and thrust it above the car to spend itself in the thin air. Thereupon, Diomedes made his cast, which was so accurately guided by the goddess that his spear pierced into Ares' belly and brought him to the ground, where Diomedes—now on foot—thrust him with his sword and withdrew his impaled spear. But, owing to his divinity, the war-god did not perish. Instead, he rushed from the plain of battle, bellowing with a brazen voice which equalled that of ten thousand men.

Stricken in his pride even more than in the flesh, the humiliated deity hastened to Olympus and, sitting beside the throne of Zeus, showed the immortal ichor flowing from his wound. Then, he bitterly complained that, through the machinations of Athena, the mortal Diomedes had been permitted to wound not only himself but also the goddess Aphrodite (Cypris). His great father, however, gave him no sympathy. Instead, he berated him as an inheritor of the unbearable and brawling spirit of his mother Hera, and concluded by remarking that if the war-god were not his own son he would, long before, have been sent down to the depths of Tartarus. Dismissed with this lack of consolation, Ares was sent to the Olympian physician Paeon, whom Zeus directed to heal the wound. This was done with divine celerity; and the unhappy deity regained some measure of comfort when his sister Hebe bathed him and clothed him with fresh raiment. He was not at all pleased, however, when he soon saw Hera and Athena returning from the earthly battlefield unscathed where he had recently been wounded.

---

[37] Ares partiality for the Trojan cause was due to his jealousy of Athena—partisan of the Greeks—who was accustomed to outdo him in warlike efforts. Another and perhaps cogent reason was because he was Aphrodite's lover. It may be noted (and not necessarily as a paradox but as additional proof of his hateful character) that Ares' sons, Ascalaphus and Ialmenus, fought on the Greek side as joint leaders of the Minyan forces.

[38] Oresbius was a Boeotian reputed to possess great wealth.

[39] The goddesses went to Olympus in the chariot of Hera, which was coupled to the horses with the assistance of Hebe.

[40] When Hera's horses were unhitched, the river Simois made ambrosia to spring up for them to graze upon.

[41] Hence, our "stentorian."

[42] To appreciate the point, it should be borne in mind that the Dardanian gate was at the eastern side of the Trojan wall—opposite to the plain where the fighting occurred.

24

The Trojan War IV

The Iliad

Book VI. RELIEVED of the active participation of the gods, the battle continued in its bloody course with the Greeks in the ascendency. Telamonian Ajax drove his spear through the forehead of the tall Thracian Acamas; Diomedes slew Axylus from Arisbe, who dwelt "by the high-road and was wont to give entertainment to all"—and, with him, his squire Calesius also met his death. Euryalus slew Dresus and Opheltius and followed by destroying Aesepus and Pedasus, borne to Laomedon's son Bucolion by the fountain-nymph Abarbarea; Polypoëtes slew Astylaus; Odysseus killed Pidytes of Percote; Teucer slew Aretaon; Antilochus slew Ablerus; Agamemnon slew Elatus; Leitus slew Phylacus; Eurypylus accounted for Melanthius; and Adrastus was murdered by Agamemnon, although taken captive by Menelaus.[1]

At this low ebb in the Trojan fortunes, Priam's son, Helenus, who was endowed with the gift of prophecy, came to Hector and Aeneas with the advice that they should encourage their men to stand fast, after which Hector should go into the city and join with his mother, Hecuba, and the other aged women of Troy in praying to Athena for protection against the Greeks—but especially against Diomedes. They followed his bidding, their forces rallied and the enemy were forced to give ground and cease from the earlier almost uninterrupted slaughter.

While Hector was on his way into the city, Diomedes met Glaucus (the son of Hippolochus and grandson of Bellerophon) in the space between the two armies. Observing his noble bearing, he asked if he were a god, and added that he was not minded to fight with an immortal because of the fate which had befallen Lycurgus when he had once opposed the wine-god Dionysus.[2] Upon this, Glaucus gave his lineage and related the story of Bellerophon (see chapter 6). When he had finished speaking, Diomedes planted his spear in the ground and extended to him the hand of friendship—saying that, of old, his father Tydeus entertained Bellerophon for twenty days in his house and that, upon parting, they exchanged gifts in token of their mutual admiration.[3] Following this narrative, the two men leapt from their chariots and, after clasping hands, pledged their amity by exchanging armor.[4]

Meanwhile, Hector came to the Scaean gate and was quickly surrounded by the wives and

---

[1] Menelaus had spared the life of his captive when the latter promised that his wealthy father would pay a great sum for his ransom.

[2] The story of Lycurgus and Dionysus is related in chapter 15.

[3] The gift of Oeneus was a scarlet belt and that of Bellerophon was a golden cup which Diomedes related was still at his palace when he left for Troy.

[4] The poet gravely comments that Zeus must have taken away Glaucus' wits, because he exchanged golden armor for bronze—"the worth of an hundred oxen for the worth of nine."

daughters of his comrades, seeking news of their sons, brothers, friends, and husbands who had engaged in the great battle. And to many he was forced to impart sorrowful tidings. Proceeding onward, he came to Priam's palace with its fifty chambers for his sons and twelve chambers for his daughters.[5] There, in the company of her fairest daughter Laodice, Hecuba greeted him and, with motherly solicitude, offered to bring him a cup of wine, but he replied that he feared it would deprive him of his valor, and bade her go to the temple of Athena with the other Trojan women to pray that the onslaught of Diomedes might come to an end. This she did, taking with her a richly embroidered robe, which had been brought from Sidon by Paris and dedicated to Athena at her altar which was presided over by Theano, wife of Antenor and daughter of Cisseus.

As the old women prayed, Hector went on to the palace of Paris, where he found his amorous brother idly handling his curved bow and other arms as he sat with Helen and her serving women who were busied at their embroidery. At this sight, the great warrior exploded words of recrimination which, following a conversation in which Helen voiced her feelings of guilt, resulted in the promise of Paris that he would again engage with the Greeks on the field of battle, where he said that he would be upon Hector's own return. Though Helen bade him sit for a while, Hector hastened on to his apartment, but found that his wife Andromache had gone, with his young son Astyanax (surnamed Scamandrius) to the top of the city's wall, where they were anxiously awaiting news of him. Hastening there, Andromache came running to meet him, followed by the nurse with her baby, and she pitifully announced her fear that her husband's prowess would be his own doom.[6] So saying, she implored him to stay on the wall to repulse the onset of the Greeks, who thrice before had attempted to scale it.

Hector replied that he knew in his heart that the day would come when the victorious Greeks would not only conquer Troy but would also take Andromache herself away as a captive, but he added that he had no choice except to fight on.[7] With an affected gaiety, he now stretched out his arms to his young son, who shrank back into the arms of his nurse—afraid at the sight of the horsehair which waved from the crest of his father's helmet. His childish action broke into his parent's mood of tragedy and, laughingly, Hector departed as his dear wife and son returned to their apartment. But, when she had returned, Andromache sat among her handmaidens and lamented because she had a foreboding that her husband would nevermore return from battle. Meanwhile, he was joined by Paris, and together they went back to the plain where the opposing armies were.

Book VII. Upon their return, the fighting was renewed with double ardor—especially by the Trojans. Paris led off by slaying Menesthius, the son of the mace man, Areithous; Hector followed suit by spearing Eioneus through the neck. When the Lycian leader, Glaucus, smote down Iphinous, Athena could no longer contain herself and darted down from Olympus to stem the Trojan tide. From his seat on Pergamus, however, Apollo spied the goddess and, meeting her beneath an oak tree, they agreed to put off the general engagement for the rest of the day but to incite Hector to propose a single combat. Understanding the spirit of the plan, the seer Helenus communicated it to his great brother who, giving his assent, stood up between the opposing hosts and gave the challenge.

At first, the Greeks were silent, for shame that none dared to meet the redoubtable Trojan. But, at length, Menelaus sprang up and, putting on his armor, would have gone forward—had not Agamemnon persuaded him that he could not gain the victory. Upon this, ancient Nestor arose and—again citing his youthful triumph over huge Ereuthalion at Pylus—chided all of his fellows with effeminate

---

[5] Although the names of Priam's fifty (or more) sons are recorded, the names of eight of his daughters do not appear to have been preserved by the mythographers.

[6] Andromache related how her father Eëtion, king of Cilician Thebes, had been slain—with her seven brothers —by Achilles, and her mother had been slain by the goddess Artemis, for some undisclosed reason.

---

[7] The action of Hector perhaps prompted the immortal phrase of Richard Lovelace in "To Lucasta, Upon Going to the Wars" which says: "I could not love thee, dear, so much—loved I not honor more."

cowardice. Stung by his words, nine of them leapt to their feet. They were Agamemnon, Diomedes, the two Aiantes (who, seemingly, acted in unison), Idomeneus, Meriones, Eurypylus, Thoas, and Odysseus. From these, Ajax was chosen by lot and went forth to meet Hector—bearing among his other arms a shield of eight layers which had been made by the artisan Tychius, who was considered to be the most expert of all workers in hide. And it was well that he had such a shield, because the first cast of Hector's spear carried through the six outer layers, but was stayed by the seventh. Ajax' own spear then pierced cleanly through Hector's buckler and would have proved fatal had not his adversary bent aside. Thereafter, when the victory was about to be won by Ajax—who had drawn blood from Hector's neck and had knocked him to the ground with a huge stone—the Greek herald Talthybius and the Trojan herald Idaeus jointly came to them and announced that the fight should cease, as night was come. Obediently, they parted—but before doing so exchanged gifts to evidence their mutual admiration.[8]

After retiring to their encampment, the Greeks sacrificed a bull to Zeus and, in honor of his prowess, gave its long chine to Ajax, while the rest ate food which was less delectable. When the meal was over, Nestor arose and proposed that their dead warriors should be burned on a single pyre with a large barrow erected over the ashes[9] and that, thereafter, the Greeks should build a moated wall for the protection of their ships.

At the same time, the Trojans were also holding a council, in which Antenor suggested that Helen and her treasures be given up—so that the grievous war might be brought to an end. But Paris refused to part with his fair love, although he agreed that the treasures taken from the palace of Menelaus should be returned. After he had spoken, Priam urged that Idaeus be sent to the enemy with the compro-

mise proposal and with a request that a truce be given in which to burn the dead. This was done, but when the herald carried his message to the Greeks, Diomedes leapt up and stated that, even though Helen should also be returned, the fight must continue until Troy should be utterly destroyed. And Agamemnon gave the same answer, although accepting the proposal for an armistice.

At dawn, the dead of both armies were gathered and burned in respectful silence and, on the following morning (without mention of the intervening night), the Greeks built a great mound over the ashes of their slain warriors and erected a wall about their ships, with gates for exit and entrance and surrounded by a deep ditch. Upon viewing these activities, Poseidon gloomily complained to Zeus that the newly built fortifications of the Greeks would, in after times, cause the walls of Ilium, built by himself and Apollo, to be forgotten; but his supreme brother promised him that, after the siege was over, he would be at liberty to demolish them with his floods. Following this, the sun went down and the Greeks feasted and drank wine which had just come in from the island of Lemnos on ships sent by Euneus (one of the twin sons borne to Jason by Hypsipyle). In the walled city, the Trojans likewise took their meal, but when they were done, they went to sleep with an uneasy feeling of impending doom.

Book VIII. Mindful of his promise to Thetis, Zeus now assembled the gods on Olympus and threatened them with the danger of being hurled down to Tartarus if any of them should help either of the warring forces, but he could not resist the plea of his favored daughter, Athena, that she should be permitted to give the Greeks her counsel. Thereupon, he mounted his car and went to the peak of Gargarus on Mount Ida where, taking his seat, he sent blazing thunderbolts into the army of the invaders as they marched in battle upon the Trojans—to whom the supreme god had decided that the day's victory should be given.

Frightened by this sign of divine disapproval, the Greeks broke ranks and fled back toward their ships, with Nestor remaining to face the enemy—and he only because one of his horses had been wounded by an arrow from the bow

---

[8] Hector gave Ajax his silver-studded sword and, in return, received his adversary's scarlet belt.

[9] The bones were to be carefully segregated so that they might be taken back for burial in the native homes with which they were identified.

of Paris. While the old man was cutting the traces from his stricken animal, Hector came upon him, and he would surely have perished had not Diomedes seen the danger which was threatening. Driving up in his chariot, he induced his aged friend to leave his horses in charge of his squires, Eurymedon and Sthenelus, and to take a seat in his own car. Then, driving furiously, the two Greeks charged upon the oncoming Hector, at whom Diomedes cast his spear—which missed its aim, but struck the Trojan's driver Eniopeus, who fell dead from the chariot. However, he was quickly replaced by Archeptolemus, and Hector was about to continue the fight when Zeus threw a thunderbolt before the horses of Diomedes. Knowing this as an omen of divine disapproval, Nestor wheeled about and—despite the protestations of his comrade that his action would stamp them for cowards—took flight back to the Grecian encampment. In hot pursuit Hector urged on his four horses—Xanthus, Podargus, Aëthon, and Lampus—asking that they now pay back to him the past favors of Andromache in feeding them well with "honey-hearted wheat and mingled wine."[10] The chariot bearing Nestor and Diomedes, however, arrived safely within the recently raised wall, where the Greeks were huddled in terrible fear that the gods had decreed their annihilation.

Seeing the misery of her favorites, Hera was restrained from interfering only when Poseidon pointed out that the supreme will of Zeus was not to be thwarted. In the alternative, she put it in the mind of Agamemnon to pray to her great spouse, and he—as a sign that the Greeks would not perish—sent an eagle with a fawn in its talons, which was dropped at the altar where they were wont to offer their sacrifices. Encouraged by this manifestation of divine approval, Diomedes sallied forth from behind the walls and fixed his spear in the back of Trojan Agelaus. Following him, in order, came Agamemnon, Menelaus, the two Aiäntes, Idomeneus, Meriones, Eurypylus, and Teucer—the last named using the shield of Ajax as a cover from

which to dart out and shoot his arrows at the puzzled enemy.[11] So, using this device, he successively brought down the Trojan warriors Orsilochus, Ormenus, Ophelestes, Daetor, Chromius, Lycophontes, Amopaon, and Melanippus. At his unerring performance, Agamemnon was so elated that he promised to give him a choice of treasure when Troy should be taken, but Teucer replied that he needed no such encouragement—he wanted only to lodge one of his arrows in the breast of Hector. So saying, he shot at the Trojan leader, but his shaft missed its mark and, instead, brought down the warrior Gorgythion, a son borne to Priam by Castianeira. He followed with another which also missed and lodged in the breast of Hector's charioteer, Archeptolemus, who had taken the place of the slain Eniopeus. Upon this happening, Hector wrathfully leapt from his car and, turning over the reins of his team to his brother Cebriones,[12] he smote Teucer with a stone which so stunned him that Ajax was forced to stand guard over his prostrate body until he could be carried back to the Greek ships by his comrades Mecisteus and Alastor.

As the Trojans, under Hector, pressed on until the Greeks were forced to take refuge behind the wall which they had built around their ships, Athena and Hera prepared to descend to the battlefield to succour their proteges. But, when Zeus perceived their intention, he sent Iris from his seat on Ida to Mount Olympus with a message that he forbade them to engage in the combat.[13] Thus prohibited, the goddesses could only sit down upon their celestial thrones and hope for the best.[14]

Meanwhile, the day was coming to its end and, having driven the Greeks behind their walls, Hector called off his attacking forces. He

---

[10] In his book *Homer and the Epic*, Andrew Lang points out that in no other instance is a battle chariot described as being pulled by four horses.

[11] Since Ajax was skilled only in the weapons used at close range, the Trojans were mystified at the rain of arrows shot by his half brother Teucer.

[12] Cebriones was a half brother of Hector, whose mother's name is not given by the mythographers.

[13] Without explanation, Athena mentions at this point that she could have thwarted Zeus' son Heracles in his emergence from the realm of Hades, where he had been sent to capture the hound Cerberus.

[14] Zeus threatened that, if they disobeyed his injunction, they would both receive wounds which would take ten years to heal.

left behind, however, a whole army of watchers[15] to make certain that the enemies—whom he was now confident of overcoming—would not leave during the night.

Book IX. The tired Greeks were not permitted to remain long at rest for—stricken with dismay at the thought that the gods had deserted his cause—Agamemnon called them into assembly and, weeping, proposed they they should all go home. And his men sat silently with grief until Diomedes leapt to his feet and announced that, whatever course the rest might take, he and his comrade Sthenelus intended to remain until Ilium should be taken. Thereupon, Nestor arose and suggested, with his accustomed sagacity, that the Greek chieftains should decide what best should be done, and when his suggestion was approved, sentinels were sent out to guard the convocation. They were: Nestor's son Thrasymedes; Ascalaphus and Ialmenus, the sons of Ares and Astyoche; Meriones, Aphareus, Deipyrus, and Lycomedes. Nor were the sentinels unaccompanied, for each of them took a hundred warriors with him, who sat between the trench and the protecting wall.

When the chieftains were alone, Nestor proposed that atonement be made to Achilles for having deprived him of the woman Briseis, and, confessing his proud folly, Agamemnon agreed to make amends by sending gifts of gold, horses, and women and he added that he would give back Briseis as she had come to him.[16] Furthermore, he said that—if it was fated that the Greeks should return to their native land—he would reward Achilles with the hand of one of his three daughters and with the government of seven Peloponnesian cities.[17] Taking him at his word, Nestor advised that the emissaries carrying the proposal should be Phoenix, Telamonian Ajax, and Odysseus, and that they should be accompanied by the heralds Odius and Eurybates. Pursuant to his suggestion, the men he

named came to the great hero's hut, where they found him singing to the accompaniment of a lyre—with only his comrade Patroclus.

Although Achilles warmly greeted his old friends and, with the assistance of Patroclus and his squire Automedon, fed them bountifully, he rejected the proposal which they had brought from Agamemnon—implying that he had been so humiliated that he could never be induced to return to the conflict on the side of the Greeks until he had received a personal apology from their haughty leader.[18] Nor was the sulking warrior swayed by the entreaty of his old friend Phoenix who, in a long discourse[19] sought to induce him to change his mind. Following this, Ajax and Odysseus departed to report the failure of their mission; but Phoenix remained in the tent of Achilles who had threatened to leave on the morrow and go, with his Myrmidons, back to his home in Thessalian Phthia. For the moment, however, he was content to retire beside his captive Lesbian maiden, Diomede. Patroclus, following suit, rested with "fair-girdled" Iphis.

Book X. After learning of Achilles' refusal, the Greek leaders retired to sleep, but Agamemnon was so distraught with worry that he arose and, while dressing, was joined by Menelaus—unable to rest for the same reason. Going their separate ways, they awakened and called into midnight council Nestor, Odysseus, Diomedes, Telamonian Ajax, Meges, Meriones, and Nestor's young son Antilochus. As they sat in a space near the moat, out of hearing of their sentinels, it was decided that Diomedes and Odysseus should make a scouting expedition into the midst of the enemy to ascertain both the physical arraignment of their army and their

---

[15] Before a thousand fires, the Trojans watched—with fifty warriors attending each flame.

[16] Although Briseis was not a maiden when he received her, Agamemnon vowed that she had never entered his bed.

[17] The three daughters were Chrysothemis, Laodice, and Iphianassa, and the seven cities were Cardamyle, Enope, Hire, Phermae, Antheia, Aepeia, and Pedasus.

[18] In a politely heated controversy, during the latter part of the last century, between Walter Leaf and Andrew Lang, the latter contended that it was a primary purpose of the poet to depict "the Wrath of Achilles" as continuing until such time as the Greeks were about to be overcome by the Trojans.

[19] In the course of his conversation, Phoenix related: how he was seduced by his stepmother and had to flee to the home of the centaur Cheiron, where he was reared with Achilles; how he was made king of the Dolopians; how the hunt for the Calydonian boar developed from a fight between the Curetes and the Aetolians; and how, as a result of it, Meleager came to his death.

plans for battle. After the two men were armed[20] they started on their mission, and were led through the darkness by following the cry of a heron which Athena sent to precede them.

On their way, they encountered the Trojan Dolon who had been sent to spy on their own encampment—bribed by Hector with the promise that, for his efforts, he should receive the immortal horses of Achilles. Seizing him, they learned not only how the allies of the Trojans were aligned for battle but also that they had just been bolstered by the accession of a Thracian tribe led by Rhesus.[21] After obtaining this information, Diomedes summarily cut off the spy's head and, proceeding on to the place where the Thracians were sleeping, he successively slew twelve of them while Odysseus pulled their corpses aside so that their horses might have an unimpeded passage of exit.[22] As the thirteenth, and last, Diomedes now murdered Rhesus while he lay dreaming, and following the bidding of Athena, he and Odysseus drove the Thracian steeds back to the Greek camp, where—after reporting the success of their undertaking to inquisitive Nestor and their other comrades— they gave the animals fodder at the manger from which the horses of Diomedes were accustomed to feed. Meanwhile, Apollo, becoming aware of what had happened, awakened Rhesus' kinsman Hippocoön, and the remainder of the Thracians, who indignantly gazed with their Trojan allies upon the carnage that the two stealthy Greeks had brought about.

Book XI. Stirred by Eris, the goddess of strife, Agamemnon armed himself for battle, wearing a beautiful corselet that had been given to him by the Cyprian king, Cinyras, and carrying his shield in whose center was set an image of the fearful Gorgon Medusa. Opposing his forces, the Trojans mustered about Hector, Polydamas,[23] and the three sons of Antenor named Polybus, Agenor, and Acamas. Until noon, the two armies seem to have fought an even battle in which no individual was outstanding. But then Agamemnon went on a one-man rampage and successively slew Bienor, Oileus, Isus, Antiphus,[24] Peisander, and Hippolochus.[25] Meanwhile, Hector was forced to withhold the strength of his arm, because Iris had been sent by Zeus to direct that he should not go into action until after Agamemnon should have been wounded and be about to depart in his chariot from the battlefield.[26]

Continuing with relentless fury, the Greek king now slew Iphidamas and Coön, two sons of Antenor, but before the latter expired, he was able to wound his attacker with a spear thrust below the elbow, and—even though the flow of blood soon ceased—Agamemnon was so pained that he leapt into his chariot and ordered that he be driven back to his headquarters. Thereupon, Hector gave a loud shout to encourage his ranked Trojans, Dardanians, and Lycians; and, showing his own enthusiasm, waded into the Greek host and successively felled Asaeus, Autonous, Opites, Dolops, Opheltius, Agelaus, Aesymnus, Orus, and Hipponous.

Alarmed at this turn in favor of the enemy, Odysseus called to Diomedes who—though gloomily announcing that he felt the gods were on the side of the enemy—proceeded with his accustomed vigor to slay Thymbraeus, while Odysseus accounted for the dead man's squire,

---

20 Before they left, Nestor's son Thrasymedes gave Diomedes a sword, a shield, and a helmet of bull's hide, without a crest; and Meriones gave to Odysseus a bow, quiver, sword, and the famous helmet which—first stolen by Autolycus (Odysseus' maternal grandfather)—had passed down as a family heirloom.

21 Although the father of Rhesus is named as Eioneus in the Iliad, later writers—including Euripides, who wrote a tragedy entitled by his name, called him a son of the god of the river-god Strymon and the Muse Terpsichore.

22 According to legend (mentioned in chapter 4), an oracle had prophesied that Troy could not be taken if the horses of Rhesus were permitted to pasture on the plain lying between the city and the sea.

23 Polydamas was a son of the Trojan elder Panthous, and is said to have been born on the same night with Hector.

24 Isus and Antiphus were two of the sons of Priam who, during his raids about Troy, had earlier been taken captive by Achilles as they were herding their sheep. But, having been set free for ransom, they were enabled to take part in the later fighting.

25 When Agamemnon attacked Peisander and Hippolochus, as he overtook their chariot pulled by runaway horses, they pleaded with him to take them alive and to hold them for ransom; but, recalling that their father, Antimachus, had bade the Trojans slay Menelaus and Odysseus when they first came as emissaries, he mercilessly cut them down.

26 At this point, the Trojans had been driven back and had taken their stand before the Scaean gate.

Molion. The son of Tydeus then killed and stripped the two sons of Merops of Percote (Amphius and Adrastus), and Odysseus followed suit by slaying Priam's two bastard sons Hippodamus and Hypeirochus. Following this, Diomedes slew the Trojan Agastrophus and, as Hector came charging upon him, knocked the great leader senseless with such a blow of his spear that, when he revived, he was forced to draw back into the midst of his comrades. But, while victorious Diomedes was engaged in stripping the armor from Agastrophus, Paris wounded him with an arrow in the foot and he was forced to retire—leaving Odysseus alone to stand off the foe. Nor was Odysseus daunted at his plight, because—assuming the burden of the battle—he took the lives of Priam's sons, Deiopites and Chersidamas, and then proceeded to slay their comrades Thoön, Ennomus, Charops, and Socus—the last named being renowned for his wealth but more renowned because before he fell he forced his spear into the side of his Ithacan opponent.

Seeing the blood gush from their companion's wound, Menelaus and Ajax went to the assistance of Odysseus and led him out from the battle; but Ajax remained to slay Priam's bastard son Doryclus and his fellow Trojans Pandocus, Lysander, Pyrasus, and Pylartes. Meanwhile, on the left side of the engagement, where the revived Hector was fighting against the Greek battalions led by Nestor and Idomeneus, Paris aimed a three-barbed arrow which pierced the right shoulder of the leech Machaon—a man so invaluable that Nestor raised him to his chariot and speedily drove him back to the ships for medical attention. As he left the field, Cebriones noted the rout which Ajax was causing in the center and went with his brother Hector to oppose the warriors led by the huge son of Telamon; but although Hector brought great slaughter to the rank and file of the Greeks, he avoided hand to hand combat with their mighty leader.

Zeus now brought a daze upon Ajax, which caused him to give way and become so hard pressed that Eurypylus came to his assistance and smote down the Trojan warrior Apisaon with his spear. However, while he was stripping his victim, Eurypylus was wounded in the right thigh with an arrow from the bow of Paris which broke off, but its point remained so deeply imbedded that he was forced to limp toward the rear as the protecting shield of Ajax kept the Trojans from following in pursuit.

In the interim, Achilles marked the chariot of Nestor bringing in the wounded Machaon and commenting, with some touch of malice, that it seemed the Achaeans would soon be begging for his help, he directed Patroclus to go to Nestor's tent and inquire the identity of his maimed passenger. When he arrived, he found that the squire Eurymedon had loosed the horses from the chariot and that Nestor and Machaon were both drinking a potion compounded from the cheese of goat's milk and barley meal—mixed for them by Hecamede, a beautiful captive from Tenedos whom Achilles had given to his aged friend.

After ascertaining that it was Machaon who had been wounded, Patroclus would have sped back to Achilles' tent with the requested information, but Nestor stayed his return—complaining that, while Achilles and his Myrmidons lay idle, a great many of their comrades had been slain and wounds had been suffered by Diomedes, Odysseus, Agamemnon, Eurypylus, and Machaon. Not losing the opportunity for an audience, the old man detailed many of his past accomplishments—relating how, when he was younger, he had: slain Itymoneus who was trying to prevent a reprisal raid of the Pylians upon the Elean[27] cattle of Augeias; killed the spearman Mulius and a hundred other warriors in the formal engagement which followed; and how he would have also slain the two great Moliones had not their putative father Poseidon enshrouded them in a deep mist. He then went on to say how, when the Trojan War was brewing, both Patroclus and Achilles had been found by him at the house of Patroclus' father, Menoëtius, and had eagerly enlisted in the Greek cause with the blessings of their fathers.[28] Concluding, he suggested that, even though Achilles was shunning the fight because of some god-given

---

[27] As elsewhere, no distinction seems to be made between the adjectives Elean and Epeian.

[28] The story of Homer about the circumstances of Achilles' enlistment is at variance with the later, and more colorful, legend which relates that he was discovered while secreted among the maidens at the court of Lycomedes.

impulse, nevertheless Patroclus should don his armor and frighten the Trojans into the belief that the great warrior had entered the battle. Pondering this advice, Patroclus departed and, encountering the lamed Eurypylus, took him to his tent and cut the imbedded arrow from his thigh, which he tenderly washed and salved until his wound dried.

Book XII. Describing the battles beside the ships and the Greek wall, which are initiated in the twelfth book of the Iliad, Andrew Lang says that they are confused, but he adds "the story is brief, the skirmishes are few, and the account is lucid" compared with the battles of the commentators on the subject.[29]

Looking to the Iliad itself however—without benefit of scholarly interpretation—we learn that, when the Greeks were driven back behind their wall[30] by the forces of Hector who were unable to cross the moat, Polydamas suggested to the Trojan leader that they should leave their chariots and manage the attack on foot. Following his advice, the Trojans and their allies dismounted and, after dividing themselves into five companies, began their assault.[31] Asius however —a captain of the third company—remained in his chariot[32] and, followed by some of his men, charged against the left gate which was defended by the Lapith warriors Polypoetes and Leonteus. And, when his onset was resisted by them in a determined stand, aided by stones

which their comrades hurled down from the walls, he appealed to Zeus in baffled anger at not finding the entrance which Hector was destined to first make.

As the fighting continued about the gate, Polypoëtes slew the Trojans Damasus, Pylon, and Ormenus; and Leonteus brought down Hippomachus, Antiphates, Menon, Iamenus, and Orestes. In the meanwhile, an eagle flew over the first company of the attackers and dropped into their midst a snake which it had borne in its talons. Thereupon, Polydamas suggested to Hector that this should be taken as an omen directing their withdrawal, but his great comrade answered in noble words: "One omen is best, to fight for our own country." So saying, he led on and the Greek walls were injured; but their wall of shields remained unbroken, as the two Aiäntes ranged all about and aroused their companions to strong resistance. Nor would a breach have been made had not Zeus spurred his son Sarpedon to attack with Glaucus the section of the wall which was being defended by the Athenians. When Menestheus saw them coming, he shuddered from fear and forthwith sent his herald Thoötes to summon the aid of the Aiantes. Telamonian Ajax quickly responded, accompanied by Teucer and his squire Pandion bearing the latter's great bow, but he left the Lesser Ajax and his friend, Lycomedes, to defend the place of fighting whence he had come.

Arrived at the side of the Athenians, Ajax crushed with a stone the head of the Lycian warrior Epicles, who had mounted to the top of the wall, and his brother Teucer wounded the onrushing Glaucus with an arrow so that he was forced to leave the battle. But they were unable to resist the might of Sarpedon who—first slaying Alcmaon with his spear—caught hold of the wall in his strong hands and pulled down a large section which laid bare the way. And, although the sons of Telamon were permitted, for a while, to hold the Lycians from entering, they were powerless to stay off Hector, to whom Zeus vouchsafed the glory of being the first to leap within the protective enclosure—for he burst in the central gates with a heavy stone and the Greeks were forced to retire back to the sterns of their ships.

---

[29] In the words of Lang: "Lachmann wars upon the left, and Nutzhorn on the right. Benicken and Baeumlein, Holm and Duntzer, Gerlach and Cauer, Kochly, Jacob, Kiene, Giseke, Genz, Bernhardy, Bergk, are but a few of the heroes in this conflict, every man fighting gallantly for his own hand over the prostrate body of Homer."

[30] A prophetic interpolation in the poem relates that, in after times, the Greek wall was swept away at the bidding of Poseidon and Apollo by the combined flow of the rivers which took their sources on Mount Ida, namely: Rhesus, Heptaporus, Caresus, Rhodius, Granicus, Aesepus, Scamander, and Simois.

[31] The leaders of the five companies were in order: first led by Hector, Polydamas, and Cebriones; second led by Paris, Alcathous, and Agenor; third led by Helenus, Deiphobus, and Asius; fourth led by Aeneas with Antenor's sons Archelochus and Acamas; and fifth led by the Trojan allies Sarpedon, Glaucus, and Asteropaeus.

[32] Asius was a son of Hyrtacus and Priam's first wife, Arisbe. The men who followed to the left gate with him were Iamenus, Orestes, Adamas, Thoön, and Oenomaus.

25

The Trojan War V

The Iliad

Book XIII. HAVING BROUGHT the opposing forces into desperate battle, and feeling that his earlier threat would keep the other deities from interfering, Zeus—apparently for no particular reason—turned from the Trojan scene and amused himself by gazing upon other lands, including those occupied by "the lordly Hippemolgi that drink the milk of mares" and "the Abii, the most righteous of men." But Poseidon came down from the topmost peak of Samothrace[1] where he had been watching the fighting, and—assuming the form of Calchas—urged the Aiäntes and many of the other Greeks to hold firm.[2] Spurred by his encouragement, the onslaught of Hector was stayed in a struggle where many feats of valor were performed on both sides.[3]

Becoming more enraged at the death of Amphimachus, who was reputed to have been his grandson, Poseidon now assumed the form of the Aetolian king, Thoas, and encouraged Idomeneus to arm himself and fight.[4] With his kinsman Meriones, who had obtained a new spear, Idomeneus hastened to the left flank[5] and quickly killed Othryoneus—a man come from afar to fight with the Trojans in the hope of winning the hand of Priam's daughter, Cassandra. And, when Asius came up to keep him from stripping his victim's corpse, the greying, Cretan king slew him also, while Nestor's son, Antilochus, assisted by piercing the Trojan's charioteer with his spear and driving off his horses into the Greek lines. Upon this, Deiphobus cast his spear at Idomeneus, but the weapon missed its mark and struck Hypsenor, who was carried—groaning heavily—back to the ships by his comrades Mecisteus and Alastor.

The next victim of Idomeneus was more illustrious. He was Alcathous, son of Aesyetes

---

[1] Instead of proceeding directly to the Trojan plain, which was overlooked from the peak of Samothrace, the sea-god went to his watery palace at Aegae and drove back in his chariot, drawn by steeds which were tethered in the deep between the islands of Imbros and Tenedos.

[2] In addition to the Aiäntes, Poseidon spoke separately to Teucer, Leitus, Peneleos, Thoas, Deipyrus, Meriones, and Antilochus, relating that—notwithstanding Agamemnon's treatment of Achilles—it was up to them to defend the honor of their country.

[3] As highlights of the engagement: Meriones broke his spear on the shield of Priam's son, Deiphobus, and went back to his hut for another weapon; Teucer slew Imbrius, a Trojan who was wedded to Priam's daughter Medesicaste; Hector brought down Amphimachus, son of Cteatus, but was barred by Telamonian Ajax from stripping the corpse, which was taken into the Greek lines by Stichius and Menestheus—together with the

body of Imbrius who had been previously slain by Teucer; and, in rage at the death of his friend Amphimachus, Ajax the Lesser cut off the head of Imbrius and sent it rolling in the dust before Hector's feet.

[4] It seems rather odd that Idomeneus was not already armed; and, perhaps stranger still, it is related that he was assisting an unnamed comrade from the battlefield when Poseidon approached him in the form of Thoas.

[5] Before entering the battle on the left flank, Idomeneus observed that the middle of the Greek line was well-protected by the two Aiäntes and the mighty bow of Teucer.

and brother of Antenor, who was married to Anchises' daughter, Hippodameia. After he fell, the raging Cretan challenged Deiphobus to come out. Priam's wary son, however, first obtained the assistance of his great kinsman Aeneas[6] and, in the meanwhile, his challenger brought up his comrades Ascalaphus, Aphareus, Deipyrus, Meriones, and Antilochus to his own aid. With the battle raging around the corpse of Alcathous: Idomeneus avoided the spear of Aeneas, but his own pierced Oenomaus and, withdrawing it, he stood back to avoid the cast of Deiphobus, which smote down his comrade Ascalaphus; Meriones wounded Deiphobus in the upper arm and, retrieving his weapon, leapt back into the throng of his comrades while Polites led his injured brother to the Trojan rear; Aeneas slew Aphareus; Antilochus slew the Trojan warrior Thoön, and would have stripped him of his armor, but Adamas set upon him—only to lose his life when Meriones speared him as he shrank back to avoid his own fated end; Priam's prophetic son, Helenus, killed Deipyrus with a stroke of his sword which rolled the Greek warrior's helmet in the dust; Menelaus retaliated by thrusting his spear through the hand of Helenus, who retired to the midst of his comrades where the weapon was removed and his wound was bound by Agenor; and Menelaus also slew Peisander after a furious duel and stripped his body of its armor.

Harpalion, a son of the Paphlagonian leader Pylaemenes, now assaulted Menelaus but his spear thrust was stopped by the Spartan's shield and he shrank back to save himself—only to be slain by an arrow from the bow of Meriones. In wrath at the destruction of one who had once been his host among the Paphlagonians, Paris loosed an arrow which pierced Euchenor beneath the jaw and caused his death.[7] This incident brings to a close the poet's recital of the day's events on the left flank, where the

Greeks seem to have had the better of the fighting.

Meanwhile, Hector fought on within the wall which he had broken through in the center —unaware how the fortunes of his comrades were elsewhere; and he stood his ground strongly against the Aiäntes and other Greek warriors[8] until his forces were so harassed by missiles from the concealed Locrian archers and slingers that he accepted the advice of Polydamas to hold a council of war, lest Achilles might possibly be induced to come forth from his sulking inactivity. But, before retiring to the council, Hector rushed to the left flank to collect his leaders and discovered that of them Paris was alone unwounded. Dismayed at the news, the Trojan chieftain upbraided his younger brother —even though he had been fighting valiantly.[9] But Paris gave him a soft answer and the two of them reentered the battle where the struggle was fiercest.[10] Telamonian Ajax now approached and added to his challenge the prediction that the day was not far distant when the Greeks would gain the victory—a prediction which caused his men to shout aloud when it was followed by the appearance of an eagle soaring high above on the right of their band.[11]

The thirteenth book ends as the opposing forces are about to clash again, with Hector apparently forgetting about the council which he had earlier agreed to call.[12]

---

[6] Upon approaching Aeneas, Deiphobus found him standing aside in apparent sulk that Priam had not originally offered him a post of honor befitting his rank as the son of Aphrodite and of Anchises—his Dardanian father of the same degree as the Trojan king.

[7] Before going to the war, Euchenor had been told by his seer-father Polyidus that he was destined to perish either in his own halls or in the Trojan fighting.

[8] Among those named as standing with the Aiäntes against the onslaught of Hector were the Boeotians, the Ionians "of trailing tunics," the Locrians, the Phthians, the Epeians, and the Athenians. Of the Athenians: Menestheus was leader with Pheidas, Stichius and Bias as captains; of the Epeians: Meges was leader with Amphion and Dracius as captains; and the Phthians were led by Podarces and Medon.

[9] In chiding his brother, Hector called him Evil Paris ("Dysparis").

[10] Those joined by Hector and Paris are named as being Cebriones, Polydamas, Phalces, Orthaeus, Polyphetes, Palmys, Ascanius, and Morys.

[11] Because the eagle was sacred to Zeus, its appearance was considered to indicate the god's approbation of the prediction of Ajax.

[12] The somewhat confused account of the fighting given in book thirteen, which has led some scholars to question its authenticity, is defended by Andrew Lang on the ground that the activities of the five separate Trojan companies are necessarily related in successive order although many of them were contemporaneous at different positions without and within the Greek wall.

Book XIV. The increasing clamor of war reached Nestor's ears, as he was sitting at a table with the wounded Machaon who was tended by his slave-maid Hecamede. Going out to learn the reason, he was so alarmed to see the Greeks in flight[13] that he hastened to the hut of Agamemnon. On the way he encountered the chief commander in the company of Odysseus and Diomedes—all three of them limping with the aid of their spears as crutches.[14]

In his despair, Agamemnon proposed that the ships should be made ready for flight, but he was chided so severely by both Odysseus and Diomedes that he agreed with them that—wounded though they were—they should go back to the fighting and encourage the army. At this point, Poseidon miraculously joined them in the form of an old man[15] and, shouting with the combined voice of ten thousand warriors, he heartened the Achaean forces.

The scene now changes to Olympus where Hera is determined to keep Zeus unaware of Poseidon's forbidden assistance. Firstly, going to Aphrodite, she obtained the use of her irresistible zone of love—upon the pretense that it was for the purpose of repairing a marital rift between Oceanus and Tethys.[16] Secondly, she went to the island of Lemnos, and induced Hypnos (Sleep) to aid her design. Finally, she went to her great lord on Mount Gargarus, who was so overcome by her charms—and the sly influence of Hypnos[17] that he caused a great cloud to envelop the mountain and, in her arms, went peacefully to sleep.

Hypnos hastened down to the battlefield and, when he told Poseidon that the eyes of his supreme brother were closed, the sea-god urged the Greeks on against the enemy.[18] At the initial onslaught, Hector cast his spear at Telamonian Ajax, but it could not pierce the two-fold baldrics of his shield and his sword, and the huge Greek retaliated by smashing his adversary with a stone which made him spin around like a top and collapse unconscious. But their leader's inert form was protected and carried to the banks of the river Xanthus[19] by his comrades Polydamas, Aeneas, Agenor, Sarpedon, and Glaucus—an incident which encouraged the Greeks to attack with renewed vigor.

In the resultant fighting, Ajax the Lesser wounded the Trojan Satnius; Polydamas slew the Boeotian leader Prothoënor; Telamonian Ajax slew Archelochus with a spear intended for Polydamas;[20] Acamas, protecting his brother's corpse, slew the Boeotian leader Promachus; Peneleos, in revenge for the deaths of his kinsmen,[21] slew the Trojan Ilioneus and exultantly exhibited his severed head aloft on the point of his spear; Telamonian Ajax now slew the Mysian Hyrtius; Antilochus slew Phalces and Mermerus; Meriones slew Morys and Hippotion; Teucer slew Prothoön and Periphetes; Menelaus slew Hyperenor; but Ajax the Lesser (the swift son of Oileus) accounted for more of the foe than any other Greek warrior.

Book XV. In the opening lines of book fifteen, Zeus awakes in the arms of Hera to see Hector wounded and the Trojans driven in rout back across the moat surrounding the Greek wall. He rebukes Hera for her guile and reminds her of the earlier occasion when she was punished by him for a similar trick.[22] His wrath is

---

[13] Since book thirteen ends with the Greeks being heartened by the eagle of Zeus and apparently on the offensive, the close-following statement that Nestor saw them in rout has given rise to a scholastic controversy, whose solution is beyond the scope of this compilation.

[14] The hut of Agamemnon was located near his ship which, like those of his lieutenants, was nearest to the water and farthest from the inland protecting wall.

[15] The Iliad does not name the "old man" whose form Poseidon assumed, but a later interpolation into the story relates that he assumed the likeness of Achilles' companion Phoenix.

[16] As related in chapter 3, Hera was reared by Tethys and Oceanus, and this fact gave a measure of plausibility to her solicitude for their continued happiness.

[17] Before Hera could obtain the help of Hypnos, she had to allay the misgivings which he had about the probable wrath of Zeus which had been exhibited on the previous occasion when the goddess drove the ship of Heracles to the island of Cos while her great lord slept.

[18] For some obscure reason, Poseidon had the bravest of the Greeks take from their comrades the best of their armor before making the attack on the Trojans.

[19] Although Hesiod says that Oceanus and Tethys were the parents of all the streams on earth, it is related in the Iliad that the river-god Xanthus was begotten by Zeus.

[20] After slaying Archelochus, the son of Antenor, Ajax remarked that his fallen foe was not "of mean descent."

[21] Promachus and Prothoënor were first cousins of Peneleos and, with him were co-leaders of the Boeotians.

[22] When Hera drove the vessel of Heracles in a great storm to the island of Cos while Zeus slept, he

appeased by her submission, and he announces that Iris shall be sent to call off Poseidon's assistance of the Greeks and that Apollo shall be sent to revive Hector—to the end that the Trojans shall again drive the fighting to the sterns of the Greek ships and bring about the situation, promised to Thetis, wherein Agamemnon would be forced to humbly call upon Achilles for help. He further announces that Patroclus will be slain and the Greeks will eventually be victorious after Achilles shall have slain Hector.

Following this, Hera whisked herself to Olympus and, with a somewhat foolish change of mind, sought to incite the assembled deities against the supreme rule of Zeus. Indeed, Ares took her words so much to heart that he would have gone forthwith into the battle on the side of the Trojans had not Athena dissuaded him. The feeling of revolt, however, was temporary and Hera sent Iris and Apollo down to Zeus on Mount Gargarus to receive their instructions. Having done so,[23] Iris bade Poseidon leave the battle and he plunged into the sea—but only after consenting in a speech filled with reluctance and passion. As soon as he disappeared below the waves, Zeus sent Apollo down to inspire Hector, who eagerly led his men back to the fight, with the archer-god himself in the van carrying the dread aegis of Zeus.

Alarmed at the return of their great foe, whom they had but recently seen carried from the battlefield in a state of unconsciousness, the Greeks decided (upon the advice of Thoas) that their rank and file should retire to their ships while the strongest of their chieftains should stand off the attackers. The operation was accomplished, but in the fighting: Hector slew the Athenian leader Stichius and the Boeotion leader Arcesilaus; Aeneas slew Medon, the half brother of Ajax the Lesser, and the Athenian captain Iasus; Polydamas slew Mecisteus; Priam's son Polites slew Echius; Agenor slew

Clonius, another Boeotian leader;[24] and Paris slew Deiochus.

Following this great slaughter of the Greek chieftains, the wall protecting their ships was cast down by Apollo "even as when a boy scattereth the sand by the sea"; and the Trojan horde rolled in. At this juncture, Neleus prayed to Zeus, and the god answered by sending a clap of thunder which the Trojans took as encouragement for their cause and continued their relentless onslaught.

The story now goes to Patroclus, who had long been tending the wounded Eurypylus in his hut. Upon seeing the enemy rushing through the fallen wall, he hastened to the tent of Achilles to urge him to the battle. Meanwhile, the fighting continued: Telamonian Ajax and Hector again tangled; the former's spear missed his antagonist, but brought down his cousin Caletor; Hector's return cast also missed, but pierced through the head of Lycophron the squire of Ajax; an arrow from Teucer's bow knocked Cleitus from his chariot and his horses were given by Polydamas to Astynous to hold; but a second arrow aimed by Teucer at Hector did not leave the string, which was broken by the will of Zeus even as it was tautened. Thereupon, he dropped his bow and reentered the fighting with shield and spear—to the comparative joy of the Trojans who more greatly feared the cruel punishment theretofore brought upon them by his unerring arrows.

In the struggle which followed: Hector slew the Phocian leader Schedius, the son of Perimedes; Telamonian Ajax slew Antenor's son Laodamas; Polydamas laid low the Epeian Otus; Meges slew the Trojan Croesmus and, with the help of Menelaus, brought down Laomedon's grandson, Dolops; Antilochus slew Melanippus and would have stripped him of his armor but he was forced to flee at the approach of Hector and, slaying Periphetes on the way, the raging Trojan chief would almost single-handed have set the Greek ships afire had they not been valiantly defended by Telamonian

---

awakened to punish her by suspending her from the heavens with two anvils tied to her ankles, and when Hephaestus sought to intervene, he was hurled down to the island of Lemnos.

[23] Contrary to the account of Hesiod, which makes Zeus the youngest son of Cronus, the Homeric story relates that he was the eldest.

---

[24] The ancient valor of the Boeotians was attested not only by the fact that they were named in the Catalogue first among the Greek forces, but also by the brave fighting of their leaders in the Trojan conflict.

Ajax who, leaping from deck to deck, took his stand on the bark of Protesilaus, where he ringed himself about with the corpses of twelve slain enemies.

Book XVI. While the Greek fortunes were reaching this crucial state, Patroclus came to the tent of Achilles and obtained the permission of his great friend to don his armor and lead his Myrmidon forces into battle, so that the Trojans might be led to believe that the sulking hero had at last become reconciled with Agamemnon. However, permission was given with the condition attached that Patroclus should content himself with the rescue of the Greek fleet, without further pursuit of the enemy—for Achilles intimated that he wanted to participate with his friend in the final overthrow of the Trojan citadel. Following this, smoke was seen to rise about the Greek ships, where the point of Telamonian Ajax' spear had been sheared off by Hector's sword and Achilles set about gathering his men, while Patroclus arrayed himself in the borrowed armor[25] and ordered the charioteer Automedon to yoke the swift horses—Balius, Xanthus, and Pedasus.[26]

When the Myrmidon host had been drawn up and divided into companies under their five captains,[27] Achilles exhorted them to fight bravely. Then, withdrawing to his tent, he poured a libation to Zeus and prayed to the supreme god[28] to give success to his men. Thereupon, Patroclus led them in to battle and the Trojans, believing him to be Achilles, were so stricken with terror that each man of them felt his own destruction to be imminent. And it was for many, because Patroclus slew the Paeonian leader Pyraechmes and also the Trojan Areïlycus; Menelaus slew Thoas; Meges slew Amphiclus; Antilochus slew Atymnius; Thrasymedes slew Maris;[29] Ajax the Lesser slew Cleobulus; Peneleos slew Lyco; Meriones slew Acamas; and Idomeneus slew Erymas. At this low ebb in the Trojan fortunes, both Telamonian Ajax and Patroclus charged upon Hector, but his swift horses carried him beyond reach and, turning back, Patroclus had to content himself with successively bringing down Pronous, Thestor, Erylaus, Erymas, Amphoterus, Epaltes, Tlepolemus, Echius, Pyris, Ipheus, Evippus, and Polymelus.

Seeing the wholesale slaughter of his Trojan allies, the Lycian Sarpedon—who was a son of Zeus—attacked Patroclus[30] and, after a furious combat in which his squire Thrasymelus was slain, lost his own life at the hands of the raging Greek.[31] As he fell, he urged his kinsman Glaucus to stir up the Lycians against his destroyers[32] and Glaucus, healed of his wound by Apollo,[33] rallied both the Lycians and the Trojans to fight over the inert corpse. In the subsequent fighting, the Myrmidon Epeigeus lost his life; Patroclus slew Trojan Sthenelaus; Glaucus slew the Greek Bathycles; Meriones slew Laogonus, who was a Trojan priest of Zeus, and bandied words with Aeneas until Patroclus called upon him to strip the armor from Sarpedon's body. Upon

---

[25] Patroclus did not attempt to use the spear of Achilles, given as a wedding present to Peleus by Cheiron, because it was of such bulk that none but the owner could wield it.

[26] Balius and Xanthus, the immortal equine offspring by Poseidon of the Harpy Podarge and Zephyrus (the west-wind), were given to Achilles' father, Peleus, as a wedding present. The third horse, Pedasus, was mortal, and had been taken by the hero from King Eëtion after the sack of Asiatic Thebes in one of the raids preceding the events related in the Iliad.

[27] The five captains of the Myrmidons were. Menesthius, a son of the river-god Spercheius; Eudorus, a son of Hermes; Peisander; Phoenix, the son of Amyntor who was reared with Achilles; and Alcimedon.

[28] In his prayer to Zeus, Achilles called him "thou King Dodonaean, Pelasgian, thou that dwellest afar, ruling over wintry Dodona—and about thee dwell the Selli, thine interpreters, men with unwashen feet that couch on the ground." This reference to the Selli is converted by some eminent philologists into "Helli," and is cited as being the ancient source of the name Hellenes, by which the Greeks were later known.

[29] It is related that Atymnius and Maris were sons of Amisodarus, "he that reared the raging Chimaera, a bane to many men."

[30] In his attack, Sarpedon initially cast his spear at Patroclus but it missed and buried itself in the right shoulder of the horse Pedasus and, as he died, he was cut loose from the traces by Automedon.

[31] Before Sarpedon was permitted to be slain, Zeus and Hera had an interesting conversation on Olympus in which she pointed out that if he should be minded to save the life of his son, other deities, who also had sons engaged in the battle, would feel free to follow his example.

[32] Glaucus was the nephew of Laodameia, who was the mother of Sarpedon by Zeus.

[33] As related earlier, Glaucus had been wounded by one of the arrows of Teucer.

this happening, Hector (who had returned to the battlefield unarmored) was again impelled by Zeus to flee, and was followed in such a rout by Trojans and Lycians alike that the Greeks were able to strip the corpse of Sarpedon of its bronze armor without being bothered. They bore it then back in triumph to their ships. However, they were not permitted to mutilate the body—for, at the bidding of Zeus, Apollo carried it from the battlefield and, after anointing it with ambrosia and clothing it in immortal raiment, gave it in charge of Sleep (Hypnos) and Death (Thanatos) to convey back to Lycia.

Pursuing the fleeing enemy, Patroclus continued in his carnage by slaying Adrastus, Autonous, Echeclus, Perimus, Epistor, Melanippus, Elasus, Mulius, and Pylartes. And, despite the admonition of Achilles, he would have raged on into the city had not Apollo thrust him back with his immortal hands. The god then assumed the form of Hecuba's brother Asius[34] and incited Hector to attack in his chariot driven by his half brother Cebriones. As they approached, Patroclus leapt from his chariot and cast a jagged stone which caught Cebriones in the forehead and he fell lifeless to the ground. There followed a furious tug of war in which Hector tried to protect his driver's corpse by holding fast to the head while Patroclus pulled mightily by the foot. Finally, with the help of his men, Patroclus was successful and again turned to the attack as the Greeks drew the dead body to their rear and stripped it of its armor. Thrice he leapt upon the enemy and thrice he slew nine men; but, when he rushed on for the fourth time, he was smitten down by Apollo and the glorious helmet of Achilles rolled in the dust. As he arose and stood in a daze, his back was pierced by the sharp spear of Euphorbus and he attempted to draw back into the ranks of his comrades; but, seeing his injured condition, Hector rushed upon him and completed the kill by a spear-thrust through the belly. Then, withdrawing the weapon as the dying

man prophesied that Achilles would take vengeance, the Trojan leader set out in vain pursuit of Automedon drawn by the immortal horses of his master Achilles.

Book XVII. When Menelaus saw Hector leave the prostrate form of Patroclus, he hastened to bestride the corpse to protect it from the enemy and was successful in slaying Euphorbus as he tried to take the armor to which he felt entitled by reason of his earlier spear-thrust in the dead man's back.[35] He was forced, however, to retreat in search of help from Telamonian Ajax when Hector, inspired by Apollo in the form of the Ciconian leader Mentes, charged in furiously and stripped the armor of Achilles from the body of his slain friend. The two Greek chieftains, however, returned before Hector was able to drag away the corpse itself and the Trojan leader was driven back to his own men, where he was chided for being a coward by his Lycian ally Glaucus. Stung by the charge, he donned the armor which he had taken and rallied his men to help him in driving off Ajax and Menelaus from their defense of Patroclus' corpse.[36] And Zeus fired his heart with courage, although decreeing that he should not live to carry the armor of mighty Achilles to exhibit before his loving wife, Andromache.

As the enemy host came upon them, Ajax and Menelaus called upon their comrades for help and were gratified when they were reinforced by many of the Greeks—among whom Ajax the Lesser, Idomeneus, and Meriones were in the van. Zeus was not minded to permit the corpse to be taken, but the result was not determined until after a bloody engagement was fought. The Trojans first drove back the Greeks, and the Pelasgian Hippothous was dragging away the dead body, when Telamonian Ajax roused his companions to a counter charge by slaying the would-be despoiler. Hector retaliated by a cast of his spear, but Ajax stepped aside and

---

[34] In the Iliad, the father of Hecuba and Asius is named as "Dymas, that dwelt in Phrygia by the streams of Stangarius," but on our genealogical charts we have followed the more popular legend that Hecuba was a daughter of the river-god Sangarius.

[35] Euphorbus was a son of the Trojan elder Panthous, whose name does not appear on our genealogical charts because there is no extant reference which mentions his undoubtedly noble lineage.

[36] Among those rallied by Hector, the following are specifically named: Mesthles, Glaucus, Medon, Thersilochus, Asteropaeus, Deisenor, Hippothous, Phorcys, Chromius, and Ennomus, the augur.

the weapon brought death to the Phocian leader Schedius, a son of Iphitus. Ajax now slew Phorcys as he tried to protect the body of the slain Hippothous and, when the Trojans gave ground, the Greeks drew off the corpses of both men and stripped them of their armor.

As the Trojan fortunes again waned, Apollo took the form of the herald Periphas and urged Aeneas to resist, lest the walled city be soon brought to destruction. Recognizing the divinity, Aeneas shouted to Hector that their cause was succoured by the gods and, leaping to the forefront, rallied his discouraged countrymen. In the melee which followed, he wounded Leocritus. Lycomedes, the comrade of Leocritus, retaliated by slaying the Paeonian Apisaon, whose fall brought his tall companion Asteropaeus rushing in to the battle; but Telamonian Ajax ranged to and fro among the fighting Greeks, and they stood firm over the corpse of Patroclus in a defense so furious that it seemed as though darkness had fallen.

Meanwhile, Nestor's sons, Antilochus and Thrasymedes, were warring in a distant sector, unaware of the death of Patroclus; Achilles sat in his tent and awaited news of his dear comrade's anticipated success, but the immortal horses, Balius and Xanthus, stood weeping at a distance from where the corpse of Patroclus was being fought over, and refused to budge despite the entreaties and lashings of Automedon. As they mourned, Zeus took pity upon them and, at his bidding, they were bearing Automedon from the field of battle when they were halted by Alcimedon, who chided Automedon for fleeing. When Automedon said that his flight was not from cowardice, but because he could not control the steeds, Alcimedon leapt into the chariot and—taking over the lash and the reins—they swept back to the conflict. Seeing their approach, Hector and Aeneas (accompanied by Chromius and Aretus) advanced to meet them, for the Trojan leader was eager to capture the immortal animals as complementary renown to the armor of Achilles which he had already obtained and donned. Calling upon the two Aiäntes and Menelaus for help, Automedon cast his spear, which cleanly passed through the shield of Aretus and brought him to death. In return, Hector threw his weapon

at Automedon, but he avoided its thrust and, with the arrival of the Aiäntes and Menelaus, the Trojans were forced to give ground somewhat.

At this point, the mind of Zeus "turned" and he sent Athena down to encourage the Greeks fighting about the corpse of Patroclus. Taking the form of elderly Phoenix, she encouraged Menelaus so that he slew and stripped Podes, the son of Eëtian and comrade of Hector. But Apollo, espousing the cause of the Trojans, came to the side of Hector in the form of Phaenops and, by shaking his aegis, caused the Greeks to lose heart.[37] With this change in the fortunes of the combatants, the Boeotian leader Peneleos lost his life when pierced by the spear of Polydamas, and Hector wounded Leitus on the wrist so sorely that he had to cease fighting. While the Trojan leader chased his injured victim, Idomeneus ineffectually smote his corselet with a spear and the return thrust of Hector brought death to Coeranus, the comrade and charioteer of the Cretan Meriones.

Realizing that their state was critical, Telamonian Ajax and Menelaus decided that it was at last necessary to call upon Achilles for help and, searching out Antilochus and conveying to him the news of the death of Patroclus, the young son of Nestor (first doffing his armor and leaving it in the keeping of his comrade Laodocus) at their request leapt into his chariot and hastened to deliver the sorrowful message of entreaty. And, as he went, Menelaus and Meriones started back toward the Greek lines with the corpse of Patroclus, while the two Aiäntes mightily fought off the Trojan onslaught which would have frustrated their effort.

Book XVIII. When Antilochus came to the hut of Achilles and told him that Patroclus had been slain, the great warrior groaned so loudly[38] that Thetis, his mother, came up from the

---

[37] It is not within the province of this compilation to resolve the classical argument as to whether Zeus, Athena, or Apollo was the preeminent deity in the Greek mythology. Many learned treatises have been written on the question, and suffice to say that, on occasion, each of them seems to have been preferred.

[38] Added to the groans of Achilles were the anguished shrieks of the handmaidens who were wont to attend Patroclus in the hut which they shared jointly.

depths with her sister-Nereids[39] and inquired the reason for his grief. After a tender scene, in which she prophesied that he would meet his own death after slaying Hector, the goddess plunged back into the sea with the promise that she would return on the morrow with a new suit of armor, made by Hephaestus.

Meanwhile, the Greeks were having their troubles in bringing the corpse of Patroclus back into their lines and were successful in their efforts only because at the bidding of Iris, sent by Hera, Achilles accoutered himself in the dread aegis of Athena and—otherwise unarmored—went to the moat and shouted thrice so loudly that the Trojans fled in a stampede in which twelve of their warriors were trampled to death. The Greeks thus were enabled to complete taking their dead comrade from the field of fighting and, as the sun went down, they thronged weeping around his bier. The most tears of all, however, were those shed by Achilles as he gazed upon the form of his dear friend whom he had sent forth to death in the chariot drawn by his own horses.

On the Trojan side, Polydamas—a son of Panthous born on the same night with Hector—urged that they retire within the protection of the city's walls, lest on the morrow Achilles should take the field. Hector, however, spurned the suggestion and announced that he would again attack the Greek ships, and added that he was not afraid to stand face to face with their great warrior in single combat. Meanwhile, throughout the night, Achilles mourned before the corpse of Patroclus and vowed that it should not be buried until a ceremony at which the head and armor of Hector should be offered, together with twelve Trojan warriors whose throats would be cut before the funeral pyre.

As Zeus and Hera talked over the day's events, Thetis came to Olympus and entered the palace of Hephaestus, where she was greeted by his wife, Charis,[40] and led to a silver-studded chair in which she sat until the fire-god entered and clasped her by the hand.[41] After she had related the purpose of her visit, he readily agreed to fashion a new suit of armor and, soon returning to his anvil and twenty bellows, went to work without delay. Soon he had completed a wondrous shield,[42] corselet, helmet, and greaves. These he gave to her and she sprang down from Olympus like a falcon, bearing the flashing equipment to her great son on earth.

---

[39] The attending Nereids named in the Iliad were: Glauce, Thaleia, Cymodoce, Nesaea, Speio, Thoë, Halia, Cymothoë, Actaea, Limnoreia, Melite, Iaera, Amphithoë, Agave, Doto, Proto, Pherousa, Dynamene, Dexamene, Amphinone, Callianeira, Doris, Panope, Galatea, Nemertes, Apseudes, Callianassa, Clymene, Ianeira, Ianassa, Maera, Oreithyia, and Amatheia. It will be noted that the list is not the same as that of Apollodorus which is given in chapter 1.

[40] Although Charis (considered a surname for Aglaia, the youngest and most beautiful of the Graces) is named as the wife of Hephaestus in the Iliad, the conventional legend (preserved in the Odyssey) related that his wife was Aphrodite.

[41] When Charis summoned Hephaestus from his anvil with the announcement of Thetis' presence, he recalled how the Nereid and the Oceanid Eurynome had graciously lodged him for nine years in a hollow cave after he had been thrown from Olympus by Hera for shame of his lameness.

[42] The marvelous designs which Hephaestus worked on the shield of Achilles are related in too much detail to be here repeated. In general, they followed the pattern of those on the shield of Heracles, which have been mentioned at length in a footnote of chapter 14.

26

The Trojan War VI

The Iliad

Book XIX. At dawn, Thetis came with the armor to the Greek ships and delivered it to Achilles, whom she found wailing aloud as he clasped the body of his dead friend. As his Myrmidons shrank from the sight of the immortal equipment, Achilles announced that he was minded to don it at once and give battle, but he expressed a doubt that, before he should return, the corpse of Patroclus might still be preserved from decay. Assuring him that she would protect it in sound flesh, even though it should lie for a full year, his Nereid mother bade him call the Greeks to a gathering and publicly renounce his wrath against Agamemnon before going to the attack. Pursuant to her bidding, the gathering was called and was attended by all of the Greeks, of whom Agamemnon last took his seat —still burdened with the wound which had been given to him by Antenor's son, Coön.

Forthwith, Achilles arose and made open apology for his sulking wrath—saying that it would have been better if Briseis had been slain by the goddess Artemis before he had taken her as part of the spoils from the sack of the town of Lyrnessus. Agamemnon followed with his apology—not so frank, because he blamed his impetuous action upon the goddess Ate, and cited the instance of her deluding Zeus into making the boast which resulted in the bondage of Heracles to Eurystheus.[1] But he concluded by offering the same gifts of requital that he had previously tendered through the offices of Odysseus.[2]

Having received Agamemnon's public submission, Achilles was eager to avenge the death of Patroclus, and would have hastened to the attack immediately, but Odysseus gave counsel that it would be better to fight with full stomachs and the army scattered for breakfast after the gifts of Agamemnon were taken to the hut of Achilles.[3] The great warrior, however, refused to eat, although urged so to do by the principal Greek chieftains,[4] and continued his mourning until, at the bidding of Zeus, Athena shed upon him the nectar and ambrosia of the gods. Then donning his newly made armor and grasping the great spear of Peleus—which he alone could wield—he mounted his chariot, to which Automedon and Alcimus had harnessed the immortal horses, Balius and Xanthus, and adjured the

---

[1] The complete story of how Zeus was deluded by Ate has been related in chapter 14.

[2] The essence of Agamemnon's offer was that he would return Briseis to Achilles, together with a dowry consisting of the rulership of seven Argive towns, seven tripods of gold, and twelve horses.

[3] In detail, the gifts of Agamemnon were carried to the hut of Achilles by Antilochus, Thrasymedes, Meges, Thoas, Meriones, Lycomedes, and Melanippus; and consisted of seven tripods, twenty cauldrons, twelve horses, and seven maidens to attend Briseis.

[4] The chieftains attending Achilles before he entered the battle were Agamemnon, Menelaus, Odysseus, Nestor, Idomeneus, and Phoenix. While they were seeking to comfort him, Briseis—seeing the corpse of Patroclus—wailed with her women and, tearing herself, lamented the day when the dead man had promised her that she should become Achilles' bride.

steeds that they should not permit his charioteer Automedon to suffer the same fate that had befallen Patroclus. Upon hearing this, the horse Xanthus bowed his head and, excusing the death of Patroclus on the ground that he had been slain by divine Apollo, prophesied that Achilles himself was fated to lose his life—notwithstanding the fact that he should be pulled in his chariot with the speed of the west-wind Zephyrus.[5] But Achilles, already knowing from Thetis that Xanthus spoke the truth, proudly drove forward to the attack.

Book XX. Upon seeing the move of Achilles, Zeus had Themis summon the gods to Olympus and, save only ancient Oceanus,[6] they all responded to the call. Questioned by Poseidon about the purpose of the assembly, the supreme deity announced that, if the forthcoming engagement should be fought only between the Greeks and the Trojans, the might of Achilles would certainly prevail, and he added that each of the immortals was now at liberty to take sides actively as he or she should be minded, while he himself would gaze down passively from his seat in the skies. Thus freed from the previous divine prohibition, Hera hastened to the assistance of the Greeks, accompanied by Athena, Poseidon, Hermes, and Hephaestus. And the forces of the Trojans were joined by Ares, Apollo, Artemis, Leto, the river-god Xanthus, and Aphrodite.[7]

In the raging combat which followed, Poseidon stood against Apollo; Athena stood against Ares (Enyalius); Hera stood against Artemis; Hermes stood against Leto; Hephaestus stood against the river-god Xanthus (Scamander); and the earth quaked so furiously that Hades (Aïdoneus) became fearful that it would be so cloven as to reveal to the upper view his dread and dank realm below.

As Achilles looked about in search of Hector, Apollo assumed the form of Priam's son Lycaon and urged Aeneas to do battle with the great Greek but, having had a previous and almost disastrous encounter with him,[8] Aeneas refused until the god heartened him by pointing out that his mother Aphrodite was a daughter of Zeus, while Achilles' mother Thetis was of lesser divine degree. At this point, the opposing deities made a tacit compact to refrain from active participation in the fighting, and those favoring the Greeks proceeded to the Trojan wall and sat down, while those favoring the Trojans retired to Mount Callicolone on Ida.

When Aeneas and Achilles came together, they first paused for an interchange of boasting in which Achilles recalled their earlier meeting on Mount Ida, and Aeneas spoke in detail of his high descent from Dardanus. Having done with talk, Aeneas made the first cast of his spear, which was unable to pierce the shield wrought by Hephaestus. The thrust of Achilles was likewise warded off, although it pierced two circles of Aeneas' sheltering shield. The two warriors then came to closer grips—Achilles with his drawn sword and Aeneas with a stone of such size that no two mortals could have borne it; and death surely would have come to one of them had not Poseidon leapt down from his seat on the wall and wafted Aeneas away while he covered the eyes of his adversary with an

---

[5] The miracle of the speaking horse, Xanthus, is naturally reminiscent of the colloquy between Balaam and his ass, which is related in the Bible at Numbers 22: 28 et seq.

[6] The river-god Oceanus was excused from attending the call because of the dignity accorded to him in the Homeric theogony as the first created of the divinities.

[7] The leading reasons for the respective alliances of the immortals with the opposing sides seem to have been as follows: Hera and Athena were still burning with wrath because Paris had preferred Aphrodite to them in awarding the golden apple which was dropped by Eris at the wedding of Peleus and Thetis and labeled "to the fairest"; Poseidon was still angry because the Trojan king, Laomedon, had refused to pay him for his labor in building the walls of the city; Hermes was the maternal great-grandfather of the Greek hero Odysseus and was also the father of Eudorus, who was one of the leaders of the Myrmidons; Hephaestus was doubly tied to the cause of the Greeks as the deity from whom the Athenians claimed their descent and because Thetis had given him lodgment when he was cast down from Olympus by Hera; Ares took the part of the Trojans out of love for his paramour Aphrodite; Apollo, Artemis, and Leto were incensed against the Greeks for the original ravishment of Chryseis by Agamemnon; the river-god Xanthus was considered a native of the Troad and thus obliged to fight for its protection; and Aphrodite, of course, naturally favored the cause of Paris—to whom she had given Helen in return for his having awarded her the golden apple.

[8] In one of the raids about Troy which preceded the main engagement, Achilles captured the cattle of Aeneas which were feeding in the mountains of Ida, and would have slain their owner had he not been miraculously wafted off by Zeus.

impenetrable mist.[9] With a warning that he should not again engage with the great son of Peleus, the sea-god deposited the Dardanian leader at the uttermost verge of the field of battle and, returning, raised the mist so that Achilles might continue the fighting against others of the enemy.

Hector now wanted to attack Achilles, but was warned by Apollo not to take the offensive and, knowing the voice of the god, shrank in fear back into the midst of his comrades. And well he did so—for the raging Greek successively slew the Trojans Iphition, Antenor's son Demoleon, Hippodamas, and Priam's young son Polydorus.[10] When he saw his brother disemboweled, Hector could no longer stay himself and, forging to the front, cast his spear at Achilles but, by the intervention of Athena's breath, it miraculously returned to him and fell before his feet. Thereupon, Achilles rushed upon him with his spear—only to face nothingness when Apollo carried away his intended victim under cover of a thick mist. Again thus thwarted by divine interposition, he turned upon the remaining forces of the Trojans and, in quick succession, put to death Dryops, Demuchus, Laogonus and Dardanus (both sons of Bias), Tros,[11] Mu-

lius, Agenor's son Echeclus, Deucalion, the Thracians Rhigmus and Areïthous, and many others who fell before his spear without the small consolation of being identified by name.

Book XXI. Having driven the Trojans back to the ford of the river Scamander[12] with such slaughter that the waters of the stream were red, Achilles fished out twelve youthful warriors alive to offer as sacrifices at the burial of Patroclus and gave them to his comrades to lead to the Greek ships. Returning to the fighting he next slew Lycaon, son of Priam and Laothoë and full brother of Polydorus—in spite of the fact that he had taken the youth captive[13] and he now begged to be held alive for ransom. Tossing his lifeless body into the river, he followed up by dealing a like fate to Asteropaeus[14] and to the Peonians Thersilochus, Mydon, Astypylus, Mnesus, Thrasius, Aenius, and Ophelestes, and he would have slaughtered many more but the river, choked with dead bodies, leapt from his bank in great waves and gave such furious chase that Achilles was forced to call upon Zeus for help. Poseidon and Athena heard his cry and gave to him words of encouragement, but he was relieved from his predicament only when Hera bade Hephaestus to pour forth his fires upon the waters so that, seething like a cauldron, the god of the river was forced to plead for mercy before his aqueous domain should become a mere trickle.

When his plea was granted, Hera stood apart, but the other gods fell into strife and the earth rang with the din of their contention and the heavens pealed as though with the sound of a mighty trumpet.[15] Ares leapt at Athena and, vowing revenge because she had permitted him

---

[9] The reason why Poseidon—a proponent of the Greek cause—was led to save Aeneas is alleged to be that it was ordained that Aeneas should survive the Trojan conflict in order to become the divine ancestor of the Romans.

[10] According to a different legend, related in the "Hecuba" of Euripides, Polydorus was sent with a store of Trojan treasure for safekeeping to Priam's friend Polymestor, king of the Chersonesus in eastern Thrace. After the Greeks had overthrown Troy, he was killed by the Thracian, who appropriated the treasure—only to meet the reward of his perfidy when his eyes were put out by Hecuba and other captive Trojan women. Another tradition, related by Hyginus, states that Polydorus was entrusted to his sister Iliona, who was married to Polymestor. He was brought up as her son, while she made others believe that her actual son was Deipylus. The Greeks, wishing to exterminate the race of Priam, bribed Polymestor to kill the lad and, mistakenly, he killed Deipylus. Later, the Thracian king was murdered by his own Trojan wife. Still a third version of the story, mentioned by Dictys Cretensis, relates that Polymestor gave up Polydorus to make peace with the Greeks and the youth was stoned to death beneath the walls of Troy when the Trojans refused to exchange Helen for his live body.

[11] The young warrior Tros was slain in cold blood, notwithstanding that he clasped the knees of Achilles and begged to be taken captive.

---

[12] In the Iliad, the Scamander (Xanthus) is described as begotten of Zeus.

[13] In an earlier raid, Achilles had taken Lycaon captive and had sold him as a slave to the island of Lemnos; but the youth had ransomed himself twelve days earlier than that on which he met his death, after reentering the Trojan forces.

[14] Asteropaeus was the tallest man in the Trojan conflict. Before his death at the hands of Achilles, he proudly boasted of his lineage as a grandson of the Macedonian River-god Axius, and had been able to wound Achilles slightly.

[15] The portion of the Iliad describing the fight between the deities is generally referred to as the "Theomachy."

to be wounded by the mortal Diomedes, smote upon her tasselled aegis, but she struck him with a jagged stone and laughed as his inert form slumped to the earth and stretched out over seven roods.[16] As Aphrodite tried to lead the moaning war-god from the field, Athena (bidden by Hera) smote her also to the ground. Upon this happening, Poseidon challenged Apollo to combat and ridiculed him upon taking the part of the Trojans, since both of them had been defrauded long since by Trojan Laomedon.[17] But Apollo did not want to contest with his father's brother and turned back from the contest, despite the scolding of his sister Artemis, who chided him for being a coward. Hearing her words, Hera challenged the virgin goddess of the chase and so soundly boxed her ears that she fled in tears from the plain, leaving behind her bow and arrows, which her mother Leto picked up and carried back to Olympus, where her weeping daughter complained to Zeus of the treatment accorded her by proud Hera. The supreme god, however, just smiled indulgently as he saw that the harmless internecine fighting which he had permitted had come to its close.

Meanwhile, Apollo returned to the Trojan city which was about to fall before the onset of the Greeks and, encouraging Antenor's son Agenor to stand before Achilles, moved an image of him back and forth across the plain so that it was fruitlessly pursued by Achilles, and his enemies were given an opportunity to herd themselves behind their protecting walls.

Book XXII. Leaving the pursuit of the delusive guise of Agenor, Achilles now returned to the Scaean gates which had closed upon all of the Trojans save only Hector. Seeing his approach, both Priam and Hecuba entreated their great son to come within the protecting walls; but, with "courage unquenchable" (?), he remained outside until Achilles neared—and then

fled. He was chased three times around the walls, with never a respite offered to enter either the Scaean or the Dardanian gates. Meanwhile, Apollo sought to come to his aid, but Zeus had tilted the scales in favor of Achilles and, as he rested breathless from the pursuit, Athena came to Hector in the form of his brother Deiphobus and counseled him to stand and fight.

The end was not long in coming, for after each of the great heroes had wasted his spear upon the other, and Hector became aware that Deiphobus was only a delusive shade, Achilles (whose weapon had been returned to his hand by Athena) pierced the gullet of Hector with the ashen spear of Peleus and, falling to the dust, his adversary died even as he begged that his body not be left as carrion to be preyed upon by birds and dogs.

Withdrawing his spear, Achilles wanted first to follow up his victory by an attack on the Trojan walls; but, remembering Patroclus, he decided to drag his victim's corpse back to the ships of the Greeks. And, after stripping off its armor, while his comrades crowded around in awful admiration, he tied the dead man's body to his chariot by the feet and touched his horses, who raced past the walls with their added and ghastly tail piece, while Priam and Hecuba wept and Andromache fainted.[18]

Book XXIII. When the Greeks had triumphantly returned to their ships, they scattered to their several quarters, save only the Myrmidons whom Achilles ordered to pay honors of mourning to Patroclus before they should unyoke their horses and take of food. And before the bier of his slain friend, he placed the corpse of Hector face down in the dust, while he repeated his promise to cut the throats of the twelve Trojan warriors as a burial offering. After this, the rest of his comrades feasted; but Achilles laid himself down unwashed on the seashore and groaned at the loss of his friend, until at last sleep overtook his weary limbs.

As he slept, the ghost of Patroclus appeared and demanded the rites of burial, supplemented

---

[16] The bulk of Ares may thus be determined, since the rood was measured as being one-quarter of an acre.

[17] At the same time when Poseidon was spending his unpaid year in building the walls of Troy for Laomedon, Apollo—as a result of their joint conspiracy against Zeus—was punished for the same period by being forced to serve as the keeper of the Trojan king's cattle and, like Poseidon, he was summarily dismissed without receiving his promised reward.

---

[18] Unaware that Hector had remained outside the walls, Andromache arrived on the scene with her handmaids just as her husband's corpse was being dragged through the dust behind the chariot of his conqueror.

by the request that eventually their bones should lie together in token of their joint rearing at the house of the centaur Cheiron.[19] Eagerly reaching to clasp the dreamed phantom, Achilles awakened as the dawn broke, and continued to mourn on the morrow while, under the direction of Agamemnon, Meriones, and the Myrmidons built a great funeral pyre for Patroclus. When the pyre was built, Achilles placed in the hand of the corpse a lock of his own hair[20] and, bidding Agamemnon draw aside all but the leaders of the Greeks, he conducted the funeral rites, which included the slaughter of two dogs and the cutting of the throats of the twelve Trojan warriors whom he had promised. But he refused to place the dead body of Hector on the fire—saying that it was his purpose to feed it to the dogs.[21] And when, after some delay, the winds Boreas and Zephyrus had fanned the flames to burn away the fleshy parts, the bones[22] were placed in a golden urn to be later mingled with those of his great friend. Thereafter, a small[23] barrow was raised and Achilles set forth prizes for the funeral games, which consisted of cauldrons, tripods, horses, mules, "strong oxen," "fair-girdled women," and "grey iron."

Modestly (?) stating that he would refrain from the contests in order to give his comrades a chance, he announced that the first event would be the chariot race. This was umpired by Phoenix and was won by Diomedes, but only after a competition replete with thrills, spills, and claims of foul in the best tradition of mod-

ern times.[24] Next, Epeius, the son of Panopeus,[25] won the prize in boxing against Euryalus, the son of Mecisteus.[26] In the third contest, wrestling, Telamonian Ajax and Odysseus struggled to a tie—the strength of the one being offset by the guile of the other so that neither was able to obtain a clear fall. And so they were awarded equal prizes.

In the footrace, Odysseus was aided by Athena, who caused the lesser Ajax to slip and come in second, while Nestor's son Antilochus ran third.[27] Next, Telamonian Ajax and Diomedes contended in single combat so evenly that their comrades bade them cease and take up equal prizes; and they divided between them the armor that Patroclus had stripped from Sarpedon. But Achilles, judging that Diomedes had an advantage in the contest, awarded to him as an additional trophy the great Thracian sword which had been taken from tall Asteropaeus.

---

[19] In the Iliad, it is intimated that Patroclus fled to the house of Peleus after his accidental slaughter of Clitonymus (the son of Amphidamus) and was there reared with Achilles.

[20] When Achilles left for the war, Peleus made a vow to dedicate the hair of his son to the Thessalian river Spercheius if he should return in safety. In placing one of his locks in the hands of his dead comrade Patroclus, Achilles did so with the knowledge that he was not fated to return.

[21] The vengeful determination of Achilles that Hector's body should be fed to dogs was thwarted by the divine will of Aphrodite and Apollo, who kept the corpse fully preserved until the later time when it was delivered to Priam.

[22] The corpses of other slain warriors were burnt at the same time, but that of Patroclus was placed in the middle of the pyre and his bones were easily identified.

[23] Subsequently, the originally small, commemorative barrow was raised to greater proportions.

[24] The racing contestants were: Eumelus, the son of Admetus, driving the horses which had been tended by Apollo; Diomedes, the son of Tydeus, driving the horses of Tros which had been taken from Aeneas; Menelaus, driving his own horse Podargus, coupled with the mare Aethe, which had been given to Agamemnon by Anchises' son, Echepolus, as the price for remaining undisturbed from war; Antilochus, the son of Nestor, driving steeds which his father had bred at Pylus; and the Cretan Meriones, whose coursers seem to have been undistinguished. In the back stretch, the chariot of Eumelus shot to the front with that of Diomedes pressing closely; but Apollo deprived Diomedes of his lash, only to have Athena restore it as she broke the yoke from the horses of Eumelus and caused their driver to plunge from his car. Menelaus, at this point, pressed forward; but was passed by Antilochus, who furiously drove through an opening on the outside while his elder comrade cursed him for his recklessness. And thus, at the finish, it was Diomedes to win, Antilochus to place and Menelaus to show; while Meriones came fourth and Eumelus ended last. In view of the mishap, however, which had overtaken the son of Admetus, he was given the corselet of Asteropaeus as a consolation prize; and, when Menelaus and Antilochus got into an argument about the propriety of the youth's driving, which gave Nestor an opportunity to expatiate on his own past exploits, the garrulous old man was quieted by the gift of an urn.

[25] In the post-Homeric legend, Epeius gained much greater fame as the builder of the Wooden Horse, which the Trojans gullibly drew within the walls of their city.

[26] As related in chapter 8, Euryalus was one of the Epigoni who took part in the overthrow of Thebes.

[27] In gracefully acknowledging the victory of Odysseus, Antilochus said that the older man could outrun everyone except Achilles; and, for his flattery, received an added prize of a half talent of gold.

The contestants in the shot-put event[28] were: Polypoëtes, son of Peirithous; Leonteus, son of Coronus and grandson of the famed Caeneus; Telamonian Ajax; and Epeius, son of Panopeus. At the first throw—made by Epeius—the Greeks were forced to laugh aloud because of his weak effort, which was far exceeded by the following competitors, of whom Polypoëtes gained the victory.

As a target in the archery contest, a dove was tied by the foot with a cord leading to a tall mast which was placed upright in the sands at a great distance. Teucer first loosed his shaft which cut the cord, and the dove soared into the air, where it was shot on the wing by Meriones, who proudly accepted the prize for his rare marksmanship. When the javelin throw was announced as the last event, Meriones first arose; but when he was followed by Agamemnon, Achilles forthwith awarded the victory to the latter without contest, saying that all knew he was by far the best of all the Greeks in handling the weapon. However, with the consent of Agamemnon, he gave a spear to Meriones, who handed it over to the herald Talthybius.

Book XXIV. For eleven days following the funeral games for Patroclus, the Greeks rested, but on each morning Achilles dragged the corpse of Hector behind his chariot three times around the barrow of his dead comrade. On the twelfth morning, the gods took pity and contemplated sending down Hermes to steal the cruelly treated body, but Zeus summoned Thetis and sent her to Achilles with word that he should surrender the remains of his victim for ransom, and he sent Iris to Priam with word that he should go to the Greek ships with gifts for Achilles and ask for the return of his slain son. When Achilles heard from his mother of Zeus' will, he acquiesced; but, when Priam received the message from Iris, he first consulted with his wife, Hecuba. Although she shrilly prophesied that his mission would be in vain and voiced fears that his life, like that of many

of his sons, would be taken by the vengeful Greek, the aged king—knowing the speech of Iris to be that of a goddess—determined to proceed, no matter what the risk.

Opening his treasure chests, he took out twelve each of robes, cloaks, coverlets, mantles, and tunics; and added to these ten talents of gold,[29] two gleaming tripods, four cauldrons, and a precious cup which had been presented to him while on a visit to the Thracians. While he was engaged in setting these valuables apart, his curious family so crowded about him that, in deep anger, he drove them from the room; and, chiding nine of his remaining sons by name,[30] ordered them to draw up a wagon and load into it the treasures which he proposed to take as gifts of ransom. After his command was obeyed, and an eagle appeared following a libation to Zeus suggested by Hecuba, the herald Idaeus drove the laden wagon forth from the gateway and the Trojan king followed in his own car, bravely plying the lash to his horses with a show of bravado that concealed his inner feeling. But the old man's sons and the husbands of his daughters followed with anxious forebodings of his death until they were forced to return to the city as the slim caravan lost itself in the darkness of the Trojan plain.

At the bidding of Zeus, Hermes appeared to the travelers as they halted in the night to water their mules and horses[31] at a place beyond the barrow of Priam's grandfather Ilus. Idaeus, thinking him an enemy, urged flight; but the messenger-god, claiming to be a squire of Achilles,[32] quieted their fears by saying that the corpse of Hector was intact[33] and that he would lead them safely to their destination. Thereupon, he leapt into the chariot of Priam and,

---

[28] The "shot" used in the contest was a mass of rough-cast iron which had been taken from King Eëtion, the father of Andromache, by Achilles when he sacked Cilician Thebes in one of his early raids.

[29] As a weight, the Greek talent is said to have been the equivalent of about 57.85 English pounds.
[30] The sons to whom Priam called were Helenus, Paris, Agathon, Pammon, Antiphonus, Polites, Deiphobus, Hippothous, and Dius.
[31] The chariot of Priam was drawn by horses and the wagon driven by Idaeus was drawn by mules which had been given to the Trojan king by his Mysian allies.
[32] Hermes (here described as Argeiphontes) represented himself as the son of a Myrmidon named Polyctor.
[33] Although often cruelly dragged in the dust, the corpse and flesh of Hector had been preserved unmutilated by the divine intervention of Apollo.

breathing strength into his horses and the mules which drew the treasure wagon, they soon came to the trench which surrounded the ships of the Greeks. Shedding sleep upon the sentinels, the deity forthwith opened the gates and led on to the hut of Achilles, where he opened the door and carried in the gifts of ransom. Then, revealing his divinity to Priam, he bade him go into the hut alone and make his entreaty to Achilles. So saying, he departed for Olympus.

Leaving Idaeus to tend the mules and horses, Priam entered to find Achilles as he had just finished his meal, waited upon by Automedon and Alcimus. Clasping his hands about the knees of the great warrior, the old king pleaded that he be permitted to ransom Hector's corpse;[34] and likened his plight to that of Achilles' own aged father with such tender speech that they both wept. Achilles, however, soon overcame his emotion, and ordered Idaeus to be brought in, while Automedon and Alcimus wrapped the dead body in two of the robes and a tunic from among the gifts of ransom and placed it on a bier in Priam's wagon. When this had been done, he told his aged suppliant that he might depart at dawn with his cherished load but, citing the example of Niobe,[35] suggested that they should now partake of food. After eating, Achilles had couches laid for Priam and Idaeus beneath the portico outside his hut[36] and

promised that he would hold back the battle for twelve days, in order to give the Trojans ample time within which to bemoan Hector and give him decent interment.

When all had retired, and Achilles lay in sleep beside his restored Briseis, Hermes came down from Olympus and awakened Priam with a warning that he should depart at once, lest the other Greeks should discover his presence and take his life; and the deity himself yoked the mules and horses and drove the Trojan suppliants to the ford of the river Xanthus, where he wafted himself back to Olympus as the dawn was beginning to break.

As Priam and Idaeus continued toward their city in cart and wagon, their approach was noted only by the prophetess Cassandra; but she let forth a shrill cry so that all were aroused to meet the sad sight of their aged king and his herald returning with the wrapped corpse of Hector. In the general lamentation which followed, the dead man's wife, Andromache, and his mother, Hecuba, first spoke aloud with sorrowing words, which were joined in by Helen as she recalled that, notwithstanding her shame, she had never been reproached by him for having brought on the disastrous conflict.[37]

Having dismounted, Priam related the promise of Achilles to grant an armistice for the funeral rites and ordered his subjects to begin bringing in wood for the pyre.[38] This they did for nine days and, on the tenth, Hector's body was placed upon the lighted heap outside their city, while the grieving Trojans retired within their walls to mourn at a glorious feast (?).

---

[34] Although Priam had just left (at least) nine of his sons behind the walls of his city, he related to Achilles that of the fifty borne to him (nineteen from Hecuba and the rest from other women in his palace) all had been slain by the Greeks.

[35] In referring to Niobe, the Iliad states that she had six daughters and six sons, all of whom were slain by Apollo and Artemis for her slur on their mother, Leto. To bring home his example, Achilles is described as relating that, after grieving for three days, Niobe paused to eat and was thereafter changed into a stone on Mount Sipylus.

[36] The reason, assigned by Achilles for couching his visitors outside his hut, was that their presence might not be detected by someone who would relay the information to Agamemnon and bring about his interference in the ransom of Hector's corpse.

---

[37] In her speaking, Helen announced that it had been twenty years since she had been taken from her native land—an incident of chronology which had a tremendous, and confusing, effect upon the narratives of lesser mythologists, to whom the word of Homer was not to be gainsaid.

[38] Since Troy was situated on the (treeless) plain, the bringing of wood for the funeral pyre was a matter of considerable difficulty.

27

The Trojan War VII

THE ILIAD ENDS with the cremation of Hector upon his huge funeral pyre. As mentioned in chapter 21, the more ancient sources for the subsequent events of the Trojan War were the separate works of the Epic Cycle known as the "Aethiopis," the "Little Iliad," and the "Sack of Ilium." However, they have been preserved to us in only fragmentary form, and the following account has been largely taken from the "Fall of Troy," composed in the fourth (or fifth) century by Quintus Smyrnaeus.[1]

Penthesileia

After the death of Hector, the Trojans fortuitously gained a new ally in the person of the Amazonian queen, Penthesileia, who—urged on by the hope of cleansing herself for the accidental killing of her sister Hippolyte[2]—brought her band of warrior women from the mouth of the river Thermodon to fight against the Greeks. Among them, the more important were Clonia, Polemusa, Derinoë, Evandra, Antandra, Bremusa, Hippothoë, Harmothoë, Alcibia, Derimacheia, Antibrota, and Thermodosa.

At their coming, Priam rejoiced—for he felt that the host led by the war-god's daughter would prove invincible, but the widowed Andromache intuitively knew that no woman could prevail against the might of Achilles, who had so easily vanquished her beloved Hector. Penthesileia, however, was stricken with no such misgiving. On the contrary, while she slept, Athena sent a deceptive dream to augur her victory over the powerful Greek; and, at the next dawn, the proud Amazon—vainly succoured by the prayers of ancient Priam—led forth the Trojans and her own followers to renew the battle.

As she rode in the van, on a fleet steed which had been given to her by Oreithyia, the bride of the north-wind Boreas, the Greeks marveled at the sight; because, with Hector's death, they had hoped that the Trojan spirit had been completely humbled. But they quickly learned that their hope must be deferred, as the Amazonian queen successively slew Molion, Persinous, Eilissus, Antitheus, Lernus, Hippalmus, Elasippus, and an unnamed son of Haemon. Meanwhile, as the tide of battle capriciously changed: Derinoë slew Laogonus, Clonia slew Menippus, Podarces slew Clonia, Penthesilea slew Podarces, Idomeneus slew Bremusa, Meriones slew Evandra and Thermodosa, the lesser Ajax slew Derinoë, and Diomedes slew both Derimacheia and Alcibia.[3]

---

[1] The narrative of Dictys Cretensis, entitled "De Bello Trojano," and fabulously claimed to have been taken from the diary of a companion of the Cretan leader Idomeneus, is followed in the text in connection with certain incidents of lesser significance.

[2] The story mentioned in the text is, of course, at variance with the legend that Hippolyte was slain by Heracles in his quest for her girdle.

[3] In the same engagement (besides the activities of the Amazons): the Greek Sthenelus slew Cabeirus; Paris slew Evenor; Meges slew the Milesians, Itymoneus and Agelaus; and Polypoëtes slew Dresaeus.

Unaware of the furious fighting, Achilles and Telamonian Ajax stood apart, still mourning at the grave of Patroclus.[4] Lacking their help, the Greeks seemed to be getting so much the worst of the engagement that a foolish Trojan maiden, named Tisiphone, encouraged her sistren to emulate the daring of the Amazons but she was dissuaded by Antenor's wise wife, Theano, who pointed out that the women led by Penthesilea had been reared to war from youth while those of Troy had been trained only in the arts of domesticity.

When the Greeks had been driven back to their ships, Achilles and Ajax finally awakened to the realization that a major battle was under way and, donning their war gear,[5] they joined their comrades—with the heartening effect that one might have anticipated. Ajax forcefully announced his presence by successively slaying the Trojans Deiochus, Hyllus, Eurynomus, and Enyeus; and Achilles—concentrating on the Amazons—brought down Antandra, Polemusa, Antibrota, Hippothoë, and Harmothoë.

With all of her principal lieutenants now gone, Penthesileia hurled her javelins against both Achilles and Ajax; but they were easily turned aside by the shields of the Greek warriors and, knowing well that his comrade needed no help against them, Ajax insultingly turned aside to battle with the Trojan men. Nor was he mistaken, for Achilles first pierced the Amazon's breast with his spear and followed by impaling the body of her steed so that she fell, face down and lifeless, into the dust. Seeing her fall, the Trojans fled in fear back to their city, while the Greeks gathered round as Achilles removed the helmet from a face of such beauty—even in death—that, with his comrades, he grieved at the passing of the war-god's daughter, for her features were flawless and she was "most divinely fair."[6]

As he gazed upon his beautiful victim, Achilles was jeered as having a soft heart by Thersites and, in a precipitate burst of anger, killed the miserable man with a blow of his fist below the ear. Upon this happening, his comrades applauded—except Diomedes, who was the slain man's kinsman.[7] But his wrath was cooled by the words of his fellows; and, at the request of Priam the body of the Amazonian queen and that of her war horse were interred in the barrow of old Laomedon, while those of her slain band were buried in the plain nearby. With like dignity, the Greeks attended to the corpse of Podarces, but that of coward Thersites was thrown uncovered into a pit, and they returned to their ships to feast their victory.

Memnon

After the death of Penthesileia, the Trojan elder Thymoëtes suggested that it might be well to take counsel whether the city should be further defended;[8] but Priam urged that the resistance be continued and that succour would soon be forthcoming from the Ethiopian hordes of his nephew Memnon.[9] Upon this, Polydamas (the son of Panthous, who had been born on the same night with Hector) advanced a third alternative by suggesting that the conflict be brought to an end by surrendering Helen and the treasures of Menelaus to the Greeks. His words met a hearty acquiescence from the rest of the Trojans save only Paris; but, as the two of them spoke heatedly, the argument was brought to an end by the entrance of the giant Memnon and his equally modeled troops. In their honor, a great banquet was laid and after much boasting[10] about what he would do on the

---

[4] It should be remembered that Aegina, daughter of the river-god Asopus, was the maternal grandmother of Achilles, Ajax, and Patroclus.

[5] The facility with which the combatants at Troy were accustomed to doff and don their armor has been gravely commented upon with scepticism by many classical scholars.

[6] At this point in the story, it is related that Ares would have blazed down from Olympus to avenge his daughter's death but that he was deterred by the thun-

derbolts of Zeus, who had permitted his own son, Sarpedon, to suffer his destined fate.

[7] Agrius, the father of Thersites, and Oeneus, the grandfather of Diomedes, were brothers.

[8] A son Menippus, born to Thymoëtes and his wife, Cilla, on the same night with Paris, was mistakenly exposed to the elements by Priam following a prediction of the seeress Cassandra which referred to her own brother; and the actions of Thymoëtes were reputedly referable to his natural resentment.

[9] Memnon was the son of Priam's brother Tithonus and the dawn-goddess Eos, whose abode was believed to be in the Ethiopian country, of which Memnon was king.

[10] Although Memnon boasted that he had destroyed

morrow the Ethiopian king went to his rest.

When the dawn came, the Trojans sallied forth from their gates under his leadership and were met by the Greeks in head-on conflict, wherein Achilles first slew Thalius and Mentes. But, on the other side, Memnon made short shrift of the Pylians Pheron and Ereuthus, and then rushed upon Nestor's young son Antilochus and pierced him through the heart with his spear.[11] And, although Nestor called to his aid his elder son Thrasymedes and the warrior Phereus, they were unable to hold back the Ethiopian giant from stripping the armor from his victim's body, or from continuing in his slaughter of the lesser Greeks. However, when he came to single combat with Achilles, a more even contest was waged. Although they were able to wound each other, the cuts were so slight that they were able to indulge in boasting about their respective pedigrees, and followed by closing in with their swords in a furious encounter (of more than one hundred poetic lines) which ended when Achilles brought death to Memnon by thrusting his weapon through his breast bone. When he fell, the Trojans retired in dismay and the triumphant Myrmidons stripped the armor from his giant body, but the corpse itself was miraculously wafted through the air by the winds, and the Ethiopian host, changed into winged fowl, followed high above in its wake back to their own land.

The Death of Achilles

On the next day, Achilles was so enraged at the death of his young friend Antilochus that he seemed to run amuck among the Trojans and soon choked the streams of Simois and Xanthus with the gory corpses of many of their best warriors. Seeing the terrific slaughter, Apollo leapt down from Olympus and, with a terrible shout, ordered him to turn back but, although he recognized the immortal voice, the raging Greek defiantly bade the deity to get himself away to his own heavenly mansion lest he be killed like an ordinary man. So saying, he moved away and sped after the Trojans as they sought frantically to obtain the protection of their city's walls. This affront was too great for the god to take and, vanishing into a cloud, he sent an arrow from his divine bow that imbedded itself in Achilles' mortal ankle and brought his great frame crashing to the ground.

Realizing that he was approaching his foretold end,[12] the fallen man drew the shaft out and indignantly hurled it from him, as the blood gushed forth from his wound and, caught by a sudden gust of wind, the arrow was swept back to the quiver of Apollo as he was returned to Olympus. There, he was upbraided with bitter words by Hera and sat ashamed as she prophesied that, although Achilles should die, his son Neoptolemus would soon come from the island of Scyrus and prove to be as great a scourge to the Trojans as his mighty sire.[13] Meanwhile, the awed Trojans stood at a distance and stared at the dying man—afraid to draw near. Their timidity was warranted because, with a last burst of courageous strength, Achilles leapt into their midst and slew Orythaon, Hipponous, and Alcathous. But then, as his blood ran out, the mightiest of the Greeks toppled in death down to earth like the fall of some great mountain cliff.

Although many of his comrades still trembled from memories of the great havoc which Achilles had wrought upon their armies, Paris exultingly rallied them to hale the fallen corpse within the walls of the city. But they failed to reckon the strength of Telamonian Ajax, who bestrode the inert form of his friend and, in a furious defense, slew Agelaus, Thestor, Ocythous, Agestratus, Aganippus, Zorus, Nessus, and the Lycian Erymas. At the death of his countryman, Glaucus rushed in and exchanged boastful words with the battling Greek, but he

---

the Solymi, an earlier legend relates that they were exterminated by Bellerophon.

[11] Before he lost his own life, Antilochus cast his spear at Memnon and slew his comrade Pyrrhasus.

[12] Thetis had told her son that he was destined to die before the Scaean gates from an arrow of Apollo. A different version of the legend, related by Apollodorus and others, was that the arrow was shot by Paris and guided to its mark by the deity.

[13] In her verbal castigation of Apollo, Hera recalled how the Trojan king Laomedon had cheated him of the wages promised for his year's service and how, at the wedding of Peleus and Thetis, he had played on his divine lyre while singing good wishes for the fortune of their offspring.

too lost his life and only through the super-human efforts of Aeneas was his body retrieved for decent burial.[14] Elated at his success, the son of the love-goddess tarried to fight for the corpse of Achilles. He soon sustained a wound, however, in his right forearm from Ajax' spear, which caused him to hasten back to the city for medical treatment, as strong Odysseus came upon the scene of action to succour the defense. Nor was his aid slight, for he fended off and slew the attacking warriors Mehaelus, Atymnius (borne to Ethiopian Emathion by the nymph Pegasis), and Alcon, and despite a wound in his knee made by the spear of his last named victim, continued to fight vigorously until he and Ajax were reinforced by others of their comrades.

At last, after Ajax had felled Paris with a stone—as the Trojan prince sought to draw his bow—the attackers fled to their city and the Greeks, scorning to strip the armor from the many whom they had slain, drew the corpse of Achilles back to their ships. As it lay, stretched out on the ground like Giant Tityus,[15] the Myrmidons wailed aloud with Telamonian Ajax, and ancient Phoenix clasped its form with voiced lamentation for the happier days when they dwelt sweetly together in the house of Peleus.[16] Agamemnon, too, came forward, but the sincerity of his sorrow at the death of the hero was tinctured by his own dismay (engendered by the thought that the cause which he was leading had now been deprived of its most powerful support). Not so with Nestor, who genuinely grieved at the loss of his friend almost as much as for his slain son, Antilochus. But, stemming his tears, he counseled the Greeks to wash the corpse of their lost champion and place it upon a quiet couch. And, when this was done, Athena showered upon it the ambrosia of the gods so that the great frame seemed to the awe-struck onlookers as though it were only wrapped in sleep.

When, with Briseis at their head, the captive maids raised their moans—meanwhile rending their flesh in sorrow—they were joined by the Nereids, who came up from their dwelling in the depths, and the Muses came from Helicon to add their sweet dirge to the sad cavalcade which restlessly surged around the bier. In her grief, Thetis thought to go again to Olympus and upbraid Zeus for permitting her brave son's death, but the Muse Calliope restrained her by pointing out that Fate[17]—and not Zeus—determined the end of every mortal, and that her own son, Orpheus, had passed on when his alloted time expired, despite his mother's own immortality. Thetis was persuaded by the Muse's urging to forego her fanatic purpose; but, while the Greeks slept, she and her sister-Nereids sat by the sea and, during the whole night long, continued to mourn as Calliope and the other Muses sought to assuage their sorrow with soft words.

After many days, during which a great pyre was built with wood brought down from the mountains of Ida, the corpse of Achilles was tenderly placed on the heap with solemn gifts—which included the shorn hair of all the Myrmidons and of Briseis—and, as Aeolus sent the winds to blow, the lighted flames burned with such intensity that their fuel soon became embers and the white bones of their slain champion were tenderly lifted by the Greeks into a silver casket.[18] This was enclosed in a golden vase, which Hephaestus had made for Thetis, and over it a great barrow was heaped, while the immortal horses, Balius and Xanthus, added their mourning voices to the general lamentation. Poseidon now arose from the sea and comforted Thetis by saying that her son was not destined for the realm of the lower world but,

---

[14] According to a different legend, the body of Glaucus (like that of his uncle Sarpedon) was miraculously wafted back to Lycia.

[15] When Apollo slew Tityus for his assault upon Leto, the giant's body was taken down to Tartarus where, stretched out over nine roods, it was continuously preyed upon by vultures.

[16] According to a different legend, Phoenix and Achilles were reared together in the home of the centaur Cheiron.

[17] Fate is plurally described as the gods of the lower world.

[18] According to the legend related by Euripides and Ovid, Achilles was buried by the Greeks in Thrace on their return from Troy and Priam's daughter, Polyxena, was sacrificed on his tomb. A different version of the same incident is that Polyxena (having fallen in love with the Greek warrior on the occasion of his surrender of the corpse of Hector) slew herself on his Troad barrow.

like Heracles, should dwell in the company of the gods on a holy island of the Euxine Sea.[19] Thus speaking, he returned to his watery element and was followed by the Nereids; and the Muses went back to their home on Mount Helicon.

As soon as the burial ceremony was over, the impetuous Diomedes arose and suggested that the Trojans be attacked immediately, but he was stayed by Telamonian Ajax, who related that Thetis had promised to return on the morrow to preside over funeral games for her son. When she arrived, Nestor took the floor and eulogized so about the valorous achievements of Achilles that the Nereid smiled and gave to him "fleetfoot" horses which had—years before—been brought by Telephus as an offering of thanks for the healing of his wound.[20] This done, the funeral games followed.

In the footrace, Telamonian Ajax bested his half brother Teucer but, apparently, only because the latter twisted his ankle when one of the gods made him step upon the root of a tamarisk tree.[21] In wrestling, Diomedes and Telamonian Ajax contested furiously to a happy tie—happy because each of them received two beautiful handmaids and ended the encounter by exchanging kisses. In boxing, all were afraid to meet Idomeneus and, unchallenged, he was awarded the prize. Upon this, Phoenix chided the younger men, and Nestor seized the opportunity to declaim about the exploits of his younger days. Their words so roused the spirit of emulation in Panopeus' son, Epeius, and Jason's son, Acamas, that they leapt up and, donning their gauntlets, fought a furious contest—which was so even that it was called off as a tie, and each was awarded a silver bowl as a prize.[22]

Then they kissed, and Podaleirius impartially tended their respective bruises.

Disregarding his injured foot, Teucer entered the archery contest against Ajax the Lesser and gained the arms of Troilus for his victory when he shot away the plume from a helmet placed at a distance, after his adversary's shaft had missed the target by a narrow margin. Following this event, Thetis produced a massive bar of iron which Heracles had taken from the Libyan giant Antaeus and had later given to Peleus for his help in overcoming Laomedon. Transmitted to Achilles, the weight had been brought by him to Troy and was now to be used to test the strength of lesser men. None but Telamonian Ajax, however, could do more than lift it from the ground, but he threw it quite far. For his effort, he received from the sea-goddess the resplendent arms of Ethiopian Memnon.

In other contests: the Arcadian Agapenor was awarded the armor of Cycnus for his excellence in leaping; the Argive Euryalus was awarded a silver oil flask for making the farthest throw with the javelin; Telamonian Ajax was awarded two talents of silver when none would accept his challenge "to strife of hands and feet;[23] Menelaus was awarded a golden cup for his victory in the chariot race;[24] and Agamemnon was awarded the silver breastplate of Polydorus for his victory over Sthenelus in the horse race.[25]

Meanwhile, Odysseus was forced to sit aside and look upon many of the trials of skill and strength which he would surely have won but that he was denied entry by the sore wounds suffered in his defense of Achilles' corpse.

---

[19] As noted in chapter 7, a variant of the legend related that Achilles was transported to the Isles of the Blest and there became the husband of Medeia.

[20] As earlier related, the wound which Telephus received from the spear of Achilles was healed when salved with an ointment made from the weapon's rust.

[21] Because Thetis and her sister-Nereids were among the spectators, Ajax and Teucer did not race naked but modestly placed on their loin cloths.

[22] The silver bowls, fashioned by Hephaestus, had previously been given to Achilles as ransom for Lycaon, the captured son of Priam and Laothoë, who was later overcome a second time and slain by the Greek warrior.

[23] Since Ajax and Diomedes had previously wrestled to a tie, one can only conjecture the nature of the contest thus denominated.

[24] Those who competed with Menelaus were Eurypylus, Eumelus, Thoas and Polypoëtes. The order of the finish is not related by Quintus Smyrnaeus, but it was necessary for Podaleirius to spread salves over wounds which both Thoas and Eurypylus suffered in falling from their chariots.

[25] The victory of Agamemnon was due to his superior horsemanship, because Sthenelus was riding the immortal steed Arion—the offspring of Poseidon and Demeter ridden to safety by Adrastus after the rout of the famous Seven Against Thebes.

The Madness of Ajax

When the athletic contests were done, Thetis laid down the armor of Achilles and announced that it should be given to him who had rescued the body of her dead son from the grasp of the Trojans. At her words, Odysseus and Telamonian Ajax both arose and agreed that the issue should be judged by Idomeneus, Nestor, and Agamemnon but, upon the advice of Nestor, they refused the office—because they well knew that, no matter what their decision might be, the loser would likely be taken with a fit of disruptive anger. In this impasse, they agreed that the question of priority should be put to the vote of the Trojan captives—a determination which promptly evoked from both Ajax and Odysseus speeches of mutually jealous recrimination and braggadocio that did credit to neither of them.[26] After they had spoken, the captives—with apparent unanimity—brought in their verdict in favor of Odysseus, and Ajax was so visibly stunned that his friends led his bewildered hulk back to the ships.

The last award being thus disposed of, Thetis took her sister-nereids back into the deep and the Greeks went to their rest; but Ajax, smitten with madness, put on his armor and set out with the intention of setting the ships afire and hewing Odysseus with his sword limb from limb. As he raged with foaming mouth, Athena directed his crazed attack against the sheep, which he slaughtered right and left until, as he stood over a slain ram that he thought was the body of Odysseus, the cloud lifted from his brain. Then, seeing the innocent fruits of his carnage, he realized that he was doomed by the gods and died by thrusting the sword of Hector through his own throat.[27]

As the great corpse lay stretched out on the plain, the mourning Greeks gathered about it, and Teucer was so stricken with sorrow that he would have followed the self-inflicted death of his half brother but his comrades wrested the sword from his hand. Thereupon, he fell in anguish upon the dead body and was joined by Tecmessa, who bemoaned her lord's passing[28] with a seeming selfish accent on the future fate of herself and her young son Eurysaces.[29] But Agamemnon assured her that they should be protected as long as either he or Teucer should live and, after a speech of self-condemnation from Odysseus, Nestor sagely announced that no amount of lamentation could awake the dead and suggested that the funeral pyre be laid. This was done, the fire was lit and—fanned for a night and day by sea winds sent by Thetis—burnt furiously until it consumed all except the bones of Ajax. These his comrades reverently laid in a golden casket and buried beneath a headland mound, after which they retired.

Eurypylus—the Grandson of Heracles

On the next morning, Menelaus called the army to assembly and, seeking to try the temper of his comrades, suggested that the deaths of both Achilles and Ajax made it inadvisable to continue the fight. When he had done speaking, Tydeus' strong son Diomedes arose and, spurning the cowardly suggestion, urged that battle begin again with an even fiercer determination. Although these bold words were greeted with silence, the Greeks leapt to their feet with shouts of joy when Calchas, their seer, followed by recalling that he had theretofore prophesied victory in the tenth year, and suggested that Diomedes and Odysseus should be sent to the island of Scyrus to bring Achilles' son Neoptolemus to assist their cause.[30] On

---

[26] Ajax chided Odysseus for attempting to shirk service in the Trojan War by feigning insanity; having counseled the Greeks to destroy Palamedes; and having been of no assistance in the battle about the ships when the walls had been broken through by Hector. Replying, Odysseus bragged that he had brought Diomedes into the war; had secretly spied upon the Trojan citadel; and as proof of his strength, he had won the prize for wrestling at the funeral games for Patroclus.

[27] Ajax had received the sword from Hector when they exchanged gifts following their duel, as related in book VII.

[28] Tecmessa was a daughter of the Phrygian king, Teleutas, who had been taken captive in one of the predatory raids about Troy. Allotted as a prize to Ajax, he became so fond of her that he made her his wife.

[29] Quintus Smyrnaeus and Sophocles mention only Eurysaces as a son of Ajax and Tecmessa, but Herodotus names another—Philaeus—whom the Athenians claimed as a progenitor of one of their distinguished families.

[30] A legend mentioned by Dictys Cretensis, and others, relates that Odysseus contrived to capture Helenus, the prophetic son of Priam, and learned from

behalf of the two heroes, Odysseus promptly accepted the mission and they set forth in a boat manned by twenty rowers and with an authorization from Menelaus to offer to Neoptolemus the hand of his daughter, Hermione, as an added inducement for his services.[31]

Now missing the strong arms of two more of their greatest champions, the Greeks came to still another peril—for their Trojan enemies were bolstered by the addition of Eurypylus the grandson of Heracles, who brought up his host of Mysian warriors to the beleaguered city.[32] After being enthusiastically greeted and feted, he donned his armor and, taking up his great shield,[33] came upon the plain of battle at the head of the combined armies, in whose van he was attended by Paris, Aeneas, Polydamas, Pammon, Deiphobus, and the Paphlagonian Aethicus. In opposition, the Greeks leapt forth from their ramparts under the leadership of Agamemnon with a force which caused their attackers at first to give way but, as the Trojans and their allies rallied, Eurypylus slew the handsome Nireus[34] and, when Machaon sought to hinder him from stripping the prone corpse, slew him also with a thrust of his lance through the right thigh. Yet, his second victim did not die until he had prophesied that his destroyer

would soon come to his own death on the same battlefield.

Summoning his comrades to join him in protecting the corpses of Nireus and Machaon, Teucer went to the fore—accompanied by Machaon's brother Podaleirius, who quickly brought down the Trojans Cleitus and Lassus. And, though many of the Greeks lost their lives, the rest were successful in bringing the dead bodies of their comrades back to the ships. During the withdrawal, Ajax the Lesser stood off the enemy and slew the Trojan Polydamas,[35] while Menelaus pierced Deiphobus through the right breast, and Agamemnon rushed upon Aethicus so furiously with his spear that the Paphlagonian shrank back into the midst of his own men.

In the later fighting: Eurypylus, Paris, and Aeneas charged upon Ajax the Lesser, who was hit by a stone from the hand of Aeneas and would have been overcome except that his comrades Teucer, Idomeneus, Thoas, Meriones, and Thrasymedes came to his assistance; Teucer thrust back Aeneas with a spear thrust, but failed to pierce his buckler; Meriones slew the Macedonian Laophoön, who had come to Troy with tall Asteropaeus; Alcimedes slew Pammon's unnamed charioteer and the Trojan prince would have lost his own life had not one of his comrades leapt into the driverless car and taken over the reins; Nestor's son Thrasymedes plunged his spear through the knee of Acamas and caused him to retire into the ranks of his own fellows; Echemmon was wounded by the squire of Eurypylus and, in flight, was overtaken and slain by Heracles' valiant grandson; Thoas wounded Paris, who fled to the rear in anguish; and Idomeneus dashed a huge stone ineffectually upon Eurypylus' arm. But, following these perhaps equal turns of fortune, Eurypylus rallied his men to take the iniative, and himself brought death to Bucolion, Nesus, Chromion, Antiphus, and countless other Greeks. And, ranging with him, Aeneas slew Antimachus and Pheres, while Agenor brought

---

him that, before Troy could be taken: firstly, Neoptolemus must be brought to the assistance of the Greeks; secondly, the arrows of Heracles must be used against the Trojans; and thirdly, the Greeks must obtain possession of the image of Athena known as the Palladium.

[31] According to Euripides, Menelaus had previously bethrothed Hermione to Agamemnon's son Orestes before setting out on the Trojan expedition.

[32] The alliance of Eurypylus—a grandson of the greatest of all Greek heroes—with the Trojan cause seems to be somewhat of a paradox until we note that his mother, Astyoche, was a daughter of the Trojan king, Laomedon.

[33] The shield of Eurypylus, minutely described by Quintus Smyrnaeus, was embossed with depictions of many events in the life of his grandfather Heracles. Among them were: the Twelve Labors; the shooting down of the eagle of Prometheus; the fight with the centaurs; and the destruction of the centaur Nessus as he sought to violate Deianeira.

[34] Nireus, who led three ships manned by the Symaeans to Troy with the Greeks, was acknowledged—next to Achilles—to have been the most handsome warrior among the contesting forces. In Lucian's "Dialogues of the Dead" it is intimated that his beauty exceeded that of all men.

[35] Polydamas was a son of the Trojan elder Panthous —an important personage who was undoubtedly of divine descent, but whose genealogy has not been preserved in the writings of ancient authors.

down the Argive Molus, who had come to the war with his friend Sthenelus.[36] Inspired by the leadership of Eurypylus, Paris now returned from the rear, whence he had slunk after being wounded by Thoas and (perhaps from behind some unnamed protection) sent forth his winged arrows which brought death to Phorcys, Mosynus, Cleolaus, and Eëtion. Following these losses, the hopes of Greek success seemed lost, but night came, and they were permitted to retire to their ships without molestation, while their Trojan enemies and Eurypylus exulted before a great campfire on the plain.

Neoptolemus

Refreshed by sleep, the main body of the Greeks went forth on the next day to meet the forces led by Eurypylus, but Podaleirius stayed behind and mourned at the tomb of his brother Machaon until he was assured by Nestor that the dead man's spirit had come to quiet rest as an associate of the immortals in the heavens.[37] The ancient consoler then raised up his sorrowing comrade and they proceeded together to the ships, where they found Eurypulus again on the rampage. For two days and nights he slaughtered right and left, and did not cease until the Greeks sent an embassage to ask for an armistice while they buried their dead—among whom they chiefly mourned the Boeotian leader Peneleos.

Meanwhile, Odysseus and Diomedes arrived at Scyrus and marveled when they saw Neoptolemus, for in countenance, build, and carriage he was scarcely distinguishable from his great father Achilles.[38] After explaining the purpose of their mission, and offering Neoptolemus the shining armor of his sire, they were gratified at his ready acquiescence—given despite the forebodings of his mother Deidameia;[39] and with him they set out on the return journey. Nor was their arrival untimely. For, as they came to the Trojan shore where the Greek ships were beached, Diomedes saw that Eurypylus was about to breach the protecting wall[40] and called upon all to follow, as he disembarked and hastened to Odysseus' tent.[41]

There, Odysseus put on the dependable armor which he had brought from his island of Ithaca; Diomedes donned that which had been taken from the body of the wealthy Trojan Socus; and Neoptolemus was arrayed in the arms of his mighty father—made by Hephaestus and fitting him perfectly. As they came forth to join in the battle, the Greeks were overjoyed to see them speed to the place where Eurypylus and his men were scaling a tower, exultant in the hope that triumph was near at hand. But, inspired by Athena and reinforced by the aid of the Gyrtonian leader Leonteus,[42] Neoptolemus ranged over the wall like a lion and stemmed the assault, so that the forces led by Eurypylus were forced to retreat. In his raging, he slew Celtus and Eubius (sons of Trojan Meges) and so many others of the enemy that old Phoenix rushed forward to kiss his head and breast.[43] And, at dark, a feast was laid in honor of Achilles' worthy son, at which Agamemnon added words of eulogy and Briseis marveled while she looked upon the filial image of her slain lord.

On the next morning, while Eurypylus was preparing to lead his forces in a renewed attack on the walls, Neoptolemus took the initiative and, riding behind the immortal horses of his

---

[36] The Argive Molus is not to be confused with the Cretan father of Meriones who bore the same name.

[37] "There is a saying among men that to the heavens unperishing mount the souls of good men, and to nether darkness sink souls of the wicked."

[38] The son of Achilles and Deidameia was first called Pyrrhus from the name Pyrrha assumed by his father while disguised as a maiden at the court of Lycomedes. At the time when he was first seen by Odysseus and Diomedes, he was approximately twenty years old—according to the Homeric legend wherein Helen states that she had been away from Sparta for that period.

[39] Deidameia recalled how the selfsame pair—Odysseus and Diomedes—had initially discovered Achilles in his maiden disguise and had taken him to the wars in which he lost his life.

[40] Apparently the previous breach, made by Hector, had been repaired.

[41] In addition to the rowers who serviced the vessel Odysseus and Diomedes, the returning force included twenty men sent by Lycomedes to attend his grandson Neoptolemus.

[42] As a grandson of the great warrior Caeneus, Leonteus might properly be designated as a Lapith.

[43] In the narrative of Quintus Smyrnaeus, Phoenix recalls how he held Neoptolemus in his arms as a babe; but, according to the Homeric legend, Achilles (and, ergo, Phoenix) never saw his son.

father (driven by his inherited charioteer Auto-medon), led his Myrmidons out from behind the protecting wall. As the armies met on the plain, he—staying in the van—struck down Melaneus, Alcidamas, Menes, the Phrygian spearman Morys, and two Trojans named Poly-bus and Hippomedon. Meanwhile, Aeneas slew Aristolochus; Diomedes slew Eumaeus; Aga-memnon smote the Thracian Stratus; Meriones slew the Lycian Chlemus; and Eurypylus suces-sively killed Eurytus, Menoëtius, and Harpalus. When Harpalus had fallen, Antiphus hurled his spear against the strong descendant of Hera-cles, but it missed the mark and pierced his comrade Meilanion. Upon this, Eurypylus rushed in to retaliate, and Antiphus escaped with his life only by leaping back into the pro-tion of his own ranks.[44]

Finally, the fated encounter came on as Eurypylus and Neoptolemus met each other in single combat. After an interchange of proud words, they rushed furiously together and, while the gods looked down with varying emotions, the son of Achilles gained the victory by thrust-ing the great spear of Peleus through the throat of his adversary who, with blood gushing from his body in torrents, toppled dead to the earth. With their leader fallen and his corpse stripped by the youthful conqueror, the Trojans raced in a rout back to the city; but the war-god Ares came down with his female companion Enyo; and his rallying voice was recognized by Priam's seer-son Helenus, who urged on his comrades to offer stiff resistance. Again, many lives were lost as: Neoptolemus slew Perimedes, Cestrus, Phalerus, Perilaus, and Menalces; Deiphobus slew Lycon; Aeneas smote Dymas; Euryalus hurled a dart through the breast of Astraeus; Agenor slew Teucer's comrade Hippomenes; and Teucer, strangely missing his object, shot down the Trojan Deiphontes with an arrow aimed at Agenor.

Enraged at the fight which Neoptolemus continued to wage despite his godly opposition, Ares was minded to cast aside the veil of cloud in which he had secreted himself and meet the youth face to face; but Athena swooped down to thwart her mad brother's design, and Zeus parted them with a thunderbolt, so that the battlefield was again tenanted only by the forces of contesting mortals. Now deprived of divine aid, the Trojans retreated behind their walls and fought bravely against the Greek assault; but it became so furious, as Meriones shot down Phylodamas and winged an arrow at Polites that, at the behest of Ganymedes (the fair son of Tros who served as cup bearer on Olympus), Zeus was induced to cover the city with a mist, whose protecting cover was a sign to Nestor that the attack of the Greeks should be foregone and, following his advice, they retired to their ships.

When dawn came, Priam sent his herald Menoetes to Agamemnon to ask for a truce and, it being granted, both sides buried their dead. While, on the Trojan side, Eurypylus was being entombed before the Dardanian (eastern) gate, Neoptolemus went with old Phoenix and his Myrmidons to weep at Achilles' barrow. Arising from their lamentation in an ecstasy of rage, they attacked their enemy's walls with such fury that the assault would have succeeded had not Deiphobus, Priam's son, rallied his comrades to resist.[45] In so doing, he led the way and slew Nestor's charioteer; but the old warrior's plight was noted by Melanthius, who leapt into the car and drove it to safety. Yet, Deiphobus continued with his slaughter of the Greeks, which was matched only by the exploits of Neoptolemus, who successively smote down the Trojans Ami-des, Ascanius, and Oenops. In another part of the field, Agamemnon and Diomedes were fighting a losing battle until Neoptolemus, at last, came head on with Deiphobus. But the expected duel was not consummated, because Apollo poured a dense cloud about Deiphobus, and he was borne within the protecting walls—causing his foe to swear loudly as he found him-self futilely stabbing at the empty air. When Zeus dispersed the cloud, however, and the forms of the Trojans were revealed about the Scaean gate, Neoptolemus threw himself into

---

[44] Antiphus was saved for a more spectacular death when, as one of the companions of Odysseus, he was later eaten alive by the cyclops Polyphemus.

[45] According to the legend, preserved by both Dictys Cretensis and by Hyginus, Deiphobus became the hus-band of Helen after the death of Paris.

the fight again and slew so many of the enemy that Apollo would have smitten him had not the young warrior been warned off by words of Poseidon, which were accompanied by birds of omen and other signs sent down from the heavens. At this stage, the seer Calchas realized that the city was not destined to be taken without the help of the arrows of Heracles and, at his suggestion, Diomedes and Odysseus were sent to fetch them from the island of Lemnos where they had been left with Philoctetes, years before when he was put ashore with his gangrened foot.

Philoctetes

Arriving at the island, they were grieved to find the stricken man as he lay groaning from the pain of his wound in a rocky cavern where the feathers of numberless birds were scattered, upon whose flesh he had been forced to subsist during the long period since he had been abandoned by his comrades. As his visitors approached, Philoctetes sprang to his bow but, when he learned their identity and received their promise that his wound should be cured, he readily promised to go with them back to Troy.[46]

After a pleasant sailing, urged on by a breeze sent by Athena[47] and during which their craft was accompanied by playful dolphins, the voyagers returned to the Trojan coast and disembarked among the Greek ships. Here, their comrades joyfully greeted them, but noted sorrowfully the wasted form of Philoctetes who had to lean on Odysseus and Diomedes for support. The physician Podaleirius, however, lost no time in spreading a healing salve over his wound and, with mythological celerity, it was healed so that—even as his erstwhile fellows looked on— the flush of health came over his bloodless face, and full strength returned to his withered limbs.[48]

Thus requickened, Philoctetes was taken to the tent of Agamemnon, where he received a public apology for the treatment accorded in leaving him stranded at Lemnos. And, with promise of greater rewards to come after Troy should be taken, the Greek commander gave him gifts which consisted of seven handmaidens, forty chariot horses, and twelve tripods.[49] In addition, he vouchsafed to his restored comrade the privilege of thereafter always eating at the royal table.[50] Thoroughly appeased by such magnificent treatment, the son of Poeas[51] announced that he freely forgave all past mistreatment and suggested that, rather than feasting, all should retire to rest, in order to be ready for the fighting next day. This advice was cheerfully followed and, after a night of easy sleep, the Greeks went forth at dawn against the enemy—encouraged by the knowledge that in their van marched their old comrade Philoctetes, who was armed with the bow and unerring arrows of divine Heracles.

The Trojans were still burying their dead outside the walls of their city when they saw the oncoming host, rushing forward with renewed determination. Perceiving that some new and

---

[46] In the tragedy "Philoctetes" of Sophocles, Odysseus is represented as having been responsible for the abandonment of Philoctetes on Lemnos, and Neoptolemus—instead of Diomedes—is named as the companion who accompanied him to bring back the wounded man. Knowing that Philoctetes hated him for having been responsible for the abandonment, Odysseus stayed out of sight and induced Neoptolemus to go forward with a guileful story designed to make the wounded man believe that he too had been mistreated by the Greeks and that he was on his way back from Troy. By this trick the confidence of Philoctetes was obtained and, when he fell asleep from painful exhaustion, he willingly gave his bow and arrows to Neoptolemus for safekeeping. The arms were useless, however, without their owner and, in addition, Neoptolemus became so conscious stricken at his own doubtful participation that the mission was about to fail. At this point, the shade of Heracles appeared above and announced that it was the divine will that Philoctetes should go to Troy. Accepting his destiny, he consented—despite the fact that, in the meanwhile, he had realized the identity of hated Odysseus as one of his escort.

[47] In the version by Quintus Smyrnaeus, Athena caused the rage to die out from the heart of Philoctetes as soon as Diomedes and Odysseus approached his cave on Lemnos.

[48] It may be noted that Podaleirius and his slain brother Machaon, who attended as physicians to the Greeks, were grandsons of Apollo—the chief divinity supporting the Trojan cause.

[49] The tripods—often given as prizes—were considered valuable because often made of precious metals.

[50] In view of his long period of hunger on Lemnos, the boon of eating at the king's table must have been highly acceptable to Philoctetes.

[51] As earlier related, Philoctetes' father, Poeas, had received the bow and arrows of Heracles for his service in kindling the great man's funeral pyre.

heartening addition must have been made to the forces of the enemy, the Trojans retired within the invulnerable[52] walls, behind which had been gathered sufficient provisions for subsistence during a prolonged siege but, at the bidding of Aeneas, his comrades chose to stand and meet the Greek onslaught.

In the holocaust which followed: Aeneas slew the Boeotian Harpalion and the Cretan Hyllus; Neoptolemus slew twelve Trojan warriors with his father's great ashen spear;[53] Meges slew the Dardanian Eurymenes and, as Deileon and Amphion rushed in to strip his armor, Aeneas smote them down; Diomedes slew Menon and Amphinous; Paris slew Demoleon, who had come to the war from Laconia; Teucer slew the Phrygian Zechis; Meges drove his spear beneath the heart of Alcaeus; Ajax the Lesser cruelly wounded the Lycian warrior Scylaceus;[54] and Philoctetes, after slaying Deioneus and Antenor's son Acamas, brought down so many others of the enemy that others in the Trojans' rank and file dared not come within the range of the great bow which he wielded.[55]

Paris, however, came up from the rear and loosed an arrow which would have pierced Philoctetes had he not swerved aside; and the shaft, although missing its mark, lodged itself above the breast of the Rhodian Cleodorus and brought on his death. Marking his attacker, Philoctetes in turn shot at him an arrow which merely grazed the flesh of his wrist;[56] but the barbed point of a second arrow plunged squarely into Paris' body between the flank and groin, and, stricken with both agony and terror, he fled back to the Trojan leeches, who vainly sought to relieve his pained frenzy with their salves. In the meanwhile, night came on and the opposing armies retired to sup and sleep.

Recalling the prophecy that he might escape the doom of death only at the hands of his forsaken wife, Oenone, Paris trudged through the darkness to her mountain home and fell suppliant at her feet. Resorting to the oft-used mythological excuse, he pleaded that the Fates —and not his own free will—had led him to desert the nymph for Helen's embraces and tearfully asked that he might be forgiven and healed of his wound. But his entreaty was futile, because the heart which he had broken was now steeled and, mocking his agony, Oenone bade him go back to Helen and whimper beside her bed.

The Death of Paris

As the doomed man stumbled down through the brakes of Mount Ida, Hera spied him from on high and, speaking to her handmaidens,[57] told them of other things which were fated to come.[58] Even while she spoke, Paris gave up the ghost on the montainside and the Oread nymphs, who—years before— had smiled at his childish prattle, set up a loud wailing which reverberated sorrowfully through all the glens around.

Soon after, a herdsman brought to Hecuba at Troy the news that her son was dead, and she wept with an intensity matched only by the tears of Helen.[59] But each of them inwardly mourned mainly for herself—Hecuba, stricken with a foreboding that her city was doomed to fall and that she would be haled into captivity; and Helen, feeling that she was destined to suffer for having brought on the war, whether

---

[52] Because the walls of Troy had been built by Poseidon, they were thought to be invulnerable.

[53] The names of the Trojans slain by Neoptolemus were Cebrus, Harmon, Pasitheus, Hysminus, Schedius, Imbrasius, Phleges, Mnessaeus, Ennomus, Amphinomus, Phasis, and Gelenus.

[54] After the war was over and Scylaceus returned to Lycia, a throng of women met him and inquired about their sons and husbands. When he told them that they all were dead, the women stoned him to death and he was buried in a grave beside that of Bellerophon.

[55] According to Quintus Smyrnaeus, Philoctetes also had inherited the great shield of Heracles and carried it into battle, but the conventional accounts credit him as being possessor only of the hero's bow and arrows.

[56] It was mythologically important that some part of Paris' anatomy should be hit because the arrows of Heracles were fated never to miss their mark.

[57] According to Quintus Smyrnaeus, the four handmaidens of Hera were daughters of Helios and Selene who represented the four seasons of the year.

[58] Hera foretold that Helen should marry Deiphobus; disappointed Helenus should reveal to the Greeks that Troy could not be taken so long as it contained the Palladium; and how Diomedes and Odysseus, after slaying Alcathous at the temple, were able to bear away the sacred image.

[59] The reaction of Priam is not related, because when the news of the death of Paris was received at Troy the old king was still weeping beside the barrow of Hector.

she remained among the Trojans or fled to the camp of the Greeks. Only the grief of Oenone was unfeigned, as she lay moaning on her lost husband's bed and repented her refusal to heal his wound—for she truly loved him despite the cruel treatment which she had received. When night came and her sister-nymphs slept, she raced down the mountain to the place where neighboring shepherds had laid the corpse of Paris upon a burning funeral pyre. Then like Evadne, she leapt into the flames; and, when the burning heap was quenched, the mingled ashes of the two lovers who had been made mere pawns in the great mythological game were tenderly enclosed and buried in a golden vase.

Since Paris did not die on the field of battle, no truce was made for his burial, and the opposing forces continued in their murderous conflict. Still leading on the Greeks, Neoptolemus slew the Lycian Laodamas, and followed by smiting down the Trojans Evenor, Iphition, and Hippomedon. Aeneas slew Bremon and the Cretan Andromachus. Philoctetes shot down Peirasus and, leaping on his fallen body, sheared the neck through with his sword. Trojan Polydamas struck down Eurymachus and Cleon with his spear. Grecian Eurypylus laid low the Phrygian Hellus, and his shorn arm twitched like the severed tail of a serpent. Odysseus slew the Ceteians Aenus and Polydorus. Sthenelus smote Trojan Abas with a javelin cast through the throat. Diomedes slew Laodocus. Agamemnon slew Melius. Deiphobus smote down Alcimus and Dryas, and the Trojan Agenor slew Hippasus.[60]

As the fighting continued: Thoas slew the Trojans Lamus and Lyncus; Meriones slew Lycon; Menelaus laid low Archelochus; Teucer shot down Menoëtes; and Euryalus shattered the head of Trojan Meles with the casting of a great stone. At this low ebb in the Trojan fortunes, Apollo assumed the shape of Polymestor[61] and so encouraged Aeneas and Euryma-

chus, that they leapt upon the Greeks with the fury of madden wasps. Their surprise attack caused the enemy to retreat in a rout shared in by all except an unnamed son of Anthalus but, when he sought to stand, Agenor struck the bone of his shoulder with his sword, and Aeneas completed his destruction by hurling a spear through the navel. The rout was stemmed, however, when Neoptolemus came charging in with his Myrmidons and caused all, save the forces of Aeneas, to retreat in turn.[62] With the tacit acquiescence of Zeus, Athena now came to the aid of the Greeks and they drove the Trojan survivors back within their city's walls—discouraged because they had been deprived of the leadership of Aeneas, who had again been enveloped by Aphrodite in a great mist and carried away from the danger.

The emboldened Greeks, led by Sthenelus and Diomedes, sought to storm the Scaean gate; but were held back by the arrows and huge stones precipitated from the walls by Deiphobus, Polites and their comrades. And a similar defense of the Idaean gate was made by Helenus and Agenor against the charge of Neoptolemus and his Myrmidons. At another place,[63] Aeneas repulsed an attack led by Odysseus and Eurypylus, the son of Evaemon, in which the Greeks came forward with their locked shields raised as a roof over their heads. Even though the cleverly designed stratagem of Odysseus was effective in warding off the missiles of the lesser Trojans, it could not withstand the force of the huge stones thrown down from the walls by the son of Aphrodite, whose mighty casts were directed by the war-god Ares.

A short distance away, where Ajax the Lesser was creating havoc among the enemy with his arrows, the Locrian warrior, Alcimedon, sought to scale the walls on a ladder but, as his head appeared above the parapet, Aeneas crushed it in with a stone and the bold man's lifeless body

[60] Quintus Smyrnaeus relates that Agenor slew Hippasus, without naming the allegiance of either man but, since he adds that the slaying took place "far from Peneius' river," it may reasonably be conjectured that the slain man was a Greek.

[61] This Polymestor is described as a seer-son borne to a priest of Apollo, and is not to be confused with the

Thracian king who married Priam's daughter, Iliona.

[62] For some unstated reason, Quintus Smyrnaeus says that Thetis—revering Aphrodite—caused Neoptolemus to refrain from attacking Aeneas.

[63] Troy was reputed to have a number of gates in its walls, but only the Scaean (western) and Idaean (eastern) were given names which have persevered in classical literature.

was dashed to the ground. Upon this happening, Philoctetes shot one of his arrows at Aeneas, which grazed his buckler and, being thus turned aside, pierced the brow of Medon, who toppled dead from his towered perch. Enraged at the death of his friend, Aeneas threw down another stone, shattering the skull of Philoctetes' comrade Toxaechmes, but he was too clever to accept the challenge of Philoctetes to come down and fight in single combat—and the battle appeared to be at a stalemate.

The Wooden Horse

Calchas now assembled the Greek chieftains and, relating how he had seen a falcon swoop down upon a dove from his hiding place in a bush, advised that thought be given to some method of trickery which might accomplish the end which they had been unable to gain by force. Pondering this advice, Odysseus suggested that a great horse should be fashioned, in whose hollow interior a number of the strongest warriors should be secreted; the rest of the army should then sail away to the nearby island of Tenedos, and some man, unknown to the Trojans, should be left behind to relate that the image had been constructed as an offering to appease the wrath of Athena for the theft of the Palladium.[64] Thus, it would secure for the Greeks the protection of the goddess on their homeward voyage. He further suggested that the gullible Trojans would inevitably draw the horse within their town and that, when this should have been done, the armed warriors could issue from its belly in the dead of night while the waiting army on Tenedos were being recalled to their assistance by the flash of a torch.

The crafty plan was applauded by all except Neoptolemus and Philoctetes, who fiercely protested that they preferred to continue the fighting openly but, when Zeus sent down a great clap of thunder, it was taken as a sign of his disapproval of their mutterings and they reluctantly joined their comrades in gathering tim-

bers for the construction of the horse—under the supervision of Epeius, the son of Panopeus. In three days' time, the huge wooden image was completed.[65] After Sinon[66] offered himself as the prospective Trojan captive, the mightiest of the Greek warriors entered the hollow belly—Neoptolemus being given the honor of going first.[67] When the ladder had been drawn up and the secret door was closed, the rest of the army sailed at night to Tenedos under the leadership of Agamemnon and Nestor.

On the following morning, when the Trojans looked from their walls and saw that the Greek ships were gone, they joyfully rushed to the shore and came upon the Wooden Horse, beneath whose form they spied cowering Sinon. With brave restraint he permitted himself to be cruelly tortured—even to the loss of his nose and ears—before, with seeming reluctance, he related that the image had been left to propitiate Athena, and that he himself had fled into hiding because it had been proposed that his life should be given as an additional sacrifice to assure a safe homeward voyage to the Greeks.[68]

Given under such circumstances, Sinon's story was believed to be true by most of the Trojans, and they prepared to take the horse within their city's walls. But Laocoön, nephew of Anchises and a priest of Apollo, suspected

---

[64] According to the legend related by Virgil and other later mythographers, Odysseus and Diomedes had earlier entered Troy through a subterranean passage and had carried off the Palladium by stealth.

[65] In a dream sent to Epeius, Athena announced that she would be his invisible helper in the construction. During the three-day period, it is related by Quintus Smyrnaeus that the Olympian gods again gathered on the Trojan plain and were about to engage in open warfare among themselves, but were dissuaded and dispersed by Themis, who pointed out that their persistence would certainly bring down the wrath of Zeus and cause their own destruction.

[66] Owing to the deceptive role of Sinon, it was sometimes fancifully related that he was a son of Sisyphus.

[67] Following Neoptolemus, those who entered the horse were: Menelaus, Odysseus, Sthenelus, Diomedes, Philoctetes, Menestheus, Anticlus, Thoas, Polypoëtes, Ajax the Lesser, Eurypylus, Thrasymedes, Idomeneus, Meriones, Podaleirius, Eurymachus, Teucer, Ialmenus, Thalpius, Antimachus, Leonteus, Eumelus, Euryalus, Amphimachus, Demophon, Agapenor, Acamas, Meges and last—after unnamed others—Epeius. In a typical speech referring to his past prowess, Nestor pleaded that he also might be permitted to enter, but his claim to inclusion was lightly put aside by Neoptolemus.

[68] According to a later legend, Sinon added that if the Wooden Horse should be destroyed Troy would fall and that, if it should be taken into the city, the Trojans would always thereafter be victorious.

that a fraud was intended, and urged that the wooden image be burned. As soon as he ceased speaking, however, Athena struck him blind and, taking this as divine proof of his fallacy, the Trojans made a great breach in the walls and dragged the horse within, on the greased rollers which Epeius had thoughtfully provided. As the townspeople shouted in exultation, Laocoön continued to exhort them to "beware of Greeks bringing gifts," but this warning was again disregarded when two great sea serpents came into the city and destroyed his young sons, Thymbraeus and Antiphantes.[69] Satisfied by these portents that their city was at last saved, the Trojans now set themselves to revelry—despite the ominous predictions of the prophetess Cassandra, who shouted loudly her unbelieved words of impending calamity. And when all had retired—heavy with food and wine—Sinon first lifted a torch as a signal to the waiting army on Tenedos, and then approached the Wooden Horse to say that the clever plan of Odysseus had thus far met with complete success.[70]

The Fall of Troy

Opening the secret door and letting down the ladder which had been drawn inside the hollow image, Odysseus was the first to set foot on the ground. He was quickly followed by all of his comrades who, seizing the dying brands from the fires of the sleeping Trojans, set about kindling the city's buildings into flames. Soon after, they were reinforced by the army which had sailed back from the island of Tenedos, favored by a driving wind sent by Thetis.

In the slaughter which followed, many of the Greeks lost their lives, but all of the Trojan warriors were slain, save only Antenor and Aeneas.[71] As related by Quintus Smyrnaeus,

among the highlights included in the struggle: Diomedes slew the Phrygian Coroebus, who had come to Troy to seek the hand of the unfortunate prophetess Cassandra, and followed by slaying the aged Eurydamas[72] and the Trojan warrior Eurycoön; Ajax the Lesser slew Amphimedon; Agamemnon smote down an unnamed son of Damastor; Idomeneus slew Mimas; and Meges slew Deiopites. Rushing about everywhere, Neoptolemus successively struck down Priam's sons Pammon, Polites and Antiphonus. To them he added as his victim Antenor's brave son Agenor; and then he struck down the aged King Priam of Troy, even as he knelt by the altar of Zeus.

Elsewhere, unnamed Greek warriors hurled Astyanax, Hector's young son, down from the high walls to his death, while his mother, Andromache, wept for the cruel fate which she knew was in store for her. Only the house of Antenor was spared, because he had originally counselled the Trojans to return Helen to the Greeks. But, by the will of the gods and the advice of Calchas, Aeneas was permitted to flee from the burning city with Ascanius, his young son, and his aged father, Anchises.[73]

While the general massacre was taking place, Menelaus came to the apartment of Helen, only to find that she had fled into the palace; but drunken with wine, Deiphobus still remained and the Spartan king slew him with his sword, as he voiced regret that it had not been vouchsafed that he should have dealt the same punishment to Paris—predecessor in his false wife's affections. Pushing onward, and slaying Trojans right and left, he came to the inner chamber where Helen lay cowering, and, although it was his intent to take her life, he was debarred by a sweet longing sent upon him by Aphrodite and by the plea of Agamemnon that she should be spared.

The sack of the city continued with such fury that the gods themselves were forced to mourn its fate—save only Hera and Athena. But even

---

[69] The incident is preserved in a beautiful, and pathetic, piece of statuary which is lodged in the Vatican.

[70] An addition to the legend is that Deiphobus led Helen—to whom he was married after the death of Paris—to the Wooden Horse and had her call to the men inside with voices resembling those of their wives. Her mimicry was so true, a response would have been evoked from Anticlus had not Odysseus placed his strong hand over the young warrior's mouth.

[71] It was mythologically necessary that Aeneas and Antenor should be saved in order to preserve the stories that they later founded colonies in Italy.

[72] Eurydamas is described as a son-in-law of Antenor, but the name of his wife is not given.

[73] Aeneas' wife, Creusa, also left the city with him, but disappeared before he had proceeded any great distance.

the latter was shamed when Ajax the Lesser outraged the prophetess Cassandra, who had taken refuge in her temple on Pergamus.[74] Amidst the burning carnage, only one incident seemed to bring a breath of sweet normality— for Demophon and Acamas, the sons of Theseus, were enabled to recover their grandmother Aethra, who long ago had been enslaved as handmaiden to Helen when the Dioscuri found their beautiful, young sister in her custody at Aphidnae.

It was appropriate, however, that the fall of Troy should be concluded by a note of tragedy, and the narrative of Quintus Smyrnaeus draws near its close when Priam's daughter, Laodice, is swallowed up by an earthly chasm, as she prays to her great ancestress Electra to be delivered from the prospect of future thralldom.[75]

---

[74] Although mentioning earlier that the Palladium had been taken from Troy by Odysseus and Diomedes, Quintus Smyrnaeus relates that the image turned its face when Cassandra was ravished by Ajax.

[75] According to a different legend, Laodice bore a son named Munitus to Acamas and, presumably, in the division of spoils would have been allotted to the man whom she loved.

28

The Returns

THE LOST EPIC written by Hegias of Troezen, entitled "The Returns," is reputed to have been an account of the events attending the various Greek heroes—except Odysseus[1]—in their homeward travels after the fall of Troy. But, for the purpose of this chapter, the classical girdle has been expanded to include briefly the subsequent adventures of the more prominent actors to whom a live exodus from the battlefield was permitted, whether Greek or Trojan.

It should first be noted that, in the division of booty, Agamemnon got Cassandra, Neoptolemus got Andromache, and Odysseus got Hecuba. Upon this happening, the ghost of Achilles appeared above his grave and demanded that the daughter of Priam, Polyxena, be sacrificed to him, and Neoptolemus dutifully performed the cruel command.[2] As the maiden's corpse was given to old Antenor for burial,[3] the news of her slaughter came to the ears of Hecuba and, while the Greeks stood in amaze-

ment, the body of the Trojan queen was changed into that of a stone hound.[4]

Upon Nestor's advice, the ships were now loaded and they began the homeward journey but, foreboding disaster, Calchas and Amphilochus[5] elected to remain ashore and, proceeding southward by foot, came to Colophon in Caria. There, as related in chapter 7, Calchas died from a broken heart when he was overcome in augury by the great seer Mopsus.[6]

As the rest of the Greeks gaily weighed anchor, their captive women looked sorrowfully ashore where the only people left were the old and wounded. Under the supervision of Antenor, these were last seen as they laboriously built a huge funeral pyre upon which, side by side, they tenderly placed the bodies of all their slain men. When the wood had been lighted, they wept as the conquerors of once-great Troy sailed out of sight. Nor was it fated that any vestige of the ruined city should remain for, at a later time, Zeus permitted Poseidon to send an inundation of strong waves which toppled

---

[1] The wanderings of Odysseus, constituting the subject matter of the Odyssey of Homer, were not recounted by Hegias.

[2] According to Quintus Smyrnaeus, Polyxena was sacrificed after Neoptolemus had a dream in which his father requested that an offering be made to him of the best of the Trojan spoils. Another legend relates that she died willingly because she had long been secretly in love with Achilles.

[3] Quintus Smyrnaeus relates that Polyxena had been reared by Antenor as the prospective bride of his son Eurymachus.

[4] A different account (of Euripides) of the circumstances under which Hecuba was changed into a bitch, after blinding the Thracian king, Polymestor, has been earlier mentioned in chapter 4.

[5] According to Apollodorus, Calchas and Amphilochus were accompanied by Leonteus, Podaleirius, and Polypoetes.

[6] According to Quintus Smyrnaeus, Calchas and Amphilochus settled in cities of Cilicia and Pamphylia—east of Colophon.

the lofty walls until their intermingled essence was indistinguishable from the mud of the plain.

Approaching the coast of Euboea, the Greeks were caught in a great storm brought upon them by Poseidon and the wind-god Aeolus at the behest of Athena—who was still outraged because Locrian Ajax had defiled her temple by the ravishment of Cassandra.[7] While many ships foundered, the goddess caused a thunderbolt to strike the vessel of the impious man so that it went utterly to pieces and he was forced to swim for protection to a nearby rock. Foolishly thinking that he had been saved, he boasted that her divine intention had been thwarted. Thereupon, Poseidon angrily smashed the rock with his trident, so that Ajax fell into the sea and drowned.[8]

Although the storm now somewhat abated, many of the other Greek vessels were lured to their destruction by flares which were set on the promontory of Caphareus by Nauplius, in revenge for the destruction of his son Palamedes at the beginning of the long war. Of those who were saved, only Nestor seems to have been vouchsafed an uneventful return to his Pylian home—a boon to which his great age and past exploits undoubtedly entitled him. Among the rest: the Magnesian leader Prothous and the Elean leader Meges lost their lives; Gouneus, leader of the Enienes, was driven by the storm to Libya; Antiphus, the grandson of Heracles, landed among the Pelasgians and named their country Thessaly after his father, Thessalus;[9] his brother, Pheidippus, finally settled on Cyprus after first touching the island of Andros; and Philoctetes landed at Campania in distant Italy. Diomedes was permitted to return to

Argos but, upon arriving, was heartbroken to learn that Aegialeia, his wife, had been unfaithful to him, and according to later legends, he migrated to Italy where, at death, he was buried and worshipped as a god. Idomeneus also returned to his home to find that Meda, his wife, had been appropriated by another[10] and, being expelled from his Cretan kingdom, went first to Italy and afterward to Colophon in Asia Minor.[11]

Menelaus came out of the great storm with five of his ships, which were able to make their way to a headland of Attica but, again being driven to sea, wandered for eight years up and down the coasts of Libya, Phoenicia, Cyprus, and Egypt—until, at last, he was permitted to return with the great treasures collected during his travels.[12]

According to Apollodorus, Neoptolemus avoided the storm off the coast of Euboea by remaining at Tenedos—where the Greek fleet first stopped on their return journey—and proceeded with Andromache, Phoenix, and the Trojan Helenus to Epeirus, where he gave Andromache to his friend Helenus in marriage, after she had borne to him three sons, Molossus, Pergamus, and Pielus.[13] Afterward, he went back to Phthia and took over the rulership of his ancestral domain; but was later slain at Delphi, under circumstances which will be narrated later when the fate of Agamemnon and his son Orestes is discussed.

Aeneas

As previously mentioned Diomedes, Idomeneus, and Philoctetes were all reputed to have been eventually responsible for the establish-

---

[7] Apollodorus relates that, before they set sail, Calchas told the Greeks that Athena was angry at the impiety of Ajax, and adds that his comrades would have killed the Locrian leader had he not fled to an altar for refuge. Commenting on the same incident, Pausanias relates that Odysseus advised that Ajax should be stoned to death.

[8] Quintus Smyrnaeus relates that Poseidon dashed a huge rock down upon Ajax, and Apollodorus adds that his body was washed up on the island of Myconus, where it was buried by Thetis.

[9] A different legend related that Thessaly took its name from Thessalus, a son of Haemon and grandson of Pelasgus.

[10] As elsewhere related, the infidelity of the Greek wives was attributed to the malicious rumor spread by Nauplius that their husbands at Troy were consorting with captive maids.

[11] The tragic circumstances attending the return of Idomeneus to Crete are related in chapter 15. According to Diodorus Siculus, his tomb was shown in later times at Cnossus.

[12] According to the "Helen" of Euripides, the greatest treasure collected by Menelaus was Helen, his wife, who had been borne to Egypt by the gods while only her wraith had been fought for at Troy.

[13] The friendship between Neoptolemus and Helenus is said to have originated when the latter cautioned his erstwhile enemy to return home by land.

ment of settlements in Italy. Antenor, likewise, was considered as the founder of Venice. Among those who migrated, however, to the new country[14] after the fall of Troy, Aeneas, the Dardanian prince, is classically preeminent —immortalized by Virgil's great epic poem, the Aeneid. As the literary connecting link between Greece and Rome, it is appropriate to briefly state the highlights of the story.

Amid the confusion attending the sack of Troy, Aphrodite appeared to her son Aeneas and bade him leave the stricken city; and he proceeded with his family and household gods[15] toward a ridge of Mount Ida, where he found that a number of other fugitives had gathered. But, upon arrival, he discovered that Creusa, his wife, was missing; and, after backtracking in a vain search for her, the poor woman's ghost appeared and announced that he was destined, after a long period of wandering to found a new home in Hesperia (Italy) and there take a new wife.

When a fleet of sailing vessels had been constructed under his supervision, Aeneas first crossed with his comrades to the coast of Thrace[16]—the commencement of seven years of wandering which successively led them to Delos,[17] Crete, the island of the Harpies, the coast of Epeirus,[18] the land of the Cyclops,[19] and Sicily, where Anchises came to a peaceful death. After burying the old man, the expedition again set sail with the intention of doubling

back to the western extremity of the island, whose shores were hugged closely in order to avoid the dangers of Scylla and Charybdis. Under Palinurus, the able steersman, and the comforting words of his friend "faithful Achates," Aeneas was looking forward with pleasure to an early landing in the new country which had been promised to him. But, at this juncture, Hera sent a great storm and, when it had subsided, only seven of the vessels were able to make their way to the coast of Libya, where they came to harbor near the city of Carthage.[20]

With his friend Achates, Aeneas set out to look over the land where they had been stranded and shortly encountered Aphrodite in the disguise of a mortal. She informed them that the city of Carthage was under the rule of Dido, who had fled to Libya from Tyre following the murder of her husband;[21] and advised her son to seek the queen's protection. This he did, with the result that his personal charm won Dido's love[22] so that she offered to share her rule with him. Wearied with his long wandering, Aeneas was about to accept the proposal when Zeus sent Hermes to stir up his ambition, and—leaving Dido to destroy herself—he led his men on to their ships.

After sailing northward, a landing was made at Cumae in Campania,[23] from where the resi-

---

[14] As mentioned earlier, Sicily and the southern part of Italy had long since been colonized by Greeks, and the land was known as Magna Graecia.

[15] In his exodus, Aeneas carried his father, Anchises, on his shoulders, led his young son Ascanius (Iulus) by the hand—and was followed at a distance by Creusa.

[16] While pulling up trees in Thrace to place upon the sacrificial altar to his mother, Aeneas was amazed to hear the voice of Polydorus announce that the grove had sprung from spear handles which Polymestor had driven into his unhappy breast.

[17] At Delos, the oracle bade Aeneas seek the home of his ancestors, and he mistakenly went to Crete where a dream directed him to proceed on to Italy.

[18] In Epeirus, Aeneas was surprised to find that the country was ruled by Helenus with Andromache as his wife; and from them he obtained instructions and directions pertaining to the remainder of his journey.

[19] In the land of the Cyclops (Cyclopes), Aeneas saw the blinded Polyphemus, who is later mentioned in detail in connection with the wanderings of Odysseus.

---

[20] It is related in the Aeneid that Hera induced the wind-god Aeolus to raise the storm without the knowledge of Poseidon, who came up from his watery depths to bring on the lull which permitted Aeneas and his comrades to make their way to port.

[21] When Dido's husband was murdered by her brother, Pygmalion, she fled to Libya and the inhabitants granted her the privilege of taking over as much land as could be enclosed within the hide of a bull and, by cutting the hide into strips, she surrounded the considerable tract upon which the city of Carthage was built.

[22] In order to make Dido fall in love with Aeneas, Aphrodite had her little son Eros (Cupid) take the form of Ascanius. While the Carthaginian queen fondled the supposed mortal on her lap, she was impregnated with one of the love-god's fatal arrows.

[23] Before reaching Cumae (about 12 miles west of modern Naples), the band of Aeneas again landed in Sicily and celebrated funeral games in honor of Anchises, who had been buried there the year before. While the games were in progress, the Trojan women—afraid to again brave the perils of the sea—set fire to the ships; but, following a prayer by Aeneas, the flames were quenched by a sudden shower and, advised by the ghost of Anchises, the women were left in Sicily with the chil-

dent Sibyl conducted Aeneas into the lower world (known to the Romans as Avernus). There, he first saw the shades of his steersman Palinurus[24] and of others of his comrades who had lost their lives by drowning.[25] Then, after conversing with the shades of others whom he had known, it was revealed to him that he was destined to found a great nation—and the Sibyl lead him back to earth.[26]

Returning to his comrades, Aeneas now led them to Latium, where—after engaging in a war with the forces of the Rutulian king, Turnus— he married Lavinia, the daughter of King Latinus. And it was through Silvius, their son, that the Romans claimed the descent of their strictly local heroes, Romulus and Remus.

Agamemnon

The sad circumstances attending, and following, the return of Agamemnon from the Trojan War were the common subject matter of many stories often referred to by ancient writers, but the most comprehensive account is that of Aeschylus, preserved to us in three related tragedies which are collectively known as the "Trilogy" (or the "Oresteia") and separately known as the "Agamemnon," the "Cheophori" (libation pourers) and the "Eumenides" (the Furies).[27] The great dramatist assumes that his audience is familiar with the legends about the house of Tantalus.

The "Agamemnon" opens as news is relayed to Clytemnestra, from messages flashed by successive beacons all the way from Phrygian Mount Ida, that Troy has at last fallen and her husband's return may be shortly expected. Soon after, a herald appeared and, when he had given a rather sketchy resume of the homeward journey, Agamemnon drove up to his palace at Mycenae seated in a chariot with Cassandra by his side. Clytemnestra feigned great joy upon again seeing him after his long absence and, despite the warnings of Cassandra, both he and the captive prophetess followed his false queen into an inner chamber, where they were slain.[28] Clytemnestra now boldly appeared to her people and acknowledged that she had committed the crime to be revenged for the sacrifice of Iphigeneia; and was quickly joined by Aegisthus, who admitted his complicity, and excused it as being fully warranted by the previous murders committed by Atreus upon the children of Thyestes.[29]

As part of the plot to perpetuate their rulership, it was intended by the guilty couple that Orestes, Agamemnon's young son, should also be slain, but he was rescued, either by his sister Electra or by his nurse Cilissa, and was taken for rearing to the court of the Phocian king, Strophius, who was married to his aunt Anaxibia.[30] There, he grew up with his cousin Pylades in a beautiful friendship which has become proverbial in classical mythology. As he approached manhood, he received frequent messages from Electra urging the necessity of avenging his father's death and, after seeking advice from the oracle at Delphi, secretly repaired to Argos with his companion Pylades.[31] It is at this point in the story that the events related in the "Cheophori" of Aeschylus begin.

First going to the tomb of Agamemnon attended by Pylades, Orestes reverently placed upon it a lock of his hair. As he did so, with apology that he had not been permitted to be present at the original interment, a chorus of women were seen approaching, followed by

---

dren and aged men, while the rest proceeded on to Cumae.

[24] Palinurus had been drowned when he fell overboard while stargazing.

[25] He also saw the shade of Dido, still bloody from her self-inflicted wound.

[26] Before returning, Aeneas was told by the shade of his father how he was destined, through his son Silvius, to become ancestor of the great Roman nation.

[27] The extant tragedies of Euripides—entitled "Electra" and "Orestes"—and the "Electra" of Sophocles deal with the same general subject.

[28] There are varying legends of how Agamemnon and Cassandra came to death. Aeschylus has Clytemnestra declare that she struck down Agamemnon with three thrusts after first entangling him in a netlike garment, and intimates that she slew Cassandra also. In the Odyssey, the shade of Agamemnon tells Odysseus that he was slain by Aegisthus, while Clytemnestra killed Cassandra.

[29] According to Pausanias, Pelops and Teledamus— the young sons of Agamemnon and Cassandra—were murdered by Aegisthus on the tomb of their parents.

[30] Anaxibia was Agamemnon's sister.

[31] In the "Electra" of Sophocles, Orestes pretends that he has come to Mycenae as a messenger from Strophius—with news of his own death and bearing his own ashes.

Electra, and the two companions concealed themselves while she ascended the tomb to pour libations, after praying that Orestes might soon appear to avenge her father's death. Spying the shorn lock, she was seized with the thought that it had been offered as a sacrifice by her brother—a thought which became a certainty when Orestes appeared from his place of hiding and revealed himself as she descended from the top of the tomb.

After relating to his sister how the oracle of Apollo (Loxias) had bade him slay his father's murderers, Orestes—accompanied by Pylades—gained access to the palace on the pretext that he had been sent to bring news of his own death. First killing Aegisthus, he followed it by dragging Clytemnestra within and taking her life also.[32] But now the dread Furies were seen to arise from below and, chased by them, Orestes was forced to flee—stricken with a fit of madness which they brought upon him.

---

[32] In the "Electra" of Sophocles, the story is related with a number of variations from the plot of Aeschylus. Among them: Electra is not made aware of the return of Orestes until after he gains admittance to the palace through the ruse of pretending to be a messenger from Phocis; meanwhile, she has engaged in heated arguments with both her sister Chrysothemis and her mother Clytemnestra when they sought to defend the murder of Agamemnon; the curse on the house of Atreus is related to the action of Pelops in slaying his charioteer Myrtilus; it is Chrysothemis, and not Electra, who discovers the lock of hair which Orestes has laid on his father's tomb; Orestes slays his mother; but the story ends as he peremptorily orders Aegisthus to enter the palace to meet his doom at the selfsame spot where Agamemnon had bled.

Similarly, the "Electra" of Euripides contains other variations. Among them: Electra is represented as having been married to a peasant by Aegisthus with the thought that no danger might come to his usurped throne from her lowly children; after Orestes, accompanied by Pylades, places the lock of his hair on his father's tomb, the two companions visit the cottage of the peasant and, without revealing themselves, state that they have tidings of Orestes; as they talk, the old servant who had originally taken Orestes to Phocis comes in and, first reporting the finding of the lock on his erstwhile master's tomb, recognizes Orestes and tells his identity to Electra; Orestes is led by the old servant to a place where Aegisthus is preparing a feast for the nymphs and, after slaying the usurper, brings his corpse back to the cottage. Lured by news that her daughter had given birth to a son, Clytemnestra arrives at the cottage and is likewise slain; the shades of the Dioscuri arise and prophesy the persecution of Orestes by the Furies. Having remained a virgin during her marriage to the peasant, Electra is given by her brother as bride to his friend Pylades.

The "Eumenides" of Aeschylus opens with a soliloquy of the Pythoness at Delphi,[33] from where the distraught Orestes—followed by the Furies—fled to seek the aid of Apollo. The "Orestes" of Euripides, however, supplies several incidents of high, mythological importance which have occurred in the interim, and it seems proper at this point to make note of them.

After the madness came upon him, Orestes fell into a stupor which lasted for six days, during which Electra sat mourning by his bedside. During her vigil, Helen appeared and requested that locks of her hair be taken as an offering to the tomb of her slain sister[34]—stating that she feared to go herself lest the citizenry should assault her for having brought on the great war in which many of their best men had lost their lives. But Electra refused the mission and, at her suggestion, Helen's daughter, Hermione,[35] was sent with instructions to offer both the fair locks[36] and liquid libations at the grave. Shortly afterward, Orestes awakened and when Menelaus arrived (later followed by aged Tyndareus) it was revealed that the Argive townsmen, under the leadership of Oeax,[37] were threatening to put both Orestes and Electra to death by stoning. Upon this, Orestes asked Menelaus to assist him, but the Spartan king lamely replied that his single spear could not prevail against the multitude and, intimating that he would try to dissuade the townsmen from their purpose, retired with Tyndareus.

Subsequently, after Menelaus and Tyndareus had joined the townsmen in their meeting, decision was made that Orestes and Electra should be stoned to death—a decision silently acquiesced in by Menelaus and vocally seconded by

---

[33] In her soliloquy, the Pythoness related how the shrine at Delphi had successively been presided over by Gaea, Themis, Phoebe, and Apollo.

[34] Clytemnestra was the daughter of Tyndareus and Leda and, thus, a half sister to Helen.

[35] In addition to Hermione, borne by her to Menelaus, Helen was said to have been the mother of Bunomus, Helena, and Idaeus, borne by her to Paris; but nothing of consequence is related about them.

[36] As Hermione departed, Electra noted that she carried only the tips of Helen's hair, "sparing its beauty —still the Helen of old!"

[37] Oeax was the son of Nauplius, and brother of Palamedes who had been condemned to death at Troy by Agamemnon for an alleged treason.

Agamemnon's faithless herald Talthybius. Apparently, only Diomedes spoke in favor of the condemned pair, by proposing exile instead of death.

Apprised of the determination of the townsmen, it was agreed by Orestes, Electra, and Pylades that, in retaliation for the pusillanimous inaction of Menelaus, Helen should be destroyed and, that upon the return of Hermione, she should be held as a hostage to insure their escape. The plan was duly carried out, and the "Orestes" of Euripides concludes as Apollo appears in the clouds with Helen and—after announcing that Hermione and Orestes shall wed[38]—bids Menelaus and the Argive populace to forego their murderous purpose.

Returning to the "Eumenides" of Aeschylus, when the Pythoness retired, she last saw Apollo standing beside Orestes, who was seated on the Omphalos,[39] surrounded by the sleeping Furies —and with Hermes in the background. At the bidding of Apollo, Hermes led the suppliant Orestes from Delphi to the court of Athena at Athens, and there, inevitably followed by the chasing Furies, a trial was held which would indicate that, from it, our present-day legal procedure may have taken its source.

First, Orestes embraced the image of Athena —probably hoping to be seen by the judge and, thus, create a prejudice in his favor. Next, the prosecuting Furies entered and ridiculed Orestes —telling him that he had no chance of winning his case. Orestes countered by saying that he would rely upon the defence of laches—his actual words being: "Time, waxing old, doth all things purify." Following this conversational interplay, Athena appeared in her chariot and, after tethering her horses, daintily tripped to the seat of justice to inquire about the controversy. Thereupon, the Furies stated that Orestes was guilty of the crime for which they had immemorially been the prosecutors—the crime of shedding the blood of a kinsman—and urged that sentence be pronounced forthwith upon him.

Now, Athena showed the judicial stuff of which she was made, and answered their frenzied demands by saying: "Two parties plead, one only have I heard." To this, the Furies replied that Orestes should not be heard, because he had refused to be sworn upon his oath to tell the truth. Athena, having sat on the bench through some several thousand preceding terms, had evidently learned the fallibility of testimony given under oath and sagely announced: "Repute of justice, not just act, thou wishest. By oaths win not unjust success, I say." Thus speaking, she asked Orestes to state his side of the controversy, and he answered that the matricide was justified under the primal law of "blood for blood"—claiming that in no other way could Clytemnestra's murder of Agamemnon have been expiated. As a second defense, Orestes— anticipating the theory of nonresponsibility advanced by Clarence Darrow—pleaded: "And sharer in the blame is Loxias, who goads of anguish to my heart announced, unless the guilty found from me their due."

Athena now empaneled a jury to try the issue, in a trial packed with much legal background ordinarily considered as having roots which stem from the times of the English Magna Charta. Here, in mythological Greece— at least two thousand years earlier—we find not only the right of trial by jury, but the number of the jury is twelve, and both sides were permitted to offer evidence. One distinct difference, however, from our present system may be noted, in that Athena's jury was from her townsmen "culled the best." But, by substituting "worst" for "best," the correspondence is well-nigh perfect.

After the jury were sworn and seated, Apollo was discovered buzzing and whispering about their chairs, but the prosecuting Furies raised such a howl that he had to come out in the open before he had an opportunity to do any real serious fixing. He then tried to plead the defense, but judicial Athena, knowing her procedure, shut him up and called upon the prosecuting Furies to state their case—saying, "It is

---

[38] As related in chapter 14, Tisamenus—the son of Orestes and Hermione—was the leader of the forces which unsuccessfully sought to stem the invasion of the Peloponnesus by the descendants of Heracles and their Dorian allies.

[39] On the hearth of the temple at Delphi a perpetual fire burned, and near it was the Omphalos—or navel stone—which was supposed to mark the middle point of the earth.

yours to speak—thus I commence the suit. Since the plaintiff, taking first the word, to state the argument may justly claim."

As their first, and only, witness the prosecuting Furies called the defendant, and he freely admitted slaying his mother, but again offered as excuse the two defenses already mentioned, to wit: expiation of Clytemnestra's murder of Agamemnon and the defense of nonresponsibility because impelled to commit the murder by injunction of the god Apollo. To these defenses, he now intimated that a third might be added—his mother was not of blood kin to him, in which event the Furies would be without jurisdiction to prosecute. This naive claim was advanced by his lawyer—Apollo—in the following words:

> Not mother of her so-called child is she
> Who bears it;—she is but the embryo's nurse;
> He who begets is parent; she for him,
> As stranger for a stranger, rears the germ,
> Unless the god should blight it in the bud.

Pondering these things, the jury retired; and, when its vote was brought in—six for conviction and six for acquittal—Athena declared that the verdict was "not guilty," and the disgruntled Furies were forced to leave off the persecution of Orestes and hie themselves back to the lower world until some fitter subject should evoke their recall.[40]

---

[40] According to a different legend, related in the play of Euripides, entitled "Iphigeneia in Tauris," Orestes consulted Apollo how to be relieved of his madness, and went with Pylades to Tauris to fetch the image of Artemis to Greece. There, he discovered that his sister Iphigeneia was the priestess of the temple and, by tricking the forces of the native king, Thoas, the three were able to return with the image—which (as related in chapter 3) was placed, and worshipped with barbaric rites, at Brauron in Attica.

The conventional story is that Orestes married Hermione, the daughter of Menelaus and Helen, and that Tisamenus, their son, ruled in Argos at the time of the Dorian Invasion. The "Andromache" of Euripides, however, relates that Hermione afterward married Achilles' son Neoptolemus, who was slain at Delphi by Orestes.

29

The Odyssey I

THE LAST of the Greek heroes to reach his homeland after the fall of Troy was Odysseus, the brave and cunning king of Ithaca, whose exploits were so respected by the Trojans themselves that they voted him to be a worthy successor to the armor of Achilles. The events of his long, and roundabout, journey are narrated by Homer in the Odyssey—an epic poem conventionally divided into twenty-four books. The following is a resume, based upon the English translation of Andrew Lang.

Book I. At the time of the poem's beginning, Odysseus is being detained by the nymph Calypso, a daughter of Atlas, on her mythical island of Ogygia, from where—after losing all of his companions—he had been driven by Poseidon, because he had blinded the god's giant one-eyed son, the Cyclops Polyphemus. While Poseidon is away on a visit to the Ethiopians, Athena joins a council of the gods and obtains the consent of Zeus that Odysseus will eventually be returned to his home—despite Poseidon's displeasure.[1] To put the plan in motion, it is agreed that Hermes shall be sent to Ogygia to convey the supreme will to Calypso, and that Athena herself shall go to Ithaca to guide Odysseus' son Telemachus to Pylus and Sparta, for the purpose of seeking tidings about his father.

Assuming the semblance of Mentes, a Taphian captain, the goddess approached the gate to the Ithacan court of Odysseus, and gazed upon the wooers of Odysseus' wife, Penelope, as they were gaily engaged in playing at draughts and in feasting upon the all-too-scanty provisions of her unfertile island. Seen by Telemachus, the stranger was hospitably brought within by him and, sitting somewhat apart from the noisy wooers, was given refreshment—followed by songs from the minstrel Phemius. During the entertainment, Telemachus complained to the supposed Taphian about the uncertainty of his father's fate, and that his mother's suitors (being most of the unmarried nobles from the islands of Dulichium, Same, Zacynthus, and Ithaca itself) were about to eat him out of house and home. In the conversation, his guest related that he had heard it said on the island of Cyprus that Odysseus was still alive, but was being withheld from home on a "seagirt isle." He prophesied, however, that the wanderer would return before the passage of not too long a time, and suggested that, in the meantime, Telemachus should satisfy himself by going to Nestor at Pylus and to Menelaus at Sparta, in order to inquire the last news which they may have had about his great father. Having thus spoken, the goddess flew away in the form of a sea eagle, and the amazed youth realized that he had been visited by one of the deities.

Phemius, the minstrel, now began to sing

---

[1] As the goddess of wisdom, Athena admired Odysseus greatly for his ready wit, and on many occasions offered him her divine assistance.

about the pitiful endings which had come to many of the Greeks as they were returning from Troy and, when Penelope came from her chamber and bade him cease his sad song, Telemachus—emboldened by Athena's encouraging words—ordered her to return to her handmaids and attend to her domestic duties, asserting that it was he who was lord of the house. In a like voice of authority, he proceeded to announce to the proud wooers that they should assemble on the next morning for the purpose of collectively hearing him order that they should leave his halls. Following a colloquy with Antinous and Eurymachus—two of the more prominent suitors—he then went to his own chamber where, after his old nurse Eurycleia had hung up his clothes, he meditated all night upon the journey that Athena had proposed.

Book II. When the wooers had been assembled the next morning, Telemachus composedly took his father's seat, attended by two swift hounds and bearing in his hand a bronze spear. The first to speak was Aegyptius, an aged friend of Odysseus, whose son Antiphus had gone with the Ithacans to Troy and (as it later developed), had been eaten by the Cyclopes while stranded on his island during the return home. Aegyptius had three other sons, of whom two were continuing dutifully to till their Ithacan fields. The third, however, named Eurynomus, was consorting with the suitors of Penelope. Although weeping because his son and his king had failed to return, the old man hopefully inquired whether the assembly had been called to hear good tidings.

After the herald Peisenor had placed a staff in his hands, Telemachus replied by saying that he had received no news, and that he had called the meeting only to chide the wooers for their wantonness in continuing to devour his flocks, instead of going to the house of Penelope's father, Icarius, and asking him to bestow her hand upon one of their number. He then intimated that their continued conduct would soon bring the wrath of the gods upon their heads. So saying, he dashed the staff to the ground and broke into tears.

Antinous now answered that the fault was that of Penelope, who had promised that she would choose a new husband as soon as she should have completed a shroud which she was weaving for the day when Odysseus' aged father, Laertes, should die. For three years, she had woven the web by day, only to unravel her work secretly during each night; in the fourth year, one of her women had betrayed her ruse to the wooers and they had discovered her even as she was undoing the previous day's weaving. Having thus complained, he defiantly announced that neither he nor his competitors would depart for their own homes until the queen should make good her word by taking one of them in marriage.

As Telemachus again threatened that divine punishment was forthcoming Zeus sent down two eagles and, hovering in midair above the assembly, they "tore with their talons each the other's cheeks and neck on every side,"—after which they flew away over the city. Upon this happening, the seer Halitherses, recalling that he had previously prophesied that Odysseus would return to Ithaca in the twentieth year after embarking for Troy, now read the omen of the eagles to mean that he would soon appear and take vengeance upon those who were despoiling his house.

Belittling the seer's words, Eurymachus reiterated Antinous' demand that Penelope should immediately make choice of a husband, and renewed the threat that the wooers would not leave until she had done so. Thereupon, Telemachus bade that no more be said about the matter, and he asked to be given a swift ship and twenty men to accompany him to Pylus and Sparta to inquire concerning the return of his father—promising that, if he should hear that Odysseus was dead, he would return to Ithaca and would give his mother's hand in marriage to one of her suitors.

After making this proposal, the youth sat down, but Mentor jumped up. He was an old companion of Odysseus to whom he had given the stewardship of his house when he left for Troy. Wrathfully, he cried shame upon the wooers, and upon the people of Ithaca for their failure to drive the haughty men out by force. Deriding the old man, Leocritus replied that, even if Odysseus should return, he could not overcome the great number of the suitors, but would himself be slain and denied his wife.

Sneeringly, he added that Mentor and Halitherses should set about hastening the voyage suggested by Telemachus—which he considered to be merely a bluff. When he had finished speaking, the townspeople scattered to their homes, and the arrogant wooers proceeded to the house of Odysseus for a continuance of their wasteful feasting upon his provisions.

Going down to the shore, Telemachus first washed his hands and then prayed to Athena, who soon drew near to him in the likeness of Mentor. After speaking words of encouragement, she promised to furnish a ship for the journey to Pylus, and said that she would herself go along as his companion. She then bade him return to his house and gather provisions for the voyage, while she was rounding up a crew of his fit townsmen. In compliance, he went back to the chamber of his house where wine, olive oil and barley meal were stored and, on the way, had to pass by the reveling wooers. Nor did they overlook the opportunity to ridicule him about his plans for the voyage which they thought would never be taken.

Calling his old nurse Eurycleia into the chamber, he instructed her to gather into one place twelve jars of wine and twenty measures of barley meal, and told her that he would come for them after his mother should have retired to sleep. When she sought to dissuade him from his purpose, he bade her take heart—saying that he had been prompted to the undertaking, and would be cared for, by a god. And he made her swear a great oath that she would not reveal his departure to his mother until the eleventh or twelfth day thereafter, or until such earlier time as Penelope should miss him.

Meanwhile, Athena assumed the likeness of Telemachus and, going through the city, gathered a crew of men—instructing them to meet at the mooring of a swift ship whose use she had earlier obtained from a willing Ithacan named Noemon. This done, she went to the house of Odysseus and, after bringing sleep to the wooers, again assumed the form of Mentor and led Telemachus down to the place where his crew were waiting beside their vessel. At his bidding, they fetched the heaped provisions from his house and stored them aboard. And now, with a favorable west wind, the ship put out to sea, where drink offerings were made to the gods— but chiefly to the grey-eyed daughter of Zeus, whom none but Telemachus knew was one of their own number.

Book III. The voyagers arrived at Pylus to find on the shore nine companies of five hundred men each, engaged in offering black bulls as sacrifices to Poseidon. Stepping forth from the ship, Telemachus was somewhat abashed but, encouraged by Athena who led the way, proceeded to where the Pylian king was seated, surrounded by his sons and the rest of his company. Peisistratus cordially greeted the strangers and, placing them beside his father, Nestor, and his brother, Thrasymedes, gave them a golden cup of wine and bade them make a drink offering and a prayer to Poseidon. This they did— Athena first drinking and praying for the health of their host and for their own safe return. Nor was it a discomforting thought for her to realize that "herself the while was fulfilling the prayer!"

Upon Nestor's inquiry, made after the sacrificial ceremony was completed, Telemachus informed him that they had come to seek news of his father. In the course of a long-winded recital,[2] the old king related: that one-half of the Greeks had tarried at Troy with Agamemnon to offer sacrifices to Athena, while the other half sailed promptly from the conquered shore; that among the latter were Odysseus and Nestor himself; but that, after landing on the island of Tenedos, they sailed their different ways and had never again seen each other. Upon hearing this story, Telemachus reluctantly became resigned to the belief that his father must have perished, but as Athena (still in the form of Mentor) spoke words of encouragement, he proceeded to question his ancient host about the returns of Agamemnon and Menelaus.

In reply, Nestor related: how Aegisthus, hav-

---

[2] Among other incidents mentioned in his discourse, Nestor related: that Ajax, Achilles, Patroclus, and his own dear son Antilochus had fallen in the Trojan conflict; that Odysseus "very far outdid the rest in all manner of craft." On the return journey, he had met Menelaus on the island of Lesbos. He himself, being given a sign by the gods, had sailed directly across the sea from Lesbos to Euboea; Diomedes, Neoptolemus, Philoctetes, and Idomeneus had all returned safely to their respective homes; and that Agamemnon had also come through, only to meet his death at the hands of usurping Aegisthus.

ing seduced Clytemnestra, slew her returned husband, Agamemnon, and thereafter ruled over Mycenae for seven years; how, in the eighth year, he was himself slain by Agamemnon's son Orestes; and, on the same day when a funeral feast was being held for the usurper and the faithless queen, Menelaus arrived, bringing great treasures which he had collected in his wanderings through Egypt and other distant places.[3] The ancient concluded by offering to furnish his young guest with a chariot and horses for the journey to Sparta—intimating that he there could perhaps obtain information about the fate of his father, which Menelaus might have acquired while traveling in strange lands.

Evening having now descended, offerings were made to the gods and the visitors were about to return to their moored vessel. However, Nestor persuaded Telemachus to spend the night in his palace, and Athena left by herself—but not in the form of Mentor, for her departure was in the semblance of a sea eagle and thus revealed her divine identity to the wise old Pylian king, who reverently made a prayer to her for the happiness of his household. He then led the way into his palace and, after a bowl of sweet wine was drunk in honor of the goddess, all retired to rest—Telemachus being conducted to an echoing gallery where he occupied a jointed bedstead beside Peisistratus, who was his host's only unwed son.

On the next morning, Nestor arose and, occupying the seat of his departed father Neleus, gathered about him his six sons, who brought in Telemachus to join them.[4] Breakfast was not forthcoming until after Stratius and Echephron had fetched a heifer and the goldsmith Laerces had gilded its horns. Even then, the meal was not ready until the animal had been slaughtered in a bloody ritual which caused Nestor's daughters and his wife, Eurydice, to cry aloud. But, finally, the meat was roasted (with a basting of red wine) and, when the cakes of barley meal

were well-done, all fell to eating with appetites that were possibly sharpened by the delay.

Meanwhile, Telemachus was bathed and anointed with olive oil by Nestor's youngest daughter, Polycaste, and came to the table "forth from the bath in fashion like the deathless gods."[5] After the meal was over, he proceeded with Peisistratus to yoke his ancient host's horses to their waiting chariot and—with perhaps a fond farewell to dainty Polycaste—set out on the road to Sparta. At evening, they came to Pherae, where they rested for the night in the house of Diocles, the son of Orsilochus;[6] the next day's travel brought them to the wheat-bearing plains of Lacedaemon.

Book IV. The young travelers arrived at the palace of Menelaus in the midst of a great feast which he was giving for the weddings of his daughter, Hermione, to Neoptolemus and of his son Megapenthes to an unnamed daughter of Alector.[7] Their presence was announced to the Spartan king by his steward Eteoneus, with a query as to whether they should be permitted to enter during the festivities or should be sent elsewhere. Displeased at this intimation of inhospitality, Menelaus peremptorily ordered his foolish servant to unyoke the tired horses and to lead the strangers inside to join in the feast.

They soon entered and, after marveling at the richness of the lofty palace, were bathed and anointed by the court handmaidens—after which they donned thick cloaks and doublets, and sat down at the festive table beside the king. Bidding them to eat heartily, he promised to wait until they were filled before asking who they were, but he added that it was easy to see that they were of noble blood. After eating, Telemachus first spoke—remarking that his host's house was so richly furnished that it

---

[3] For an undisclosed reason, Menelaus' helmsman Phrontis was slain during the voyage by one of Apollo's arrows.

[4] The surviving six sons of Nestor were named Echephron, Stratius, Perseus, Aretus, Thrasymedes, and Peisistratus.

[5] As previously mentioned in chapter 10, Telemachus later married Polycaste and she bore a daughter to him who was named Persepolis.

[6] Diocles had two sons, named Crethon and Orsilochus, who were slain by Aeneas in the Trojan War. His town of Pherae was located in the Peloponnesus, and it should not be confused with the Thessalian town of the same name where the palace of Admetus was memorialized by the visit of Heracles.

[7] Although Hermione was betrothed to Orestes, the son of Agamemnon, while both were still children, Menelaus had promised her hand to Neoptolemus in return for his mighty help on the Trojan battlefield.

seemed worthy of Zeus himself. Thereupon, Menelaus related that he had gathered much of his treasure during his seven years of wandering in Cyprus, Phoenicia, Egypt, and in the lands of the Ethiopians, the Sidonians, the Erembi, and the Libyans, where lambs were horned from birth and the ewes yeaned thrice each year. He then recalled the sad ending of his brother (Agamemnon) and remarked that he would willingly retain only a third part of his treasures if he could restore to life those companions who had perished at Troy—among whom, he said, the dearest to him was Odysseus.

At the mention of his father's name, Telemachus let a tear fall to the ground, and Menelaus pondered whether he should let the youth voluntarily announce his lineage or should draw him forth with questions. At this juncture, however, Helen came into the room, accompanied by her handmaidens, and the near sight of her beauty erased all mundane thoughts from the minds of those who were present.[8] Forthwith, she announced that she had no doubt of the identity of Telemachus, because he so clearly carried the features of his great father. When Menelaus acknowledged the soundness of her observation, Peisistratus interposed to confirm the fact, and stated that they had come to the Spartan king in the hope of obtaining from him some word of Odysseus' fate.

Again mentioning his love for the hapless man whom the gods had cut off from returning, Menelaus wept, and was joined in his tears by the rest. But as the grief of Peisistratus caused him to speak of his perished brother Antilochus, his wise host bade that they should all leave off weeping, and promised that on the morrow their conversation should be resumed. As he finished speaking, the squire Asphalion brought water for their hands, and the company fell to drinking their wine—into which Helen cast a drug to lull all pain and anger and to bring forgetfulness of sorrow.[9]

---

[8] The names of Helen's handmaidens were Adraste, Alcippe, and Phylo. Of these, the latter entered with a silver basket which had been given to her mistress at Egyptian Thebes by Alcandra, the wife of King Polybus.

[9] The drug had been given to Helen by Polydamna, a woman of Egypt, whose inhabitants were said to have been descended from the Olympian leech Paeon.

When the soothing drink had brought on good cheer, she related how Odysseus had stolen into the Trojan city in the disguise of a beggar, and how she, alone recognizing him, had anointed him with oil and kept his secret, after he had revealed to her the plans of the Greeks and had returned to their camp—leaving behind the corpses of many Trojans to attest the might of his long sword. Somewhat apologetically, she added that, at the time, she had come to realize the mistake which she had made in leaving her lord and her child for the embraces of Paris, and blamed her action on the blindness cast upon her by Aphrodite. As though to lay bare her pretense of naivete, Menelaus now recalled that, when the Greeks had left behind the Wooden Horse in which many of their warriors were secreted, his dear (?) Helen, in the company of her new husband, Deiphobus, had walked around the hollow image—calling on the Greek chieftains by name, in voices so simulating those of their wives that Odysseus kept Anticlus from making reply only by closing the mouth of the deluded man with his strong hands. Recital of this incident must have brought a blush of shame to his wife's fair cheeks, because—for no apparent reason—Telemachus now suggested that it was time to go to bed. Gratefully acquiescent, Helen ordered her handmaidens to set out bedsteads with purple coverlets for the use of her guests, and herself retired with Menelaus into their inner chamber—where she lay by his side and made her peace.

On the next morning, in answer to a direct query, Telemachus told Menelaus how the wooers of his mother were bringing the house of Ithaca to ruin by continuing to devour its flocks and grain; and he besought his host to tell him the truth about his father's ending. After prophesying that Odysseus would bring death to the wooers, just as he had done when he destroyed huge Philomeleides in a wrestling match on the island of Lesbos, the king related that, while he had been detained on the island of Pharos for twenty days, he had contrived to grasp the elusive sea-god Proteus, and had learned from him that Odysseus was being detained by the nymph Calypso at her island home.[10] He added

---

[10] Menelaus was enabled to trap Proteus only with

that the Old Man of the Sea had also said that he—Menelaus—was destined to live in immortality on the Elysian plain and, concluding his discourse, invited Telemachus and Peisistratus to remain as his guests for another eleven or twelve days—promising that he would then send them forth in a polished car drawn by three horses, and laden with gifts. Telemachus gratefully acknowledged the courtesy but stated that his presence was needed in Ithaca and refused the offer of the horses on the ground that his unfertile island could not provide them with proper pasturage. Respecting the youth's wishes, the king promised to give him as an exchange gift a beautiful mixing bowl, made by Hephaestus, which he had received from the Sidonian king, Phaedimus.

While these things were happening at Sparta, the proud wooers continued their feasting at Ithaca. But they were amazed when Noemon came into their midst, as they were casting weights and spears, and inquired about the return of Telemachus, to whom—days before—he had lent the use of his ship for the journey to Pylus, for this was their first intimation that he was not still on Ithaca tending his flocks and fields. In answer to his interrogation, Noemon proceeded to relate how he had himself seen the embarkation, and departure, by a crew of noble youths under Mentor's leadership. He added that he was confused by the fact that even the day before he had observed the old man among his townspeople. He then left for his home and, in a council of the wooers, it was agreed that Antinous should equip a vessel with twenty men and proceed to the strait between Ithaca and Samos, where the returning voyagers might be intercepted and put to death.

It so happened that Medon, a faithful servant of Odysseus, overheard the wooers while they were designing their plot, and he hastened to convey their intention to Penelope who now, for the first time informed of her son's journey, fell to bemoaning the fate meted to her by the gods. Yet, with true queenly courage and presence of mind, she ordered that her thrall Dolius be dispatched immediately to seek the counsel of Odysseus' aged father. At this point, the old nurse Eurycleia, being relieved from her promise of secrecy by Medon's prior revelation, proceeded to relate her assistance in gathering up provisions for her young master's voyage, and spoke encouraging words which caused Penelope to cease from weeping. Instead, she prayed loudly to Athena for the safety of Telemachus, and her prayer was heard by the goddess who, when the queen slept, sent a phantom of her sister Iphthime to bid her take courage. Meanwhile, the wooers had taken ship and, arriving at the double entranced harbor of the little isle of Asteris, laid in wait for the bold son of Odysseus.

Book V. The locale of the story now changes to Olympus where, in an assembly of the gods, Athena complains that Odysseus is being detained unjustly on Calypso's island and that the wooers are set upon slaying his son. In reply, Zeus testily pointed out that the goddess herself had placed the plan to slay Telemachus in the minds of the wooers, so that Odysseus might have greater provocation to take full vengeance upon his return. The supreme father, however, could not deny the plea of his favorite daughter, and told her to lead Telemachus back unharmed. At the same time, he dispatched Hermes to the home of Calypso, with instructions to tell the nymph that Odysseus was destined to leave her isle on a raft, which in twenty days would carry him to Scheria, where the Phaeacian inhabitants would load him with gifts and arrange for a swift passage back to his Ithacan kingdom.

Proceeding as he was bidden, the messenger-god flew over the seas to Ogygia and came to the great cave in which Calypso dwelt. All around were soft meadows and blossoming woods in which "roosted birds long of wing," and within he saw the beautiful nymph, who sang in a clear voice as she sat knitting before a blazing fire of fragrant sandal wood; but he did

---

the assistance of his daughter Eidothea who, out of pity, gave him directions about how to proceed, and secreted him with three companions in the skins of seals, whose stench she removed by giving to each man a whiff of ambrosia. So disguised—Menelaus was able to seize the "Old Man of the Sea" when he unsuspectingly approached, and he retained his grasp despite the fact that Proteus successively transformed himself into a lion, a snake, a leopard, a boar, running water, and a flowering tree.

not see Odysseus, for he sat weeping on the shore as he looked wistfully over the sea. When Calypso learned of Zeus' will, she shuddered and made complaint that the gods were jealous at her mating with a mortal man—even as they had been earlier when Artemis took Orion for her lover and when Demeter yielded to the embraces of Iasion. She realized, however, that her happy interlude was at an end and, going down to the sea, bade Odysseus build a raft for his journey—adding that she would stock it with an abundance of bread and red wine to keep hunger away. Odysseus was suspicious at the unexpected offer, but the nymph swore by the river Styx that it was not made with guile, and they went to their evening meal. When it was concluded, she suggested that, if he should remain with her, he could enjoy a life of immortality, and she coyly mentioned that the beauty of Penelope was no match for her own divine comeliness. Admitting the truth of her last remark, Odysseus replied that he was steadfast in his wish to return to his island kingdom; but, he took some of the sting from his refusal by retiring with his fair hostess to the bedchamber of the cavern, where they "had their delight of love, abiding each by other."

On the next morning, Odysseus set to work with tools supplied by the nymph, and, on the fourth day, completed his raft, which he pushed down to the water. And, on the fifth day, he started on his way—propelled by a gentle breeze that brought him—seventeen days later —within sight of the land of the Phaeacians.

At this moment, it so happened that Poseidon, resting on the mountains of the Solymi as he was returning from his visit to the Ethiopians, spied the raft and realized that, during his absence, the gods had changed their purpose— so that it was now ordained Odysseus should escape; but he angrily determined that the event should not be accomplished until greater suffering were inflicted upon the presumptuous man who had been guilty of blinding his son (the Cyclops). Thereupon, he caused a storm to arise with such fury that a great wave swept Odysseus overboard, and only by the exertion of superhuman effort was he enabled to regain the raft's protection. As he sat in the midst of its quaking timbers, the sea-goddess Leucothea came up from the waters and bade him cast off his garments and swim ashore, under the protection of an imperishable veil which she tossed to him. She then dived below, but Odysseus remained on the raft—until Poseidon sent another huge wave which broke it into bits and again threw him into the churning sea. Fortunately, he was able to bestride a single beam from the wreckage and, belatedly following the advice of the goddess, he stripped off his clothes and wound the veil around his breast. Seeing his victim in this sad plight, Poseidon (with perhaps an approving chuckle) lashed his steeds and went on to his shining palace at Aegae.

For two days and two nights, the poor man was cruelly tossed about in the surge and, even when he once reached the rocky coast whence he was driven by the north-wind at Athena's behest, his grasp was torn loose and he was again washed out to sea. But, finally, with the help of the goddess, he made his way into a smooth-flowing river and, crawling up on its banks, let loose the veil of Leucothea—which she lightly caught as a returning wave bore it to her hands. Then, going slowly into a nearby wood, the grateful man laid himself beneath the leaves, and pitying Athena brought sleep to his tired eyes.

Book VI. While Odysseus slept, Athena went to the palace of the Phaeacian king, Alcinoüs,[11] and—as a dream in the form of one of her maidens—told the king's daughter, Nausicaä, that she should go to the seashore on the next morning to wash her trousseau in preparation against the near day when she might become a bride. Upon awakening, the maiden marveled at what she had dreamed but, ashamed to speak of marriage, asked her father for the use of a wagon and mules to transport her soiled clothing to be washed, merely that they might be ready and clean when she wished to go out dancing. He willingly gave his consent and, accompanied by her handmaidens, Nausicaä

---

[11] Contrary to a normal expectation, Homer relates that King Alcinoüs was descended from Poseidon and Periboea, daughter of the giant Eurymedon; and does not attempt to derive his descent from Phaeax, the son of Poseidon and Corcyra, daughter of the god of the river Asopus.

stored her dainty unmentionables in the "polished car," and drove down to the stream near
whose banks Odysseus was lying asleep.

After the laundry was done, the princess
began to sing and fell to tossing a ball with her
companions, among whom she shone like the
goddess Artemis at play with her nymphs.
When one of the maidens missed the ball and
it fell into the water, they all screamed so
loudly that Odysseus was awakened; and, as he
came out from his leafy bed in his dirty naked-
ness—wondering whether he had at last come
among gentle mortals—the maidens all fled,
except Nausicaä. Following a short conversation
with her, he retired to cleanse himself of brine
and, having been given food and clothing, proceeded into the city in the rear of his female
escort and sat down in a grove sacred to Athena.
This he did at the injunction of Nausicaä, who
feared the gibes of her townsmen if they should
see her bringing in the handsome man, whom
they might take for her intended spouse.

30

The Odyssey II

Book VII. AFTER Nausicaä had been given ample time to return to her apartment—where she was gently tended by her old handmaiden Eurymedusa—Athena enclouded Odysseus in a mist, which rendered him invisible to the townspeople, and led him to the palace of Alcinoüs on whose doors were carved gold and silver dogs made by Hephaestus. There, the mist dissolved and he knelt at the feet of Queen Arete and begged her to send him on to his own country.[1] Prodded by one of his elders named Echeneus, the king raised the visitor to a chair and bade his steward Pontonous bring refreshment. When all had partaken, Alcinoüs directed his retainers to leave for their homes—to regather on the morrow for further entertainment of the stranger, whose high bearing indicated that he was descended from the gods.

Now, in answer to their questions, Odysseus related briefly to the king and queen the events immediately preceding his unasked deposit on their shores. He related: how he had been detained on the island of Ogygia by the nymph Calypso who, for seven years, vainly sought to gain his love;[2] how, in the eighth year, he had taken off on his raft; and how, after seventeen days' travel, he had come—tossed by storms—to Scheria.[3] It was late when his partial narrative was concluded and, with the promise of Alcinoüs that he should be speedily conveyed to his own land, the Ithacan hero retired to a welcome rest.

Book VIII. On the next morning, after fifty-two chosen young Phaeacians had drawn down a swift black vessel to the sea, a sacrificial feast was celebrated and—after it was eaten—the minstrel Demodocus was called up to play and sing. His theme was the Trojan War[4]—a theme which brought so many sorrowful memories to Odysseus that Alcinoüs noted his concealed tears, and suggested that the music should cease and that the celebration should be continued with athletic activities. In these, Odysseus first took no part, and the victors were: Clytoneus, son of Alcinoüs, in the footrace;[5] Euryalus in wrestling; Amphialus in leaping; Elatreus in

---

[1] The friendly role of the Phaeacians, as convoyers of shipwrecked persons has been noted in some detail in chapter 10.

[2] While he tarried at Ogygia, it is related that Calypso bore to her reluctant lover two sons, named Nausinous and Nausithous.

[3] Homer's ancient island of Scheria has been identified with present-day Corcyra—or Corfu—off the coast of Epeirus.

[4] In singing of the Trojan War, Demodocus related how Agamemnon had been made happy by an altercation between Odysseus and Achilles which arose during a feast to the gods—an incident which does not appear to be elsewhere mentioned by the ancient writers.

[5] Those who contested with Clytoneus in the footrace were: Acroneus, Ocyalus, Elatreus, Nauteus, Prymneus, Anchialus, Eretmeus, Ponteus, Proreus, Thoön, Anabesineus, Amphialus, Laodamas, Halius, and Euryalus. The last named was described as a son of Naubolus who was "goodliest of all the Phaeacians next to noble Laodamas," and seemingly was a descendant of Nauplius who had come to Scheria from the island of Euboea.

weight throwing; and Laodamas, also son of Alcinoüs, in boxing.

When Odysseus was asked by Laodamas whether he should like to show his own athletic prowess, he begged off on the ground that his heart was set upon returning home and not upon sports but, ridiculed by Euryalus, he angrily arose and—taking up a weight much larger than that which the Phaeacians had used—cast it many feet farther than any of them had been able to do. Having thus proven his mettle, he was courteously deterred from continuing his show of ability when Alcinoüs suggested that the trials of strength and skill should give way to a dance.[6] In this activity, Odysseus did not participate but sat and marveled at the deft feet of the Phaeacians as they kept time to the music of Demodocus, who sang of the illicit love of Ares and Aphrodite.[7]

The dancing concluded with a skit in which Halius and Laodamas, the sons of Alcinoüs, performed with a purple ball. After an interlude —during which Odysseus received handsome gifts from the Phaeacian princes and a bath from Nausicaä's maidens—he sat back to relate in more detail the adventures preceding his arrival at Scheria.[8]

Book IX. First announcing (what his host had already suspected) that he was the son of Laertes and a resident of the island of Ithaca, he recited that—after leaving Troy—he had sacked the city of the Cicones.[9] Of Odysseus' men, however, six were lost in a counter attack by the natives, which might well have wiped out his whole crew had they not taken to their ships and set sail for home. When this was done, a great storm came on and, continuing intermittently

for eleven days,[10] drove the small fleet to the land of the Lotus eaters.[11] The people of the country were thoroughly hospitable. Their food, however, was such as to make all forgetful of their own homeland; and, it was with the greatest of difficulty that Odysseus was able to persuade his men to resume their journey. Indeed, he forcibly led them back to their ships in tears and bound them to their rowing benches.

Proceeding on, a landing was made at night on an island opposite the land of the Cyclopes[12] and, during the next day, a great feast was made on the flesh of native goats, which were so plentiful that the men in each of twelve ships were able to shoot down nine of the animals for their own portion. Following this nice gorging, all of the company laid down to rest on the beach and slept peacefully until dawn, when Odysseus assembled them and announced that he and his crew were going to the mainland to learn what kind of people lived there.[13] After they landed, he went inland with twelve of his best men, taking along a skin filled with wine that had been given to him by Maro (Maron), a priest of Apollo who was descended from the wine-god Dionysus.[14] Soon coming to a great cave not far from the shore, which Odysseus intuitively knew to be the home of a monstrous Cyclops who dwelt apart from his fellows, the adventuring band entered and found that the owner was away, for he was tending his flocks at

---

[6] In his wrath, Odysseus boasted of his general athletic prowess; but modestly admitted that—in shooting the bow—Philoctetes had been his superior at Troy and that, before his time, Heracles and Eurytus of Oechalia had perhaps also been better.

[7] The incident, wherein Ares and Aphrodite were entrapped in an invisible net by the god Hephaestus, has been related in some detail in chapter 3.

[8] Before Odysseus resumed his narrative, the ladies retired after he graciously reminded Nausicaä that he should always remember her in his prayers as having been responsible for saving his life.

[9] The city of the Cicones is said to have been Ismarus on the coast of Thrace.

[10] After the first two days, the storm abated, and Odysseus thought he would be enabled to make his way home safely, but—as he rounded the promontory of Malea on the southern end of the Peloponnesus—the storm again arose with redoubled fury and drove him off his course.

[11] According to the conjecture of Gladstone, in his book *Juventus Mundi*, the land of the Lotus eaters was on the northern coast of Africa in what is now the western part of Egypt.

[12] The Cyclopes, whose land was visited by Odysseus, were descended from Poseidon and the nymph Thoösa (daughter of Phorcys and Ceto). They should not be confused with the Cyclopes, mentioned in an earlier chapter, who were descended from Uranus and Gaea.

[13] The Cyclopes were described as a lawless race who, for some unnamed reason, were permitted to exist without the necessity of planting or tilling the ground of their country where wheat, barley, and grapes grew of themselves in perpetual abundance.

[14] The chain of descent, as shown on chart 88, is Maro, son of Evanthes, son of Oenopion, son of Dionysus.

a distance. Looking about, however, they saw numbers of lambs and kids in separate pens, and all around were baskets filled with cheeses and vessels containing whey. After kindling a fire and making a burnt offering to the gods, they ate to their fill of the cheeses and sat back to await the return of their unsuspecting host, and shortly, the great creature arrived.

Leaving the males outside, the Cyclops drove the ewes into the cave, whose mouth he closed with a huge stone, and it was only after he had completed his milking that he saw his visitors. When he asked their identity and learned that they were worshippers of Zeus, he boasted that his race paid no heed to the gods and proceeded to make his supper by slaying and devouring two of Odysseus' companions. On the next day, after milking his ewes and feeding his lambs, he drove his flocks forth to pasture—but first ate another brace of his visitors, and kept the remainder penned within the cave by closing its entrance with the same stone. During the giant's absence, Odysseus had his men cut off a fathom length from a huge club that was found at hand and this was sharpened to a point at one end, which was hardened in the fire, and the weapon so fashioned was hidden beneath a dung heap.

In the evening, the Cyclops returned and, after driving all of his flocks into the cave and milking the ewes, dined upon two more of the unfortunate men. Then, persuaded by Odysseus, he drank a cup of Maro's wine and found it so delicious that he asked for more and quickly drank a second—and a third—promising that if Odysseus should reveal his name he would make him a stranger's gift. Upon this Odysseus, seeing that the wine had taken its effect, slyly declared that he was called "Noman," but was by no means overjoyed when the giant declared that for his gift he would be the last man to be eaten. So saying, the Cyclops fell with upturned face in a drunken slumber—vomiting the flesh of those whom he had recently devoured. Quickly heating the pointed shaft in the deep ashes of the cavern fire, Odysseus had four of his men plunge it into his single eye while, from a perch above, he turned it about like a drill until the eyeball was completely burned away. Maddened with the pain, Polyphemus called loudly to his fellows who lived about him in nearby caves and when, after gathering at the closed opening of his cavern, they asked what his trouble might be, he cried out that "Noman" was slaying him by guile.

Upon hearing this response, which they understood to mean that "no man" was disturbing their kinsman, the Cyclopes thought that they were being made sport of, and departed in disgust as Odysseus laughed within himself at the success of his ruse. But his hopes of escape were considerably dimmed when the groaning Polyphemus groped his way to the entrance and, after removing the great stone, sat at the mouth of the cave with his arms outstretched so that he might grasp any one who sought to pass. In this apparently hopeless situation, the cunning of Odysseus again came to the fore and, tying each of his remaining comrades beneath the belly of the middle of three sheep who were yoked abreast, they were enabled to pass unnoticed out of the cavern mouth as Polyphemus ran his hands along only the backs of his departing flock. Odysseus himself came last, hanging beneath the belly of the ram; and, when they were all safely outside, he loosed his hold and, after releasing his six men,[15] swiftly proceeded with them back to his beached ship and put forth to sea.

When the shore had been left behind just such a distance as a man's voice might carry, Odysseus could not resist the temptation to gloat over the escape and, despite the remonstrances of his company, mockingly shouted back to Polyphemus that he had been outwitted by the son of Laertes. Upon hearing this, the Cyclops recalled that the seer Telemus had prophesied that he would lose his sight at the hands of Odysseus and, first praying to his father Poseidon to bring evil days upon the man who had injured him, cast a huge stone at the retreating vessel. But it struck only the rudder and caused a huge wave which drove the ship on to the shore of the nearby island, where the remainder of Odysseus' men were overjoyed to greet their comrades whom they had given up for lost. Here, the sheep of the Cyclops were

---

[15] Of the twelve men who had gone into the Cyclops' cave, six (including Antiphus) had been devoured by him.

evenly divided and a great feast was made on their flesh, but the ram which had borne Odysseus to safety was sacrificed by him to Zeus—a sacrifice which later proved to have been unheeded. Then, after resting for the night, the voyagers took to their oars at dawn and, grieving for those of their number who had been lost to the Cyclops' maw, again put out to sea.

Book X. Making port at the Aeolian (Liparian) Islands, Odysseus went to the palace of the wind-god Aeolus where he dwelt with his six daughters and six sons.[16] He was graciously received and, after relating the details of his previous adventures, was given by his host a wallet made from the hide of an ox, in which all adverse winds were hemmed in. This, upon departure, was made fast in the hold of the ship with a silver thong, and a blast of the westwind (Zephyrus) carried the voyagers for nine days until they came within sight of their native island of Ithaca, where they could see the glowing fires of their townsmen. At this juncture Odysseus, who was managing the sail, unfortunately went to sleep, and his curious comrades took the opportunity to investigate the supposed treasure contained in the leather wallet which Aeolus had given him. Their presumption brought on calamity—for, as soon as the wallet was opened, the pent winds broke forth and raised a great storm which drove all the ships (twelve in number) back to the island where Aeolus dwelt.

After the company had gone ashore and eaten their midday meal, Odysseus went with a herald to the palace, but when the wind-king learned of what had happened he realized that his visitor was in disfavor with the gods and speedily ordered him to go away. Again rowing out to sea, without the help of any favorable breeze, the disappointed wanderers made a landing on the seventh day at the fortress of Lamus in the Laestrygonian town called Telepylus.[17] Eleven

of the ships moored within the harbor but Odysseus moored his outside, where he made his hawser fast to a rock and sent three of his men inland to learn what kind of men lived in the land. Nor were they long in finding out— for, directed by the king's daughter whom they met as she was drawing water from a well, they proceeded on to the palace of her father, Antiphates. Upon entering, they first saw the queen and had some misgivings when they looked over her ugly form, which was in bulk like a mountain peak. And their misgivings changed to terror as, answering her call, the king himself appeared and forthwith seized one of their number for his midday meal. Upon this happening, the surviving two fled back to their ship—while Antiphates raised a war cry which brought up his Laestrygones (Laestrygonians), who were more like giants than men. These stormed upon the eleven ships moored inside the harbor and, after slaying all of the crews, bore their dead victims off. Realizing that it would be useless to offer help to his doomed men, Odysseus cut the hawser of his vessel, which quickly flew out to the high seas under the strong strokes of his frightened company.

Some time afterward, a landing was made at the island of Aeaea where dwelt the goddess Circe, daughter of the Sun-god Helios and sister of the wizard Aeëtes whom the Argonauts had encountered in their quest for the Golden Fleece. After reconnoitering the island and shooting a huge stag, Odysseus returned to his ship with his quarry and a glorious feast was had —but it was not accompanied by the normally expected merriment, for all sat mourning over the fate of their comrades who had lost their lives in the lands of the Cyclopes and the Laestrygones. On the next morning Odysseus related that, in his tour of the island, he had seen smoke coming from an inland grove and, after drawing lots, Eurylochus was sent to investigate with twenty-two men, while the same number remained at the ship with their great leader. Coming to the palace of the goddess, the

---

16 In the Odyssey, the wind-god Aeolus is described as a son of Hippotes (see chart 43), but perhaps the preferable legend is that he was the son of Poseidon and Arne, who was a daughter of Hippotes' son. The names of his six sons and six daughters, mentioned in the text, are not given—save only that of his daughter Alcyone (see chart 50).

17 The interval between nightfall and daybreak in

the land of the Laestrygones is said to have been so short that herdsmen returning from their day's task were accustomed to meet their fellows driving out their flocks to graze on the following day.

band of Eurylochus were greeted by lions and wolves, which though mountain-bred had been bewitched by the goddess with drugs so that they were harmless. When the sweet voice of Circe was heard as she sang at her knitting, Polites bade his companions call to her and, as they did so, she opened her doors and asked them to enter. But Eurylochus tarried behind, for he suspected some trickery. Nor was his suspicion amiss because, when the rest passed within, the goddess fed them a meal containing drugs which made them forget their own country and then, with a stroke of her wand, changed them all into swine and penned them in sties.

Eurylochus hastened back to the shore and, when he reported what had taken place, Odysseus took up his arms and asked that he be led to the palace of the sorceress, but Eurylochus was loath to return and Odysseus set out by himself. On the way, he encountered the god Hermes who told him how to handle Circe and gave him a herb called "moly" to ward off the effects of her magic. The herb proved so effectual that he did not yield to her efforts to change him and, after bedding with the beautiful creature, he was able to persuade her to restore his comrades to their original condition. Then, at her bidding, he went back to his ship and fetched the rest of his men,[18] who thereafter lived and feasted for a whole year in the home of the goddess while their leader nightly shared her couch.[19] Having tarried for such long time, Odysseus was urged by his comrades to start again for their homeland, but when he broached the subject to Circe, she told him that he was destined to perform still another journey—a journey to the realm of Hades and Persephone, where he would receive further instructions from the spirit of the blind Theban seer Teiresias. She concluded by adding detailed instructions as to how the descent below should be

made through a rift at the banks of the great river Oceanus, and prescribed a sacrificial ritual whose performance would induce the spirit of the seer to appear.

Odysseus now proceeded to rouse his men, to whom he related the words of the sorceress, and they went down to their ship, where they found that she had tethered a ram and a black ewe nearby—to be offered later as sacrifices in the rites which she had indicated. But the thought of their grim destination brought no joy to the wanderers and their grief was increased when they learned that Elpenor, their youngest comrade, had fallen from the roof of Circe's palace and had died of a broken neck upon suddenly awakening at Odysseus' call.[20]

Book XI. When the ship was ready for sailing and the sheep had been placed aboard, Circe sent a favorable wind which, within the period of one day, carried the voyagers to the land of the Cimmerians on the banks of the river Oceanus at the ends of the earth. After running the ship ashore, they proceeded on foot through an underground opening until they came to a rock at the place where the rivers Periphlegethon and Cocytus flowed into the Acheron.[21] Here, Perimedes and Eurylochus held the ram and the ewe, which had been brought along, and (as he had been bidden by Circe) Odysseus dug a pit about which he poured offerings of mead, wine, water, and meal—meanwhile entreating with prayers the heads of the dead and promising that upon his return to Ithaca he would make other sacrifices, including the sacrifice apart of a black ram to Teiresias alone. He then cut the throats of the sheep and, as their dark blood fell into the pit, the spirits of the dead began to arise from the depths of Erebus.

First came the shade of Elpenor, who pleaded that Odysseus would return to Aeaea and bury his corpse, so that he could gain passage across the Styx.[22] After giving his promise

---

[18] Before returning to Circe's palace, Odysseus ordered that his ship be drawn ashore and that its provisions be stored in nearby caves. It was only by threat of force that Eurylochus was induced to go along with the rest.

[19] Homer mentions no offspring of Odysseus and Circe; but Hesiod names three sons—Agrius, Latinus, and Telegonus—and the Scholiast on Lycophron adds a daughter, Cassiphone.

[20] It is intimated that Elpenor may have imbibed too freely and, when he was awakened from his sleep on the roof, forgot to descend by the ladder.

[21] Odysseus was accompanied below by Perimedes and Eurylochus, but no definite statement is made with reference to others of his band.

[22] The spirits of those whose corpses were left unburied were forced to flit aimlessly about in the darkness

so to do, Odysseus wept as he saw the spirit of his mother, Anticleia, ascended from below— soon followed by that of the seer Teiresias, who drank of the sacrificed sheep's blood and prophesied his suppliant's future.[23] Odysseus asked how he might make himself known to the shade of his mother, and the seer replied that he might talk with all whom he permitted to draw near the blood. So saying, the spirit of the old Theban returned below and, as that of Anticleia drew near, Odysseus talked with her, from which he learned the state of affairs with the remainder of his family at Ithaca. When he sought to embrace his mother's spirit, however, she flitted from his hands like a shadow and bade him hasten back to the sunlight.

As other shades were seen to approach, Odysseus drew his sword and permitted them to come on singly, so that he might have an opportunity to question them one at a time about their lineage. Thus, in order, came Tyro, Antiope, Alcmena, Megara, Jocasta, Chloris, Leda, Iphimedeia, Phaedra, Procris, Ariadne, Maera, Clymene, and Eriphyle.

When Odysseus reached this point in his narrative to his Phaeacian listeners, Queen Arete suggested that his departure be somewhat deferred until he could be sent home fully laden with gifts—a suggestion which was promptly seconded by the elderly retainer, lord Echeneus, and acquiesced in by King Alcinoüs. Odysseus graciously accepted the postponement of his departure and, responding to the king's questioning, went on to relate his conversations with the shades of others whom he permitted to draw near the bloody trench. These were: Agamemnon, who told how he had been slain by Aegisthus and how Cassandra had been slain by Clytemnestra, but was unable to give any news

concerning the whereabouts of Telemachus; Achilles (accompanied by the spirits of Patroclus, Antilochus, and Telamonian Ajax), to whom Odysseus was happy to relate the great exploits performed at Troy by his son Neoptolemus; Minos, who was seen as he judged the dead; Orion, who was seen driving before him the wild beasts which he had slain on earth; Tityus, who lay stretched out over nine roods with vultures gnawing at his liver as punishment for his attack on Leto; Tantalus, who was not permitted to drink of the water in which he stood nor eat of the fruit which dangled from the trees overhead; Sisyphus, who continually sought to roll a huge stone over the brow of a hill; and, lastly, Heracles, who spoke with words of lament about the ill-usage which had been accorded to him on earth by Eurystheus.

Having seen the shades of those mentioned, Odysseus would have tarried longer in the hope of meeting others of olden times—especially Theseus and Peirithous—but, as the myriad tribes of the dead thronged up together, he ran in fear back to his ship and, after the hawsers were loosed, his men rowed down the stream of Oceanus with a fair wind as their convoy.

Book XII. Leaving the river, Odysseus and his band again voyaged to the island of Aeaea and buried the corpse of Elpenor, in fulfillment of the promise made to his pitiful shade. As their task was completed, Circe came down to the shore and invited them to refresh themselves by partaking of the meat, bread, and wine which her attendant handmaids and brought. Her invitation was gratefully accepted and all feasted for the remainder of the day; and, as darkness came on, she led Odysseus apart from his comrades in order to tell him of further dangers to be encountered.

She prophesied that, after leaving her island, the wanderers would first approach the land of the Sirens whose sweet song was accustomed to enchant and draw to destruction all within hearing—and gave instructions as to how the alluring maidens might be passed in safety. Continuing, she described the perils attendant upon the passage between the wandering rocks and, likewise, the difficulties of avoiding disaster at the hands of the sea-monsters Scylla and Cha-

---

of Erebus for all eternity, without being permitted to attain the comparative rest to which they would otherwise have been entitled in the lower world.

[23] Teiresias prophesied that Odysseus would have a hard passage home, owing to Poseidon's anger at the blinding of his son Polyphemus. Also he would lose both his men and his ship if harm should be done to the herds and flocks of Helios which grazed on the island of Trinacria; would eventually slay the wooers of Penelope; and would meet his death by drowning at a "smooth" old age.

rybdis. She then foretold that the ship would come to the island of Trinacria (Thrinacria)[24] and warned that, if any hurt should be done to the cattle or flocks of the Sun-god Helios which grazed there, Odysseus would lose both his vessel and all of his men—but that he himself would be saved to endure still more evils.

Having thus spoken, the goddess remained with Odysseus until dawn[25] when she returned to her house and he roused his men to take to sea; and, as the ship sailed onward with a favoring wind, he rehearsed to his comrades the prophecies and instructions which she had related to him. Nearing the island of the Sirens, the ship was becalmed and Odysseus had his men draw in the sail, but before he permitted them to proceed by oar he stuffed their ears with wax and had them bind him firmly to the mast. Following these precautions, which had been suggested by Circe, the unhearing men rowed safely past the sound of the Sirens' voices, even as they came to the ears of Odysseus with such sweet seduction that Perimedes and Eurylochus were forced to bind him even tighter to the mast lest he should set himself free and seek the shore.

As soon as the island of the Sirens was left behind and their wax stoppers had been removed, his comrades released Odysseus from his bonds and all breathed a sigh of relief at the narrowly averted danger. But their joy was short-lived, for presently smoke and a great wave appeared with aspect so ominous that the rowers let loose their blades and again took them up only at the strong entreaty of their leader, who recalled that their present danger was no greater than that from which they had escaped when penned within his cave by one-eyed Polyphemus. He told them to row with all their strength and cautioned the helmsman to steer a course away from the smoke and wave and to hug the rocky shore—but said nothing of monstrous Scylla, for fear that they might be paralyzed with terror. He was himself so frightened

that, despite a previous warning from Circe to face all dangers unarmed, he caught up two lances in his hands and went to the prow of the vessel. But he was powerless to contend with the mysterious sea monsters for, as the vessel sailed through the narrow strait, Charybdis sucked down and belched forth the sea water with such force that, while all looked to her for destruction, Scylla reached into the ship and snatched six men from the rowing benches. And these she devoured, while with loud shrieks they stretched forth their disappearing hands to their pitying comrades.

At such cost, the channel between the two sea terrors was finally negotiated,[26] and the ship soon approached the island of Helios. Recalling the admonition of Circe, Odysseus was minded to by-pass the island, but consented to land at the urging of Eurylochus and the rest of his company who pleaded their need of rest. He gave a stern warning, however, that the herds and flocks of the Sun-god were to be in no way molested, and put all to their oaths that they would refrain from slaying either sheep or cattle. The oaths were dutifully kept for a while but, owing to adverse winds which blew for a whole month, no departure could be made from the island harbor, and the provisions given by Circe were wholly consumed. At this juncture—while Odysseus was wrapped in sleep—Eurylochus announced that he would rather risk the wrath of the god than starve to death and, being of like mind, the rest joined him in slaying a number of the sacred cattle and greedily consuming their flesh.

As the savor of the roasted meat penetrated to Odysseus, he awakened and—realizing what had happened—prayed in anguish to Zeus, while Lampetia hastened to her godly sire and reported the sacrilege.[27] Helios now himself called upon Zeus, and the supreme deity promised to bring quick disaster to his defilers who,

---

[24] The island of Trinacria was identified with Sicily.

[25] The hours until morning are delicately passed over by the poet's statement, "So spake she, and anon came the golden-throned Dawn."

[26] Before passing through the strait guarded by Scylla and Charybdis, the voyagers successfully sailed between the wandering rocks, but no account is given of the details of their maneuver.

[27] As related in chapter 4, Lampetia and her sister, Phaëthusa, tended the flocks and herds of their divine father.

for six days, continued to feast upon the flesh of the slaughtered animals.[28] On the seventh day, they set sail with a fair wind but—as foretold by Circe—a storm soon arose in which all save Odysseus lost their lives and, driven back to the strait guarded by Scylla and Charybdis, the ship itself came apart, leaving its great-hearted master only its riven timbers for support. To these he clung for nine days and, on the tenth, came to the Ogygian island of Calypso to remain for the seven years whose attendant experiences he had previously narrated.

Book XIII. After Odysseus ceased talking and the stirrup cup had been passed around, all went to rest until morning when—after a final drink-offering mixed by the steward Pontonous —the illustrious visitor embarked on the gift-laden Phaeacian vessel and immediately went to sleep on a rug covered with a sheet of linen.[29] As he slept throughout the day and night, the rowers assigned by Alcinoüs pulled on their oars so strongly that on the following dawn they drew into a cave at the headland of a harbor of Ithaca and deposited their sleeping

passenger with the gifts which they had borne with him. Then, they started back home but, before they had reached their island, Poseidon complained to Zeus and was permitted to change their ship into stone which turned into a great mountain overshadowing their hospitable coast.[30]

Although Odysseus awakened in his native land, Athena shrouded him with a mist which made him feel that he had been deposited in another country and, looking upon his gifts, he inwardly berated the Phaeacians for depositing him on foreign shores. But, after an interchange of persiflage with the goddess,[31] she revealed her identity and opened his eyes to the fact that he had been brought back to his island of Ithaca, and suggested that he store his gifts in a nearby cave. Agreeably this was done and, while Odysseus—with the help of the goddess—was changed into a withered old man, Athena went to Sparta to bring Telemachus from the court of Menelaus.

---

[28] The men of Odysseus were forwarned of coming disaster by the creeping skins and bellowing flesh as they roasted the sacred animals.

[29] In addition to the generous gifts of the Phaeacians, Queen Arete sent down to the ship her hand-maidens bearing a robe, a doublet, and a basket of bread and wine.

---

[30] As noted previously, Poseidon was angry because the Phaeacians were in the habit of giving safe convoy to those whom he had shipwrecked.

[31] As Odysseus awakened, Athena approached him in the form of a young herdsman and, in answer to her inquiries, he replied with a fictitious story of his travels which included the alleged slaying of Orsilochus, son of Cretan Idomeneus, who—as claimed by Odysseus—was attempting to steal his booty brought back from the Trojan War.

31

The Odyssey III

Book XIV. IN HIS CHANGED FORM, Odysseus proceeded inland to the place where his old swineherd, Eumaeus, dwelt and was greeted by an attack from the latter's fierce dogs, which might have proven hurtful had not the old man driven them away. This done, he graciously invited the supposed stranger into his hut and served him a meal of young pig's flesh, barley meal, and wine—meanwhile complaining about the voracity of Penelope's suitors and expressing fears that his master (Odysseus) had perished. Touching the last point, his guest announced that Odysseus would return to Ithaca before the rising of the next new moon—a prediction which Eumaeus passed lightly by as he added that the suitors were lying in wait to murder Telemachus on his way back from Pylus, where he had gone to seek tidings of his great father.

Continuing, the swineherd asked his guest's identity and was regaled with a fictitious tale that began on the island of Crete and—after successively passing to Troy, back to Crete, to Egypt, and the land of the Thesprotians—ended by relating that in the last-named land Odysseus was seen as he embarked for home.[1]

Although Eumaeus had some doubts about the truth of what he had heard, he politely ordered his helpers to prepare supper which, after appropriate sacrifices, was served by his thrall Mesaulius, whom he had bought with his own substance from a band of wandering Taphians. After the meal was finished, Odysseus talked a bit further, saying that—in his feigned role—he had been third in command with Menelaus at Troy. And, although Eumaeus still doubted, he suggested that Odysseus get some sleep, and went outside the hut with his sword to defend his guest's slumber from being disturbed by the animals which roamed in the dark.

Book XV. While the conversation just related was happening in Ithaca, Athena hastened to Sparta and, awakening Telemachus from the couch which he occupied next to Peisistratus in the palace of Menelaus, asked him to go back to Ithaca with all haste, warning him that he should avoid the strait between Samos and Ithaca where his mother's suitors lay in wait

---

[1] In weaving his fairy story, Odysseus related that: he was the illegitimate son of a Cretan named Castor; fought for nine years in the Trojan War and returned to his wife and children in the tenth year, only to stay a month before the spirit of adventure urged him to outfit a ship and sail to Egypt; in Egypt, although his men lost their lives when they were discovered ravaging the country, its king took him under protection and lavished gifts upon him for seven years; in the eight year he was prevailed upon by a Phoenician to go to that country, but—at the end of a year—was set in a vessel for sale as a slave in Libya; on the voyage a great storm arose and he was driven to the land of the Thresprotians and, there, he was graciously received by king Pheidon, who showed him the vessel in which his alleged self was setting out for Ithaca; leaving Thesprotia, the fanciful journey continued to the island of Dulichium, from where he was sent to Ithaca by Acastus, the invented ruler of the island.

for him.[2] Learning of the desire of his guests to make an early departure, Menelaus asked them to stay longer at his palace but, as Telemachus insisted on starting right away, the Spartan king had his squire Eteoneus lay a farewell meal and ordered his son Megapenthes to bring in a mixing bowl—a previous gift from the Sidonian king, Phaedimus—which was presented to the young visitors as they mounted their chariot and started their return. Helen also gave them a robe of curious needlework which had been embroidered by her own fair hands as a parting gift. And, as they left, it was considered a good omen that an eagle flew off to the right with a goose in its talons.

After driving all day, Telemachus and Peisistratus rested at the house of Orsilochus at Pherae and, departing the following dawn, came to Pylus. Here, Telemachus feared that he might be detained by having to listen to another long-winded discourse from Nestor and, with the acquiescence of Peisistratus, he did not proceed on to the king's palace but was dropped off at the shore, where he bade his waiting townsmen make ready for a homeward embarkation. As the sails were being hoisted, a stranger appeared at the stern of the ship who turned out to be Theoclymenus, descended from the seer Melampus,[3] and—at his request—was permitted to join the departing band. With him aboard, Athena sent a favoring breeze which soon drove the vessel northward past the country of Elis on its return journey.

The locale of the narrative now reverts to the hut of Eumaeus on Ithaca. To test how long his old swineherd might feel inclined to continue his hospitality, Odysseus suggested that on the next day he was minded to go into the city and beg among the suitors of Penelope, and he was very gratified to have Eumaeus insist that he should remain—warning that a

visit to the suitors would subject him to outrage and perhaps violence. Then, in answer to questioning, the swineherd revealed how he had come to Ithaca, had become the thrall of ancient Laertes and had been reared with his master's daughter, Ctimene—and he added that he was himself the son of a king of the island of Syria.[4]

After this conversation, they slept until morning. In the meanwhile, the ship of Telemachus landed on Ithaca—after eluding the ambushed suitors—and the youth sent it on to the city under the leadership of his new friend Theoclymenus,[5] while he himself went on foot to the hut of the swineherd Eumaeus.

Book XVI. Telemachus arrived at his destination while Eumaeus and Odysseus were still at breakfast but, unlike the reception accorded his long-absent father, he was joyously greeted by the dogs and the embraces of the old swineherd. First inquiring about his mother and joining in the meal, he asked the identity of the stranger and was told by Eumaeus that he was a Cretan who wanted to serve at the palace. Telemachus then spoke frankly of his problems, and advised the swineherd's guest against working among the wooers lest they ridicule and mistreat him. Instead, he proposed to supply the stranger with a mantle, doublet, sandals, and a two-edged sword, and then permit him to choose between going his way or remaining with Eumaeus to be fed from the palace.

The stranger now boldly asked Telemachus why he had submitted to oppression by the wooers, and ridiculed him for permitting them to continue wasting his goods. Telemachus apologetically ascribed his helplessness partly to Penelope's procrastination—her prolonged refusal to either accept or refuse the hateful marriage—but largely to the wooer's superiority in num-

---

[2] Adding an extra spur to her admonition, Athena told Telemachus that Penelope was about to wed one of the suitors named Eurymachus.

[3] Through his descent, which has been related in chapter 8, Theoclymenus was himself endowed with the powers of prophecy. He should not be confused with the other of his same name mentioned in the "Helen" of Euripides, who was the Egyptian son of the sea-god Proteus.

[4] As related in chapter 6, Eumaeus was descended from the Aeolid Cercaphus. In the story which he told to Odysseus, he left his home at Sidon with his nurse, who had been seduced by a Phoenician mariner, and began service with Laertes after being shipwrecked on Ithaca.

[5] Before Telemachus left the ship, he entrusted his new friend to the hospitality of his townsman Peiraeus, after Theoclymenus announced it to be a good omen that a hawk had flown from the right with a dove in its talons.

bers. He then told Eumaeus to hasten to the palace and inform Penelope that her son was safely back from his voyage. It was further agreed, after a brief discussion, that Penelope would be asked to relay the message, through a trusted handmaiden, to Laertes who, since the departure of Telemachus for Pylus, had lamented and wasted away—neglecting his customary task of overseeing the tillage of the palace farms.

When the swineherd had gone, Athena showed herself to Odysseus, in the form of a woman fair and tall. But to Telemachus she remained invisible. The time had come, the goddess said, for Odysseus to reveal himself to his son, that they might plan death and doom for the wooers. Touching Odysseus with her golden wand, she increased his size, filled out his cheeks, darkened and freshened his skin, spread a black beard around his chin, and dressed him in a fresh linen robe and doublet.

Telemachus at first mistook his father for a god, but Odysseus convinced him of his real identity, whereupon they embraced, with tears and mutual lamentations. Odysseus explained how he had been brought to Ithaca by the kindly Phaeacians; how their ship had set him down asleep, with gifts of gold and bronze and woven cloth which he later had hidden in a cave; and how he had been guided to the swineherd's hut by Athena to await his son's arrival.

Telemachus expressed doubt that two men could defeat the whole party of wooers: fifty-two chosen lords, with six serving men, from Dulichium; twenty-four men from Same; twenty lords of the Achaeans from Zacynthus; and twelve from Ithaca; not to mention the herald Medon[6] and two squires skilled with carving knives. Odysseus countered by mentioning their own potent allies, Zeus and Athena. He then outlined the following plan: Telemachus was to show himself among the wooers on the following dawn and Odysseus, in beggar's guise, would arrive later in the morning with Eumaeus. Any mistreatment of Odysseus was to be ignored by Telemachus. Later, during the wooer's revels,

Odysseus, on a sign from Athena, would give the nod to Telemachus, whereupon the latter was to remove from the walls and secrete the old weapons of Odysseus, on the double pretext of protecting them from smoke in the great hall[7] and preventing wine-inspired bloodshed among the wooers. Only two swords, two spears and two oxhide shields were to be left—for use against the wooers after they had been brought to their ruin by Athena and Zeus. Meanwhile, Odysseus' identity would be concealed from all —even from Penelope, Laertes, and the faithful Eumaeus—since loyal people sometimes were indiscreet. Odysseus also outlined a plan for investigating the faithfulness of the maid-servants and other workers in the palace and palace farms. Those who had proven themselves untrue were to be punished.

As this plan was being laid at the swineherd's hut, Telemachus' ship landed at the harbor, his men removed their weapons, carried the gifts brought from Sparta to the home of Clytius, and dispatched a herald to Penelope to inform her of her son's earlier landing and whereabouts. The herald and swineherd reached Penelope almost simultaneously, but the latter lingered to whisper to her the latest instructions from Telemachus.

Meanwhile the wooers, disturbed by the failure of their plan to murder Telemachus, were holding council outside the gates. Eurymachus suggested sending a second ship to bring back the one captained by Antinous, but even as he spoke, Amphinomus spied it coming into the harbor. After it landed, Antinous told the wooers why his mission had failed and how the gods had protected their intended victim. He then urged the immediate destruction of Telemachus, but the wooers preferred the advice of Amphinomus that they should first seek counsel of the gods, and then went to the palace.

Informed by Medon of what was afoot, Penelope appeared before the wooers and rebuked Antinous for proposing to ambush her son— stressing his monstrous ingratitude by reminding him of how his father, Eupeithes, had once been given refuge by Odysseus from the wrath

---

[6] Here, for reasons unclear, Telemachus was wrongly assuming the faithful Medon to be on the side of the wooers.

[7] In the Homeric Age, halls did not have chimneys, so often objects were covered with soot.

of the people after he, in league with Taphian sea robbers, had harried the Thresprotians, who were then at peace with the Ithacans. When she ceased talking, the treacherous Eurymachus, after smoothly acknowledging nummerous favors from Odysseus, solemnly assured her that no harm would come to Telemachus—all the while, however, pondering how he might be slain. Penelope then returned to her chamber and bewailed her long-absent husband until Athena caused her to sleep.

In the evening, the swineherd returned to the hut where Telemachus was sitting with Odysseus, who had now resumed the guise of an old man lest Eumaeus recognize him and convey the news to Penelope prematurely. Replying to questions, Eumaeus was unable to say whether the wooers had remained in ambush for Telemachus, having come straight to the hut after receiving a possibly incomplete report from Medon. Then he said that, from a hill, he had seen a swift ship entering the harbor laden with weapons, and added that it might have been the one manned by the wooers. Unseen by Eumaeus, Odysseus and Telemachus exchanged smiling glances. The three men then feasted and slept.

Book XVII. After bidding Eumaeus to follow with the supposed stranger, Telemachus took his spear and went out the next morning to the palace, where he was welcomed affectionately in turn by the nurse Eurycleia, by the handmaidens, and Penelope. Questioned by Penelope, he delayed telling her what he had learned of Odysseus on his voyage, explaining that he must first hasten to the assembly hall and bid welcome to a stranger—the seer Theoclymenus who had accompanied him from Pylus on his ship. Meanwhile, he bade his mother pray to the gods and promise a sacrifice of hecatombs "if haply Zeus may grant that deeds of requital be made."

Proceeding to the assembly place, he talked briefly of the adventures of his trip with Mentor, Antiphus, and Halitherses, old friends of his house. Then, as Piraeus approached with Theoclymenus,[8] he went to talk with them. Piraeus

suggested that maidservants be sent to the home of his father, Clytius, to bring to the palace the gifts from Menelaus which had been stored there since their removal from the ship. But Telemachus replied that the gifts should be left with Piraeus and should become his property— and not that of the wooers if the latter should be successful in the impending battle.

Telemachus now led Theoclymenus into the palace, where they both were bathed, anointed, given fresh doublets and mantles, and fed on wheaten bread, by the servants. During the meal, Penelope sat against a pillar beside them, spinning threads from yarn, and heard her son's story of his journey to Pylus and Sparta, and of the news about his father (previously related in books III and IV).

Theoclymenus now spoke up, interpreting the omen seen upon the first landing at Ithaca (a hawk flying from the right with a dove in its talons) to mean that Odysseus was somewhere on the island even now, plotting death for the wooers; and, heartened by this prophesy, Penelope promised him rich gifts if it should prove to be true. Meanwhile, Medon appeared among the wooers before the palace, interrupting their games of weight and spear-casting, and invited them inside to help slay animals for the evening feast.

Earlier in the afternoon, Odysseus and Eumaeus had left the swineherd's hut afoot, bound for the palace—Odysseus in his beggar guise and grasping a long staff. After walking along a rugged path, they came to a fresh-water basin which Ithacus, Neritus, and Polyctor had built for the city—a basin fed by a cold stream falling from a high rock on which stood an altar to the nymphs. Here, they met the goatherd Malanthius (son of Penelope's servant Dolius), accompanied by two herdsmen and leading she-goats to the feast of the wooers. Cursing Eumaeus, the goatherd demanded to know where he was taking the plaguey beggar and, in the same breath, reviled the supposed mendicant as a shunner of work who would rather go loafing through the land "asking alms to fill his insatiate belly." Stools would fly about his head and break upon his ribs, the goatherd warned, should he venture to show his face at the palace. He then proceeded to bruise Odys-

---

8 Since the landing, Theoclymenus had been a guest at the home of Clytius, Piraeus' father.

seus' hip with a vicious kick, which the latter stoically endured in silence while Eumaeus angrily invoked the well-water nymphs to bring home avenging Odysseus for Melanthius' destruction. The goatherd countered by threatening to take Eumaeus away on a ship and sell him into slavery, and concluded with a prayer that Apollo might soon bring death to Telemachus at the wooers' hands. Following this the traitorous slave sped to the palace and sat down among the wooers to join in their continued feasting.

Proceeding somewhat more slowly, Odysseus and Eumaeus presently found themselves before the palace from whence there issued the sounds of revelry, the music of Phemius' voice and lyre, and the savory odors of the feast. Here they spied Odysseus' hound Argos, a mere pup when last seen by his master and a famed hunter in his prime; but now he lay helpless on a dung pile, near death from old age and neglect. The old dog recognized Odysseus, despite his disguise and, as he feebly wagged his tail and dropped his ears, Odysseus turned his face from Eumaeus to wipe away a tear. For, within the hour—having lived more than twenty years—the faithful beast died.

Entering the great hall ahead of Odysseus, Eumaeus was immediately seen by Telemachus and was summoned to his side to partake of food. As the supposed beggar followed, and squatted against a pillar of cyprus wood inside the threshold, Telemachus sent Eumaeus to him with a serving of meat and bread, together with permission to beg at the palace. After he had eaten, Odysseus was encouraged by Athena to go among the wooers and learn which were righteous and which unjust, although it was not fated that anyone of them should be spared from well-merited destruction.

The wooers, suddenly aware of the stranger as he moved among them, began to inquire who he was. Thereupon, Melanthius told them of his earlier encounter with the beggar and the swineherd. When he had completed his narration, Antinous rebuked Eumaeus, arguing, with unconscious humor, that the palace already had a surplusage of plaguey beggars "devouring the living of the master." Eumaeus countered by asserting that invitations to feasts seldom were issued by those of Antinous' selfish ilk except to those who could somehow serve or benefit them —craftsmen, prophets, healers of ills, shipwrights, minstrels—but never to poor beggars. Telemachus now interposed, broadly hinting that Antinous, in objecting to the beggar, had been impelled more by his own evil nature than by any honest desire to save "the living of the master." Thus chided, Antinous grasped a footstool threateningly, but made no immediate move, and Odysseus continued to walk among the wooers, collecting bread and meat until his wallet was filled.

As the disguised man returned to the threshold, he halted by the side of Antinous and gently rebuked him by mentioning his own contrasting generosity in happier days when he himself was rich, and—to conceal his real identity—told of imaginary adventures[9] in Egypt and Cyprus to explain his present poverty. Antinous now ordered him to move on lest he should "come soon to a bitter Egypt and a sad Cyprus," but the ragged one stood his ground, boldly asserting that his maligner was so closefisted that he could not even bear to give away the property of others. Upon this, Antinous caught up the footstool and struck him with it in the back below the right shoulder; but Odysseus controlled his urge to retaliate and, returning to the threshold, loudly bewailed his poor fate. Blows received for one's "wretched belly's sake" were much more painful, he grumbled, than those received in war, and he prayed that the gods might avenge the insult by bringing death to the proud suitor before his wedding day.

Antinous furiously commanded him to be quiet, lest he be dragged by hand or foot through the house and all the flesh stripped from his bones. Here, one of the other wooers cau-

---

9 Zeus-driven, in this fictional narrative, he joined and became leader of a band of sea robbers. Mooring their ship in the Aegyptus (Nile), he sent into the surrounding fields a party of scouts who, against orders, carried away the rural wives and infant children and slew the men. Horsemen and footmen from the nearby city counter-attacked in force, whereupon the robbers, made suddenly weak and panicky by Zeus, were slain or captured to the last man, and their leader taken prisoner. Later he was delivered by his captors to one of their friends, Demetor, ruler of Cyprus, and was taken to his island kingdom, from where he later escaped.

tioned Antinous for his dangerous folly in strik-ing the ragged stranger—suggesting he might easily be a god in disguise, wandering through the cities to behold the violence and the righ-teousness of men, but Antinous gave no heed to his words. In the meanwhile, Telemachus, though deeply grieved by the assault on his father, only shook his head in silence and man-aged to conceal the deep feeling within his breast.

On hearing of the quarrel, Penelope de-nounced Antinous as the worst of all the wooers and, with the house dame Eurynome assenting, implored Apollo to smite him even as he had smitten the poor beggar. She then asked Euma-eus to bring in the stranger that she might greet him and inquire whether, in his travels, he had heard tidings of Odysseus. To this, Eu-maeus replied that the stranger, describing him-self as a resident of Crete, had called himself a friend of Odysseus, who—he declared—was still alive and prospering not far away in the rich land of Thesprotia, whence he would soon return to Ithaca. As requested, he then went to fetch the stranger while Penelope, greatly heart-ened by his words, became suddenly overjoyed when she took it as a good omen that Telema-chus was heard to sneeze in the hall. On receiv-ing the queen's message from Eumaeus, Odys-seus balked at approaching her publicly, fearing the wrath of the wooers. Instead, he proposed to sit with her privately after nightfall, preferably near a fire, because of his thin and sorry gar-ments. On seeing Eumaeus reappear alone, Penelope first assumed that shame had deterred the stranger and remarked that "a shamefaced man makes a bad beggar," but after hearing Eumaeus' explanation, she admitted the wis-dom of Odysseus' suggestion and readily agreed to await his later coming.

After leaving the queen, Eumaeus went back to take care of the chores at his farm; but first talked with Telemachus, who bade him return to the palace the next morning with animals suitable for sacrifice. This the loyal swineherd promised to do and departed, but only after admonishing his young master to be unceasingly on the alert against the treachery of the wooers who—with the coming of evening—had now already begun their accustomed revelry.

Book XVIII. After Eumaeus left for his farm, a professional beggar known as Irus,[10] making a routine visit to the palace, discovered the disguised Odysseus inside the doorway. Con-fident of his ability to trounce his supposed rival, a smaller and older man, he ordered him to begone. Replying softly that there was room on the threshold for both of them, and seeing Irus unmoved, Odysseus, despite his handicap of age, threatened that if he were not left alone he would bloody the other's lips and breast. Seeing a chance for sport, Antinous proposed to match the disputants in a fight, the winner to receive a pudding (a goat's paunch filled with fat and blood) and the exclusive right to beg among the wooers. Irus eagerly agreed to this proposal but, before consenting to fight, Odysseus, with Te-lemachus' support, exacted a solemn promise that he would be struck no foul blows by Irus' sympathizers.

While getting ready for the fight, Odysseus, magically aided by Athena, exposed his mighty thighs and arms and, looking upon them, the amazed wooers muttered: "Right soon will Irus, un-irused, have a bane of his own bringing." Irus became unnerved at the muscular sight, and began to tremble as the servants girded him and led him out. His fear was so obvious that Antinous rebuked him for fearing a careworn, old man and warned that, should he lose the fight, he would be sent to King Echetus in Epeirus, "maimer of all mankind," who would cut off his nose and ears and draw out his vitals to be consumed by dogs.

As the two men squared away, Odysseus re-solved to deliver no fatal blow lest his identity be revealed by such display of power. Accord-ingly, after one futile swing by Irus, he con-tented himself by lightly (?) tapping Irus be-neath the ear, and merely crushed his bones so that his adversary collapsed in the dust, kicking, groaning, and gnashing his teeth while blood gushed from his mouth. And, as the great hall rang with laughter and applause, he completed his victory by seizing Irus by the foot, dragging him through the door, propping him upright

---

[10] Arnaeus was his name, but his practice of running errands when bidden brought him a nickname corrupted from the gods' messenger Iris.

against the courtyard wall, putting his staff in his hand, and warning him against again trying to lord it over strangers and beggars.

The wooers now congratulated Odysseus, Antinous gave him the pudding, and Amphinomus presented him with two loaves of bread while wishing him much happiness. Desiring to spare Amphinomus, if possible, from the coming slaughter, Odysseus praised him and urged him to go home before disaster should come; but, though troubled by the warning, Amphinomus was prevented from heeding it by Athena—for she was bent on total annihilation of all the wooers.

Following the contest of the beggars, Penelope was seized by an urge to appear before her suitors and, with a perhaps excusable feminine desire, to make their hearts flutter with hope—to the end that she might thus win greater honor from her husband and son. She also wished to gain an opportunity to talk with Telemachus and to warn him against continuously consorting with the hypocritical and treacherous suitors. To this last aim Eurynome, the housewife, gave her approval. She remarked hopefully that Telemachus might now heed his mother's advice, since he had recently acquired a chin beard and, presumably, had attained adult wisdom. Eurynome, however, besought her mistress first to wash herself, anoint her face, and not to appear before the wooers with tear-stained cheeks. But this suggestion Penelope rejected—calling it futile, since the gods had destroyed her beauty on the day when Odysseus sailed for Troy. So saying, she bade Eurynome summon the handmaidens, Autonoe and Hippodameia, to stand by her side in the great halls, for she was afraid to go alone among the importunate throng. Obediently Eurynome went to do her bidding and, while she was gone, Athena put her mistress to sleep, made her taller and shapelier, whitened her skin to a newly-sawn ivory shade, and "steeped her face with beauty imperishable. . ." Answering their summons the handmaidens, Autonoe and Hippodameia, shortly entered and, first commenting on her momemtary lapse into slumber, Penelope now prayed to Artemis for a soft death so that she might no longer waste her life in sorrowful longing for Odysseus. Then going

below with her handmaidens, she stood by a tall pillar and, while the wooers looked upon her with enchanted eyes each uttered a prayer that he might lie beside her.

Still mindful of the disguised beggar, Penelope now rebuked her son for letting his guest be mistreated. Replying, Telemachus doubly pleaded that the wooers' evil ways had driven him out of his wits, and that he was only one man against many. Furthermore, he said, all things had not gone as the wooers wished, as witness the stranger's defeat of Irus; and he concluded by invoking the gods that the suitors might be similarly vanquished.

Eurymachus next spoke, asserting that if all the Achaeans could look upon Penelope's extraordinary beauty, the press of wooers in the palace would be even greater. Delicately negativing the point of this remark, Penelope replied that she had lost the excellence of both her face and form on the day when Odysseus left for Troy. Then, leaving the subject, she related how, in his parting speech, her great husband had advised her, in the event of his failure to return, to marry whomever she wished after her son should become bearded. The time was now at hand for that marriage, she told Eurymachus, but she sadly deplored that the suitors not only had failed to bring her the customary wooing gifts but had devoured the goods of her house continuously over a long period without making any atonement. When Odysseus overheard these words, he rejoiced—for he knew that her heart was set on drawing gifts from the wooers by guile while still avoiding a hateful marriage with any one of them. Nor was he mistaken, because her ruse was successful, and the rich gifts long withheld by the wooers were now brought by their various squires and henchmen.[11] But the gifts were forthcoming only after Antinous had declared that none of the wooers would leave until she had wedded the man of her choice.

---

[11] From Antinous she received a richly broidered robe on which were twelve golden brooches fitted with curved clasps; from Eurymachus, a cunningly wrought gold chain strung with bright amber beads; from Eurydamas, a pair of earrings with three clustering drops; from Peisander, an exceedingly beautiful necklace. Gifts from the other wooers are not described.

Later, when the sun had gone down and Penelope had retired with her gifts, the great hall was lighted by fire-burning braziers and torches which the maidens were tending in turn; but Odysseus boldly bade them join their mistress and help her with the twisting of yarns and the carding of wools—adding that he himself would take care of the lights throughout the revels, even if the wooers should remain until dawn.

After he had spoken, his right to give orders was sharply questioned by Melantho, an ingrate daughter of Dolius who had been tenderly reared by Penelope but who had now become a paramour of Eurymachus. Why, she railed, had he lingered at the palace, begging and making trouble, instead of departing to a smithy or common lodge for sleep? Was his idle babbling caused by wine, lunacy, or exultation at his victory over Irus? Was he not aware that some better man than Irus might yet befoul him with blood and send him packing away? Infuriated at her outburst, Odysseus vowed to pass the word to Telemachus and have her torn limb from limb. And his words had such a ring of truth and authority that Melantho and the other maidens fled in terror, leaving him alone to tend the lights.

Impelled by Athena, who was bent on heating Odysseus' wrath against the wooers to the boiling point, Eurymachus made a jibe that Odysseus must have been sent to Ithaca by a god because of the radiance which shone from his head—referring to the reflection cast upon his shiny bald head by the torch which he held. And the insulting man added that he would gladly hire the supposed beggar for tree planting and rock gathering on his upland farm except for the certainty that he, being practiced only in evil, preferred begging to working. Hardly able to contain himself, Odysseus angrily voiced the wish that he could be matched in contest with Eurymachus in grass cutting, ox driving, or ploughing; or that Eurymachus could have seen him on the field of battle; and he declared that the proud wooer was fated to sing a different tune with the return of Penelope's husband.

These words so enraged Eurymachus that he followed a tirade of abuseful language by throwing a stool at Odysseus, who had sat down beside Amphinomus; but the stool missed its mark and smote the right hand of a cupbearer so that he fell back in the dust, groaning, while his jug of wine clattered on the ground. As the wooers in chorus condemned the stranger for creating so much tumult, Telemachus spoke up to politely suggest that perhaps their impatience was due to the act of a god or to too much wine; and that they should go home and rest—adding, however, that he was not driving them but merely suggesting. Further angry words would probably have followed, but Amphinomus agreed with Telemachus and—after his squire, Mulius, had mixed a final libation, the haughty wooers departed to rest for the night, each one to his own house.

Book XIX. After they had left, Telemachus arranged with Eurycleia to have the treacherous maidservants kept away from the great hall while he and his father removed the weapons of Odysseus from the walls to one of the storerooms of the palace. And their labor was made easier as Athena lighted their way with a bright radiance which caused the knowing Telemachus to declare that some god was in their midst.

When the task was completed, Telemachus retired—leaving Odysseus in the great hall which Penelope soon after entered. She sat down near the fire on a silver and ivory inlaid chair made by the artist Icmalius and, as some of her maidens began tidying up the tables, Melantho recognized Odysseus who was standing somewhat apart. She angrily demanded that he stop sneaking about the darkened palace and spying on the maids, and ordered him to leave lest he be chased out with firebrands. Replying heatedly, the disguised man mentioned his own fall from high estate and warned that she, for her sins, might fare similarly at the hands of Penelope, Telemachus, or the returning Odysseus.

Overhearing the words of the supposed beggar, Penelope scolded Melantho and told her that she wanted to honor the stranger and question him about Odysseus. At her bidding, Eurynome then placed a chair for the stranger beside the queen, who proceeded to ply him with questions. Odysseus at first refused to talk of his race or lineage, pleading that the story would be too sorrowful and harrowing. Penelope thereupon sought to encourage him by telling the sad story of her marital dilemma; and, in return, he regaled her with his old Cretan tale, adding a few embellishments.[12]

Although she wept at hearing his story, Penelope nevertheless doubted that the stranger had known her husband, and asked him to describe Odysseus as he had looked in Crete. Convinced by his reply,[13] she assured him that henceforth he would be a privileged guest at the palace. She again voiced doubt that Odysseus would ever return to Ithaca, whereupon the disguised man sought to encourage her with a mixture of truth and fiction,[14] ending with a solemn assurance that, before the new moon Odysseus would come home from Thesprotia heavily laden with treasure.

Although Penelope remained sceptical, she promised the stranger rich gifts if his prophecy should come true, and offered to have his feet washed and a couch prepared for him by her handmaidens. But, distrusting the faithless girls, he expressed an unwillingness to be ministered to except by some good and faithful old woman who had suffered as much as himself. And, as he had hoped, Penelope then summoned his ancient nurse Eurycleia. During the washing, Odysseus kept his legs in shadow, thus concealing from his old nurse a large scar above his right knee.[15] Eurycleia nevertheless recognized the scar when her hand touched it, and suddenly dropped his leg, crying in a shaky voice, "Thou art Odysseus!" Quickly clutching her throat, he ordered her to keep silent lest she share the destined fate of the worthless maidservants. This Eurycleia promised to do and, as she continued with her pleasant chore, offered to give him the names of all the faithless girls in the palace; but Odysseus said that he already knew who they were.

Although she was seated nearby, Penelope was unaware of Eurycleia's recognition of Odysseus—for her thoughts had been held on other topics by the ever-alert Athena. When Odysseus again seated himself beside her, she spoke of the difficult decision[16] which she must soon make: whether, despite his growing impatience, to remain with her son and administer the palace for her husband who might still be alive, or to marry that one of her wooers whose gifts were most splendid. She then besought Odysseus to explain one of her recent dreams—a vision concerning some partly tamed wild geese that had learned to eat her corn. In her dream, she said, an eagle from the mountains had suddenly attacked the geese and had broken the necks of twenty of them. Following this, the eagle had appeared on her window sill, telling her to be of good cheer, and adding: "The wooers are geese, and I, the eagle, am Odysseus, returning to put an end to them." The stranger declared this to be a heaven-sent vision—an accurate forecast of things to come—but, though she wished to be-

---

[12] According to his story, he was a Cretan named Aethon, the younger of two sons of Deucalion. The imaginary Aethon, in the absence of King Idomeneus, his older brother and Odysseus' friend, had the honor of entertaining the Troy-bound Odysseus for twelve days when adverse winds forced him ashore in Crete.

[13] Odysseus had worn a white linen tunic, the stranger explained, and over it a mantle of crimson wool fastened with a double-bowed brooch of gold embossed with a dog holding a writhing fawn in his forepaws. The stranger also mentioned Odysseus' companion, Eurybates, as being a curly-haired man with dark skin.

[14] According to the stranger's story, Zeus and Helios, angry at Odysseus for the slaying of the Sun-god's cattle by his men, wrecked his ship and drowned his men in the sea near Trinacria, only Odysseus surviving. Washed ashore on the island of the Phaeacians, he later refused their kindly offer to take him to Ithaca. Choosing to continue roaming, he later went to rich Thesprotia (the stranger failed to say how) for the purpose of gaining treasure and profit there before sailing for home. The stranger told how he himself was recently shown Odysseus' great store of treasure in Thesprotia by that country's king, Pheidon, who explained that Odysseus, uncertain whether to return to Ithaca openly or secretly, had gone to Dodona to hear the counsel of Zeus from the great oak tree whose voice was considered to be that of the supreme god.

[15] The history of Odysseus' scar, as here inserted by Homer, begins with a visit of Autolycus to Ithaca during which he gave a name to his newborn grandson at the request of Eurycleia, the child's nurse. Admittedly swayed by his own "plaints against many dwellers upon earth," Autolycus named the child Odysseus, meaning "a man of wrath." On reaching manhood, Odysseus visited Autolycus and Amphithea, his maternal grandparents, and accompanied their sons on a hunt on Parnassus, during which, while spearing a boar, he was wounded by one of its tusks and was left scarred above the right knee.

[16] Penelope's troubled mind quavered, she said, like the song trilled by the sylvan nightingale, daughter of Pandareos, in sad memory of Itylus, her son, whom she unknowingly slew with a sword.

lieve, Penelope could not accept his prophecy as true.[17]

The queen now declared her intention to arrange a contest on the morrow wherein the wooers should take Odysseus' bow and attempt to shoot an arrow through the holes in twelve axe heads set in line—a feat which she had seen her husband perform, and she stated that he who should be successful would be entitled to possess her in marriage. Approving her plan, the supposed beggar boldly predicted that—even before any of the wooers should have succeeded in bending and stringing the bow—Odysseus would appear and would himself shoot an arrow cleanly through the axe heads. After hearing these encouraging words, Penelope retired to her chamber and, lulled by the goddess Athena, was soon asleep—while Odysseus laid himself to rest on the bedded floor of the entrance hall.

Book XX. Although lying on fleeces and an oxhide, and covered by a mantle which the housekeeper threw over him, Odysseus was unable to sleep—so great was his wrath. And, hearing the laughter of the faithless maidservants as they left the great hall to lie with the wooers, he felt impelled to rise and slay wooers and maidens alike; but restrained himself, being one against many and not knowing—as he presently told Athena—where to flee afterward from their avengers. Remembering how he had endured in the cave of the Cyclops, he determined to remain silent; and, in mortal form, the goddess soon appeared—to dispel his fears by saying that he was under her protection and could not be conquered even though he should be assailed by fifty companies of men. After this he slept peacefully as the wise goddess leisurely returned to her home on Olympus.

Penelope awakened early, after a tantalizing dream in which Odysseus appeared to have lain beside her. Weepingly, she implored Artemis to slay her with a dart, while she still retained "the image of Odysseus unsmirched by dalliance with a baser man," and she prayed that whirl-winds would bear her away to the mouth of backward-flowing Oceanus, even as they had carried off Pandareos' daughters to destruction.[18]

Awakened by the sound of Penelope's weeping, Odysseus in the nearby entrance hall momentarily thought that she stood beside him and had discovered his identity. Disturbed, he lay aside the fleeces and went outside the palace, carrying the oxhide, and he prayed for two good omens: a sign directly from Zeus and a speech of good portent from some one within the palace. Zeus instantly responded with a clap of thunder which, coming from a clear and star-spangled sky, brought the desired mortal speech from a woman thrall in a grain mill attached to the palace. Long chained to cruel toil, that the wooers might have their fill of bread, she hailed the clear-sky thunder as a favorable portent and prayed aloud that it might foretoken doom for the wooers, and an end to their feasting, on the day now dawning.

On arising that morning, Telemachus found Odysseus absent from the halls and anxiously inquired of Eurycleia whether his father had been properly taken care of by his sometimes careless mother. But he was content with her reply when Eurycleia explained that the stranger had chosen to sleep on a pallet in the entrance hall in preference to a couch prepared by Penelope's maidens. He then set out for the assembly place, armed with a sword and a bronze-tipped spear, and accompanied by two swift dogs.

Shortly thereafter, while the maidservants and the wooers' serving men were preparing the midday meal, Eumaeus, bringing three boars, met Odysseus in front of the palace. The two men were discussing the supposed beggar's sufferings at the hands of the wooers when Melanthius appeared, bringing goats, and accompanied by two herdsmen. After tethering his goats

---

[17] Penelope here mentioned the two gates connecting the land of dreams with man's mind—the gates of horn and of ivory through which pass, respectively, the truly prophetic and the misleading dreams—and voiced doubt that her eagle and geese dream had come through the gate of horn.

[18] The daughters of Pandareos, after the gods had slain their parents, were helped by Aphrodite, who cherished them with curds, honey, and wine; by Hera, who gave them beauty and wisdom; by Artemis, who dowered them with stature; and by Athena, who taught them skill in handiwork. But while Aphrodite was journeying to Olympus to petition from Zeus a glad marriage for the maidens, the spirits of the storm snatched them away and gave them to be handmaids to the hateful Erinnyes.

under the palace portico, he reviled the stranger for lingering so long at the palace, threatened to give him a beating, and advised him to go begging elsewhere. But Odysseus answered him not a word, although he shook his head in anger.

Next, Philoetius approached, driving a heifer and goats which he had brought by ferry from the mainland. Questioning Eumaeus about the stranger, the swineherd volunteered that he somehow resembled a royal lord, though shabby. Introduced by Eumaeus, Philoetius then shook Odysseus' hand and wished him happiness, while remarking sadly that his noble master might be similarly in rags and adrift if not in the realm of Hades. He then told how, while still a lad, he had been employed by Odysseus and put in charge of his cattle in the land of Cephallenia. In recent years, however, he had been tempted, he said, to take the animals and seek a living elsewhere, and had been deterred only by the lingering hope that the kindly king of Ithaca would some day return. Odysseus then told his old servant to be of good cheer and said that it would not be long before the missing king would surely appear and slay the wooers.

Meanwhile, at the assembly place, the wooers had first schemed to slay Telemachus; but had abandoned the project after seeing an eagle flying on their left with a dove in his talons—an omen which Amphinomus interpreted to mean that Zeus disapproved of the murder plot.

The wooers now returned to the great hall and resumed their usual feasting—being joined by Eumaeus, who gave out the cups, Melanthius, who served the wine, and Philoetius, who served the bread. Odysseus again sat just inside the door where Telemachus provided him with a bench, a small table, and a serving of entrails; meanwhile promising to protect him from the wooers and boldly warning them to let the beggar alone. Mindful of the adverse omen, Antinous advised his fellows to obey the order, but Ctesippus of Same was inspired by Athena to ignore his counsel and, in mock generosity, presented the supposed beggar with an alleged gift of food—by violently hurling a cow's hoof which, when Odysseus dodged, struck the solid wall behind him. Telemachus then angrily told Ctesippus that he would have slain him with his sword had the hoof struck the stranger; and,

while admitting himself outnumbered, declared that he would choose death in preference to permitting any further mishandling of strangers or maidservants in the palace.

Agreeing with the young prince that neither the stranger nor any of the palace thralls should be misused, Agelaus arose to argue that all hope of Odysseus' returning had vanished and that Telemachus, instead of opposing, should now favor Penelope's marriage and departure with a husband, whereafter he would comfortably come into possession of his Ithacan inheritance. In reply, Telemachus said that he had never opposed his mother's marriage, but he also made clear that he would not urge her into it for the sake of possible gain to himself.

Athena caused this speech to be received by the wooers at first with laughter and later, with tears—a weird and contradictory mood which Theoclymenus, the seer, interpreted as an ominous portent of their doom. Eurymachus now called the seer witless and advised that he be guided out of the palace, but Theoclymenus retorted that he had eyes, ears, feet, and a mind, —was in no need of a guide—and that furthermore he had no wish to stay for he saw that evil was soon coming. Saying this, he departed to the home of Peiraeus where he was warmly welcomed.

After he had gone, one of the wooers derided Telemachus as a luckless host, describing his two guests as respectively, a filthy wanderer and a pseudo-prophet, and he added the suggestion that both men should be transported to Sicily to be sold into slavery. Telemachus looked toward his disguised father, half expecting a sign that the time had come to lift hands against their tormentors, but none was given. Meanwhile, Penelope had entered and, taking a chair in the hall, had heard all the men's speeches; and preparations for the noon meal were going forward amid the laughter of the wooers which gave no foretoken of what was to follow.

Book XXI. A little later Penelope, after going to the palace's treasure room appeared before the wooers carrying Odysseus' famous bow, a gift from Iphitus,[19] with quiver and arrows,

---

[19] Odysseus and Iphitus met and became friends at the home of Ortilochus when they were in Messene on

and accompanied by her maidens bearing her lord's combat gear. She then proposed a contest with the bow, and promised to wed whomever should most easily string it and shoot through the holes in twelve axes to be set in line. She next commanded the swineherd to set up the axes. At this, Eumaeus and Philoetius, moved by the sight of Odysseus' ancient weapons, began to weep. In an attempt to delay the contest, the outcome of which he feared, Antinous rebuked them for stirring the soul of a lady already overburdened with sorrow; and commanded them either to stop weeping or leave the feast.

Seeing through this ruse, Telemachus sought to hasten the contest by praising his mother's beauty in extravagant terms. On sudden impulse, he then declared his own intent to make trial of the bow as a test of his ability to rule the palace after his mother's departure. Casting off his cloak, he speedily dug a trench and set up the axes. This done, he seized the bow and strove with all his strength to string it. Three times he made the attempt, and again was straining mightily, and might have succeeded, had not Odysseus stayed him with a frown. He then modestly confessed himself a cowardly weakling, or perhaps too young, and stepped aside.

Antinous now suggested, for his own advantage, a sequence of contestants beginning from the left, so that the soothsayer Leiodes—the one and only well-behaved wooer, not given to infatuate deeds—was first to take the bow. Being delicate of build, he failed to bend it and soon gave up the attempt, while gallantly describing his failure to win Penelope as worse than death. Antinous then requested Melanthius to build a fire and bring lard, for warming and oiling the

bow to increase its resiliency. But despite this advantage, the next several contestants were also unable to string it.

While all this was going on, Eumaeus and Philoetius retired outside the palace and were followed by Odysseus, who straightway revealed his identity to the faithful pair, and confirmed it by showing his leg scar. When they embraced him with tears of joy, and readily gave their promises to aid in slaying the wooers, Odysseus gave them the following instructions: Eumaeus, while pretending to pass the bow from one contestant to another, should place it in Odysseus' hands, and should direct the maidens to bar their chamber doors and ignore all sounds of groaning from the hall, and Philoetius, for his part, should bolt, bar, and tie the outer gate of the courtyard.

Reentering the hall, they found Eurymachus vainly trying to string the bow. Forced to give up, the haughty wooer confessed himself disturbed no less by his marital disappointment than by his evident inferiority to Odysseus in might. When he had sat down, Antinous, craftily recalling that the present day was a holy feast day, requiring sacrifices to Apollo, now proposed a recess of the contest that proper time might be given to the drinking of libations in worship of the archer-god. His proposal was assented to and, after all had drunk the libations, Odysseus spoke up to ask permission to try the bow himself—saying that it was only for the purpose of testing whether he still possessed the strength of his younger and happier days.

The suitors were greatly enraged at this request, for they secretly feared that the strong beggar might be able to string the bow, and Antinous jeered at his presumptious wish to vie with his betters. Accusing the ragged one of being drunk,[20] he threatened to send him on a ship to Echetus, "the maimer of men," should he succeed in his effort. But, siding with the stranger, Penelope said there could be no harm in letting him try the bow, since he could not in

---

business: Odysseus to obtain repayment from that country for three hundred sheep and their shepherds, which the men of Messene had taken in Ithaca; and Iphitus to search for twelve mares and some mule foals which he had lost. They exchanged gifts, Odysseus receiving the famous bow which Iphitus had inherited from his father, Eurytus, and Iphitus received a sword and spear. Iphitus recovered his lost mares and foals, but shortly after, while he was a guest at the home of Heracles, his host slew him and took the animals. Thereafter, Odysseus used the bow only on his own land but never in war, preserving it as a memorial to his dead friend.

---

[20] As a warning to the stranger, Antinous told how Eurytion, a centaur, lost his ears and nose in the struggle which he precipitated in the hall of the Lapith king, Peirithous, while under the influence of wine.

any case hope to win her hand in marriage. Her remark caused Eurymachus to declaim worriedly that the whole group of wooers, if bested by a mere beggar, would suffer greatly in reputation—to which the queen replied that the wooers had already lost their reputations by dishonoring another's house and destroying his goods. She insisted that the stranger be allowed to test his strength and promised him rich gifts should he be successful in his attempt.

Telemachus now implored his mother to leave the problem to him and retire with her maids to the loom and distaff in her chambers. Though puzzled, she obeyed and thanks to Athena's magic, soon fell asleep. When she had left the hall, the swineherd picked up the bow, meaning to place it in Odysseus' hands, but his right to touch it was quickly challenged by the wooers, with threats so frightening that he dropped it. Their action was rebuked by Telemachus and, again lifting it up Eumaeus handed the weapon to Odysseus. This done, he called Eurycleia aside and relayed to her the order, earlier given by Odysseus, that the doors should be barred and no attention paid by the maidservants to the noises which might follow. Meanwhile, Philoetius went stealthily outside and fastened the gates of the courtyard.

Looking at Odysseus, as he thoughtfully fingered the bow, the wooers at first were amused, but were fearfully amazed as they saw him string it without apparent effort. Hearing at this moment a loud clap of thunder, Odysseus secretly rejoiced, for he knew it as a sign of Zeus' approval. Then, without rising from his bench, he easily pulled back the bowstring and sent an arrow cleanly through the twelve axes, touching no part of any one. He turned next to Telemachus and pointed out, with ominous portent, that his strength remained unimpaired; and remarked somewhat euphemistically that after-dinner entertainment must soon be provided for the astonished wooers. As he spoke, and made a sign with his brows, Telemachus tightened his sword belt and took firm hold of his spear.

Book XXII. Then suddenly Odysseus arose, stripped off his rags, and leaped across to the threshold. Pouring arrows from the quiver around his feet, he loudly declared that since the contest was over he would now try a virgin target—one never before smitten. So saying, he drew his bow and let fly an arrow which passed completely through the throat of Antinous who fell mortally wounded to the ground. The astounded wooers sprang up as one man, their eyes sweeping the walls on all sides. Seeing no shields or spears, they were vaguely frightened, though still unaware of the stranger's identity. Thinking that he had slain Antinous by accident, they now began cursing him, and vowed that he would pay for his carelessness with his own life.

In a loud voice Odysseus now revealed his identity and sternly announced that all the wooers were doomed to death for wasting his goods, lying with his maidservants by force, and traitorously wooing his wife while he was still alive. To this statement, Eurymachus alone made answer—the others being too stunned to speak. Seeking to shift all the blame to their dead leader, he glibly explained that the ambitious Antinous had hoped to make himself king of Ithaca by marrying Penelope and slaying Telemachus. Then he tried to bargain. If spared from death, he said, each of the wooers, in atonement for his crimes against Odysseus, would pay him twenty oxen worth in gold and bronze.

Odysseus' reply was blunt and to the point. He would not, he said, spare the wooers if offered all their possessions, and they could hope to escape only by fighting or fleeing. Eurymachus now shouted to the others to hold up the tables as shields and move against Odysseus in a body. Drawing his sword, he leapt to the attack, but as he did so, Odysseus shot an arrow through his breast and into his liver. Dying in agony, the once proud man collapsed and lay prone. Next came Amphinomus, quickly drawing his sword as he lunged at Odysseus, but Telamachus stopped him with a fatal spear thrust between the shoulders. Fearing to stoop to withdraw his spear lest he be attacked from behind, he quickly consulted with his father, and straightway was sent on a dash to the storeroom, from where he brought back shields, spears, and helmets for himself, Odysseus, Eumaeus, and Philoetius. And thus equipped, the four men continued the onslaught, killing one after the other—with Odysseus using his arrows while they lasted and then attacking with a spear.

Meanwhile, Agelaus urged Melanthius to escape, if possible, through a small postern door and bring aid from the outside. Rejecting this suggestion because the postern, set high near the main threshold, was well guarded by Eumaeus, the traitorous goatherd successfully tried another expedient. Climbing to the clerestory, he escaped to the storeroom through smoke vents and brought back weapons for the wooers by the same route. Aware that some one had blundered, Odysseus questioned Telemachus and learned that his son, in his haste, had left the storeroom door unlocked. To correct the mistake, he sent Eumaeus who quickly returned to report that Melanthius was again in the storeroom. With Philoetius, Eumaeus then sped back and seized the goatherd as he was about to leave, bearing a helmet and the old shield of Laertes. Swiftly, they bound boards behind his back and tied his feet and hands together behind him. Then, looping a rope around him they pulled him up to a position just under the roof beams, where he was left to suffer cruel torture.

After the two faithful servants returned to the hall, Athena, assuming the form and voice of Mentor, appeared before Odysseus. Although he addressed her as Mentor, Odysseus knew the goddess and begged for her aid and protection. As he did so, Agelaus loudly threatened death to the newcomer should he side with Odysseus, but Athena paid no heed, and proceeded to chide Odysseus for being fearful—in sad contrast with his valorous self of the Trojan War days. She promised, however, to aid him and, swiftly changing herself into a swallow, perched on an overlooking beam. Unaware of the metamorphosis, and knowing only that the supposed Mentor had disappeared after uttering empty boasts, Agelaus now fiercely urged the wooers to renew the attack by hurling their spears six at a time, rather than all at once. His advice was heeded, and the suitors again moved in under the leadership of Agelaus, Eurynomus, Amphimedon, Demoptolemus, Peisandrus, and wise Polybus. Their effort, however, was futile: for their spears were deflected by Athena and landed harmlessly against the doors and walls. Odysseus and his company now took aim and threw their spears—Odysseus killing Demoptolemus, while Telemachus, the swineherd, and the neathered slew Euryades, Elatus, and Peisandrus, respectively. Then, as the wooers fell back, they dashed out and withdrew their shafts from the corpses of those whom they had slain.

During the next attack of the wooers, Amphimedon's spear grazed and slightly cut Telemachus' wrist, and Ctesippus' spear grazed Eumaeus' shoulder, but no serious wounds were inflicted. Next Odysseus slew Eurydamas, Telemachus killed Amphimedon, and the swineherd slew Polybus, while the neathered Philoetius dispatched Ctesippus with a spear thrust through the breast. Odysseus followed by wounding Agelaus in a close fight, and Telemachus wounded Leocritus with a spear thrust clean through his flank. At this point, Athena held up her destroying aegis, throwing the wooers into a panic, so that they all fled wildly through the hall, vainly seeking means of escape as they were smitten right and left by their pursuers until the floor was covered with their blood.

In the midst of the carnage, the soothsayer Leiodes fell on his knees before Odysseus and begged for mercy, swearing that never had he wronged a maiden in the palace, and had always sought to restrain the others from violent deeds. But, Odysseus was unswayed by his plea and grimly declared that, if his suppliant were a soothsayer, he had doubtless often prayed that the lord of the palace would not safely return and that he himself might wed Penelope. So saying, he snatched up a sword dropped by the dying Agelaus and swung freely, so that Leiodes' head, while his mouth still pleaded, went rolling in the dust.

The minstrel Phemius then begged to be spared, insisting that he was guiltless since he had served the wooers with voice and lyre against his will. Hearing his plea, Telemachus spoke up in his behalf, and added that the henchman Medon also should be spared if he had not already been slain. At this, Medon emerged from under a high seat, heartened but still fearful, and cast off the oxhide that had hidden him and, seizing Telemachus around the knees, he besought protection from his mighty father. Seeing the poor man tremble,

Odysseus smilingly assured him that he would be spared, and dismissed both him and Phemius through the door to a safe place in the courtyard beside the altar of Zeus.

Odysseus now examined the piled bodies, and searched carefully through the house to make sure that none of the wooers remained alive. This done, he asked Telemachus to summon the nurse Eurycleia. After the old woman arrived, she cried out for joy at sight of the corpses and warmly praised her master for his great achievement. He rebuked her gently for her unholy boasting over slain men, and modestly belittled his accomplishment, explaining that it was by the destiny of the gods and by their own cruel deeds that the wooers had been overcome. Turning to the matter of the maidservants, he learned from Eurycleia that twelve of the fifty women employed in the palace had been faithless, had behaved shamefully with the wooers, and had become disobedient both to herself and Penelope. Concerning their disobedience to Telemachus, she added, there was no need for discussion, since the wise queen had never allowed her young son any authority over the girls.

She concluded by asking permission to tell Penelope that her lord had returned and had slain the wooers, but Odysseus bade her wait a bit and, instead, to bring forth the twelve shameless girls whom she had named.

When the nurse had left, Odysseus directed Telemachus, Eumaeus, and Philoetius to begin carrying out the bodies and cleaning up the hall, intending that on their arrival the faithless women would be ordered to help with the tasks, and would then be slain in the courtyard. This plan was carried out, up to the point where the frightened and weeping maidens were taken to the yard for slaying. Telemachus then argued that a "clean death" would be too good for girls guilty of pouring dishonor on his and his mother's heads by lying with the wooers. Accordingly, the maidens were hanged, all at once, with nooses dangling from a ships' cable, which was attached to a pillar and stretched just high enough to take their feet off the ground. In order to complete the punishment of all those who were guilty, Telemachus and his two helpers now brought the trussed Melanthius down from the storeroom into the courtyard and, after removing his shackles, cut off his nose, ears, hands and feet, and threw his genitals to the dogs.

After these proceedings, Odysseus ordered Eurycleia first to bring fire and sulphur for purging the hall, and then to summon Penelope and her maidens. The old nurse, mindful of his high position, suggested that he should immediately take off his rags and don a more royal doublet and mantle, but he elected to postpone the change until after the hall should have been cleansed. Her suggestions were dismissed, and she proceeded to bring the fire and sulphur, and Odysseus used them not only in the great hall but also in the courtyard and in the women's polluted chambers. When this was done, Eurycleia summoned the faithful women of the palace who presently came, bearing torches, and fell upon Odysseus with cries of joy as they embraced and kissed his head and shoulders.

Book XXIII. Entering the queen's chamber, Eurycleia awakened her and joyously announced that Odysseus had returned home and had slain the wooers. Penelope straightway rebuked her both for speaking nonsense and for arousing her from the soundest sleep that she had enjoyed since Odysseus sailed for Ilium and, declaring that the gods had made her distraught, she bade the old woman begone. But, persisting, Eurycleia related that it was Odysseus who was disguised as the ragged beggar, and added that Telemachus, long aware of his identity, had prudently kept silent until the wooers should be disposed of. Penelope was momentarily convinced, but, upon reflecting somewhat, skeptically inquired how one man could alone have slain such a great number. The nurse now vowed that she herself had seen the wooers' piled-up corpses. So Penelope, while happily accepting the slaying, nevertheless insisted that the wooers had been disposed of by a god in the guise of Odysseus who himself had not returned. Eurycleia then told of having recognized Odysseus by his scar while washing him, and how, with threats of injury, he had forced her to keep silent about his identity.

Though unconvinced—for the scar, she said, might easily be a trick played by the gods—Penelope allowed herself to be escorted into the great hall. There she saw Odysseus still in rags, and she remained silent and doubting, until Telemachus rebuked her—calling her cruel for thus standing aloof from her returned lord. Denying the accusation, she answered that she was only waiting for Odysseus clearly to reveal his identity by broaching topics known alone to herself and him. Upon this, Odysseus stepped forward and smilingly promised to identify himself later, in a private meeting, but he now switched to the more pressing problem of possible forthcoming reprisals by the wooers' kinsmen. As a partial solution, he proposed that music, dancing, and a show of celebration be immediately begun in the palace—in order to convince passersby that Penelope had finally married one of her wooers, and to postpone the townspeople's discovery of the slaughter—until time should be given within which to make definite long-range plans at Laertes' farm in the woods.

Later, while the mock revels suggested by him were in progress, Odysseus was washed, anointed and clothed by Eurynome, and was miraculously crowned by Athena with a radiant splendor so that he came forth like one of the immortals. He then seated himself on his throne opposite Penelope, and proceeded to chide her for her cruelty in failing to recognize him, and he added to the poor queen's uneasiness by suggesting that old Eurycleia should make a bed for him to lie upon all alone. Penelope seized upon this last remark to draw forth from him a statement clearly proving his identity, and additionally instructed Eurycleia concerning preparation of the requested bed. Remembering that one of the posts of their bridal couch, built years before by Odysseus, was an olive tree rooted in the earth, she now directed that it be moved and set up outside the chamber. Protesting, as she had hoped, Odysseus raised questions. How could such a bed be moved? Had it been somehow altered? Had some fool sawed through the olive post?

Hearing these, and other pertinent questions whose answers were known to only the two of them, the queen could not longer doubt her husband's identity, and she joyfully threw herself into his arms, embracing and kissing him, and begging forgiveness for her hesitancy—a wary hesitancy which she now explained as stemming from bitter experience with deceitful men, and from memories of the hapless Argive Helen, whom the gods had tricked into lying with a stranger and taking him for a lover. Odysseus now embraced and freely forgave her—as she gazed upon him no less fondly than a shoreward-swimming sailor gazes upon land after being shipwrecked. Then she again embraced him and joined him in an orgy of happy tears which lasted throughout a night which Athena kindly lengthened.[21]

Odysseus at last suggested that they retire to bed, seek rest, and gain strength for the many toils ahead, which had been foretold to him in Hades by the spirit of the blind seer, Teiresias. Questioned by Penelope, he told her how the seer's ghost had bidden him go forth to many cities, bearing a shapely oar in his hands, until he should come to men ignorant of the sea and of the use of salt; that, on hearing one of the men call his oar a winnowing fan, he should then and there fix it in the earth and make offerings to Poseidon—a ram, a bull, and a boar; and thereafter he should depart for his home and, after arrival, should offer sacred hecatombs to the immortal gods. Quoting Teiresias further, Odysseus said that he was destined to die far from the sea, and gently, at a ripe old age, with all his people prosperous around him. On hearing this, Penelope rejoiced, remarking that if he were destined to live long, he might yet escape from evil. Eurycleia now entered and led her master and mistress to the bridal chamber, which she had prepared with the help of Eurynome and, after a separation of more than twenty years, the king and queen of Ithaca again retired in each other's arms. Before they slept, however, the queen spoke to Odysseus of all that she had endured in his absence and he, in turn, related his own adventures.

Book XXIV. Carrying his golden rod, made for inducing men into and out of sleep, Hermes led the souls of the slain wooers out of the great hall and down to the fields of asphodel in the realm of Hades. And there, they found the souls of Achilles, Ajax, Patroclus, and Antilochus.

---

[21] The goddess ordered both Night (Nyx) and the Dawn (Eos) to remain motionless for a while.

These were presently joined by the shades of Agamemnon and of all who had perished with him in the house of Aegisthus. A ghostly colloquy ensued, in which references were made to many earthly events narrated at length in previous chapters. But the mood of reminiscence was abandoned when Agamemnon hailed the shade of Amphimedon and, reminding him of their past friendship,[22] asked what had brought him and so many other fine warriors to the lower world. Amphimedon's shade then briefly recounted the events leading up to the mass slaughter wrought by Odysseus and bewailed that, unknown to their kinsmen, the wooers' bodies still laid uncared for at the Ithacan palace. This recital provoked Agamemnon's shade to remark upon Odysseus' good fortune in having wed Penelope, a good and faithful wife —in violent contrast with his own wicked spouse, Clytemnestra, by whom he had been slain. The unearthly dialogue was then brought to an end.

The story of the Odyssey now reverts to the farm of Laertes on earth, where Odysseus had gone—in the company of Telemachus and the two faithful herdsman—to reveal himself to his ancient sire. First sending Telemachus and the others to kill some swine for the midday meal, he entered the house, which was well tended by an old Sicilian woman, but he found his father in the terraced garden where he was digging about a plant. Seeing how tired, sorrowful, and old he looked, Odysseus paused under a pear tree to weep, debating whether to fall on Laertes' neck and kiss him or first to test him with questions. Deciding on the latter course, he approached, praised the garden, called himself a stranger from abroad, and followed by making inquiries about his friend, one Odysseus, an Ithacan, whom he pretended to have once entertained in his own country. Disclosing his own identity, the old man tearfully replied that he knew not whether his son were dead or alive, and asked how recently the stranger had seen him.

Odysseus then introduced himself as Eperitus from Alybas and said he was son of Apheidas and grandson of Prince Polypemon; he added that some god had misdriven his ship to the shores of Ithaca from Sicania. Next, he explained that Odysseus had been his guest in Alybas five years previously, and had sailed away for parts unknown—albeit with good omens (birds on his right) at his departure. Hearing this, the old man caught up handfuls of dust and showered them on his grey head, so moving Odysseus that he suddenly embraced him, revealed himself as his long-absent son and declared that he had slain all of Penelope's greedy wooers.

Fearing trickery, Laertes asked for some more definite proof of identity and Odysseus then showed him the scar made by the boar on Parnassus, and mentioned the thirteen pear trees, ten apple trees, two score of fig trees and fifty rows of vines which he in childhood had possessed as paternal gifts. Now fully convinced, Laertes dropped in a faint on his son's breast, but soon recovering, gave thanks to Zeus that the wooers were dead—adding, however, that he was fearful that their kinsmen would attempt reprisals.

After these words, Odysseus and Laertes entered the house, where they found Eumaeus and Philoetius carving flesh. Retiring, Laertes was bathed, anointed, and dressed in a fair mantle by his Sicilian handmaid, wife of his chief thrall Dolius. In the process, Athena filled out his shrunken limbs and made him so tall and mighty that, on presently seeing him, Odysseus was amazed. Reminiscing on his might when, as prince of the Cephallenians he stormed the castle of Nericus, the old man voiced a deep-felt wish that, endowed with his early strength, it might have been vouchsafed to him to stand with his son in the battle against the wooers. As they sat down to eat, Dolius entered with his sons, who had just come in tired from their labor in the fields. Recognizing Odysseus, they stood in momentary amazement, until Dolius rushed forward and kissed Odysseus wrist. Unaware of recent developments, he inquired whether a message should be dispatched to Penelope to inform her of her lord's long-awaited return, but learning that she

---

[22] According to the Homeric story, it was in the house of Amphimedon that Agamemnon and Menelaus urged the hesitant Odysseus to join the expedition against Troy.

knew all, he respectfully withdrew and sat among his sons.

Meanwhile, news of the slaughter of the wooers had become rumored throughout the city and the angry townspeople, flocking to the palace, had removed the bodies for burial. When this was done, an indignation meeting was held at the assembly place. Eupeithes, weeping for his slain son, Antinous, arose and proposed an immediate attack on Odysseus lest he escape the country. Medon and Halitherses, the seer, now both counseled against the attack, and suggested that the gods had themselves ordained that the wooers should die for their own infatuate action—and they cautioned that Odysseus be let alone lest even further evils should befall. Their wise words were approved by a few, but the greater number, thirsting for revenge, donned their bronze armor and, led by Eupeithes, assembled before the town.

On Olympus, Athena now anxiously counseled with Zeus, asking whether he proposed to permit another evil war or wanted to bring about friendship between the Ithacans and Odysseus. After gently blaming her for the existing situation, he proposed to erase the slaughter from the memories of the Ithacan islanders so that, no longer feeling anger, they would make a binding covenant with Odysseus, which would insure a lasting peace.

At the farm, shortly after Odysseus and his companions had been fed, a son of Dolius sighted the approaching enemy and gave the alarm. Odysseus then put on his armor, as did Laertes, Telemachus, Philoetius, Eumaeus, Dolius, and his six sons. And Athena, appearing as Mentor, came up to join them into battle. Odysseus admonished Telemachus to fight well lest he disgrace his illustrious ancestors, world renowned for their courage. When Telemachus promised to do so, ancient Laertes voiced his joy at seeing his son and his son's son vying with one another in valor.

As the townsmen drew near, Athena stood beside Laertes and bade the old man to raise his spear and let fly. Obeying, he hurled the weapon with a great strength breathed into him by the goddess. Nor was the cast in vain, for the spear plowed through the cheek piece of Eupeithes'

bronze helmet and brought him to his death. Odysseus and Telemachus now fell upon the charging warriors with swords and spears, and would have slain them all had not Athena suddenly cried out, commanding them to halt and settle their differences without bloodshed. In panic, the townsmen dropped their weapons and fled homeward with Odysseus in hot pursuit. But, at this juncture, Zeus hurled a flaming bolt before Athena's feet and she admonished Odysseus to cease this beginning of civil war, lest he move the supreme god to wrath. Inwardly glad, Odysseus obeyed her warning and thereafter Athena set a covenant of peace between the contestants—which endured through all mythological time.

The Telegonia

Not content with the prospect of the divinely enforced inactivity promised by the conclusion of the Odyssey, Eugammon of Cyrene added to the Homeric Cycle an account known as The Telegonia, or the Telegony, which is described by Andrew Lang as "a silly sequel to say what became of them all."[23]

According to the fragments of the narrative preserved by Proclus: after the suitors of Penelope were buried by their kinsmen, Odysseus sacrificed to the nymphs and sailed to inspect his herds at Elis; there he was entertained by King Polyxeinus with whom he had fought against the Trojans and, having received a mixing bowl as a guest-gift, was further regaled with the local stories about Trophonius, Agamedes, and Augeias. Next, he sailed back to Ithaca and performed sacrifices which had been prescribed to him by Teiresias on the occasion of his visit to the lower world and, then, went to Thesprotia and married Callidice, the queen of the country, who bore a son named Polypoëtes to him. Subsequently, he led the Thesprotians in a war against the Brygi but, owing to the intervention of Ares, his forces were routed, and (Callidice having died) he returned to Ithaca after

---

[23] The restless spirit which would not permit Odysseus to settle down to a life of ease has been immortalized by Lord Tennyson in his familiar poem entitled "Ulysses" (the Latin name for Odysseus).

establishing young Polypoëtes as successor to the kingdom.[24] Meanwhile, Telegonus (one of the sons borne to him by Circe) had traveled in search of his father and, landing at Ithaca, was ravaging the island. In defense of his country, Odysseus came out against the invader and, in the fight which followed, was unwittingly slain by his own son. When he learned of his mistake, Telegonus now transported his father's body, together with Penelope and Telemachus, to the island of Aeaea, where Circe made them immor-

tal. And, as a finish to the "silly sequel," Telegonus married Penelope and Telemachus married Circe.[25]

But, no matter how silly the sequel or how drab its ending, the men and women of the Heroic Age were destined to remain brilliantly in the memories of all succeeding generations; and their stirring activities of long ago have become for us in later questioning times both an accurate record of man's inherent sense of justice and a trusted augury of the future.

---

[24] Following the traditional pattern, Eugammon embellishes his account of the war between the Thesprotians and the Brygi by having Athena engage with Ares until they are separated by Apollo.

[25] The "Telemachus" of the Frenchman Fenelon does not purport to be a continuation of the classical story, but is used merely as the vehicle for the exposition of his political views advanced in the 17th century.

Bibliography

Source Books

Aeschylus. *Agamenon, Cheophori, Eumenides, Persians, Seven Against Thebes, Prometheus Bound, The Suppliants.* Translated by Anna Swanwick. Bohn Library. London, 1886.

Antoninus Liberalis. *Metamorphoses.* Amsterdam, 1676.

Apollodorus. *Library and Epitome.* Translated by Sir James G. Frazer. 2 vols. The Loeb Classical Library. Cambridge, Mass.: Harvard University Press, 1921.

Apollonious Rhodius. *Argonautica.* Translated by R. C. Seaton. The Loeb Classical Library. Cambridge, Mass.: Harvard University Press, 1921.

Apuleius. *The Golden Ass.* Discourse on Magic, Florida and Cupid and Psyche. Bohn Library. London, 1913.

Apuleius. *The Marriage of Cupid and Psyche.* Translated by Andrew Lang. 1887.

Aristophanes. *The Acharnanians, The Clouds, The Knights, The Wasps, The Peace, The Birds, The Frogs, The Lysistrata, The Thesmophoriazusae, The Ecclesiazusae, The Plutus.* Translated (verse) by Benjamin Bickley Rogers. 3 vols. The Loeb Classical Library. Cambridge, Mass.: Harvard University Press, 1927.

Athenaeus. *The Deipnosophists.* Translated by C. B. Gulick. 7 vols. The Loeb Classical Library. Cambridge, Mass.: Harvard University Press, 1927.

Cicero. *De Natura Deorum.* Translated by Joseph Hindmarsh. 1683.

Clement of Alexandria. *Exhortation to the Greeks.* Translated by Rev. G. W. Butterworth. The Loeb Classical Library. Cambridge, Mass.: 1919.

Dictys Cretensis. *De Bello Trojano.* Amsterdam, 1702.

Diodorus Siculus. *Historical Library.* Vols. 1–6 translated by C. H. Oldfather. 12 vols. The Loeb Classical Library. Cambridge, Mass.: Harvard University Press, 1935.

Euripides. *Iphigeneia at Aulis, Rhesus, Hecuba, Daughters of Troy, Helen, Electra, Orestes, Iphigeneia in Tauris, Andromache, Cyclops, Bacchanals, The Madness of Heracles, The Children of Heracles, Phoenician Maidens, The Suppliants, Ion, Hippolytus, Medeia and Alcestis.* Translated by A. S. Way. 4 vols. The Loeb Classical Library. Cambridge, Mass.: Harvard University Press, 1925.

Euripides. *Scholiast of Hecuba, Orestes, Phoenicias, Medeia, Hippolytus, Alcestis and Andromache.* Basle, 1544.

Eustathius. *Commentary on Homer.* Leipzig, 1827–1830.

Herodotus. *History.* Translated by H. F. Cary. Bohn Library. London, 1904.

Hesiod. *Works and Days, Theogony, Catalogues and Eoiae, Shield of Heracles, Melampodia, Aegimius, Fragments, Homeric Hymns, Epigrams, Thebaiad, Cypria, Aethiopis, Little Iliad, The Returns, The Telegony, Cercopes, Battle of the Frogs and Mice, Contest of Homer and Hesiod.* Translated by H. G. Evelyn-White. The Loeb Classical Library. Cambridge, Mass.: Harvard University Press, 1926.

Homer. *The Iliad.* Translated by A. T. Murray. The Loeb Classical Library. Cambridge, Mass.: Harvard University Press, 1928.

Homer. *The Odyssey.* Translated by A. T. Murray. The Loeb Classical Library. Cambridge, Mass.: Harvard University Press, 1927.

Homer. *Homeric Hymns*. Translated by Andrew Lang. 1900.

Homer. *The Minor Poems of Homer*. Translated by Parnell, Chapman, Shelley, Congreve, and Hole. New York, 1872.

Hyginus. *Fabulae and Poeticon Astronomicon*. Amsterdam, 1681.

Josephus. *Antiquities of the Jews*. Translated by Havercamp. London: Blackie and Sons, n.d.

Juvenal. *Satires*. London, 1739.

Longus. *Daphnis and Chloë*. Translated by George Thornley. The Loeb Classical Library. Cambridge, Mass.: Harvard University Press, 1916.

Lucian. *Works*. Translated by H. W. and F. G. Fowler. Oxford: Oxford University Press, 1905.

Lycophron. Translated by Viscount Royston. Commentary of Joseph Sealiger, Leyden, 1599. Classical Library, 1882.

Nonnos. *Dionysiaca*. Translated by W. H. D. Rouse. 3 vols. The Loeb Classical Library. Cambridge, Mass.: Harvard University Press, 1940.

Opuscula Mythologica. Excerpts from the Mythological Writings of Palaephatus, Erotosthenes, Phurnutus, Sallust, Mazerius, Lucan, Timaeus, Theophrastus, Secundus. Amsterdam, 1688.

Ovid. *Metamorphoses*. Translated by F. J. Miller. 2 vols. The Loeb Classical Library. Cambridge, Mass.: Harvard University Press, 1916.

Ovid. *Fasti and Tristia*. Translated by H. T. Riley. Bohn Library. 1851.

Parthenius. *Love Romances*. Translated by S. Gaselee. The Loeb Classical Library. Cambridge, Mass.: Harvard University Press, 1916.

Pausanias. *Descriptions of Greece*. Translated by W. H. S. Jones. 4 vols. The Loeb Classical Library. Cambridge, Mass.: Harvard University, 1918.

Pindar. *Odes* (Olympian, Pythian, Nemean, Isthmian), *Paeans, Dithyrambs, Processional Songs, Maidens' Songs, Dance Songs, Eulogies, Dirges* and *Fragments*. Translated by Sir J. E. Sandys. The Loeb Classical Library. Cambridge, Mass.: Harvard University Press, 1927.

Pliny. *Natural History*. Translated by John Bostock and H. T. Riley. Bohn Library. 1855.

Plutarch. *Lives*. Translated by Aubrey Stewart and George Long. Bohn Library. 1914.

Quintus Smyrnaeus. *The Fall of Troy*. Translated by A. S. Way. The Loeb Classical Library. Cambridge, Mass.: Harvard University Press, 1913.

Sophocles. *Oedipus the King, Oedipus at Colonus, Antigone, Electra, Trachinae, Ajax and*

Philoectetes. Translated by E. P. Coleridge. Bohn Library. 1893.

Strabo. *Geography*. Translated by H. C. Hamilton and W. Falconer. Bohn Library. 1854.

Suetonius. *Lives of the Caesars*. Translated by Alexander Thomson and T. Forester. Bohn Library. 1845.

Theocritus. *Idyls*. Translated by Andrew Lang. London, 1889.

Thucydides. *Peloponnesian War*. Translated by William Smith. Philadelphia, 1844.

Virgil. *The Aeneid*. Translated by John Dryden. London, 1730.

Virgil. *Eclogues and Georgics*. Translated by J. W. Mackail. The Modern Library. New York: Random House, Inc., 1934.

*Digests or Commentaries
Based upon the Source Books*

Barton, Samuel Goodwin and W. H. *A Guide to the Constellations*. New York: McGraw-Hill, 1928.

Bell. *New Pantheon*. London, 1790.

Breasted, James Henry. *Conquest of Civilization*. New York: Harper, 1926.

Cary, M. et al., eds. *Oxford Classical Dictionary*. 1949.

Cox. *Mythology of the Aryan Nations*. London, 1878.

Gayley. *Classic Myths*. Ginn and Co., 1911.

Gladstone, William E. *Studies on Homer*. London: Oxford Press, 1858.

Gladstone, William E. *Juventus Mundi*. London: Oxford Press, 1869.

Gladstone, William E. *Homeric Synchronism*. 1876.

Grote, George. *History of Greece*. 12 vols. New York, 1949.

Lang, Andrew. *Custom and Myth*. 2nd ed. London: Longmans and Co., 1885.

Lang, Andrew. *Homer and the Epic*. London: Longmans and Co., 1893.

Lang, Andrew. *Homer and His Age*. London: Longmans and Co., 1906.

Lang, Andrew. *The World of Homer*. London: Longmans and Co., 1910.

Rose, Herbert Jennings. *Handbook of Greek Mythology*. New York: E. P. Dutton and Co., 1928.

Schliemann, Heinrich. *Troy and Its Remains*. New York: Charles Scribners, 1875.

Seymour. *Life in the Homeric Age*. New York: The Macmillan Company, 1907.

Smith. *Dictionary of Greek and Roman Biography and Mythology*. London, 1880.

Smith. *Dictionary of Greek and Roman Geography*. London, 1872.

Index